THE OXFORD HISTORY
OF ENGLAND

Edited by SIR GEORGE CLARK

THE OXFORD HISTORY OF ENGLAND
Edited by Sir George Clark

ROMAN
BRITAIN

By

PETER SALWAY

OXFORD
CLARENDON PRESS
1981

Oxford University Press, Walton Street, Oxford OX2 6DP

OXFORD LONDON GLASGOW
NEW YORK TORONTO MELBOURNE WELLINGTON
KUALA LUMPUR SINGAPORE JAKARTA HONG KONG TOKYO
DELHI BOMBAY CALCUTTA MADRAS KARACHI
NAIROBI DAR ES SALAAM CAPE TOWN

*Published in the United States
by Oxford University Press, New York*

© *Oxford University Press 1981*

British Library Cataloguing in Publication Data

Salway, Peter
   Roman Britain. — (Oxford history of England).
   1. Great Britain — History — Roman period,
   55 B.C.–449 A.D.
   I. Title   II. Series
   936.1'04   DA145   80-41811

   ISBN 0-19-821717-X

Reproduced from copy supplied
printed and bound in Great Britain
by Billing and Sons Limited
Guildford, London, Oxford, Worcester

PREFACE

THE Clarendon Press, by publishing in 1936 the volume in this series entitled *Roman Britain and the English Settlements* by R.G. Collingwood and J.N.L. Myres, marked a watershed in the study of Roman Britain. Revised for a second edition in 1937 the book established itself as a classic. More than forty years later it is still in print at the time of writing, an achievement in so fast-moving a subject that is quite extraordinary. 'Collingwood and Myres', as it came affectionately to be known, was not a work of collaboration. The two authors were contained within a single cover—in a friendly fashion—as a matter of convenience, neither subject at that time requiring treatment on a scale demanding a full volume in the *Oxford History*. This present book is designed to substitute for 'Collingwood' alone. That is a measure of the expansion in each field over the last four decades.

The untimely death of Sir Ian Richmond in 1965 prevented the writing of that full-scale historical study of Roman Britain which had been hoped for. When I was asked subsequently to consider revising Collingwood's work as a new edition for the *Oxford History* it immediately became obvious that the changes in Romano-British studies over the previous thirty years were so great that it could not be brought up to date without impossibly cumbrous annotation or by so tampering with the text that Collingwood's marvellous style would be ruined. In 1967 the Press commissioned me to write instead an entirely new book. This work is therefore in no sense a revision of Collingwood, nor is it based upon him, except in so far as all of us who study this period of British history have been profoundly affected by him, directly or indirectly.

I have followed Collingwood in attempting no more than a sketch of the island before the campaigns of Julius Caesar. The reasons for this I have set down in more detail in my first chapter, but in brief the problems are partly of scale and partly stem from the lack of consensus among prehistorians

at the present time, extending even to some of the fundamental features of pre-Roman Britain. The closer that one
approaches the Roman period, the greater the area of disagreement. There is, fortunately, some logic in beginning the
story where written records begin to appear in tangible
quantity, however inadequate and one-sided they may be.
Propaganda though they undoubtedly are, with Caesar's
Commentaries prehistory begins decisively to give way to
history. This present book, as a volume in the *Oxford History
of England*, is not a book about the archaeology of Roman
Britain, though it draws extensively on archaeological sources.
For the same reason I have not treated art in Roman Britain
except in passing nor have I made much use of social interpretation of architectural remains, believing that in our
present state of knowledge that subject, though full of fascinating possibilities, is too full of ambiguities to provide a
reliable major source for our present purpose.

Where to end presented me with some problems. Modern
students of the early Anglo-Saxons extend their field well
back into the fourth century, while the 'sub-Roman' or 'post-
Roman' age of Britain is now taken far into the fifth century,
if not the sixth. Down to the end of Roman rule in Britain I
have tried to treat the evidence with reasonable fullness, but
thereafter have approached the fifth century AD from an
essentially Roman angle, leaving to other hands those sources
in which Germanic and Celtic scholars can claim competence,
but not I. After about AD 450 when the insular Roman evidence shrinks to a trickle I have deliberately reduced my scale,
and I have brought the account to a close at the turn of the
century. At that point separate events in Britain and in Gaul
decisively changed the pattern of Roman and barbarian that
had developed differently but, I believe, not without relevance
to one another in these neighbouring parts of the western
Roman world.

Collingwood's brilliance made his book all things to all
men. A word or two about my more modest ambitions may
explain certain features of this present work. The *Oxford
History* assumes a well-read but not professional public; and
since its previous volumes have been widely received abroad
it is necessary to include more topographical detail than
would be normal if a readership in Great Britain alone had

to be considered. It is, moreover, no longer possible to assume a general knowledge of Latin and Greek, though there is some compensation in a more widespread occurrence of information about the ancient world at large through broadcasting and popular printed works, even if these are sometimes coloured by myth. My approach has been to build on the general interest in ancient civilization and to treat Britain as a distinctive but integral part of the Roman world. Much that is scattered and incoherent when seen from a Romano-British viewpoint alone falls into place observed in context as part of the evidence for the age as a whole.

Collingwood wrote in very different circumstances from those prevailing among professional scholars of Roman Britain today. By 1936 the work of a series of distinguished students of the period had brought order to the subject. The main outlines of political, military, and social history seemed established, with promise that further research would fill in more details and settle outstanding problems. The pattern was in fact so firmly set that in the 1950s it remained still largely unchanged. For those twenty years it was possible to conceive of definitive accounts of the period, as indeed Collingwood's largely remained. From the fifties, however, a mass of new information gradually became available, from aerial photography and out of rescue excavation on sites of all kinds, ranging from deep holes dug in cities for new office blocks penetrating far below anything before to vast areas of countryside stripped for motorways and other developments. Concurrently scholars began to question many of the apparently fixed points in the accepted picture of Roman Britain. We are now in a period when there is no agreement on many major issues and, perhaps much more important, no possibility that all aspects of the subject can ever again be comprehended by one historian.
  This book is thus one man's view at a particular time. There are occasions where I have 'chanced my arm', I hope not unreasonably. Others may as validly come to different conclusions on the same evidence, and it is certain that some ideas will be overturned by new discoveries and further research. Moreover unlike Collingwood I am not a philosopher. I have based my work on no specific philosophy of history or ideology, other than a belief that what men and women have

done in the past is worth pursuing and remembering for itself. One of the problems of Romano-British studies has been the emotional commitment of many of its practitioners, whether to 'pro-Roman' or 'anti-Roman' sentiments or to favourite theories within the subject. There has also been, outside this circle, a curious prejudice against Romano-British studies, as if they were in some way not quite intellectually respectable, though whether this was because of a distaste for the Romans themselves or belief that the subject was too well comprehended and therefore 'easy', I cannot say. If the latter, then the intellectual feat of comprehension and communication that Collingwood's work represents had ironic consequences. No one can now reasonably think Roman Britain lacking in new material or intellectual challenge. Indeed there are signs that it is particularly well suited to the newer techniques of analysis that are being imported from other disciplines, provided that we remember that they are means to a historical end, not ends in themselves.

When Collingwood wrote, most of the leading scholars of the day had had wide experience outside the purely academic, much of it in a world with features now disappeared but relevant to the study of the past. The same was broadly true of the subsequent generation that came through the Second World War. It is less true of the younger generation of Romano-British specialists. My own experience has been rather different from many of them, after starting in much the same way with ten years of full-time research in Roman archaeology. However in recent years it has only been the kindness of the Council of the Open University in granting me a total of twelve months' leave to complete this book that has released me from other affairs that have strongly influenced me in my approach to the subject and put me at some distance from the everyday preoccupations of those wholly engaged in it. This has not given me a better perspective than my friends and colleagues in the field, but a rather different one.

I cannot claim to have attempted the impossible task of being in touch with every source of information relevant to Roman Britain. It is not possible to give an absolute date after which new information has not been taken into account, but substantially this book represents my view of the subject based on the material available to me up to the summer of

1977. Some modifications have been made as and where feasible in subsequent stages of preparing the manuscript for the Press. The form of Bibliography laid down for the Oxford History—a guide to further reading rather than a list of sources used for the text—has proved an advantage in this respect as well as others, for it provided the opportunity to insert further material that had either not been published when the text itself had reached its final form or had not come to my notice at that time.

It is certain that this book would contain far more errors than I hope it now has but for the labours of Mr Anthony King and Mrs Lysbeth Merrifield, whose services I was able to retain over the last few months of the work on the second draft, thanks to a generous grant from the Research Committee of the Open University. Mr King acted as internal critic, Mrs Merrifield checked my references and translations. It is conventional to say that the credit is theirs, the remaining errors mine. In this case that is not only true, but the constraints of my everyday duties are such that without them there would have been no hope of this book ever reaching the Press, since the flood of discovery was overtaking the speed of its composition. For the same reason, the labours of my typists—first Valerie Goode and latterly my secretary Ysabel Barringer—took on an unusual importance as they patiently tackled draft after draft. Most of all this volume owes form and inspiration to the late Sir George Clark, General Editor of the series. I have met no more acute an editor nor a kinder one. For his patience and percipience I owe a debt of gratitude that I could never have repaid; but I hope the emergence from the Press of one more volume of the *Oxford History* conceived and written under his direction will go a little way to record it.

STANTON HARCOURT   P.S.
1980

CONTENTS

CONTENTS

IV. ROMAN BRITAIN AND THE FIFTH CENTURY WORLD

15. THE COLLAPSE OF IMPERIAL RULE

16. BRITAIN, THE END OF THE WESTERN EMPIRE, AND THE SUCCESSOR STATES

V. BRITAIN UNDER ROMAN RULE

17. THE ASSIMILATION OF BRITAIN

18. THE HISTORICAL GEOGRAPHY OF ROMAN BRITAIN

xviii   CONTENTS

ABBREVIATIONS

AE	*L'Année Épigraphique*
Amer. Journ. Philology	*American Journal of Philology*
Ant. J.	*The Antiquaries Journal*
Arch. Ael.	*Archaeologia Aeliana*
Arch. Atlantica	*Archaeologia Atlantica*
Arch. Cambr.	*Archaeologia Cambrensis*
Arch. J.	*The Archaeological Journal*
Bericht d. Röm.-Germ. Kommission	*Bericht der Römisch-Germanischen Kommission*
Bonner Jahrb.	*Bonner Jahrbücher*
Brit.	*Britannia*
Brit. Mus. Yearbook	*British Museum Yearbook*
Bull. Board Celt. Stud.	*Bulletin of the Board of Celtic Studies*
Bull. Inst. Arch. London	*Bulletin of the Institute of Archaeology of the University of London*
Bull. New York Acad. Med.	*Bulletin of the New York Academy of Medicine*
CBA	Council for British Archaeology
Chron. Min. see	*MGH (AA)*
CIL	*Corpus Inscriptionum Latinarum*
Cod. Theod.	*Codex Theodosianus*
Dig.	The *Digest* of Justinian
ILS	H. Dessau, *Inscriptiones Latinae Selectae*
Int. Journ. Naut. Arch. and Underwater Explor.	*International Journal of Nautical Archaeology and Underwater Exploration*
It. Ant.	*Itinerarium Antoninianum*
Jones, *LRE*	A.H.M. Jones, *The Later Roman Empire, 284–602*
Journ. Arch. Science	*Journal of Archaeological Science*
Journ. Brit. Arch. Ass.	*Journal of the British Archaeological Association*
Journ. Geol. Soc. Lond.	*Journal of the Geological Society of London*
JRS	*Journal of Roman Studies*
MGH(AA), Chron. Min.	*Monumenta Germaniae Historica (Auctores Antiquissimi), Chronica Minora*
New Phytol.	*New Phytologist*

Not. Dig.	*Notitia Dignitatum*
Not. Dig. Occ.	*Notitia Dignitatum Occidentalis*
OGIS	*Orientis Graecae Inscriptiones Selectae*
Pan. Lat. Vet.	*Panegyrici Latini Veteres*
Proc. Camb. Ant. Soc.	*Proceedings of the Cambridge Antiquarian Society*
Proc. Camb. Phil. Soc.	*Proceedings of the Cambridge Philological Society*
Proc. Prehist. Soc.	*Proceedings of the Prehistoric Society*
Proc. Soc. Ant. Scot.	*Proceedings of the Society of Antiquaries of Scotland*
Rav. Cosm.	*Ravenna Cosmography*
RCHM	Royal Commission on Historical Monuments (England)
RIB	R.G. Collingwood and R.P. Wright, *The Roman Inscriptions of Britain*
SHA	Scriptores Historiae Augustae
Trans. Archit. and Archaeological Soc. Durh. and Northumb.	*Transactions of the Architectural and Archaeological Society of Durham and Northumberland*
Trans. Birm. and Warwicks. Arch. Soc.	*Transactions of the Birmingham and Warwickshire Archaeological Society*
Trans. Bristol and Glos.	*Transactions of the Bristol and Gloucestershire Archaeological Society*
Trans. Caern. Hist. Soc.	*Transactions of the Caernarvonshire Historical Society*
Trans. Cumb. and Westm. Ant. and Arch. Soc.	*Transactions of the Cumberland and Westmorland Antiquarian and Archaeological Society*
Trans. London and Middx. Arch. Soc.	*Transactions of the London and Middlesex Archaeological Society*
Trans. Perthsh. Soc. Nat. Sci.	*Transactions of the Perthshire Society of Natural Science*

LIST OF MAPS

These maps, in common with most other maps of the ancient world, should be used with caution. Many details are approximate or conjectural, particularly ancient political boundaries. Present coastlines have been adopted throughout, in view of continuing uncertainty about changes during and since the Roman period. Place-names for Roman sites here and in the text are given in modern rather than ancient form, with a few exceptions such as Verulamium which are in common use. Similarly, the modern place-names themselves appear in whatever spelling it seems likely at the present time will be most readily recognized by non-specialist English-speaking readers.

MAP I. THE ISLAND OF BRITAIN
(*modern coastline and place-names*)

MAP II. THE TRIBES OF BRITAIN

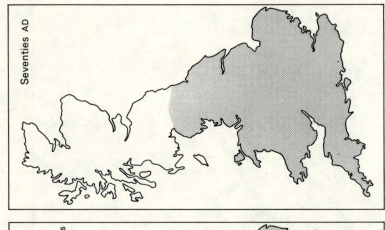

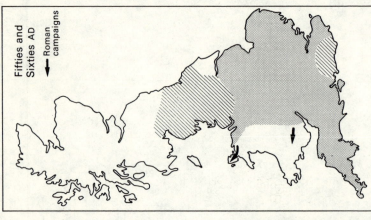

Fifties and Sixties AD

Roman campaigns

Seventies AD

Forties AD

Client kingdoms

Roman occupation

Cartimandua

Prasutagus

Cogidubnus ?

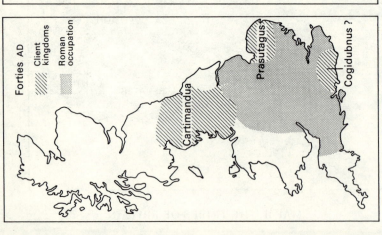

MAP III. THE ROMAN CONQUEST

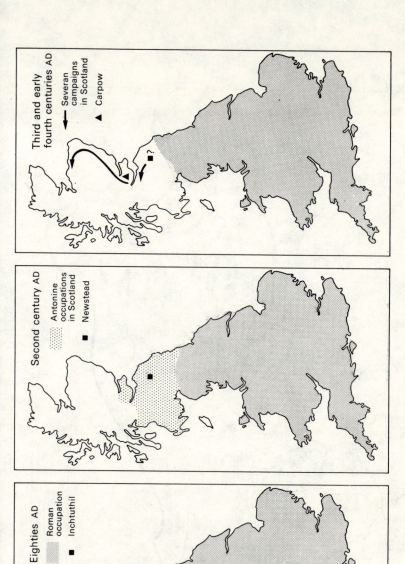

MAP III. (*cont.*)

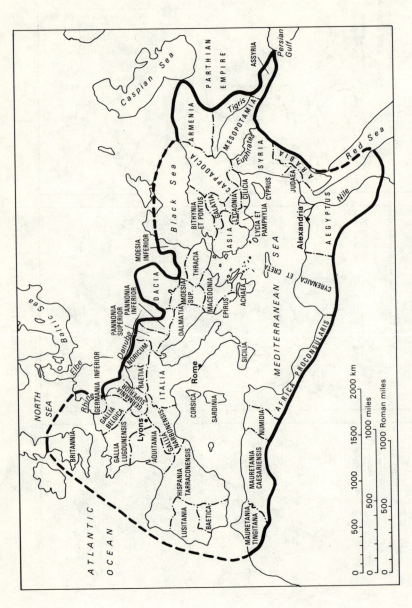

MAP IV. THE EMPIRE UNDER TRAJAN

PARTHIAN EMPIRE

Caspian Sea

ASSYRIA

Persian Gulf

Tigris

ARMENIA

MESOPOTAMIA

Euphrates

SYRIA

CAPPADOCIA

Black Sea

BITHYNIA ET PONTUS

GALATIA

CILICIA

CYPRUS

ARABIA

Red Sea

ASIA

LYCAONIA

MOESIA INFERIOR

LYCIA ET PAMPHYLIA

JUDAEA

Nile

THRACIA

DACIA

MOESIA SUP.

MACEDONIA

Alexandria

AEGYPTUS

PANNONIA SUPERIOR

PANNONIA INFERIOR

DALMATIA

EPIRUS

ACHAEA

MEDITERRANEAN SEA

CRETA

CYRENAICA ET CRETA

Danube

NORICUM

ITALIA

SICILIA

North Sea

Elbe

RAETIA

GERMANIA INFERIOR

GERMANIA SUPERIOR

Rhine

Rome

CORSICA

SARDINIA

AFRICA PROCONSULARIS

Baltic Sea

GALLIA BELGICA

GALLIA LUGDUNENSIS

Lyons

GALLIA NARBONENSIS

AQUITANIA

NORTH SEA

BRITANNIA

HISPANIA TARRACONENSIS

NUMIDIA

MAURETANIA CAESARIENSIS

ATLANTIC OCEAN

LUSITANIA

BAETICA

MAURETANIA TINGITANA

2000 km

1500

1000

500

0

1000 miles

500

0

1000 Roman miles

500

0

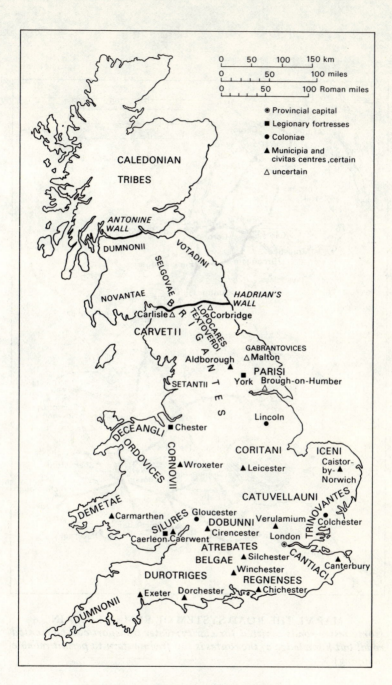

MAP V. SECOND-CENTURY BRITAIN
(lesser towns and forts not shown)

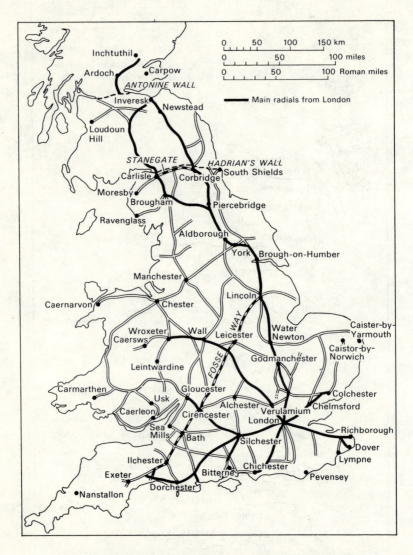

MAP VI. THE ROAD SYSTEM OF ROMAN BRITAIN
(some lesser roads omitted for clarity; water transport complemented road, but knowledge of the routes is too fragmentary to permit reliable mapping)

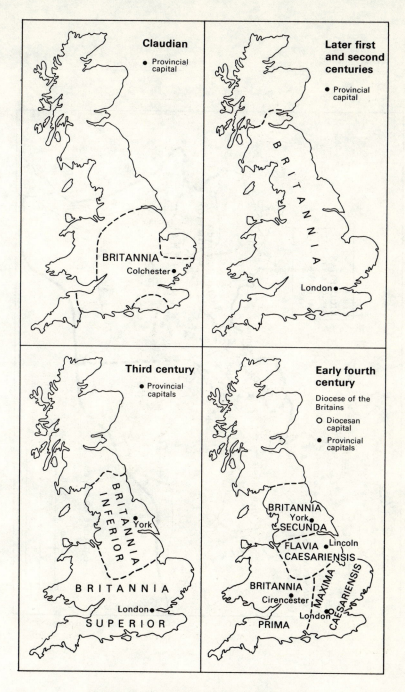

Claudian

● Provincial capital

BRITANNIA

Colchester ●

Later first and second centuries

● Provincial capital

BRITANNIA

London ●

Third century

● Provincial capitals

BRITANNIA INFERIOR

York ●

BRITANNIA SUPERIOR

London ●

Early fourth century

Diocese of the Britains

○ Diocesan capital

● Provincial capitals

BRITANNIA SECUNDA

York ●

FLAVIA CAESARIENSIS

Lincoln ●

BRITANNIA PRIMA

Cirencester ●

MAXIMA CAESARIENSIS

London ●

MAP VII. THE PROVINCES OF BRITAIN
(*probable arrangement at different periods: n.b. later fourth-century*
province of Valentia not shown)

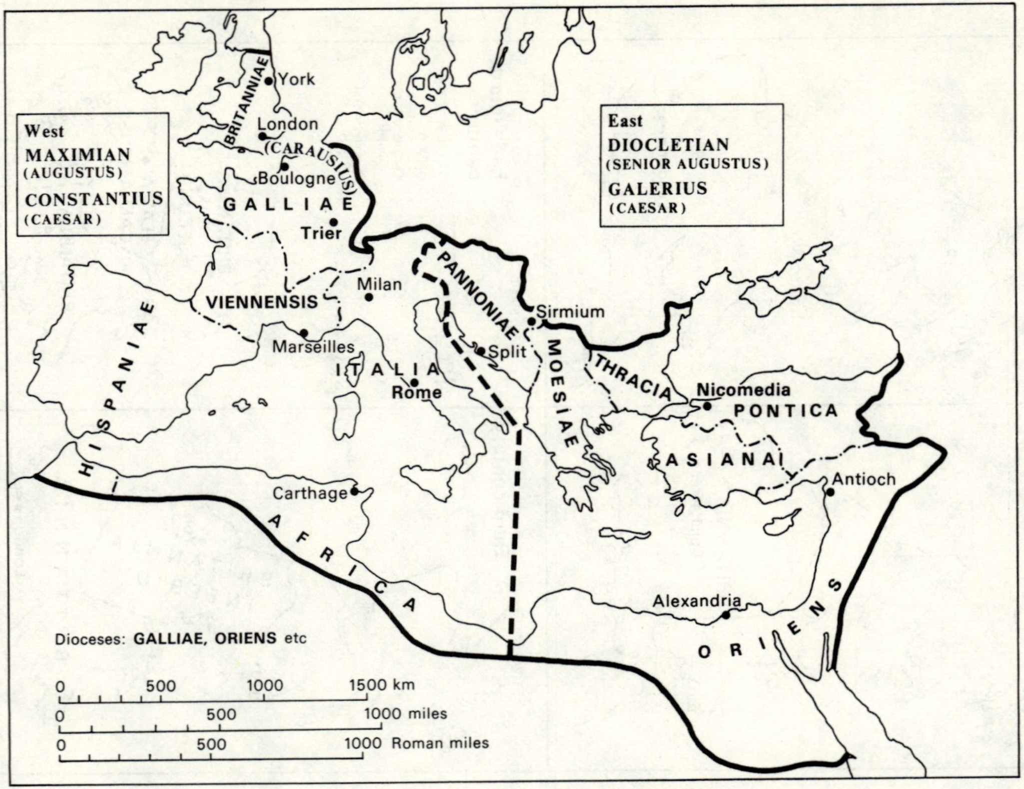

MAP VIII. THE TETRARCHY

West
MAXIMIAN
(AUGUSTUS)
CONSTANTIUS
(CAESAR)

East
DIOCLETIAN
(SENIOR AUGUSTUS)
GALERIUS
(CAESAR)

Dioceses: GALLIAE, ORIENS etc

1500 km
1000
500
0

1000 miles
500
0

1000 Roman miles
500
0

BRITANNIAE
York
London
(CARAUSIUS)
Boulogne
GALLIAE
Trier
VIENNENSIS
Marseilles
HISPANIAE
Milan
ITALIA
Rome
Carthage
AFRICA
PANNONIAE
Sirmium
Split
MOESIAE
THRACIA
Nicomedia
PONTICA
ASIANA
Antioch
ORIENS
Alexandria

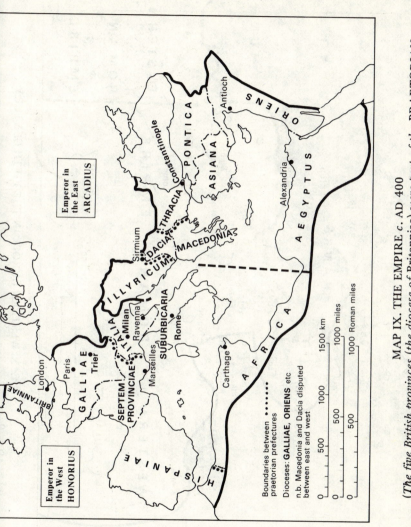

Emperor in the East
ARCADIUS

Emperor in the West
HONORIUS

BRITANNIAE

London
Paris
GALLIAE
Trier

SEPTEM
PROVINCIAE
Milan
Ravenna
Marseilles
ITALIA
SUBURBICARIA
Rome

HISPANIAE

ILLYRICUM
Sirmium
DACIA
MACEDONIA
THRACIA
Constantinople
PONTICA
ASIANA
Antioch
ORIENS

Alexandria
AEGYPTUS

AFRICA
Carthage

Boundaries between ······· prefectures
Dioceses: **GALLIAE, ORIENS** etc
n.b. Macedonia and Dacia disputed between east and west

0	500	1000	1500 km
0	500	1000 miles
0	500	1000 Roman miles

MAP IX. THE EMPIRE *c*. AD 400

(*The five British provinces (the diocese of Britanniae) were part of the* PRAETORIAN PREFECTURE OF THE GAULS, *along with the dioceses of Galliae, Septem Provinciae, and Hispaniae*)

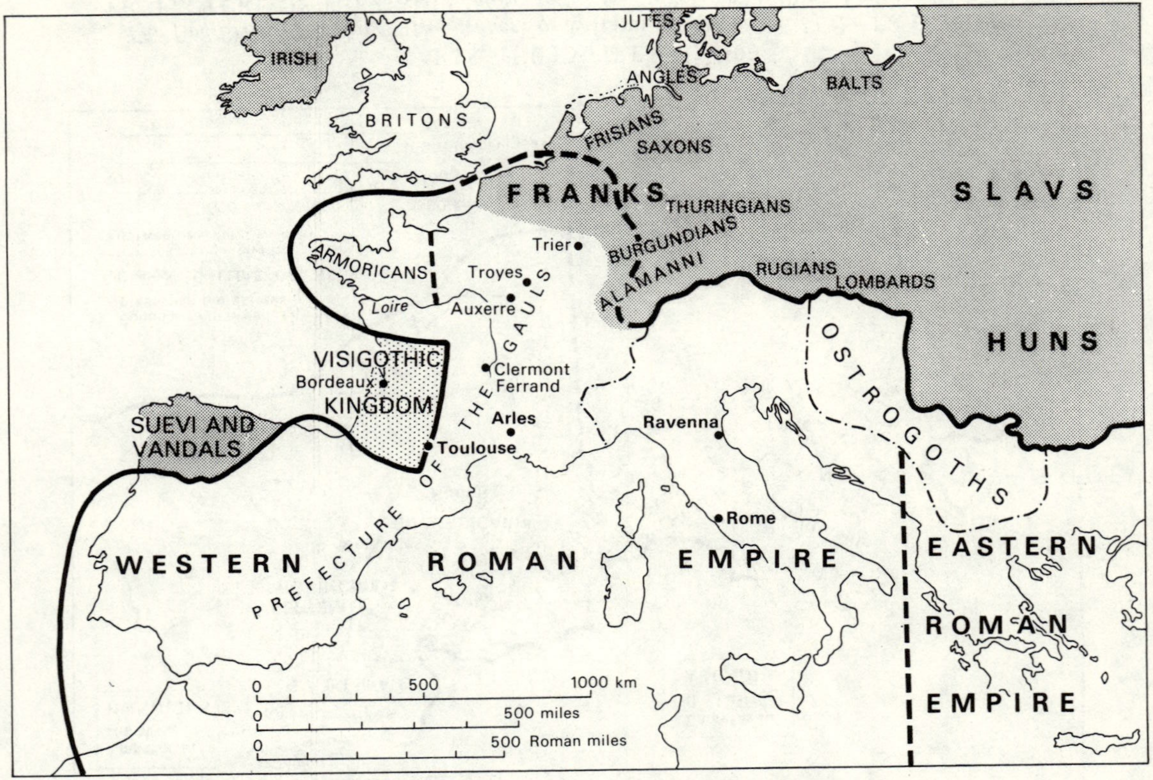

SLAVS

HUNS

BALTS

JUTES
ANGLES
FRISIANS
SAXONS

FRANKS

THURINGIANS
BURGUNDIANS
ALAMANNI

RUGIANS
LOMBARDS

OSTROGOTHS

EASTERN
ROMAN
EMPIRE

IRISH

BRITONS

ARMORICANS

Trier

Troyes
Auxerre

Clermont
Ferrand

Arles

Toulouse

Bordeaux

VISIGOTHIC
KINGDOM

Ravenna

Rome

WESTERN ROMAN EMPIRE

PREFECTURE OF THE GAULS

SUEVI AND
VANDALS

Loire

0   500
0   500 miles
0   500 Roman miles

1000 km

MAP X. WESTERN EUROPE IN THE FIFTH CENTURY

(a) c. AD 420

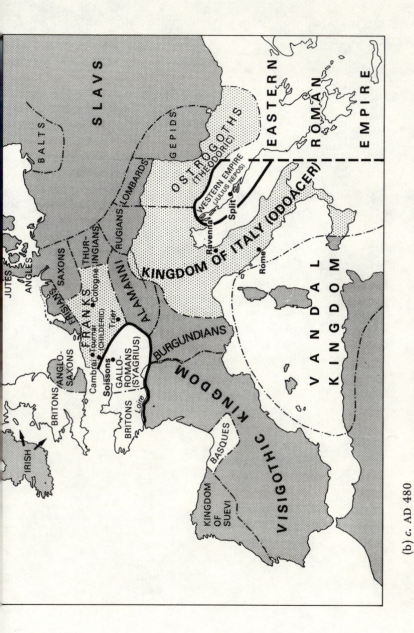

(b) c. AD 480

(n.b. the western Roman empire ended with Julius Nepos in 480, and Childeric was
succeeded by Clovis in 481)

I
THE FIRST ROMAN CONTACTS

1
THE BRITISH BACKGROUND

THE study of Roman Britain has taken various forms. Sometimes it is regarded as a period of interest only to antiquarians and archaeologists, sometimes as one of many elements in local studies, but in either event without wider significance. Many historians have seen it as no more than a passing phase in the history of Britain, of some curiosity value in itself but of little general importance. Yet we shall be looking at a period of some five centuries, as long a stretch of time as from the Wars of the Roses to the present day. This is the age not only for which we first have contemporary or near-contemporary written sources—in itself a matter of crucial historical relevance—but for the greater part of which Britain was absorbed into an empire based on the Mediterranean and subject to the direct impact of classical culture. For the whole of this period the island was closely involved with the fortunes of Europe at one of the most formative periods of its history. 'The toga was often to be seen among them': with these words the Roman writer Tacitus describes the Britons adopting the Roman way of life at an early stage of their long history as Roman provincials. The purpose of this book will be to chart this process and to see how far it went, to examine Britain as an integral part of the Roman empire, to inquire how it resembled other provinces and how it differed from them. From this will emerge its own particular character.

Rome herself never underestimated Britain. For Caesar's first expedition across the Ocean the Roman senate decreed a lengthy period of thanksgiving, very dubious though the real extent of his success may have been. Augustan propagandists constantly foretold the subjection of Britain to imperial control or claimed it as already accomplished. Gaius' last-minute cancellation of the invasion seemed all the more striking because of the magnitude of the enterprise in Roman eyes. Claudius' splendid triumphal procession through Rome for the British victories gained by the armies under his command performed a vital role in confirming him

3

on that throne to which he had been elevated in such an unexpected and undignified manner. Command in Britain was
time and time again felt to require the appointment of some
of Rome's greatest generals. Hadrian authorized the construction here of the most elaborate of all Roman frontier
defences. Septimius Severus in person led his armies in what
was perhaps the last real attempt to conquer the whole island
for the empire. The forces stationed in Britain were exceptionally large, powerful, and sometimes notorious. On several
occasions they intervened in imperial politics in a major way,
and in proclaiming Constantine the Great emperor perhaps
made their greatest impact on world history. It is a measure
of the weight Rome attached to Britain century after century
that, so long as it could physically maintain control, the central imperial government thought it worth tying down substantial forces in its defence, not hesitating to expend scarce
resources on successive restorations after civil wars and barbarian incursions. Even after the remnants of the imperial
government in the west had lost political control of Britain
we shall see that there is reason to think Roman interest in
Britain was not dead; and Britain remained in its own way
within the orbit of the Late Roman world even after the
western empire was extinct.

The framework on which the Roman province was constructed has customarily been defined by reference to the
division of Britain geographically into highland and lowland
zones, differentiated by relief, soil, climate, and communications. Very broadly speaking, the lowland zone is that part
of Britain which lies south and east of a line drawn from the
mouth of the River Tees to the mouth of the Exe, geologically
characterized by comparatively young rocks and whose
countryside is marked by fairly low hills and large areas of
flat ground, much of it gravelly river valley highly suitable
for settlement and agriculture. The highland zone to the
north and west is characterized by the bleak hills of Dartmoor,
Exmoor, and Bodmin Moor in the south-west, by the mountains of Wales, the Lake District, the Peak District, the high
moors of the Pennines and Cheviots—and most of Scotland,
'Lowlands' as well as 'Highlands'. There are, of course, patches
of the opposite sort of landscape in each zone, for example
the Cleveland Hills in the lowland zone and the Cumberland

Plain in the highland, and some highland land is better for agriculture than contiguous lowlands. All in all, however, there is a broad distinction between the two. The lowland zone was particularly suitable for settled, arable agriculture; and the relative ease of communications made both the spread of new ideas and actual conquest comparatively easy, while the highland zone was more naturally pastoral country with communities comparatively isolated and resistant to change. These are substantial differences and have had a very considerable influence on the history of the country. Frank Noble, in an unpublished critique of the classic expression of this approach to British history has summarized it for us thus: '(In this theory there is a) boundary between the "Lowland Zone" where new cultures tended to be imposed and the "Highland Zone" where new cultures tended to be absorbed, transformed or lost. Even if cultures from the lowlands crossed to dominate the highlands the long-term influence of physical factors would re-assert the actual line of division.'[1]

We shall return in a later chapter to this concept, which has tended to obscure other equally important factors in the process of determining where and how man settled in ancient times. Important as it is, these other factors could modify or override it. When we come to the Roman period we have to take into account the intervention of men whose decisions might be determined by considerations which had little or nothing to do with the conditions of a particular locality and who had the physical and technological resources to carry out projects that would have been impossible or unrewarding for a local community. Forest, we are often told, was another major determinant in deterring ancient settlement. There is a good example in the persistence of the Ciminian Forest north of Rome as an unoccupied area in Etruscan and early Roman times. It was opened up as the result of the driving through it of a major Roman highway, underlining the fact that the Romans were entirely capable of overcoming natural difficulties when there seemed positive advantages to be gained, in a way few of their predecessors could approach. If the Romans failed to exploit certain areas we may confidently assume rather that they did not think the probable return

---

[1] Unpublished M.Phil. thesis (Open University, 1977).

worthwhile, whatever it might be, than that they were unable or unwilling to tackle the problems if they so wished. Roman occupation sometimes spread into areas which seem to have been completely empty in the Iron Age. One such area is the Fenland of East Anglia, where, assisted by a change in relative sea-level, they opened up virgin lands, engineering drainage and introducing population.

A factor of great importance, at least in the early stages of Romanization, was the character and existing culture of the various peoples absorbed into the province. The *degree* of material prosperity in each case may have depended to a large extent on the terrain and how it could be exploited, but by the time of Caesar's expeditions the cultures of the inhabitants of Britain had been formed to a greater or lesser extent under the influence of the later Iron Age cultures of the Continent, though prehistorians disagree on how much independent development occurred in Britain itself. In some areas this was probably the result of the arrival of strangers, whether individually or in large groups and whether arriving peaceably or as invaders, in others by the exchange of material objects by way of trade or gift and by the spread of ideas. It seems most unlikely that we shall ever be certain to what extent there had been significant changes of population in the immediate pre-Roman centuries, and prehistorians are becoming much less confident in asserting that there was one substantial invasion after another in the British Iron Age. In the 1960s, as has recently been observed, the debate among prehistorians was between proponents and opponents of the 'invasion hypothesis'; while in the later 1970s it was over the methods by which the material we have on the period should be classified and analysed. Some practitioners of the art would now have us go so far as to ignore—at least for the present—such slight historical sources as we have while they develop 'socio-economic' interpretations based on the archaeology alone. This approach constructs pictures of the successive societies in prehistory by studying the changing character of the artefacts associated with them in the light of models drawn from the social sciences, notably modern geography and anthropology.[1] Specialist opinion on this period

[1] e.g. John Collis, 'The European Iron Age', *Current Archaeology*, 61 (1978), 51 ff.

is at present so fluid that anything more than a bare outline is likely to be obsolete as soon as it is written, and certainly by the time it is published. Nor is it any part of the duty of a Roman historian to decide between the differing views of prehistorians; but some attempt must be made to sketch in a picture of Iron Age Britain if the varying conditions of the British tribes[1] at the time of the Roman arrival are to be understood.

In the 1960s the invasion hypothesis was challenged by a view that saw Continental traits in British cultures of the Iron Age as exotic importations, probably not implying substantial immigration (except in certain restricted areas) and often modified by the cultures into which they were received. This approach emphasized the continuing native element in the British tradition and related the Continental imports to their Continental origins rather than to a British classification of Iron Age cultures based on a notion of successive invasions. A central feature of this new view was the use of a technique involving 'type-fossils', in other words, of isolating groups of characteristics which, when found together, could be recognized as identifying the presence of one particular culture rather than another. The weakness of the approach has been that the only 'type-fossils' which seem with certainty to mark a British Iron Age culture have been three—the use of round houses, of bone weaving-combs,[2] and of ring-necked pins[3] — all of which may have been of relatively minor importance at the time and individually subject to rebuttal by other archaeologists.

What has, however, come out of this debate is a much greater willingness to see Britain as part of a European Iron Age picture and to acknowledge that the position was complex and changing, susceptible to no single theory of development and change. Here we are concerned to recognize the

---

[1] 'Tribe' is an unsatisfactory word: 'state' might be better if it did not have overtones of sophistication which are probably too great for most of Late Iron Age Britain.

[2] The actual use to which these 'combs' were put is uncertain.

[3] The culture identified by these 'type-fossils' has been entitled the 'Little Woodbury Culture' by Professor F.R. Hodson, proponent of the approach, after the 'type-site' on which they were found. A 'type-site' is, in archaeological jargon, the site after which a culture is named, often the site at which it was first discovered or recognized as distinct.

characteristics of the population which faced the Romans rather than to give an account of British prehistory. It will therefore be useful to start where these characteristics seem to begin emerging. It is uncertain, indeed, how far back in time we can follow the history of the inhabitants of Britain known to the Romans, but there is reason to think that characteristic ways of life that persisted into the Roman period, particularly in agriculture, were already present in Britain in the Late Neolithic period. The arrival of peoples from the Low Countries using the so-called Beaker pottery (so-named after a particular type of vessel), possibly in quite small numbers, may have introduced by conquest the pattern of social organization the Romans encountered. In the early stages of the British Iron Age the type-fossils we have already noted seem widely present, at least in the lowland part of the island. Some prehistorians think that the adoption of iron by these people was simply a change of habit by a long-established population, since many of the features of their culture can be shown to belong to a tradition reaching back to the Middle or Early Bronze Age. The round house and weaving-comb are already associated at the Bronze Age site of Shearplace Hill, Dorset, and the idea of agriculture based on small, rectangular 'Celtic' fields which is a striking feature of the Roman period is present in the late Middle Bronze Age at such sites as Itford Hill and Plumpton Plain on the Sussex Downs. Even more striking is the fact that at Gwithian in Cornwall it has been shown that ploughing with ards (primitive ploughs, themselves already known to the Neolithic inhabitants) on the criss-cross system in small lynchetted[1] fields—essentially an agricultural tradition that survived into the Roman period—was being practised in the period of transition from the Early to Middle Bronze Age. It has been suggested that this practice was initiated by the Beaker intruders.[2]

This reinterpretation of British prehistory was worked out with reference to southern Britain, largely 'lowland'. The idea

[1] Lynchets in archaeological terminology are scarps or banks formed between adjacent fields lying upon a slope. 'Strip lynchets' are narrow, terraced fields on a hillside and are generally thought to be post-Roman. There is, however, much controversy on this whole subject.

[2] This is based on Professor J.G.D. Clark's observations in *Antiquity*, 40 (1966), 185.

of a cultural tradition—and a population—settled before the beginning of the Early Iron Age and continuing through into the Roman period had already helped to explain the situation in the north and Wales. It has long been recognized that the Iron Age cultures of northern England, Wales, and Scotland were immediately based on Bronze Age antecedents, though in some areas it looked as if they acquired exotic characteristics from elsewhere—perhaps from the Iron Age south—habits such as the building of hill-forts, those defensive earthworks that still survive in many parts of Britain. Now, however, the main British hill-fort tradition itself seems to go back earlier than was formerly believed and large-scale Iron Age invasions of the north have never been postulated in a way that carries conviction. If an essentially Bronze Age population survived in the south as well, we are quite a long way towards identifying a substantial element in the population of Roman Britain that had been settled in the island for a very long time when the Romans arrived.

The 'invasion hypothesis' saw the picture rather differently. The main Iron Age cultural divisions were first distinguished, by Professor Christopher Hawkes, as 'A', 'B', and 'C', and will still be met by the reader under those symbols in many works on British prehistory. It should be emphasized that these are *cultural* and not chronological divisions, though they do in general seem to start in that order. This cultural pattern was further refined by identifying regional differences within it, first in the south and more recently in the north, and by subdivisions of the main categories. In this view of events in the Iron Age, a scatter of 'Iron Age A' people of Hallstatt[1] traditions entered the country by the sixth century BC, and by 500 this was already a regular settlement. In the middle of the fourth century the southern and eastern parts of England were thoroughly colonized, with outliers to the north-west. In the fourth and third centuries fresh and probably more warlike invaders introduced the distinctive 'B' culture in the south based on Continental La Tène fashions, but large areas retained their Iron Age A traditions. The interaction between the two cultures was at that time

[1] The Hallstatt and La Tène cultures are named after 'type-sites' in Austria and Switzerland respectively.

thought to have set off the main wave of hill-fort building. In due course the 'B' peoples penetrated north and west before the arrival of 'C' intruders in the late second and first centuries BC, about whom as actual immigrants there is rather less doubt.

Although it is no longer safe to postulate general conquest by Iron Age A and B invaders, there are two areas where there certainly seem to have been actual intrusions of groups of people fairly early in the pre-Roman Iron Age. When the Continental Iron Age was in its 'La Tène I' phase there appeared in East Yorkshire the so-called 'Arras Culture', the first distinctively Continental culture in Britain in the Iron Age, even if not an exact reproduction of its Continental relative. This culture is characterized archaeologically by burials containing wheeled vehicles and by burial-mounds or 'barrows' with square-plan ditches.[1] The culture's origin has been attributed to the district of Marne in northern France, but seems to have affinities further east. The part of Yorkshire in which it appears was known in Roman times as the district of the Parisi, a tribe which has its parallel in Gaul.

The second invasion or series of invasions is much later. Some slight doubt has recently been thrown on the reality even of these, but we have clear archaeological evidence of the importation of La Tène III culture over a large area of south-eastern Britain by some means or another, coupled with Julius Caesar's statement[2] that the tribes of the seaward part of Britain were recent 'Belgic'[3] arrivals who had come as raiders or in war and retained the names of the people from whom they had originated. It is certainly true that the names of the Catuvellauni or the Atrebates, tribes known in the south in Roman times, can be paralleled in Gaul. Historical theories on the precise movements of the peoples which created this situation in Britain however depend largely on

[1] See in particular the important report by I.M. Stead, *Ant.J.* 56 (1976), 217 ff.
[2] Caesar, *Bell. Gall.* v. 12. Dr D.W. Harding has argued that Caesar's 'seaward part' (*maritima pars*) should include Essex as well as the south-east, in J. Collis (ed.), *The Iron Age in Britain—A Review*, Sheffield (1977), 63.
[3] The meaning of the term is disputed and is avoided by many archaeologists. It is uncertain what it means when applied to one side of the Channel or the other—see R. Hachmann, *Bull. Inst. Arch. London*, 13 (1976), 117 ff., for a recent discussion of the difficulties. The use of 'Belgic' and 'Iron Age C' as synonymous terms is common but subject to challenge.

interpretation of the coin evidence. There are at present some difficulties in pushing the other archaeological evidence[1] for the Belgic intrusions back as far as the coin evidence may suggest. The 'Aylesford–Swarling' group of archaeological material which represents the middle phase of the Kentish Belgic culture is now, for example, dated later than Caesar, to the period 50/30–10 BC. Some doubt has been thrown on whether the waves of Gallo-Belgic coins which appear in Britain really represent migrations, but it is somehow necessary to account for the fact that Caesar represents the Belgae as well established in Britain in his time. It would need powerful contrary evidence from the archaeology to reject a statement of this kind *by a contemporary observer* without a discernible motive for falsifying the record.

If we are right in seeing the 'waves' of imported coins as representing actual movements of people—and it might be safer but unhelpful in constructing a hypothesis simply to record the coins without interpretation—then it was probably in the later second century BC that Britain first began to feel the effects of pressure from Germany on the people known to the ancients rather vaguely as the Belgae. There were two main groups of Continental Belgae, which had been forming in the Low Countries from the fifth century BC and in northern France from the third. The first Gallo-Belgic coins appear in Britain in the mid-second century, but it is entirely uncertain whether they were brought by raiders or individual settlers or simply came in, as we have already observed, as gifts or in the course of commerce, however primitive. In the last years of the second century BC the situation in Gaul was rendered critical by the wanderings of the Cimbri and Teutones. These powerful tribes invaded Gaul in 109 BC from Germany and in a few years had penetrated so far south that they threatened Italy. This awakened ancient memories of the sack of Rome by the northern barbarians centuries before, and heightened the popular effect at Rome of the two great victories by the Roman general Marius in 102 and 101 BC. But as well as the effect on Roman politics and the part it played in renewing Roman interest in the northern barbarians, the havoc the Germans had wreaked in their

[1] The characteristics of the culture include a distinctive style of wheel-made pottery.

years in Gaul before being annihilated by Marius was almost
certainly responsible for a substantial movement of northern
Gauls into Britain. We do not know whether they came in
large groups or in small numbers as a dominant warrior aristocracy, but their traces appear in Kent, Essex, Hertfordshire,
Cambridgeshire, and the south-east Midlands. This period is
marked by the appearance of the first distinctively British
coins and it is clear that tribal identities were now being felt,
if not before. These people were, strictly speaking, probably
not all Belgic. It has been argued that the tribes north of the
Thames, despite their general cultural appearance, were not
Belgic, if defined as being among those groups who were
recent immigrants when Caesar landed—and this doubt extends to include his chief opponents the Catuvellauni—or
arrived after he finally withdrew. Nevertheless, there is the
strong probability that these tribes were formed out of elements related to the Belgae that had come in at an earlier stage
in the influx of Iron Age Continental people.

Certainly the cultural change spread over a substantial
period of time, with movements making themselves apparent
in Sussex and Kent in the first half of the first century BC,
reaching a climax marked numismatically by the largest wave
of Gallo-Belgic coins about the middle of the century. This
was probably caused in part by further German pressure on
Gaul and partly by Caesar's own Gallic wars. It is not, however, clear to what extent we owe this archaeological material
in Britain to movements before Caesar's inconclusive British
campaigns, rather than to migration immediately after Caesar's
subsequent and final victory over the great Gallic confederation of tribes that had come together under their chosen war-
leader Vercingetorix. This dramatic end to Gallic resistance
presented a clear prospect of Gaul now being permanently
subject to Roman rule, a sharp contrast to a Britain that
might well remain unconquered.

Whether or not the Catuvellauni and certain other tribes
were technically Belgic, many of the southern and eastern
tribes reveal some markedly different patterns of life from
their predecessors and neighbours. The strongly tribal organization of these peoples implies a form of central authority
and perhaps a reasonable degree of peace within the tribal
boundaries. It has been argued that there was thus less need

for hill-forts, to account for their relative scarcity in these areas. Yet there is less and less reason to suppose that all hill-forts were built for the single purpose of serving as refuges for the local population in time of war or civil disturbance. It is now clear that they have a very long history, extending back beyond the Iron Age, possibly even into the Neolithic. Until recently it was thought that hill-forts were normally unoccupied in peace: it is now certain that there were not only small fortified settlements but that some large hill-forts, such as Danebury in Hampshire, were intensively settled, even to the extent of a simple form of street system. Other hill-forts may indeed have been normally occupied only by a few people, either serving as a community refuge or as a chieftain's castle into which he could bring his dependants in time of war. Just as the distribution of hill-forts is extremely uneven over Iron Age Britain, we probably have no need to assume the same purpose for all of them or at all periods in their individual histories. Nor is the term 'hill-fort' entirely satisfactory, since some of the major earthworks are on relatively low ground. Indeed, though it is often said that it was the Romans who forced the Britons to abandon their hill-fortresses and move to new towns in the valleys, it is clear that in some areas this had already occurred before the Roman occupation, while in others it did not occur till considerably later, if at all.

It was at one time believed that in the Belgic areas the introduction of a heavier plough allowed the cultivation of stickier soils and permitted valley agriculture. This is no longer thought certain. On the other hand it is now known that there was very heavy occupation of valley gravels (much of which is covered by relatively light and easily worked soil) by agricultural settlements in the Iron Age, a situation that we shall see becoming even more intensive in the Roman period. It was perhaps unfortunate that the classic excavation of an Iron Age farmstead should have been at Little Woodbury in Wiltshire.[1] The new standards set by this excavation in 1938-9 encouraged archaeologists to take the site as typical, and to see the isolated single farm working upland country as typical of the Iron Age—indeed a concept it has been difficult to shake even when extended into the Roman

[1] G. Bersu, *Proc. Prehist. Soc.* 6 (1940), 30 ff.

period. It was aerial photography that made it clear that on the gravels the Little Woodbury type of isolated single farm was only one of a number of different settlement patterns. Exploration of the broad valley gravels of the east Midlands and the Upper Thames, for example, has revealed large numbers of settlements of varying type and size, often in clusters and set in an open landscape marked by hardly any hill-forts at all. Further aerial photography has shown in the hill-fort country of the Welsh border and the Severn that the valleys, previously thought not to have been settled in the Iron Age, contain numerous settlements of village size, among which the excavated site at Beckford, near Tewkesbury, shows, for example, a densely packed group of individual farmsteads with continuous occupation over the period between about 250 and 50 BC.[1] It is now certain that there was a whole range of types of agricultural settlement in Britain on both upland and lowland, from the single farm to the hamlet or village.

Many of these settlements continued to be used into the Roman period or can be distinguished from Roman-period sites only by their datable small finds. In places there seems to be continuity of settlement boundaries and by the late first or early second century AD under Roman rule some Iron Age farmsteads were replaced on the same site by modest Roman villas,[2] as if only the ownership or perhaps simply the standard of living had changed but the unit of farming remained constant. Evidence has been accumulating in the Thames Valley that the decisive change in land use there occurred not at the Roman Conquest in the 40s of the first century AD but in the hundred years before it.[3] This is marked not only by alterations in the shape and appearance of the farmsteads themselves but, more importantly, by a switch from agriculture based on the grazing of livestock over uninterrupted pasture between the farms to the development of enclosed meadows with fixed boundaries. This suggests

[1] *Current Archaeology*, 45 (1974), 293 ff.
[2] e.g. at Park Street and Gorhambury, Hertfordshire.
[3] 'After Little Woodbury: Village and Farm in Iron Age Oxfordshire', *Current Archaeology*, 63 (1978), 106 ff. Cf. M.A. Robinson, in Susan Limbrey and J.G. Evans (eds.), *The effect of man on the landscape: the Lowland Zone*, CBA Research Report No. 21 (1978), 35 ff.

that a much more settled form of land-ownership was being introduced on the Thames gravels under 'Belgic' influence and we should not be surprised to find the same sort of pattern emerging elsewhere. In fact at Odell in Bedfordshire we can again note the employment of fixed boundaries in the years just before the Conquest, and the excavations there have shown no distinction in the types of activity there that can be equated with the arrival of the Romans.[1] Positive developments do not occur at Odell till considerably later in the first century. It is now becoming clear that there was a major change late in the pre-Roman Iron Age in Britain, at least in these densely populated agricultural river-valleys. The Roman Conquest accelerated the development of this new way of life, rather than initiated it.

In many respects, too, the pattern of labour was changing in the later pre-Roman Iron Age. There is a much greater use of wheel-made pottery, for example, in place of the generally handmade wares of earlier periods, and signs of a professional pottery industry emerging, making some excellent products which strongly influenced Roman factory production when it got under way. Life was becoming more specialized and more organized. It was to become more so. Slave-chains from the pre-Roman hoard of metalwork at Llyn Cerrig in Anglesey and from the Iron Age site that preceded the villa at Park Street may relate to the known slave-trade from Britain to the empire but they may also reflect a local slave-using society, as in the Classical world. Both in some hill-forts— long before the Roman occupation—and perhaps in some of the larger valley-settlements there were the beginnings of urbanization, and there was an apparent division between a tribal aristocracy chiefly interested in the arts of war and a farming peasantry. This seems reflected in the art of late Iron Age Britain. This art is an aristocratic one. It is marked by splendid weapons, mirrors, and personal ornaments of the highest artistic merit and technical achievement but these occur in small quantities only, as is characteristic of an art essentially confined to a restricted class in society. In Gaul the tribes were to prove admirably suited to Roman ways, however politically unreliable they might sometimes be.

[1] Brian Dix, 'Odell: A River Valley Farm', *Current Archaeology*, 66 (1979), 215 ff.

They, too, were tribal societies essentially of nobility and commons, and by Caesar's time these were not only being governed by their upper classes but a loose inter-tribal organization of leading Gauls had emerged. Out of the controversy surrounding the British Iron Age we can at least extract the probability that by the time Claudius came to form the Roman province, and perhaps already before Caesar, influential sections of some of these tribes had moved to Britain. They, and the people who fell under their influence or followed their examples, were to become among the most successfully Romanized under imperial rule.

Beyond the 'Belgic' areas, though life continued in many respects much as before, some developments in settlement types now appear. Many of the features which emerged in southern Britain are also found in Wales and the north, including Scotland. Comparable hill-forts appear in many areas and the settlements on artificial islands in Scotland known as *crannogs* can perhaps be equated with the Iron Age lake villages of south-west England. Perhaps more important, there is an over-all similarity in the minor settlements, however many differences of detail may be found, and it may well be that variations between the highland and lowland zones, where they appear, are as much due to the size of population the differing terrain could support and the variations in type of agriculture or other forms of support dictated by the land, as to inclination or cultural tradition. Terrain indeed was not the only cause of differences in standards of life: certain of the peoples of the south, for example, also controlled the trade routes with the Continent in such commodities as Cornish tin and Irish gold.

The over-all picture emerging is that by the time of the Roman conquest of Gaul (and certainly in the years immediately after it) a culture with very many common elements spread over most of Britain and that in many ways it closely resembled that which by now had come to dominate continental Europe from the Danube to the North Sea. We have so far avoided the terms 'Celt' and 'Celtic', since they have modern and misleading overtones, but there are no other convenient words to describe this phenomenon, and the area in Europe with which we are dealing is so vast and the peoples so varied that—like the ancient writers—we can only use the term with a very vague idea as to its limits. It can, however, with some precision be applied to the language spoken by the Britons. In the post-Roman period two main versions of the Celtic language were spoken in Britain, and from these the modern Celtic languages of Britain and Ireland are descended. These were distinguished by the use of a *p* sound in one where a *q* sound occurred in the other. The first ('Brythonic' or 'Brittonic') is now represented by Welsh and Cornish, the second ('Goidelic') by Irish, Gaelic, and Manx. Since Scottish Gaelic derives from late immigration from Ireland, it is clear that historically these versions represent two blocks, one centred on mainland Britain, the other on Ireland. Except where explicable by subsequent Irish immigration, Celtic place-names in England and Wales fall wholly into the Brythonic group. Goidelic was, it seems, an Irish variant of the common tongue and for our purposes we can ignore it as beyond the area that ever came under Roman rule. It has been argued that Celtic remained in general use as the common tongue in Britain throughout the Roman period, particularly in the countryside.[1] The widespread occurrence of Celtic place-names in Romanized forms and the virtual absence of place-names obviously deriving from another language strongly support the hypothesis that by the time of the Roman conquest most of Britain was speaking Celtic. In Caesar's account we find that all names that occur are Celtic and there is no sign that the conquering Roman armies a century later encountered anything else, even when they penetrated far into the north of Scotland. Certainly in Caesar's time the south and east were therefore speaking Celtic and by the second half of the first century AD this seems to be true of the whole island, even if we are relying to some extent on negative evidence.

Almost every cultural movement identified archaeologically in Britain from the Beaker period onwards has been associated by some specialist with the introduction of the Celtic language. The relative smallness of the differences between

[1] K. Jackson, *Language and History in Early Britain,* Edinburgh (1953), 76 ff.: his conclusions are, however, somewhat modified by D. Greene in 'Some linguistic evidence relating to the British church', in (eds.) M.W. Barley and R.P.C. Hanson, *Christianity in Britain 300–700,* Leicester, 75 ff. The main point, however, continues to be generally accepted.

Brythonic and Goidelic suggests that their period of separation was not particularly long, and it therefore seems bold to push the introduction of Celtic into Britain as a whole as far back as the Beaker folk, perhaps fifteen hundred or two thousand years before our period, or even the Neolithic. On the other hand, not only is the whole 'invasion' hypothesis now under fire, but it is anyhow difficult to find evidence for a universal change of population or total conquest that would account for the ubiquitous appearance of the language. The Late La Tène or 'Belgic' cultural, and eventually political, domination of southern Britain is clearly too late and insufficiently all-embracing to account for the almost total obliteration of any possible trace of other linguistic traditions. Only the few otherwise inexplicable place-names may suggest survival of occasional words from an earlier tongue or tongues,[1] fossilized by this means but whose original significance was not necessarily any longer comprehended. On current evidence we are left without any reliable indication of when the Celtic speech was introduced or became common. Yet, whatever the other differences between them, this Celtic language does seem to have been a common feature throughout the tribes of Britain when the Romans arrived.

We do not know to what extent the peoples of the interior contributed to the forces which opposed Caesar, but they are likely to have been indistinguishable to him as far as their language went. Overall it is likely that Caesar's own experience of Britain was largely of a country under strong La Tène influence and therefore very similar to what he had met in Gaul. At least by the time of the Claudian conquest a hundred years later 'Celtic' culture was widespread in Britain, with broad similarities of society and practice perhaps now more important than differences in standards of life, surroundings, and ways of making a living. Indeed, we shall probably be better able to appreciate how Britain came to be absorbed into the Roman empire—in particular how it became part of, in broad terms, a common Romano-Celtic culture embracing the Roman provinces of north-western Europe—if we go further and abandon any rigid conceptions of a major cultural divide in the later Iron Age between the

---

[1] Cf. Margaret Gelling, *Signposts to the Past: Place-names and the History of England* (1978), 19.

peoples on either side of the Channel.[1] Differences there
certainly were between Britain and Gaul in pre-Roman times,
but they were perhaps more of degree than of kind, just as
there were between the Gallic and the Danubian Celtic
regions. In the same manner we shall see that the Roman
provinces of the north-west differed from one another in
various ways, but within a developing common tradition
under Roman rule.

[1] A move in this direction among prehistorians is now beginning to appear—
e.g. T. Champion, *Arch. Atlantica,* 1 (1975), 127 ff.

2

THE EXPEDITIONS OF CAESAR

B Y the 50s of the first century BC the old republican system of government at Rome was in an advanced state of decay. Theoretically the Republic was still governed by annual magistrates, elected by the citizen body and advised by the senate. The latter was a body whose legal powers were limited but which had exercised enormous authority by virtue of its composition, since it was composed of men who had held major public office and led by those who had occupied one of the two annual consulships, the supreme offices of state. Most of those elected to office came from families that had produced previous office-holders, and it was this 'senatorial' class that had come to dominate the state for generation after generation. Competition between families was keen, but there had been certain conventions within the game and there was much political intermarriage. Poorer relations and lesser families attached themselves to the greater, and a powerful network of patronage grew up, in which the great commanded the allegiance of their 'clients' (*clientela*). Landed property was central to the position of the senatorial aristocracy. Not only were high property qualifications required for office but the acquisition by the great families of vast holdings of land brought with it the inevitable web of obligation and influence. Some families dominated whole regions of Italy—Pompey the Great was to boast that he had only to stamp his foot in his home district and legions would spring from the ground to follow his command—and as public lawlessness increased these senatorial clans began to form states within the state, to whom lesser men looked for protection and advancement rather than to the public institutions.

Magistrates' powers were theoretically unlimited within their sphere of competence, on the principle of absolute delegation of power for a limited period common in ancient elective systems of government, but at Rome the holders of office had been controlled not only by the pressures of public opinion (especially from their colleagues in the senate) and by the traditional code of behaviour, but also by the principle of collegiality, under which magistrates were appointed in pairs (as the consuls) or in greater numbers, each having the power of veto over his fellows. Military command normally went to former holders of the highest offices, and as Rome's foreign wars gradually acquired her an empire piecemeal in the second and first centuries BC provincial governorships came to be allotted by the same system. Opportunities for gaining glory in war—the greatest of spurs to the ambitious Roman—and for enriching oneself overseas under the very lax control over the provincial administrations exercised by the Republic made these commands much sought after. By the first century BC the great senatorial families were making a normal practice of manipulating the electoral system, by corruption of the common electorate and violence in the streets of Rome as well as through the more traditional use of the *clientela*. At the same time a new element had entered politics with the creation of, in effect, a permanent professional army. Until the time of Marius armies had normally been raised as and when they were required, theoretically by conscription of ordinary citizens who returned to normal life after the emergency. By the end of the second century BC there were so many landless peasants and unoccupied city-dwellers glad of employment that it was not difficult to attract men to serve in one campaign after another for pay. Marius reformed military tactics and welded these men into a professional army; and the Republic made the crucial mistake of failing to attach the troops to the Roman state rather than the individual generals, largely through senatorial unwillingness to commit the treasury to regular provision for troops disbanded after a campaign or retired after long service. These professionals thus had to look to their own old commanders for support. Rome now not only had the best professional army in the world, but also one whose troops would follow their own commander rather than the legitimate government if it came to the choice. This extremely dangerous extension of the old principle of patron and client was a fatal error on the part of the Republic that certainly formed a very large element in its own downfall. Subsequently the Roman state made thorough provision for veterans, but the pattern of loyalty had by then been set:

we shall see how it contributed to the long-drawn-out failure of the Empire.[1]

The fall of the Republic had its particular origins in the upheavals of the latter part of the second century BC and the early first. The period was marked both by violent politics at Rome and turmoil in Italy as other communities demanded rights in the Roman state that now dominated them. At the turn of the century bloody civil war broke out between the followers of the two great generals of the day, Marius himself and the ruthless Sulla. The latter, successful militarily, attempted to revive the antique Republic and its aristocratic virtues by force, curbing the powers of the commons whom the party of populist aristocratic politicians that gathered around Marius had courted. Yet, by making the mistake of persecuting the Marian leaders and their families, Sulla utterly failed to ensure that his reformed Republic had any chance of survival at all after his own presence was removed. Among those aristocratic families that had supported Marius was that of Julius Caesar himself, who narrowly escaped.

By the 50s the traditional curbs on political behaviour were largely ineffective. Magistrates' colleagues were intimidated, courts were bribed or overawed by force, and every constitutional trick was played. Power had largely fallen into the hands of three men, Caesar, Pompey, and the immensely wealthy Crassus, who jockeyed with one another for power, sometimes in uneasy alliance, sometimes near to civil war. Caesar himself, like Oliver Cromwell, came comparatively late to military command, but had shown a natural genius for it in Spain. His command in Gaul gave him the opportunity to show a capacity for large-scale conquest which he proceeded to demonstrate with extraordinary speed, overrunning that vast country and reaching the Rhine. His combination of daring and attention to detail brought success in the field and the devotion of his troops. Good fortune, whether the product of luck or the taking of carefully calculated risks, was of

---

[1] The term 'Empire' as used here refers to the period when Rome was ruled by emperors and the attendant political system rather than the area of the world governed by Rome. This period conventionally begins with Augustus' assumption of constitutional powers in 27 BC and ends (in the west) with the deposing of Romulus in AD 476, though it might in practice be taken from the battle of Actium in 32 BC and more properly end with the murder of the rival western emperor Nepos four years after Romulus lost his throne.

immense importance to a Roman commander, since it demonstrated that the favour of the gods shone upon him.
Sulla had taken it so seriously as to take the surname of 'the
Fortunate' (*Felix*). In times of wavering loyalties a lucky
commander tended to be a secure one.

The question by 55 BC was no longer whether Caesar was
an outstanding commander as well as politician but where he
would go next. There is much debate on whether he had a
long-term plan in life, always intent eventually on supreme
power, or was essentially an opportunist. For the moment,
however, the use of his troops to seize power was not feasible,
even if he had wished it. Germany and Britain lay beyond but
contiguous to Gaul, and arguably, since they were not within
the commission of any other Roman commander, he might
extend his operations in either direction. Some of the Germans were to argue that he had no right to cross the Rhine,
that they had been forbidden to enter Gaul themselves and
that therefore Rome in its turn had no authority across the
Rhine. This is an argument Caesar reports without comment
as if it needed no reply. He judged there was a threat from
the Germans and had a further excuse in a request from one
German tribe for assistance. Britain presents a very similar
picture. What Caesar's precise intentions were is something
we are never likely to know. He himself does not tell us
whether he aimed at conquest or punitive action. His only
illuminating comment is that in most of his Gallic campaigns
up to the time of his first British expedition he had found
British contingents fighting against him, and even this he
brings forward as a reason for hastening the invasion, not as
a motive for the enterprise in the first place.[1]

To Romans the unconquered barbarian tribes beyond those
Caesar had already subdued must have seemed to have much
in common with them. Indeed the cultural evidence for close
connections between Late La Tène Gaul and Britain was
clearly borne out by the presence of Britons in Gallic armies.
It is probable that the connections were made obvious by
tribal and even family links among the Belgic peoples on both
sides of the Channel. Caesar noted, for example, that within

[1] See Caesar, *Bell. Gall.* iii.9; iv.20. Gallo-Belgic coins seem to indicate payments by the Gauls for help from south-eastern Britain (see J.P.C. Kent, in
*Collectanea Londiniensia : Studies in London Archaeology and History presented
to Ralph Merrifield* (1978), 53 ff.).

living memory one Diviciacus 'the greatest man in Gaul' had held sway not only among Gallic tribes, including the Belgic Suessiones (around Soissons) but also in Britain.[1] In 57 BC those nobles of the Bellovaci who had unsuccessfully urged an anti-Roman policy on their tribe fled to Britain.[2] Moreover the most powerful political force among the Gauls, Druidism, had, according to Caesar, originated in Britain and spread to Gaul.[3] There is reason to believe that in fact the Druids were less politically influential in Britain than in Gaul, but what matters in this context is what Caesar thought *at the time*—or chose to let be believed at Rome.

It is not possible to say when Caesar first conceived the idea of invading Britain. There is some cause to think that the revolt of the Veneti, the major seafaring nation on the Atlantic coast, whose ships were accustomed to cross to Britain in large numbers and who dominated the other peoples engaged in sea trade in that area,[4] was due to a fear that a Roman invasion of Britain would bring their lucrative enterprise to an end, though the immediate cause was a dispute over hostages. If Caesar had the idea of invasion already by the beginning of 56, it was probably much strengthened by the successes of that year which seemed then to have procured the total pacification of Gaul. He was now free to look round for further fields to conquer, and indeed was almost obliged to do so by the extension of his provincial command following the Conference of Luca in 56. At that meeting Pompey, Crassus, and Caesar had joined in an uneasy alliance to dominate Roman politics. In 55, as a result of this agreement, Pompey and Crassus were the two consuls in Rome and Caesar needed new conquests to keep his name before the Roman public.

A case has, moreover, been made for thinking that there was an even more pressing reason for further military adventure than the mere need for personal publicity: that in fact he could be recalled if the purpose for which he had been

---

[1] Caesar, op.cit. ii.4.
[2] Ibid. ii.14.
[3] Ibid. vi.13.
[4] The scarcity of Venetic coins in Britain compared with those of other tribes of Armorica (Brittany and lower Normandy) suggests that the Veneti themselves were carriers rather than merchants (see, for example, *Ordnance Survey Map of Southern Britain in the Iron Age,* Chessington (1962), Introduction, 31).

sent to Gaul had been completed.[1] A Roman magistrate enjoyed something analogous to diplomatic immunity while he
retained office, and this applied to provincial governors as
well as magistrates at Rome. Once he laid down his command
Caesar would both lose his troops and be vulnerable to prosecution on real or trumped-up charges brought by political
opponents. If he was now threatened with recall, then Caesar
certainly was in a difficult position, for with Gaul apparently
pacified it could be said that there was no further reason to
keep Caesar in his command. An extension of the war to
Britain, particularly if it could be argued that this was for the
security of Gaul, would be a good reason for retaining his
commission.

In Gaul, however, the military situation was not entirely a
happy one for Caesar. On the one hand he could hardly afford
not to attack Britain, if it was acting as a refuge for dissident
Gauls and supplying help for Gallic revolts, but on the other
it might prove dangerous to take a large proportion of his
army away from the newly conquered lands to an island from
which it would not be easy to return speedily in the event of
trouble behind him. Nevertheless, it seems likely that Caesar
had decided on an invasion of Britain in time for the beginning
of the campaigning season of 55. He was diverted from this
purpose by news that two German tribes, the Usipetes and
the Tencteri, had been expelled from their homes by the
powerful Suebi and had forced a crossing of the Rhine. Some
of the Gauls were said to be in correspondence with them.

By the time he had dealt ruthlessly with this threat to the
peace of Gaul and followed up with the punitive expedition
across the Rhine, the end of the summer was approaching
and there was little time left for an expedition to Britain.
Ancient armies were rarely able to mount campaigns in winter, even by land, and the transport of men and supplies by
sea was normally halted for long periods of the year. That he
proceeded with an expedition to Britain now rather than

---

[1] The case is made out by C.E. Stevens (*Amer. Journ. Philology*, 59 (1938),
176; *Antiquity*, 21 (1947), 3 f.) and J.P.V.D. Balsdon (*JRS* 29 (1939), 73 and
170 ff.). Both authors argue that this is what L. Domitius was threatening to do
at the beginning of 56 BC (on the basis of Suetonius, *Div. Jul.* xxiv). This is quite
likely, though the text of Suetonius is not specific as to the method of depriving
Caesar of his command that Domitius proposed to use.

waiting for the following season emphasizes the urgency of the operation in his eyes. On the other hand, the fact that he only took a small force in 55 may possibly indicate his uncertainty about conditions in Gaul but more probably stems from a realization on his part that there was no time for more than a reconnaissance and a show of force. Nevertheless such a reconnaissance was probably made worth undertaking immediately by the inability of the merchants who traded with Britain to tell him anything of military value. In particular it is notable that they could not indicate any harbours suitable for large fleets, suggesting that even the Veneti had customarily employed single ships or at the most small flotillas. Caesar was thus facing an unprecedented enterprise if he was to transport a whole Roman army across the Channel, and had good reason to want direct information if a major invasion was to be launched. The lack of coastal information was in fact to prove nearly fatal to the Roman expedition, even on the limited scale undertaken in the first year. But this limited operation had to be carried out: Caesar himself implies that a landing seemed to him a worthwhile precursor for successful large-scale action in a future season, even if it proved to be too late to do anything more.[1] He was determined to go ahead in 55 and, supreme opportunist that he was, would exploit any chances that presented themselves.

The resolve to invade having been formed, an essential preliminary was the discovery of a suitable landing-place. Caesar's method was to send Gaius Volusenus, a military officer for whom he had a high regard, to scout along the English coast with a single ship and report back. This operation took four days and historians have deduced that he coasted along till he discovered open beaches with good anchorage in front in the region of Deal. At this point Volusenus may have turned back, for it is a feature of both of Caesar's campaigns that he did not use the great natural harbour that once lay protected by the isle of Thanet.[2] This harbour was to prove perfect for the invasion fleet of Claudius and it has been stated categorically that the failure to find the port of Richborough was

[1] Caesar, op.cit. iv. 20.
[2] Cf. S.C. Hawkes in Barry Cunliffe (ed.), *Fifth Report on the Excavations of the Roman Fort at Richborough, Kent* (1968), 224 ff.

the major blunder committed by Caesar. However, though our knowledge of sea-level and coastline changes is at present fragmentary, it is sufficient to make one hesitate before saying that a harbour suitable for a large fleet in the mid first century AD was necessarily as good a hundred years earlier. It is enough to say that Caesar did not use Richborough, without passing judgement on his intelligence service or his assessment of its reports.[1]

In the meantime Caesar was concentrating the forces to be used for the expedition and assembling his transports. The fleet was made up of ships which had earlier been engaged in the war against the Veneti and apparently also some Gallic vessels commandeered from the coastal tribes. Altogether about eighty transports and a number of warships were assembled, probably at Boulogne, and a further eighteen transports, detained by a contrary wind, loaded cavalry at another port which seems to have been Ambleteuse. The main force consisted of two legions, Roman regulars, and some native auxiliary troops, sufficient for a powerful reconnaissance but hardly intended for serious conquest.

These preparations, however, seemed formidable enough from the other side of the Channel. Several tribes in Britain sent envoys to Caesar offering submission. Caesar accepted their offers and sent back with them a Gaul named Commius. The latter he had made king of the Gallic Atrebates and commanded great respect not only with Caesar himself but also in Britain. Commius was dispatched with orders to contact as many tribes as possible and, by spreading the news of the impending Roman arrival, to encourage adherence to the Roman side. Neither the Britons nor, in the long run, Commius himself were to prove faithful.

After completing various arrangements in Gaul, Caesar set sail for Britain. The main force crossed the Channel successfully and anchored, waiting for the cavalry transports to come up. They, however, had taken too long over embarkation and their ships were carried back to Gaul by the tide. They were to be prevented by the weather from ever joining Caesar in Britain, and lack of their support was to prove a serious handicap in the campaign. Meanwhile the main body of the

[1] Similarly, we do not know yet if Lympne, subsequently used regularly by the Roman fleet, would have seemed suitable at this time.

fleet was waiting off the cliffs of Dover, watching the Britons assembled on the heights and realizing that this was not a suitable place to force a landing. Caesar took this opportunity to summon the legates (generals commanding the legions) and the military tribunes, their senior subordinates, in order to explain his plans. He impressed upon them the need for immediate reaction to orders. The fact that he delayed revealing his intentions till the fleet was at sea may have been out of regard for security, but more probably because, from Caesar's own words, it seems he did not decide where to land until he had seen the coast at Dover for himself.[1] When he had observed that the cliffs were strongly held, he decided to move along the coast to the less formidable beaches around Deal which had presumably been reported to him by Volusenus. The Britons followed suit on land as soon as they realized the Roman intention.

By the time Caesar was ready to disembark his forces the Britons were in position, not only with their cavalry and chariots but also with the rest of their troops. This opposed landing presented the Romans with grave difficulties. The transports were unable to beach and Caesar had not provided them with assault boats. Faced with the prospect of wading ashore in some depth of water laden down with equipment and in the face of vigorous opposition the Roman troops hesitated. In this emergency Caesar's ingenuity did not desert him. To relieve the pressure he ordered the warships to run aground on the enemy's right flank, thence to harass the Britons with the fire that they could then bring to bear from their archers, slingers, and artillery. The infantry were still holding back when the famous incident of the standard-bearer of the Tenth legion occurred. He, with a shout of 'Jump, comrades, unless you wish to betray our eagle to the enemy: I at any rate intend to do my duty to my country and my commander', promptly leapt from the ship clutching the standard. Thus encouraged, the others in his own vessel followed and the men from the rest did the same. This heroic action did not, however, immediately win the success it deserved: the men were unable to form up correctly in their own units[2] and the Britons were able to surround them as

---

[1] Caesar, op. cit. iv. 23.
[2] This was vital for disciplined manœuvres in battle: hence one reason for the

they disembarked in small groups. Caesar now had the warships' boats and his scout-vessels filled with soldiers, and by sending them to the points where reinforcement was needed gradually brought the situation under control. Immediately the legions were formed up on the beach they charged and routed the Britons at once. This, however, was the point at which the absence of the Roman cavalry first made itself felt: Caesar was unable to follow up his success and turn it into complete victory.[1]

The Britons nevertheless were overwhelmed by their reverse and sent envoys to ask for peace. With them came Commius, bearing the Britons' excuses for arresting him when he had first arrived. Caesar, having first reproached them for opposing him after sending an embassy to Gaul offering friendship, pardoned them but demanded hostages. Some of these the Britons produced immediately, at the same time dispersing their own troops back to their homesteads. 'From all parts', as Caesar says, chiefs were now coming in to his camp suing for peace. For two or three days it looked as if Caesar had achieved his ends with a single battle.

On the fourth day after Caesar's landing the disaster occurred. It was in two stages. First the fleet of transports which was making a second attempt to bring the cavalry to Britain was caught by a violent storm when already in view of Caesar's camp and scattered. All the ships were forced to return to the Continent. The same storm also struck at the fleet which had brought the main body over, and, combined with the exceptionally high tide at full moon—a phenomenon which Caesar says was unknown to the Romans—wreaked havoc among the ships. Not one was left seaworthy. The army was now in a very serious situation. They had brought no stores with them for winter, the intention having been to return to Gaul, and, perhaps even more frightening to the Romans, they were now isolated beyond the limits of the known world. The Britons reacted immediately. The chiefs in Caesar's camp could see how small his army was, they realized the magnitude of the

importance attached in the Roman army to the legion's eagle and other unit standards that allowed men to rally to their proper stations on the field.
[1] The advantage of a victory in battle was often lost through inability to follow it up: thus Agricola was unable to prevent large numbers of the enemy melting into the Highlands at night after his final battle at Mons Graupius.

disaster and they saw a possibility of finishing with Rome once and for all if they prolonged the war into the winter. They therefore secretly renewed their mutual vows of alliance and slipped away from the camp one by one, recalling their men from home to war.

Caesar seems to have had no direct information of what was going on. He rightly inferred from the cessation of the supply of hostages what was about to happen, but apparently not how soon. By salvaging equipment from the worst-damaged ships and by sending to Gaul for naval supplies he was able to save all but twelve of his vessels. The problem of food supplies he tackled by sending his soldiers out daily to collect corn from the fields of the native farms around, in order to be prepared for anything that might occur. So far there was still an air of peace. The Britons were still working in their fields and coming and going in the Roman camp. The Seventh legion was engaged in cutting corn. Its men were scattered and had laid aside their arms. They were working near a wood and had nearly finished when the Britons came out of the trees in force and took them by surprise. It was only the fact that the dust of battle was visible from the Roman camp, bringing Caesar up in person at the head of a relieving force, that saved the Seventh. Even so, Caesar was able to do no more than relieve the pressure and withdraw his united force to the camp. The Britons, now in good heart, spent the next few days of bad weather in assembling an army from far and wide. Eventually Caesar, assisted now by a very small cavalry contingent which Commius had brought across, was able to bring them successfully to battle in front of the camp. This was normally the paramount aim of a Roman commander fighting a barbarian enemy, since his best hope of securing victory was the use of his armoured and disciplined troops in the dense, hand-to-hand combat for which they were specially trained. On this occasion, however, though the weight of the legions soon overwhelmed the enemy, the pursuit had to be on foot and was once more incapable of clinching the victory.

This time when the Britons came suing for peace Caesar demanded twice the number of hostages and ordered them to be brought to the Continent. He had already decided to sail back as soon as possible in order not to expose his damaged ships to the winter seas, and we may surely assume that he announced his intention of returning the following year since otherwise his demands would have had no force. Apparently the same day, the day of the battle, he took advantage of a favourable wind and crossed the Channel with his whole army.

This was little less than a precipitate withdrawal and typifies the whole campaign. In the first place Volusenus had failed to find better havens and in the second Caesar had been let down by the officers responsible for embarking the cavalry, but thereafter the mistakes were all his own. He deserves credit for not glossing them over. However, despite them, his dispatches must have been impressive for the senate decreed a quite exceptional period of thanksgiving. He had after all achieved two of his probable objectives. He had made a substantial military impression on public opinion at Rome, and he had seen the Britons and their mode of fighting for himself. He was now in the position to estimate the size of force required for an effective campaign and had learnt the absolute necessity of an adequate cavalry contingent. Yet he does not seem to have learnt the lesson of the disaster to his ships, for he appears to have made no serious attempt to find a safer harbour. Nor had he succeeded in cowing the Britons—only two tribes bothered to send the hostages required. On balance the expedition had been a qualified success, but it needed to be followed up by a much more decisive campaign if any lasting advantage was to be won.

Caesar had made little permanent impression on the Britons in this first campaign and the security of Gaul must have remained a problem. We shall probably never know whether he intended conquest in the second campaign, and if so, of how much of the island. It is possible that he had not made up his mind himself but left the decision to be taken in the light of events in Britain and Gaul. He gives us no statement of his intentions and our inferences can be little more than guesses.

During the winter, while Caesar was in northern Italy and Illyria holding assizes and ordering the affairs of those parts of his command, his legionary legates in Gaul were engaged in building new ships and repairing the old ones. This work was pressed forward so energetically that when Caesar returned he found 600 new transports and 28 warships. The transports were constructed to a special design, low and broad, workable by sail or oar. Caesar had learnt the military lesson of the first landing itself, that it was essential to get his men ashore rapidly and in good order. These new ships could be easily manœuvred and run right on to the beach.

The new expeditionary force was much more formidable than the old. This time Caesar had 5 legions and 2,000 cavalry, a force that could hit hard and follow up its victories. Three legions and a further 2,000 cavalry were left under the command of Titus Labienus to keep Gaul under control. That this latter task was expected to be no sinecure, even before the great rising of the French national hero Vercingetorix, is proved by Caesar's statement that he took most of the Gallic tribal leaders with him to Britain lest there should be a rising in Gaul during his absence,[1] a fear fully justified by the attempted flight of the Gaulish chief Dumnorix from the camp before the expedition left. Dumnorix, leader of the anti-Roman party among the Aedui, one of the most influential tribes, had previously conspired against Caesar. This time he was pursued and cut down.

Despite the fact that sixty of the new ships were prevented from joining the invasion fleet, Caesar eventually sailed with over eight hundred vessels. He tells us that these included some private ships, implying the presence of camp followers. Clearly it was no longer reckoned an expedition of extreme danger beyond the confines of the known world. The safe return of the previous year's expedition and the magnitude of this year's force must have reassured these civilians. Some of these may have intended to trade with the natives or benefit by exploiting the conquered lands, others, one may be sure, meant to live off the Roman soldiery, after the manner of their kind. But there is no need to assume they were all petty adventurers. It was normal practice for a Roman magistrate to be accompanied by a group of respected friends and some of these may have had their own ships, whether for comfort or with an eye to profit. War was expected to produce not only the glory of military success to the victors in the ancient world but also a handsome financial return. The greater the immediate booty, the more substantial the prospects for future exploitation of the conquered lands, the higher the prestige conferred on the general. The historian Tacitus was

---

[1] Caesar, op.cit. v.5: nevertheless, Labienus was left with a relatively small force for the enormous area he had to cover.

later to employ in connection with Britain the memorable and revealing phrase 'the wages of victory', *pretium victoriae*.

After a troublesome crossing the landing was unopposed, apparently being made at a point not far from the previous year's landfall. With a confidence surprising after the events of the year before, Caesar left his ships at anchor and marched by night inland. After a skirmish at a river, probably the Stour, the Britons withdrew into a fortress in a thick wood, perhaps Bigbury, near Canterbury. The entrances were all blocked with felled trees. The men of the Seventh piled earth against the defences and, locking their shields over their heads in the classic 'tortoise' (*testudo*), took the place by storm with only a few casualties. The Britons fled from the wood, but Caesar forbore to pursue, wishing to fortify his camp.

The next morning Caesar had already sent out a mixed force of cavalry and infantry in three columns to pursue the enemy when he received serious news from Quintus Atrius, commanding the base camp. Once again a storm had struck the fleet in an unprotected roadstead, causing the ships to drag their anchors and run foul of one another. Caesar immediately called off the pursuit and returned to the coast where he found forty of the ships hopelessly damaged and the rest in a poor state. He took vigorous measures to have as many as possible repaired and sent to Labienus with orders to build more. At the same time he decided to beach all the ships and to enclose them together with the camp in a single fortification.[1] This proved to be a major undertaking, occupying the troops day and night for ten days. Such a serious break in the campaign encouraged the Britons, so that when Caesar returned to his former marching camp he found a much larger British force assembled under a new leader. This is the point at which Cassivellaunus, king of the Catuvellauni, enters the story. The Catuvellauni seem to have been the most energetic and powerful of the southern tribes and were now settled in Hertfordshire perhaps already pursuing a policy of all-round aggression against their neighbours. That the Britons appointed the king as their leader by common consent shows how

---

[1] This site has not yet been found and may have been lost because of subsequent coastal change. However it is strange that so far none of Caesar's temporary camps inland has been identified, unlike the large numbers known from later Roman campaigns.

alarmed they were by Caesar, and this appointment was to prove only a temporary intermission in the history of Catuvellaunian expansion at the expense of other Britons.

Caesar's first contacts with the new enemy were not too happy. An attack on the Roman line of march was repulsed successfully but with unnecessary casualties caused by too eager pursuit. This was followed by a surprise attack on Caesar's troops as they were fortifying their marching camp. The action was fought in full view of the Roman camp and was disturbing. The first assault pushed in the outposts that Caesar had stationed at the edge of the woods. The first cohorts[1] of two legions sent to their relief were unable to join up and the enemy escaped between them, the legionaries being too startled to take effective action. Further cohorts were thrown in, but their heavy armour and their unwillingness to break ranks made them unsuitable for dealing with this mobile enemy who fought in open order and with frequent feigned retreats. Caesar's Gallic cavalry, too, was no match for the British charioteers, who could dismount and fight as infantry when they had drawn the Gauls away from the legions. In the end the Britons pulled back, but they had proved how effective they could be under a good commander.

Caesar was not slow to learn the lesson of this engagement. The next day he did not allow a small force to be detached but sent out three whole legions and all his cavalry on a foraging expedition. This tempted the Britons into an attack on this major force which was to prove a turning-point in the war. As on many other occasions, a less disciplined enemy made the fatal mistake of taking on in pitched battle a good Roman army that was expecting attack. Though the British thrust penetrated as far as the standards of the legions, it was repelled vigorously by the legionaries who pressed hard on the heels of the retreating enemy. Emboldened by the sturdy support of the legions the cavalry charged and shattered the resistance of the Britons. A great many were killed in the rout and the rest were unable to halt their chariots to make a

---

[1] The Roman legion was divided into ten cohorts, each made up of six centuries or companies normally of 80 men, and by Caesar's time in regular use as a compact tactical unit in the field. The term also came to be used for a regiment of auxiliary infantry, a unit of approximately the same size. The first cohort of a legion was double-sized.

stand. The defeat broke the British confederacy under Cassivellaunus and the contingents from the various tribes who had joined him dispersed. The Britons were never again to oppose Caesar with their full strength.

The country was now clear of enemy forces as far as the Thames, where the Britons next made a stand. Caesar states that the river was only fordable at one point. There has been much discussion of the whereabouts of this ford and opinion has generally come down in favour of Brentford, but the place where Caesar forced the passage is in fact unknown. Despite a palisade on the British side, heavily manned, and the report of stakes concealed in the river-bed, the Roman troops, infantry and cavalry together, crossed the river and took the enemy position in one rush, a considerable feat. Once more the Britons were put to flight.

Cassivellaunus now abandoned all hope of winning a pitched battle and disbanded the greater part of his forces, retaining only four thousand charioteers whom he used to harass the line of march. Caesar was forced to draw in his outriders and concentrate on making a desert of everything within reach of the legionaries. It is not clear for what Caesar was heading on this march. It is certain from what he says that he did not yet know the whereabouts of Cassivellaunus' base.[1] It is probable that he hoped to force a surrender by doing the maximum damage and instilling terror into the countryfolk. Cassivellaunus' guerrilla tactics seem to have been fairly effective in limiting this operation and it is likely that Caesar would have achieved little but for one of those lucky diplomatic incidents which often favoured Rome.

A young prince of the Trinovantes of Essex, one of the most powerful of the southern British tribes, had come to Caesar in Gaul as an exile. The Trinovantes were no friends of the Catuvellauni: in the ensuing period they were to be annexed by them; and it seems likely that it was Catuvellaunian pressure which had led to Mandubracius, the prince, being exiled. Roman territory often provided a haven for such political refugees. They were as often used by Rome as pawns in her relations with neighbouring states, sometimes, when it suited their book, as an excuse for direct intervention. The Trinovantes now saw their chance and appealed to Caesar for

[1] Caesar, op.cit. v.21.

help against the Catuvellauni and the return of Mandubracius as king. In exchange for hostages and grain for his troops Caesar sanctioned this arrangement, which had the added advantage of placing a pro-Roman power in Cassivellaunus' rear. This action by the Trinovantes, doubtless linked with the apparent failure of Cassivellaunus' anti-Roman policies, brought a number of other tribes over. These were the Cenimagni, the Segontiaci, the Ancalites, the Bibroci, and the Cassi. None can be certainly identified with tribes known later in Roman Britain, but if the Cenimagni were the Iceni of East Anglia, this may be the beginning of their early pro-Roman policy. Almost certainly these tribes were strongly influenced by fear of the growing power of the Catuvellauni. Their surrender brought Caesar a vital piece of information, the whereabouts of Cassivellaunus' base. It says much for the ability of the British leader to inspire loyalty that this information was not forthcoming till this late stage. Caesar's reaction was to march straight at this stronghold, perhaps Wheathampstead in Hertfordshire (the identification is not universally accepted). He now had something less elusive than guerrilla bands at which to strike. Despite the strong fortifications, Caesar's attack on two sides soon persuaded the defenders to abandon their position by a back entrance. Many Britons were killed or captured and a quantity of cattle was taken.

This was not the only action fought at this time. While these events were going on Cassivellaunus made one last attempt to strike at Caesar. His name was still sufficiently influential to persuade four Kentish kings, Cingetorix, Carvilius, Taximagulus, and Segovax, to make a surprise attack on Caesar's base where his ships lay ashore. The troops in the camp managed to beat this off by a highly successful sortie in which they captured one Lugotorix, a Briton of high birth. Caesar does not make much of this attempt on his base, but there is a possibility, from the fact that he is known to have been on the coast in person at about this time, that he took it rather more seriously than he admits.[1]

This British reverse finally made Cassivellaunus, alarmed

[1] T. Rice Holmes, *Ancient Britain and the Invasions of Julius Caesar*, Oxford (1907), 348f.; Caesar, op.cit. v.22.

that his allies were falling away, decide to sue for peace through Commius. The surprising feature of these events is that Caesar tells us that he accepted these overtures from the enemy because he himself had *already* decided to return to Gaul for the winter lest there should be an uprising there.[1] Caesar had won the war and the whole of the south-east was in his hands, but it was a Pyrrhic victory. It looks as if he would have withdrawn—or at least kept no more than a token force in Britain—whatever the outcome. His terms were moderate: hostages, an annual tribute, and an undertaking not to attack Mandubracius or the Trinovantes. The subsequent history of the Catuvellauni does not suggest that the last promise was kept for long. We do not know if the tribute was paid[2]—the presence of hostages in Roman hands may have ensured it for a limited time—but the real importance of the terms may have been, as we shall later see, the fact that Caesar had been able to dictate them, not their immediate effectiveness.

For Caesar himself, there can be no doubt that it was fortunate he withdrew now. That winter saw the beginnings of the great Gallic revolt which was to involve him in some of the hardest fighting of his military career and threaten not only his conquests but the reputation on which his political survival depended. For Rome it was equally providential, for a total victory by Vercingetorix would not only have wiped out the enormous gains made by Caesar in central and northern Gaul but might well have threatened her hold on the Rhône valley and the Mediterranean coast, the bulk of which had been under Roman domination, if not a fully organized province, for three-quarters of a century and commanded the vital land route to Spain. Indeed, it is difficult to see how Rome's pretensions in north-western Europe could have survived such a tremendous blow to her prestige. Whether Caesar would have withdrawn if he had not scented rebellion in the air is a moot point. The second reason he gives for accepting Cassivellaunus' overtures is not conclusive, for he simply says that the Britons could easily have held out for the short part of the summer still remaining. This might imply

---

[1] Ibid.

[2] It is clear that in Strabo's time, probably not many years later, it was not being paid: Strabo, *Geography*, II.v.8.

that he would have taken his forces back to Gaul anyhow for the winter, or just that they would soon be immobilized in winter quarters in Britain, unable to take offensive action.

Caesar's stated reasons for accepting peace and withdrawing his army do not help us to divine the underlying motives for his campaigns. One may suspect that with modern eyes we are looking too hard for a motive. To Roman observers it may have seemed obvious that the glory to be gained by such a prestigious foray across the Ocean was a perfectly sufficient objective that needed no explaining. It is quite a different matter to try to extract the immediate military, as opposed to political, aims of Caesar in Britain and to judge his achievements against them. If the major intention of the British war was to deter Britons from sending reinforcements to rebellious Gauls, then, in the medium-term at least, he was successful.[1] The British campaigns would thus fall into line with his two German expeditions—the weakening of hostile tribes and the strengthening of friendly ones in consolidation of the conquest of Gaul. If, however, he had in mind the permanent occupation of Britain, then even his friends could only have argued that he had at least pointed the way. But the momentous fact that he had opened up the whole possibility of conquest by demonstrating that it was possible to transport a large Roman army across the dreaded Ocean and defeat the fabled Britons, would have seemed less impressive in the hands of his contemporary political enemies than it was to prove to subsequent generations of Romans. Indeed, if an intention to conquer was known at the time, then for the present the moral victory was Cassivellaunus'. Caesar is perhaps deliberately concealing consciousness of failure when he refrains from saying what he really intended. The senate certainly decreed no thanksgiving for the second campaign, unlike the first, but this may have been due to the influence of his many enemies at Rome rather than to public disappointment at victory apparently thrown away. The writer and politician Cicero may provide a hint of the arguments that could be used in the senate against Caesar. Two occasions in

---

[1] Strabo (op.cit. II.v.8) writing later, under Augustus or Tiberius, said that the Britons were too weak to make expeditions across the Channel. In 58 BC, Caesar's second crossing of the Rhine was partly provoked by German reinforcements being sent into Gaul.

54 he reported having had letters both from Caesar and his own brother Quintus who was serving as an officer in Caesar's expeditionary force.[1] The first time he records that they tell of a complete lack of silver in Britain and no hope of booty except slaves, the second confirms the failure to acquire booty and reports that the army is returning home only with hostages and the imposition of 'tribute', tax exacted from peoples subdued. Nothing is said of the expected slaves in the second report, and it looks very much as if Caesar's expedition had failed to come up to financial expectations that had been widely put about. Oddly enough, the intelligence about lack of silver was wrong: it started to be mined in Britain almost immediately after the Claudian conquest a century later, but not from the parts of Britain penetrated by Caesar. It is interesting, therefore, to speculate whether the belief that Britain was rich in silver was based not on direct information but arose from the circulation of British coins in Gaul, a number of which have been found in modern times. Whatever the origin of the hopes, their disappointment probably served to diminish Caesar's achievements sufficiently where they mattered most.

There is very little doubt, therefore, that profit in cash and kind was very much to the fore among Roman motives for these campaigns in 55 and 54 BC and there is no reason to think Caesar did not share them. His actions in Britain can be interpreted in terms of the probable reaction of almost any leading Roman of the period given the chance of a military success, let alone such a potentially spectacular one. Caesar's later biographer Suetonius emphasizes that in Gaul he missed no opportunity or pretext for war, however dangerous or unjust.[2] What he did in Britain fits his character as a tactical opportunist, but tells us nothing of his deeper intentions here or elsewhere, if indeed he had any.

[1] Cicero, *Letters to Atticus* (*Ad Atticum*), IV.xvi.7; IV.xviii.5.
[2] Suetonius, *Div. Iul.* xxiv.

3

FROM CAESAR TO CLAUDIUS

W HEN we compare our picture of the country Caesar found with the state of knowledge about Britain just before the Claudian invasion a century later, we must be struck by the difference that for the later period it is possible to construct a reasonably complete map of the tribes and to people it with the names of a substantial number of rulers at whose policies we can in some cases make reasonable guesses. In Caesar's account of Britain not many tribes are actually named, and most of those that are named cannot be located. There are, moreover, very few identifiable personalities. By the time of the Claudian invasion many individual tribes can be located and named, however uncertain the boundaries between them may be, and something of their relations with one another can be deduced and discussed.

The apparent clarity of our picture of the Britain that emerged in the period between the invasions must not, however, blind us to the fact that our knowledge rests on foundations that may be radically modified or eroded by future advances in scholarship. It is partly based on the fact that certain of the tribes maintained their identity under Roman rule, as was normal in Roman provincial administration, and so are known from literary sources and inscriptions. This is at best an uncertain guide to the pre-Roman pattern, since the centres of tribes were often shifted by the Romans, boundaries were altered for administrative and political reasons, tribes were divided or amalgamated, even created by the central authorities. This source is a retrospective one and no substitute for contemporary evidence. There is, however, another source of material in the work of recent years on British coinage which, for example, has resulted in the publication of series of maps showing the distribution of coins of different tribes and rulers.[1] This gives us some picture of the

[1] For example, in the introduction to the Ordnance Survey *Map of Southern Britain in the Iron Age*. Subsequent work has cast some doubt on whether coinage was exclusively issued by tribes or their rulers and the means by which they were distributed is uncertain.

area of influence of the various tribes. The basic uncertainty in this form of evidence is that we cannot be sure to what extent the areas of contact represented by spreads of coins correspond to tribal boundaries. Indeed, it has been suggested that the manner in which the densities of particular types of coin diminish with distance from central points indicate distribution not restricted by political boundaries. Moreover, we know little about how coins were used in pre-Roman Britain—whether as the internal currency of a tribe, as a means for inter-state trade, or as precious objects chiefly employed as gifts between princes or offerings to deities. Nevertheless, if we ignore the most peripheral finds, the blocks of coins on a distribution map may produce a blurred aproximation to a tribal picture. It cannot tell us whether this means political power or a spread of influence, but it should indicate where the effective centres of a tribe lay and from which districts its influence spread out to be felt by others.

Much more precise is the information about the changing scene between Caesar and Claudius which can emerge from the study of the successive names that appear on coins and possibly, too, of the adoption of particular coin types by individuall tribes. These political changes had repercussions on the Roman empire: when we find persons appearing in Roman literary sources whose names are recorded on British coins we know for certain that British archaeology is at last emerging from the prehistoric world.

The tribes of Britain between the invasions of Caesar and Claudius may be classified in various ways, none of them entirely satisfactory. Perhaps the simplest is geographical. To a Roman trader or envoy coming from the Continent the peoples with whom he would first come into contact were those of the south and Essex and there is little evidence that many Romans penetrated further. However in this area a considerable amount of Roman material has been found on sites of this period, and it seems likely that Caesar's invasions opened up the country for direct trade. The private persons who accompanied Caesar's second expedition perhaps made good use of their time. Britain was no longer a land beyond the confines of the known world, communications with which were in the sole hands of the Veneti. With that Breton people destroyed, Britain twice penetrated in force by a

Roman army, and the British tribes at least formally constituted as tribute-paying kingdoms or Roman allies, trade and the carrying of trade probably now passed to Romans, to other Gauls, to people from other parts of the Roman world, and perhaps to Britons themselves. Strabo, writing at this time, describes the exports of Britain as grain, cattle, gold, silver, iron, hides, slaves, and hunting-dogs.[1] Some of these commodities must have originated with the inland tribes but the main contact of the Roman world with the Britons still seems to have been with the peoples of the south and east, who probably benefited greatly from the traffic passing through their territories. They themselves acquired pottery, wine or oil, and other items[2] from the Roman empire. In this way the upper classes of southern England were drawn into the cultural orbit of Rome, however inimical they may have felt to Roman power.

From the course of the Roman invasions of Britain it is likely that one route into Britain at this time was through Kent.[3] Caesar considered the people of *Cantium* to be the most civilized of the Britons (*humanissimi*).[4] There is no evidence that in pre-Roman times these people constituted a single tribe. In Caesar's time there were four kings in that area,[5] which might possibly indicate a multiple magistracy, as was sometimes known in Gaul, but more probably means that there were four separate minor kingdoms. The area was strongly under 'Belgic' influence and we shall see it apparently falling under the control of aggressive neighbours.

Moving westward the next group of peoples, for whose organization we have no evidence, was fairly thinly scattered over the area broadly known as the Weald, in south-west Kent, east Sussex, and east Surrey. These people, in their forested land, seem to have escaped conquest or even much

[1] Strabo, *Geogr.* IV.v.2. At first sight this may look an odd list, but all the items were reckoned goods of substantial value in the Roman world. We lack, as usual, any figures from which to estimate the value of the trade overall or the respective importance of the different commodities. Note that the slave trade was active *before* the Roman conquest.

[2] Cf. Strabo, *Geogr.* IV.v.3. which mentions ivory, amber, and glass, but not pottery or its contents, perhaps considered too common to be worth recording.

[3] Cf. Caesar, *Bell. Gall.* v.13.

[4] Ibid. v.14.

[5] Ibid. v.22.

influence from their Belgic neighbours and had a form of society making greater use of hill-forts.

West of the Weald came the kingdom of the Atrebates, occupying west Sussex, west Surrey, Hampshire, Berkshire, and north-east Wiltshire. It was apparently centred on Silchester and Selsey. It had strong connections with the Atrebates of north-western Gaul, of whom Commius had been king under Caesar, and was a fully Belgic state. The connections of the British Atrebates with the Gallic tribe are emphasized by the fact that it is here that Commius is found striking coins after his flight from Gaul.[1]

Proceeding northwards and crossing the Thames a Roman traveller would enter the broad territories of the Catuvellauni, the most powerful of the tribes of southern Britain. They had originally been centred on Hertfordshire, but in the period between the invasions they expanded outwards to dominate Cambridgeshire, Northamptonshire, Bedfordshire, Buckinghamshire, Oxfordshire east of the Cherwell, Middlesex, and north-east Surrey. We shall look at them later in more detail, and we shall see this great 'Belgic'[2] power occupying the lands of the Trinovantes in Essex, which they had sworn to Caesar not to do. Their coins appear in Kent and they seem to have gained some sort of influence over the northern part of the Atrebatic kingdom. Their ascendancy has also been detected in the territory of the Dobunni which lay west of the Catuvellaunian realm proper in west Oxfordshire, Gloucestershire, north Somerset, Avon, parts of Hereford and Worcester and Warwickshire. The Dobunni were essentially a non-Belgic people, organized round an impressive series of hill-forts, but showing considerable signs of Belgic influence.

Across their other frontiers, too, the Catuvellauni had substantial cultural, if not political, influence. To the north lay the Coritani, based on Leicester and Old Sleaford, and inhabiting Leicestershire, Nottinghamshire, Lincolnshire, and perhaps part of South Yorkshire. An interesting feature of their coinage is that it was regularly struck by two rulers at once, and at one time by three, apparently colleagues. Another, and at least later monarchic, state was situated to the

[1] Frontinus, *Strategemata*, II.xiii.11.
[2] The Catuvellauni are among those peoples about whose Belgic label there is disagreement.

east of the Coritani and separated from them by the practically uninhabited Fenland.[1] This was the tribe of the Iceni of Norfolk and north-west Suffolk who were to play an important part in the early history of Roman Britain. The true extent of the political power of the Catuvellauni cannot be known, but it is certain that none of these varied peoples could ignore them.

Turning now to the tribes beyond Catuvellaunian influence we come first to the Durotriges of Dorset. They had no recognizable centre, unless perhaps the mint at Hengistbury Head is an indication, but display a quite unusual density of powerful hill-forts which were to be the scene of stubborn resistance against the Romans. The impression here is of a number of fiercely independent groups or baronies rather than a closely unified state. The territory extended into south Wiltshire and south Somerset, where they met the Dobunni, and on the west they were bordered by the Dumnonii along a line probably represented by the River Exe.

The Dumnonii were basically a people with strong traditions reaching back unusually unmixed into the Bronze Age. In the eastern half of their territory, Devon west of the Exe, they appear to have used hill-forts of the common type, with some alien elements from further west, but across the Tamar these practically disappear and their place is taken by fortifications whose parallels can most easily be traced in Brittany and Spain.[2] Diodorus Siculus, who wrote after Caesar's campaigns in Britain and before 30 BC (but, it is believed, basing himself on information gathered by Pytheas of Marseilles who sailed to Britain at the end of the fourth century BC) said that the people living around Land's End were friendly to strangers and had become civilized through contact with traders. This situation had grown because of the attraction of the Cornish tin-mines: whether it was still true in Diodorus' own times we have no means of knowing, but in the absence of contrary evidence we may accept that the western Dumnonii were especially influenced by their Continental connections. It seems quite likely that the eastern and western

[1] It has been argued that if the coast of the Wash lay much further south even in Roman times than has previously been thought, then the territory of the Catuvellauni may have extended between them to the sea.

[2] As was pointed out by A.L.F. Rivet, *Town and Country in Roman Britain* (1958), 52.

Dumnonii were rather different in many ways, and there is no obvious tribal centre.

Similarly without a tribal centre were the Cornovii, who chiefly inhabited Shropshire, but also extended into Staffordshire, Cheshire, Clwyd, and the eastern part of Powys. As in the country of the Durotriges, also without a clear centre, there were many hill-forts, though the cultural affinities of the people remain uncertain.[1] West of the Cornovii and the Dobunni lay the wild country of Wales. Tribal boundaries here are, if anything, more uncertain than in England, but broadly speaking the Deceangli occupied the extreme north, comprising north-west and north-east Clwyd and northern Gwynedd; the Ordovices were chiefly situated in southern Gwynedd; the Demetae spread over south-western Dyfed; and the Silures were settled in the Glamorgans and Gwent and perhaps extended into southern Powys. Hill-forts are fairly common throughout most of Wales, and in the territories of the southern tribes, the Demetae and the Silures, styles of fortification show affinities with south-west England.

The whole of the north of England except Humberside was occupied by a people known as the Brigantes. It has generally been assumed that this must have been a federation rather than a single tribe. However, the known existence of factions among the Brigantes at a later date is no evidence for this, for such political troubles are known in other tribes in Britain and Gaul. Subdivisions going back to pre-Roman times do seem to be recorded on the northern fringe in Northumberland, where there is a Roman inscription recording the *curia Textoverdorum*. This may refer to the Celtic *corie*, a host or tribe.[2] Perhaps a more certain instance of this sort of subdivision is preserved in a name which appears in the Ravenna Cosmography, perhaps for Corbridge—*Corielopocarium*. The Brigantes had few hill-forts and their settlements are mostly in the form of small hill crofts. Despite the existence of the vast earthworks at Stanwick in North Yorkshire there is no obvious pre-Roman centre, for the greater part of those earthworks may have been thrown up in the last stages

[1] The fact that in Roman times (not particularly early) the centre was adjacent to the hill-fort of the Wrekin and seems to derive its name therefrom does not prove that the pre-Roman Cornovii had a single predominant centre.

[2] *CIL* VII, 712 (= *RIB* 1695, where an alternative explanation is offered). For the theory see C.E. Stevens, *Arch. Ael.* 4th ser. 11 (1934), 138 ff.

of the resistance against the Romans.[1] The absence of hill-
forts cannot be taken to indicate a people that had reached
the sophisticated organization of the Belgic states which similarly lack them. In fact they do not seem for the most part
to have reached the hill-fort stage or perhaps found them unnecessary for political or social reasons.

By comparison the very different people of Humberside,
the Parisi, were insignificant in the extent of their territory,
but there is some evidence that their rather more advanced
culture had an effect on their massive neighbours. How this
area was characterized by an intrusion of La Tène people
from the fifth century BC has been already described, with
the distinctive marks of chariot-burials and barrows with
square-plan ditches. However in the western part of the area
there appear probably from the late first century BC sings
of a new intrusion characterized by graves containing swords.
This is the so-called 'North Grimthorpe Culture'. These two
elements presumably went to make up the historical tribe of
the Parisi. There is again no certain centre, and it has been
suggested from the Celtic name of Brough-on-Humber in the
Roman period[2] that the area was divided into four sections.

Of the tribes and political divisions of Scotland and north
Northumberland this is not the place to speak, for there is no
known direct Roman contact with the peoples beyond the
Brigantes for forty years after the Claudian invasion. As far
as the areas eventually conquered by Rome are concerned,
their state of development was in some ways parallel to that
of the Brigantes—a basically Bronze Age culture with some
Iron Age features, notably, in the Scottish case, hill-forts.

The literary evidence for the political history of Britain in
this period and its relations with the Roman world consists of
tantalizingly brief references in a number of authors, some
contemporary, others writing considerably later but presumably drawing on earlier sources. The coin evidence fills some
of this in with further names of rulers otherwise unattested
and confirms some of those already known from literature.
As political evidence it has to be used with considerable caution, though it can sometimes reasonably be suspected that

---

[1] Doubts have recently been cast on the interpretation advanced by Sir Mortimer Wheeler.

[2] *Petuaria* from the British *petuario-* meaning 'fourth'.

the coins of one ruler have superseded those of another.

For the period immediately after Caesar's second campaign the coins do not display a clear pattern and this probably reflects confused conditions. We do not know how long Cassivellaunus remained ruling the Catuvellauni, Mandubracius the Trinovantes, or the four kings their lands in Kent. The first move for which we have any evidence is that in 52 BC Commius the Atrebatian fell out with Caesar and led a powerful contingent to join the forces of Vercingetorix. Efforts were made to capture or murder him, but he escaped to Britain. The appearance of coins struck by him among the British Atrebates strongly suggests he became their king, though whether by invitation or war we do not know. There is more certainty about his son Tincommius, who undoubtedly held the Atrebatic throne subsequently. The latter's reign seems to go down to the end of the century or a little beyond (when his coins are displaced by those of Eppillus). It is probably he who appears as the enigmatic *Tim* . . . who is recorded as a suppliant king from Britain in Augustus' biographical and self-laudatory account of his own reign.[1]

In the other kingdoms of south-east Britain we have only hints of complicated political events taking place in the course of the latter part of the first century BC. Cassivellaunus' powerful kingdom came, perhaps around 15 BC, into the hand of one Tasciovanus. The latter's coinage is widespread, not only in the area already described as the territory of the Catuvellauni, but also beyond, particularly in Essex, where it has been found apparently contemporaneously with a ruler named Addedomaros, possibly suggesting some sort of Catuvellaunian overlordship, or perhaps close economic, dynastic, or diplomatic links. In the same period a king named Dumnovellaunus appears prominently in Kent, though there were other rulers there as well, continuing the tradition of Caesar's day. Around the end of the century coins of Dumnovellaunus appear also in Essex, where he may have held land like a medieval king in another kingdom than his own, or actually supplanted Addedomaros. His coinage disappears around the end of the century, apparently at the same time as Tincommius', and it is a reasonable assumption

---

[1] *Res Gestae*, xxxii.

that he was the Dumnobellaunus or Domnoellaunos who is named as a second suppliant British king in the Augustan record.

Roman policy towards Britain in this period falls into three distinct phases. For twenty years after Caesar's second expedition no action seems to have been taken to follow up his expeditions. Yet in the nine years from 34 BC there were no less than three occasions on which preparations for an invasion proceeded some way before being cancelled. That there were serious intentions seems to be implied for 34, 27, and 26 BC.[1] It was certainly public belief that an expedition was being prepared. The Roman poets persistently spoke of the conquest of Britain as imminent or even accomplished.[2]

By 34 it was a very different Roman world from that to which Caesar had returned in 54. In 49 the split between Caesar and the dominant party in the senate, which had eventually won over a reluctant Pompey, the only other Roman general who could challenge Caesar's military reputation, had become irreparable. Caesar's series of overwhelming victories in the subsequent civil war put him into supreme power, with the permanent position of *dictator*, a post previously only used as a very temporary appointment in moments of national emergency. The Roman Republic was effectively dead. Even Caesar's murder in 44 brought only a momentary flicker of life, for renewed civil war put power almost immediately back into the hands of the Caesarian party, with the Roman world divided between the three great magnates, Mark Antony, Lepidus, and Caesar's youthful but utterly ruthless great-nephew Octavian. By the date of 34 BC which we are considering, these had been reduced to two, with Octavian commanding the western half of the empire and Antony the east. Octavian's relations with Antony were uneasy. In 37 differences had been patched up, but relations subsequently worsened. Octavian had won so far no real military reputation, and Antony's was uncomfortably brilliant. The reason for the first projected invasion of Britain given by Dio is interesting. He says that Octavian intended to emulate his adoptive father, Caesar. A campaign in Illyricum went

---

[1] Dio, XLIX.xxxviii.2; LIII. xxii.5; LIII. xxv.2.
[2] e.g. Virgil, *Georgics,* i.30; Horace, *Odes,* I.xxxv.29–30; and perhaps Virgil, *Georgics,* iii.25.

very well and he was free to seek further fields for military glory. Despite the fact that he was planning conquests on the Danube, Britain seemed a feasible interlude. However dangerous revolts in Pannonia, Dalmatia, and in North Italy among the Salassi and perhaps other tribes diverted him from this purpose. Relations with Antony, moreover, rapidly worsened, and in 32 erupted into open war. In the great battle of Actium, Antony, deserted by Cleopatra's fleet, was decisively defeated and by the summer of 30 Octavian was the undisputed master of the Roman world.

At this point and until he offered in 27 to lay down all his powers Octavian's position was based on very dubious legal authority. Essentially, and in spite of ingenious pleading on his behalf, it lay in the rights of victory and the absolute loyalty of the troops to their triumphant commander. But, however much they might break the law, the Romans had a deeply rooted need to find legal and constitutional forms for the exercise of authority. Octavian's formal offer to resign power in 27 and his assumption of new authority at the hands of Senate and People was an essential part of his consolidation of his own position and a prerequisite for any return to stability. The Republic was on the surface restored: Octavian himself, henceforth accepting the name Augustus, merely the leading citizen. In practice his concurrent holding of the key offices of state, including the command of practically all the armies, meant that his power was irresistible if he chose to exercise it. Over many aspects of state he held actual legal power, *imperium,* by virtue of the offices he held at a particular time; over any area in which he chose to intervene he held sway because of his personal 'weight' (*auctoritas*)— the respect traditionally given to men of great seniority and reputation in public life. This *auctoritas* could, for example, be used to determine who was elected to public office simply by indicating which candidates he supported, without the necessity to appoint direct, or to rig the elections. The holding of these public offices were required steps in a career that led to the most coveted military and civil posts. On the surface this was no more than the exercise of traditional Republican aristocratic practice. The difference, however, was that there was now one man and one family that held such a position unchallenged. Any ambitious Roman now needed the support of that single family and as the system became ever more pervasive practically every office of consequence came to be occupied by persons who were in effect placemen of the emperor, however both sides liked to dress it up. The position of the imperial family was crowned by the fact that the troops would, again as a logical extension of Republican tradition, still obey Augustus as the victor in war and the heir of Julius Caesar, not in the final event because of the legal authority of the offices he held. This *auctoritas*, therefore, was the central element in his power, each part of it consciously rooted in Republican tradition but adding up to the overwhelming dominance which Republican magnates may have dreamed of but never achieved. From now on there is no doubt that Rome had an emperor, however much constitutionalists might explain it away. It is clear that Augustus came fairly soon to feel sufficiently sure of his own position to risk formally handing back power to the old Republican institutions, secure in the knowledge that no one would seriously use them to challenge him.[1]

By 27, therefore, Augustus was obviously sufficiently free of worries about the Roman state to think about fresh conquests abroad.[2] What, moreover, could better mark the restoration of the Republic than a spectacular victory by its armies—under the supreme command, of course, of its first citizen?[3] Dio gives us no specific reason for this projected British campaign, but we really do not need any more. In the event it was called off, because, according to Dio, not only was Gaul still in an unsettled state but also the Britons seemed likely to propose a treaty. Presumably nothing came of the latter, for in 26 we hear that the Britons had refused to come to terms. What the emperor had been demanding is not recorded—possibly the tribute which had been imposed by Caesar. The campaign was revived, but cancelled again because

---

[1] Augustus took the unofficial title *'Princeps'* to emphasize his public stance that he was 'first citizen' rather than master of the Roman state. The Early Empire is often for this reason referred to as the 'Principate'.

[2] Professor C.M. Wells has argued persuasively that Augustus was a convinced traditional Roman militarist. See Wells, *The German Policy of Augustus,* Oxford (1972), to whose analysis of Roman imperialism and the references to ancient sources on which it is soundly based I am greatly indebted here and elsewhere in this book.

[3] See Note, p. 61 below.

of the further and last revolt of the Salassi, who commanded a vital position in the western Alps, and trouble in the Pyrenees. Henceforth no further plans seem to have been made public in the reign of Augustus for the invasion of Britain.

Somehow into this account of Roman policy towards Britain under Augustus we have to fit Strabo's two notices which are undated. In the first he says that though they could have held Britain the Romans had scorned to do so, because they saw that the Britons were too weak to cross over and harass them and because the cost of holding the country and exacting tribute would be such that the profit would be less than was already brought in by taxes on commerce.[1] It is not clear whether Strabo is referring to Augustus' failure to carry out his invasion or to Caesar's letting Britain slip from his grasp. It may be that he did not think it expedient to be too explicit. The most interesting point in the present context is that Roman dues on traffic with Britain were so profitable. The same point is made in the second passage from Strabo, where he says that the Britons submitted to heavy duties on imports and exports with Gaul, and that if Britain were occupied the tribute would be offset by the cost of the occupying army (there is an interesting if rather wild estimate of one legion and some cavalry) and the customs duties would have to be lowered.[2] In the same passage Strabo tells us that some of the leading men of the Britons had paid court to Augustus and dedicated offerings at Rome on the Capitol—indeed they had practically made the whole island Roman property. Even allowing for substantial exaggeration this suggests the existence of a powerful pro-Roman party in Britain whose influence was widespread. Strabo's Britons at Rome are clearly not fugitives but persons of weight at home. The period is, it would appear, one in which Rome and Britain in general are not overtly hostile, and must then be attributed to a time before 34 BC or after 26.

Though Augustus seems to have made no more plans for warlike intervention in Britain there is a slight hint of some diplomatic activity when he visited Gaul in 16 BC.[3] In an

---

[1] Strabo, II.v.8.
[2] Strabo, IV.v.3.
[3] The point is strongly argued by C.E. Stevens in 'Britain between the Invasions' (below, Note, p. 61).

Ode[1] written probably not before 15 BC Horace seems to list
the Britons among those who 'pay attention to' the emperor,
and it is about this time that Tincommius started to strike
coins of a distinctly Romanizing type. The evidence seems
too thin to talk of any regular treaty, but it seems quite
likely that good relations[2] were established with Tincommius
'son of Commius' despite his family history. If so, it was a
considerable success, and may have achieved much of what
Augustus had been aiming at when he planned to launch an
invasion earlier against the Britons who 'would not come to
terms'.

Although Augustus proudly recorded receiving the two
suppliant British kings, there is no sign that he took any
effective action to replace them on their thrones. Their reception may have approximately coincided with Augustus'
disastrous attempt to press ahead with the conversion of Germany beyond the Rhine into a regular Roman province at
too great a speed for its inhabitants.[3] If successful, this would
have brought the empire permanently up to the Elbe. As it
was, it all ended in AD 9 with the Roman general Quinctilius
Varus' loss of three legions in the infamous disaster of the
Teutoburgerwald. Henceforth Augustus' policy was reversed.
Unlimited expansion was replaced by a decision to consolidate the empire within the boundaries as they existed after
that defeat. The conquest of Britain could have no place in
the new programme. After Augustus' death in AD 14 this
policy was carried on by his successor Tiberius, who treated
it as a sacred trust.[4] In the case of Britain the policy seems to
have brought good relations, since it is recorded that in AD
16 some Roman soldiers cast ashore on the coast of Britain
were returned to the Continent by the British princes.[5] A
quarter of a century was in fact to pass before Rome again
turned her military attention towards Britain.

Why, however, did the Romans have this obsession with
war and conquest? It was certainly in Augustus' immediate

---

[1] Horace, *Odes,* IV.xiv.47–8.
[2] Stevens, op. cit., thinks that Propertius, IV.iii.9, may refer to these negotiations.
[3] See C.M. Wells, op. cit.
[4] Tacitus, *Agr.* xiii.
[5] Tacitus, *Ann.* ii.24.

political interest to concentrate attention on the concepts of
Roman invincibility and its embodiment in himself. But he
illustrated an abiding strand in Roman tradition when he
erected statues of great Roman commanders of the past alongside his own in Rome 'in order that the lives of these men
should be, as it were, a standard which would be required by
their fellow citizens both of himself and of the emperors of
succeeding ages.' Cicero, who had gained the consulship
under the Republic, expressed in his writings and career the
ethics and political aspirations of the ancient aristocratic
circle at Rome into which he had come from a provincial
Italian background and consciously inserted himself. In the
course of a speech he summarized the public face of the
Roman obsession succinctly: 'Glory in war exceeds all other
forms of success: this is the origin of the Roman people's
reputation, this is what ensures our City will have eternal
fame, this has compelled the world to submit to her rule.'[1]
Cicero had studied closely the ways in which personal success
was gained in the political arena he had entered: 'Who can
doubt that for a man who hopes to achieve the consulship
the possession of a military reputation is much more useful
than successful practice at the Bar?' It is, he says, in addition
much more advantageous to have been engaged in enlarging
the bounds of Roman rule (*in propagandis finibus*) than in
administering territories already won (*in regendis*). This order
of priorities is fundamentally important in understanding
Roman actions and the motives behind them.

The desire for military glory and the scramble for office
are features which are not difficult for us to recognize from
our experience of the present and the recent past. Yet behind them in the Roman world was a tradition based on
foundations largely alien to the modern western mind. Central to Roman religion (as we shall examine in more detail
later) was the cult of the family, living and dead, and this was
at its most intense among the oldest senatorial clans. The
holding of the highest office in the state in succeeding generations was an act not only of personal ambition but also of
piety, and the acquisition of military glory shed added lustre
on the family name and did honour to the ancestors by recalling their own achievements and keeping their reputation

[1] Cicero, *Pro Murena,* ix.22.

alive in the public eye. Even those who privately scorned religion and publicly misused it for political ends moved in a society imbued with this tradition, and while they acted in the crudest self-interest could appear to be following the highest path of honour. Under the Late Republic, as we have seen, any method of gaining the desired end had become acceptable; and from those days there was always an uneasy tension between loyalty to reputation and family honour and loyalty to the state. Augustus had hoped to restore stability by encouraging the readoption of the ancient restraints, but this was never more than partially successful at best. The most successful emperors were those who managed to hold the competition under control and harness the energy to the good of the state, but rivalry was never far under the surface. Those emperors who managed to identify themselves with the traditions of the upper class of the day and, as it were, to hold the ring in the competition between the leading contestants for honour were in many ways the most secure, but their own position was itself an object of the same forces of ambition. Loyalty to the state—and the emperor as embodying the state—could never be relied upon above loyalty to self and family.

This basic weakness in Roman society was never overcome, and the more the empire assimilated other peoples and imbued them with its attitudes and ideals the wider this fault extended. In many ways it is surprising Rome did not collapse from within centuries before the actual end of the empire in the west. But there were two factors that undoubtedly sustained her. One was that the overriding spirit of competition was at its worst—or at least most effective—among a relatively small group of people, those in a position to hope for high office or supreme power—in other words chiefly among the senatorial order under the Early Empire, and, as the older nobility was gradually excluded from military careers, among the professional officer-class of the Later Empire. Though the Roman army gained an evil reputation for indiscipline among the ranks, a reputation cultivated by ancient historians mostly drawn from the upper classes, relatively few army revolts actually started with mutinies of ordinary soldiers. Most were generated by dissatisfied middle or senior officers, often by feuding members of the imperial house itself. Troops were certainly still prepared to follow their commanders when someone appealed to their personal loyalties and interests, but for the most part the initiative came from above.

The second factor was the Roman genius for organization. Something in the Roman character enabled them to create systems that continued to work effectively despite the political instability. To understand the Romans it is necessary to draw a distinction between their innate sense of order when they were engaged in any professional activity and their political indiscipline. This explains how they were both able to forge the Roman army into an unparalleled military force by the imposition of strict order in its everyday affairs and to retain acceptance of that discipline by the troops almost without break, yet be prepared to use those troops for personal ends. Similarly the legal system could from time to time be misused shamelessly for political and personal ends, yet the normal processes of justice be maintained by the very same men in the daily round of cases that came before them in the courts. There is no doubt, too, that throughout the empire and over the centuries enormous numbers of men at every level of public and private business carried on a conscientious and reasonably competent administration of the affairs of everyday life. Indeed, from the topmost levels of society downwards there were many who believed that public service was an absolute duty, however bad the current emperor and whatever the depth of corruption among the immediate holders of power. In this they were able to appeal to the better side of the old Republican tradition; and there is no doubt that this contributed greatly to the survival of the empire despite the not infrequent incompetence and occasional criminality of its leading citizens.

While Rome's military attention was diverted elsewhere in the last years of Augustus and during the reign of Tiberius, the political pattern in Britain underwent considerable change. The first sign is the appearance of coins being minted at Colchester by a member of the house of Tasciovanus, named Cunobelinus, better known to most English readers as Shakespeare's Cymbeline. The long struggle between the Catuvellauni and the Trinovantes had evidently ended in victory for the former. Soon afterwards Cunobelinus started striking coins at Verulamium (St. Albans) as well. It is clear that he had achieved a united kingdom, with its centre moved east-wards to Colchester. In the territory held formerly by Commius and Tincommius there seems to have been a complicated series of events in which the family of Tasciovanus again played a part. Eppillus, having apparently supplanted Tincommius, did not last long, but rather surprisingly reappears in Kent alongside a shadowy figure named Iovir. His successor among the Atrebates seems to have been Verica, whose coins have been found over the whole area thought to be Atrebatian. However at some point the coins of Epaticcu, apparently a brother of Cunobelinus, appear in the northern part of the territory of the Atrebates, the district centred on Silchester, near Reading. It seems probable that Catuvellaunian influence had won yet more territory. Nor was Eppillus' new sphere in Kent free from Catuvellaunian penetration, for in due course the coins of Cunobelinus appear there as well.

An interesting feature of the Atrebatian coinage of Eppillus and Verica is the word *REX* which appears on some of it. There seems no reason to accept the theory that this is not the Latin for 'king' but some Celtic word. Its exact significance is another matter. It has been suggested[1] that Eppillus and Verica were the British rulers who dedicated offerings on the Capitol and that the title implies that they were in regular relationship with Rome as 'client-kings', subject to considerable control. This would certainly justify Strabo's description of Britain as virtually Roman, but it is equally possible that Eppillus and Verica were simply adopting Roman fashions. Moreover the fact that written Celtic is extremely rare, even in Gaul—and more or less non-existent in Britain—makes it the more likely that if titles needed to be written they should be translated into Latin. The language in itself need have no political significance. That the title *rex* need not necessarily mean a *client*-king is surely demonstrated by its appearance also on the coinage of Cunobelinus, of whom nobody has ever suggested that he was in any way subject to Rome. The finds from the famous tumulus or burial-mound at Lexden near Colchester show how the rulers of a sometimes strongly anti-Roman state were accepting Roman culture, and there is no reason why the adoption of Latin titles should not have been part of the same movement. Fashion and politics did

[1] C.E. Stevens, op. cit. 340 f.

not necessarily go hand in hand in the ancient world and it is most unsafe to assume that political or religious affiliation can be automatically deduced from style or taste. The Catuvellauni, one may observe, never showed any disinclination to import either *amphorae*, the great jars in which wine was commonly carried, or other luxury items of Roman origin, however far they may have been moving in a direction sure to incur Roman hostility.

A much more substantial basis for hypothesis is offered by a remarkable change in the pattern of *distribution* of goods from the Continent. Prior to Caesar's time the chief port of entry seems to have been Hengistbury Head, but following his destruction of the Veneti and expeditions to Britain this ceases. It is very noticeable that in the period we are now considering the bulk of Roman goods in Britain are found in the 'Catuvellaunian area'.[1] One cannot help wondering whether the origin of this lay in Caesar's friendship with the Trinovantes and support of their king Mandubracius. Was it followed by the transference of a virtual monopoly of the traffic in goods from the Continent from Hengistbury to the south and east, particularly Essex? This might well explain why the resurgent Catuvellauni wanted Colchester enough to risk Roman wrath and why Cunobelinus moved the royal centre of his people there when they had gained it.

The nature of the goods exchanged points to a predominantly aristocratic interest, at least on the part of the Britons. On the Roman side, of course, material goods were much more widely distributed among the classes and even the ownership of slaves was by no means confined to the rich. There is no reason to doubt that private enterprise took the opportunity of profit offered and we may be sure that this included not only individual merchants, some probably in business in quite a modest way, but also those in public office, including the emperors themselves. But we may also suspect that the involvement of the Roman state was not confined to the lucrative operation of taxing the Britons on the passage of goods in both directions. The commodities mentioned by Strabo as being derived from Britain are of

---

[1] See D.P.S. Peacock in D. Hill and M. Jesson (eds.), *The Iron Age and its Hillforts,* Southampton (1971), 172.

two kinds. The first—gold, silver, slaves, and hunting dogs (used not only for the chase but also the arena)—were exactly the sort of spectacularly valuable prizes which a Roman general traditionally flaunted if he brought them back as booty. It is probably going too far to guess they might represent the tribute imposed by Caesar and which we have speculated Augustus may momentarily have managed to revive. Nevertheless they certainly fell into the class of goods particularly attractive to members of the Roman upper classes, led by the imperial family itself. In that sense, the bulk of the trade in these commodities was probably in the end between aristocrats on each side, most likely at the highest level, even though we are quite ignorant of the mechanism of exchange.[1]

It is perfectly possible that some of the objects found in Britain arrived as diplomatic gifts from Rome, and equally that the commodities in the first category above included presents sent to Rome by British leaders. The second category suggests a rather different area of contact between Rome and Britain at the official level. Grain was always a political commodity in the Roman world: control of the grain supply to the capital was at all times politically vital. It seems improbable that any British grain reached Rome, but it is not unreasonable to suspect that—as in later centuries—a major customer was the Roman army. This supposition is strengthened when one adds in the remaining goods in Strabo's list: hides, cattle, and iron, all essential military supplies. It is perhaps not too fanciful to see the Catuvellaunian princes paying for their luxuries at least in part by supplying the procurement agents of the Roman army. Control of the Thames and the east coast estuaries was essential if the Catuvellauni were to have a firm grip on the direct sea route to the Rhine, where Roman forces were massed under Augustus and Tiberius, while expansion into Kent would capture the shortest crossings to Gaul as well. At the same time, we may perhaps detect in the changes in the pattern of agriculture in Belgic Britain to which we have alluded the response of

---

[1] A possibility not to be discounted is that the slave trade mentioned by Strabo represents prisoners taken by the expanding Catuvellauni and sold to Roman merchants. A gang-chain with six neck-fetters, for example, has been found at Lord's Bridge, Cambridgeshire (see Derek Roe, *Prehistory* (1970), 213, fig. 127 for an illustration).

British farmers and landowners to the demands and opportunities of the new market. The wider the Catuvellauni spread their influence in Britain, the more vital reasonable working-relationships between them and Rome must have become, not only to the Roman authorities but also to those Britons who valued the exchange of goods we have examined. By the early years of the first century AD the Catuvellauni may have been in a position to supply or withhold the luxuries or status symbols desired by the leaders of other British tribes more or less at will.

It has been argued that in western Britain there was a strong movement against any form of alignment with Rome, political or cultural. The Durotriges of Dorset were certainly implacable in their hostility at the time of the Claudian campaigns and this may not have been unconnected with a tradition of resentment following a transfer of wealth and power from Hengistbury and its hinterland to the east. The Dobunni, who apparently coalesced as a Belgicized group first in north Wiltshire and south Gloucestershire, later expanded into north-east Somerset and perhaps Hereford. In the latter part of the first century BC the Atrebates had reached their border and their coinage seems to be found parallel with that of Commius and the earlier years of Tincommius. Not later than 30/20 BC they in fact adopted a coin type strikingly similar to that then in use by their Atrebatic neighbours. They failed, however, to follow Tincommius subsequently when he changed to a Romanizing coinage at the time of his putative agreement with Augustus; and it is significant that these coins of Tincommius were themselves apparently being rejected by the independent peoples of Salisbury Plain.

This does not, however, seem to be the end of change among the Dobunni. There may have been an alliance or understanding between the Dobunni and the Catuvellauni when the latter, in the person of Epaticcu, were penetrating the lands of the Atrebates. Bagendon, in Gloucestershire, the centre and mint of the Dobunni, is a fortification of Belgic type and has produced at this period large quantities of Italian, Gaulish, and Gallo-Belgic pottery. The rulers of Bagendon could clearly tap the same sources of supply as the Catuvellauni, and may have received the goods from or through them. There does not yet seem to have been a

powerful direct penetration of the Dobunni by the Catuvellauni, since the coins of Cunobelinus stop short at the
River Cherwell and another Belgic people, establishing itself
in west Oxfordshire, seems to have acted as a buffer between
the two powers. Nevertheless we may have discerned the
beginnings of two tendencies—or factions—among the
Dobunni. In the next stage, from about AD 20/25 the amount
of contact with the Catuvellauni appears to have increased
and the coins of the Dobunni spread over the territory in
west Oxfordshire. The Dobunni were clearly still independent
and presumably on friendly terms with the Catuvellauni,
though now sharing a border with them.

In AD 39/40 an upheaval occurred among the Catuvellauni
which was to draw Britain once more to the attention of
Rome. Suetonius,[1] who describes Cunobelinus as king of the
Britons (rex Britannorum), tells us that the Catuvellaunian
ruler expelled his son Adminius, though we are not told for
what offence. Adminius fled to the Continent with a small
band of followers and surrendered to the Romans. The eccentric emperor Gaius (Caligula) treated this as a famous victory
and wrote a fulsome dispatch which he insisted on being
delivered to a full meeting of the senate. More important, it
may have implanted in his head the idea (and pretext) for an
expedition across the Channel.

It is impossible to disentangle the truth about Gaius'
proposed expedition from the ridicule and invective of the
historians.[2] According to them he assembled his army on the
Channel shore complete with siege equipment, gave the signal
for battle and suddenly ordered the troops to gather sea
shells which were later sent to Rome as spoils of war. There
has been an ingenious attempt to explain the shells as a misunderstanding of the technical term musculi or sappers'
huts.[3] Whatever the truth of the matter it seems quite likely
that the poor state of military discipline at that time may
have had some influence on the decision to call off the

[1] Suetonius, Gaius, xliv. For possible coins of Adminius, see Brit. 7 (1976),
96 ff.
[2] Suetonius, xlvi; Dio, LIX. xxv (Xiphilinus, 166–7).
[3] J.P.V.D. Balsdon, JRS 24 (1934), 18. But would they have been taken to
Rome? This is, however, only found in the later authors and may have been an
embellishment to the story.

attempt. Three years later the next emperor was to have a hard time persuading the troops to embark and they may have been no more enthusiastic in AD 40 than they were in 43. The only concrete mark of the attempt recorded by the ancient writers was the lighthouse which Suetonius says Gaius had erected as a monument of victory, but the real legacy must have been the plans and military preparations for a full-scale operation across the Channel. The presence of troops on the coast of Gaul indicates not only that the necessary planning had been done but that the actual movement of units required to assemble the invasion force had been carried out. From what is known archaeologically of Roman military supply-bases in the first century it is reasonable to suppose that extensive construction work had been completed in Gaul and that there was intense naval activity as preparations were made to transport the troops and supplies. One may speculate that two or three years later, with a more determined emperor on the throne, all this may not yet have been dismantled. The paperwork at least had been done and perhaps the supplies lay ready. Most of all, public attention had been drawn to a venture which had lain dormant for so long. War was of course still thought of in terms of glory and profit: Britain in the first century may have had for many Romans the golden attraction that America held for sixteenth-century Europe.

NOTE

Augustus and Britain, 27 BC. In an early stage of the planning for the campaign of 27 it seems as if it was not intended that the emperor take the field in person, for in the *Panegyricus Messallae*, 147–9 (written before 27 BC) C. Valerius Messalla Corvinus seems to be designated as commander for a British expedition. Horace, *Odes*, L.xxi. 15 may look forward to this campaign. C.E. Stevens, 'Britain between the Invasions', in W.F. Grimes (ed.), *Aspects of Archaeology in Britain and Beyond* (1951), 335 ff., thought that Dio is mistaken in recording *two* campaigns, for 27 and 26, because Augustus was busy in Spain in 26, but there seems no reason why he should not have made contingency plans and preliminary dispositions in case his hands should become free before the end of the campaigning season.

II

THE ROMAN CONQUEST

4

THE CLAUDIAN INVASION

WHILE it is not really true that the Romans acquired their empire in a fit of absent-mindedness, much of it came under their rule as the incidental result of wars whose causes and motives were very varied, or as a consequence of the absorption of foreign peoples in a variety of ways, more or less peaceful, including the bequest of neighbouring kingdoms in the wills of their rulers or becoming involved in nominating princes to their thrones. Most of these processes were illustrated in the history of Roman contact with Britain in the five centuries from Julius Caesar. It has been doubted, with justice, whether Roman emperors could be said to have 'policies' in the modern sense, due to the enormous burden of daily response to immediate problems that fell on them personally. There is little sign that the many efforts made to share the burden of the imperial position made a significant improvement. Indeed, the consequent increase in the complexity of the governmental machine on each occasion it was attempted probably cancelled out the advantages, and the threat to stability caused by splitting power at the top more often than not brought with it even more immediate problems to preoccupy the holders of imperial authority. Nevertheless we shall see, within particular reigns or periods, emperors and their advisers attempting specific objectives, however often they may have been diverted from them by circumstance.

Much more important than 'policy' are the trends that consistently underlie Roman action. These were remarkably persistent through the centuries. Some we have already seen, others need identifying before we can understand much of what Rome and individual Romans did or did not do. We have already seen something of the behaviour of Caesar and Augustus towards the Britons and other foreign peoples and touched on their possible motives. We need now to see them in the context of Rome's general attitude to the world, and what lay behind it in the beliefs and traditions of the Romans about their nation.

Professor C.M. Wells has focused our attention on certain critical passages in Roman literature of the end of the Republic and the Augustan period.[1] Virgil, the poet of Augustan power, makes the supreme Roman god Jupiter declare 'I set upon the Romans bounds neither of space nor of time: I have bestowed upon them empire without limit';[2] and the contemporary historian Livy similarly: 'Go and announce to the Romans . . . that the gods desire my city of Rome shall be the capital of all the countries of the world. To that end they shall cultivate the arts of war and transmit their knowledge to their descendants so that no human power shall be able to resist the military might of Rome.'[3] Virgil hammers the doctrine home in the lines he gives to the father of the legendary founder of Rome:

> Forget not, Roman, that it is your special genius
> to rule the peoples; to impose the ways of peace,
> to spare the defeated, and to crush those proud men
> who will not submit.[4]

There was, as Professor Wells points out, no third condition. If you were a non-Roman people, you were either dependent (*subiecti*) or proud and recalcitrant (*superbi*). The Romans felt they had absolute moral right on their side. This overrode any possible obligations to other peoples. It is this doctrine that explains why, for example, the Romans felt they could treat minor kingdoms in their power ('client kingdoms') exactly as they wished, or why it was entirely permissible to exterminate whole tribes who proved intractable. Later we shall observe the 'ideal' governor of Britain Julius Agricola praised for killing practically all the Ordovices of North Wales.[5] An earlier governor, Ostorius Scapula, intended similar action, it seems, against another Welsh tribe, and even the philosopher-emperor Marcus Aurelius was prepared to destroy the Sarmatians of the Danube. Complete ruthlessness—and, if necessary, unhesitating breaking of faith—were entirely justifiable means to the furthering of

---

[1] Wells, *German Policy*, 3 f.
[2] Virgil, *Aeneid*, i. 278 f.
[3] Livy, I.xvi.7.
[4] Virgil, op. cit. vi. 851 ff.
[5] Tacitus, *Agr.* xviii: *caesaque prope universa gente.*

the divine mission, whether they were applied to barbarians outside the current limits of Roman rule or to rebellious non-Roman communities within it.

The Romans did not recognize that there were areas of the known world where they had no legal or moral right to be and where Roman authority did not run if they could physically enforce it. The gods had given them 'empire without limit' (*imperium sine fine*) and Augustus and the writers of his age expressed in precise form an attitude that had formed long before them and was to run through the history of the Empire. Even when the western empire was failing, we shall see examples of total disregard for non-Romans when it was expedient—even for barbarians within the Roman forces. Indeed, this tradition was to become a serious liability when Rome no longer had the overwhelming military strength to back it up.

In the days of the Late Republic and under the Early Empire, however, there was a good chance of success for any Roman general who sought military glory in foreign lands, and any peoples likely to succumb were considered fair game. There is, indeed, even some evidence that campaigns were sometimes undertaken for as little motive as the training of troops and the testing of commanders for greater operations to come. In the first half of the first century AD, however, Britain was undoubtedly classified as one of the fields in which a major campaign would be required for success and where the reward in terms of glory would be the greater. The prospects in the period immediately following Gaius' abortive project became more and more promising as various events in Britain altered the political situation there. The most important of these changes was set off by the death of Cunobelinus somewhere between 40 and 43.

Despite the latter's expansionist policy and the anti-Roman tradition of his people, there is no evidence that he ever clashed with Rome. The nearest he seems to have come to a quarrel with the Romans was when his own son Adminius took refuge with them, but he was saved from a direct confrontation by the failure of Gaius to follow his plans for invasion through. Under the successors to Cunobelinus, his other two sons Togodumnus and Caratacus, the story was to be different. Togodumnus seems to have succeeded

Cunobelinus in the lands north of the Thames and may have been involved in an extension of Catuvellaunian pre-eminence northwards toward the Humber, though that had perhaps already come in his father's time. For territory controlled by Caratacus we have only one dubious piece of evidence, a single coin from near Guildford.

Further west there were changes among the Dobunni. The early stages are not certain, but by about AD 43 the tribe was divided in two, between a ruler called Bodvoc with a Romanizing coinage in the north-eastern part of the kingdom, stretching from the southern side of the Stroud valley to north-east Gloucestershire and west Oxfordshire, and another ruler called Corio with coinage of native type in Avon and south Gloucestershire. If the Bodunni of Dio[1] are rightly identified with the Dobunni, then the Catuvellauni had gained some sort of control over the tribe. Dio's words may mean that Bodvoc and Corio themselves were Catuvellaunian, or more probably that the Catuvellauni were in some sense their overlords. Whatever the exact truth of the matter, it is clear that this represents an advance from the position in Cunobelinus' day, when the limit seems to have lain on the Cherwell, and probably indicates westward expansion by Togodumnus.

Within the Roman empire, Gaius' increasingly erratic behaviour encouraged conspiracy against him, answered by a reign of terror. Early in AD 41 his brief reign was ended by a plot engineered by army officers and senators, no longer confident that imperial favour offered them a sure basis for success and prosperity and deeply alarmed for their families, their properties, and their lives. For a moment it seemed the Republic might be restored, but the praetorian guard, the élite troops who at this time represented the only major garrison in Rome, elevated to the throne the surprised and for the moment terrified Claudius. The assassinated emperor's uncle was the most unlikely member of the imperial house to succeed to power but possessed the magical Julian name, sole focus of the army's loyalty and hopes since the days of Augustus. The soldiers had now demonstrated with absolute clarity that their allegiance was to the imperial family, not

[1] Dio, LX.xx.2: '. . . part of the Bodunni, who were subjects of the Catuvellauni.'

the Senate and People, and in successive struggles in the subsequent course of Roman history the issue of which contender could most legitimately claim to represent the imperial line was a vital one. Claudius, like some later emperors, found himself having to execute some of those who had murdered his predecessor and put him on the throne, in order to demonstrate his family loyalty and retain the allegiance of the army as a whole. At the same time he set out on a course of reform, to restore stability in the state and to raise the prestige of the imperial family from the low point to which it had sunk. Just to stay alive he needed to establish a reputation as a sound ruler. For continued stability he required the respect that only undeniable success in the most prestigious fields could offer.

Gaius' abandonment of his invasion of Britain must have been fresh in everyone's mind. Moreover further trouble was brewing in Britain, not actually in Catuvellaunian territory though possibly due to Catuvellaunian intervention. It was Tacitus who coined that classic phrase 'divide and rule' which so aptly describes a cornerstone of the Roman system of controlling other peoples, and this gives added edge to his summary of the political character of first-century Britain:[1]

Once the Britons were obedient to kings: now they are torn apart by the warring parties of different leaders. There is, of course, from our point of view nothing more useful than if, when we are facing more than one strong enemy, they do not act in concert. It is very rare that two or more British tribes will come together to repel a common danger. They fight separately and separately are defeated.

In the distant future barbarians acting in concert were to present deadly problems to Rome. In the first century, however, the ball was firmly in Rome's court, and she meant to keep it that way. A fresh outbreak of the endemic strife among the British princes gave an excuse for Claudius to intervene. However, there was more to the matter than that: there was a real threat that Britain would be united under one power, entirely contrary to Roman interests. Dio reports that one 'Bericus' had been expelled from Britain in the course of an 'internal revolt' (the plain meaning of the words),[2] presumably in his own tribe. This is surely the Verica of the

---

[1] Tacitus, *Agr.* xii.   [2] Dio, LX.xix.1: κατὰ στάσιν.

Atrebatic coins. It looks as if the anti-Roman party in his kingdom had risen and driven him out, perhaps with the aid or encouragement of Caratacus. Suetonius, while not mentioning Verica by name, tells us that there was uproar in Britain because certain fugitives had not been returned,[1] and it seems probable that this refers to Verica and companions and perhaps to Adminius and his friends as well. It seems clear that Togodumnus and Caratacus had not only by this time gained control of, or were in alliance with, most of the south and east of Britain and part of the west but were also approaching a state of open hostility with Rome. Claudius had every reason to deal with a potential nuisance on his frontier.

It is very probable that the Roman motives for invasion were in fact more than one. Even the ancient authors do not agree exactly. Suetonius tells us that the emperor Claudius wanted to earn the right to a triumph at Rome legitimately by victory in war and not merely by the vote of a fawning senate.[2] Indeed Claudius went so far as to be present at the final victory of the campaign and to enter the enemy capital at Colchester in style. Some people said that his commander in Britain had been told to hang back to allow the emperor to assume command at the last, safe stage. As Dio does credit him with a victory[3] that story is unacceptable, but it emphasizes the emperor's eagerness for a military reputation. Dio's reason for the invasion is rather different from Suetonius'. He says Claudius was persuaded into it by 'Bericus'.[4] Perhaps the emperor did not need much persuading, but the plea from the British exile provided a pretext, pointed to an opportune moment for attack when the Britons were disunited and warned him of the probability of unchallenged Catuvellaunian ascendancy if nothing were done.

The new emperor did not have much time in which to consolidate his precarious position. His reputation was as the buffoon of the imperial family and his elevation could rapidly seem as foolish as it had been unplanned. If he did not gain

---

[1] Suetonius, *Div. Claud.* xvii: *Britanniam . . . tunc tumultuantem ob non redditos transfugas.*

[2] Suetonius, *Div. Claud.* xvii.

[3] Dio, LX.xxi.4.

[4] Ibid. LX.xix.1.

the loyalty of the army and the respect of the Roman people quickly, the temporary relief at the downfall of the dreadful Gaius would turn to disorder and his own death, followed by the elevation of a more promising candidate as emperor.[1] Acutely aware and respectful of Roman tradition, Claudius' personal inclinations and immediate safety were best served by emulation of Julius Caesar and fulfilment of the repeated expectations of Augustus' time. The day had not yet come when the army would look beyond the Julian family for an emperor. It took Nero to destroy its credit finally.

While this was almost certainly the prime motive, there may have been still others we have not yet mentioned. To establish an effective defence against disturbance in Gaul from Britain would have meant stationing a powerful force on the coast of Gaul. This would not only be expensive, it would also upset the delicate balance of power inside the empire by concentrating an undue number of troops in the north-western provinces, making it too easy for a potential rival for the throne to gather military strength. If this new northern frontier force were stationed actually in Britain it might by its conquests pay for itself. More certainly it would be much more difficult for an usurper to bring it back across the Channel to link up with the army on the Rhine. Gaius, it appears, had recently added two new legions to the Rhine garrison.[2] The concentration of too large a number of troops in the hands of provincial governors who might be potential pretenders to the throne became a matter of constant concern to emperors. Indeed, Augustus' deliberate reduction of the number of legions to the absolute minimum must have been as much for political reasons as economic. Yet Tacitus' remark that it was the Year of the Four Emperors (68–9) which revealed that emperors could be made outside Rome implies that it had not yet become generally obvious that the final power to make and unmake emperors lay with the provincial armies. After all, it had been the praetorian guard that had been both one of the sources of the conspiracy against Gaius and the means by which it was carried out. Their presence in Rome itself was the crucial element in putting Claudius on the throne. Claudius' own personal acumen and

[1] Cf. Suetonius, *Div. Claud.* xiii.
[2] See J.P.V.D. Balsdon, *JRS* 24 (1934), 13 ff.

historical research may have made him well aware of the power of the provincial armies, but it may also have made him realise this was not widely recognised.

A further need was money. Gaius had been wildly extravagant, yet there was the necessity to maintain the loyalty of the soldiers with cash. A simple desire for booty from Britain may have played a real part. It is a cardinal difference, as we have seen, between the ancient world and the modern that victory in an external war usually brought a handsome profit to the victors, especially when prisoners could be sold as slaves. Tacitus mentions gold, silver, and other metals as the 'wages of victory' (*pretium victoriae*)[1] and comments on British pearls, though deprecating their quality. It does not matter that we do not know whether the Claudian invasion brought an immediate profit.[2] What is relevant is what Romans at the time *thought* they might gain. As Tacitus says of the pearls: 'I am more inclined to think that the deficiencies are natural than that we are lacking in innate greed or the skill to take them.'[3] It is most unlikely that any serious attempt was made to estimate the probable economic gain to the empire. In Augustus' time it had been thought that conquest of Britain would not be financially worthwhile, but the growing prosperity of Britain and much wider knowledge of the island brought by increased trade may have modified opinions at Rome. The British exiles doubtless exaggerated the wealth of Britain to the emperor, but it is likely that this was only one element in a decision already assured by more immediate concerns.[4]

The army that Claudius assigned to the British expedition was a formidable one. Its commander was Aulus Plautius, who had been consul as far back as AD 29 and was brought from the governorship of the turbulent frontier province of Pannonia, on the middle Danube. Under him were, significantly, some first-rate legionary commanders. These included

---

[1] Tacitus, *Agr.* xii.6.

[2] See ch. 20 below for our lack of economic data; also p. 3 f. for Roman persistence in holding on to Britain. It is irrelevant to Claudius' decision that it soon proved necessary to extend conquest far beyond prosperous lowland Britain or that a large garrison had to be maintained for centuries.

[3] This discussion is partly derived from my earlier notes on the subject in the Open University Course Unit A291, 12, Milton Keynes (1974), 22 ff.

[4] On Claudius' possible motives see also Note p. 98 below.

the future emperor Vespasian, whose elder brother Flavius Sabinus was serving with him, and Gnaeus Hosidius Geta, possibly the same person as an officer who had recently performed with distinction in Mauretania.

The backbone of the force was probably four legions of citizen troops, II Augusta from Strasbourg, XIV Gemina from Mainz, XX Valeria Victrix from Cologne—all from the Rhine frontier—and IX Hispana from Pannonia which may have accompanied Plautius on his journey to take up his new post.[1] Under the Early Empire the commander of a legion, the legionary legate (*legatus legionis*), was a senator who had already held the praetorship at Rome. He was thus a man of considerable seniority. The legionary legates could be of very variable talents—by no means all were primarily military men —but all would have served at an earlier stage in their public careers as staff officers in a legion with the rank of military tribune. These young senatorial tribunes were known as *tribuni laticlavii*, from the broad stripe on the toga of a senator, distinguishing them from the *tribuni angusticlavii*, the 'narrow-striped' military tribunes who were career officers of equestrian status. In the ranks, the legions at this time still contained a very substantial proportion of Italian-born soldiers, though the extension of the franchise to selected individual provincials—even to whole communities—as well as the establishment of citizen colonies at places outside Italy meant that an increasing number of legionaries came from the provinces. The legion had a nominal strength of just over 5,000 men and was divided into ten cohorts, each of 480 men except the first which probably had 800. Each ordinary cohort comprised six centuries of 80 men. The bulk of the legion was infantry—there were a few mounted men who acted as scouts and messengers but not sufficient to make up a substantial cavalry wing. Many of the legionaries were specialists—engineers, architects, masons, clerks, medical staff, and other trades. Except when legions had to be brought up to strength hurriedly in an emergency, these soldiers were

---

[1] Only II Augusta and XX Valeria Victrix are actually attested as taking part in the invasion itself, though all four legions are recorded early in Britain. The fact that three of them were drawn from the Rhine army could suggest that Claudius took this opportunity to break up a group there that had proved difficult to control in the past.

highly trained long-service professionals whose skills were as important to the Roman administration in peace as in war.

The personal equipment of the legionary underwent some evolution during the first century. The simple bronze helmet with a flat neck-guard and a ridge at the front was being replaced by a more elaborate headpiece made partly of iron and designed with better protection for the neck. However a fairly wide range of variation is known, even in infantry armour, and cavalry had their own versions.[1] The leather corselet strengthened with metal was giving way to flexible body armour made of strips of metal which is commonly shown on the best document for the appearance of the Roman army under the Early Empire, the historical reliefs in Rome on Trajan's Column, which chronicle the Dacian campaigns at the beginning of the second century. Under his armour the soldier wore a sleeved tunic. The only protection below the waist was a group of metal-bound thongs which was carried like a sporran. On his feet he wore studded boots like heavy sandals. His shield, generally rectangular and curved to fit the body, was made mostly of wood, but fitted with a metal boss which could be used to throw an enemy off-balance by being thrust into his face. As offensive equipment the legionary carried a pair of javelins, equipped with a soft metal shaft below the head which was designed to bend when the missile stuck in an enemy shield. It could thus not be thrown back, and being difficult to pull out, rendered the shield useless. As his main personal weapon the soldier carried a short stabbing sword. Legionary tactics were based on in-fighting, with closely packed disciplined ranks, where the short sword was more effective than the long slashing weapon used by the Celts. In siege warfare and sometimes in open battle the Roman infantryman was backed up with an assortment of catapults and other missile-throwing machines, some on wheels and fully mobile, and, for attacking towns and other fortified places, with all manner of ingenious devices.

The 'auxiliaries' had originated under the Republic as non-Roman troops, often ill-disciplined, unreliable, and likely to desert. However the acquisition of immense provincial territories as well as the surrender of whole warlike tribes created

---

[1] A major factor is probably the fact that under the Early Empire soldiers had to purchase their own equipment out of their personal savings.

in the days of Caesar and Augustus vast new resources for the regular recruitment of soldiers within the empire. Under Augustus these non-Roman soldiers were organized into regular units, in the main with Roman officers. Many, however, retained their national differences of equipment and mode of fighting. In particular they supplied the Roman army for the first time with satisfactory forces of archers and cavalry, but there were many infantry as well. In Claudius' time they were all organized in units of about 500 men, some entirely mounted, some part and some all on foot. It may have been under Claudius himself that the automatic reward for an honourable career in the auxiliary forces became the grant of Roman citizenship. It had the further consequence that the sons of these men were eligible for service in the legions. The Claudian army for Britain is likely to have had approximately the same number of auxiliaries as legionaries, bringing the total force to about 40,000 men.[1]

A notable product of the discipline of the Roman army was the regularity of its encampments. Each soldier carried two stakes which were used for the palisade inside a ditch which was dug at each overnight stop. Within this the tents were drawn up in orderly form according to a fixed pattern. As the army settled down into regular garrisons these patterns, in elaborated and adapted form, were adopted for the standard fort whose classic playing-card shape evolved in the course of the first century AD. At first it still had tents inside the defences, then it was furnished with wooden buildings and eventually with stone. Even in garrison the troops were sometimes set to dig practice works or to assist the civil authorities with building projects, and on campaign kept up their tradition of digging themselves in at night. This regular practice and experience in construction work made it possible for Roman armies on campaign to construct siege-works, build bridges, and lay roads at a remarkable speed. Josephus describes how in the siege of Jerusalem the 8,580 yards of circumvallation and thirteen forts were completed in three days by four legions.[2]

---

[1] To arrive at this figure involves two assumptions—that there were in fact four legions in the actual invasion (see p. 73 above) and that there was about the same number of auxiliaries. But these are reasonable assumptions.

[2] Josephus, *Bellum Judaicum*, v.508–9; cf. *JRS* 52 (1962), 153.

Both to achieve such operations and to carry out its routine tasks the Roman army evolved a complex organization for stores and transport. This was dramatically demonstrated in Sir Ian Richmond's excavations of the late first-century legionary base at Inchtuthil in Scotland. Three-quarters of a million iron nails were elaborately concealed in a pit in order to deny a possible enemy a source of raw material for weapons when the fortress was closed. The sheer quantity gives some idea of the scale of the stores that could be held in one base. The whole *modus operandi* of the Roman army depended on its capacity to evolve systems for recording and utilizing information, and those in their turn would have been useless but for the theoretical knowledge and practical experience of the long-serving men in the ranks and among the career officers.

On the British side the picture could hardly have been more different. There were no standing armies, only the levies of tribes who might or might not feel inclined to join in a common cause. Since the vast majority of the British troops are likely to have been farmers the needs of agriculture must have made lengthy campaigns almost impossible. Indeed, failure to sow the crops in the expectation of being able to loot Roman granaries was later in the century to reduce Boudicca's rebel supporters to grievous straits.[1] It seems the Britons were seldom able to keep an army in being for very long. It is notable that when Cassivellaunus had been faced with a drawn-out war against Caesar he had dismissed the main body of his men and kept only 4,000 chariots. The latter, aristocratic mobile troops, were professional warriors. They are likely to have been in the main the owners of land rather than workers on it. British chariots still appear in the narrative of the Claudian and later campaigns, but their use may have died out in the course of the second century AD.[2] It is possible that they were more common and convenient in the lowlands, which were quickly overrun by the Romans, than in the more difficult terrain of the north and west. These chariots were light vehicles basically intended for carrying troops rapidly into and out of battle, conferring

[1] Tacitus, *Ann.* xiv.38.
[2] In Gaul they do not seem to have been used at all in Roman times, and their use had apparently ceased long before Caesar's Gallic campaigns.

mobility and causing confusion in the enemy ranks by the panic induced by their rushing horses and hurled missiles. They were not armoured or heavy enough to crash through determined infantry. On the contrary, one of their favourite strategems was the feigned retreat, to draw off small parties of the enemy who could then be tackled by the chariot-borne troops leaping down to fight hand-to-hand.

Apart from the professional charioteers, there was a lack of daily training and an absence of the discipline conferred on the Roman army by drill and a permanent structure of command. This meant that the Britons could not carry out complicated manœuvres in battle. Roman troops could execute pre-arranged movements at the command of the trumpet, could be detached and sent to different parts of the field as required, and could operate either *en masse* or as trained and resourceful individuals. A British commander had to rely upon the success of a relatively simple original plan—he had little chance of carrying out alternatives if the needs of the moment seemed to demand them.

The equipment of the British warrior was fairly scanty. His basic weapon was the long Celtic sword, designed for fighting in open order where it could be swung effectively. He had no body armour, and, if he was anything like the Gauls and Dacians portrayed on Roman beliefs, he probably usually went into battle dressed only in a pair of loose trousers. From archæological finds it appears that some of the Britons were equipped with helmets and elaborately decorated shields, but these may have been confined to the nobility. Of the cavalry, who appear to have been numerous as in Gaul, we know very little. Their status probably came somewhere between the chariot-owning aristocracy and the infantry. Celtic cavalry served both Caesar and Aulus Plautius extremely well and it seems likely that British horsemen were very similar. The probability is that they too belonged to an upper class that could practice regularly and perhaps supply their own horses. Their prime weakness must have been that large numbers could hardly have assembled together for manœuvres very often. These deficiencies seem very obvious in the British armies: the surprising feature is that they were to present the Romans with so much hard fighting.

This is the more remarkable in that the power now con-

fronting the Britons was much more formidable than in Caesar's day. Then they were admittedly faced by one of history's
great commanders leading an army hardened in battle and
flushed with victory, but his hold on Gaul was precarious and
continued political support at Rome very uncertain. In the
meantime the organization and internal strength of the Roman
empire had made immense strides, despite serious misgovern-
ment at home. Gaul and Germany west of the Rhine were no
longer half-conquered tribal lands watched over by scattered
Roman forces in temporary quarters but organized Roman
provinces, possessing powerful garrisons in permanent bases
on their borders and advanced civil administrations. This had
not been achieved without great efforts. It was not till Augustus' time that the Alpine tribes were finally conquered and
communications with Italy secure, and permanent military
occupation along the Rhine was step by step established.
Serious risings had again occurred among the Gauls and more
were to come. Even the central control of the armies of the
empire, which was perhaps the greatest change since Caesar's
time, had been shaken by major mutinies. However these
were passing disorders. From the Alps to the North Sea,
north-western Europe was now united under Roman rule. A
whole empire could mobilize its resources at a word from the
emperor to launch an invasion across the Channel.

The Roman government now had at its command the administration to support the military operations and to
organize the lands won by military conquest. The system
of provincial administration was already well developed and
a central civil service was evolving out of the imperial household. From the time of Augustus' assumption of power the
emperors had extended what was in origin the normal domestic and estates administration of a great Roman family to
take on more and more public business. This was entirely
natural. Indeed, in this as in so many other aspects, the
emperors never quite lost the tendency to treat the empire
as if it were part of their own private domain. They were
only following on a greater scale the practice of the senatorial
magnates of the Republic, who, as we saw earlier, could command the allegiance not only of their own immediate family
and dependants but vast sectors of the population through
the intricate system of tenancies, patronage, and obligation.

By Claudius' time the emperor's administration needed re-organization: his household was no longer adequate for the task. Claudius himself, through his secretaries, took the process of constructing a full-scale imperial civil service much further than before. It still, however, remained in appearance the administration of a private household. The immense powers wielded by the former slaves who headed the emperor's departments created deep resentment among Romans whose dignity would never have allowed them to take instructions from the freedmen in their own households, yet were now expected to take orders from men of the same class in the emperor's. It took reforms later in the century which largely replaced the freedmen in the top positions with men of the second rank in the state, equestrians or 'knights', who were much more acceptable to the senatorial aristocracy, to turn the Claudian system into something approaching a true civil service. Nevertheless it always retained direct responsibility to the emperor and many of its characteristics derived from its origins in his private household. Yet, while this enshrined some of the weaknesses inherent in the central position of loyalty to an individual and a family, it increasingly put into the hands of the emperors the means to ensure their will was carried out. At the same time it established posts and procedures that enabled continuity of administration by professionals in a way that had hardly been possible under the annual magistracies of the Republic and the *ad hoc* arrangements of the first years of the Empire.

In another way, too, the Roman empire had become more formidably organized, though many would have said at the expense of liberty. As the emperor from the beginning had controlled almost all the armies and most of the principal provincial appointments, his patronage was immense. Progress in a public career for a member of the senatorial order now meant retaining the favour of the emperor: indeed emperors found themselves obliged to control (if by oblique means) election to the magistracies from which the holders of military commands and provincial governorships continued to be drawn. Both at the senatorial and to some extent the equestrian level there was an ordered succession of posts (*cursus honorum*), and under the Early Empire the same men would occupy in turn military and civil appointments, though there was an increasing tendency to specialization according to aptitude and some emperors deliberately kept good men in particular posts well beyond the normal tour of duty. In order to secure the best men or to honour obligations, to reward friends and relatives, or to exert political pressure emperors not only indicated which candidates for office they wished elected but also accelerated the promotion of individuals by waiving age limits, or gave them gifts that raised their private fortunes to the level where they could fulfil the property qualifications. This was a continuous process in which emperors needed constantly to be on the look-out for promising young men who might be raised gradually to provide the next generation of senior officers. In effect, therefore, though they would have strenuously denied it, the vast majority of men in public life with any ambition were clients of the emperor. Under Augustus himself the affront to senatorial dignity was largely contained, partly through the emperor's undeniable personal *auctoritas* and partly through his deliberate pretence at retaining the Republic. The succession of Tiberius to the throne in AD 14 made it clear that the Empire was not a passing phase; and a series of plots and treason trials, not to mention the appalling behaviour of the emperor's favourites, made the powerlessness of the senate only too clear. When in 37 Gaius followed Tiberius, who had at least been a leading military commander and a serious administrator before his distaste for political life drove him into self-imposed seclusion, the youthful emperor's excesses alienated the senatorial class yet further. Nevertheless, the process of developing a career structure in the public service at every level went steadily on and there was apparently no shortage of men to fill the posts.

At first sight this may seem surprising. Though it is clear that very large numbers of holders of public office at all levels were mere placemen, nevertheless it is clear from the surviving literature of the Empire and from what was achieved by it that many of those in public life were men not only of great ability but also of personal dignity and self-awareness of the role they played. Some, indeed, were never reconciled to the existence of the emperors, some spoke out against the system and from time to time paid the extreme penalty for it, but even these were not entirely inhibited from following

a public career. We have already noted the overriding importance of family honour and we shall later look at the
philosophical and religious concepts behind the notion of service to the state. There is, however, another very strong element in the Roman character which it is important to understand. From the letters they wrote one another and from
Latin poetry it is clear that the Roman upper classes set great
store on the opportunity to cultivate the respectable arts in
dignified leisure (*otium cum dignitate*). Yet, at the same
time, they were driven by a restless urge to activity in both
private and public affairs (*negotium*). This tension permeated
the Roman way of life and helps to explain why even those
who could well afford to rest on their laurels were frequently
unable to resist the labours and perils of public affairs, even
under emperors they despised.

Claudius himself—without success—tried to mollify the
senate, but this did not hold him back from accelerating the
process of centralization in government. By the middle of
the first century the Roman state had the essentials of a first-
rate system with which to administer the empire it already
controlled and capable of absorbing new territories as they
were conquered. In Caesar's time this was almost completely
lacking: under Claudius the Britons faced an administrative
machine that could organize and exploit them as soon as they
were militarily subdued.

The potential advantages of incorporating Britain in the
empire were not, however, all on the Roman side. This put a
further, more subtle weapon in the Roman armoury. Across
the Channel the Britons could observe peace taking the place
of tribal warfare and must have known that Gauls who had
co-operated with the Roman government had achieved
wealth, influence, and, in a few cases, high rank in Roman
society.[1] At the more ordinary level, the material comforts of
the Roman way of life were there for all to see, by now being
widely enjoyed by native as well as Roman, and the dazzling
products of Mediterranean art and fashion which were already
entering Britain in small quantities were readily available on
the Continent. Roman policies towards barbarians were based
on the fundamental principle enunciated in Tacitus' 'divide

---

[1] Cf. Appendix IV, pp. 750–1 below.

and rule' but in the case of Britain it was almost superfluous
for the Romans to encourage political divisions among the
princes to ensure the country would not be united against
them. There may well have been more Britons ready to welcome the Romans than there were ordinary Romans keen to
go adventuring in the strange land across the Ocean.

It was indeed on this point that the Roman campaign ran
into trouble at the very outset: the troops refused to embark.
Despite Caesar's expeditions, doubtless better known to the
well-educated senior officers than to the rank-and-file, and
despite the established trade with Britain, the troops felt
they were being sent beyond the known world. Many tales
must have been running through the camp of the terrors of
the Ocean and the mysterious island.[1] Nothing Aulus Plautius
could do would persuade them to move. Eventually he was
forced to send a message to Claudius, probably at Rome, and
await an imperial envoy. If the emperor was indeed at Rome
it could have meant a two-month delay, and it is known that
it was late in the campaigning season before the crossing was
made. The imperial commands came back in the form of the
freedman Narcissus, one of that group who had already risen
very high in the emperor's personal administration. At first
the troops were outraged when Narcissus dared to address
them from the commander's tribunal. Then they saw the
funny side, and greeted him with cries of '*Io, Saturnalia!*',
because at the festival of Saturn it was customary for the
slaves to change clothes with their masters and to give the
orders. Whether it was because they were put into a good
humour by this incident, whether as a result of shame at
having to be persuaded by an ex-slave or out of respect for a
direct communication from the emperor is not clear, but the
troops now obeyed orders without giving further trouble.

We are told that the crossing was made, not without difficulty, in three divisions, in order to make opposition to the
landing less likely.[2] The delay caused by the mutiny was not
entirely disadvantageous, for the Britons, believing now that
the Romans would not come, had failed to keep an army

[1] Gaius may have had exactly the same problem with the army, but his Roman
detractors had no interest in supplying so reasonable an explanation for his
failure.

[2] Dio, LX.xix.4.

waiting on the coast. It seems quite likely that any force they had assembled at the time of the original date for the invasion had by this time dispersed for the harvest. The location of the three landing places, if indeed in the end the divisions landed separately, is not known for certain. One division certainly made its base at Richborough, where the great Claudian camp is a witness to it and where there was a perfect harbour, the factor Caesar had lacked. Another, it now seems likely, landed in the neighbourhood of Chichester, perhaps as has been suggested to link up with friendly native forces in that region. There may well have been elements here loyal to the exiled Verica and hostile to Catuvellaunian influence. The position of the third landing is quite unknown: it may have been a mere feint with actual disembarkation at one of the two other points.

Plautius, once disembarked, had considerable difficulty in making contact with the enemy. In the hope that the Romans would exhaust their supplies in fruitless endeavours the Britons sensibly retreated to swamps and forests and refused to give battle. They were evidently not assembled into a single host, for when Plautius finally succeeded in flushing them out he defeated first a force under Caratacus and then one under Togodumnus. The details are completely obscure, but it is not impossible that this account conceals separate victories in Kent and in Hampshire by two main wings of the Roman army. After these British kings had been put to flight Plautius seems to have received the surrender of a section of the Dobunni, probably by means of envoys,[1] in defiance of their Catuvellaunian overlords and perhaps representing the Romanizing Bodvoc.[2] Immediately after this Plautius established a fort and moved on.

The Britons however were not yet beaten. A substantial force disputed a river crossing, under whose command we do not know. This river was almost certainly the Medway. The battle was the turning-point of the campaign. What further marked this engagement out from the others in the campaign was that it was a two-day affair, a comparative rarity in

[1] Alternatively, it may represent the surrender of a section of the British army in the field.
[2] See Hawkes, in E.M. Clifford, *Bagendon—a Belgic Oppidum*, Cambridge (1961), 69.

ancient warfare indicating that the Britons had committed a substantial and determined force. At first the Britons thought themselves protected by the river and encamped rather carelessly. They were taken by surprise when a unit described as 'Celtic'[1] succeeded in crossing the river and shot down the horses of the British charioteers, causing such chaos that even the fighting men on the chariots were unable to escape. After this initial success Plautius sent across Vespasian and his elder brother Sabinus, his lieutenant. Rather strangely the Britons were again taken by surprise. The reason is probably that Vespasian's men were legionaries and the Britons had not expected such heavily armed troops to make the crossing. There is a note of slight surprise in Dio's account, as if he too could not be sure how they had managed it.

Despite the considerable success of Vespasian's assault, this did not finish the matter. The following day the Britons joined battle again and for a time the outcome was uncertain. The Britons all but captured one of the leading Roman officers, Hosidius Geta. The latter however retaliated by attacking and defeating the Britons so effectively that they broke off the action and retreated towards the Thames. For his outstanding services in this battle Geta was awarded the high honour of triumphal insignia, unusual for one who had not been consul.

The retreating British forces made their way across the Thames, apparently into Essex. At first the Romans had considerable difficulty in following them, but eventually the 'Celtic' auxiliaries again swam across and another detachment made use of a bridge further upstream.[2] Roman troops were therefore able to fall on the Britons from several directions and inflicted substantial losses. This action was not an unqualified success on the Roman side, for in the pursuit they lost a number of men in the marshes.

[1] Dio, LX.xx.2 describes how these men were trained to swim the strongest streams fully armed.

[2] This bridge has caused much discussion. Surprise has been expressed that the Britons should have left it unguarded and elaborate explanations offered. But this implies that it was an existing bridge. Could it not have been a temporary bridge thrown across by the Romans? They were quite accustomed to bridging rivers in the course of campaigns (cf. Caesar, *Bell. Gall.* iv, 17–18). There is no indication in Dio of the length of time these operations took. Caesar managed to construct a semi-permanent bridge across the Rhine in ten days and Plautius may have had plenty of time for a less elaborate structure.

Shortly after this the Britons suffered a grievous blow, for Togodumnus was killed, how or where we do not know. The effect, however, was surprising. It seems to have united the Britons for revenge as nothing had done before. The alleged consequence on the Roman side is puzzling, for Dio tells us that Plautius was so alarmed at this new spirit among the Britons that he halted to guard what he had won and to send for the emperor, as he had been instructed to do if he ran into particularly stiff resistance.[1]

This has provoked disbelief among modern historians. The usual reaction has been to explain it by saying that Claudius wanted to be present at the final stage of the campaign and that Plautius had orders not to make the triumphant entry into the enemy capital which he was now nearing without the presence of his emperor. But this is not what Dio, our chief authority, says.[2] He emphasizes that to accompany the emperor a considerable armament, including elephants, had been made ready for just such a moment. Nor is it entirely out of character for Plautius to ask for assistance in the face of a new combination against his advance. He had already appealed to the emperor for help in the case of the embarkation mutiny, and apart from his own inclinations he may have been under orders not to take too much responsibility upon himself.

After what may have been another delay of two months, and therefore now very late in the campaigning season indeed, Claudius arrived to take direct command of the forces awaiting him near the Thames. Suetonius does his best to play down this personal campaign of Claudius. He describes it as 'of little importance' and says that he fought no battles and suffered no casualties but received a large part of the island into submission.[3] The Jewish historian Josephus, though a younger contemporary of Vespasian, cannot be relied upon when he gives all the credit for the successes in Britain to the latter, stating that Claudius consequently gained his triumph without any effort on his own part.[4] Josephus owed his own life and his prosperity in his later years to the clemency and

---

[1] Dio, LX.xxi.1–2.
[2] Ibid.
[3] Suetonius, *Div. Claud.* xvii.
[4] Josephus, *Bellum Judaicum*, III.i.2.

favour of Vespasian and his family and cannot be regarded as an independent witness, much as Vespasian certainly contributed in Britain. Dio's account is completely different and is clearly based on a different source.[1] He makes Claudius defeat a British army which had assembled at his approach, capture Colchester (Camulodunum), and go on to gain the surrender of other tribes, some by diplomacy and others by force. This is perhaps based on the official account, justifying the splendid triumph which the emperor held on his return to Rome, but Dio adds a further scrap of information which perhaps supports his account of the emperor's part in the war. He tells how against precedent Claudius was hailed as *imperator* several times. It was traditional that a victorious general should be hailed in this way by his troops: he had to win the title by fighting a successful action. The unusual feature was that Claudius received this acclaim several times in one campaign. This indicates that there were in fact a number of incidents that could be represented as victories, probably implying that the campaign involved real fighting and counterbalancing Suetonius' estimate of the importance of the imperial expedition. The contemporary line was undoubtedly to emphasize the magnitude of the gain and the smallness of the price. Of the two triumphal arches voted by the senate to record Claudius' success—one in Gaul and one in Rome—fragments of the inscription on the latter survive. This proclaims it was erected 'by the Roman Senate and People because he had received the surrender of eleven British kings defeated without loss and brought barbarian peoples beyond the Ocean for the first time under the rule of Rome.'[2] This cannot be used to prove that Claudius himself engaged in no serious fighting. While the reference to the absence of loss probably does relate specifically to Claudius' own brief period in Britain, the phrase would have made much greater impact if the emperor were known to have commanded his troops in real action. Indeed, it falls into that category of special praise given to Roman commanders who won victories without losing Roman troops of which we shall encounter further examples, and its

---

[1] Dio, LX.xxi.4–5. Claudius was altogether in Britain for only sixteen days (Ibid. xxiii. 1), but this does not make genuine action in his presence impossible.

[2] *ILS* 216 (*CIL* VI, 920). A tableau of the surrender of the British kings was presented on the Campus Martius in Rome (Suetonius, *Div. Claud.* xxi).

appearance on the monument makes most sense if it were deliberately included in that context.

How much of the organization of the conquered territory was planned by Claudius himself we do not know, though his keen interest in Roman tradition and law make it likely that he laid down guide-lines in some detail. We have the statements of Dio that he disarmed the tribes which had surrendered to him and handed them over to Aulus Plautius,[1] and of Tacitus that under the first two governors the part of Britain nearest to the Continent (*proxima pars Britanniae*) was gradually transformed into a regular province. Writing probably in 97–8 Tacitus says:[2]

The first of the men of consular rank appointed as governor was Aulus Plautius and after him Ostorius Scapula, both excellent at war. Little by little the part nearest (*to the Continent*) was reduced into the usual form of a province, and a colony of military veterans added (*Colchester*). Certain *civitates*[3] were given to Cogidumnus to be king over them. He survived, ever most loyal, to within our own memory. This was in accordance with the ancient and long accepted Roman habit of making even kings instruments for the imposition of servitude.

The formalities by which the conquered territories—or those closest to the Continent—may have been 'reduced into the usual form of a province' (*in formam provinciae*) are worth a little attention for what they could tell us both about Claudius and about Roman provincial organization.

Under the Republic, when the situation in a new province had been sufficiently stabilized its organization was given legal form in a set of statutes, the 'provincial law' or *lex provinciae*. The authorization of such statutes was a privilege that had been reserved to the senate and they were normally prepared by a drafting commission of ten senators. Oddly enough we do not have conclusive evidence that this practice of devising a *lex provinciae* was continued under the Empire (though it is often assumed to have been),[4] but in the case of Britain Claudius' antiquarianism may well have led him to insist on the old procedure even if it had generally fallen into

---

[1] Dio, LX.xxi.5.
[2] Tacitus, *Agr.* xiv.
[3] 'Tribes' or 'native states'—in Roman contexts 'cities' or 'local government units'.
[4] I owe this interesting and important point to a lecture by Mr Mark Hassall.

disuse. We certainly know that the senate formally ratified any agreements made by Claudius or his lieutenants in Britain 'as if they had been undertaken by the Senate and People.'[1] This, and Claudius' other elaborate observations of ancient ritual on his return to Rome, underline his determination to emphasize that he had carved for himself a niche in the edifice of Roman history, in true Republican style. On the other hand, it perhaps also reveals a slight unease about the constitutional propriety of the way arrangements had been made in Britain. There is a hint of retrospective permission, suggesting that, though he had enough senators (among the friends who accompanied him and the senior officers of the expeditionary army) to constitute a senatorial commission if it had been essential, the emperor and his lieutenants had in fact made formal arrangements on an *ad hoc* basis as and when one of them found it expedient.

Whether or not there was ever an all-embracing *lex provinciae* drawn up to cover the organization of Britain, and if so, whatever the means it came into being, there is no doubt that Britain fell generally into line with other provinces. In those provinces directly responsible to the emperor (broadly speaking those with significant military garrisons) the main division under the Early Empire was between local administration on the one side and the imperial administration on the other. The latter was represented by two main arms, the governor himself[2] (in Britain an ex-consul, in deference to the size of its garrison and the importance of the province) with a considerable staff, and the financial secretary (*procurator provinciae*), drawn, unlike the governor, from the equestrian class. The equestrians at this time were strengthening their position as the second tier in the Roman upper class. They had traditionally been men of business as opposed to the land-owning senatorial nobility but were now coming to include many regular army officers, administrators, and the lesser landowners who tended to make up the governing class in the cities of Italy outside Rome and in the provinces. The procurator of an imperial province had his own staff and was directly responsible to the emperor, not the governor, a potent cause of friction within the provincial administration but

[1] Dio, LX.xxiii.6.
[2] The formal title under the Early Empire was *legatus Augusti pro praetore*.

a means by which the emperor could keep his governors under surveillance.

We can deduce something of Claudius' dispositions in Britain, though his curious combination of devotion to Roman tradition with a strong streak of originality make it hazardous to rely too much on analogy. It is not necessary to assume that most of Britain within the area under Roman control was in these early days included in the part 'transformed into a regular province'. There is some evidence that over-hasty imposition of provincial institutions in Germany between the Rhine and the Elbe under Augustus had led to the rising that destroyed Varus' legions and caused the emperor to abandon most of the territory won. Claudius must have been keenly aware of this, if it is indeed true. It is therefore all the more ironic that his pride in the new province (which induced him to add 'Britannicus' to his son's names) determined him to establish an ostentatious capital at Colchester, pointedly replacing the very hub of the Catuvellaunian realm. Just how deliberate an act this was can be judged from the fact that the fort constructed after the victory seems to incorporate the great earthen banks that had screened the entrance to the central part of the native site.[1] It was almost certainly placed there because of the location of the former royal enclosure, and the chief tribal precinct, a symbolic gesture of total victory that can have hardly been lost on the defeated Britons.[2] A few years later the symbol of Roman domination that the new Colchester became was to be a prime cause of the Boudiccan rebellion that nearly swept the Romans from Britain. However it is only fair to put in a reminder that that rebellion, inflamed by intolerable behaviour against the Britons by the colonists and by Roman military and civil officers, occurred under the rule of Claudius' successor Nero and not in his own reign.

It looks as if direct rule from Colchester by no means extended over the whole of the territory brought under Roman

[1] D.R. Wilson, *Brit.* 8 (1977), 185 ff. It is just possible that the fort dates from AD 61 rather than 43, but the earlier date is more likely.

[2] Professor G.D.B. Jones has drawn attention to apparent traces of Roman land division of the Invasion period outside the gate of this fort, suggesting deliberate confiscation and allotment to Romans or their friends of land at the centre of former British power. It had perhaps been Catuvellaunian royal property (as such it would pass straight to the emperor and be in his gift) or sacred ground.

control in these early campaigns. On the other hand, now that we know there was a Claudian legionary fortress as far west as Usk in South Wales we do not have to suppose that permanent occupation was at first confined to the south and east of Britain and co-terminous with the area fairly easily converted into a normal province. Large areas are likely to have remained under military rule for a considerable time.

To the north, the great tribe of the Brigantes showed by their subsequent actions that they considered themselves independent, though they were liable to Roman intervention (as was any state bordering on Roman territories) and may have had some treaty arrangement already. More directly under Rome but perhaps not yet within the jurisdiction of the provincial governor was the kingdom of the Iceni in Norfolk.[1] It is possible that they remained technically outside the province and geographically they were on the fringe with only the sea beyond. However, Augustus had made it clear that Rome considered client kingdoms as part of the empire, whatever they may have thought themselves.[2] Misunderstandings could arise. In AD 47 by attempting to disarm the Iceni the second governor, Ostorius Scapula, was to provoke a serious uprising. We do not know whether Prasutagus, husband of Boudicca, was already king of the Iceni at the time of the Claudian invasion: he may have been established in 47 after the Icenian war was over.[3] Nevertheless the initial friendship of the Iceni was important. Not only were they the immediate northern neighbours of Colchester but they also controlled the important sea routes into the Wash and the lesser estuaries of the Norfolk coast. This meant it was not necessary to tie down to guard these routes large Roman forces who would be better employed in more forward areas or watching the surrendered tribes.

The 'certain tribes' (*quaedam civitates*) that were given to

[1] They were still armed in AD 47 (Tacitus, *Ann.* xii.31) and were therefore not among those that had surrendered to Claudius after being subdued by force of arms, but they may have accepted his diplomacy.

[2] C.M. Wells (*German Policy*, 249n.) draws our attention to Suetonius, *Div. Aug.* xlviii, referring to such allied kingdoms (*reges socii*) as 'integral parts of the empire' (*membra partesque imperii*).

[3] See a study by D.F. Allen (*Brit.* 7 (1976), 276 ff.) of a coin type, possibly of Prasutagus, partly Roman and partly British in style, probably of the period 54–61.

'King Cogidumnus' establish conclusively that the policy of client kingdoms was actively pursued by Claudius in Britain. It is unfortunate that Tacitus does not tell us which *civitates* these were and is rather vague about dates. The whole situation surrounding 'Cogidumnus' is one about which a good deal less is known than is commonly supposed. It will be remembered that Verica of the Atrebates played an important part in the decision to invade. Control of the Southampton area meant commanding another of the major sea routes into Britain. Yet there is no sign of a return of Verica to his domains in Hampshire. By now he was perhaps dead or had served his turn and been discarded in favour of other policies better suited to the times. Victory had been accomplished: reconciliation was desirable. The origins of Cogidumnus—or Cogidubnus, as he has become better known and which I shall for convenience call him—are quite unknown and almost everything about him and his kingdom tantalizingly imprecise.[1] However it seems reasonable to accept provisionally that his realm was centred in the Chichester area, and the discovery of early military structures at Fishbourne and Chichester itself strongly suggests that the object was to secure the loyalty of this vital base area, without tying down troops on surveillance or officers in civil administration in these critical early days of the province's history. This client state, including at least part of the old territory of the Atrebates, will, one assumes, have formed an enclave within the Roman province—certainly as soon as the army started to move westwards, as was clearly intended. It may therefore be guessed that the kingdom was intended to be a fairly short-term arrangement. Indeed, though Tacitus makes it certain that Cogidubnus himself remained loyal for a long time, this does not necessarily imply that the kingdom itself survived equally long. It is consistent with the early and tentative stages of organizing new Roman territory. Even where client kingdoms were more in the nature of buffer states beyond the borders of the empire, the Roman government became increasingly disillusioned with them after the reign of Nero and inclined to replace them with direct rule. Nevertheless, the kingdom of Cogidubnus, however temporary a political

---

[1] See Appendix IV, p. 748 below.

expedient, seems to have had substantial success, probably extending well beyond its own life. The eventual development of a string of fine country houses or 'villas' in this coastal area, quite exceptional for first-century Britain, suggests both an unusual initial impetus and the presence of persons in high favour with the authorities or able to make particular use of the opportunities afforded by the Roman peace. The Roman intention itself was—as we shall see was normal—political and military. The governor was freed from the day-to-day responsibility for part of his territory while he pursued the war, and one may assume the king and his subjects had ample opportunity to profit from the support of the Roman authorities and the markets presented by the transit bases of the Roman army in their territory. We may perhaps detect the hand of this client-state at the town of Silchester, near Reading, where in an early phase we find buildings going up that are in the Roman fashion but no regular street-pattern has been imposed.[1] One guesses that this may have been due to enthusiastic but not entirely sure Romanization under a native princedom: at least it indicates peace. In the meantime, the work of military conquest was progressing.

While Claudius was still in Britain the future emperor Vespasian was campaigning separately westward. Suetonius tells us that he conquered the Isle of Wight, fought thirty battles, subjugated two warlike tribes (*validissimae gentes*) and captured more than twenty native centres (*oppida*).[2] We know that this was partly carried out under Claudius and partly under Aulus Plautius: we do not know whether this campaign had started before Claudius arrived. It has generally been assumed that Vespasian took with him the legion he commanded at the battle of the Medway, but he may have been transferred to a force which had already landed on the Hampshire coast, one of the original three divisions. At any rate, from its later history, it seems likely that the backbone was the Second legion. The 'warlike tribes' pose some problems. It seems certain that one was the Durotriges of Dorset, where

---

[1] G. Boon, *Roman Silchester*, (1957), 66f. Native traditions could die hard. In a town like Dugga in Tunisia the buildings could be Roman (even if displaying native influences in their style of masonry) but the streets remain irregular to the end.

[2] Suetonius, *Div. Vesp.* iv.

there are signs of violent attack at hill-forts such as Maiden Castle, Hod Hill, and Spettisbury Rings; and the presence of forts occupied from this period at Hod Hill, Waddon Hill, and probably Ham Hill suggests that the area remained restive for some years to come.[1] For the second warlike tribe the western part of the Atrebates has been suggested. This seems later to have been formed into the Roman local authority (*civitas*) 'of the Belgae', centred on Winchester. In the pre-Roman period this region appears to have been occupied by a number of small groups which did not form a single tribal unit and there is some reason for thinking them anti-Roman. Their lands may well have been resettled by more reliable elements after their conquest.[2] However they do not sound like one of the *validissimae gentes* of Suetonius and the campaign would have been more satisfactorily rounded off if Vespasian had defeated the Dumnonii of Devon and Cornwall, even if he did not occupy their territory. Now that we know there was a legionary fortress at Exeter occupied in the period c.55–75 and have strong reason to believe its garrison was Vespasian's own legion, II Augusta,[3] it becomes a distinct possibility that his successful war in the west extended well beyond the region previously been assumed to have been its theatre, primarily Wiltshire and Dorset, and that he made an initial penetration far into the south-western peninsula of Devon and Cornwall. The discovery that a permanent fort was constructed at Nanstallon, near Bodmin, between AD 55 and 65[4] makes it clear that Devon and Cornwall were effectively incorporated into the province no later than the reign of Nero. It is therefore a reasonable hypothesis to suppose that Vespasian's thrust westwards in the Invasion period established his wing of the Claudian forces in firm control at least as far west as Exeter before the end of the first governor's

[1] Shapwick, alongside Badbury Rings, seems on the contrary to have been abandoned early. (*Brit.* 7 (1976), 280 ff.).

[2] Vivien Swan has suggested that the immediately post-Conquest pottery of the Oare/Savernake area was made by 'Belgic' potters following the Roman army as it moved westwards (Swan, *Brit.* 6 (1975), 45). Anthony King, in drawing my attention to this reference, raises the question whether a whole community vaguely called the Belgae may not have moved from somewhere further east. The possibility of deliberate resettlement seems worth noting.

[3] See Note, p. 98 below.

[4] *Brit.* 1 (1970), 297 f.; 3 (1972), 56 ff.

tour of duty, even if they had not moved into their new fortress there at that point.

Vespasian's personal success was certainly rated very highly, since, like Hosidius Geta, he too received great rewards at the hands of the emperor, being granted triumphal insignia, elected to two of the priesthoods that ranked at Rome like orders in an honours list, and subsequently in AD 51 advanced to the consulship, thus qualifying his family for inclusion among the leading senatorial houses.[1] It must, indeed, be admitted that Claudius was decidedly lavish with triumphal honours for this his only campaign—granting them even to the senators, some of doubtful loyalty, who had accompanied him—but the case of Vespasian was different. For a man whose origins were equestrian, he had thus by AD 51 already achieved a notable eminence, and although he undoubtedly owed much of his preferment to the favour of the great imperial freedman Narcissus, there can be no question but that his brilliant performance in Britain confirmed Narcissus' judgement of him in the eyes of the emperor and won for Vespasian the respect which was to stand him in good stead years later in the struggle for the throne.

For the operations in other sectors carried out in the four years of Aulus Plautius' governorship after Claudius' departure from Britain we have no literary evidence and have to rely solely upon archaeology. The heart of the former Catuvellaunian kingdom was secured by stationing a legion at Colchester and this was almost certainly the Twentieth.[2] Other forts included one at Verulamium. Thus the centres of the old kingdom were secured.

From its later appearance at Lincoln it seems probable that the Ninth legion operated northwards, and the discovery of a camp of half-legionary size at Longthorpe on the Nene

[1] Suetonius, loc. cit.

[2] Tacitus, *Ann.* xii.32 indicates that when the colony was founded at Colchester in 49 it was intended to take over from the legion the function of surveillance (*subsidium contra rebelles*) of the conquered tribes. The fine tombstone of the centurion Marcus Favonius Facilis at Colchester, almost certainly dating before the Boudiccan rebellion of 60-1 (and apparently associated with a burial with pottery of the period of about 50-60) gives his legion as the Twentieth (*RIB* 200). However it is not at all impossible that he was on temporary duty at the provincial capital after the legion had moved out, and does not in itself prove that the garrison of the original fortress was in fact the Twentieth.

near Peterborough suggests that part of it was stationed on that river, perhaps first prior to entering the territory of the Coritani. It is likely that by the end of Plautius' term of office the Ninth had pushed the frontier up to the Humber or beyond. The discovery of tombstones of men of the Fourteenth at Wroxeter in Shropshire, apparently early in date, suggests that this legion drove westwards through the further parts of the territory of the Catuvellauni and their dependents. Thus by 47 the lowlands of south and east England were under Roman control, either directly garrisoned or in the hands of friendly kings.

The picture of how the main forces of the Roman army in Britain were disposed once the initial battles had been won has been transformed by the discovery in recent years of a dozen legionary bases of approximately half the normal size for a full legion,[1] of which Longthorpe is one. These are very widely scattered, from Great Chesterford near Cambridge, to Lake north of Poole Harbour, to Clyro in Powys on the edge of the Welsh mountains, and as far north as Malton in North Yorkshire. It seems highly likely that the legions were subdivided into large 'vexillations' (detachments) and placed in strategic positions that depended partly on purely military considerations and partly on political and administrative requirements.

One of the dominant concepts in the thinking of modern scholars on Britain in the early years after the invasion is the idea of a 'Fosse Way Frontier', sometimes in the slightly different guise of a 'Severn–Trent' line. The Fosse Way is the major Roman road which runs diagonally across Britain from Topsham in Devon to Leicester and Lincoln. This line can be carried on by the line of the road from Lincoln to the Humber. Romano-British specialists fell into the habit of speaking of it as a deliberate frontier, delimiting the early province more or less from sea to sea. Gradually, however, a realization that there were not only early forts on or near the line but on both sides, led to a shift in thinking towards a broad frontier zone served by a lateral line of communication.[2] Now, however,

[1] S.S. Frere and J.K. St. Joseph, *Brit.* 5 (1974), 1 ff. including an invaluable map on p.7. These 'vexillation fortresses' are probably not all of one date: it is pointed out for example that Great Chesterford is likely to be associated with the Boudiccan revolt.

[2] See, for example, Dudley and Webster, *The Roman Conquest of Britain*

the discovery of more and more forts in the south and Midlands (in particular the vexillation fortresses) combines with
the difficulties of precise dating to make it clear that the
situation is a complicated one. The idea of a linear frontier
is distracting. It is easy to be misled both by modern notions
of national boundaries and by Hadrian's Wall and other physical barriers erected for military purposes by the Romans
but not introduced here for another three-quarters of a century. It may well be that the Fosse Way indicates the general
limit that secure control had reached by about AD 47, but in
essence it is better thought of as a cross-country link that
eventually connected the various lines of military communication radiating from the south-east. One may guess that its
construction and safe operation depended on the presence of
strong forces already well to the north and west of it, as well
as the posts on the line itself. We have already seen that the
political arrangements in the part of Britain to the south and
east of the Fosse Way were at this stage complex and included
client kingdoms as well as the beginnings of the province
proper. It therefore requires too many qualifications to continue to talk of the Fosse Way as a 'frontier' without causing
more confusion than gain in understanding mid first-century
Britain.

Apart from this major matter, there is a further point that
must make us look again at the idea of the Fosse Way being
from the first a link right across Britain. At Cirencester, where
an early fort is known under the later Roman city centre and
where it is possible there was one of the vexillation fortresses,
it has been convincingly demonstrated that the road from the
south coming from Chichester and Silchester and heading towards Gloucester was earlier than the Fosse Way from the
north-east.[1] Moreover the south-western section of the Fosse,
to Bath and Topsham, was a later addition still. Two things

(1965), 117 ff. Since that was written, many forts have been found by aerial
photography or excavation. It must be emphasized that caution should always
be exercised when a site is identified as military by the discovery of odd pieces
of military equipment. In all ages military equipment has tended to go astray,
even when not disposed of quite legitimately as surplus. The same problem will
face us later when we consider the nature of the evidence presented by finds of
Late Roman military equipment in Britain.
    [1] I.D. Margary, *Roman Roads in Britain* (1967), 146 ff.

stand out from the arrangement of roads at Cirencester. One is that there is no need at all to postulate a linear frontier south-west of Cirencester based on the Fosse Way, even if that were true further south. Indeed it would have been superfluous from the earliest time if the Dumnonii were in fact conquered by Vespasian. The second is that the road-builders plainly envisaged heavy traffic to and from the south at Cirencester, the head or terminus of the original section of the Fosse Way. The early routes to the south led variously to the base at Chichester, to Silchester which we have above suggested may have come under the client-king, and to the heavily garrisoned and turbulent territory of the Durotriges. The movements expected at the Cirencester junction must have been communications traffic between the garrisons in Dorset and the forward units, and army supplies coming up from the client-kingdom and its south-coast port. Subse-quently a new road was constructed by extending the Fosse Way for access to the south-west, Exeter and a new sea-haven at Topsham.

At the earliest stage, then, the fort at Cirencester is at the head of a line of communications back to the south coast. Forward of it lies the line of penetration to Gloucester and to Usk. It is joined by the lateral road from Lincoln and Leicester, and finally by the extension south-westwards, to link up with the westward thrust by Vespasian's corps, eventually the legionary base at Exeter, with its own access to the sea on the estuary of the Exe. While, therefore, the Fosse Way should no longer be seen as an early linear frontier, it does represent the spine of a very broad and well-garrisoned band of territory from the Humber to the Severn behind which, by the middle of the first century, the process of reducing the south and east of Britain into provincial form was well under way.

Aulus Plautius had surely earned the rare tribute of a triumphal ovation which he received on his return to Rome by his successful direction of operations and laying the foundations on which this province could be constructed.[1] But we have to remember two things in assessing the extent of Roman achievement at this point. One is that it could very

---

[1] Suetonius, *Div. Claud.* xxiv: the emperor went out from the City to meet him and showed him other extraordinary signs of favour.

nearly all be lost again by Roman stupidity under Nero. The blame for that lay on many more people than the emperor alone, some of them men of considerable experience in the army and government. The other is that the part yet conquered by no means encompassed all of lowland Britain, nor was the eventual development of successful Roman provincial life confined entirely to this section of the island. It would therefore be wrong to give the first governors the credit for conquering all of Britain that would one day respond to Roman rule. But whether the Romans might not better have remained content with what was won under Claudius is quite another matter, one that lies in the profitless historical realm of the 'might have been'.

NOTES

Motives for the Invasion: a geographical theory. One other possible reason not mentioned above has been suggested by some scholars—the widespread belief still common in Tacitus' day that Britain not only lay north of Gaul (which is broadly correct) and west of Germany but also *east* of Spain. This meant that it seemed encompassed by Roman provinces on three sides, with only the ocean on the fourth. This notion might be relevant both to the inconvenience of having a hostile Britain and also to thoughts of neatness and common sense in including it in the empire. However there is no evidence that it had any bearing on Claudius' decisions.

Exeter, II Augusta, and the transfer of legions. Until the discovery of the legionary fortress at Exeter it was commonly assumed that the second-century geographer Ptolemy made a simple error in locating the Second legion at *Isca Dumnoniorum* (Exeter) rather than *Isca Silurum* (Caerleon, in South Wales) where it is well attested later. The legion's presence at Exeter is supported by the appearance of a stamped roofing-tile there (in a layer dated in the region of AD 60: *Brit.* 7 (1976), 278 ff.; 358 ff.). We do not know precisely where Ptolemy's information originated, but it seems likely that it had been accurate but was well out of date by the time he used it. Certainly the legion made at least one move before it finally arrived at Caerleon, where it had long had its main base in Ptolemy's day. As it happens, detachments of the legion are in fact attested in his period on a number of assignments in other parts of the country, but that is a different question from the siting of the principal station of the unit. It is now clear from archaeological evidence that moves from one permanent base to another were often gradual as sections of the new fortress were built. It seems reasonable to surmise that the transfer of individual duties and responsibilities of legions from one part of the province to another were also frequently carried out piecemeal, especially when another legion was not being

brought on to the site vacated but the area turned over to other purposes. We shall probably confuse ourselves, therefore, if we assume
there was necessarily a clean break on a particular site at a particular
date.

5

RESISTANCE AND REVOLT

'AULUS Plautius was the first of the consulars appointed to govern Britain, and immediately after him came Ostorius Scapula, both of them excellent in the art of war: little by little the nearest part of Britain was reduced into the form of a province.'[1] If the later years of Aulus Plautius' governorship seem to be a period of military consolidation within which a new province could be shaped, the period immediately following is marked by violent reaction from the Britons. The Romans were manifestly in Britain to stay: this was not to be a repetition of the expeditions of Caesar. After the initial Roman victories the Britons seem to have been temporarily stunned, allowing the setting up of a regular system of garrisons without apparent resistance. Indeed, one may wonder from subsequent events whether there would have been internal resistance but for Roman policy itself.

The change of governor in 47 was marked by an attack by hostile tribes from outside the conquered territory, thinking to take a new commander by surprise with the onset of winter and the end of the normal campaigning season upon him. Publius Ostorius Scapula,[2] however, was not the man to hesitate in the face of such a situation. He marched at speed at the head of a number of lightly armed cohorts and stamped out all opposition. However he followed this by an action that may have made military sense but showed a lack of political judgement. An attractive emendation of an apparently corrupt text of Tacitus, if correct, gives us the information that Ostorius 'prepared to tame everything this side of the Trent and the Severn'.[3]

While this may in particular refer to the establishment of

[1] Tacitus, *Agr.* xiv.
[2] For Ostorius' governorship see Tacitus, *Ann.* xii. 31–40.
[3] For *castris Avonam (inter) et Sabrinam fluvios* (Tacitus, *Ann.* xii. 31) should probably be read *cis Trisantonam et Sabrinam fluvios*: cf. Dudley and Webster, *Roman Conquest,* 137 ff. This emendation led Collingwood to associate his postulated Fosse Way frontier with Ostorius' operations.

some of the later Claudian forts, it is probable that it also refers to the disarming of tribes within the south and east of Britain that had so far been allowed to keep their weapons and whom the new governor felt to be suspect. The decision may have stemmed from an intention to move more troops forward in preparation for further conquest, but it can be envisaged as part and parcel of the general policy of 'reducing the nearest part of Britain into the form of a province'. It proved a costly mistake.

This is the point at which the Iceni of East Anglia rebelled for the first time, bitterly resenting the governor's action since they had voluntarily acceded to the Roman side. Indeed this may be the actual beginning of that hatred of Rome that later fired the followers of Boudicca, probably already wife of their king. The Iceni rose in revolt and took with them certain neighbouring tribes who are not specified. The Trinovantes were certainly allies of the Iceni subsequently in the much worse upheaval under Boudicca, though at this early stage they may have been inhibited from full participation by the presence of the fortress of the Twentieth legion at Colchester. A hoard of early Roman silver plate found at Hockwold in Icenian territory on the eastern edge of the Fens perhaps reflects some unfortunate Roman officer or official caught up in the rising.[1] The native confederation was defeated by Ostorius after a stiff fight, who once again used auxiliary troops. It has recently been suggested that the battle was at Stonea Camp, on a small natural island in the peat fens near March in Cambridgeshire.[2] The Roman road from Peterborough to Denver known as the Fen Causeway is almost certainly of later date, but even if a forerunner had already existed, the island of Stonea would probably still have been difficult of access in a maze of watercourses and

---

[1] *JRS* 53 (1963), 138.

[2] *Brit.* 5 (1974), 5 f. The hypothesis is that the establishment of the 'vexillation fortress' at Longthorpe may have been in 48 as a direct result of this affair, and that it was not yet in being when the rising broke out, explaining the use of auxiliaries only. However, as suggested below, it may have been chiefly the topography that led Ostorius to choose an auxiliary force. Nevertheless a date of 48-9 for Longthorpe does fit in with the removal of the Twentieth from East Anglia when the colony was founded at Colchester in 49. See *Proc. Camb. Ant. Soc.* 66 (1976), 24 and C.W. Phillips (ed.), *The Fenland in Roman Times* (1970), 218 for references to surface finds of pre-Flavian pottery and an Icenian coin hoard at Stonea Camp.

meres. The use of auxiliaries rather than heavily armed legionaries makes good military sense.

Ostorius had scored an unusual success for a Roman general operating against such an opponent, for he had defeated a British enemy without actually forcing him to fight a large-scale pitched battle in open country or being obliged to employ the full effort of Roman siege tactics and heavy equipment to storm a major fortress. This is the second time we have seen him using light-armed troops, indicating some originality of mind as a soldier. Caesar himself during his second campaign in Britain, harassed and unable to bring the enemy to battle, could only burn settlements along his line of march till he was at last able to discover the crucial British fortress. Three decades after Ostorius, Agricola used extermination as his method of dealing with such a foe. If Ostorius was able to win a decisive victory in such difficult landscape as the southern Fenland by the intelligent use of light-armed troops, then he deserves special credit. Stonea Camp is no massive fortress but protected by treacherous ground and quite unsuited to the sort of attack that Vespasian had mounted against the great hill-forts of the south. On the other hand, Ostorius was to be less successful later in his governorship in using auxiliaries, and it may be that overall it was less a matter of good tactical judgement that guided him in his choice than a reluctance to risk the expensively trained legionaries. The latter not only formed the crucial element in the governor's civil as well as military strength but were also, as Roman citizens, reckoned politically much less expendable than auxiliaries, at this time still mostly non-citizen. Nevertheless, though he may have understood Roman feelings, he had not shown the same acumen in relation to the Iceni. It had been their disarming that had, after all, made the fighting necessary in the first place. Romans had a dangerous propensity for making this sort of mistake, out of an insensitivity to the feelings of other peoples, which obliged them to fight unnecessary wars.[1] Ostorius was to make another error in relation to the Silures that had serious consequences, not least for himself.

---

[1] Hadrian, for example, proposed to turn Jerusalem into a Roman citizen colony glorifying himself and the Roman state gods.

For the moment, however, his victory decided other tribes who had been contemplating rebellion to desist from their enterprise and Ostorius was left free to campaign beyond the borders his army currently held. His first drive was against the Decangi or Deceangli of north-east Wales. He fought no pitched battles but defeated the enemy whenever they tried to harass his column, ravaged their territory and collected extensive quantities of booty. The Roman fortress discovered at Rhyn Park in Shropshire, on the English side of the River Ceiriog opposite Chirk, is at 17½ hectares (42 acres) as large as the permanent legionary fortress at Lincoln and may have been built as the base for his campaign—or it may date from slightly later military activity in this area.[1] At the time of writing there is very little dating evidence from this site, but what pottery there is indicates a mid first-century context. At any rate, Ostorius himself was unable to pursue this profitable operation against the Deceangli further, being recalled by an outbreak of violence among the Brigantes, whose vast territories stretched north from the then limits of the Roman-occupied part of Britain and whose friendship was a prerequisite for its continued peace. With the execution of the few who had taken up arms this revolt subsided, but the existence of an anti-Roman party in what was already amounting to a client-kingdom had now been revealed. The omens were bad for the future, and this was indeed not to be the end of serious trouble from that quarter.

At this point Cunobelinus' pugnacious son Caratacus comes back into the picture, first as a leader among the Silures of South Wales and then a little later, as general commander of the opposition to Rome, in the territory of the Ordovices of central Wales. It is probably due to the defective nature of our written sources that we know nothing certain of his adventures in the years since the invasion, but it has been suggested that the great earthworks known as The Bulwarks on Minchinhampton Common in Gloucestershire represent the stronghold of Caratacus and his followers in the intermediate stage before he joined the Silures. There is some reason for thinking that this was in the territory of the anti-Roman part of the Dobunni, and an intended stand by Caratacus seems quite likely. He cannot have remained there till the end of

[1] *Antiquity,* 51 (1977), 55 ff.; *Brit.* 9 (1978), 436.

Plautius' governorship, since it is almost certain that this district was by that time included in occupied or supervised territory.

The rising of the Silures was hard to deal with, neither harsh nor lenient treatment having any effect. It had important consequences. Tacitus tells us that it required the establishment of 'legionary fortresses' to bring them under control.[1] He also tells us that in order to make this possible a 'colony' of military veterans was established at Colchester, to act as a bulwark against revolt and to familiarize those natives who were friendly with the rules of Roman government.[2] This gives us a date—AD 49—for the foundation of the first Roman *colonia* in Britain and a hint of the major troop movements which accompanied it. It seems likely that now, six years after the invasion, there were many legionaries due for discharge, and the establishment of a colony was an appropriate way of providing for them. Under the Early Empire a *colonia* was a deliberate foundation, all of whose members were Roman citizens, generally time-expired soldiers. It held the highest rank in the hierarchy of provincial cities and, where planted in conquered territory, was the clearest gesture of Roman power. It was frequently accompanied by land-allotments to the colonists, and the provision of these from the lands of a defeated enemy (*agri captivi*) was a simple method. The confiscated royal estates of the house of Cunobelinus will, like all such captured royal domains, have automatically been added to the private property of the emperor. Of itself, this may not have given much offence to the local Trinovantes, who seem to have been taken over by the Catuvellaunian kings not many years earlier. However, that the land settlement was not restricted to these royal estates is suggested by the amount of ill will it was to create among the natives. Indeed, if the Trinovantes were among those unnamed tribes who had recently joined in the revolt of the Iceni, then private properties around Colchester may have been seized in retribution just before the foundation of the colony and we shall see there is reason to think the colonists went on expanding their occupation of tribal lands. Each

---

[1] Tacitus, *Ann.* xii. 32: ... *castrisque legionum premenda* ...
[2] Ibid. *colonia Camulodunum valida veteranorum manu deducitur in agros captivos, subsidium adversus rebellis et imbuendis sociis ad officia legum.*

incident added fuel to the fires of resentment building up in eastern Britain.

We have noted that Tacitus spoke of the establishment of 'legionary fortresses' to quell the Silures. While it was always possible that this was the simple Latin usage of plural for singular, it was more difficult to explain before the discovery of vexillation fortresses and the realization that movement from one legionary base to a new one could be a piecemeal affair.[1] The possibilities now opening up make any firm statements here inappropriate. Further excavation at Clyro, Usk, Gloucester (Kingsholm), and perhaps Cirencester, is obviously relevant, but changes in other areas consequent on these operations under Ostorius and potentially detectable in excavation may well give us yet more information. In particular the movements of the Fourteenth legion towards central Wales remain extremely obscure, and we need to know more about Wroxeter, Leighton, Wall, and perhaps Leicester —and maybe other sites not yet identified.

Central Wales was in fact soon to become a major theatre of war. Caratacus' position among the Britons is interesting. He had no apparent difficulty in switching the war from the lands of the Silures to those of the Ordovices and was joined by all the opponents of Rome. It is clear that he had a supranational authority, in the tradition of Cassivellaunus or Vercingetorix. Doubtless the lustre of being a son of Cunobelinus had much to do with his success in welding together the British tribes. All who dreaded a Roman peace came to his side.[2] The pacification that they feared was to become notorious in Britain: 'they make a desolation and call it peace'.[3]

The site of the battle remains uncertain, though it seems fairly clear that it lay on the Severn. The British had taken up a position on a range of steep hills above the river and fortified with a crude stone rampart the places where the gradient was easiest. Behind the British position the country was so difficult that they could not easily be surrounded. Recent discussion on the location of the battle has centred on Cefncarnedd and Dolforwyn as possibilities. The exact site, though interesting, is not vital to the story. The strength of

---

[1] See, for example, *Brit.* 7 (1976), 278 ff.
[2] Tacitus, *Ann.* xii.33: *qui pacem nostram metuebant.*
[3] Tacitus, *Agr.* xxx.6: *ubi solitudinem faciunt, pacem appellant.*

the position and the difficulties of crossing the river and engaging the very formidable warriors facing him rather surprisingly dismayed Ostorius, but in true heroic literary fashion the eagerness of the Roman soldiers and their officers as described by Tacitus overcame his doubt. In the event the crossing of the river proved easy and the tactics and equipment of the legionaries and the auxiliaries combined to produce an overwhelming superiority over the Britons. Caratacus' wife and daughter were captured, his brother surrendered, and he himself fled to the shelter of the Brigantes.

The respite gained by Caratacus was a short one. He may have hoped that all the opposition to Rome among the Brigantes had not yet been crushed. He was to be disappointed. The pro-Roman queen Cartimandua, conscious of her status as an allied monarch and of the rebellion among her subjects that the governor had recently put down, promptly handed him over in bonds to the Romans.[1] This was treated as a very special success at Rome. Not only did the senate meet and equate the capture of Caratacus with the most famous captures of kings in ancient days, but Claudius staged a great display of the captives in front of the Praetorian Camp at Rome. The speech of Caratacus at this occasion as reported by Tacitus is one of those set pieces by kings and commanders so well known in the pages of the Roman historians,[2] but whatever Caratacus did or did not actually say his bearing so impressed the emperor that with a show of clemency the latter pardoned both the Briton and his family. This was something Julius Caesar had not done in the case of Vercingetorix, despite his reputation for mercy. With Caesar, clemency was always a calculated political act. Claudius had once again outdone his great ancestor. Living up to the destiny Virgil had proclaimed for Rome in Augustus' time, the emperor's armies had 'put down those barbarians who would not submit to Roman rule and shown mercy to the defeated'.

Ostorius himself was honoured with triumphal insignia, but this was to bring him little pleasure. The defeat of Caratacus was by no means the end of the war, either because the Britons longed for revenge or the attention of the

---

[1] Tacitus, *Hist.* iii.45, says that she captured him by a trick, a slightly different story from *Ann.* xii.36.

[2] Tacitus, *Ann.* xii.37.

Romans slackened. The situation soon developed into continual harassing of the Roman forces. The worst area was that of the Silures, whom Ostorius had forced into desperation by incautiously saying that they must be annihilated or transplanted. His lack of political judgement had once again done him harm. A substantial force of legionaries under a camp commandant (*praefectus castrorum*) engaged in building forts in Silurian territory was cut off.[1] It was only with difficulty rescued, and suffered the loss of the prefect and eight centurions, a considerable defeat.[2] Other incidents included the putting to flight of a Roman foraging party and then in turn the cavalry and auxiliary infantry which had been sent in to restore order. In the end Ostorius had to commit the legions before bringing the situation under control. In another serious incident, two auxiliary cohorts fell into a trap prepared by the Silures and were apparently taken prisoner. By distributing their prisoners and booty among other tribes the Silures were able to bind the latter to the cause, and a new British confederacy began to form. In this moment of crisis Ostorius died, worn out with care (*taedio curarum fessus*)[3] and the Silures were saved from extinction. Rome however was left with an extremely turbulent frontier and a half-pacified province.

A new governor was appointed with unusual speed. There was danger that the image gained by the Claudian victories would be tarnished. A man with an impressive record was chosen: Aulus Didius Gallus, who had recently been decorated for a successful campaign in south Russia to place a Roman nominee on the troubled throne of the client-kingdom which controlled the Crimea. Tacitus however does not seem to like him. He is scornful of his governorship and accuses him of leaving the action to his subordinates, inferring, probably unfairly, that he preferred the quiet life. By the time he arrived, the Silures had already inflicted a remarkable defeat on the Romans by winning a victory over a legion, presumably the Twentieth, and at the time of his arrival were ranging far and wide. The fact that the governor's arrival was apparently

[1] The incident may have occurred on the Wye, at Clyro or Clifford.
[2] Tacitus, *Ann.* xii.38.
[3] Ibid. xii.39.

sufficient to bring the situation again under control indicates that he had more energy and military skill than Tacitus would allow.[1]

This was not the end of Didius' difficulties, for fresh troubles now broke out among the Brigantes. Venutius, husband of Queen Cartimandua and 'now that Caratacus had been captured the most outstanding Briton in the field of military science'[2] had in the *previous* disturbance among the Brigantes been among the party that was confirmed in power by Roman arms. Now, however, he was alienated by his wife and had taken up arms against the pro-Roman party. Cartimandua cunningly laid hold of Venutius' brother and others of his relatives and he retaliated by invading her kingdom with a strong band of young warriors. It has been conjectured that the Brigantes were more of a federation than a single tribe, and suggested that Venutius ruled over a separate section of the Brigantes in the north-west.[3] He may, however, have collected his war-band in exile and returned to invade the kingdom. Cartimandua's exact status in relation to this alleged confederation is obscure, but the fact that one of the reasons for the support given to Venutius was abhorrence of feminine rule suggests that she was claiming a wider supremacy at this time than before.[4] Perhaps because of this, Venutius' move was foreseen by the Romans. They sent in auxiliary cohorts at first, then a legion, probably the Ninth but possibly the Fourteenth. These forces fought successful actions and confirmed Cartimandua on her throne. Venutius, however, was to cause further trouble in the future.

In AD 54, while Didius was still governor, and perhaps while these events were happening in Britain, the Emperor Claudius died in suspicious circumstances and his stepson Nero, later to be so notorious, came to the throne. Suetonius

[1] Tacitus, *Ann.* xii.40. In *Agr.* xiv he says that Didius merely 'established a few forts in the hinterland.' This, however, implies a positive policy. This may have been early in his governorship. Frere, in the first edition of his *Britannia* (1967, 84) suggested that he may have been the governor responsible for the vexillation base at Usk, and excavation has indeed confirmed that it was constructed about AD 54. (W.H. Manning, *Current Archaeology*, 62 (1978), 71 ff.) It may also refer to support later for Cartimandua and imply new forts constructed in his governorship in or near her territory.
[2] Tacitus, *Ann.* xii.40.   [3] I.A. Richmond, *JRS* 44 (1954), 50.
[4] She had already increased her power as a result of handing over Caratacus (Tacitus, *Hist.* iii.45).

states that Nero at one stage considered abandoning Britain[1] and it is possible that with this uncertainty Didius did not feel justified in doing more than containing the troubles on his borders. With the death of Claudius came the fall of most of his leading advisers, including the freedman Narcissus, who had been prominently associated with the British adventure. It is typical of the ambivalent attitude of the regime to the dead emperor and his policies that it arranged his deification but permitted literary fun to be poked at the new god.[2] It is however indicative of the importance of the military reputation of Claudius to the imperial house that the reason given for the young Nero's decision not to withdraw from Britain is that it would have reflected upon Claudius' glory. Nero clearly had no intention of seeking a military reputation for himself but he and his advisers could not afford to let a notable success of the Claudian house seem to end in failure.[3]

The choice made in appointing the next governor is convincing evidence for a firmer policy. Quintus Veranius had been marked out early for promotion and had built up a distinguished military reputation by his conduct of war in the Near East, in the mountains of Lycia and Pamphylia.[4] It was clearly intended at the least that a punitive expedition should be undertaken into Wales and probably, in the light of the actions of Veranius' successor, that conquest was envisaged. Veranius, however, had time only for a few minor raids into Silurian territory before he, too, died in office. Tacitus reports with more than his usual brevity the phrasing of Veranius' will, which he must surely have dictated as he was dying.[5] The result is Delphic in difficulty of interpretation. Tacitus says that Veranius swore that he would have subjected 'the province' to Nero if he had been granted two more years of life.[6] The historian's implication is that this was an idle boast. If 'the province' means 'the island' then

---

[1] Suetonius, *Nero*, xviii.   [2] Seneca, *Apocolocyntosis*.

[3] It seems as likely that Suetonius' reference to Nero's idea of abandoning Britain refers to the latter part of Aulus Didius' governorship as to the period of the Boudiccan rebellion, an alternative explanation of the passage.

[4] For Veranius, see E. Birley, *Roman Britain and the Roman Army*, Kendal (1961), 1 ff.

[5] Tacitus, *Ann.* xiv. 29.

[6] Birley reminds us that this was the residue of the normal three-year term of office.

Tacitus is justified. But might Veranius not have meant that he would have secured the total pacification of the province *as it then was,* by the subjection of the tribes of Wales whose persistent intrusions stirred up unending trouble in Roman territory?

The next governor, C. Suetonius Paulinus, was again a man of high military reputation. He too had had outstanding experience of mountain warfare when as a praetorian legate he had been the first Roman to cross the Atlas mountains of Mauretania. From his arrival in Britain, probably in the early part of 58, he had two highly successful years in the field. In 60 these campaigns were ending with an all-out assault on the island of Anglesey, a fact which suggests he had been fighting his way through the difficult country of North Wales. It is often alleged that this attack was in order finally to extirpate the Druids, thought commonly to have had their major centre there. Yet for this there is little evidence. Tacitus describes the island as 'heavily populated and a sanctuary for fugitives' and 'a source of strength to rebels'.[1] These were the same sort of reasons we have seen involved in the original decision to invade Britain in 43. To take Anglesey would make a logical continuation of the original policy. In addition, Tacitus goes out of his way to impute to Suetonius another reason for launching this difficult attack which is entirely believable in its social context. The historian claims that Suetonius was driven by jealousy of the foremost of his contemporaries, Suetonius being 'a rival general to Corbulo, both in fact as a professional soldier and in popular belief (in which every prominent man has to have a rival), and he wanted a victory to set against Corbulo's reconquest of Armenia.'

Tacitus has left us a dramatic picture of the savage force that defended the shores of Anglesey—fierce warriors, wild women, and praying Druids. The countervailing savagery of the Roman response, sketched in a few words by Tacitus, cannot be doubted.[2] Yet while Suetonius was engaged on this operation, the most bloody episode in Romano-British history for which we have detailed literary evidence was taking shape behind him. For Suetonius the Boudiccan

---

[1] Tacitus, *Ann.* xiv. 29; *Agr.* xiv. 4.   [2] Tacitus, *Ann.* xiv. 30.

rebellion was to provide extreme peril, great military success, and in the end discreet removal from office. For Britain, it came close to being the finish of her history as part of the empire.

A large proportion of a governor's problems arose from his dealings with the local communities. Winning and maintaining the confidence and co-operation of the provincial upper classes was crucial to the peace, administration, and financial structure of the empire, for the relatively small Roman army compared with the enormous area of the empire could not possibly have controlled the provinces without them. Only by delegating large areas of business to local men who could be trusted (and in the end this was only achieved when they had turned themselves into good Romans) was long-term government assured. The Boudiccan rebellion essentially arose from the disastrous failure of the early governors of Britain to get these relations with the local inhabitants right. Until the advantages of being within the empire were patently clear to a large proportion of the men of influence within the local communities there could be no real security. By the period we have so far reached this had not come about. On the contrary friends were being turned into enemies and the initial advantage by which the Britons were divided within themselves was being lost. Worse still, the Roman government seems to have had no inkling of what was happening. Suetonius' political sensitivity seems to have been no better than Ostorius', and the acute and original mind of the Emperor Claudius was no longer on the throne to interpret reports coming back to it. Nor, as we shall see, was the government at Rome likely to have had intelligence from the provincial procurator then in office such as might have alerted it to impending disaster, for his own stupidity and foolishness were among the causes of the uprising.

Roman provincial arrangements were varied and flexible and changed with time and circumstances. By AD 60 we may expect a number of the British tribes to have been formally recognized as *civitates*, or non-citizen but regular local authorities on the Roman pattern, to whom various functions were delegated, and it is likely that the kingdoms of Prasutagus of the Iceni and of Cogidubnus and perhaps others were similarly regulated, with individual arrangements being set out for each. The governor's main administration was almost certainly at Colchester at first, but may have moved from there when the Claudian *colonia* was established in 49, or soon after.[1] It is not certain that the provincial procurator's office was ever at Colchester, and at an early date there was probably already a drift of officials or even whole departments to London, which was much more convenient for communications and, as a hive of commerce, a natural centre for financial administration. Colchester, however, was a focus for imperial prestige, containing the hub of the Imperial Cult and probably providing the meeting-place of the provincial council, the loyal assembly of provincial aristocracy, if, indeed, one had yet been set up.

While there is no doubt that substantial towns, in some cases with monumental public buildings, were by this time already in being, Mr Wacher has pointed out that even at Colchester, and at Verulamium, probably the first and possibly the only British town to be given privileged status as a *municipium*—a native city raised to chartered status—the regular pattern of central administrative buildings, notably the *forum* and *basilica,* seem to be absent at the time of the Boudiccan rebellion,[2] though Colchester certainly and Verulamium probably had attained their chartered status as early as the governorship of Ostorius Scapula. Many towns, in fact, were developing on comfortable but as yet fairly irregular lines, in many cases on sites recently vacated by the military. At Verulamium and Silchester, to take two instances where there is reasonable certainty about a very hazy subject, earthwork defences were provided at this time, but we may be sure it was at the expense of the inhabitants. In the Roman world, amenities for civilians, even defences, were almost always expected to come out of the pockets of private citizens and usually at their initiative, either collectively or individually. In effect this usually meant that public works came out of the pockets of members of the local council or

[1] This is perhaps reflected in the Claudian redevelopment at London in the period *circa* AD 50 on the site of the later forum. (Cf. B.J. Philp, 'The Forum of Roman London,' *Brit.* 8 (1977), 1 ff.)

[2] J.S. Wacher, *The Towns of Roman Britain* (1975), 205 f.: however he goes on to point out that 'the age of the monumental, unified complex of forum, basilica and sometimes capitolium had not yet reached Britain, and had by no means spread universally elsewhere.' Cf. Philp, op. cit. 1 f.

of some great magnate with an interest in the district, often because estates in the locality formed part of his landed property. The role of government was a matter of permission and occasional supervision, perhaps with the provision of skilled advice but very rarely indeed with money. 'Romanization' in the commonly assumed sense of a conscious spreading of Roman amenities at Roman expense to provincials is a misunderstanding: pressure and the offering of advantages to men of local influence was the method of attempting to ensure loyalty and it was as these leading provincial families came to emulate and identify themselves with Roman political and social culture that the Romanization of the provinces which we can recognize archaeologically followed. The merging of these people with the Roman official classes, military and civil, and the creation of a unified substructure of urban society that served this 'establishment', were the mainsprings of the provincial cities now developing, which in their turn influenced the economy and ambitions of the countryside around them. But it all depended on the native aristocracies being convinced and remaining convinced that their interests lay with Rome. By 60 we are at the critical point where pacification seemed to have reached the stage where the south and east of Britain could largely be trusted, where the main Roman forces were being withdrawn or split up and civil towns and normal civil life were developing in their place. It was clearly judged that massive concentrations of troops in the south and east were no longer necessary: Suetonius had ambitions for spectacular conquest in Wales and the distribution of legionary vexillations, supported by auxiliary forts were still deemed necessary, should be enough to deal with any local difficulty.

The rebellion of Boudicca[1] has been one of the most written-about events in Romano-British history, but perhaps the most interesting feature about it is the causes related by the historians, where are very revealing of the conditions

---

[1] I have adopted the spelling 'Boudicca' in preference to 'Boadicea' which still survives in popular use but seems to derive from miscopying of the text of Tacitus during its transmission from Roman times. There is evidence from inscriptions and philology for a form 'Boudica' as a personal name in ancient times, but no direct association with the queen of the Iceni herself. Tacitus is the only contemporary rendering of her name we have.

which could prevail in a Roman province.[1] The seat of the rebellion was again the state of the Iceni in Norfolk, whom we have seen in previous trouble in 47 when they objected to being disarmed. Now their prosperous client king Prasutagus had died and the land was wide open to the worst elements in Roman provincial administration. That these had not been restrained must be laid in large measure at the door of Suetonius. He may have been engrossed in his Welsh campaigns, but never in his career in Britain did he show the slightest feeling for the provincials. The constitutional position may not have been clear, but that is no excuse. Tacitus states that Prasutagus had left the emperor co-heir with his two daughters, hoping to keep his kingdom and household safe from harm. It is quite clear that the whole kingdom was not left to Rome in the way that Attalus III had left the kingdom of Pergamum in Asia Minor in 133 BC. It must surely mean that the king left the emperor a share of his personal possessions and royal estates, a common device by which wealthy Romans ensured the secure carrying-out of their wills. Under this arrangement part of the Icenian territory should have become imperial estate and the emperor will presumably have received a proportion of the royal treasure.

The local officers of the governor and of the provincial procurator, Decianus Catus, took a completely different view. They treated the whole territory of the Iceni as if it had been handed over in surrender to Rome. The general complaints of the Iceni and their friends were that the governor tyrannized over their persons, the procurator over their possessions. They were being despoiled of homes and children and impressed into the Roman service. Centurions serving Suetonius were plundering the kingdom. Icenian nobles were being evicted from their ancestral properties. Members of the royal house were being treated as slaves, while the procurator's own servile officers were looting the king's household. It may be assumed that the royal family put up some resistance: at any rate the late king's widow was flogged and his two daughters raped. The result was rebellion,

---

[1] The surviving ancient accounts of the rebellion are Tacitus, *Agr.* v.3; xv-xvi. 2; *Ann.* xiv. 29–39; Dio, LXII, i-xii.

led by the insulted queen Boudicca. She was joined by certain tribes unspecified in the sources 'who had not yet been broken by servitude' and by the Iceni's southern neighbours, the Trinovantes of Essex.

The Trinovantes had their own particular reasons for detesting the Romans. They had a special hatred of the discharged soldiers settled in the colony at Colchester. These veterans had driven the native inhabitants from their homes and lands and treated them as captives and slaves, with the encouragement of the Roman garrison[1] which hoped for like opportunities in the future. The original land allotments to the colonists may, as we have seen, indeed have been taken chiefly from the royal domain lands of the house of Cunobelinus, but it seems likely that the colonists were now expanding well beyond their original territory.[2] Tacitus may perhaps be compressing grievances arising over a long period, but the impression is that they were recent occurrences and do not refer to the original foundation of the colony in AD 49.

Tacitus had good reason to know the causes of the rebellion, for his father-in-law Julius Agricola was serving on the governor's staff at the time, and on general grounds his account is to be preferred to Dio, who wrote long after.[3] Yet if there is any truth in the reasons detailed by Dio—who makes the rebellion arise almost entirely out of financial causes—then a little of the blame may be lifted from Suetonius. Dio not only alleges that the procurator was demanding the return of money that had been given to prominent Britons by Claudius, but also that the statesman, playwright and moralist Seneca was recalling all at once and in an unfeeling manner huge loans that he had previously forced on to the unwilling Britons.[4] If this is true, then a lead in the exploitation of the provincials was being given at the highest

[1] Tacitus, *Ann.* xiv.32: these troops may not have been a regular garrison but a few men detached from their units on special duty. However it is quite likely that they were a small force attached to the provincial capital.

[2] The question of the *territorium* of Colchester is obscure. It is unknown how much of the tribal area of the Trinovantes it took; nor is it clear whether the remaining parts of the tribe were treated as *attributi*, attached to the colony in a subordinate situation or had their own local government organization as a *civitas*.

[3] He was probably born about AD 163 or 164 and held the consulship in 229.

[4] Dio, LXII.ii.1.

level. Seneca, once tutor to the boy Nero while Claudius lived, had since Nero came to the throne dominated the young emperor in collaboration with his friend, the praetorian prefect Burrus. It has been generally agreed that they were a moderating influence on Nero, but that their power over him waned till it finally came to an end with the death of Burrus and retirement of Seneca in 62. If these allegations had a basis in fact—and much doubt has been cast upon them[1] —then we may have both an explanation for the behaviour of Suetonius and Decianus and a contributory cause in the decline of Seneca from his position as virtual co-regent at Rome. Even if not strictly true, they reflect attitudes to the provincials among Romans that are significant and underline the impression that a general financial discontent was an important factor in the uprising. It has been suggested that the British nobility, accustomed to older ways, may have misunderstood the meaning of the offers of money made to them. Yet there seems no reason to underestimate the comprehension of the Britons a considerable number of years after the Invasion: indeed Dio implies in their unwillingness to accept the loans that they understood Roman financial enterprise only too well. There is no doubt at all that northern barbarians conquered by Rome could distinguish between just and unjust taxation.[2] Before the Conquest they may have been used to a world where princes and nobles exchanged gifts as a matter of course, but there is no reason to think that after it they could not judge financial enterprise on the part of Romans as shrewdly as they could estimate fairness in taxation, even when the approaches might come from the rulers of the empire themselves. Indeed, if they had come from the emperor in person it would have caused no surprise in the Roman world: we have already noted how deeply the imperial household and the government were interwoven and that emperors often behaved as if the empire were their own property.

There has been some discussion of the exact date of the

[1] For an extreme expression of distrust of Dio as a source see R. Syme, *Tacitus,* Oxford (1958), 762 ff.

[2] The Frisii on the lower Rhine had been driven to revolt in AD 28 by excessively zealous collection of taxes (Tacitus, *Ann.* iv. 72). Elsewhere Tacitus says that the Britons bore taxation with equanimity, provided that it was justly applied and administered (*Agr.* xiii; ibid. xix).

rebellion.[1] Though Tacitus places it firmly in the consulate of Caesennius Paetus and Petronius Turpilianus (AD 61) yet we have to fit into this year not only the rebellion itself and its complicated aftermath but also Turpilianus himself arriving as the next governor. It seems probable that Boudicca was in the field in AD 60 and that the subsequent events extended through that winter into 61.

The course of the rebellion has been often told, yet the horror of the events does not pall. In true Roman style the ancient authors build up the atmosphere with prodigies and portents: more interesting to the modern reader is the fact that there was a 'fifth column' inside the colony of Colchester, doubtless native residents (*incolae*), who successfully confused the Roman colonists and prevented any serious measures for the defence of the city. It had no walls,[2] but was well equipped with public buildings—a council chamber, theatre, and the huge temple of the Imperial Cult.[3] The latter was a particular object of hatred to the Britons, symbolizing their servitude. Tacitus also tells us that 'those who had been chosen as its priests found themselves obliged to pour out their whole fortunes in its service.' A prime purpose of the cult was to bring together influential provincials and encourage them in loyalty to the emperor and integration into the Roman governing classes, yet it seems to have been so mismanaged as to have had the opposite effect. One cannot help suspecting that these were among those who were privy to the conspiracy and their prominent position would have rendered them particularly able to spread confusion in the city.

As a consequence of the confusion in their counsels no attempt was made by the colonists to evacuate the non-combatants, even though they had enough warning to send to the procurator for assistance. All they received was two hundred 'semi-armed' men. There were also a few regular troops in the neighbourhood, but the city was overrun and

---

[1] e.g. Syme, op. cit. 765 f.

[2] Tacitus, *Ann.* xiv. 31. There is some evidence that the defences of the legionary fortress were deliberately dismantled when the colony was founded. (See Philip Crummy, 'Colchester: the Roman Fortress and the Development of the Colonia', *Brit.* 8 (1977), 65 ff.)

[3] There is dispute about whether the Temple of the Divine Claudius was actually dedicated to him during his lifetime: D. Fishwick, Brit. 3 (1972), 164 ff.

destroyed almost immediately. Only the small band of soldiers was able to barricade itself in the temple where it held out for two days. Very soon the British horde was on its way towards London, a city without colonial or municipal status but already a flourishing mercantile centre and a rich prize for a vengeful and plundering army.

However before they could fall upon London, the Britons had to deal with a force which was marching to the rescue under the command of the legate of the Ninth legion, Q. Petillius Cerialis, a man whose career is remarkable for the number of times he escaped from the brink of military disaster. It now seems highly likely that he had with him only one of the vexillations into which his legion was probably at this time divided, in accordance with the pattern we have discussed. Nevertheless he did not hesitate to meet the Britons in battle. His infantry was cut to pieces and he escaped with only the cavalry part of his force to take shelter behind the defences of his base. Lincoln seems too far away; and Professor Frere has made a case for regarding the apparently hasty work of about this period discovered at the vexillation fortress of Longthorpe near Peterborough as the product of a desperate attempt by the remnants of this Roman force to put themselves into a position of defence if the Boudiccan army came after them.[1]

This disaster to the Ninth shattered the confidence of the procurator who was by now thoroughly frightened by the intensity of the hatred shown against him. At this point in his narrative Tacitus puts the blame for the rising squarely on Decianus and his greed, though it is in fact clear that the governor's own officers and the colonists at Colchester ought also to bear large shares in the immediate responsibility. The procurator forthwith wisely fled to Gaul.

The governor, on the other hand, made for London with all speed, apparently without the bulk of his troops. He does not seem to have realized that there were no troops at London. He may have expected the other legionary vexillations to have gathered there, and he appears to have had ideas of

---

[1] 'Longthorpe II' has a reduced perimeter and apparently no refurbishing of the internal buildings, which might be expected if a proper new garrison was being installed. Professor Frere suggests that Cerialis may have been left with (at the most) 1,000 cavalrymen. (*Brit.* 5 (1974), 38 f.)

defending it.[1] However, in view of Cerialis' defeat, he made
the unpalatable decision to regroup elsewhere:

He decided to sacrifice the one town to save the general situation. Un-
deflected by the prayers and tears of those who begged for his help he
gave the signal to move, taking into his column any who could join it.
Those who were unfit for war because of their sex, or too aged to go or
too fond of the place to leave, were butchered by the enemy. The same
massacre took place at the city of Verulamium, for the barbarian British, happiest when looting and unenthusiastic about real effort, bypassed the forts and the garrisons and headed for the spots where they
knew the most undefended booty lay. Something like 70,000 Roman
citizens and other friends of Rome died in the places I have mentioned.
The Britons took no prisoners, sold no captives as slaves and went in
for none of the usual trading of war. They wasted no time in getting
down to the bloody business of hanging, burning and crucifying. It was
as if they feared that retribution might catch up with them while their
vengeance was only half-complete.[2]

This account records the explosion of a remarkable amount
of pent-up loathing, the accumulation of only seventeen
years of Roman rule. It is all the more remarkable when it is
recalled that of the two tribes that led the rebellion, one had
joined Rome under Claudius as a free ally, the other had
been released by his conquest from subjection by the Catuvellauni who had usurped their old capital. It reflects ill on
the Roman administrations of the day and cannot be blamed
on Nero himself, since in 60 his government was still largely
in the hands of those 'good men', Seneca and Burrus. There
was much that needed to be changed if Britain was to become a loyal part of the empire. But first the rebels had to
be defeated, and whatever Tacitus may hint, it was by no
means certain that this was going to be possible.

Suetonius' march brought him back to his main force,
which numbered about 10,000 men and comprised the Fourteenth legion, detachments of the Twentieth, and auxiliaries
drawn from the nearest garrisons. A severe shock was the
non-arrival of the Second, then under the temporary command of its camp commandant, Poenius Postumus, who refused to move. No reason was given for his conduct and it is

[1] There is some sign at London of military occupation earlier than the stone
fort built around AD 90, but not in this period. (See Philp, op. cit.)
[2] Tacitus, *Ann.* xiv. 33. Dio gives a highly coloured but perhaps not too inaccurate account of the atrocities: Tacitus confines himself to a few evocative
words (*caedes patibula ignes cruces*).

possible that he was afraid to leave the west unguarded rather than that he acted out of terror of Boudicca. He may, too, have remembered too vividly the *praefectus castrorum* who had been caught unawares and killed by the Silures during Ostorius' governorship. In the event his disobedience probably pinned down some of the most dangerous tribes and prevented them from joining Boudicca, but this does not seem to have been taken into account subsequently. Meanwhile Suetonius was preparing to give battle on ground of his own choosing,[1] presumably somewhere in the Midlands.[2]

Suetonius drew up his legionary troops in close order in a defile, protected in the rear by dense forest. Auxiliaries were stationed on the flanks and cavalry on either wing. Boudicca's enormous force (Dio puts it as high as 230,000)[3] assembled in loose array. Behind the British army were its wagons, loaded with women and children, like grandstands at a Roman spectacle. One notes with interest that the Britons were still using chariots and with surprise that the Romans had not deprived them of their traditional weapon of war. Chariots can hardly have been so easy to conceal as small arms nor as quick to manufacture. Perhaps the Romans believed they were now no more than of ceremonial significance, but this curious feature provokes the speculation that the trouble in AD 47 over disarming had decided the Romans to pursue this policy no further. Tacitus gives the impression of a fairly brief battle, Dio that it was more prolonged. The essential feature of the engagement seems to have been the shock effects of the discharge of javelins by the Romans after they had lured the Britons into attacking up the slope, followed by the disciplined charge of the legionaries in wedge formation, backed by the *auxilia* and cavalry. This broke up the British army and forced it back on to the wagons. These now proved a trap, the draught animals being slaughtered by the Romans. The battle henceforth turned into a massacre, the women being killed with the men, and Tacitus, without committing himself on their accuracy, quotes 80,000 British

[1] Dio says that Suetonius gave battle unwillingly but was forced into it by shortage of supplies, and by being pressed hard by the Britons. Being so short of legionaries this is hardly surprising. He may have hoped that the British confederate army would break up, as in Caesar's day, if he delayed giving battle.

[2] Webster (*Boudica* (1978), 97; 111 f.) discusses the possibility of Mancetter.

[3] This seems an impossible figure, particularly as it omits the non-combatants.

as against 400 Roman dead. As he says, it was a victory to set alongside those of former days.[1]

Boudicca herself seems to have escaped from the field, but her death followed soon after, by poison according to Tacitus, from illness in the account of Dio.[2] Poenius Postumus, the camp commandant of the Second legion, also killed himself when he heard of the victory. That legion itself, together with the Ninth, now joined Suetonius in the field, and further reinforcements were received from Germany. These consisted of 2,000 legionary infantry, who, Tacitus tells us, brought the Ninth up to strength,[3] and eight cohorts of auxiliary infantry with a thousand auxiliary cavalry. The auxiliaries were placed in new winter quarters,[4] the legionaries apparently remained on active operations. The nature of these operations shows Suetonius at his most active and unpleasant. With fire and sword he set about vigorously laying waste the territory of all the British tribes that had either joined the rebellion or stayed neutral. Bodies, weapons, and signs of violent destruction by fire at the hill-fort of South Cadbury in Somerset may well be material traces of Suetonius' consuming vengeance ranging far from the original centres of the revolt.[5] Despite all, Dio says there were Britons who were ready to fight again after the battle and they now received support in their resistance to the governor from an unexpected quarter. They were in desperate straits, having failed to sow their crops earlier in the year while they prepared for war, in the expectation of capturing the Roman military granaries. Now they were being pressed hard by Suetonius and faced with a winter without supplies, promising famine for those who survived the punitive actions of the governor. Yet they were encouraged in their resistance by a new figure on the scene, Julius Classicianus, the new provincial procurator sent out to replace the runaway Decianus Catus.

---

[1] Tacitus, *Ann.* xiv. 37: *clara et antiquis victoriis par ea die laus parta.* For the numbers compare Agricola's victory at Mons Graupius: 10,000 British dead for 360 Romans (Tacitus, *Agr.* xxxvii).

[2] Dio also says that the Britons gave her a rich burial, an archaeologically tantalizing piece of information.

[3] This indicates that the infantry under Cerialis destroyed by Boudicca can certainly not have been the whole infantry force of the Ninth.

[4] These camps ought to be archaeologically identifiable.

[5] See *Antiquity*, 53 (1979), 31 ff.

He is an interesting figure.[1] It is very likely that he was by origin from the area around Trier on the Moselle, and that he was the son-in-law of Julius Indus, a distinguished provincial from the same region. The latter had raised a cavalry regiment and supported the Roman authorities at the time of a dangerous rebellion there in the reign of Tiberius. The new procurator is thus likely to have had considerable insight into the motives of such rebellions and the consequences of their repression. Tacitus alleges that his support for the refusal of these Britons to surrender was due to dislike for Suetonius; yet even if more generous motives were not present, he may at least have been considering the disastrous consequences to his own tax-collecting department that would follow from continued devastation of the tribal lands. His intervention was of the highest importance for the future of the province.

The procurator's adverse report to Rome on the governor was nothing new in imperial administration. In this case it provoked a commission of inquiry, in the person of the powerful ex-slave Polyclitus. Such freedmen were under Nero still in positions of great power in the emperor's secretariat. This fact seems not to have been appreciated by the Britons (which reveals an interesting lack of knowledge of the realities of power within the empire on the part of the Britons) but was well understood by the governor and the army. Tacitus does not bother to conceal the prejudices of his own senatorial background:

Nero had great hopes that Polyclitus' personal authority would not only heal the rift between governor and procurator but also persuade the rebellious barbarians to accept the idea of peace. Nor did Polyclitus fail: burdening both Italy and Gaul on the way with his vast retinue he managed, after crossing the Channel, to strike terror even into our own army. The enemy thought him comic: themselves still imbued with notions of liberty they had not yet realized the power of degenerates. They were amazed that a general and an army who had successfully brought to a close such a great war should give obedience to mere servants. However everything was played down when reported to the emperor. Suetonius was retained in office, but a little later when a few ships had been wrecked and their crews lost he was ordered, just as if wartime conditions were prevailing,[2] to hand over his command to Petronius Turpilianus who had at this moment completed his term as

----

[1] His massive funerary monument was found in London and is in the British Museum (*RIB* 12).
[2] See Note, p. 123 below.

consul. The latter neither provoked the enemy nor was harassed by them and thus gained the honourable name of peace for what was disgraceful inactivity.[1]

The traditional Roman upper class which was Tacitus' primary audience hated the freedmen who had gained so much power; did not much love civilian equestrians; liked to contrast the noble savage with contemporary Rome, fallen from the virtues of her legendary past—and despised governors of frontier provinces who preferred peace to war. Yet it is difficult not to conclude that Polyclitus carried out a very delicate mission with success and that the subsequent events were to the benefit both of Britain and Rome. Tacitus is scornful of Turpilianus' alleged lack of action, but it may fairly be argued that quiescence on the part of the governor was what was now required. Certainly Turpilianus and Classicianus seem in due course to have achieved such a satisfactory settlement that the south never rose again: later governors were able to plan forward movements and carry them through with reasonable confidence that there would be no commotion in the rear.

NOTE

The recall of Suetonius Paulinus.[2] The translation 'just as if wartime conditions were prevailing' of the phrase *tamquam durante bello,* used by Tacitus of the context in which Suetonius was ordered to hand over his command to Petronius Turpilianus, was suggested to me by Anthony King. The usual rendering is on the lines: 'as if he were prolonging the war'. The latter translation implies that the imperial government thought the war was being unnecessarily drawn out. Mr King's translation, however, leaves the matter open. It simply implies that the imperial authorities chose to treat the war as still active and withdrew Suetonius on the grounds of a defeat. We are therefore left not knowing whether this attitude was adopted merely in order to be able to recall Suetonius unobtrusively as soon as a convenient pretext offered itself or whether, at least till this point, Suetonius' policy in Britain had received continuing imperial approval. This would carry with it the assumption that Classicianus' arguments had been discounted. Suetonius' reputation was certainly not permanently damaged. Nero awarded him a second consulship a few years later and he was still a prominent figure in the Year of the Four Emperors.

[1] Tacitus, *Ann.* xiv. 38-9.   [2] Tacitus, *Ann.* xiv.39: see p. 122 above.

6

RECOVERY AND ADVANCE

LITTLE is yet known of the progress of Romanization and the development of Roman institutions immediately after the pacification of the province. In due course archaeology may tell us more than the very little so far revealed of how quickly the towns struck down by the rebels recovered, how other towns developed in this period, and whether new towns were started. The sole structural evidence for new public buildings comes from London, where the first phase of the forum, a relatively small complex by later standards, dates from this period. It is not surprising to find restoration beginning here, and perhaps significant that the new city centre is cast in a civil mould, in contrast to the buildings of military type destroyed by Boudicca on the same site which may well have housed the governor's administration before the great rebellion. It is not fanciful to see a reflection of the changed style of government under Petronius Turpilianus and Julius Classicianus. Elsewhere there is little evidence for the founding of urban centres in the later years of Nero. One may conjecture that the experience of Colchester had made the imperial government and its legates in Britain chary of pressing the British aristocrats to take on new public burdens while old grievances were fresh in their minds. Nor can we ignore the probability that the war and the reprisals carried out subsequently by Suetonius had left in many areas a decimated and impoverished native upper class. In the majority of cases their personal wealth must have lain in the land, and we may remember that Tacitus reported the Britons in a state of famine after their defeat, because they had failed to sow the crops in the year of the campaign expecting to feast on Roman supplies after their expected victory.[1] Neglected farms, a whole year's harvest lost and, we may reasonably assume, a sizeable proportion of the agricultural work-force lost in battle, wounded, sold as slaves by their Roman captors, or simply run away in the confusion of war must have brought

---

[1] Tacitus, *Ann.* xiv. 38.

very low the fortunes even of those families who had escaped personal retribution in the punitive operations carried out by Suetonius before he was recalled.

In the countryside itself this period is, as one would imagine, as difficult to identify as in the towns. A pointer to the probable state of things is the history of the site at Gorhambury near Verulamium. A Roman villa had replaced Iron Age huts in the years before the Boudiccan war, but seems to have reverted to a hutted settlement for a period after it before eventually being rebuilt once again on Roman lines. Here we have a rare example of positive evidence for the period. Except for the development of a very few villas in stone, mostly on the south coast, it is so far largely a blank, a fact in itself not without significance. The literary record, which for all practical purposes is that of Tacitus, presents almost total silence on the achievements of the new administration. Tacitus himself was eager to give the credit of civil development in Britain to his father-in-law's governorship nearly twenty years later and anything done in the decade or so after the rebellion we would expect to be played down. Further illumination is only likely to come from archaeology, and the question of what happened in this period is one that has to be posed to the archaeologists. We may suspect the response can only be the accumulation of negative evidence, of itself inherently inconclusive. The period is, however, a vital one for the history of Roman Britain and any further pointers as to its character are of the utmost importance.

There can be no doubt that the winning of the general support of the native aristocracy in these years after the defeat of Boudicca was crucial to the recovery of the province. Without it, the problems of security and administration would have been, as a long-term proposition, extremely difficult to bear. A substantial number of Britons had favoured Rome in 43, but we have seen how very many were alienated in the years that followed, including leaders once friendly to the imperial power. Now the Britons had to be won back. As to how it was done, we have a hint in Tacitus' reference to the way in which, under Trebellius Maximus who was governor from 63, the Britons learnt the pleasures of peace and civilization,[1] even though the historian chose to regard it as

[1] Tacitus, *Agr.* xvi: *didicere iam barbari quoque ignoscere vitiis blandientibus.*

degeneracy. We can learn in greater detail of the sort of arguments that Rome used to persuade leading provincials that Roman rule was in their interest from a remarkable speech Tacitus puts into the mouth of Petillius Cerialis. This speech is represented as being Cerialis' address to the Treviri and Lingones of north-east Gaul, the occasion being the most critical point of the great provincial revolt on the Rhine which was stirred up in the civil wars of 68–69. It has special interest in that it is attributed to Cerialis just before he was sent back to Britain as governor, and, whether or not it was delivered in the words reported, undoubtedly represents a contemporary and well-informed Roman view of the reasons that swayed the provincials in their favour. Though it is disingenuous in its account of the original Roman intervention in Gaul and Germany (much the same gloss could have been put on the invasion of Britain), it appeals revealingly to the provincials' self-interest, and in particular to their upper classes' past experience of participation in the Roman system:[1]

I have no capacity for public speaking and have always maintained that the worth and excellence of the Roman people lies in its courage and skill at arms, but I feel I must make a few points . . .

The reason why Roman generals and emperors came into your territories and those of the other Gauls was not a desire for gain but at the invitation of your forefathers. They had become so exhausted by internal strife that they were close to collapse, and the Germans whom they had called in to help had seized power over friend and foe alike. It is well enough known how many battles we fought against the Cimbri and Teutones, how great were the exertions of our armies in the German wars and what was the final outcome. We did not occupy the Rhineland to protect Italy but so that a second Ariovistus should not impose his rule on the peoples of Gaul[2] . . . Until you conceded to us the right to govern you, there were wars constantly among you and local despots in control all over Gaul. Yet, though we have often been provoked, we have used our victories to impose only those burdens that are unavoidable if peace is to be preserved. Peace between nations cannot be maintained without armies; armies need paying and that means taxes. Everything else is shared with you. You and your fellow countrymen frequently command our legions and govern these and other provinces of the empire. You are not excluded from anything. In fact in one way

[1] Tacitus, *Hist.* iv.73–4, here abridged.

[2] Ariovistus of the Suebi, leading a German confederation, won considerable power in Gaul in the first century BC. He was in fact recognized as an ally of Rome by the senate, but Gallic leaders appealed to Caesar who found an excuse for fighting and defeating him.

you benefit especially: the good that flows from popular emperors reaches everyone, far and near alike, but the evil wreaked by tyrants falls on those closest to them. Just as you put up with natural disasters such as too much rain or poor harvests, so should you look upon extravagance and greed among those who are in power over you. There will be faults so long as there are men, but they are not with us all the time and better times compensate for bad. But do you really expect a milder regime if (*the rebels*) Tutor and Classicus take over? Or that they will reduce the taxes necessary to support the army that protects you from the Germans and the Britons?[1] If the Romans are expelled—which Heaven forbid!—what else can follow but world-wide conflict in which each people will fall on its neighbours? Good fortune and discipline have over the past eight hundred years gone hand in hand to build this structure which destroyed will bring down all together . . . At present, victor and vanquished enjoy peace and the imperial civilization under the same law on an equal footing. Let your experience of the alternatives prevent you from preferring the ruin that will follow on revolt to the safety that is conferred by obedience.

Cerialis also pointed out that his particular hearers, prosperous and by now extensively Romanized, were in particular danger from the very fact that they were so well-off. This was at the heart of the matter: the more that provincials became Romanized, acquired Roman amenities, and became identified with Roman rule themselves, the more they needed the protection only Rome could give them. At one point Germans hostile to Rome appealed to their kinsmen living in the great Roman city of Cologne to make common cause with them, as Britons seem to have done in Boudicca's day at Colchester. The Germanic inhabitants of Cologne, however, replied that they were now so intermingled with the Romans that they were one population. Both sentiment and self-interest tied provincials closer and closer to Rome and to one another, and while it was at their own expense that they developed their local manifestations of Roman culture Cerialis was surely correct in pointing out that it could not have happened or continue without the presence of the Roman system and most of all the Roman army.

The success of the work of Trebellius Maximus and his colleagues in Britain can be measured by what happened—or

---

[1] The reference to the Britons is interesting. Is Cerialis (speaking at the *colonia* of Trier) trying to scare them with memories of the Boudiccan revolt and the fate of cities like Colchester? Or were the northern Britons considered a real menace to the north-western provinces as a whole? He might almost be laying the grounds for his own subsequent campaign against the Brigantes.

rather did not happen—in Britain when news came of the shattering events of AD 68 which led to the deposition and suicide of Nero and to the civil wars that followed. Britain was on the sidelines throughout[1] but troops of the Roman army in Britain took part in some of these upheavals and there were various political repercussions among the Romans in the province. However, the cardinal fact of the British situation in this troubled period is that no general uprising occurred among the conquered peoples inside the province of Britain. Although every Roman's attention must have been on the news from the Continent, no provincials, even if restive, seized the opportunity. This reflects great credit on the despised administrators who succeeded Suetonius Paulinus. Indeed already, probably in the previous year, 67,[2] the emperor had been able to withdraw for service elsewhere the famous Fourteenth legion, victors in the final battle against Boudicca. Nero had begun to feel insecure on the unmasking in AD 65 of a plot against his life, led by C. Calpurnius Piso and one of the two praetorian prefects who commanded the élite troops normally stationed in Rome. The actual train of events that was to unseat Nero began in 68 with the abortive revolt of Vindex, governor of Gallia Lugdunensis, which, though quickly crushed by the Rhine army who believed it to be a native uprising, implicated the governor of Hispania Tarraconensis, the elderly but military Servius Sulpicius Galba. In its turn the Rhine army itself became disaffected and offered the throne to its own commander, Verginius Rufus, who had already shown some tendency towards sympathy with Vindex. He was too cautious to accept the offer. In the meantime, however, the praetorian guard went over to Galba. Nero was deposed by the senate and driven to suicide.

Galba's reign was firm, tactless, and brief. A major error was the recall from Germany of Verginius Rufus, the only man who could restrain the army of the Rhine. On January 1 69, the Rhine legions mutinied, probably at the instigation of two of its legionary legates, Caecina and Valens. At Rome, Galba was murdered by the praetorians who now preferred one of Nero's former courtiers, M. Salvius Otho, once husband of Nero's notorious empress Poppaea. Rather surprisingly,

---

[1] Cf. Tacitus, *Hist.* i.9.   [2] Tacitus, *Hist.* ii.66.

perhaps because he could be represented as heading the legitimist party, Otho was supported by Suetonius Paulinus, the ex-governor of Britain, who emerges from obscurity at this point, and by Verginius Rufus himself. Simultaneously the Rhine legions formerly commanded by Verginius Rufus put up another candidate, A. Vitellius, governor of Lower Germany, a man very willing to be led but unfitted to lead. Everything was thus set for a major civil war.

In the meantime the disturbed state of the Roman world was having some effects in Britain. Military sympathy in the province seems to have been on the side of the Vitellians,[1] though the former governor Suetonius and their old comrades of the Fourteenth (whose overweening pride may have made them unpopular) were in the Othonian army. The governor then in office, still Trebellius Maximus, had for a long time been at odds with the commander of the Twentieth legion, Roscius Coelius, and this now came to a head. Coelius complained of the impoverished state of the British troops, which suggests that Trebellius had been restraining their natural tendency to despoil the natives. In the end the auxiliaries joined the legions in following Coelius' lead and the unfortunate Trebellius[2] was forced to flee to Vitellius, leaving his province in the hands of a committee of legionary legates dominated by Coelius, which nevertheless adhered to the Vitellian cause.

Though the support of the army of Britain was held to have immensely strengthened the Vitellian side, the legions remaining in Britain did not take any active part in this campaign. While Vitellius was still assembling detachments summoned from the Second, Ninth, and Twentieth,[3] his two supporters Caecina and Valens had already descended on Italy and fought a great battle at Bedriacum near Cremona. Their victory won the war and brought about the suicide of Otho. The only actual unit of British troops known to have taken part in the campaign is a single cohort of Britons in the army of Caecina.

[1] Ibid. i.59.
[2] Tacitus' two accounts of the governorship of Trebellius Maximus (*Agr.* xvi; Hist. i.60) do not entirely agree: the former says that Trebellius returned to his command and governed on sufferance. The two versions *may* refer to different incidents, but it is more likely that the latter is a correction of the former.
[3] Totalling 8,000 men (Tacitus, *Hist.* ii.57).

In the intervals of the round of riotous living with which he now celebrated the victory which had been won for him, the new emperor found time to deal with some of the outstanding problems left by the war. Trebellius Maximus was not sent back to Britain but was replaced by Vettius Bolanus, at that time at the imperial court. The state of the Fourteenth legion, still in Italy, constituted a serious problem. Living up to its proud reputation it refused to acknowledge that it had been defeated on the Othonian side, saying that only an advance party had shared in the débâcle at Bedriacum. At one point the legionaries picked a quarrel with some Batavian auxiliaries with whom they had long had bad relations, possibly since service in Britain. More serious trouble with the Batavian nation will enter our story later. The Fourteenth also burnt part of the city of Turin. Vitellius took the only possible course and sent them back to Britain, where they are hardly likely to have been greeted with enthusiasm by their old colleagues who had supported the other side.

Suetonius Paulinus and Verginius Rufus were spared by the new regime at Rome, but the brutal execution of Othonian centurions sparked off considerable discontent and alarm in the legions stationed in the Balkans which had sympathized with Otho. These executions proved to be a fatal error. Cautious moves against the Vitellian government began to be made in the east by Mucianus, governor of Syria, and Vespasian, now in command of operations in Palestine against a Jewish revolt. Both of them had nominally been supporters of Otho and were watching events. The two legions stationed in Egypt proclaimed Vespasian as emperor and the garrisons in Syria and Palestine followed their example. Steps were then taken to assemble an expeditionary force for war against Vitellius, but events were already moving faster on the Danube, where, as we have seen, the legions were already restive.

Antonius Primus, commanding the Seventh, and Fuscus, imperial procurator of Illyricum, were already in communication by letter with the irrepressible Fourteenth in Britain. Primus now organized a lightning march on Italy, equal to the most brilliant in ancient military history. To meet this threat Vitellius called for reinforcements from Gaul, Spain, and Britain. Vettius Bolanus in Britain hesitated, considering his province not thoroughly pacified and in genuine doubt which side to support.[1] Among his considerations must have been the facts that of his four legions one was the Fourteenth and another II Augusta which Vespasian had commanded with great distinction in the original invasion. His legions were also seriously depleted: it is reported that an important consideration in the debate between Antonius Primus and his friends was the fact that Vitellius was in Italy with 'the flower of the army of Britain'.[2] However they also considered Britain an important source of reserves for the Vitellians,[3] within striking distance of north Italy, the inevitable theatre of war. Vettius Bolanus was obviously not going to obstruct the orders of Vitellius for ever.

The leaders met in conference at the base of the Thirteenth legion at Poetovio, in modern Yugoslavia. The impetuous Primus eventually had his way, and the march on Italy with the Danubian legions continued. Advancing from his temporary base at Verona Primus was met by the Vitellians coming up from the lower Po valley near the site of the previous battle of Bedriacum. This time the detachments from the British legions formed the centre of the Vitellian army. The outcome of the battle was a crushing victory for the Flavians, with heavy casualties on the Vitellian side. There was little mercy and it may be assumed that the troops from Britain took their share of the losses. The Flavian army, by this time thoroughly out of hand, went on to loot and destroy the city of Cremona, which became a prime example of what Roman troops could do to Roman civilians in time of civil war. The final stages of the war included a bloody entry to the city of Rome, the storming of the praetorian camp, and the lynching of Vitellius himself. All was now set for Vespasian to assume his throne. It had been demonstrated clearly in this 'Year of the Four Emperors' not only that emperors could be made outside Rome but also that men of comparatively obscure family could hope for the throne. Henceforth every provincial governor and army commander was a potential emperor and the loyalty of the frontier armies became a precarious thing, assiduously

---

[1] Tacitus, *Hist.* ii.97.
[2] Tacitus, *Hist.* iii.1: however these may possibly have been the 8,000 men summoned from Britain before the *first* battle of Bedriacum.
[3] Ibid. *Hist.* iii.2.

to be cultivated by every emperor who wished for stability and a long reign. The British garrison had played its part, and had been shown to be a formidable reserve of military power that would have to be taken into account in any future calculations of this sort. It had not yet produced an imperial candidate of its own, but the possibility was now open. Britain came over to the Flavian side when it finally became clear who had won the war, but not without reservations. Vettius Bolanus was still governor, but fortunately, as we have seen, though appointed from those around him by Vitellius, he had not been unswerving in his support. The Second legion, once commanded in Britain by Vespasian himself, was eager to advance the Flavian flag. The new emperor's eldest son, Titus, whose later military exploits earned him a great reputation, had served a few years earlier as a tribune in one of the legions in Britain. Suetonius tells us that his industry and modest conduct had earned him considerable respect, marked by the erection of numerous statues and inscriptions.[1] These doubtless dated from after the Flavian achievement of supreme power, but it is not unreasonable to assume that his conduct had reinforced sentiment in Britain favourable to his father, particularly amongst the army. It is not surprising, therefore, that the general balance of opinion was on Vespasian's side. Nevertheless the fact that a high proportion of the career officers and ordinary soldiers in the other legions in Britain had been promoted by Vitellius caused some hesitation among them.[2] In particular the Twentieth and its commander were doubtful quantities. Vespasian therefore decided to replace that legionary legate with Gnaeus Julius Agricola, whom we have already encountered as father-in-law of Tacitus, and who knew Britain well from serving on Suetonius Paulinus' staff during the Boudiccan rebellion. He had recently proved his efficiency and political sympathies in raising levies in the Flavian cause. For the moment Bolanus, whose lack of positive action on the Vitellian side now stood him in good stead, was continued as governor of Britain, ruling with a light hand.

Despite the undoubtedly conventionally exaggeration of the eulogies of Vettius Bolanus in remarks directed to his

---

[1] Suetonius, *Div. Tit.* iv.1.   [2] Tacitus, *Hist.* iii.33; *Agr.* vii.

son by the poet Statius, there may be elements of truth behind the reports of successful campaigning northwards during his governorship. It is difficult to believe Statius' assertion of conquest in Caledonia, but it is not impossible that Bolanus' Brigantian war—which we must examine next—is conflated by the poet with an exploration of Scottish waters by the fleet.[1] The Brigantian affair was serious, and may have begun before the victory of Vespasian was complete. Cartimandua, the queen of the Brigantes who had ended the career of Caratacus when she handed him over to Claudius nearly two decades earlier, now divorced and deposed her consort Venutius in favour of his armour-bearer Vellocatus. The infuriated Venutius replied by fomenting revolt within their scandalized tribe and summoned help from outside.[2] The Britons, Tacitus tells us, were encouraged by the turbulence in the Roman army and the news of the civil wars, even though, as we saw, the provincials did not rise when the struggle for the imperial throne broke out. Bolanus intervened in the Brigantian dispute by sending in a force of auxiliary cavalry and infantry. In spite of some bitter fighting, they could do no more than rescue the queen: Venutius was left master of the kingdom.[3] The situation in Britain was thus transformed. The province was no longer protected from the north by a friendly client-kingdom, but immediately threatened by a determined foe of Rome who might also prove a rallying point for dissident elements in regions apparently pacified. The old policy of occupying the south alone (if it ever was a conscious policy) had collapsed—and a governor who preferred the quiet life was no longer suitable. A complete reassessment of the Roman position in Britain was required.

Fortunately there was a promising candidate for the governorship to hand, if the emperor was willing to risk appointing a man in whom rashness and good luck seemed closely balanced. One of the devices adopted by Antonius Primus to harass the Vitellians had been to encourage Civilis, the chief of the Batavians situated in Holland to rise against

---

[1] Statius, *Silvae*, V. ii. 53 ff.;142 ff.   [2] Tacitus, *Hist.* iii.45.
[3] Tacitus, ibid.: *regnum Venutio, bellum nobis relictum.* It has been suggested that the Roman intention was at some stage to house Cartimandua under protection at Chester.

the Roman garrisons on the Rhine. The Batavians had been a first-class source of cavalry for the Roman army (we have seen them in action in Britain). This rising got out of hand and engulfed the whole of the Rhine area. One of Vespasian's first problems was to put down what his own supporters had stirred up. The commander who bore the brunt of this task was the extraordinary Petillius Cerialis, whose escape from total defeat when in command of the Ninth legion was one of the notable events of the Boudiccan rebellion. This had been followed in the civil wars by a series of adventures marked by daring bordering on foolhardiness. Nevertheless luck was a characteristic the Romans took seriously in a general—and he had the added advantage of being a close relative of the new emperor. Tacitus strongly disliked him: 'He was given to improvisation with brilliant success—luck made up for what military skill was lacking. Hence neither he nor his army worried about discipline.'[1] How unlike the revered Agricola.

To strengthen the expeditionary force placed at Cerialis' disposal against the Batavi, a force that included former Vitellian troops as well as Flavians, the Fourteenth was summoned from Britain again. This time it was never to be sent back. The task force thus made up must have needed a man of Cerialis' unconventional flair to hold it together. The Batavian campaign turned out to be extremely hazardous, Cerialis coming very near to defeat several times, saved again by his genius for improvisation, clever diplomacy, and his extraordinary luck. He was finally triumphant, and soon afterwards, now with a very considerably enhanced reputation, was appointed to the governorship of Britain, to replace Vettius Bolanus. His main task was, unavoidably, to deal with the menacing situation on the northern frontier.

The choice of this dynamic man as governor was a clear sign that the new government intended a forward policy in Britain. The army in Britain was in poor shape: Bolanus had declined to enforce discipline and there had been an attitude of unwillingness to act in the face of hostile incidents.[2] Now,

---

[1] Tacitus, *Hist.* iii.45: for Tacitus' attitude to Cerialis see A.R. Birley, *Brit.* 4 (1973), 179 ff.

[2] It is noticeable that Cartimandua was rescued by a force of auxiliaries: the legions did not move. Tacitus, *Agr.* xvi, imputes a certain lack of response, *inertia erga hostis*.

however, came 'a succession of great commanders and excellent armies',[1] a succession opened by Cerialis with a re-
juvenating effect upon the morale of the British army, ably
supported by Agricola as commander of the Twentieth and
sometimes of larger forces.[2]

This is perhaps a convenient point at which to review the
changes in the disposition of the legions in the second half of
the 60s. At the beginning of this period the Fourteenth was,
it would appear, at Wroxeter, the Ninth at Lincoln, the Second
at Exeter, and probably the Twentieth at Usk. Nero's recall
of the Fourteenth in 67 does not seem to have left Wroxeter
unoccupied: on the other hand by the end of Nero's reign
Usk had been evacuated, if not actually demolished. It is
therefore highly likely that the Twentieth was transferred to
Wroxeter in place of the Fourteenth. This would have left a
serious gap in the notoriously unstable region of the Silures.
In fact we find a new legionary fortress being constructed at
Gloucester shortly after 64–6 and there is good reason to
think that the Second was transferred here from Exeter. Yet
at Exeter itself the legionary baths were themselves undergoing substantial work as late as 60–5, not long before the
site ceased to be a legionary base. Direct evidence is lacking,
but it is not unreasonable to guess that relatively little notice
was given for the move from Exeter to Gloucester. The
troop movements consequent on the removal of the Fourteenth would supply a context. At all events, by the Year of
the Four Emperors the new pattern of legions was probably
complete.[3]

Whether this pattern was temporarily disturbed when the
Fourteenth was sent back to Britain in 69 we do not know.
Troops had been detached from the other legions during the
wars, and the troublesome Fourteenth was perhaps briefly
divided to strengthen the garrisons that remained. A substantial part, possibly the core of the legion, may have been
moved into the territory of the Parisi to outflank the Brigantes

---

[1] Ibid. *Agr.* xvii. Tacitus himself may not have intended to include Cerialis
(see A.R. Birley, op. cit. 180).

[2] Tacitus, *Agr.* viii.

[3] Professor M.G. Jarrett argued as early as 1964, long before the discovery of
the fortress at Exeter, that the Second was only at Gloucester from AD 67 (*Arch.
Cambr.* 113 (1964), 47 ff.).

on their eastern side, since a vexillation fortress has been found at Malton. However, this fortress may date to the next phase in the Brigantian war, and the legionary situation in the province was anyhow short-lived. Within a year the Fourteenth was again removed from Britain, and after the defeat of Civilis by Cerialis it became a part of the Rhine army, never subsequently returning to Britain.

To bring the army of Britain back to its full complement of four legions for the war in the north that now clearly had to be fought, Cerialis was allocated a new legion on being posted to the province. This was II Adiutrix, recently formed from marines during the civil wars and perhaps intended to act in Britain as a reserve. This latter conjecture gains some credence from the fact that the legion was moved into Lincoln when the Ninth was subsequently advanced to York. And it was the Ninth, we may be sure, Cerialis' old command, that the new governor intended from the first to be the spearhead of the campaigns he was to carry out in his years of office. Malton may indeed be an early step in the progress of the Ninth northwards, while the Twentieth under Agricola advanced in the west, operating, if Tacitus' words are not deliberate embroidery, often more or less independently.

Traces of these campaigns have been thought to be identified at Brough-on-Humber as well as Malton, at York, in marching camps in the Stainmore Pass, at Carlisle, and at the immense British fortification at Stanwick, near Richmond, long thought to be the scene of Venutius' last stand but now the subject of some doubt.[1] We may imagine a strategy that moved the main forces across the Humber, consolidated a hold on eastern Yorkshire and established its main base at York. A pincer movement closed on the southern Pennines, with Cerialis himself advancing through the Stainmore Pass to join Agricola's force moving up the western side of the country. The final stage would be a probe at least as far north as Carlisle with the whole army now united. Just how far the Romans penetrated during the governorship of Cerialis and

---

[1] See Sir Mortimer Wheeler, 'The Brigantian Fortifications at Stanwick, York-shire', in R. Bruce-Mitford (ed.), *Recent Archaeological Excavations in Britain* (1956), 43 ff. Subsequent doubt has been cast on the 'Battle of Stanwick', (See B. Dobson in 'Roman Durham', *Trans. Archit. and Archaeological Soc. Durh. and Northumb.* n.s. 2 (1970), 31 f.).

the extent of actual conquest at that time has long been a matter of debate, but Cerialis campaigned over most of the territory of the Brigantes, if not with complete success. It has been assumed that at some point there was a major battle with Venutius' forces; but, whether or not that actually happened, we hear nothing more of him thereafter and his power must have been broken, and with it that of the Brigantes. All this was not achieved without loss on the Roman side, nor on the British. Tacitus' curt phrase 'many battles, some not unbloody,' leaves its own impression, certainly not unintentional.[1]

On the recall of Cerialis in 74—his tour of three years was more or less the typical length—Sextus Julius Frontinus was appointed in his stead. The latter was not only a versatile soldier but also the author of several treatises on military and engineering matters. Frontinus clearly regarded the problems of the northern frontier as solved, at least for the time being, no mean compliment to Cerialis, for he turned his attention to the uneasy situation of II Augusta facing the Silures. He followed Cerialis' example by pursuing a forward policy— with considerable difficulty but in the end triumphantly— subduing this awkward tribe and their rugged terrain. The Ninth had been moved forward to York. Now the next stage in the establishment of the early Flavian legionary pattern was put into effect. Gloucester was evacuated and a new legionary fortress constructed at Caerleon, in the valley of the River Usk and much closer to the Bristol Channel than the old site at Usk itself. Easy communication was now established both inland to central Wales and by land and sea with the fertile Vale of Glamorgan, the best land of the Silures. Frontinus also seems to have established auxiliary forts in central Wales itself and it is recorded that he pushed his outposts right into the territory of the Ordovices. Tacitus talks of a cavalry squadron 'operating in their territory'.[2] This does not necessarily imply a network of forts actually established in their lands, but implies that there were Roman bases reasonably near at hand. The vexillation fortress at Rhyn Park which we noted earlier in connection with Ostorius Scapula was certainly succeeded by a smaller fort, and this

[1] Tacitus, *Agr.* xvii.   [2] Tacitus, *Agr.* xviii.

may have been the occasion of the latter's construction. More important, however, we know that in the latter part of his governorship Frontinus was in the process of completing the new disposition of the legions by starting the construction of a fortress at Chester. If, as seems likely, his purpose was to transfer II Adiutrix here from Lincoln, then Wales was to be faced by three legions, a remarkable concentration. The attention of the Roman authorities was undoubtedly now fixed on this sector.

Collingwood acutely observed that under Frontinus, distinguished as an engineer, lawyer, and administrator, the Romanization of the province went forward as it may not have done under Cerialis, though he underestimated the latter as no more than a pure soldier. The movement of the centre of the Silures from their fortress in Llanmelin Wood to a new Roman town at Caerwent has long been thought probably to belong to Frontinus' governorship and it seems likely that with his interest in administration he was responsible for rounding off his conquest by forming the Silures into the *respublica civitatis Silurum* known (much later) to epigraphy.[1] It is at least certain that, unlike Ostorius Scapula's, his policy towards them was not extermination. It is possible that we may now detect Frontinus' hand elsewhere too in the surge of civic projects which has sometimes been attributed exclusively to his successor Agricola. It seems almost certain that the forum at Verulamium with its great public buildings was planned and probably started under Frontinus, at Exeter the forum and basilica were begun about AD 75 and it is highly likely that the forum at Cirencester should also be attributed to him.[2]

The exact year in which Frontinus' successor arrived has long been a subject of debate. We know that Julius Agricola was consul for part of the year 77, that he subsequently gave his daughter in marriage to the historian Tacitus, and that he arrived in Britain late in the campaigning season. We do not know whether all these events took place in the same year. The most straightforward reading of Tacitus' biography of his father-in-law would suggest that they did, but there are difficulties. The balance of probability is that Agricola's governorship started in AD 78.[3]

[1] RIB 311.   [2] See Note, p. 167 below.   [3] Ibid.

Although Agricola arrived half-way through the summer he surprised everyone by going into action straightaway, to avenge the destruction of the cavalry squadron we have noted among the Ordovices. He had, of course, commanded the Twentieth legion under Cerialis, when its home station was most likely Wroxeter; and during that command had probably learnt much about the Welsh Marches and the tribes facing Rome in that region. There was, of course, a long history of trouble with the Ordovices themselves. We do not know whether Agricola used Wroxeter or Chester as his principal base for this campaign. Chester was still in the process of construction in 79, but the probability now established that legions often carried out moves from one base to another in stages makes it impossible to be sure of the position at this moment. It is interesting to note that Tacitus specifically refers to the use of vexillations brought together for this campaign.[1] This may not only refer to troops brought from the other legions of Britain but also to concentrating in one place parts of II Adiutrix from each of its two sites before striking at the enemy. Indeed, the very fact that the army was currently engaged in a major change of permanent base should have added to the surprise created. Like Cerialis, Agricola may have deliberately chosen to use his old legion as the prime instrument of his first field operation as governor, and this is not without significance. A newly arrived governor, keen to make an immediate impression, may well have preferred to rely on troops he knew well and who knew him. Indeed, the location of that legion itself may have influenced his choice of where to act first.

Agricola struck at once, against the advice of many who thought it better to watch how the situation developed.[2] One may guess that this advice came from the group of friends who normally advised a magistrate as well as from senior officers. Tacitus would leave us with the impression that Agricola overruled opinion based on hide-bound unwillingness to act rapidly and out of the normal campaigning season, but there may have been those who thought the extermination of the Ordovices and the inevitable commitment to

[1] Tacitus, *Agr.* xviii 2: *contractisque legionum vexillis et modica auxiliorum manu.*

[2] Tacitus, *Agr.* xviii 2.

a larger war unwise in view of past history in Britain. In the event the outcome was near annihilation of the Ordovices[1] — the settlements in their area did not recover till the third century—and the annexation of Anglesey, the task from which Suetonius Paulinus had been deflected during Agricola's first term of duty in Britain. To some such action Agricola realized he was committed once he had attacked the Ordovices.[2] The two operations were militarily distinct, for the first was carried out with legionary detachments and a few auxiliaries, the second by a force of auxiliaries specially picked for their ability to swim with their arms and equipment, possibly Batavians or other units drawn from the Low Countries. With these he achieved complete surprise over an enemy that had been expecting ships and the whole elaborate business of a Roman invasion by sea. Agricola had from the first gained a psychological advantage over the Britons. He had struck before anyone, including even his own troops, had expected any positive action and had made conscious use of terror. He had now established his position with his troops, his province, and his potential barbarian enemies. He had also, in a climate where Vespasian had so recently rehabilitated the name of Corbulo, spectacularly completed the work that Suetonius Paulinus had been engaged upon while attempting to rival the achievements of the latter, and done it with maximum economy of men and effort. Tacitus does not hesitate to remind us that Suetonius had been recalled from the conquest of Anglesey by the rebellion.[3] Agricola had now joined that league of generals which Corbulo and Suetonius had represented in their day.

Unlike Suetonius, however, Agricola was not to throw away the advantages of military capability of a high order by inability to ensure just government of the provincials under his jurisdiction or to understand when the application of terror was counter-productive. Tacitus' aim in the *Agricola* is to present his subject as the ideal governor and this involves some implied denigration of his immediate predecessors. But Tacitus' purpose is not just to enhance family reputation— vital though that was—but also to instruct his contemporaries on proper behaviour and how to serve the state, even under

---

[1] Ibid. xviii 3: *caesaque prope universa gente.*
[2] Ibid.   [3] Ibid.

an evil emperor. We have to remember that Agricola's governorship in Britain started under Vespasian, continued under Titus, but was brought to an end under Domitian, whom Tacitus is at pains to represent as the ogre he appeared to the writer's own class and political faction in Roman society. For such a purpose some adjusting of the balance of fact was held to be permissible.

It is difficult to believe that the abuses in taxation that Agricola is said to have put down in his first winter were really rife under Frontinus: it is more likely that stray instances of malpractice are being interpreted as a general malaise. Yet they give some idea of the disadvantages of Roman rule. We hear, for example, of provincials having to buy back grain that they had already supplied as taxation in kind in order to fulfil their quotas, and at inflated prices, and being ordered to deliver it to military stations far away — often not served by roads — doubtless to persuade them to bribe the officials to avoid the burden.

The following summer Agricola again took the field, incorporating new territory, receiving hostages, and throwing a network of forts around the tribes whose surrender he accepted. The mention of 'estuaries and forests' in Tacitus' account of these operations[1] suggests that the north-west of England is meant, and it is probable that Agricola was here following up the work he had carried out as a subordinate of Cerialis a few years earlier. Archaeology is confirming the Flavian date of the first military occupation of many of the Roman sites in this area, for example at Ambleside at the head of Lake Windermere.[2] The pattern of garrisons reveals the classic Roman method of control of areas with difficult terrain, in which the natives were split up into relatively small units which could be supervised and prevented from making common cause. The surrender of many tribes was doubtless due to Agricola's complementary policies of continuous harassment of the recalcitrant and displays of the advantages of peace to those who co-operated.

In the winter of 79, at the time when the basilica at Verulamium was being completed, Agricola can be observed

---

[1] Tacitus, *Agr.* xx.
[2] Watercrook, however, has been shown by excavation not to be Agricolan, (*Brit.* 6 (1975), 233 f.).

turning his attention to the extension of these policies:

The following winter was taken up with the soundest projects. In order to encourage rough men who lived in scattered settlements (and were thus only too ready to fall to fighting) to live in a peaceful and inactive manner by offering them the pleasures of life, Agricola urged them privately and helped them officially to build temples, public squares with public buildings (*fora*) and private houses (*domus*). He praised those who responded quickly and severely criticized the laggards. In this way competition for public recognition took the place of compulsion. Moreover he had the children of the leading Britons educated in the civilized arts and openly placed the natural ability of the Britons above that of the Gauls, however well trained. The result was that those who had once shunned the Latin language now sought fluency and eloquence in it. Roman dress, too, became popular and the toga was frequently seen. Little by little there was a slide towards the allurements of degeneracy: assembly-rooms (*porticus*), bathing establishments and smart dinner parties. In their inexperience the Britons called it civilization when it was really all part of their servitude.[1]

Agricola's true achievement seems to have been to obtain the right balance between persuasion and pressure. Even in such advanced areas as Asia Minor the establishment of citizen colonies was deliberately carried out to spread Roman ideas and the Latin language and to inculcate and supervise loyalty to the Roman state. In local communities undergoing transformation into Roman form it was, as we have earlier noted, normal practice to expect private individuals or the local aristocracy as a whole to bear the costs. We may imagine Agricola providing both professional advisers and probably military architects and engineers for public works, but grants are very much less likely. That being so, the encouragement of construction projects was attractive to the governor, since the comparatively low cost of labour meant that the relatively modest sums the British aristocracies were likely to be able to find in these early days would provide a spectacular return in terms of propaganda for the Roman way of life.

The education of the heirs of Asiatic and African princes at Rome had long been a deliberate weapon of Roman foreign policy: now the nobility of the conquered tribes were being educated in the Roman fashion, presumably in the new cities of the pacified province, though some may have travelled to Gaul or elsewhere in the empire. It is important to realize

[1] Tacitus, *Agr.* xxi.

that the regular medium of communication in Roman administration down to the humblest level was the Latin
language. Moreover, the essential ingredient of Roman higher
education was rhetoric and this was a training for public life
as much as a cultural exercise. The emphasis on rhetoric has
often been criticized by modern classicists on the grounds
that it was obsolete after the end of the Roman Republic and
that it adversely affected Latin literature. These views are
perhaps the outcome of the concentration by historians on
the senate and public assemblies of Rome and by literary
critics on Latin texts in isolation from Roman life. It misses
the point, that rhetoric was an essential tool in the conduct
of affairs. Even at Rome, public speaking retained real importance, particularly but not exclusively in the law courts.
The latter were now a primary forum not only for the simple
prosecution of maladministration but also for the pursuit of
politics. In its new role as a supreme court the senate itself
played a major part in this area of Roman life, and provincial
communities placed great importance in having as 'patrons'
influential senators who could speak out for them at Rome,
in the senate, in the courts, and to the emperor and his
ministers. In the provinces themselves the huge development
of imperial administration and of local government on Roman
lines under the Early Empire multiplied enormously the
requirement for people capable of effective public speaking
and skilled in the conventions of Latin oratory. A fine speech
was not only admired as a work of art: it could also prove,
like most things Roman, of immediate practical use. The
methods of teaching, based on the composition of practice
pieces on set themes, meant that the Britons were learning
the rudiments of classical public life and culture at the same
time as they were being instructed in the Latin language. The
acquisition of a common framework of ideas and ideals was
central to the coming together of Roman and native. Moreover, insomuch as language itself shapes attitudes as well as
being shaped by them, the spreading of the Latin tongue
carried with it a subtle means for the absorbing of subject
populations into the Roman system. This education was, in
short, an essential step in the establishing of the civil mechanism of a Roman province.

In the next campaigning season Agricola made a very

notable advance. It is emphasized that he was opening up and
ravaging the territory of fresh nations,[1] and the pattern of
roads later established suggests very strongly that he advanced
in two columns, one through Corbridge across the Tyne and
on to the Tweed, finally reaching the Forth at Inveresk, the
other through Carlisle and Crawford, before swinging north-
east to meet the first column at Inveresk. The Twentieth
legion will most likely have formed the core of the western
force and the Ninth that of the eastern. When the two arms
of the advance had met, the joint force pressed on to the
Tay.[2] Garrisons were settled in the rear of the advance. At
some point, it now seems likely, the Twentieth may have
started to prepare a new fortress at Carlisle for themselves;
and on the eastern line of march the Agricolan base discovered
at Corbridge on the Tyne must be associated with his campaigns in Scotland.[3] Tacitus makes a particular point of
claiming that this admirable governor so placed his forts that
none of them was ever taken, abandoned, or surrendered to
the enemy, and that because they were provisioned for a year
units could winter in them however hostile the territory.[4] Indeed, it proved possible to harass the enemy continually from
them throughout the winter, a powerful inducement to them to
sue for peace. The Britons were used to regaining their
strength and their ground during winter, and probably still
had difficulty in keeping forces together throughout the year.

The summer of 81 was employed in consolidating the gains
of the previous year as far north as the Forth–Clyde isthmus.
Tacitus is emphatic that the isthmus was garrisoned,[5] but
archaeology has been slow in demonstrating substantial occupation of Flavian date. However it has for some time been
known at Camelon at the eastern end and in 1978 an undoubted Agricolan fort was found, slightly to the south of
the later Antonine Wall, at another point on the isthmus. The

[1] Ibid. xxii.

[2] The reading *Taus* in certain of the manuscripts of the *Agricola* seems convincing, even though it is a marginal variant rather than part of the text. The fact
that Agricola spent the following summer consolidating on the Forth–Clyde line
makes it obvious he had previously penetrated beyond and the Tay is a likely
halting-point on the far side of the isthmus.

[3] Identified at Beaufront Red House in 1974 and in size large enough for half
a legion.

[4] Tacitus, *Agr.* xxii.   [5] Ibid. xxiii.

existence of a string of forts has yet to be established, and it is possible that long-range patrols were employed from fewer bases than in later days. The country to the south was safe in Roman hands, at least in the east. The temporary camp known as Chew Green I, in the Cheviots alongside Agricola's Dere Street, probably represents the previous year's thrust northwards. Now, we may conjecture, the first period of occupation of the permanent sites, such as Newstead on the Tweed, began.

The emphasis of the fifth season was on a future conquest of Ireland, and we are told that the campaign started with a 'crossing' by ship and that the whole coast facing Ireland was occupied by the Romans.[1] It seems certain that these operations were in south-west Scotland, where forts are known inland, for example at Dalswinton in the Nith valley, on the south coast at Glenlochar and Gatehouse of Fleet, and towards the west coast at Loudoun Hill. It is less certain that total occupation of the area rather than containment of its tribesmen was intended. The discovery of a fort at Annan on the south-facing coast[2] strongly suggests that the 'crossing' was a sea-borne assault across the Solway Firth from the Cumbrian coast, an action in itself embodying an element of surprise and suggesting that strong resistance was expected from the tribes against a movement westwards along the coast from Carlisle. Whether Agricola made any serious preparations for an invasion of Ireland, we do not know. The consolidation of the Forth–Clyde line may suggest that the intention was indeed to move against Ireland rather than the Highlands. In view of Agricola's belief that Ireland could be conquered with one legion and a few auxiliaries,[3] the fact that the invasion was not proceeded with was perhaps fortunate. Nevertheless, in typical Roman style he kept this card in the game. Agricola was particularly interested in the psychological advantage which might be gained by removing the spectacle of a free island so close to Britain, though in fact there is no sign that the existence of unoccupied Ireland ever had any effect on the loyalty of the Britons.

In the event Agricola's attention was diverted to the more pressing problem of Scotland north of the Forth–Clyde line.

---

[1] Ibid. xxiv.
[2] Norman Hammond, *The Times*, 17 January 1978, 17.
[3] Tacitus, *Agr.* xxiv.

In the summer of 83, to forestall a possible general rising of
the tribes of the north, he launched a general advance by land
and sea. He seems to have established forts as he went, for
the first sign of enemy reaction was an assault on a fort somewhere north of the Forth. Agricola's answer to an intended
attack by the enemy in several columns was to divide his own
army into three. This proved nearly disastrous, for the Britons
promptly concentrated their forces for a night assault, which
was almost successful, on the Ninth legion. The Ninth was
only rescued by Agricola coming up in the nick of time with
the rest of his army. The particular camp involved in this
action is not known, though air photography and excavation
are gradually enabling us to distinguish the marching camps
of different periods beyond the Forth.[1] At the end of the
season both sides were eager to fight to a finish.

We do not know for certain where Agricola and his army
wintered in 83, but there is good reason to think a large camp
known at Carpow on the Tay was the point from which the
next year's campaign was launched. In that decisive summer
he entered the field determined to force the enemy to give
battle. Once again the fleet was sent ahead to raid the coast
and spread terror, and this time the army was accompanied
by British allies.[2] They came up with their enemy at a place
named *Mons Graupius*, where the Britons had at last clearly
chosen their place to turn and fight, barring further Roman
advance.[3] The location of this famous battle has been the
subject of endless debate, but the discovery of a very large
Roman camp at Durno, near Inverurie in Aberdeenshire,
makes it very likely indeed that the mountain now known as
Bennachie is rightly to be identified as Mons Graupius. Durno
itself has every appearance as being the site where Agricola's
forces finally concentrated, having advanced in two columns
represented by separate series of marching camps, one larger
than the other. We are told that the British host, under a
Caledonian named Calgacus, amounted to more than 30,000
men. We know that Agricola had 8,000 auxiliary infantry
and between 4,000 and 5,000 auxiliary cavalry. The size
and number of his legionary detachments is uncertain,
though a phrase in Calgacus' speech as reported or invented

---

[1] Cf. J.K. St. Joseph, JRS 67 (1977), 143 ff.; *Brit.* 9 (1978), 271 ff.
[2] Tacitus, *Agr.* xxix.   [3] St. Joseph, op. cit.

by Tacitus[1] suggests that he did have the main strength of his legions with him in the field.[2] His army was perhaps also around 30,000 in all. The Roman battle order was arranged with the auxiliaries forming the front with their infantry in the centre, and the legions in reserve drawn up before the camp. The glory would be greater if no Roman blood was shed.

The Britons had the advantage of the slope, as befitted the side that had chosen the ground, and placed their chariots in front of the main body. Agricola spread out his line and, sending away his own horse, led his auxiliaries into battle on foot. To lead in person was a gesture often made by ancient generals for the sake of morale. It may be remembered that as late as the eighteenth century European kings were leading their troops into battle. It emphasizes how little in the way of control a general could exercise once a battle was under way. There was little point in holding back on occasions when real advantage might be gained from being seen to be in the van.

Tacitus gives Calgacus a speech comparing British unity with what he likes to portray as the motley and unreliable nature of the Roman forces:

You are united: you Caledonians have *never* been slaves. From here there is no retreat by land and even the sea offers no escape because of the Roman fleet . . . There are no more peoples behind us. There is nothing but rocks and waves—and the Romans are more menacing than them! . . . They rob, kill and rape and this they call Roman rule. They make a desert and call it peace.

We the unconquered are not yet touched by subservience . . . At the very first assault let us show what heroes Caledonia has hidden in her bosom. Do you really think the Romans will be as brave in battle as in bed? Their fine reputation rests on our discord. The glory of their army has been built on the faults of their enemies; and it is a ragbag of many races, united by success but sure to collapse if repulsed. Do you really consider for a moment that these Gauls and Germans and (to our eternal shame) Britons too are really bound to Rome by ties of faith and affection? . . . They were foes of Rome for much longer than they have been allies: fear is a poor bond—remove it and hate will take over again. Every real incentive to victory is on our side . . .[3]

[1] It was the understood practice for ancient historians to put in the mouths of opposing generals speeches appropriate to the occasion. The convention allowed the historian to set out dramatically arguments and analysis of motive that a modern writer would include in his own comments or consign to a footnote.

[2] Tacitus, *Agr.* xxxii: *vacua castella . . . hic dux, hic exercitus.*

[3] Tacitus, *Agr.* xxxi–xxxii.

Calgacus was right in pointing to the multi-national character of the Roman army. He was probably disingenuous in contrasting this with an alleged unity among his own forces, made up of Highland clans and doubtless many fugitives from further south. He was wrong to assume no common cause on the other side, no merging of Roman and provincial, but he pointed to the vital ingredient in the Roman army, its reputation for success. To some extent that success was based on fear, on a ferocious code of discipline, but whatever the reason revolts by units of non-Roman troops were rare. Discipline and training won battles and campaigns. Mons Graupius was to be no less than a Culloden, and for some of the same reasons.

The battle fell into two stages. In the first the preliminary exchange of missiles was followed by hand-to-hand fighting, ordered by Agricola so that the Batavian and Tungrian infantry, it would appear equipped in Roman fashion, could make use of their superior arms and training in close combat. At the same time the cavalry engaged and routed the British chariots and then turned to join the infantry battle. At this point the rearward sections of the British army slowly moved down the slope and began to encompass the Roman rear. This opened the second phase of the battle. Agricola promptly threw in four squadrons of cavalry which had been held in reserve. These broke the British ranks, then rode round to take them from behind. The result was complete chaos on the British side, and Tacitus writes in triumph:[1] 'Some 10,000 of the foe had fallen: our losses were 360, among whom was numbered Aulus Atticus, prefect of a cohort, whose youthful keenness for battle and the ardour of his horse had carried him deep amongst the enemy.'

It is perhaps more significant, however, that two-thirds of the British army disappeared completely in the night, presumably back into the Highlands from which they had come, and the next morning the Roman scouts could find no trace of them. In these 20,000 angry men may be the reason for the massive concentration of garrisons, now to be established in eastern Scotland north of the Forth. Alternatively it may have been the prospect of being bottled up in the glens that

[1] Ibid. xxxvii.

had itself provoked the Britons to give battle, a battle which it was essential to Roman policy should be fought.

It is difficult to estimate the point in the history of the Roman conquest of Britain at which long-term security made complete victory over all Britain essential, if indeed it ever was. Certainly Agricola's apparent intention to establish permanent occupation beyond the Tyne–Solway line must have made this battle vital, but it may go right back to the original decision not to stop at control of south-east England. Whatever the truth, Agricola's failure to destroy or capture such a large number of the fighting men of the northern Britons ought perhaps to be recognized as crucial in the history of Roman Britain.

Most of the elements by which the Highlands were to be controlled are now known. The system hinged on a new legionary fortress at Inchtuthil on the Tay. This was supported by auxiliary forts north-east at Cardean and Stracathro and south-west at Fendoch, Strageath, Dalginross, and Bochastle. The discovery in 1977 of a fort south of Loch Lomond on Drumquhassle Ridge[1] makes complete the series that closed off the Highland massif. North of this was campaigning country. Agricola had continued his advance northwards after Mons Graupius, but despite Tacitus' proud statement that all Britain had been conquered—*perdomita Britannia*—it is clear from his own account that not all the operations Agricola had in mind were in fact carried out that season. Tacitus says that because it was late in the summer the war could not be extended,[2] and it is clearly implied that further operations in future seasons were a possibility and it was maybe in anticipation of these that Agricola sent his fleet on a circumnavigation of Britain.

Perdomita Britannia et statim omissa: Britain was completely conquered and immediately let go. Tacitus is deliberately creating a picture of a province completely conquered and handed over safe and sound by Agricola to his successor[3] and immediately let slip by the wicked emperor Domitian. We have already seen that the picture of a completely conquered province was false—the truth of the second part of the

---

[1] *Brit.* 9 (1978), 411.

[2] *Perdomita Britannia*: Tacitus, *Hist.* i.2; the war: *Agr.* xxxviii.

[3] Tacitus, *Agr.* xl: *provinciam quietam tutamque.*

statement will bear examination. It should be noted that there is one complaint Tacitus does not make. He does not say that Agricola was recalled too soon. It would spoil his picture if he implied that there was more to do. Indeed Agricola had had an unusually long run, and Tacitus' contemporary audience would know it. Instead he implies that Domitian deliberately cheated Agricola of the coveted governorship of Syria he had earned and subsequently out of malice failed to appoint him to one of the great proconsulships, Africa or Asia. Even in Agricola's death there is a hint of poisoning arranged by the emperor. Whatever the truth of these innuendoes, there is an objective test of Tacitus' veracity in the archaeological evidence for how long Agricola's dispositions in Caledonia were allowed to stand. Of the governors of the period from the recall of Agricola to the murder of Domitian in 96 we know very little. Agricola may have been followed by Sallustius Lucullus, to whom we shall return shortly. Whoever he was, it seems reasonably certain that Agricola's immediate successor had every intention of completing the permanent conquest of Scotland and likely that the forts closing off the Highland glens were in fact constructed under him. Excavation has of course demonstrated that both Inchtuthil and the auxiliary fort at Fendoch were deliberately dismantled not long after construction and evacuated, but it is important that the coin evidence proves that this did not happen before 87.

The immediate reasons for the withdrawal of the legion have been the subject of much discussion. Though it is not completely certain which legion occupied Inchtuthil, it is most probable that it was the Twentieth. If II Adiutrix was transferred from Chester to Moesia before 92, probably in 86 or 87 for Domitian's Dacian war (where the emperor was facing a serious situation, two Roman generals having been defeated in quick succession), then a move back south by the Twentieth may have become imperative. The fort at Forden Gaer in Wales is thought to have been burnt about AD 90, and a permanent reduction in legionary strength in the Welsh sector may have seemed premature. Or it may have been that a shortage of auxiliaries made permanent occupation of the whole of Scotland seem less and less feasible. In either case, the Twentieth will have moved directly into Chester. But even without the legion or the forts blocking the glens, military occupation north of the Forth–Clyde isthmus was not immediately surrendered. The concept of total occupation may have been given up or deferred, but for a short while a series of watchtowers was maintained. It is indeed not impossible that Agricola had done his work so well that the Highlands now seemed so cowed that larger numbers of troops appeared unnecessary. Under any interpretation of the evidence it is not true to say that northern Scotland was given up immediately after Agricola's withdrawal: certainly, till these watchtowers themselves were abandoned around AD 90, there was still a Roman military presence in the area. Moreover it was at a level that would suggest no serious threat was expected. Pacification, we may presume, seemed sufficiently complete that control could be exercised at a distance from a command centered probably on the large fort of Newstead in the Scottish Lowlands, as it was to continue to be into the early second century. Such peace in Scotland underlines the magnitude of Agricola's achievement in war, while it fails to support Tacitus' thesis against Domitian.

The activity south of the isthmus was indeed intense in this period, and beyond it Ardoch was reconstructed as an outpost fort. All the known Agricolan forts in southern Scotland were reconstructed, some on the grand scale. Newstead itself was increased to nearly 6 hectares (14.3 acres) and remodelled to take a detachment of legionaries and a squadron of auxiliary cavalry. The coin evidence suggests that this reconstruction was contemporary with the evacuation of Inchtuthil. Another large fort was the reconstructed station at Dalswinton, apparently designed to house two cavalry units and probably intended as a headquarters fort for south-west Scotland. Yet other forts saw modifications and improvements, which all adds up to a very substantial reorganization consequent upon the decision to vacate the forward position and to concentrate Roman forces in southern Scotland.

The withdrawal of the legion from Inchtuthil is a certainty, the date of departure of II Adiutrix from Britain is not. If the latter did not occur till some time after the former, then there was a period, however short, when the concentration of

legions in the south was restored to the same high level as
before Agricola started on his northern campaigns. The problem of accommodation was not insuperable. Wroxeter had
not been demolished when its legion was removed: it was
probably not finally abandoned till a new permanent disposition of legions in Britain seemed settled. Such a concentration, if it happened, will have occurred sometime not long
after 87. It is not impossible that one consequence was to
throw suspicion on the governor Sallustius Lucullus, for he
was executed around AD 89. The reason was ostensibly that
he had named a new lance after himself. This may have been
the immediate cause in the paranoiac atmosphere with which
Domitian had by then surrounded himself, but the background may have been some supposed (or real) connection
between the troop movements in Britain and the conspiracy
against the emperor in 89 led by Saturninus, legate of Upper
Germany.

By the end of the century the long series of changes in the
location of legions in Britain was over. Henceforth, for a
century or more, there were three permanent fortresses, at
Chester, Caerleon, and York, occupied at this time by the
Twentieth, II Augusta, and the Ninth respectively. Two
other important developments, apparently in this same
period of the last few years of the century, also have a bearing
on the over-all military situation. Both were foundations of
citizen colonies, almost certainly consisting of discharged
legionary soldiers. The first was founded at Lincoln on the
site of the disused legionary fortress. Its precise date is uncertain, though it is known to be Flavian.[1] It seems unlikely
that under Agricola legionaries were being discharged in any
number—or, for that matter, under his immediate successor—
and Tacitus would surely have mentioned so important and
prestigious a piece of work as the foundation of a colony if
it had occurred in Agricola's governorship. It seems almost
certain that the foundation was within the years 84–96 and
we may conjecture it was towards the end of that period, in
the latter part of Domitian's reign. It is possible it took place
in the governorship of Nepos (probably P. Metilius Nepos)

[1] On *CIL* XIII, 6679 a man whose place of origin was Lincoln is given the
voting tribe *Quirina* in which Flavian foundations were enrolled.

who may have been appointed before the close of Domitian's reign, as he is mentioned as a recent incumbent of Britain in a *diploma* or army discharge certificate dated to AD 98.[1]

At about the same time another colony was established, at Gloucester, on or near the former legionary fortress. The date in this case can be determined more exactly, as the city had the honorific title *Nervia* or *Nerviana*, thus establishing its foundation in the short reign of Nerva, 96–8.[2] It is noticeable that in both cases the new cities were established on land which had been within legionary territory. There is some evidence that such land sometimes reverted, perhaps unofficially, to the local civil authority when abandoned by the army,[3] but reoccupation of such land by the state may have caused less resentment than had the taking of the best tribal land by the colonists of Colchester half a century earlier. Moreover near both Lincoln and Gloucester there was riverine land that could be reclaimed by Roman drainage methods and may previously have been of little use to the locals. It is therefore quite possible that the bulk of the land taken for redistribution to the colonists had not previously been settled by Britons. As a reserve of military strength and a centre of loyal influence Colchester had been a failure, but this time not only were the colonies more tactfully situated but they were provided with walls. There is every sign that the imperial government had learnt its lesson.

Until the conspiracy of Saturninus the reign of Domitian had, *pace* Tacitus, been stern but on the whole just. His provincial administration was particularly fair, and he vigorously suppressed abuses. Unfortunately his strong personal inclination to absolutism aroused opposition among the Roman aristocracy, particularly those with a lingering desire for the return of the Republic. This was by now perhaps more an attitude of mind than a real belief in its practicality. However, in his early years as emperor Domitian had unwisely tended to ignore the senate as far as serious matters of state were concerned. At the same time his use of his power to draft into it many provincials and members of the equestrian

---

[1] *CIL* XVI, 43.   [2] *CIL* VI, 3346.
[3] See *RIB* 1049 where in AD 216 a military unit is apparently reasserting the boundaries of a military *territorium* after a period of evacuation.

order, unpopular at the time, had important long-term effects in accelerating the growth of an empire-wide senatorial class. From 88 he became more and more suspicious of individual senators and from 93 this developed into a reign of terror. At the same time heavy expenditure made the confiscations of the property of condemned senators very convenient. Finally in 96 Domitian's own wife, Corbulo's daughter, in fear for her own life led a conspiracy in concert with both praetorian prefects. This time the plot was real and the assassination successful.

The opportunity now presented to the senate to try to restore the Republic was not taken, but they came as close to it as they dared by proclaiming as emperor a fairly elderly but moderate and capable senator, Marcus Cocceius Nerva. This marks the beginning of the period often known as 'the Five Good Emperors', the reigns of Nerva, Trajan, Hadrian, Antoninus Pius, and Marcus Aurelius. Lasting from AD 96 to 180, it is regarded, in many ways reasonably, as the golden age of the Roman Empire. It is too simple a view to regard this happy outcome solely as the consequence of a revulsion against the hereditary principle in choosing emperors, but that was a major element. The new pattern was for an emperor to mark out his successor within his lifetime and usually to associate him with himself in office. This allowed the measured choice of men of experience and moderation, likely to win acceptance among the governing classes to whom they were personally well known. There can be little doubt that the system did play a great part in ensuring stability and good government over this long period. Nor can it be doubted that Marcus Aurelius' choice of his own dreadful son Commodus as colleague towards the end of his life did much to bring this fortunate age to an end. Yet even at the elevation of Nerva there were disquieting signs. The army was anything but happy at the loss of an emperor who had both shown military aptitude and raised their pay. The senate was unable to resist pressure for the execution of Domitian's murderers and Nerva was more or less forced to indicate a military man as his chosen successor at an early date. It was fortunate that his choice fell on Trajan, who had the confidence of the troops: in fact it had been he who had suppressed the revolt of Saturninus against Domitian. He thus bridged the parties of senate and army and was careful to keep this balance. This was true, too, of his family background. He was indeed patrician, but this had been due to his own father's rise to the consulship and appointment into the ranks of the patricians by Vespasian.[1] Vespasian himself had represented a new breed of emperor. Till the murder of Nero the throne had remained in the hands of the Julio-Claudian family, heirs of Julius Caesar and Augustus, who happened to descend from the most ancient and prestigious Republican aristocracy. However, both Vespasian's father and his mother, though still Italian, were equestrian, not senatorial, and he rose by himself through the system to senatorial and consular rank. Trajan had been born in Spain, where his father was a citizen of the Roman *municipium*[2] of Italica and his mother was Spanish. This was a further change. There were now emperors who, though Roman by citizenship and career, had origins in the provinces. This had been the background of Agricola too: men like him could now hope for the supreme position in the empire. The prospects and status of the great provincial families consequently continued to increase.

The advantages of merging with the new imperial aristocracy were becoming more and more obvious to the ambitious provincial, and with the upward mobility between the classes that is an outstanding feature of Roman society this attitude spread far beyond the leading families of a province. In AD 98 the first provincial came to the throne: after only two years' reign Nerva died and Trajan unostentatiously but firmly assumed power, backed by army and civilians alike.

We may now see how Britain stood at the end of the first century AD and assess the achievements of the Flavian regime in the island. From being a relatively small province encompassing only the south of England and part of Wales and still shaken by the Boudiccan upheaval, Britain was now all but entirely conquered. We have already seen that soon after the crushing of Boudicca quiet attempts were being made to

---

[1] The 'patricians' were the highest social class, a group within the senatorial aristocracy. Under the Republic membership was hereditary and restricted to certain ancient families. There were some political offices that could only be held by patricians (and some that could not). Many of these families had died out by the Early Empire, and emperors took the power to raise other families to this rank.

[2] A chartered Roman town, often of native origin (as opposed to a *colonia*, under the Republic and Early Empire a deliberate Roman foundation).

encourage the Britons to settle down into Roman ways; that by the time of Frontinus' governorship major public works were under way; and that Agricola is credited with a very large and deliberate campaign to turn Britain into a region of the empire that would fully accept the Roman way of life. It is when one turns to the archaeology that one begins to appreciate also the monumental scale on which building construction was now proceeding in Britain, representing a real enlargement in the way people thought about public life.

Flavian propaganda liked to use architecture to depict a government dedicated to the public quite unlike the egocentric regime of Nero and his erratic Julio-Claudian predecessors. The vast gesture of demolishing Nero's fabulous Golden House in the centre of Rome and replacing it with the Colosseum devoted by contrast to the pleasure of the populace of the capital was an enterprise started by Vespasian and completed by Titus and probably Domitian. In Britain, while there may be legitimate doubts about attributing the Flavian flowering of 'temples, civic squares and private houses' (*templa, fora, domos*) to Agricola alone, its reality is clear. A few examples will show the pattern, and we may start with London. We noted there was reason to think that the provincial procurator had some offices there before the Boudiccan destruction of the city and a strong probability that his main administration was sited there from the time of Classicianus. But until recent years archaeology has been able to show us little that befitted a provincial capital. It is now clear, however, that there was a period of intense building activity during the period from about AD 70 to 125, much of it under the Flavian emperors. A report on excavation at the site of the Flavian governor's palace, which places the construction of that building as not earlier than AD 80, refers to the theory that the already recognized growth of London had caused it to be granted the status of a *municipium* and its citizens to begin the construction of appropriate public buildings. Peter Marsden, the excavator of the palace, presents us with an interesting and important theory. Referring to the fact of an apparent much wider spread of major buildings than the usual municipal centre, he writes:

From this distribution it would seem that the provincial government was not only concerned with the construction of the palace, but also

with a more general programme of public building. And it is interesting
that wherever the buildings have been dated they fall into the late
first–early second century date range of the great period of public
building in London. It is generally agreed that the construction of the
basilica and forum in the City began during the Flavian period, thus
indicating the period at which Londinium received her municipal
charter; but the suggestion that this was a result of the prosperity and
general progress towards romanization rather than because the City was
elevated to the status of provincial capital is hard to justify in the light
of these latest studies. Judging from scattered traces of occupied Flavian London it is fairly clear that during this period the city had probably doubled in size, and that, at the same time, important public
buildings were constructed not just by the City itself, for the stamped
tiles in some of them indicate that there was some central provincial
government aid. These are surely the effects of Roman government
policy in actually creating a capital city, not only by massively enlarging its population, but also by constructing at least some of its
administrative buildings on a huge scale in keeping with the new status
of Londinium.[1]

The point is a convincing one, at least where the buildings
of the provincial administration itself were concerned and
these are likely to have been many. And indeed in such a
show-piece, the Flavian emperors may have considered it
worth subsidizing the city council's own building programme
for the propaganda effect it would have. Yet one cannot
help wondering whether the tile-evidence is conclusive—or
whether, particularly where official architects were seconded
for local works, materials might not have been supplied from
government sources but paid for by the local community.
Other cities showed spectacular development in the same
period. We have already noted the foundation of two new
coloniae, Lincoln probably at the end of Domitian's reign
and Gloucester under Nerva. Both occupied the sites of
evacuated legionary fortresses. The former was given a new
set of walls almost straight away, doubtless to impress as well
as to defend, for there was no general programme of town-
wall building at the time, even for London. Gloucester had
private houses for its ex-soldier colonists carefully designed
to fit the areas vacated by the former barrack blocks. There
at least it appears certain there was central planning. At

---

[1] Marsden, 'The Excavation of a Roman Palace Site in London, 1961–1972',
Archaeology in the City of London, No. 4, Museum of London (reprint from
Trans. London and Middx. Arch. Soc. 26 (1975) 1 ff.). Cf. Philp, *Brit.* 8 (1977),
1ff.

Gloucester, however, the main public buildings, the forum and basilica, were probably not actually erected till Trajan's reign, but at Cirencester and Verulamium we have seen them under construction as early as the governorship of Frontinus. Inspired by state or individual, each development contributed to the transformation of Britain. This emphasizes how necessary it is for us to see the whole of the last twenty-five years of the first century (and probably the early years of the second) as a single, more or less continuous period of growth in the scale and quality of urban life in Britain—at least as reflected in its public architecture.

This should prompt us to reflect in turn on how the countryside fared in this period, whence many of the local notables who took part in this town life must have come. It does not appear that Agricola's encouragement of the Britons to build houses in the Roman manner was, at least as far as Tacitus' report of it goes, related to the construction of villas, or 'country houses' in modern terms. Tacitus uses the word *domus*, the normal word for town houses, and we may be sure that this is what he means. It reflects the stated objective of getting the Britons to come in from their scattered dwellings, become educated in Roman ways and take part in public life, which in Roman terms was a city-based concept. It was important that they should have a stake in the town, even if they retained houses on their country properties. No one would dream of suggesting that they give up their country estates altogether, since the possession of land was an essential ingredient of being a Roman gentleman, but the city was the proper focus of life.

We might expect Agricola's policy to be reflected in the archaeology of the Flavian towns. This makes the results of a recent study particularly interesting.[1] In the countryside of Roman Britain there are very many examples of farmsteads changing relatively little from their pre-Roman style and indeed continuing so throughout the Roman period. On the other hand, there is a fair amount of archaeological evidence that as the province recovered from the Boudiccan revolt other country properties gradually began to be rebuilt in

[1] C.V. Walthew, 'The Town House and the Villa House in Roman Britain', *Brit.* 6 (1975), 189 ff. See p. 614 below for a discussion of the term 'villa'.

Roman style and to Roman standards of amenity, if in a fairly modest way. This was a process that seems to have gained momentum in the Flavian period and be well established in the first half of the second century. Yet the Flavian *towns* seem to produce only the simplest sorts of Roman private buildings, and most of these have a predominantly commercial rather than residential look. An exception may be the *coloniae*, but even there the house-types have a tendency to follow closely, even to be built upon the foundations of, the de-molished barrack-blocks of previous legionary occupation. These buildings, too, are not particularly grand, and the possibility has to be borne in mind that at least some of the colonists preferred to live on land they farmed outside the city. For the other towns a quotation from the study cited excellently summarizes its position:

If the main hypothesis of this paper is correct, namely that in planning, construction and decoration villa houses were more advanced than town-houses until roughly the mid second century, this clearly has important social and economic implications. It is difficult to conceive of the Catuvellaunian, Silurian, Cornovian or Dobunnic nobles occu-pying the Insula xiv timber buildings at Verulamium, the strip-houses of Caerwent and Wroxeter or the Insula v shops at Cirencester, although it is perfectly possible that they owned such property and drew the revenue from it. It would rather seem that they continued to live on and invest in their country estates. This is surely what one would ex-pect from the nature and pattern of Iron Age settlement and there are some villa sites where the evidence for continuity of occupation from the late Iron Age into the Roman period is reasonably convincing . . . Can we then say that Agricola's attempts to win the Britons over to town life failed? In terms of attracting the wealthy to build themselves town-houses the answer is probably yes, at least initially.[1]

Dr Walthew is right to define his terms closely in the last sentence from the quotation. In terms of that narrow object-ive it does look as if Agricola failed in his policy, or, to be absolutely fair, the policy Tacitus attributes to him. But, leaving aside the fact that even the simple private buildings so far identified in the towns of the period are in the main superior to the Iron Age dwellings these British notables had presumably previously inhabited, there is the very important point that if they were becoming landlords of town properties, commercial or otherwise, they were going far to fulfilling the

[1] Ibid. 203 f.

wider objectives of the policy—to get the Britons to have a personal stake in the city. Once they had a financial interest in the city and its prosperity and once there was physical property to be attended to from time to time, their links would be much stronger. Private business as well as public was likely to bring them into the cities and they would gradually be drawn into social life there. They could, of course, enjoy Tacitus' 'smart dinner parties' in their new villas by inviting in the owners of neighbouring estates and, as they came to build bath-houses, which were becoming increasingly common in the countryside, they could equally enjoy the peculiarly Roman social pleasure of the baths on a small scale, but hardly any villas of the period in Britain could provide *porticus,* and for the full life of the public baths and the forum they had to come into town. They may even have soon realized the advantages of a town *pied-à-terre* (and for this reason we should perhaps not be too hasty in dismissing the apparently humble town-houses of the period as unworthy of the landowning class) and the appearance of better houses towards the middle of the second century would be a natural progression. The architectural pattern does seem to be the reverse, as Dr Walthew points out, of that in northern Gaul, Germany, and Switzerland, but we should perhaps beware of assuming a very wide difference in social life. It is indeed difficult to see how the Britons became so fluent in Latin and so imbued with Roman culture as Tacitus claims if they mostly stayed at home in the countryside, though we must make allowance for Tacitean hyperbole as he steadily builds up the eulogy of Agricola. A Latinized culture, nevertheless, does not mean the Romano-British aristocracy of this generation could not have regarded themselves as primarily resident in the countryside—a way of life in tune with the ideals of the Roman authors they had doubtless been set to read. They may well have preferred to spend their money on villas rather than in setting up elaborate establishments for themselves in the cities, while still making use of urban facilities when it suited them to do so.

The much-discussed site at Fishbourne is in some ways out of line with the pattern so far emerging, but has important features that fit in with it. The site originally seems to have been military. Then, still under Claudius, appeared a timber-framed villa. This was replaced in the 60s by the first stone villa, which is in line with the scatter of stone villas on the south coast built in the years after Boudicca (though at Fishbourne one cannot be sure of the exact date). It is out of line in that it is of a particularly high standard for the period in Britain, including use of imported materials. The enormous 'palace' itself was constructed some time after AD 73, probably about 80. It certainly is very large: it is bigger than the known fourth-century villas of Britain—the great age of the grand country mansion—and matched in nearby northern Gaul chiefly by the vast villas of the third century. For Flavian times it has been measured against imperial houses and has been compared with Nero's Golden House and Domitian's palace on the Palatine Hill in Rome. These, however, are urban houses—and at the heart of the capital of the empire, where the same size of dwelling may confidently be assumed to represent much greater wealth than in the countryside. When we know more about the house attributed to Nero's wife Poppaea at the site known as Oplontis on the Bay of Naples we may have a better comparison for a country—or rather, like Fishbourne, seaside—house at that social level. Indeed, renewed archaeological interest in the Roman villas of Italy—a subject long neglected—suggests that an establishment on the scale of Fishbourne may be nothing out of the ordinary viewed against the standards of the senatorial aristocracy of the period.

Whether or not Fishbourne belonged to Cogidubnus is a debate that has unduly overshadowed the important point that, though on a larger scale, it stands with a few neighbours on the coast in representing the beginnings of revival after Boudicca, and in its enlarged and revised form coincides with the powerful surge in building in the province in mid to late Flavian days.

Peter Marsden's remarks quoted above, dating the Flavian governor's palace at London not earlier than 80 and advancing the idea of a wide programme of public building there in the late first century and early second, make one wonder whether Fishbourne may not have been part of the same movement. It may come as early in date as the start of construction of the town centres at Cirencester and Verulamium in the earlier 70s, or it may be Agricolan. If it was not the residence of the elderly Cogidubnus[1] it is possible to think in terms of an official seaside residence, perhaps matching the Flavian palace at London. One may probably discount the idea that it was a purely private residence—unlikely on such a magnificent scale in Britain at this time—but we do not have to assume that it was provided for the governor himself. We know, for example, of the presence in Britain on temporary assignments of no less than two of the new grade of special legal commissioners introduced by Vespasian—*legati iuridici*—in the period immediately after AD 80.[2] Both were senators of great distinction. One was Salvius Liberalis, the other the outstanding jurist Javolenus Priscus himself. The latter had already held legionary commands by this time and was to go on from this post to hold the consulship. Subsequently he held three major provincial governorships including Syria and the most prestigious of all, the proconsulship of Africa, both posts of which Agricola himself was disappointed. Men of this standing would hardly be out of place in such a setting as Fishbourne. Nor is it fanciful to imagine that in that grandiose period it might have been felt appropriate to have a villa on this scale to house visiting dignitaries situated close to one of the ports of entry to Britain. It is likely to have had a highly important role by example in stimulating private villa development. It is, in a sentence, an anomaly in scale and luxury among the Flavian villas of the province, but of a piece with the over-all trends of the age in Britain.

The exceptional importance attached to Britain (and perhaps again with the need to impress) is indeed underlined by another, undoubtedly official piece of construction. Archaeology following the devastation in central London by bombing in the 1939–45 war has revealed the construction of a fort in the Roman city around AD 100 or soon after. Such a fort is extremely rare in the Early Empire. It is possible but very unlikely that it housed an 'urban cohort', one of the special units of gendarmerie otherwise only known outside Rome itself at Lyons and Carthage and originally transferred there from Rome. Its troops almost certainly included the legionaries and other men on headquarters duty on the governor's staff and in his guard. Indeed, the cessation of active campaigning in the north is of a piece with London extensively

---

[1] See Appendix IV below.   [2] *ILS* 1011; *ILS* 1015.

rebuilt on the assumption that from now on the governor was normally going to be resident in the provincial capital and not spend most of his time on campaign far away. In this situation the military as well as the civil administration would be run permanently from there. Whether such a policy was established in the peaceful days when Inchtuthil could be given up or after the abandonment of southern Scotland (which will be discussed shortly) does not affect this argument: Trajan had great military projects elsewhere and in the context of a lack of intention of further campaigning in Britain the rounding off of the Flavian rehousing of the administration of Britain by the provision of such a fort at the provincial capital would make good sense and—if a rather unusual arrangement—be entirely in line with the originality of many of Trajan's initiatives in government.

At about the same period there was a general move to replace timber buildings in fortresses and forts with stone, no doubt partly because the structures put up by Frontinus and Agricola were reaching the end of their useful life, but also implying the prospect of fairly stable military conditions.[1] At Caerleon the process had already begun in AD 100,[2] at Chester it was at least partly carried out after 102,[3] and at York either at the end of 107 or during 108.[4] The same process of reconstruction is also known from auxiliary forts. The general implication seems to be that the army was settling down to be a garrison army and campaigns were no longer likely as the normal way of life. The military stations were not now to be thought of primarily as winter quarters but as the year-round homes of permanent garrisons.

It is possible that the first of Trajan's appointments to the governorship of Britain was T. Avidius Quietus.[5] He may already have been in office when Nerva died, and held the post till perhaps 100 or 101. His immediate successor was probably L. Neratius Marcellus,[6] who was governor by 103. These men are of particular interest, for, like their contemporary the

---

[1] Professor M.G. Jarrett is surely right that this was a gradual process, not an intensive programme (see V.E. Nash-Williams, *The Roman Frontier in Wales*, 2nd ed. Cardiff (1969), 31 and 38).
[2] *RIB* 330. [3] *RIB* 464. [4] *RIB* 665. [5] *CIL* VI, 43.
[6] See A.N. Sherwin-White, *The Letters of Pliny: A Historical and Social Commentary*, Oxford (1966), 229 f.

Younger Pliny, in whose letters they are recorded, they belong
to that group of prominent senators who were coming to
terms with the permanence of the Principate and supported
Nerva and Trajan as the next best alternative to the restoration of the Republic. What we know of them exactly charac-
terizes the spirit and practices of the governing class of their
time. Their appearance in Britain, apparently one following
the other, reflects the high prestige which the governorship of
Britain then held in the senatorial career.

The intellectual climate of the party now in power is typified by Quietus. In his youth he had been a member of the
aristocratic circle of Thrasea Paetus, most distinguished of
the traditionalist opposition to Nero and put to death by
him. This circle professed devotion to the old Republic and
their ideals were enshrined in the Stoic philosophy, though,
as we have seen, many were ready to draw back from the extremes of open opposition in favour of survival or from a
belief that the service of the state was best promoted by continuance in public life, however bad the emperor. Quietus'
friendship with the historian Plutarch and an apparent particular interest in Greece help to fill in the picture of this
man.[1] He was a personal friend of Pliny, in whose support
he spoke in the senate when the latter was attempting to obtain justice for the surviving relatives of Helvidius Priscus, a
family that had suffered much under the Flavians for continuing the senatorial opposition to the emperors.[2]

Neratius Marcellus was also personally known to Pliny.
The influence the latter now wielded among the closest adherents of the new regime is clear. From Marcellus Pliny was
able to obtain for his slightly younger contemporary Suetonius, the historian, a commission as a military tribune.[3]
Particularly interesting for our purposes, however, is that this
piece of patronage was not only clearly routine, but that
when Suetonius declined the opportunity to go to Britain
Pliny had no difficulty in transferring the post to someone
else whom Suetonius wished to advance. Thus we see a
governor of Britain at this time not only able to make appointments in his army without prior reference to the

[1] Ibid. 388.   [2] Pliny, *Letters,* IX.xiii.15; cf. VI.xxix.1.
[3] Ibid. III.viii.1.

emperor but also quite content, as it were, to issue a friend with a blank cheque.[1]

It is, of course, true that such appointments often entailed little real responsibility, but in general the existence of such an apparently casual system only avoided causing the rapid military and administrative collapse of the Roman provinces by the fact that it was operated by a fairly close-knit ruling circle, made up of men of experience in government who could in general be relied upon not to promote hopeless men into positions of responsibility, if only to protect their own credibility. The weaknesses are obvious, and it is not surprising that imperial supervision of postings became tighter. However, while the emperors themselves continued to be drawn invariably from the same social group the system was not unsuccessful in providing for the staffing of the empire.

It is a curious coincidence that among the fragments of writing tablets found in the early fort at Chesterholm in Northumberland (now often referred to by its Roman name, *Vindolanda*) is one in which Neratius Marcellus' name has been read, a draft, it would seem, of a private letter to be sent from that place.[2] Chesterholm, by a further coincidence, lay on a road, the Stanegate, which, as we shall see became of particular importance soon after AD 100. Indeed, it may well have been within Neratius' governorship itself that a major change came over the situation in the northern frontier region. Some time not long after 100/105 Newstead and probably Corbridge were destroyed and Dalswinton, Cappuck, Glenlochar, Oakwood, and High Rochester all burnt. It has been suggested that the burning of the latter five forts was part of a strategic withdrawal due to the need for troops for the Dacian wars of Trajan (101–2 and 105–6), but since the destruction of Newstead looked in excavation like the result of a military disaster and that or Corbridge very likely so, it is possible to argue that all the forts went that same way.[3]

[1] The literal truth of this is borne out by the fact that he seems to have sent Pliny a blank warrant for the commission, the name to be filled in and the document forwarded to military records.

[2] Tablet no. 31—Robin Birley, *Vindolanda: A Roman frontier post on Hadrian's Wall* (1977), 136; A.K. Bowman and J.D. Thomas, *The Vindolanda Writing Tablets*, Newcastle (1974), 26.

[3] In this we may perhaps see the hand of the hostile chariot-borne British chieftain Argiragus, mentioned in Juvenal, iv. 126–7 (published sometime after AD 100).

Trajan's Dacian wars may well have been, however, the reason why the ground lost was not permanently reoccupied. Some action was certainly taken, for the mess left at Newstead was cleared up by a Roman working-party, implying the temporary return of Roman forces to the northern part of the area. As yet however there was no reoccupation of the forts.[1]

The Trajanic frontier thereafter seems to have lain in the Tyne–Solway gap, along the Stanegate road. This east–west highway acted as a link between the western high-road to the north, through Carlisle, and the eastern one, Dere Street, where it crossed the Tyne at Corbridge. How the extremities of this line were held remains uncertain. At the western end the subsequent Hadrianic system was carried on down the coast and the discovery of a new fort at Burgh by Sands, probably of slightly earlier date and of a length of road between that and Kirkbride fort to the west suggest that the Trajanic *limes*[2] was carried some distance along the Solway Firth.[3] At the eastern end the Stanegate may in this period have turned across the Tyne over the Dere Street bridge and continued eastwards along the south side of the river. The fort discovered at Washing Well, Wickham, in the country south-west of Newcastle, could prove to have Trajanic origins. However, we still know relatively little for certain about the northern border of Trajanic Britain. This has been emphasized in a recent work on Hadrian's Wall, which makes some tentative suggestions useful to record here:

Rebuilding the legionary fortresses in stone, in itself perhaps no more than was necessary some thirty years after their construction in timber, may have been the occasion for a decision that Britain, like Germany, was to stay as it was, without significant expansion. Such stability made necessary some system of border control. Observation towers had already come into use under Domitian and existed on the Danube under

[1] Punitive action at this stage may be reflected in Juvenal, xiv.196, when forts of the Brigantes are mentioned as being stormed. On the other hand the reference may be to some Hadrianic activity. The Brigantes seem to have extended into south-west Scotland (e.g. *RIB* 2091). For evidence of action under Trajan see Birley, *Roman Britain and the Roman Army*, 22 ff.

[2] The word *limes* meant either 'road' or 'boundary' or sometimes both. It took on the sense of fortified boundary or frontier, including both a road or path with forts or posts spaced along it and an actual physical barrier such as a palisade or wall.

[3] See Norman Hammond, *The Times*, 17 January 1978, 17.

Trajan. Fortlets of milecastle[1] size appeared on the Germany frontier under Trajan. In the light of these the Stanegate towers and small forts almost as big as those in Germany, based like them on a lateral road, may indicate the extension of the German type of frontier control to Britain. At the same time strengthening the numbers of fighting troops on what now became the frontier road by stationing them at half-day instead of day intervals gave it a special military importance and made possible more intensive patrolling.[2]

Despite the uncertainty over the circumstances in which Scotland was given up by 100 or soon after, Roman Britain had attained what in the perspective of history may seem like its natural boundary. This may not have seemed so at the time. Tacitus, when he used the phrase *statim omissa* and left the reader with the impression that the recall of Agricola had allowed the total conquest of Britain to be thrown away by the jealous Domitian, may well have been deliberately concealing that in fact Scotland had been evacuated in the reign of the hero–emperor Trajan under whom he was writing, whether this had been because of disaster or simply a prudent withdrawal. It may have been sensible but did not fit the image of the conqueror. In the long run, however, the Tyne–Solway boundary was, with minor adjustments, to prove the best that could be found.

NOTE

The date of the arrival of Agricola and of the forums at Verulamium and Cirencester. Against accepting AD 77 are two difficulties. One is that a cohort of Usipi figures in the account of the sixth year of Agricola's governorship, and that tribe was not annexed till 83. In this period auxiliary units were raised from among non-citizens under Roman rule, not from peoples outside. On the other hand, this argument is not conclusive since the Usipi were close to the border of Roman military occupation, and the exact distance beyond within which Rome could exert effective power is uncertain. The other difficulty is that, as Professor E. Birley pointed out to Collingwood, it is clear that Agricola's final battle, in his seventh year of office, took place *after* the Emperor Domitian's triumph granted for the war in Germany against the Chatti, which seems to have been awarded in 83 (compare Tacitus *Agr.* xxxix with *Camb. Anc. Hist.* 9 (1936), 164, n.2 where the dating of the triumph is implied from numismatic evidence). Neither piece of evidence is conclusive, but 78 seems the more likely.

---

[1] This is the term applied in the modern literature to a type of post on Hadrian's Wall.

[2] D.J. Breeze and Brian Dobson, *Hadrian's Wall* (1978), 25.

There is a further ambiguity in the *Agricola* that helps those who support the later date. The destruction of the *ala* by the Ordovices (*Agr.* xviii) is not firmly placed in the governorship of Frontinus, so there may in fact have been a gap between Frontinus' departure from Britain and his successor's arrival. For a fuller discussion of the dates of Agricola's governorship see R.M. Ogilvie and Sir Ian Richmond's annotated edition of the *Agricola* (Oxford, 1967), 317 ff.

The dedication inscription of the forum at Verulamium (*JRS* 46 (1956), 146 f. no.3) erected *on completion* of the building is dated to the second half of 79. If Agricola in fact arrived in the second half of 78, there is hardly enough time within his governorship for both planning and construction. Moreover the heavy buttressing in one corner of the forum is perhaps due to the known presence of an earlier ditch. At Cirencester the principal building of the forum, the basilica, which is dated in general terms 'mid-Flavian', subsided into a similar earlier ditch. It looks as if the Verulamium designers had had time to learn from the mistake at Cirencester, which would certainly put the latter structure back into Frontinus' governorship at the latest.

7

HADRIANIC BRITAIN

THE death of Trajan in 117 on the way home from his
eastern conquests marks a turning-point in Roman, indeed in European, history. In Britain as we have seen
Trajan's reign was a period of military withdrawal and consolidation, in sharp contrast to this emperor's brilliant career of
expanding the empire elsewhere. In Dacia and Mesopotamia
his energetic campaigns won great new areas, and that alone is
reason enough why no forward policy was adopted by him in
Britain. It is reasonable, too, to assume that Britain benefited
from Trajan's careful attention to the appointing of provincial governors and other officers. In many ways Trajanic
Britain seems to foreshadow the general imperial policy of
Hadrian, who gave up the expansionist policy and abandoned
Trajan's new territories in the east. In the military sphere
Hadrian concentrated on restoring order in the various parts
of the empire where there was violent disaffection and in
consolidating the frontiers. A great part of his reign was spent
in personal tours of inspection of the provinces, strengthening each part of the empire, one by one. The renewed respect
for the Principate which had been won both at Rome and
with the army by Nerva and Trajan permitted the new emperor to concentrate his energies away from Roman politics
and towards the largest schemes of civil and military reconstruction. His constant presence among the frontier armies
encouraged their loyalty and his keen interest in the provinces underlined the fact that he was the second provincial
to come to the throne (from the same city as Trajan) and
emphasized the oneness of the empire—or at least its communities of Roman citizens, wherever they might be within
its territories. Italy was no longer regarded as mistress of the
Roman world and the provinces as her inferiors, and though
she always retained a special social status she gradually lost
her political privileges.

Yet, though a provincial like Trajan, Hadrian was a very
different person. The former had seemed a personification of

all the old Roman virtues: a deliberately modest style of life, a devotion to the ancient ideals of the family, a grandeur in his public works essentially based on utility, and a conviction that the glory of Rome was best served in the extension of the empire by wars of conquest. Hadrian shared Trajan's devotion to duty, his incorruptibility, and his scale of vision but he broke away completely from the ideal of military glory by conquest. His personal tastes were for Greek culture, his character complex. His building works were as vast as Trajan's, but they were motivated as much by aesthetics as utility. His devotion to the Greek youth Antinous and the extravagance of his grief at his untimely death reveal an emotional and restless nature. Yet, though he did not share Trajan's affinity with the senate, a fact that was to sour his relations with society at Rome, he was probably the emperor most suited to the needs of the empire at that time. Constant expansion and internal stresses in the immediate past required that attention should now concentrate on continuing and expanding the work of the Flavians and of Nerva and Trajan in reforming the system and welding the peoples within the Roman frontiers together into a single nation.

From this time forward, the Roman empire effectively stopped expanding. From time to time there were limited movements which rationalized a frontier at one point or another, but the emphasis in practice was on defence. Looked at from the long perspective of history, it is sometimes argued that the loss of dynamism involved in the conversion from offence to defence was the first sign of 'decadence' in the empire. Nevertheless the immediate effect was three-quarters of a century of peace in most corners of the empire, and the consequent development of its general prosperity and its institutions to their highest peak. This was such an achievement that the decision cannot fairly be criticized on any grounds based on hindsight. To people alive at the time close on a century is a long time, and the achievement of peace and restrained government over a huge area for such a period is something that few statesmen in world history have to their credit.

It should not, however, be imagined that there was any change of heart among Romans at large on their nation's role in the world. Even Hadrian could show by his insensitivity to the Jews that he conceived as Rome's task the extension of the classical way of life to the whole empire, not the governing of the Roman world in terms of a multitude of nations with equally valid cultures. Nor was the carrying forward of this task by glorious conquest generally regarded as an obsolete ideal. On the contrary Britain itself finds Hadrian's immediate successor, Antoninus Pius, launching a new forward movement, and we shall have to beware of assuming this was merely to achieve a more economical frontier or to deal with a local difficulty with neighbouring barbarians. It was force of circumstance that held the limits of the empire no larger than the first quarter of the second century left them. Indeed one may even question whether some of Hadrian's own decisions to retreat from military adventure were not more due to outside pressures than to his own inclinations.

At the very beginning of his reign he was in severe difficulties. Not only were there major uprisings within the empire to be put down, notably that of the Jews in the east, but his own succession had been in odd circumstances. The peace of the empire in the second century has often been attributed to the practice of nomination of their successors by the emperors. However, there were suspicions that Trajan had not in fact named Hadrian, and there was considerable discontent among some of the late emperor's most senior generals. Hadrian had in practice been a member of Trajan's family, since being made his ward many years before, when his own father died under Domitian. He was popular at the imperial court and he had risen steadily to the highest offices and received important honours. There is probably little reason now to doubt that Trajan intended him as his successor to the throne, but whatever may have been known to the imperial family there was sufficient public uncertainty to present an opportunity to those who disliked him. As these included leading generals and senators this was an extremely hazardous moment. Hadrian dealt with this by rapid changes in some of the senior posts. This action was immediately followed by the unmasking at Rome of an alleged conspiracy against the emperor by four of the most distinguished ex-consuls, who were promptly condemned in the senate and executed. Hadrian had not yet returned to

Rome and blamed the praetorian prefect for excessive zeal, but despite all his protestations and lavish gestures of good-will to Senate and People, suspicions lingered and were never entirely dispelled. This was a black mark on the beginning of his reign, particularly among the senatorial aristocracy. The latter had been the chief victims of the dark days of Domi-tian's closing years. In many ways Domitian's rule had been excellent but it was the senatorial aristocracy that still pro-duced the governors and generals who administered the empire and formed the society to which the provincial upper classes aspired. These executions demonstrated that the good times that had seemed to have returned with Trajan were pre-carious and lay at the mercy of the emperor and the army. Peace and moderate government in fact were to continue for a long time, but the warning note had been sounded.

The 'Conspiracy of the Four Consulars' reminds us that ambition was by no means dead among the most influential men in the empire, and raises the very real question as to whether Hadrian could have afforded the continued acqui-sition of military reputations by leading senatorial generals which would have followed from extending Trajan's policy by further unnecessary wars. Moreover, to deal with the widespread provincial disturbances and at the same time to launch new foreign conquests would almost certainly have meant increasing the army very considerably. It is therefore perhaps not surprising that Hadrian followed Augustus' advice to Tiberius to maintain the empire within its existing borders. Yet one remembers that Augustus' advice was quite contrary to Augustus' own personal ambitions and those of his class.

The political executions and the moves to placate public feeling were, however, sufficiently successful in that Hadrian was able, unlike any emperor before him, to spend a very large part of his reign away from Rome. His protracted tours of inspection and reform in the provinces are of major im-portance, not least in Britain where they left their mark in the most pronounced way in both civil and military affairs. These absences established incidentally but finally that the *de facto* capital of the empire was wherever the emperor might be. Tacitus had remarked that the 'Year of the Four Emperors' revealed the basic truth that emperors could be made by the frontier armies: Hadrian made it abundantly

clear that the empire could be run from outside Rome and
Italy, not just for short periods while the emperor was on
campaign, but for years at a time. This combined with
Hadrian's intense interest in the welfare of the provinces to
accelerate the process by which the provincials came to
identify themselves with the empire. A major step had been
taken in creating a unified governing class and it also looks
forward to the almost universal extension of the Roman
citizenship to the free inhabitants of the empire at the beginning of the next century.

Though a good deal of the credit for this imperial peace
and uniformity of sentiment must go to Hadrian, Britain was
certainly one of the places where all was not well at the
beginning of Hadrian's reign. When in the course of one of
his early tours he arrived in Britain in 122, the province had
recently been the scene of serious warfare, probably in the
governorship of Q. Pompeius Falco (118-22). This was
most likely caused by invasion from outside the province,
though the epigraphic evidence is not entirely certain.[1] It is
also possible there was collusion with rebels within the
province, of which a fourth-century description of Hadrian's
intention in building the Wall—that it should divide the barbarians from the Romans—may be an echo.[2] The governor
had brought the situation back under control,[3] and the
emperor bent his mind to seeing that this sort of trouble
should not happen again.

In the year of his visit Hadrian appointed his friend Aulus
Platorius Nepos governor to succeed Pompeius Falco and it
seems likely that emperor and governor were closely associated in the design of the new frontier. It is also almost
certain that Hadrian brought a new legion with him, VI
Victrix, since it is recorded on what was probably one of the
first works of the great building operations now put in

[1] See *RIB* 1051: if *diffusis* [*barbaris*] is the correct restoration then invasion
from outside must be implied.

[2] SHA *Hadr.* xi, 2: *Britanniam petiit, in qua multa correxit muramque per
octoginta milia passuum primus duxit, qui barbaros Romanosque divideret.*

[3] 3,000 men brought to Britain as detachments from legions in Germania
Superior and Hispania Tarraconensis, probably in 122 (*ILS* 2726, 2735: see
Jarrett, *Brit.* 7 (1976), 146 ff.) may have been directly for the purpose of building work on the Wall, but may also indicate there had been serious legionary
casualties in Britain that needed replacing.

hand.[1] Whether the Sixth was brought specifically for the Wall project or as a replacement for IX Hispana is not known. The unlucky Ninth legion is last recorded in Britain at York in AD 107/8. Many theories have been advanced, notably destruction in battle or cashiering after a disgraceful defeat. These two possibilities have been connected with the trouble under Falco, with which has been associated a remark by the orator Fronto that many Roman soldiers had been killed by the Britons under Hadrian.[2] However Professor Eric Birley has pointed out that we know of officers of the Ninth who can hardly have served with it before about 120 and one whose service would most happily be placed nearer 140.[3] It had certainly disappeared by the time geographical lists of legionary dispositions were compiled about AD 170.

The discovery of stamped tiles of the Ninth at Nijmegen in Holland suggested that it had been transferred to the Lower Rhine before it disappeared from the army list. This could have occurred under Trajan, or after pacification of the province by Pompeius Falco. Professor E. Birley, while accepting a transfer to Nijmegen, argued for a rather later date, under Hadrian around 126, the original intention being to transfer it to a new base at Carlisle.[4] This would have put a legion in the centre of the northern linear system. Birley sees the Ninth as then having been sent to the east, to disappear in the Jewish wars of the 130s or against the Parthians in 161. Whatever the precise details of its end, however, we no longer have to seek for its disappearance in Britain. Whether there was a short period when the legionary establishment in Britain was reduced by one legion depends on which of the dates for the transfer of the Ninth is accepted:[5] early in Hadrian's reign—probably as early as 122 itself—the new

[1] *RIB* 1319, 1320: see also D.J. Breeze and Brian Dobson, *Hadrian's Wall* (1978), 53 ff.
[2] Fronto, ii. 22 (ed. Haines): *Hadriano imperium optinente quantum militum ab Iudaeis, quantum ab Britannis caesum.*
[3] E. Birley *Roman Britain and the Roman Army*, 20 ff.; and in R.M. Butler (ed.), *Soldier and Civilian in Roman Yorkshire*, Leicester (1971), 71 ff.
[4] Tiles of the Ninth from Scalesceugh: see E. Birley, op. cit. 76.
[5] There are various permutations on the theories: the Sixth could have arrived before Hadrian's visit to replace the Ninth; or both may have been in Britain under Hadrian before about 126.

legion, the Sixth, has appeared on the British scene and taken over the fortress at York.

The new frontier, on whose works the Sixth together with the Second and the Twentieth were employed, was the most elaborate in the Roman world and much modified in the course of construction. We have noted above that under the Late Empire it was believed that the purpose had been to divide the barbarians and the Romans and we have mentioned the suggestion that there had been recent collusion between rebels within the province and barbarian enemies without, but too much should probably not be read into it. The presence of outpost forts shows that imperial territory went beyond the line of the Wall in Hadrian's day and for long after. Such a situation indeed was legally recognized on the German frontier where imperial estates are recorded on both sides of the military line. The remark is more revealing of Roman attitudes in the third and fourth centuries when almost all the people within the empire were Romans, than the Hadrianic period when there were still many *peregrini* or non-citizens living within the frontiers who had not yet received Roman status, centuries before large settlements of whole barbarian peoples within the borders became regular imperial policy.

Drs Breeze and Dobson have summarized the contemporary military thinking which formed the background to the emperor's visit in 122:

Hadrian had come to Britain from Germany, where he appears to have initiated an artificial barrier, a timber palisade, apparently the first of its type in Roman history. There had been a frontier defensive system on the Taunus, Wetterau and Odenwald sections of the German frontier from the time of Domitian. This was most developed on the Taunus and Wetterau. Here the frontier system consisted of a road linking turf and timber forts. Also along the road were timber towers some 540 to 650 yards apart. This is not so dissimilar from the contemporary Gask Ridge system in Perthshire where the watch towers, often rather closer together than in Germany, lay along—and on either side of—the road leading north from Ardoch to Bertha. Under Trajan some new forts were built on the Taunus and Wetterau and fortlets were added to the frontier. The startling new development under Hadrian probably took place during the visit of the emperor to the area in 121–2. The reign of Hadrian saw the construction of such barriers not only in Upper Germany, Raetia and Britain but also perhaps in Africa, where the frontier complex known as the Fossatum Africae was possibly built at this time. Hadrian's Wall, however, is the best known, best preserved, and most explored of all the artificial barriers of Hadrian's reign or any other.[1]

The new frontier works took advantage of the fortunate configuration of the ground. The valleys of the Tyne, Irthing, and Eden form an almost continuous trough from sea to sea, near the bottom of which ran the Stanegate road on which the existing forts lay. The new line followed the northern edge of this Tyne–Solway gap, along which for about two-thirds of its distance a ridge gives a generally commanding view northwards and at its centre rises to the heights of the basalt cliffs known as the Whin Sill. Only at the western end of the Wall was it apparently thought necessary in Hadrian's day to provide outpost forts to the north.[2] A convincing explanation is that those were not outposts in the normally understood sense of the word, but garrisoned a part of the territory of the conquered Brigantian tribe that lay beyond the physically most convenient line for the Wall.[3]

The order in which the various elements of the Wall system were built and the modifications introduced has been deduced from excavation and from observation of their relation to one another. The original scheme was to provide a lightly held line ahead of the main garrisons: a raised sentry-walk rather than a barrier against determined attack. It was probably intended to act as a fence like the German palisade to stop easy unauthorized movement and communication between disaffected elements north and south of the Wall. The Wall itself (the 'curtain' or continuous wall) was begun at the eastern end, and was originally planned to be in stone ten feet wide and about fifteen feet to the rampart-walk, as far as the Irthing, and from there onwards where good building stone is harder to come by, in turf twenty feet wide and about twelve to the walk, perhaps as an interim measure. In front of the Wall was a ditch, of varying width and depth.[4] The patrolling garrison was housed in small forts at intervals of one Roman mile, known today as 'mile-

---

[1] Breeze and Dobson, op. cit. 54.   [2] Birrens, Netherby, and Bewcastle.
[3] Breeze and Dobson, op. cit, 43; cf. Salway, *Frontier People of Roman Britain* (revised 1967), 182 f.
[4] Whenever it has been excavated the ditch has appeared as flat-bottomed, not V-shaped, but this may be due to later cleaning-out.

castles,' with two turrets between each pair. The turrets throughout were in stone from the beginning, the milecastles in the Turf Wall sector only being in timber and turf. The 'broad' foundation of the stone wall was carried through to the Irthing and the 'Broad Wall' to its full height taken through as far as the crossing of the North Tyne. The continuous base laid, the milecastles and turrets were constructed on the foundation before the curtain wall was brought up, presumably to provide shelter and look-out posts for patrols protecting the working parties at this early stage.

As its western end the frontier works were continued for something like another 50 miles down the Cumbrian coast, where crossings to and from the shore of south-west Scotland are quite easy.[1] Here there was no curtain wall, but the same plan of forts and minor works, known nowadays as 'mile-fortlets' and 'towers' to distinguish them from the works of the Wall proper, has been discovered and must be considered an integral part of the system. Though at least one of these forts was being built in or after 128,[2] it is now considered that the coastal stretch was part of the original plan. The fort at Maryport was apparently at first built for a larger unit than occupied it eventually, and may well have been designed as a local headquarters for this sector.[3] In 1975 a pair of shallow parallel ditches were picked up at several points along the first section beyond the end of the continuous curtain wall at Bowness-on-Solway, clearly connecting the towers and mile-fortlets as far as Cardurnock on the River Wampool and at one point at least were associated with stakes or a palisade.[4] Preliminary excavation suggested that this work was part of an early stage in the evolution of the system. Despite several attempts at repair, this particular work seems to have been abandoned within the Hadrianic period in the face of coastal flooding problems, but it indicates clearly the intention to mark a continuous barrier of some sort. It is not

[1] The dating of the permanent fort at Ravenglass, a further 15 miles south of St. Bees Head, to about AD 125 by excavation (*The Times*, 18 August 1976, 14) suggests we must extend our view of the Hadrianic dispositions on this coast.

[2] Moresby (*RIB* 801), where Hadrian is given the title 'Father of his Country' (*pater patriae*), not acquired till 128.

[3] M.G. Jarrett, *Brit.* 7 (1976), 148 f., citing R.L. Bellhouse, *Trans. Cumb. & Westm. Ant. & Arch. Soc.* 2nd ser. 70 (1970), 40 ff.

[4] G.D.B. Jones, *Brit.* 7 (1976), 236 ff; *Arch. J.* 132 (1975), 20 ff.

known so far if this ditch-system was ever continued south of the Wampool: the first section may have been thought enough and the sea a sufficient marker beyond. Elsewhere in the empire water was employed as the continuous line, supported by forts and other works, as on parts of the Rhine and Danube. The Vallum, the rearward earthwork to the Wall, has not yet been found behind the coastal section, even in the Bowness to Cardurnock section, but the fact that it turns sharply southwards before it is lost suggests at least that a further stretch was in mind when the Vallum was planned and may yet be found.

While the central sector of the Wall was being built, the first major modifications were introduced. The width of the curtain wall was reduced to eight feet (two and a half metres) and—a much greater change of plan—the fighting garrisons were brought up on to the Wall. The forts of the old Stanegate line were now mostly abandoned. At certain of the new forts, for example Chesters and Housesteads, the Broad foundation and the demolished remains of a turret have been found beneath the superimposed fort. Another large-scale change is represented by the rebuilding in stone (to the eight-foot gauge) of the Turf Wall from the Irthing to the 'Red Rock Fault' five miles to the west, where the limestone ends and red sandstone becomes the underlying rock. This latter reconstruction occurred after the main garrisons were moved up on to the line, as is demonstrated at Birdoswald. The new stone wall was there carried on a fresh line in front of the old Turf Wall, which Birdoswald fort had already spanned and obliterated, and was taken up to the front corner of the fort which previously projected beyond the curtain line.[1]

The reduction in gauge of the curtain wall may have been made possible by a change in the composition of the core which has been noted, giving a greater strength for a given thickness, but a direct design connection has not been satisfactorily demonstrated. It may rather have been due to a need

[1] The forts added to the Wall are in two groups, the earlier like Chesters and Birdoswald spanning and projecting beyond the Wall where physically possible, the later, such as Carrawburgh, constructed with their fronts flush with the curtain. It had presumably been found undesirable or unnecessary to have three of the four main gates of a fort in front of the Wall. The reconstruction of the curtain in stone at Birdoswald represents the taking of an opportunity to convert that fort to the latest pattern.

for economy and speed of completion. The rebuilding of the Turf Wall in stone in its first sector from the Irthing was probably intended from the first. In the event, the rest of the Turf Wall was also replaced in stone, though to a nine-foot width that has been called the 'Intermediate Wall'. In this sector the change in the local rock meant greater difficulties in obtaining good building material, and this further phase in the development of the structure must have meant a proportionately greater expenditure.

Beyond Newcastle, to the east, there was one more fort which lay at Wallsend. On grounds of the spacing of the forts, this seems to fit in with the first decision to move the garrisons up to the Wall, but the curtain Wall itself is to the eight-foot gauge and seems to have been built late in the sequence of construction.[1] It may be that at least for the time being the river was felt to be sufficient of a linear barrier, and low priority given to the curtain. When actually built, the curtain was carried on beyond the fort and down to the Tyne.

Most of the modifications seem to have been decided upon and indeed substantially carried out during the governorship of Platorius Nepos. It is reasonable to assume that the main purpose of moving the garrisons on to the Wall was to allow rapid deployment of troops along and in front of it. It was not a decision to take lightly, since, as well as what must have been major problems of redesign and rescheduling, there was substantial demolition of work completed or half-done. As Professor Jarrett has pointed out, it must have become obvious very soon to the commanders of the units in the Stanegate forts that the existing situation was absurd.[2] The day-to-day manning, supplying, and maintenance of the Wall itself must have been extremely awkward and probably weighed much more heavily on the officers on the spot than distant prospects of battle conditions in some hypothetical war. If planning errors on the largest scale were not a commonplace of life in complex civilizations, it would be surprising that this was not realized when the Wall was first designed. On the other hand, we could perhaps give Hadrian and Platorius Nepos the benefit of the doubt and assume

[1] Breeze and Dobson, op. cit. 70.   [2] M.G. Jarrett, *Brit.* 7 (1976), 150.

they decided to tackle the task in stages; deliberately choosing to see by experience whether it was possible to avoid moving the garrisons even if it meant expensive alterations if the gamble did not come off. One may wonder, too, whether at first they were avoiding trouble with the troops. Some everyday tasks may have become easier when the garrisons were actually moved on to the Wall, but the men had been comfortably settled in relatively sheltered forts well down the slopes behind the Wall. In the end, however, the balance of advantage must have been clear, at least to senior officers.

A further modification, representing an enormous expenditure of labour, was the addition of the rearward earthwork known to us as the Vallum. It swerves from the direct route to avoid certain of the forts and was thus certainly constructed after the decision had been taken to move the main forces up on to the line. It was a continuous ditch twenty feet wide and ten deep with a flat bottom eight feet wide, flanked on either side by twenty-foot mounds set thirty feet back.[1] This huge work cut a swathe a hundred and twenty feet broad practically from sea to sea.[2] It was constructed without breaks, unlike the ditch in front of the Wall which was omitted where conditions made it difficult to cut or where a steep drop rendered it unnecessary. The Vallum was obviously felt essential throughout its length. Its purpose has been much disputed, but Sir Ian Richmond's idea that it formed a barrier preventing unauthorized access to the military zone with the risk of damage to official buildings outside the forts and the theft of bulky stores and equipment such as wagons which had to be left outside the crowded forts, is eminently reasonable. It would also have provided protected overnight camping grounds for units and supplies in transit along the Wall, thus obviating the normal need to construct temporary camps for what must have been a very frequent event. There is no reason at all to accept the oft-repeated

[1] The approximate metric equivalents are: ditch 6m x 3m; bottom 2½m; mounds 6m high; berm (space between a rampart or wall and its ditch) 9m; total width 38½m.

[2] The two ends of the Vallum are not precisely known. See p. 177 above for the western end. At the eastern end of the system it seems to have turned down to the River Tyne a little short of the fort at Newcastle. This is in itself some evidence that the Vallum was built before the extension of the Wall to Wallsend.

theory that the Vallum formed the boundary of the civil province. It was not felt necessary to delimit any other frontier province in this way, and there are no structures on the line of the Vallum that could have served as control posts. Crossing was nevertheless severely limited: the through roads were opposite the forts on the Wall just to the north. There were indeed causeways also provided south of the milecastles in between the main forts, but these only gave on to the south berm[1] of the Vallum and did not penetrate the south mound. Their function was to provide access by men from the Wall itself, probably for maintenance purposes but perhaps for patrolling duties as well.

The most extraordinary feature of the Vallum is undoubtedly its immense scale. It reflects the extravagant ideas abroad at the time in imperial circles, and there can be little doubt that it was intended to impress and overawe. If we may, also with Richmond, assume a purpose connected with the day-to-day working of the Wall system, then it emphasizes the seriousness with which pressure from the south was taken. There is no need to imagine that a major assault by rebels from within the province was expected. Modern armies have become very conscious of the effects of harassment by a disaffected local population and even a tradition of intercommunal raiding and disorder can be extremely inconvenient to a power attempting to impose peace, even when there are no political factors involved.

Platorius Nepos' record for expenditure on frontier works cannot often have been exceeded by a single Roman governor anywhere. He fell out of favour with the emperor, perhaps for this reason. Expenditure on construction grew and grew and there must have been those who wondered where it would end. The assessment of requirements seems consistently to have been faulty and the magnitude of the modifications involved very considerable. Yet the errors of judgement may have been Hadrian's own, and he did not like his acumen in such matters questioned. Trajan's brilliant architect Apollodorus, for example, was exiled on a mere pretext—eventually executed—for displeasing Hadrian by doubting his architectural abilities. Money was therefore perhaps not at the heart of the imperial disfavour that fell on Platorius Nepos: Hadrian

[1] See note 1, p. 180 above.

himself was by nature incredibly lavish on building projects, as the numerous new cities bearing his name, his enormous villa at Tivoli, and the elaborate monuments to his sorrow at the suicide of Antinous most emphatically testify. Indeed we cannot be sure that Nepos' tour of duty in Britain was in fact deliberately cut short, whatever the point at which the emperor ceased to think well of him, for his replacement around 125 (by a governor whose name we do not know)[1] is not particularly early.

Until recently the appointment of Sextus Julius Severus in about 131 as governor was thought to imply that there had been serious fighting which required the presence of one of Hadrian's most distinguished generals. This fighting, it was conjectured, might have been provoked by the building of the Wall and the cutting of traditional contacts between the people north and south of the line. However there is no archaeological evidence yet to support such a theory, and Professor Jarrett has recently shown that not only is the epigraphic evidence formerly called in support better associated with the original visit of Hadrian in 122 but also that in a period of peace, as now existed, the command of a province with a large army was exactly what one would expect of such an officer at the particular stage he had then reached in his career.[2] It is very much to the point that in 132 or 133 he was transferred to deal with the extremely serious revolt of Bar Kochba in Judaea. The over-all military situation in the empire had now changed abruptly with the outbreak of a major war. The writer Fronto's report of heavy Roman casualties in Hadrian's reign at the hands of the Jews certainly refers to this war, which needed stiff fighting and a large army to win; but the same author's reference to the other substantial loss of men, in Britain, can as I have already mentioned perfectly well be associated with the fighting at the beginning of Hadrian's reign and there is no need to assume that he is speaking of the same period in both cases.

To succeed Severus in Britain after transferring him so soon to the east Hadrian drafted in P. Mummius Sisenna. It is

[1] *RIB* 995 bears the name of a governor, but it is illegible and Mr R.P. Wright points out that it may be that of Nepos himself. It is also possible that Nepos' successor was himself succeeded by M. Appius Bradua, alternatively dated to 115–18.

[2] M.G. Jarrett, *Brit.* 7 (1976), 145 ff.

possible that this was the governor responsible for carrying out some of the latest stages in the development of the Wall under Hadrian. Yet more modifications had certainly been approved and work on them started by the time he arrived. It had become apparent that there were sections which were difficult to control from the new forts. This problem was tackled by adding extra forts in one or two places. One example of these forts is Carrawburgh, which has yielded an inscription of the governor Julius Severus,[1] but whose relatively late position in the sequence of construction could be deduced independently by simple logic from the fact that it overlies the filled-in Vallum which had here run parallel to and a little way behind the Wall. A more curious situation is that of the fort at Carvoran, where the fort lies south of the Vallum. The separation of Carvoran from the Wall is more apparent than real, for the reason for its construction well to the south was quite probably the presence of a marsh which the Vallum had already been diverted to avoid. It does, how-ever, appear to have been a late addition in its Hadrianic form, since a dedication[2] which can be dated to the years 136–8 was set up at Carvoran by the actual unit commander who supervised the building of the fort wall.[3] On the other hand it is possible that the placing was influenced by the existence of an earlier fort, not yet found but which it would have been logical to site here to guard the junction between the Stanegate and the road southwards to the Pennine lead-mining area near Alston which lay under the protection of the fort known as Whitley Castle.

It will by now be clear that the building-history of the Wall under Hadrian is extremely complicated and extends over a substantial period. We cannot be confident that we yet understand it all, and the changes of archaeological opinion over the years are a clear warning against accepting any par-ticular theories as immutable. It is not without its ironies that the Romans themselves obviously could not make up their minds what best to do. In some ways its scale, complexity, and modifications are symbolic of the vast and restless imagi-nation of Hadrian himself. On the other hand it is fair to remember that much of the system probably represents ideas

---

[1] *RIB* 1550. [2] *RIB* 1778. [3] *RIB* 1818, 1820.

that were new and untried, at least on this scale. In the end it looks as if practical considerations of manning, operation, and administrative convenience forced reappraisal and detailed improvement. Nevertheless the conception proved in the long run effective and Hadrian's choice of a frontier here, despite all the fluctuations and changes of detail over the centuries, proved decisive.

In the short run, its primary effect was to divide native from native, indeed probably provincial from provincial, for the better maintenance of order. It presumably made easier the development behind the Wall of settled conditions in which the economy of the tribes to the south could develop unhindered by raids from their neighbours and laid the foundations for a peaceful reign. The development of a heavily settled agricultural area in the Cumbrian Plain was recognized some time ago[1] and has recently been reinforced by further air photography.[2] One may confidently assume that the presence of so many troops, and in due course their families and an associated trading community,[3] further stimulated the economy. The maintenance of peace and good order was to the advantage of everyone settled there, Roman and native. The largest fort on the Wall was at Stanwix, part of modern Carlisle, where the western route into Scotland ran through the Hadrianic line. It almost certainly indicates that the most senior unit commander on the Wall was stationed there and probably implies that the immediate headquarters for the system lay here, with responsibility to the legionary legate at York. Stanwix in fact lies not far off the centre of the Wall system considered as a whole, from Ravenglass in the south-west to Wallsend in the east. It is not surprising that the locality around eventually developed into a civil civitas, with its own city at Carlisle.[4]

---

[1] Salway, op. cit. 113 ff.

[2] G.D.B. Jones, *Arch. J.* 132 (1975), 16 ff.

[3] Salway, op. cit. 101: similarly, for example at Housesteads, early civil settlements are known associated with the forts, even if in the second century they were kept at a distance by the Vallum.

[4] The earliest civil settlement on the site of the city may be Trajanic/Hadrianic or even earlier (judged from the amount of early samian pottery found there), if it does not originate from a putative legionary fortress. The town may predate the Wall, but the establishment of Stanwix must have ensured its long-term growth.

While I believe it is nonsensical to talk of the Wall as having an economic, not a military purpose, the role of the army in the second century became, through force of circumstance, essentially the keeping of order, both internally and against the incursions of foreign invaders. It was now only rarely used to win new territory but it still served to further the careers of the upper and in many cases the lower classes. From time to time it gratified the personal ambitions for glory of emperors. It had not yet evolved into a largely self-sufficient institution that could make its own interests paramount in the Roman state. It had not challenged the government since the elevation of Trajan. Hadrian's decision to eschew further conquest and to employ this loyal army to establish the strongest possible frontiers gave Roman Britain along with other parts of the empire a crucial period of stability, in which to consolidate the foundations laid down under the Flavians and Trajan but which might have come to little if the ceaseless military expansionism had not for a while been halted.

The Flavian period in Britain had been marked by spectacular advances in Romanization, but the great public buildings and the widespread adoption of Roman fashions were very recent impositions on a province of which much had not long before been in savage rebellion and was still in part being brought to heel. It is interesting to note that some Flavian initiatives may have been stillborn. Wroxeter, if one could be sure of the interpretation of its central area, would provide a striking example. In brief, the position in that city is that a large Flavian bath-house was incomplete when it was abandoned at the end of the first century. It was subsequently demolished and replaced by a forum under Hadrian, and a new set of public baths built on the opposite side of the main street. The neatest solution to the historical problem presented is the one that was long accepted, that the first impetus for the creation of a grand civic centre failed, and it was not till Hadrian's visit to Britain that a completely new start was made. This may still be the truth, but there are alternative explanations.[1] However, the great dedication inscription of

---

[1] See Wacher, *The Towns of Roman Britain,* 358 ff. for a discussion of this and related problems, and p. 376 for the possibility that something similar happened at Caerwent.

AD 129-30 set up by the *civitas Cornoviorum* over the entrance to the newly completed forum leaves us in no doubt as to the purpose or date of that structure.[1] It is reasonable to assume that Hadrian's visit to Britain was as much a spur to civil development in Britain as it was to military. It is also perhaps reasonable to observe that, just as it took most of the decade and many changes to complete the work on the Wall, much the same may have happened to civil enterprises he set in motion. The latter, we must once again remind ourselves, had largely to come out of the pocket of the local inhabitants, however clearly the imperial will may have been made manifest.

In London it is possible that the fort was built as late as the beginning of Hadrian's reign in preparation for his visit to Britain[2] (it was fitted into a grid of city streets that was already in existence) and probable that other public works were undertaken in the capital in this connection. It is reasonable, too, to assume that fairly rapid action was taken to restore the city after the major fire which happened during his reign,[3] presumably from accidental causes. Elsewhere, however, there is more direct evidence for a renewal of enterprise in the cities. Leicester's impressive forum was building at the end of Hadrian's reign and Caistor-by-Norwich also received its city centre under him, though on a much smaller scale, as befitted a *civitas* that had been severely retarded by its great rebellion in the previous century. Mr Wacher has also argued that Hadrian was obliged to create some new urban centres as a consequence of the decision to build the Wall:

The greatly increased troop concentration required by the new frontier work was only achieved by withdrawing units from forts in Wales and Brigantia. As earlier, under the governor Agricola, it could only be done if suitable civilian administrations could be established to replace military government. In taking this action, Hadrian to some extent gambled on the continued peacefulness, after military control had been removed, of potentially troublesome areas. It proved a gamble which did not entirely succeed.[4]

He cites Caerwent, Carmarthen, Aldborough, and Brough-

---

[1] *RIB* 288.
[2] Peter Marsden, *Roman Palace Site*, 70.
[3] This occurred c. AD 125-30. For recent traces see *Brit.* 7 (1976), 345.
[4] Wacher, op. cit. 375 ff.

on-Humber as examples to support this thesis. Yet there are real difficulties in the argument. One is that so far none of these towns (and even the exact site of the last is problematic, as he demonstrates) is certainly Hadrianic in origin, though they may be. The second is what I suspect to be a major misconception, that military government was normal in areas containing permanent garrisons. It is much more probable that the routine administration of the civilian population was a burden transferred from the army to the local communities as speedily as possible. This, of course, left the army itself with the option of intervention if an emergency arose. Equally, it could be sent in by the governor as his local agent whenever he had some specific task he wished undertaken directly rather than through a *civitas*—or a client chieftain, where such yet retained some recognized authority. It might be, for example, that the provincial procurator had asked the governor for troops to assist in the collection of taxes. Otherwise, it was only where there was a standing risk of rebellion and the tribes so un-Romanized as to be unfit to run their local affairs in accordance with Roman ideas that the local military commanders had to carry out direct administration on top of their ordinary duties. An alternative in difficult areas was to appoint a Roman commissioner (*praefectus regionis* or similar official), often a centurion, to run the affairs of the district. But the normal pattern was local responsibility. Under the Early Empire this was in general a tolerable arrangement, but it left dangerous precedents that came to fruition in the third century. The way the army had been used had divorced it from the day-to-day running of the community while developing in it a tradition of intervention at the behest of central authority. It was only a short step in the third century to intervention—indeed arbitrary intervention—in its own interest. The seeds of conflict between civilian and soldier were sown.

The theory of military government as a normal feature under the Early Empire has, however, a further assumption contained in it, one which, as Professor Jarrett has pointed out in another context, has no certain basis and is on the face of it positively unlikely. It is regularly assumed without question that forts were occupied or left empty in response to the peacefulness or otherwise of the region in which they lay.

Yet this ignores the real problems of finding suitable accommodation for particular units, with a given size and composition of total forces in a command at a particular moment,
a situation which is familiar to modern military planners. In
peacetime, without the overriding priorities of hostilities,
many factors other than purely operational ones weigh
heavily in the choice of location for individual units. On the
other hand, Mr Wacher may well be right in seeing the opportunity for troubles in the Pennines in the middle of the
second century as created by a gamble on Hadrian's part in
withdrawing troops from that area. This argument would be
strengthened if in fact, as now seems possible, it is proved
conclusively that there was no corresponding major reduction
in the garrisons in Wales, since no similar uprisings seem to
have occurred there.

Despite these uncertainties, one is still left with the strong
impression that Hadrian's interest in the province provided an
impetus that spread widely and deeply and started developments that may only show up in the archaeological record in
the succeeding period. The depth of the effect on the cities is
perhaps best indicated by the way in which the town-houses
seem, as we have seen, now to catch up in scale and standard
with the villas. The latter, too, continue to flourish and increase, and a more uniform spread of Romanization seems to
be emerging. Both in town and country the adoption of Roman ways and tastes and the increasing complexity of local
and central administration meant a growth in service industries and occupations. This brought in more and more Romans
in official posts at every level on varying lengths of tour of
duty, and Romanized people from many corners of the empire in the way of trade and business. It also opened up
opportunities for local men in larger numbers and further
and further down the social scale. In particular the countryside must have been affected directly by many industries depending on natural resources—for example iron deposits or
potters' clay—for in many ways industry was a rural rather
than urban phenomenon in the ancient world. Indirectly the
development of a money economy and the multiplication of
opportunities for marketing must have had a profound effect
on rural economies and the involvement of the rural population in the Roman way of life.

There is at least one rural area where a much more direct intervention by Hadrian is highly likely, and on a very large scale. The emperor is known to have had a lively interest in the problem of formerly cultivated land within the empire which had for one reason or another been abandoned. The same problem was to be particularly acute in the Late Empire and still troubles modern governments who try to tackle marginal land. Research in the Fenland of East Anglia has shown that, probably as a result of natural changes in the relative level of sea and land in the region of the Wash, large areas of potentially highly productive land were becoming available for settlement in the first century AD.[1] We have already noted the gravel island of Stonea as the possible site of the stand of the Iceni against Ostorius Scapula in 47, but the very remoteness of the Fens at that time was perhaps the reason for the location of that battle. Certainly there are very few pre-Roman Iron Age finds from the Fens and it is only in Flavian times that there is a first trickle of settlement. Somewhere around 120, however, there is apparently a sudden and very large influx of population, associated with 'straight-line features'—waterways, drove roads, and some long-distance boundaries—that indicate public works. The settlements themselves seem at first sight highly haphazard, but their form is largely dictated by the innumerable natural watercourses, and there are clear signs that at least the broad areas of settlement were decided by a central authority. The nature of the settlement is part farming (apparently chiefly pastoral), part industrial—almost certainly salt-making. The likelihood that the Hadrianic administration saw the opportunity demonstrated by small-scale private enterprise in the latter part of the first century and decided to exploit it with the emperor's authority, if not at his direct command, is very probable indeed. It is a great temptation in archaeology of the historic period to connect archaeological data of about the right date with a known person or event. Without a direct link we cannot be sure we are right, and a shift of opinion on the dating will destroy the theory. But with this caveat, the Fenland development (particularly that of the 'Silt Fens', the new alluvial land towards the sea as opposed

[1] See C.W. Phillips, (ed.), *The Fenland in Roman Times,* Royal Geographical Society Research Series 5 (1970).

to the 'Peat Fens' inland) is consistent with a perception that the enormously elaborate and permanent new frontier system of the Wall would require an equally permanent and regular source of supplies of just the sort the Fenland could produce. It would be like Hadrian to see the possibilities and to produce a scheme on a grand scale to seize the opportunity. The fact that many of the settlements went out of use after only a short life was almost certainly due to drainage problems that it may have been impossible to foresee. On the other hand the Wall has already shown how spectacular schemes of the Hadrianic period could require expensive modification and leave one with doubts about the judgement of the men in charge.

In a way, too, the early abandonment of many of these Fenland settlements is symbolic of the attitude of the succeeding regime to Hadrian's work in Britain once he was dead. A new emperor was to bring almost immediately changes which must have surprised the men who had spent two decades laboriously constructing what they must have assumed was to be the permanent framework within which the governors of Britain were henceforth to work, the frontier and military system on which their administration largely hinged, and behind which the civil province would continue to develop. But they might have had a suspicion that the death of such an unusual Roman emperor as Hadrian would bring a return to more conventional ways of thinking at the level where the highest policy decisions were taken.

NOTE

Hadrian's Wall and Offa's Dyke. Frank Noble's fundamental reappraisal of Offa's Dyke, the Dark Age linear earthwork in the border country between England and Wales which is almost certainly correctly attributed to Offa, King of Mercia, in the second half of the eighth century, ought to draw attention to features that provoke thought on the siting and operation of ancient linear frontier works, particularly Hadrian's Wall. Offa's Dyke did not mark the limit of Offa's kingdom. It runs in places across existing 'townships' (local administrative areas), which display the same boundaries before and after the construction of the Dyke and appear to be little affected by it. Secondly, Mr Noble has observed that passages through the Dyke were required at intervals of not more than a mile in pastoral country (perhaps as little as half a mile in arable), permitting normal agriculture to continue.

I have already indicated that I believe that Hadrian's Wall was neither the border of the Brigantes nor regarded as the frontier of the province.

In the first phase of the Wall, the milecastles with their gates would provide just such passage (suitably supervised) as would serve a local pastoral native community needing immediate access to grazing grounds on both sides of the Wall. This could have continued when the first series of forts was constructed on the line of the Wall itself. Once, however, the decision was taken to build the Vallum, in effect creating a continuous military zone, then this practice would have to stop. As we noted, the Vallum had the regular points where passage through was possible opposite forts. At milecastles, access was from the northern, or military, side only. Such a change would not have seriously affected long-distance transhumance, the movement of cattle at the change of the seasons from one sort of pasture to another, but would have stopped everyday freedom of movement by shepherds.

8

THE ANTONINES

IN 136, two years before his death, Hadrian had prepared for the succession by adopting one of the consuls for that year, under the name of L. Aelius Caesar. However the latter's own premature death forced a new choice on the emperor. This time he settled upon the man whom we know as Antoninus Pius, a distinguished member of the senate who had already acquired a reputation for honesty and devotion to duty. He had been a consular since 120, and towards the end of Hadrian's reign became a member of the emperor's *consilium,* the advisory committee which was analogous to the group of senior friends which it was customary for a Roman magistrate to invite to give him counsel. Hadrian had made this *consilium principis* more formal than before, and there can be no doubt that Antoninus' long previous career in the public service and his closeness to the emperor towards the end gave him intimate knowledge of the workings of the empire and Hadrian's own policies in matters of state. Indeed, in the emperor's last year Antoninus largely administered the empire on Hadrian's behalf. He thus came to the throne exceptionally well prepared. To extend further the principle of adoptive succession Hadrian had also required Antoninus to adopt both Marcus Aurelius, nephew of Antoninus' wife Faustina, and L. Verus, son of the original intended successor L. Aelius. Hadrian was making sure there would be no repetition of the uncertainty over his own elevation.

Nevertheless, it may in truth have been the respect in which he was held by the senate that ensured Antoninus' untroubled accession in 138. This respect he retained throughout his life. The exact reason and significance of the title 'Pius' bestowed on him by that body is uncertain, but it reflects their recognition of his devotion to the Roman state, the quality that Roman moralists liked to think was the mark of the ancient figures of the Republic. Though he, too, came from a provincial family, Gallo-Roman on both sides, his father and his mother had been of consular stock and he was himself a great landowner in Italy. He preferred to live in the villas on these estates as much as possible, and unlike Hadrian showed no signs of wanting to travel the empire.

The respect and affection in which he was held by the members of the senate and the fact that he so clearly seemed one of them allowed him unobtrusively to continue the policy of strengthening the grip of the imperial administration on the empire. The measures he took to stop abuses by equestrian procurators and by freedmen were doubtless popular with senate and provinces alike, while conducive to good government. His tendency to keep efficient provincial governors in office for longer periods was perhaps more difficult to reconcile with senatorial opinion, for it reduced the opportunities for promotion in the senatorial career. Yet it may have been welcomed by some individual senators and assisted continuity in provincial administration.

His foreign policy was deliberately unadventurous and in general followed Hadrian's line of resisting expansion of the empire. Unlike Hadrian, however, he largely avoided grandiose projects and had a keen eye for financial economy, while at the same time engaging in considerable building operations. It was, in fact, Hadrian's memory that gave Antoninus some of his most difficult problems. It proved not at all easy to persuade the senate into proclaiming the deification of his predecessor, a notable sign that the old resentment had not died with him. It may also help to explain Antoninus' surprising change in imperial policy in Britain, the one notable example of deliberate expansion by war in his reign. Indeed, even if Hadrian's Wall had been immensely costly to construct, one might have expected that with the modifications completed, the expenditure would now have been regarded as best written off and the new system allowed to settle down. In fact, Antoninus' decision on the British frontier was as dramatic and perhaps as sudden as Hadrian's own disavowal of Trajan's conquests in the east.

It may have been one of the very first acts in office of the new emperor to appoint to the governorship of Britain the energetic Q. Lollius Urbicus, previously governor of Lower Germany. He is found as early as 139 reconstructing the base at Corbridge where Agricola's old road to the north crossed the Tyne.[1] This is a sure sign of an interest in Scotland, for as in Agricola's day it made an ideal point from which to prepare for a campaign—and now permitting the preliminary work to be done without disrupting the routine of the Wall garrisons. Reconstruction here would make no sense unless forward action was contemplated, since the garrisons had only just been moved forward on to the Wall from this and the other Stanegate sites. As a guard for the Tyne bridge a mere fortlet would have been quite adequate, if it had become apparent that the crossing had been left vulnerable. Something larger was afoot. The Greek topographer Pausanias, writing in the second century, says that Antoninus Pius never willingly made war:[2] it seems likely that the pressures which had led to the strengthening of the Hadrianic frontier had now reached such a pitch that a drive into southern Scotland would have been justifiable on purely military grounds.[3] In 140 Lollius Urbicus was still building at Corbridge;[4] by the end of 142 or the beginning of 143 coins announced a victory in Britain. It therefore seems certain that the reoccupation of southern Scotland occurred between these dates. That this victory was in a Scottish campaign is attested by Capitolinus' statement that Antoninus Pius 'conquered the Britons through the agency of the governor, Lollius Urbicus, and having driven off the barbarians built another wall in turf'.[5]

The new frontier *limes* across the Forth–Clyde isthmus is dated by inscriptions to the reign of Antoninus Pius: its commencement under this governor is attested by two of them and we may suppose that it was started at the latest in 143.[6] The details show it to have been basically similar in concept to Hadrian's Wall but conceived on more economical

[1] *RIB* 1147. See also John Gillam, 'The Roman forts at Corbridge', *Arch. Ael.* 5th ser. 5 (1977), 47 ff.

[2] Pausanias, VIII. xliii. 3.

[3] I do not believe that this was the occasion when Antoninus Pius deprived the Brigantes of the greater part of their territory for making war on Roman subjects. (Pausanias, VIII. xliii. 4. See Salway, *Frontier People*, 184 ff.)

[4] *RIB* 1148.

[5] SHA *Ant. P.* v, 4: it has long been noted that *submotis barbaris* seems a conscious echo of Tacitus, Agr. xxiii (*summotis velut in aliam insulam hostibus*).

[6] *RIB* 2191, 2192. Construction seems to have occupied the whole of the Second legion and about half of each of the other two legions now in Britain, the Sixth and the Twentieth.

lines. This time the continuous barrier was constructed from
end to end in turf, on a stone base generally about 14 feet
wide, and fronted by a ditch normally about 40 feet across
and 10 feet deep.[1] There is good reason to think that as
originally conceived the Antonine Wall closely followed the
developed pattern of Hadrian's Wall, with forts on the line
but comparatively widely spaced, interspersed with smaller
stations.[2] Economy was also served by omitting the Vallum
and providing the forts with defended annexes, which might
serve the same military purpose at less expense in construction
and supervision.[3] Subsequently more forts were added,
bringing the main garrisons much closer together than on the
southern Wall. The length of line held was itself shorter, and
the final result was a system held in considerably greater
strength, the forts being an easy march apart and the concentration of troops approximately double that on Hadrian's
Wall. The new line was therefore more capable of resisting
powerful thrusts than the old, which was primarily fitted to
act as a base for patrols and an obstacle to casual crossing. By
the time the second stage of the Antonine frontier had been
completed a significant step had been taken towards the concept of a static frontier held in great strength, though it is
doubtful whether this was by conscious decision. It is more
likely to have been dictated by immediate considerations of
operational convenience and economy, another step in the
process that had brought the main garrisons up on to Hadrian's
Wall from the Stanegate behind. The army was almost certainly expected to patrol continuously in the field and to
meet any major enemy force in open battle. The Wall could,
however, now contain substantial enemy forces without
being obliged to muster a large army, no longer depleting
other parts of the line to deal with trouble at a single point.

The reoccupation of southern Scotland was clearly intended to be permanent. This could hardly be demonstrated
more dramatically than by the fact that on the southern Wall
the Vallum was now deliberately cancelled by means of
cuttings through the two mounds, usually every forty-five

---

[1] The approximate metric equivalents are: wall-base, 4m; ditch, 12m x 3m.

[2] See B. Hanson and L. Keppie, *Current Archaeology*, 62 (1978), 91 ff.

[3] There is no convincing evidence that the annexes were civil settlements as
sometimes alleged.

yards, the material being thrown into the ditch to form cause-ways. Similarly the gates were taken off the milecastles, so that free passage was restored. The gesture was unmistakable. Moreover in purely local terms it also suggests that sinister combination by the peoples immediately north and south of Hadrian's Wall, both probably Brigantian, was no longer a current factor in influencing Roman decisions. It is further assumed from the cancellation of the Vallum that the people to the south against whose incursions the Vallum had been constructed were now apparently pacified. Yet it may simply be that there was no longer any need to have a protected area outside the forts in which to keep materials that could not be accommodated in them when fully manned or to provide a ready-ditched area for extra units on the move. There must now have been plenty of spare space even inside forts occupied by maintenance units. Nevertheless, the theory that the Pennines now seemed peaceful is generally supported by the fact that troops to garrison southern Scotland behind the Antonine Wall seem to have been obtained by evacuating forts in the Pennines, just as the garrisons of southern England had previously been reduced. It is noticeable, too, that on the whole the military posts in the newly conquered area were much smaller than those in the Pennines (though their num-ber was considerable), and some economy of troops is thought to have been practised. However, it can also give rise to the thought that the evacuation of the Pennines in the 140s may not have been as wholesale as has often been assumed. It is unwise to read too specific an implication into the occupation of a particular fort or even group of forts at a particular time, as we have previously noted. For that matter, where the dating depends solely on pottery, it is no longer wise to assume that such dating has the precision that was once thought possible in northern Britain. Views among Romano-British archaeologists on the point have now diverged too far to permit the historian that sort of certainty.

Returning to the layout of the new frontier system, it appears that as on the Hadrianic frontier it was found ex-pedient to station forts in advance of the line in some sectors. These extended much further forward at the eastern end of the system than the west, reaching as far as the Tay. Yet on this eastern side of Scotland the strategic intention seems to have been quite different from that of the first-century series of forts that blocked the mouths of the Highland glens. Now the chief purpose looks to be the supervision of the Fife peninsula and a measure of advance warning of hostile tribes gathering to the north. The western end of the Wall is marked by a concentration of larger units on the Wall itself, presumably because the high, wild country came much closer to the line than in the east. Both flanks were protected by further forts on the Forth and Clyde, but there so far seems to be no evidence for a continuous system like that of Hadrian on the Solway coast.

The reconquest of southern Scotland may be the context for the appearance of inscriptions from 145–6 recording units of Britons, *numeri Brittonum,* on the Roman frontier in Germany.[1] It was long argued that these were raised in the newly conquered areas, partly to augment the Roman army but perhaps partly to transfer a significant proportion of the fighting strength of the subdued tribes out of the area. Yet it does not seem there was any wholesale movement of peoples or depopulation,[2] and if there was any action it did not go beyond conscripting young men into these units.

So far the Antonine advance in Britain had been a spectacular success, but it is so out of character with the tenor of Antoninus Pius' reign that we cannot avoid asking what the motives really were. There is no certain answer, but some suggestions can be made. Economy can hardly be more than part of the answer. New recruiting grounds may well have been gained, but one cannot help feeling that this could have been attained by reoccupying some of the forts in southern Scotland alone. In terms of cash and manpower-time the disturbance caused by abandoning one Wall system and building an entirely new one must have been very large and the upheaval cannot but have spread wide through the province. Experienced administrators must have heard the plans with despair. In terms of Britain alone the only reasonable explanation seems that the Roman government felt the north

[1] Doubts have recently been raised: see Breeze and Dobson, *Hadrian's Wall,* 84 f.: however the fact that *numerus* forts start in Germany well before the 140s does not prove they were garrisoned by the *Brittones* from the beginning.

[2] See G. Jobey, *Arch. Ael.* 5th ser. 2, (1974), 17 ff.; and for an earlier criticism of the theory of transportation also J.P. Gillam in I.A. Richmond (ed.) *Roman and Native in North Britain,* Edinburgh (1958), 66.

would be more secure if the tribes of southern Scotland were brought back under direct control and a shorter frontier held more intensively. Indeed, the area between the two Walls was also now more heavily garrisoned than at any other time. But one cannot help suspecting that there was a much wider motive. Antoninus Pius came to the throne without a military reputation and he also needed to demonstrate that he was going to be a very different emperor from Hadrian. The army of Britain was large, it had completed the task of building Hadrian's Wall and, now that there is no need to accept the theory that there had been heavy fighting in Britain late in Hadrian's reign, it was probably restless with inactivity. Moreover Antoninus was a traditionalist and there could be nothing more traditional than extending the empire by war. In Britain there was a chance of a tremendous propaganda victory, by winning back what had been lost under Trajan or before, abandoning Hadrian's grandiose Wall which had been shown to be consistently the subject of poor planning and replacing it with a simple but effective frontier. It might even leave just a hint of a further advance to come, to regain all of what Tacitus had recently claimed had been thrown away by the recall of Agricola. The effect would be all the greater if it could be achieved at once, and it looks as if Antoninus must have had this plan in mind at the very beginning of his reign.

Looked at from a Roman point of view, one might suggest that the British frontier was one of the few where military adventure, if it went badly wrong, would not threaten either the real security of the empire or the home districts of its most influential inhabitants. It has been suggested that in the days before the Balkans became regular Roman provinces parts of that region were used from time to time to give fighting experience to Roman armies and reputations to Roman officers. The Roman record in Britain sometimes seems to reflect the same attitude. It had the particular advantage of being remote: failure could perhaps be the more easily concealed while success was undoubtedly enhanced by the aura of distance. Antoninus' prompt initiative paid off handsomely against this background. In less than five years all the propaganda victories he might need had been won. If indeed it was at this time that the British units which appear on the Rhine were raised by enrolling captured barbarians

from the newly won territories, then he had added the ultimate traditional touch to his victory, doubtless greatly im-
pressing opinion both at Rome and among the important
garrisons in Germany. It was an ancient custom dating from
the days of the Republic that Roman generals were only ac-
claimed as *imperator* after winning an actual victory in the
field. Under the Empire, emperors had assumed the practice
of accepting such a salutation themselves after any victory
won in their name. Antoninus Pius accepted this honour only
once, and that was in 142 for the invasion of Scotland. The
point had been made, and the mild-mannered emperor had
no further need to launch foreign wars during his reign.

He was not, however, able to avoid further fighting altogether. Externally he was able to restrict Roman intervention almost entirely to diplomacy, but there had already
been serious risings inside the empire in two of the North
African provinces and also by the Jews and the Egyptians
before trouble broke out on a serious scale in Britain. In the
years following the reconquest of southern Scotland, the
process of military evacuation in the Pennines which had
started under Hadrian was perhaps completed. The Roman
authorities presumably expected a long period of peace
during which the region would gradually become Romanized
under the administration of the tribal aristocracy centred on
the Roman town of Aldborough. These hopes were almost
immediately disappointed. Coins of Antoninus Pius of 154-5
show Britain subdued and it seems likely that Pausanias'
account of the punishment of the Brigantes for an attack on
'the Genounian district', territory of subjects of Rome, refers
to this period. The whereabouts of the Genounian district remains unknown, nor do we know whether the trouble was a
war started by the Brigantes attacking Roman subjects outside their own territory or whether it represents a recrudes-
cence of the old internal warfare from the days of Cartimandua and Venutius.[1] Whatever the details, it seems to have

---

[1] See Salway, op. cit. 183 ff. for a brief discussion of the problem and references. J.G.F. Hind (*Brit.* 8 (1977), 229 ff.) argues persuasively that the name
'Genounian' is due to a confusion in the mind of Pausanias between the Brigantes
of Britain and the Brigantii of Raetia and their neighbours the Genauni. This does
not, however, invalidate Pausanias as a source for the fact of a raid by the Brigantes in Britain, only for the name of the district attacked.

set off a serious train of events. Archaeologically it appears that the Antonine Wall forts were evacuated and burnt—whether by the enemy or the retreating Romans is unclear—and at Newstead at least some slaughter apparently was involved. It is not improbable that the Roman forces involved were severely mauled in the process of putting down this revolt, even if they were finally successful, for an inscription from Newcastle upon Tyne records reinforcements for all three legions from the armies of Upper and Lower Germany under a new governor, Cn. Julius Verus.[1] It is not clear whether Julius Verus was sent to put down the rising or whether he arrived with these replacements after the rebels had been subdued. It seems quite likely that he came direct from the governorship of Lower Germany, possibly bringing these men with him. His date of arrival is uncertain, but he was still in office in 158. Although there were apparently small legionary maintenance units in forts on Hadrian's Wall during the early years of the Antonine period these were clearly kept at a very low level. It is therefore most unlikely that the replacements were primarily for these. It is therefore possible that the British legions themselves had been committed to battle and suffered losses, or perhaps more likely that a task force consisting of vexillations from the three legions had met with substantial resistance.

The Brigantian upper class had been found wanting in its duty to run the *civitas* in peaceful obedience to Rome, and the emperor replied by breaking up the administrative unit that had so signally failed. In Dacia his reaction to an unruly province had been to subdivide it under imperial procurators. We know here from Pausanias that he 'deprived the Brigantes of the greater part of their territory'[2] but not in specific words the authority to which it was transferred—though I believe the meaning is clear. One certainly cannot say that it is beyond the bounds of possibility that it was at this time the *civitas Carvetiorum* came into being. It occurs on two inscriptions[3] and almost certainly had its centre at Carlisle. Another *civitas* may have been created at the same time around Corbridge, both carved out of Brigantian territory. My own preference,

---

[1] *RIB* 1322.   [2] Pausanias, VIII. xliii. 4.
[3] *RIB* 933; *JRS* 55 (1965), 224, no. 11.

however, is for an imperial estate. Pausanias says that Antoninus took away most of the territory of the Brigantes 'for himself'.[1] Certainly the civilian population of the lands taken from the Brigantes cannot have been left without administration, and by the middle of the second century it is improbable that in a country which had been a properly organized province for so long the area would have remained for long under direct military rule, however closely it may have been watched by the local garrisons. An imperial procurator is recorded on two inscriptions found on the Antonine Wall at Inveresk.[2] His main task—assuming him to have been the provincial procurator—was probably, like counterparts known in the third century, assisting the governor by supervising building work on military installations while the governor himself was heavily engaged in other duties—as he certainly would have been in Antonine Scotland. However the presence of a very large area newly seized by the Crown would be an added and very important reason for his personal presence in the north.

It is only fair to say that alternative explanations can be provided for all the individual pieces of evidence that make up the picture of a Brigantian war at this time, and Drs Breeze and Dobson have recently summarized them. But the succeeding period is even more difficult to disentangle. I can only agree with their conclusions:

The history of the sixty years from the building of the Antonine Wall and its associated structures in the 140s to the reign of Caracalla in the early third century is most confused. Certain events are known from literary evidence, and there is a sprinkling of building records and other inscriptions, though their relevance is not always clear. Some time in the century a second occupation of the Antonine Wall and a second occupation of Hadrian's Wall have to be fitted in. There is no consensus among scholars as to how a meaningful history of the Roman north can be constructed. All that can be done is first to detail the evidence relating to events real or imaginary, secondly to describe the structural

---

[1] ἀπετέμετο.

[2] Altar discovered in December 1976 (*Brit.* 8 (1977), 433 no. 30). It is incomplete, and was reused in antiquity for a secondary inscription. Quintus Lusius Sabinianus describes himself simply as 'procurator Augusti'. I am much indebted to Gordon Maxwell of the Royal Commission on the Ancient and Historical Monuments of Scotland for a copy of the text before it was published. It confirms a damaged inscription from the same site (*RIB* 2132) recorded in the sixteenth century and subsequently lost, also naming Q. Lusius Sabinianus as 'proc. Aug.'

evidence and the varying conclusions of ceramic and numismatic experts, and finally to put forward the interpretation that seems best to reconcile all the evidence.[1]

There is no space in this book to list and discuss all the evidence which, for a period so hotly disputed among scholars, ought really to be presented if an author is to produce the detailed basis for any sort of a narrative. Fortunately Breeze and Dobson survey the material admirably and accessibly, and what follows is only one way of looking at the possible course of events, and very tentative at that.

On Hadrian's Wall the archaeological sequence shows a general recommissioning of the system, even to the extent of removing the causeways from the Vallum (though the gaps in the mounds were not filled),[2] and it must almost certainly have occurred as the direct consequence of an abandoning of southern Scotland at about the time of the Brigantian war which I have put in the 150s. Similarly under Julius Verus and later many forts in the Pennines were reoccupied and this too should be read in the context of 'depriving the Brigantes of the greater part of their territory'. This would indicate, if all this hangs together, that the so-called 'Period IB' on Hadrian's Wall began in or about AD 158 and that the frontier effectively lay on that line. The idea that for a substantial period in the history of the two Walls both were held together has been argued from pottery studies to be highly unlikely.[3] In the second century the position of the *limes* fluctuated according to circumstances between the Tyne–Solway and Forth–Clyde lines, but at no time do I think it likely that southern Scotland was treated as a zone cut off by solid fortifications in front and behind. That would have been an immensely expensive and elaborate scheme. It was either incorporated behind the *limes* or left outside, subject

[1] Breeze and Dobson, op. cit. 105. For an alternative scheme of dating see in particular M.G. Jarrett and J.C. Mann, 'Britain from Agricola to Gallienus', *Bonner Jahrb.* 170 (1970), 178 ff.

[2] This, incidentally, suggests that the ditch and not the mounds was considered the essential element of the Vallum.

[3] Mr. B.R. Hartley's study (*Brit.* 3 (1972), 15 ff.) of the dies for the makers' stamps on samian pottery reveals that the amount of samian bearing the same stamps which comes from the two Walls is negligible. This does not make some occupation of both Walls simultaneously for a short time impossible, say while one or the other was being made ready for a move, but any substantial occupation at the same time is on present evidence ruled out.

only to surveillance by outposts and patrols.

In 158 or 159 Verus was succeeded as governor by one Longus, Longinus, or Lentulus (the reading is uncertain)[1] and in 161 or 162 by M. Statius Priscus Licinius Italicus, a man of considerable distinction in provincial and central affairs. As in the first century, the emperors were continuing to send some of the best men available to Britain. One may guess that from the career point of view it was still regarded in senatorial circles as a plum among postings. Not later than 163-4 another governor appears, Sextus Calpurnius Agricola, well-known from building inscriptions on Hadrian's Wall and further south.[2]

In the meantime there had been a greater event. Early in 161 Antoninus Pius died and was succeeded by Marcus Aurelius, now known much more widely for his reputation as a philosopher than his acts as emperor. Yet in many ways the power of his most famous work, his *Meditations,* is due to the personal stress caused by his intense devotion to the twin ideals of Stoicism as recognized by the Roman aristocracy—service to the state and withdrawal into self. Marcus Aurelius suffered the extremity of the characteristically Roman conflict between *otium* and *negotium*, having a passionate feeling for philosophy but a reign tormented by almost continuous and bitter warfare. We tend to think loosely of the 'Antonine Age' (by which is generally meant the period from the death of Hadrian to the accession of Septimius Severus) as an unbroken unity, in many ways the Golden Age of the Empire. Yet the pressures on the imperial government were very different under Marcus from those that faced Antoninus. The relatively peaceful frontiers of Antoninus Pius' reign were now struck by major attack from outside: on the Rhine, in the east and, by far the worst, on the Danube. Thereafter Rome was rarely to be free from serious pressure on her frontiers.

Marcus' reign continued the process of extending the hold of the imperial administration over local as well as central affairs, and the constant warfare had serious consequences for

[1] *CIL* XVI, 130.
[2] *RIB* 589 (Ribchester), 1137 (Corbridge), 1703 (Chesterholm), 1809 (Carvoran), and possibly 793 (Hardknot).

imperial finances. In other important ways Marcus' government foreshadows later developments. Marcus himself had been high in favour both with Hadrian and Antoninus Pius and was clearly intended as the successor to the latter, but it will be remembered that Hadrian had insisted on Antoninus' also adopting Lucius Verus. The latter was kept as second choice throughout the reign of Antoninus, but on his death Marcus compelled the senate to give Verus the full titles of an emperor, in parallel with himself. For the first time the empire had a pair of co-emperors, declared as such from the outset, not as on those occasions when previous emperors had associated their favoured sons with themselves in their formal powers. In practice Marcus remained the senior, and Verus died early, in 169. Yet a precedent had been set.

Another precedent was set in the course of Marcus' military operations on the Danube. From 166 the position was constantly difficult, sometimes critical. In 166 itself a German invasion had actually penetrated north Italy, and at one stage Marcus was apparently contemplating a major war of conquest across the Danube. Antoninus' break with the Hadrianic approach to frontier policy had quite clearly restored traditional Roman responses. In the end Marcus made the interesting and important decision to transfer barbarians from outside the empire into abandoned lands south of the Danube in return for an obligation on their part to provide military support for the frontier. The settlement by the Romans of large groups from outside in new homes within the empire was nothing new (a hundred thousand barbarians had, for example, been brought across the Danube in the reign of Nero) but the requirement to act positively as an internal military buffer for the frontier was a device that was to be employed frequently under the Late Empire[1] but was something of a novelty in the second century.

In Britain Marcus seems to have been faced with problems at the outset of his reign. As late as 163 war was still threatening in the island[2] but the appointment of Statius Priscus mentioned above may suggest that there was already important work to be done when Marcus came to the throne.

---

[1] Not to be confused with the *limitanei,* as will be discussed later.
[2] SHA *Marcus*, viii. 7.

However, Breeze and Dobson make the intriguing point that each of the emperors from Hadrian to Commodus is said in the ancient sources to have found a difficult situation in Britain, which he subsequently solved. It may, therefore, have become part of the 'stock-in-trade' of imperial biographers. Indeed, the fact that Statius Priscus was transferred to the east in less than a year to take charge in an undoubted emergency should remind us of the very similar case of Julius Severus in 133.

The reconstruction of forts in the Wall region and elsewhere in the north of England that began under Julius Verus is recorded again under Calpurnius Agricola. At first sight this might seem to show a continuing process, but the dates span a critical period. It is, as Drs Breeze and Dobson rightly observe, not till 213 that we can really be confident we understand the position on the northern frontier, but this short period at the end of Antoninus Pius' reign and the beginning of Marcus' is crucial. The best that can be done in the extreme uncertainty which now prevails about this phase is to give here a summary of the events as they seem at the time of writing most likely to have happened, with a brief note on an alternative way of looking at the evidence as a warning that scepticism is particularly appropriate in considering this period.[1] The sequence and dating currently suggested by the archaeology is in many ways very attractive. It has simplicity and is consistent with the way Romans behaved. It has been conjectured that Julius Verus' withdrawal to Hadrian's Wall was unpopular with Antoninus Pius, whose one great military success had been the reconquest of southern Scotland and the establishment of the Antonine Wall. I find it difficult to believe that Verus could have taken this step without imperial authority, but think Antoninus may well have accepted its necessity with reluctance and hoped to reverse it at the earliest opportunity. The reoccupation of the Antonine Wall, known to archaeologists as 'Antonine II', would then be the result of the emperor ordering a forward movement once more and should date from about 160.[2] The

[1] For the evidence in detail, there is no better recent source than the outline and references given by Breeze and Dobson themselves. See also a collection of papers, *Scottish Archaeological Forum*, 7 (1975).

[2] Traces of 'Antonine II' thought to have been identified at the forts of Came-

archaeology certainly indicates that the reoccupation was to simpler standards than before, and may reflect both a more realistic appreciation of what was necessary and possible within the resources available and perhaps the passing with time of urgent pressure to rival the splendours of Hadrian.

The next stage in the story would coincide with the accession of Marcus, who had no personal involvement with the Antonine Wall but a growing need for troops elsewhere. This would be consistent with a second abandonment of the northern Wall in about AD 163,[1] though it looks as if certain forts in Scotland, particularly Newstead, continued to be held till at least the 180s. Under this view Calpurnius Agricola could have been sent out to implement the new policy, and recommenced the restoration of Hadrian's Wall where Julius Verus had left it. The chief differences from the frontier in Hadrian's time are that important garrisons were now retained in Scotland but the Cumbrian coast system was held much more lightly than before. Nevertheless it is Hadrian's Wall and not the Antonine Wall that is the linear system henceforth occupied.

An alternative but currently less likely framework for this whole period is to assume that the Antonine Wall remained out of use after Julius Verus' withdrawal to the Hadrianic line till renewed troubles in the 180s made it expedient to bring the Antonine Wall back into operation. This would mean 'Antonine II' starting around 185. It will then have lasted probably till 207, in the context of events which will be discussed in the next chapter. In this view Hadrian's Wall will have been in use for the second time from about 158 to 185, and out of use around 185 to 207. The root of the problem is that the sources are so unsatisfactory. The literary evidence mentions 'the Wall' but fails to specify which Wall, the inscriptions can be interpreted in several ways, the coin material tends to give only the date *after which* events must have happened, not *at which,* and the opinions of the pottery experts have had to shift so much as new data from excavation and new theories have appeared that pottery datings

lon, Ardoch, Strageath, and Bertha north of the Antonine Wall suggest Roman intentions included the renewal of close supervision of the area immediately north-east of the Wall, particularly the approaches to Fife.

[1] One published coin analysis may support such a date: see D.C.A. Shotter, *Proc. Soc. Ant. Scot.* 107 (1975–6), 81 ff.

can only be regarded as provisional and liable to change again at any time.

Returning now to the early years of Marcus Aurelius' reign, it appears that Calpurnius Agricola was recalled in about 166 and we know nothing of the governors for the next ten years and little of events in Britain, except that there was a threat of war in 169.[1] The imperial government is likely to have had little time to devote to Britain in this period. From 163 to 166 L. Verus was campaigning in the east, and his troops are said to have been responsible for bringing back the plague that went through Europe in 166–7. At about the same moment the Germans broke through the Danube frontier and reached Italy. It was not till 168 that the joint emperors were able to secure the withdrawal of the Germans, and in the following year Verus died, leaving Marcus sole emperor to face the problem of the Danube, which had now been shown to threaten the security of Italy itself. It was a very long time indeed since hostile barbarian armies had been seen in Italy, and Marcus was never to be really free of this problem again. He hoped to counter-attack by reviving the old idea of the conquest of Germany and central Europe north and east of the Danube. This was not to be. The plans for Germany were set back by a revolt in the east of one of his own senior generals, Avidius Cassius, and then by renewed German aggression. Subsequently the eastern half of the empire claimed his chief energies.

Sometime in the period 169–80 Q. Antistius Adventus was appointed to Britain, and it may have been in his term of office that one incident took place that is particularly interesting. Marcus had been campaigning across the Danube against the Sarmatians, a tribe famous for their armoured cavalry and proving extremely troublesome to the frontier. It was Marcus' intention to solve this difficulty, like Julius Agricola with the Ordovices, by wholesale extermination. However the proclamation of Avidius Cassius as emperor in Syria and Egypt caused him to break off the campaign, which was going well—from his point of view. In haste he made terms with the enemy, one of the details of which was the supply of 8,000 Sarmatian cavalry for enrolment in the

[1] SHA *Marcus*, xxii. 1.

Roman army. Of these, 5,500 were sent to Britain.[1] They were doubtless no more willing than other units raised compulsorily and transferred deliberately to another part of the Roman world, but in being drawn from outside the empire they foreshadow later Roman practice. Unlike the Frisii and the Usipi of the Lower Rhine, where regiments were raised before the areas had been formally incorporated in the empire but Roman influence was already dominant, these were from a region over which the Romans did not at that time exercise *de facto* rule, though the inhabitants had been Roman clients in the past. It is relevant that this happened at the same time as Marcus was settling barbarians south of the Danube, as we have noted, on abandoned lands to strengthen the frontier.[2] New ideas were appearing, even if in the form of *ad hoc* solutions to special problems. What exactly was done with the Sarmatians sent to Britain is not known. As veterans they are found later settled in the neighbourhood of Ribchester on the Ribble, still under special supervision and therefore presumably remaining a doubtful quantity. However they represented a substantial reinforcement to the auxiliary forces in Britain, wherever they were stationed on arrival and however subdivided. The possibility of a reoccupation of Scotland may have been assisted by this windfall for the army of Britain. Moreover, despite the triumphant return of Marcus to Rome in 176 after the collapse of the usurping regime of Cassius and the pacification of Egypt, such a celebration was an uncomfortable one. The Roman world never took kindly to victories in civil wars, and there were always Roman families, particularly among the most prominent, who were involved or whose friends suffered the consequences. A genuine victory against a foreign enemy would be very welcome, and it is not impossible that a forward movement in Britain was one of the moves contemplated at this time.

[1] Dio, LXII. xvi.

[2] The Marcomanni, Quadi, and Sarmatae-Iazyges were at the time settled in the middle Danubian region: they had each had a long history of conflict and semi-subjection to Rome and changed their homelands several times. There had been relative peace since the end of the first century, but in the time of Marcus Aurelius they seem to have been set moving against the empire by pressure of other barbarians behind them. They were to continue to give serious trouble from time to time in the third and fourth centuries and some of them were caught up in the great barbarian occupations of large parts of the empire in the fifth.

The recovery of the Antonine Wall would be a most satisfactory event.

In 177 war broke out again on the Danube. This time
Marcus did not leave the rest of the empire unsupervised. It
may have been the revolt of Avidius Cassius that persuaded
him that he could not trust someone outside his own actual
family by continuing the policy of choosing an established
figure as his successor. He may, too, have been disillusioned
by the relatively unimpressive performance of his late colleague Lucius Verus. Possibly hoping that the benefits of a
Stoic education would bear fruit if his own son actually
assumed the responsibilities of empire, he made the disastrous
decision to have the dissolute young Commodus invested
with the full imperial titles.

Modern commentators have often expressed surprise that
the Romans should have abandoned the system that had produced such a successful series of emperors and reverted to the
hereditary pattern. Yet in many ways the success had been
accidental. We have seen that the system had not in fact
worked as smoothly as a superficial look suggests. But, just
as important, there was no guarantee that the choice would
prove to be right. The position of emperor was unique, and
no amount of previous experience in high office or apparent
suitability could ensure that the candidate would fit the
office once he was on the throne. Tacitus' comment on Galba
demonstrates the Roman awareness of their dilemma with
absolute clarity. Galba, as he says, was universally agreed to
have presented all the appearance of ability to wield the
supreme power—until he was actually invested with it.[1]
Marcus' decision was an error of judgement of the first magnitude, but far more intelligible if we can forget hindsight
and look at his situation through Roman eyes. The fact is
that he made the decision; and may reasonably have expected
to shape his son to fit his responsibilities by sharing the burden of everyday duties with him. At the same time he himself
would be set free to turn to solving once and for all the
terrible problem of the Danube by a final campaign. This, in
fact, was precisely what he proceeded to do, with great success, and in 180 was on the point of making a major addition

[1] Tacitus, *Hist.* i. 49: *omnium consensu capax imperii nisi imperasset.*

to the empire by incorporating some of the most dangerous of the barbarian peoples that lay beyond and constantly harassed this critical frontier. Marcus' death at this moment deprived Rome of a probable solution to a major problem that was never to be settled thereafter. It also put one of the most worthless of her emperors on the throne.

In Britain Antistius Adventus had probably been replaced around 178 by a governor who may have been Caerellius Priscus.[1] It is unfortunate that we do not know anything about events during his governorship, for major warfare broke out around the time of the death of Marcus in 180, said to have been the most serious war of the new reign.[2] The exact date of this war is uncertain, making it impossible to be sure whether the next governor, Ulpius Marcellus (already in post before the end of 180)[3] was sent out to deal with it or was in the province when it broke out. Dio states that the enemy tribes crossed the Wall that divided them from the Roman garrisons, ravaged widely and cut down a 'general' and the troops he had with him. Within either historical outline rehearsed above the Wall occupied at this time this ought to be Hadrian's Wall, though the text gives us no guidance. It is just possible that Dio is referring to the abandoned Antonine Wall, since there were substantial garrisons still stationed between the two Walls. However, the effect was the same. Signs of destruction recorded from a number of sites in the north and previously, as we shall see, attributed to a hypothetical invasion in 197 are probably to be placed here in the 180s. The general was perhaps a legionary legate, but since there is no sign of heavy legionary reinforcement in Britain at this time to make up for losses, the destruction of a legionary fortress or the disappearance of a legion from the army list, we can reasonably assume either that his accompanying troops included relatively few legionaries or that it was a fairly small force overall.

Commodus seems to have authorized action against the barbarians, probably in the form of permission to the governor to proceed outside his province which always required imperial agreement, though it is an interesting question how much of the territory formerly garrisoned was felt in

---

[1] CIL XIII, 6806.   [2] Dio, LXIII. viii.
[3] *RIB* 1329. Cf. M.G. Jarrett, *Brit.* 9 (1978), 291 f.

formal terms to lie beyond the authority of the provincial governor of the time. Ulpius Marcellus was a man of austere incorruptibility and an extreme disciplinarian, and, we are told, exacted a terrible retribution from the enemy. This implies a punitive campaign at least in southern Scotland and probably north of the Forth–Clyde isthmus. Pursuit in the far north would perhaps more certainly be beyond a governor's authority and need the emperor's fiat, and it is from the Highlands that the barbarians may have come. Coins suggest that the first major successes were won by 184 and the campaigning continued into 185. The victory may have been felt to be enough in itself, without once again assuming the burden of permanent occupation of a large part of Scotland which had brought little return.

It is, however, worth looking a little deeper into what was now the situation. The outpost forts of Birrens, Newstead, Risingham, and probably Cappuck and High Rochester, which had been retained in use after the Antonine Wall was given up, had been lost in the war and not reoccupied after the victory. Marcus Aurelius had presumably felt them necessary to screen Hadrian's Wall after his withdrawal to that line, and in the next century Caracalla clearly came to the same conclusion. Why not now? The answer may lie in the characters of the governor in office at this moment and his emperor. A clear-sighted emperor might have seen the strategic sense of regaining these forward positions, but immediate glory was to be won by the slaughter of barbarians, and generals anxious to impress a brutalized emperor may have been keener to win victories than to consolidate them by unspectacular programmes of repair. Armies, too, could be readier to enjoy the socially most acceptable pleasures of victory and pillage than the manual labour of the construction-site. A less negligent emperor might have insisted, but left alone Ulpius Marcellus was dangerously hindered by lack of that quality in a commander which inspires men to do out of affection and respect what they would otherwise be disinclined to attempt—and was constitutionally incapable of cajoling them to it. The mood of the army in Britain under Commodus was rebellious. To what extent Ulpius Marcellus himself was to blame for this state of affairs we cannot judge, but what is certain is that a tone was now set that was to outlive his governorship, with the most serious consequences. Despite his successes in battle his behaviour towards his officers was judged to be intolerable, and at one point the disaffection reached such a pitch that the army attempted to put up a pretender to the imperial throne, one Priscus, apparently a legionary legate.[1] This candidate refused the perilous honour, but the temper of the troops is clear. They were prepared to revert to the old game of emperor-making. The revolt of Avidius Cassius under Marcus had shown the tradition was not dead, even though several generations of soldiers had passed through the Roman army since there had been a successful military coup. The common soldier and his officers were deeply imbued with the ethic in which personal and family reputation and ambition were supreme, and loyalty was a matter of ties to patron and commander. The system held together while the emperor could retain the network of respect and obligation which bound his commanders to himself and his troops to the imperial house, but it was a precarious structure in which a weak or neglectful emperor could introduce an almost immediately fatal flaw. Loyalty to the Roman state counted for little without the right man as emperor to personify it. Now, as units were stationed in particular provinces for very long periods, sometimes for centuries on end, being recruited more and more from the local population, the likelihood of provincial armies backing their own candidate became stronger and stronger. If the central government lost its grip, then the probability was that different frontier armies would put up rival candidates for the throne. The British army had now shown it was prepared to enter the field.

Like Nero, Commodus started under moderate influence. He had been gradually associated with his father in government and must have known the men and policies Marcus had favoured very well. However he soon fell out with the senate, where the men with the greatest influence and experience in government and war were concentrated, and his own behaviour became increasingly eccentric. In 182 he appointed a praetorian prefect named Perennis, to whom he left most of the government of the empire. Among the unpopular acts of Perennis was the replacing of senatorial commanders of legions

[1] Dio, LXXIII. ix.

by equestrians.[1] As part of the surge of protest against Perennis' measures the army of Britain adopted the extraordinary manœuvre of sending a deputation of 1,500 men to Rome in 185, who managed to persuade Commodus into abandoning Perennis.[2] This can only have added to the self-confidence the British garrison had already demonstrated.

In 185 P. Helvius Pertinax, later for a short time emperor, was sent to govern Britain where he had previously served, perhaps as a military tribune.[3] He started well. He quelled the disaffected leaders of the army,[4] and prevented the troops from setting up another pretender even though he himself was their favourite candidate.[5] However he does not seem to have avoided trouble for long, since a legion is reported to have mutinied, killing a number of people (perhaps his bodyguard or his *amici*) and leaving him for dead. Recovering, he punished this mutiny very severely.[6] It was perhaps this that gained him his reputation as an extreme disciplinarian, for in the end he was forced to resign on the grounds that the legions were hostile to him because of the discipline he imposed.[7] The delicate balance of forces that had kept the Roman army in check since Trajan's reign—a well-judged degree of discipline and personal respect for the emperor and the governors he appointed—was visibly breaking down, and the garrison of Britain was well to the fore.

The removal of one praetorian prefect as effective ruler of the empire was followed by the successive elevation of others to the same position. The emperor, however, careless as he was of public duty, nevertheless did not keep out of the limelight. His behaviour became odder and odder. He turned in

---

[1] See Frere, *Britannia* (1978), 190 for references showing that the commander of two British legions sent to Brittany to put down a revolt was an equestrian officer, L. Artorius Castus, *praefectus castrorum* of the Sixth. We shall see how, even when the appointment of equestrians to regular legionary commands became normal from the mid-third century, it was still a sensitive issue.

[2] Dio, LXXIII. ix, describing the men rather curiously as 'javelin-men'—this may mean legionaries. It sounds like a technical term translated into Greek. They were just possibly *beneficiarii consularis* (p. 522 below) but if so, the number seems extraordinarily high.

[3] SHA *Pertinax*, ii. 1.   [4] Dio, LXXIII. ix.   [5] SHA op. cit. iii. 6.

[6] SHA op. cit. iii.8–9. This was probably the 'great revolt' mentioned by Dio (LXXIV. iv).

[7] SHA op. cit. iii. 10.

vicious attack on the senate and came to believe himself
divinely inspired as the reincarnation of Hercules. Finally he
went too far even for the most tolerant by announcing that
he would appear publicly on 1 January 193 as Hercules returned, assuming the dual roles of consul and gladiator and
proving his divinity by invincibility in the arena. The latest
of his praetorian prefects successfully arranged his assassination and proclaimed Pertinax, now prefect of the City, as
emperor. The reactions of the army in Britain to the news of
the usurpation and the name of the new emperor are likely
to have been mixed but not difficult to imagine.

III

IMPERIAL CRISIS AND RECOVERY

9

CIVIL WAR AND ITS AFTERMATH

T HE name of the governor who had succeeded Pertinax in
Britain is unknown, but by the end of 192 the province
was under the command of Decimus Clodius Albinus,
another provincial of aristocratic Roman family, this time from
North Africa. He was in post when the murder of Commodus
set off a train of events that were to alter the life of the Roman
world irrevocably, mostly, it must be said, for the worse. The
first consequence, however, was a false dawn of reform, for
Pertinax attempted too much too quickly. He treated the senatorial order with scrupulous courtesy and restrained both the
imperial freedmen and the praetorian guard. Unfortunately
he had already proved unable to carry opinion in the legions
in Britain in support of the discipline he imposed there, and
the praetorians at Rome, accustomed to even greater privileges, liked his approach no better. The same praetorian
prefect who had arranged the murder of Commodus caused
his men to assassinate the new emperor. In perhaps the most
cynical act in their history, they put the throne up for auction
to the highest bidder, whereupon it was purchased by the
immensely wealthy senator Didius Julianus. However the
chain reaction of mutiny could not now be stopped. The
legions in Pannonia proclaimed as emperor their commander
Septimius Severus, also of North African origin. At almost
the same moment Pescennius Niger was proclaimed in Syria
and Clodius Albinus himself in Britain. All the elements of
prolonged civil war were now present.

The first move was a march on Italy by Severus, nearest in
distance to Rome, which provoked the praetorians into
declaring for him. The senate condemned Didius Julianus,
who was forthwith murdered in the palace, only six months
after the death of Commodus. Severus now had control of
the central machinery of government as well as a powerful
army. He had already shown Machiavellian shrewdness by
offering Albinus the title of Caesar,[1] an act which also has

---

[1] Dio, LXXIV. xv. 1. If the reading is correct, SHA *Sev.* vi. 10 says that Severus

constitutional interest for the future in designating as Caesar a junior emperor with proper imperial rank who at least on paper was a genuine working colleague. Albinus certainly seems to have been persuaded that he was to be a partner in government with Severus,[1] and it prevented a flank attack while the latter dealt with Niger.

In the following year Severus defeated Niger's army in the east, pursued him and killed him. Severus, having disposed of Niger, was no longer inclined to allow the title of Caesar to Albinus, who for his part was now aspiring to the supreme rank.[2] It must at this point have become clear that another civil war was inevitable: the two sides must certainly have spent the next two years before the war actually broke out in making their preparations. Among these it has often been suggested that the earthwork defences which have been discovered around many urban sites in Britain should be included. The argument is that Albinus foresaw the likelihood of having to take the bulk of the army on to the Continent to face Severus and wanted to avoid the destruction of the towns by barbarian invasion. This is indeed a possibility, though there is no reason, if the initiative was his, why he should not also have been thinking in terms of delaying Severus' invading forces if he lost a Continental war. But since the cost of such defences fell on the provincials, it is more likely, if this dating were correct, that local communities were thinking of their own security in times of civil war, whichever side won, and particularly of the disorder that would inevitably follow locally if the army were occupied elsewhere. Under these circumstances a petition to be allowed to build defences from the *civitas* councils is highly likely. This vexed question of the context and dating of town defences will be dealt with later in this book: if the earthworks do date from the time of Albinus, the choice of this method of construction rather than stone walls may be due to shortage of money, time, or trained stonemasons. But perhaps the most interesting examples are where, as at Cirencester, fine

---

sent an emissary to secure Britain, possibly implying an attempt to overthrow Albinus.

[1] The report (SHA *Sev.* vi.9) that Severus considered abdicating in favour of Albinus seems improbable. For Albinus' belief see Herodian, II.xv.

[2] Dio, LXXV.iv.1.

stone gateways were erected *before* the earth rampart was brought up to them. It may well be that undefended communities that already had had the intention of providing themselves with walls were now prompted into accelerating work already in hand by completing the circuit with temporary ramparts. We shall later see that the larger British cities provided themselves with defences in the course of the second and third centuries and almost every urban settlement was walled in the fourth century. This is in striking contrast to Gaul, where the majority of towns seem to have been unwalled till they had already been devastated by the German invasions of the middle and later third century. This ought to tell us something important about differences between the provincial communities of Britain and Gaul. Unfortunately we do not know what that is. Was Britain, even in the relatively unmilitary south, always less secure than Gaul? Was it the fashionable way in which communities competed with one another in Britain but not in Gaul? Did the emperors consider the finances of the British communities better handled and therefore were more ready to give permission for such expenditure?[1] Was Britain felt to be so remote that there was much less political danger in allowing the construction of fortifications not manned by regular troops? This matter of earthworks and stone walls is one to which we shall return, for it has important implications beyond the particular crisis we are here considering.

In 196 the discord between Severus and Albinus finally came to a head. Though the other sources are unclear, the historian Herodian represents Severus as making the first military move, after dispatching agents on an unsuccessful attempt to assassinate Albinus.[2] Herodian implies that Albinus was in a poor state of readiness,[3] but he nevertheless seems to have acted fairly rapidly in transferring himself to Gaul.[4] It may be at this point that he was proclaimed Augustus. Severus, having for his part induced the senate to

---

[1] Trajan and his successors were constantly worried about the extravagance and financial incompetence of local authorities, and often put in special commissioners to put matters right.

[2] Herodian, III.vi. For the plot see Herodian, III.v, SHA *Cl. Alb.* viii.

[3] Herodian, III.vii. this perhaps invalidates the arguments for the date of the town defences, but only if they were part of a grand strategy on Albinus' part.

[4] SHA *Sev.* x; Herodian, III.vii.

pronounce Albinus a public enemy, set out in person to bring him to battle, an act sufficiently unusual in him to cause remark.[1]

Albinus won an initial success, an engagement in which he defeated a Severan commander named Lupus, perhaps the Virius Lupus later appointed governor of Britain. The campaign culminated when the two main armies met near Lyons in 197. Dio claims that there were 150,000 men on each side in this battle, figures which it is difficult to credit, at least for Albinus' army. The whole army of Britain was not much more than a third of this number. If the figures are right Albinus must have won over very substantial numbers of regular Roman troops stationed on the Continent, as well as raising new forces from the territories he now controlled. The fight put up by his army indicates that it could not have been made up largely of raw recruits. Unlike the first century BC or even AD, Spain, Gaul, and even Britain no longer had a recent tradition of continuous native warfare to supply experienced warriors for enrolling into new auxiliary units. We do know that he gained one legion, VII Gemina, from Spain and the single urban cohort stationed at Lyons itself, but the Rhine armies are generally believed not to have supported him.

A more probable explanation is that the figures are considerably exaggerated. This is by no means unknown among ancient historians, often because they inevitably drew on the propaganda put out by the victors but also from the sheer difficulty of obtaining reliable information, particularly where in civil war hurriedly raised units and temporary allies were involved. Yet there is no doubt that Albinus had substantial forces with which to oppose Severus. Some he must have drawn from Britain, some were freshly recruited on the Continent, and we have already noted the two regular units which joined his cause. Even so, the tally still seems rather small, and one cannot help suspecting there was not absolute solidarity among the Rhine troops. Indeed, it is difficult to see how Albinus could have risked committing the bulk of his army at Lyons if the whole of the Rhine forces were free to move on his rear. Certainly something like seven or eight

---

[1] Dio, LXXV.vi, says that this was the first battle at which Severus was actually present.

years later detachments of legions from both Upper and Lower Germany were still in action against 'deserters and rebels.'

Albinus' forces were not easily overcome at Lyons, for the fortunes of the battle wavered for a long time before they finally came down in favour of Severus. There is some doubt about whether Albinus managed to commit suicide, the honourable end for a defeated Roman, but there is no question that he did not survive.

Despite the uncertainties about the size and composition of Albinus' forces at Lyons, there is little reason to question the assumption that the bulk of the British garrison supported him.[1] It does not however follow that most of it accompanied him to the Continent. Till recently it was generally accepted that hardly any of the auxiliary forts in Britain were occupied by the same unit under Severus and later as before 197, and that this indicated a substantial upheaval at this time. This, however, was not true of the legions and it seemed that at the least basic legionary cadres must have been left behind. Yet the fact of the matter is that we know hardly anything of the identity of the garrisons in the auxiliary forts in the years between the 180s and the Severan occupation of Britain.[2] Thus the changes could have occurred, either all together or piecemeal, at any time in this period which we have already seen was as turbulent in Britain as elsewhere.

Having accepted Albinus' alleged withdrawal of the garrison of Britain to fight on the Continent, Romano-British historians long believed that the result was a disastrous invasion of the province from beyond the northern frontier.[3] It was realized some considerable time ago now that this was not reflected by any archaeological sign of damage in the legionary base at York. However, this could be explained away as

---

[1] Severus may have deliberately misled his own men on the size and quality of Albinus' army—he particularly called it small and 'insular' (Herodian, III.vi.6). On the other hand, he may not have expected that Albinus would meet him in battle on the Continent at all—or, if he did, that Albinus would have success in recruiting there.

[2] See M.G. Jarrett, *Brit.* 9 (1978), 291 f.

[3] A revised version of the old theory of a barbarian invasion in 197 has been presented with some cogency by Professor A.R. Birley ('Virius Lupus', *Arch. Ael.* 4th. ser. 50 (1972), 179 ff.), but I am inclined to think it is not strong enough to restore the case.

consistent with the apparent difference in the garrisoning record of the legionary and auxiliary stations. It was maintained by some Romano-British specialists that whatever had happened at York, at least Hadrian's Wall fell, since there was a destruction level consistently recognizable in association with material of this period at all excavated Wall forts. However, Professor Wilkes's excavations at Housesteads showed no signs of this destruction and indeed as we have seen one of the interpretations of the period places the frontier at this time on the Antonine Wall. There is absolutely no clear literary report of frontier trouble on the scale implied by the older view of 197, unlike the slightly earlier or slightly later events to which the destruction levels, where they occur, should perhaps be attributed. The alleged epigraphical evidence depends on disbelieving what at least one inscription actually says.[1] All in all, it seems more likely that the widespread repairs indisputably attested for the reign of Severus, and some of those alleged to be so, were needed because there had been no large-scale reorganization for two decades at the least. It is of course quite likely there had been vandalism and looting during the temporary dislocations of the local civil war, particularly if some of the stations were for a short period left empty. Nor is it unlikely that, like many regimes newly come to power, the new administration started off with a 'new-broom' attitude.

At a later stage it will be necessary to discuss Herodian's statement that Severus immediately divided Britain into two provinces.[2] This would have been in line with his general policy of trying to reduce the risk of further attempts on the throne by cutting down the number of legions at the disposal of any one provincial governor. However there are difficulties in accepting that this happened straightaway in Britain, but for the moment it will be enough to mention that one explanation of the evidence is that the north first became a

---

[1] It is sometimes maintained that statements of the sort recorded on *RIB* 1234 (Risingham) '. . . restored from the ground up a gate with walls fallen into decay through old age' (*portam cum muris vetustate dilapsis . . . a solo restituit*) cover up the effects of hostile action, but it is difficult to see why a Severan governor or his master should be eager to conceal the results of Albinus' actions: they would surely be more likely to have emphasized the glory of repelling the barbarians and restoring Roman forts, if that was what actually occurred.

[2] Herodian, III.viii.

separate province of consular rank—in other words being governed by an ex-consul—and only later was re-formed as a province which ranked an ex-praetor in command. It would therefore be as legates of this putative north British province that we come across men of consular rank in office at this time, not as governors of all Britain as in the past. That there should be no corresponding inscriptions for the southern province is not surprising, since the greater part of Romano-British inscriptions come from the northern parts of the country where stone is plentiful and official Roman activity was intense.

It is perhaps significant that the first dated rebuilding inscriptions of this period from the Pennines[1] come immediately after the Severan occupation of Britain in AD 197, while those of Hadrian's Wall and further north date from 205 or later. The most urgent task may therefore have been restoration in the Pennines, where something seems to have wreaked havoc with the military installations. The damage may perhaps have been caused by locals still nursing old grievances from Antoninus Pius' days, or even during possible operations by Severan forces to eliminate pockets of resistance by troops who had become too deeply involved in the cause of Clodius Albinus to hope for clemency. The more routine restoration of forts further north which had not apparently suffered in this way could be left till considerably later. The process of restoration in the frontier region proceeded more or less steadily from south to north, and it is inconceivable that so active an emperor as Septimius Severus would have left the frontier *limes* itself unrestored for nearly ten years, if it had been severely damaged. Whatever the historical background, however, the sort of restoration in the forts north of Hadrian's Wall, when it came, was of the kind carried out by an army that had peaceful conditions in which to work, since it included the restoration of cavalry exercise-halls and the like.

We do not know whether Albinus had appointed a governor

---

[1] *RIB* 757, 637, 730 (and perhaps 591). None of these mention decay through old age, unlike 1234 (Risingham). 730 (Bowes) records the rebuilding of a bath-house 'destroyed by the force of fire' (*vi ignis exustum*), but this is inconclusive. It might reflect enemy action, but bath-houses were particularly vulnerable to accidental fires.

of Britain to take over the local duties when he himself assumed the purple. However on his defeat Severus appointed Virius Lupus to the post. This man, as we have mentioned, may have been the Lupus defeated by Albinus early in his campaign in Gaul. It is likely that a programme of confiscation of property and execution was carried out against the former supporters of Albinus in Britain as in Gaul and Spain, though there is no literary evidence and not much archaeological sign of disruption. The evidence from *amphorae*, the containers in which wine and other liquids were transported, does indicate a major interruption of the wine trade, but this is perhaps chiefly due to Severan measures against enemies with properties in Spain[1] rather than in Britain. The sending to Britain in 197 of an eastern equestrian, Sextus Varius Marcellus, as provincial procurator, a man who happened to be related to the new emperor, was doubtless intended to ensure that the financial affairs of the province were in completely reliable hands and that taxation was exacted without mercy. It is interesting that in a similar situation in the fourth century the victorious emperor was to send the head of the establishment records office at Rome (the *primicerius notariorum*) to hunt out those who had supported a British pretender to the empire. I suspect that in both cases these men were peculiarly appropriate to the task because they were experts in the imperial systems of record-keeping. The provincial procurator, with his control of the tax records, was in a particularly good position to carry out a programme of confiscation, and his responsibility for the junior procurators in charge of crown properties in the province—estates and industrial enterprises of many kinds, including mines and probably salt-production—should have reduced the administrative problems of absorbing confiscated property into the emperor's possessions. There are possible signs of such a change of ownership in some of the British villas at this time:[2] the Severan victory marks one of the large steps forward in the process by which more and more of the property in the empire came into the possession of the emperors, weakening the upper classes in general and greatly strengthening the centralizing of power. Yet overall the comparatively

[1] See Frere, *Britannia*, 195; 330.
[2] Frere, op. cit. 275; Salway, in C.W. Phillips (ed.), *Fenland*, 16.

small amount of evidence for punitive action in Britain may suggest that Albinus received less support from civilians in Britain than he did in parts of the Continent, and any slowing down of improvements to property archaeologically detectable in the early third century is probably more due to general economic uncertainty and indeed to the soundness of work done in the second century than to political persecution of owners.

As we have seen, it is reasonably certain that one of Lupus' first tasks was the reconstruction of Pennine forts. This he was already doing as early as 197. It is quite likely that assistance to the governor in this task was a second reason why Severus sent out his relative as procurator in the same year, as was suggested earlier in the case of the Antonine procurator Sabinianus and will be discussed in connection with later Severan procurators. This would be consistent either with Britain being as yet undivided or with the arrangements for separating it into two provinces being in an embryo state, leaving both Virius Lupus and Varius Marcellus—and probably their successors for some time to come—with responsibilities throughout the whole of Roman-controlled Britain. Neither the rehabilitation of a politically suspect administration nor the enormous task of reorganization inherent in splitting the island into two provinces could happen overnight, and it would be surprising if we were to find the full paraphernalia of two provincial administrations in being at an early date at the heart of Albinus' old realm where the political problems must have been greatest, even if Severus had taken the decision to divide Britain immediately it was gained.

Virius Lupus certainly had external problems, and assistance with the administrative side of reconstruction will not have come amiss while the governor concentrated on war and diplomacy. The Caledonians are said to have been breaking treaty agreements and preparing to aid the Maeatae.[1] These agreements were perhaps obligations that had been laid upon them by Ulpius Marcellus, but equally might have been part of precautions taken by Albinus before his Gallic campaign. If so, this may be further evidence against a major invasion

[1] Dio, LXXV.v.

in 197 before the Severans took over in Britain, since it appears the problem was only now becoming serious. Dio tells us that the various tribes of the Britons (he must be talking about those outside the province) had by this time become subsumed into two main groupings, the Caledonii and the Maeatae.[1] He further tells us that the Maeatae dwelled 'next to the cross-wall that divides the island in half'. The Maeatae, as far as we can ascertain, lived north of the Forth–Clyde isthmus. On the face of it, therefore, Dio's statement would seem to support the alternative theory that the Antonine Wall, not Hadrian's, was occupied at this time. One is uncomfortably reminded of Sir Mortimer Wheeler's remark in another context: 'In the assessment of an active and constricted phase in which the written record is absent or confusedly patchy, the translation of archaeological evidence into history must always be a hazardous operation, not least when, with a seeming perversity, it involves the rejection of written statement.'[2] Yet we cannot safely use Dio as proof of which Wall was in use at the time. His own source may have been ambiguous, or he may be making a geographical rather than a military reference. In either case, there need be no inconsistency between this statement and the employment of Hadrian's Wall rather than the Antonine one as the linear barrier at this time. There may, too, have been an added source of confusion in the information available to Dio, in that at least one fort on the Antonine Wall—Castlecary—has produced evidence of occupation well after the abandonment of the Wall itself in the 160s.[3] Certain forts between the Walls had continued to be held, and it seems probable that Castlecary was maintained (for how long we do not know) as an outlier to the main system further south without the Antonine Wall as such remaining in commission.[4]

The situation facing Virius Lupus now seems to have been a threatened attack on the Wall (Hadrian's Wall, in our scheme of things), and it appears the unfortunate Lupus did not feel he had the strength to fight it off. Dio's wording is

[1] Dio, LXXVI.xii.
[2] Foreword to Grace Simpson, *Britons and the Roman Army* (1964), vi.
[3] Cf. Breeze and Dobson, *Hadrian's Wall*, 2nd ed. (1978), 122 f.
[4] A similar source seems to have informed Herodian, III.xiv. 10. (cf. p. 229, n. 3 below).

again unclear, but the Maeatae would seem already to have risen.[1] Severus was unable to send reinforcements, owing to commitments elsewhere. Lupus bought the Maeatae off with a very large bribe, clearly with the emperor's approval. In return he obtained peace and the return of a few prisoners, presumably previously taken by the Maeatae and handed over at this time. Virius Lupus' troubled governorship came to an end in 201 or 202. He may not have been immediately succeeded by a new governor, for it seems likely that this was the time at which M. Antius Crescens Calpurnianus, *iuridicus Britanniae*, acted as temporary governor.[2] The presence of a *iuridicus* in Britain at this time suggests that additional help had recently been needed on the judicial side of the governor's duties, perhaps because of a rush of work in the courts while former adherents of Albinus were being brought to trial, but perhaps also while replanning in connection with the dividing of Britain into two provinces was in progress.

Later on in the year 202, or in 203, C. Valerius Pudens became governor and remained in post at least till 205. He was succeeded by L. Alfenus Senecio not later than 207 and perhaps in 206, and it may have been Senecio who had some military successes in 206.[3] It is not clear whether these were gained inside or outside Roman territory, but further trouble with the Maeatae and Caledonii seems quite likely. Senecio is recorded carrying out restoration on Hadrian's Wall and in one outpost fort, in two cases in collaboration with the provincial procurator, now Oclatinius Adventus, an excellent example of such collaboration on military building-work.[4] Once again the probability is that the governor was occupied by some exceptional demands on his attention. Something had indeed happened out of the ordinary, for the governor appealed to the emperor for reinforcements *or an imperial expedition*.[5] Few governors can have welcomed an imperial

---

[1] Dio, LXXV.v.   [2] *ILS* 1151.
[3] Dio, LXXVI. x. 6 which records success in 'the wars of Britain'. Cf. *RIB* 1337.
[4] *RIB* 1234 (Risingham), 1462 (Chesters).
[5] Herodian, III.xiv.1: 'The governor reported that the barbarians there were in revolt, overrunning the country, carrying off booty and destroying most things'. Professor A.R. Birley has argued (*Arch. Ael.* 4th ser. 50 (1972), 179 ff.) that this is merely a stock situation inserted by Herodian as appropriate for an imperial expedition and a 'just war'. I prefer to let it stand, in the absence of strong and specific evidence to the contrary.

visit, so a very serious situation must have threatened. It is too long after Severus' accession to have been staged as an excuse for a campaign in Britain for the propaganda reasons suggested at the beginning of previous reigns: Severus had by now no need to prove a capacity for military success. Virius Lupus' bribe to the northern barbarians had probably only bought a few years' peace, though in the disturbed state of the Roman world immediately after the civil wars that was well worth having. Herodian's account certainly implies that Senecio now judged the situation was out of control.

Both Dio and Herodian represent Severus as welcoming the opportunity to campaign, chiefly in order to provide employment for his unruly sons, but also (according to Dio) because of indiscipline among an army that had been in idleness for some time. This cannot refer to the troops in Britain, unless the whole business of the barbarian rising was a sham. In fact Severus clearly decided to use a substantial proportion of troops from other provinces on his campaign, for on his journey to the island the emperor collected troops from the areas through which he passed[1] and must have crossed the Channel with substantial reinforcements for the army of Britain in the campaign to come. On arrival he gathered together the forces already available in the island. It is alleged that Severus refused offers of peace from an enemy now alarmed by the size of the army thus collected.[2] This may indeed be so. It is just as likely that Severus had decided a salutary victory over the unreliable barbarians in Britain was required as that he merely wished to delay returning to Rome or going back without the laurels of war. The emperor was accompanied to Britain by his empress, the formidable Julia Domna, and his two quarrelling sons, Caracalla and Geta. The first son he took on campaign, the younger he left 'in the part under Roman control' to dispense justice and administer the affairs of the empire.[3] It seems certain he did not trust Caracalla. He kept him where he could watch him, and it might well be argued that he gave the more responsible task to Geta. He certainly left Geta with an advisory council,[4] but

---

[1] Herodian, III. xiv. 3.   [2] Ibid. III. xiv. 4.
[3] Ibid. III. xiv. 9. The wording suggests that Geta carried out the normal day-to-day functions of the emperor (for which see Professor Millar, *JRS* 57 (1967), 9 ff.). There seems no reason for thinking he was acting as provincial governor.
[4] Ibid. III. xiv. 9.

this was normal practice in Roman administration, as we have seen before, and it is more significant that he took with him on campaign his praetorian prefect, the great jurist Papinian whom he might have left behind to assist Geta if the latter had appeared to need it.[1]

It seems probable that the campaign did not start in earnest till Severus was beyond the Forth–Clyde isthmus. The literary sources are unclear. Dio simply states that Severus invaded Caledonia.[2] Herodian seems at first sight more specific, for he tells us that skirmishes and battles occurred after the army had crossed 'the rivers and earthworks that formed the defence of the Roman empire.'[3] Yet this is probably no more than a vague description of the frontier region culled in conversation from those who had once been there or from some inaccurate or out-of-date written source. If it is more, then it does seem more likely to refer to the Antonine Wall and the estuaries of Forth and Clyde than the Hadrianic line, but it would be wholly unsafe to use this as evidence that the northern of the two walls was occupied or reoccupied at this time. The striking absence of Severan coins from the Antonine Wall[4] makes it very unlikely that there was more than, at the most, some tidying-up carried out by the Severan army on the Antonine Wall.

Carpow in Fife was probably the real jumping-off point for the campaign. A Severan legionary fortress has been discovered there, but it is uncertain whether it was established at the beginning of this first campaign or later:[5] indeed, once across the isthmus Severus may have run into opposition before he could set about the construction of this base. In the first campaign successes are recorded and the accounts emphasize the engineering side of the operation, which the emperor prosecuted with great vigour despite his own ill-

---

[1] Dio, LXXVI.xiv. The whereabouts of Geta's headquarters (and palace) is a fascinating question. If the Sixth legion went on campaign, as is probable, he may have taken over the principal buildings of the fortress at York, but not necessarily. He would also have needed accommodation for the officers and men of his guard, as well as his military, civil and household staff, not to mention his advisers and their own establishments.

[2] Dio, LXXVI. xiii. 1.   [3] Herodian, III. xiv. 10.

[4] *Proc. Soc. Ant. Scot.* 107 (1975–6), 81 ff.

[5] Excavations at Carpow have been undertaken for many years and continue: at the time of writing the latest reference is *Brit.* 8 (1977), 361.

health, cutting through difficult terrain and approaching the extremity of the island. Some of the temporary camps recorded east of the Highlands must certainly be Severan.[1] The terrain, however, assisted the Britons. Severus, unlike Agricola, was unable to tempt them to a decisive battle and before returning into friendly territory had to be satisfied with forcing upon them terms by which they agreed to surrender a considerable area.[2]

The peace was not long kept. The Britons rose again, probably in the summer of 210, and Severus immediately ordered a punitive campaign with the purpose of slaughtering everyone encountered by the expedition. This was carried out[3] and may have been the time at which command was given to Caracalla, for the emperor was now very ill.[4] However Severus seems to have spent the winter preparing a further major expedition which he would lead in person. By now the Caledonians had joined the Maeatae, who seem to have been alone in the revolt till Caracalla's punitive campaign had been carried out. Severus was perhaps now considering total conquest. If not, the punitive campaign may have been a very serious misjudgement, ensuring long-term hostility to Rome of both the great combinations of tribes in Scotland. On 4 February 211 the emperor died. His last reported words characterize the new century. Addressing his sons, he urged on them unity between themselves, enrichment of the troops, and scorn for everyone else.

Immediately after Severus' death, Caracalla attempted to suborn the army to recognize him as sole emperor. When this failed he made a treaty with the enemy, accepting their promises of good faith, and evacuated their territory, returning south to meet his mother and brother, at York or possibly London. The political situation was too tense to let him risk staying in the far north. Not only was he at odds with his brother, but the emergence of rival claimants to the throne from elsewhere in the empire was an only too likely possibility in view of the events that had put his own father on it.

---

[1] See *JRS* 63 (1973), 231; 67 (1977), 144; *Brit.* 9 (1978), 277 f.

[2] The land surrendered by the Britons was possibly Fife, and the actual establishment of Carpow could have been at the end of the first campaign in conquered territory.

[3] Dio, LXXVI.xv.   [4] Herodian, III.xv.1.

The actual evacuation in Scotland does not everywhere seem to have been immediate. Dio notes that Caracalla abandoned forts,[1] but the decision to make the evacuation permanent and total may not have been taken straightaway. Part of II Augusta was undertaking building work at Carpow in 212[2] (possibly in conjunction with a vexillation of VI Victrix, though that legion may have been concentrated once again at York on the departure of the imperial family thence, whose presence must have made accommodation for the regular garrison difficult). It is even possible—though I think it more unlikely than not—that Caracalla did carry out the campaign Severus had planned in 211.[3] But whatever the precise truth about this brief period at the beginning of Caracalla's reign, abandonment of Scotland became a reality after a very short time.

It was very probably as part of Caracalla's settlement of the affairs of Britain that the administration of the island was definitively rearranged into two provinces.[4] The Upper province (the south, or *Britannia Superior*) held legions at Chester and Caerleon, and was administered by a consular governor, probably from London. The north, *Britannia Inferior*, under a governor of praetorian rank, had only one legion but a large number of auxiliary troops, with its centre at York. It is recorded that the joint emperors, Caracalla and Geta, took back with them a quantity of troops,[5] but these were probably chiefly those brought over with him by Severus. Thus the over-all establishment was largely maintained. The basic military and administrative pattern for third-century Britain had now been broadly fashioned.

The uncertainties of the military and political history of Britain from the middle of the second century to this point, where we can perhaps feel we are on slightly firmer ground, have compelled us to concentrate on the sequence of events

---

[1] Dio, LXXVII.i

[2] *JRS* 55 (1965), 223. Mr R.P. Wright very kindly sent me an offprint of his paper to the Fifth Epigraphic Congress held in 1967.

[3] Despite the celebratory coins of 212 it is difficult to forget that on other occasions strategic withdrawals and successful treaties have been regarded as victories. Otherwise we have to assume that both Dio and Herodian suppressed a successful campaign from their accounts of the period. Frere, op. cit. 203, notes the arguments for a Caracallan campaign.

[4] Map VII.   [5] Herodian, III. xv. 8.

lest the tenuous thread be lost in the complexities. But it is now a convenient moment to look back at the general picture of Antonine Britain, before the empire was almost shaken to pieces by the terrible events of the third century.

It is not easy to convey the character of a century in a few paragraphs, but some examples and quotations will give an impression of the age. Overall it is one of developing and deepening prosperity after the spectacular if somewhat superficial beginnings in the Flavian period and the new impetus under Hadrian. It might be supposed that all the activity on the northern frontier, much of it apparently ill-judged or short-lived, would have drained its resources and stunted its growth. But this is to look at matters in too parochial a light. Military expenditure fell largely on central government, and it is quite possible that all this movement stimulated rather than depressed the economy of the province. When we look at the towns the picture is of continued development in a fairly relaxed and unhurried fashion. Cirencester was not the only town to build grand city gates and delay constructing the walls themselves. Much the same may have happened at Verulamium, while the Nervan colony of Gloucester went to the trouble of filling in the old legionary ditch at its east gate early in the second century and building a stone gate and a length of the curtain wall, but then waited another century before continuing the circuit.[1] Structures built purely for show continued to be erected. It is, for example, perhaps towards the end of the second century that Verulamium decided to mark the limits of the first-century *municipium*, by now much outgrown, with monumental arches. Another such arch and a sculptured screen from the western end of Roman London may date from the same period.[2] Verulamium, however, gives us another way of estimating development in the Antonine age and distinguishing it from Hadrianic, because around AD 155 there was a major fire that destroyed much of the town. Mr Wacher's summary of what then happened is useful to quote. He describes the prosperity of Hadrianic Verulamium and then goes on:

---

[1] *Brit.* 6 (1975), 253.
[2] *Current Archaeology*, 57 (1977), 311 ff.: they may, however, be third century.

Nevertheless this picture of uniform prosperity was seriously marred by a disastrous fire in the town *c.* AD 155 which, however, may have assisted development by clearing away old buildings. Since almost all private houses and shops were still timber-framed structures, the fire must have spread rapidly and Frere has estimated that at least 52 acres (21ha) were consumed. But circumstances had changed since the Boudiccan fire and the sluggishness that followed it. There must have been sufficient accumulated capital for rebuilding to have started almost at once, and this was apparent not only in the private sector but also in public works. Some slight changes in the town plan can also be discerned such as the new street which was driven obliquely through Insula XIV from the forum to the theatre, and another between Insulae XVII and XIX. Then it was that the theatre and forum temples were probably constructed. Changes were also made in the methods of construction of private houses, giving rise to a combination of masonry and solid clay walls, which were altogether more fireproof.[1]

We have to be cautious, however, in pushing this argument further. We must not assume that these new methods of construction taken by themselves alone imply a higher standard of living, for excavation in the City of London has revealed a second-century *timber* building with a mosaic and painted wall-plaster. [2] In other words, timber houses in towns do not by themselves prove low standards of amenity and stone ones a higher level, nor should the replacement of timber by stone be assumed without question to imply increasing urban prosperity and comfort. But in the case of Verulamium we can observe the whole town becoming grander. There is no clear-cut end to the second-century expansion. It can no longer be assumed that the process of urban improvement halted everywhere with the civil war between Severus and Albinus and failed to re-start due to economic recession and political upheaval in the third century. I shall look elsewhere at the continued construction of town walls in the third century. One might argue that these were necessity, not an amenity. However, how else than as urban improvement—or ostentation—can we account for the total reconstruction (in stone and on a new, entirely classical plan) of the fine theatre at Canterbury, in the period 210–20?[3] Septimius Severus

[1] Wacher, *Towns of Roman Britain*, 210.
[2] *The Times,* 9 September 1977, 16, reporting on excavation of a site at the corner of Milk Street and Russia Row.
[3] S.S. Frere, *Brit.* 1 (1970), 83 ff. The original gravel-bank theatre (which probably doubled as an amphitheatre) was constructed before 100 and was

himself had a taste for magnificence in architecture which was shared by his immediate successors, and the imperial taste was followed locally elsewhere in the empire. One must assume that where there was still money—and in Britain that probably implies communities or individuals who had been sympathetic to the Severan party—expenditure on public facilities continued, still providing donors with the public recognition and honour that had always been so prized.

It is possible of course to concentrate too much on the towns. Marcus Aurelius' personal physician, the medical writer Galen, spent his boyhood under Hadrian and thus had an experience of life that spanned the Hadrianic and Antonine ages. Writing of the country people in the Roman empire he tells us:[1]

The famine prevalent for many successive years in many provinces has clearly displayed . . . the effect of malnutrition in generating illness. The city-dwellers, as it was their custom to collect and store enough corn for the whole of the next year immediately after the harvest, carried off all the wheat, barley, beans and lentils, and left to the peasants various kinds of pulse—after taking quite a large proportion of these to the city. After consuming what was left in the course of the winter, the country people had to resort to unhealthy foods in the spring; they ate twigs and shoots of trees and bushes and bulbs and roots of inedible plants . . .'

Is this, however, a fair picture to apply to Britain? Galen may be presumed to have learnt much in conversation at the court of Marcus, but his own experience was largely of Asia Minor, Egypt, and Rome, and one wonders whether it really reflects conditions in the north-western provinces of the empire. One can, however, imagine something of the sort being true of the war-torn regions of the Danube where Marcus was forced to spend so much of his reign. Moreover one is aware of the tendency of medical men to find instances to fit a theory of the cause of disease. In the Romano-British countryside, though life certainly altered at least outwardly little from the pre-Roman Iron Age on thousands of individual small farms, there were changes in the country-

---

probably part of the Flavian urbanization. The date of 210–20 above is based on convincing archaeological evidence.

[1] Galen, *De probis pravisque alimentorum succis*, i. (Transl. Fergus Millar, *The Roman Empire and Its Neighbours* (1967), 208.)

side overall that add up to something quite substantial. The stability of life, the existence of excellent main roads and a network of minor roads, the development of market towns, and the use of money as a matter of course meant that by the second century many farmers could regularly sell their surplus output and buy slaves, hire servants and labourers, and obtain the services of the expert craftsmen needed to build to Roman patterns and in Roman materials. The fame of the best-known Romano-British villas has obscured the fact that under 10 per cent of the total so far known can be classed as really grand, and the majority of those date from the fourth century. The truth of the matter is that there were now many hundreds of substantial farmhouses, often replacing Iron Age dwellings. They were certainly very much in the minority, but they represent a real change in the standard and style of living out of all proportion to their absolute numbers.

We have already seen that there is good reason to think an increasing number of the villa-owners in the second century were also town-dwellers, but there is little evidence in Britain for a substantial group of essentially town-dwelling absentee landlords. If there were some, they were more likely to be great men living in other provinces or at Rome, or the emperor himself. A clear division between those who actually lived in the British towns and the British countryside cannot be demonstrated. Yet those who had town houses as well as country properties are likely to have been largely the members of the so-called 'curial' class, the men with the property qualification to let them stand for local office and to become 'decurions' or members of the local *ordo* or *curia*, the council that ran the affairs of the *civitas* or the chartered city. Perhaps, then, any division is a matter of class? We have so far heard little of the lower classes, since the literary sources are relatively uninterested in them and they are less likely to have been able to afford commemorative inscriptions. Indeed, Professor Peter Brown, the historian of the later Empire who has done much to illuminate the life of the Late Roman world, has written of what had developed by the end of the Antonine period:

Like many cosmopolitan aristocracies . . . men of the same class and culture, in any part of the Roman world, found themselves far closer to each other than to the vast majority of their neighbours, the 'under-developed' peasantry on their doorstep. The existence of the 'barbarian' exerted a silent, unremitting pressure on the culture of the Roman Empire. The 'barbarian' was not only the primitive warrior from across the frontier: by 200, this 'barbarian' had been joined by the non-participant within the Empire itself.[1]

Nevertheless Professor Brown's view is largely from the standpoint of the eastern half of the empire and looks back from a study of the succeeding centuries. From our standpoint in Roman Britain it therefore becomes imperative to ask what we really mean when we use the terms 'native', 'native settlement', or 'peasant'. 'Native settlement' in particular is by now an accepted technical term among Romano-British specialists, though I confess to a long-standing dislike of it. This is partly because of its misleading modern overtones, partly because we have very little idea of how many of these settlements in the countryside of Britain were still occupied in the Roman period by an unmixed population directly descended from the pre-Roman inhabitants. 'Peasant' similarly has associations from more recent periods, and there is so far no term in use in the literature of Roman archaeology that is wholly satisfactory. The Romans themselves would have understood *casa*, a hut, cottage, or small country house (in the Late Roman period this had been extended to mean a small estate or farm) and possibly *casarius*, a cottager.[2] We need words we can apply specifically to the Roman period. Certainly the survival of at least the *appearance* of the same sort of life into and often throughout the Roman period as before does occur on many sites, though nowhere can life really have been unaffected. Rome imposed relative peace by preventing inter-communal warfare, but the very presence of a large army and civil establishment and the attractions that the new society held for local leaders cannot have left even the humblest British family untouched. Even in the most remote or stubborn communities the imposition of taxes, the

[1] P. Brown, *The World of Late Antiquity* (1971), 14.
[2] Anthony King has drawn my attention to this group of words as a possible solution. *Casa* is fairly common: *casarius* only survives in literature in the feminine form (*casaria*), defined in the eighth-century abbreviation of the late second-century writer Festus (Paulus Diaconus, *Epitoma Festi*, p. 48M).

search for recruits, and perhaps most of all the appearance of a money economy, new markets, and the availability on a large scale of cheap manufactured goods must have made their mark, even if families and their traditions persisted in the same homesteads they had occupied before the Romans came.

We have already noted that even where older theories had seen a deliberate policy of forced transportation of British peasantry to other provinces in the middle of the second century—from the region lying between the two Walls—Mr Jobey's intensive studies have shown the native settlements continuing and flourishing under Roman rule. In the Cumbrian Plain there is much evidence for a great expansion of native settlements and native agriculture under the stimulus of the market and protection offered by the presence of the Roman army. And in an area where the *local* urban or military market was small but the number of peasant settlements enormous, the Fenlands, a remarkable phenomenon is the vast quantity of Roman factory-made pottery, apparently thrown away with as little thought as nowadays we discard containers (which much of it was). Simple materials and vernacular styles of building do not necessarily mean a low standard of living any more in the country than in the town. What caused one farmer to rebuild in Roman style while his fellow did not was clearly a complex matter, not the least being the twin factors of availability of materials and local fashion. In the case of tenant farmers the policy of the landlord may also have had much to do with such decisions. This doubtless included whether his tenants felt they were likely to retain their lands for long periods, since Roman practice was regularly to re-let at fairly short intervals, often of the order of five years.

Verulamium may suggest that there was a decrease in the Antonine period in the humbler urban shopkeeping and craftsman class as their properties were replaced by grander private town-houses,[1] but this may have been balanced by the development of the smaller market towns. The richer Britons are much less likely to have wanted town-houses there, as little public business or social life at their level is

[1] See Wacher, op. cit., 213.

likely to have taken place in such towns. It was compensated, too, by the growth of great industrial centres such as the Castor potteries outside the small town of Water Newton, which were in large-scale production in the later second century. It was further made up by the special opportunities for superior craftsmen—sculptors, architects, and the like—in the luxury centres of Roman provincial society such as Bath, where the demands of religion, healing, and society demanded crafts to serve them. While the masters and many of the men in these industries were undoubtedly well above the lowest classes—and this particularly applies to the freedmen—much of the prosperity must have meant employment and opportunity for the humblest. And, just as in the Cumberland Plain the presence of the army seems to have stimulated native agriculture, many of the towns of the later first century and the second had developed on the sites of, and sometimes perhaps from, the civil settlements around former forts. These extra-mural civil settlements themselves were being reproduced in the second century in the areas to which the army had now moved, developing in many cases into little market towns outside the fort walls. They bridged the gap between civil and military with their mixed populations of immigrants and local-born, though perhaps less between native and Roman than might be expected. There can of course be no doubt that there were many, slave and free, whose life was miserable and whose prospects were hopeless and many whose culture and way of life was closer to the 'barbarian' than the Roman. But class or even urban and rural distinctions are, unqualified, misleading for Roman Britain, while the part the barbarian was to play in the west is a fascinating and complex story.

10

FROM CARACALLA TO DIOCLETIAN

As one contemplates the third century, the feeling that a real change has come over the Roman world is overwhelming. In the first half of the second century the empire was still expanding, in the second, despite the pressure on the Danube which at times looked very dangerous, the empire stood triumphant and unshaken. In the third century all seems changed. Inflation, military insurrection, one murdered emperor following hard on the heels of another, open autocracy, and the simultaneous breaching of the imperial defences in both the east and west look like the beginning of the end. Yet we are powerfully conditioned by hindsight. We know that under barbarian invasion and internal discord the political and military structure of the western empire disintegrated in the course of the fifth century—though that was by no means the end of Roman society in the west, an important distinction—and it is easy but unreasonable to suppose that people should have been able to recognize in the third the seriousness of events whose significance only begins to appear in the light of later centuries.

It is, however, true that the revitalizing of Rome's old eastern enemy Parthia (in the guise of the new Persian empire of the Sassanians) after the middle of the third century, and the regrouping of the German barbarians in the powerful confederation of the Alamanni with other barbarians behind them, represent fresh and dangerous versions of the old threats to the empire from without. These are joined, too, by northern people raiding by sea. Nevertheless there was no reason at the time to believe that these were other than variations on the frontier problems Rome had for centuries been used to facing and overcoming. Roman generals had defeated barbarian confederations before and the great victories over Vercingetorix, Caratacus, and Calgacus featured high among the battle honours of the Roman army. It is tempting for us to see the movement of the barbarians westward as inevitable and irresistible—and perhaps in the long run they were, though that is debatable—but the situation was constantly changing and highly complex. Even in the simplistic terms of Roman versus barbarian the balance was by no means always swinging in one direction. Many Romans still expected, as we shall see, that there would be successful wars of conquest by Rome in the future, and few behaved as if they felt the empire could fall. There is another side, too. A recent writer remarks of the fifth century:

The collapse of the Western Empire itself was incidental, a series of misjudgments and unfortunate coincidences . . . The decline and fall are seen through Roman eyes—inevitably, for almost all the eyewitnesses who have left records were Romans. But it is only half the story, for it concentrates on Roman stagnation and not upon the steadily growing numbers, unity and sophistication of the barbarians themselves.[1]

It had suited Roman moralists to see the barbarian as the noble savage, struggling to save his native virtues against the corruption of Roman civilization. Even if this had ever been generally true of Rome's enemies in the west—and it is very doubtful—there are many pointers that later barbarians, far from rejecting Roman civilization, envied the comfort and wealth that it represented. We shall later observe the merging of Roman and barbarian in the west during the Late Empire and after. Here we have to note the growing desire to share in the wealth of the Roman world, whether by raiding and piracy or by entering and dwelling in Roman territory. In the one case the target was movable goods, in the other land and what could be won from it by permanent settlement. Nor shall we find these movements always treated as hostile by Romans, when it suited them to make use of the barbarians for their own ends, and many barbarians came as individuals to seek careers and riches within the empire. Overall, however, Roman attitudes to the barbarians were still based on the assumptions that they were both a menace to be guarded against and fair game for generals ambitious to make their names and fortunes. This was to remain the dominant approach of Rome to her barbarian neighbours, long after the realities of power had decisively changed.

[1] Philip Dixon, *Barbarian Europe,* Oxford (1976), 9.

In Britain we have already seen what looks like a new confederation of old enemies under the name of the Maeatae,
joining in action the older-established grouping long known
as the Caledonii. Before the end of the third century Rome's
northern foes have taken to the sea and are harassing the
provinces on both sides of the Channel and the North Sea,
chiefly those two groups of Germanic peoples known as the
Franks and the Saxons who were to play such an important
part in the history of the west in the next few centuries.
They are also joined by further sea-borne raiders from
Ireland, less well known but equally dangerous. But the view
of events is that of Romans long after the third century. As
late as the 370s Roman frontier commanders were taking
little serious notice of the vast movements among the barbarians caused by the defeat of the Goths by the Huns, so
used were they to such conflict among the barbarians which
in the past had generally worked to Rome's advantage and
never produced results that could not in the end be contained.[1]

A century and a half earlier there was even less reason to
think the situation desperate. The third century is certainly
not an inspiring one in which to contemplate the Roman
world, but it is quite anachronistic to see in it the irreversible
collapse of the empire or even an age of unrelieved gloom.
Indeed, there were fine achievements—for example the
splendours of Severan architecture in many parts of the
empire—and in some provinces a surprising stability. It is
against this very varied background that we have to envisage
Britain in the third century.

Behind many modern assessments of the changing external
policies of the Severan House in Britain lies the individual
historian's attitude to the frontier question. From Rome's
point of view, was the right policy in the north to attempt
complete conquest or to establish some kind of frontier defence that accepted that not all of north Britain would ever
be held by Roman garrisons? It is, of course, another question
whether the choice was so clear to the Romans themselves.
Certainly it is not reasonable to judge Caracalla and his successors on the events of three-quarters of a century or a
century and a half ahead. Few defensive systems can be

---

[1] See Dixon, op. cit. 13.

expected to be effective for more than a generation or so, and only the foreshortened view of history encourages wider judgements.

The question of whether to attempt the conquest of the whole of Britain was one that could never be avoided, certainly not after the Roman armies moved on after the initial conquest of the south and east. However, the circumstances were never identical in any two periods, and the 'right' answer was not necessarily always the same. Moreover we have to remember that Britain did not stand alone. The security of Britain was only part of a complicated pattern dominated by much wider interests and heavily influenced by the expediencies of imperial politics. We cannot forget Tacitus' great phrase *'perdomita Britannia et statim omissa'* but have to remember that Tacitus was intent on purveying the image of good governor and bad emperor, not laying down a policy for the control of Britain. Yet, again, one may fairly wonder whether Romans who held positions in later periods at the level where they could take decisions of this sort or advise upon them were themselves influenced by what Tacitus had said. Certainly he was expressing in a particularly vivid way one of the strongest threads in Roman attitudes to foreign peoples and war, and he was addressing an audience that made a virtue of tradition.

The fact remains that Caracalla's dispositions in Britain were for their period highly successful. The northern frontier remained unbreached for, at the least estimate, something like 85 years—in an age when other frontiers were being overrun, some never to be held again. In the financial, administrative, and military troubles of the third century it is unlikely that it would have been possible to hold Scotland effectively while maintaining strong garrisons further south. Since the Roman government clearly deemed such garrisons now necessary, it is difficult to avoid the conclusion that Caracalla was right to consolidate the Roman position on a strengthened version of the Hadrianic frontier.

It is, indeed, all the easier now to give Caracalla the credit he deserves in this respect, as it becomes increasingly difficult to maintain the older view that the third century was a period of universal stagnation in the civil life of Britain. Of course, in that the fostering of the arrogance of the army was a major factor in the disorders and disasters of the third century, then the Severans, through the consequences of their policy on the affairs of the empire at large, were indirectly responsible for the seeming inability of the central government to deal with such major problems in individual provinces as the flooding of the Fenland. This is the sort of problem that Trajan or Hadrian would have seen was tackled and which they would have expected to be solved. In the third century there were other priorities. Nevertheless, the evidence suggests that where civil life was bypassed by such natural disasters (and we may reasonably suppose this was the norm) it continued in fair prosperity. Certainly there is little sign of such enormously destructive inroads of barbarians as those which characterize this century in Germany and Gaul (to mention only the neighbouring areas of the empire) or of the frightful horrors of mutiny, brigandage, and civil war which broke out from time to time in many parts of the empire. We shall have later to account for a remarkable period of prosperity in the earlier part of the following century, and we shall find that it is much easier to understand if it was based on sound foundations little disturbed in the third century rather than springing overnight from reforms instituted under the new imperial order imposed by Diocletian.

It is not, however, easy to form a general impression of the third century, due to a shortage of contemporary sources. Literary material is comparatively scarce and many of the leading personalities of the age consequently shadowy. In the middle of the century emperors come so thick and fast that it becomes more than usually difficult to associate such subdivisions of the period as we think we can detect archaeologically with known historical figures. A reduction in Britain of the number of Roman inscriptions (a phenomenon long recognized) combines with a decline in the import of samian pottery, a decline that becomes an almost complete cessation some time in the century.[1] Together, these factors make it much more difficult to have any confidence in dating phases

[1] Samian is a reasonably accurate source of dating evidence for the first century and the first half of the second, much less so thereafter. Coarseware *mortaria* (mixing-bowls) may eventually prove more reliable for this purpose.

within the third century archaeologically than for the first and second centuries. Coin hoards, too, a notable feature of the period and generally indicative of political and military instability and monetary troubles, are nowadays seen to be subject to so many factors affecting their individual make-up that one is inclined to use them for historical purposes only with extreme caution.

One cannot properly appreciate the remarkable phenomenon of a relatively undisturbed and moderately prosperous Britain in the third century without looking at the state of the empire in general and of the neighbouring provinces in particular. Yet our evidence for the empire at large, scrappy though it is, allows considerably more chronological precision than is possible in Britain. This means that we are frequently unable to determine with what events elsewhere—or even with what part of the century—trends that we can isolate in Britain are really contemporary. This makes it very difficult either to judge their significance or to guess at their cause.

In brief, the broad periods in the west relevant to us here are four. They are, firstly, the period from the departure of Caracalla from Britain to launch his great campaign of 213 into Germany to the death of Severus Alexander, the last of the Severan emperors, in 235; next the period of rapid turn-over of emperors in the middle of the century; then the German invasions of the empire together with the establishment of the so-called 'Empire of the Gauls' (*Imperium Galliarum*) in AD 260 (when the central administration lost control temporarily of the north-western provinces); and finally, the restoration of strong central authority by the emperors Aurelian and Probus from 274 and the accession of Diocletian in 284 with prosecution of major structural reform in the imperial system. These broad divisions will need some refining in detail but provide a general framework. In Britain, however, it is extremely difficult to go much further than imprecise subdivisions, consisting of 'Severan' (though the consolidation under the Severi from Caracalla to Alexander Severus does form a distinct feature, at least in military affairs); 'mid-third century'; 'later third century' or 'around AD 270'; and 'late third–early fourth'.

We shall see that the second half of the century presents particular problems in Britain, since its inclusion in the

Imperium Galliarum from 260 to 274 was followed by a second period of independence from the central government, from 287 to 296 under Carausius and Allectus. The features of that odd episode and of the recovery of Britain by the centre will be examined in the next chapter, but here we have to take into account that it is extremely difficult to distinguish archaeologically in Britain between the period that began with the recovery of Britain in AD 274 by Aurelian and the similar recovery in 296 for Diocletian by Constantius.[1]

As usual in Britain, such chronology as we can construct has to be largely built on military events and military remains. On Hadrian's Wall, the restoration begun by Septimius Severus continued in a fairly gradual fashion in many parts of the northern frontier area over the next quarter of a century or so. We can, for example, probably construe the refurbishing of the old outpost forts in the west at Netherby and Bewcastle as parts of a gradual renewal of the system as occasion and convenience dictated. There is little sign of urgency or any fear that the Caracallan arrangements might break down. Indeed, an unhurried programme for the putting of the military installations into good repair may well have been incorporated by Caracalla into the decisions he took on the future of Britain. At Bewcastle we seem to be able to observe new ideas emerging when we see how the rigidly planned second-century fort was now abandoned in favour of a shape better adapted to the terrain. This greater flexibility of approach in the design of military works had already appeared elsewhere and was now having its effect on the Hadrianic frontier. By the latter part of the first century a series of more or less standard plans had emerged from the very varied designs found earlier. There is a certain intellectual pleasure to be gained from contemplating the classic regularity then achieved—and Romans were rarely so stupid as to impose without modification solutions straight out of the textbook—and such standardization doubtless greatly simplified the problems of construction and supply, not to mention decision-making with its consequent difficulties and delays. However it is not surprising to find this gradually giving way

---

[1] The Emperor Constantius I, father of Constantine, is often known as Constantius Chlorus in modern writers, following Byzantine accounts, but earlier sources do not give his name in that form.

to experimentation and economy. The process was to accelerate in the third century, and one is justified in wondering whether this was not only a response to new military and economic problems but also reflected the presence in the army of more and more officers in senior positions who had risen from the ranks or came of families that had been producing career soldiers for generations.

The rebuilding of Bewcastle and the renovation of other forts were only part of the strengthening of the Wall system. In the Hadrianic period the Wall had lacked forward positions in the east. Under the Antonines Risingham and High Rochester had been built on Dere Street as hinterland forts on the vital route to Newstead and the Antonine Wall and retained when the Antonine Wall was abandoned for the second time. Risingham and probably High Rochester as well had been lost with the other outpost forts, as we saw above, in the troubles of the 180s, and it looks as if they had been left empty ever since. Now, however, strong new forts were built on both sites, and the third-century Wall was thus provided with powerful forward garrisons in both east and west.

On the Wall itself some of the turrets were abandoned on the crags in the central sector where they can never have had much practical value,[1] most of the milecastle gateways were narrowed, and sections of curtain-wall rebuilt. It has been suggested that tactical ideas had changed, that signalling along the Wall intended to allow the surprise issuing forth of Roman forces from any of a great number of gates was now abandoned in favour of interception far in advance of the line. However it is highly unlikely that the Wall was ever used as an obstacle against which to roll up large enemy forces and perhaps improbable that it was so designed. It is more likely that the original design was basically over-elaborate and the product of untried theory. Moreover it had insisted on regularities such as turrets even where they had no particular purpose. It may well have proved extremely awkward to man all the turrets, and excessively uncomfortable as well as unnecessary on the central crags. It may also have been discovered

---

[1] It is interesting that the legionary base at Carpow seems still to have been occupied in AD 215 or even 216 (R.P. Wright, *Brit.* 5 (1974), 289 ff.). This indicates either that the new arrangements were being phased in gradually or that Caracalla had not taken irrevocable decisions about Britain.

that the double-doors to the north on the milecastles were in fact hardly ever used, either by cavalry or vehicles, and that when the wooden leaves themselves decayed it was cheaper and more convenient to reduce the apertures and provide a small postern door. Indeed long ago Hadrianic regularity had been abandoned in the design of the Antonine Wall, and by the early third century the consequences of the tidy mind were probably all too obvious.

A major feature of the Hadrianic Wall which had not been repeated on the Antonine Wall was the Vallum. It has been suggested elsewhere that the function of the Vallum was served more economically on the latter Wall by the annexes to forts—and that both the Vallum and the annexes normally excluded civilians other than those legitimately attached to the officers' households. The Vallum itself had been restored at some stage in the retreat from the northern Wall to the Hadrianic line, but in the Severan period it seems not to have been kept up. Instead, substantial civil settlements were permitted to spread over the Vallum and approach the forts themselves.[1] Here and there along the Wall these settlements had already begun to develop in the course of the second century, but had been kept apart from the military installations by the Vallum. Now only the fort defences themselves delineated the strictly military domain.

It is difficult not to associate this particular change with Septimius' permission to soldiers to have lawful wives.[2] There is no reason to think that this impaired the fighting ability of the troops. They had for a very long period been contracting permanent attachments in the provinces in which they served and this fact was recognized in their discharge documents. Nor is it necessary to think it implies a peasant militia, half soldier, half farmer. The evidence for allotments of land to individual serving troops is thin and unconvincing. All that the disuse of the Vallum does imply is that for immediate tactical purposes it was no longer felt essential. The military authorities clearly decided they either could not, or need not, any longer prohibit civilian buildings close to fort walls, at least behind the Wall itself. Remains of civil settlements never extend north of the Wall curtain, and one may

[1] Salway, *Frontier People*, 66 ff.
[2] Herodian, III.viii.

suspect it still felt safer to dwell behind than in front of the Wall itself. Nevertheless there is no evidence yet that the civilians were settling into the forts themselves or that the troops were other than full-time soldiers, however wide the duties of a Roman soldier might stretch. The evidence from the Wall forts in the late fourth and early fifth centuries remains equivocal. Yet even if they then became small walled towns or walled villages with a mixed population of soldiers and civilians, we have no right to project that situation back two centuries.[1]

The lessons of the past few years had been learnt. Pertinax's attempt to impose the strictest military discipline had been a disaster and on his deathbed Severus had, as we saw, charged his sons above all else to placate the troops. There had been a decisive change of power in the direction of the common soldier. The abandoning of the most exposed turrets on the Wall may not have been solely out of greater solicitude for the comfort of the troops, but the development of the civil settlements is directly in line with Severan policy towards them.

It is legitimate to ask why the Severan government was sufficiently confident of peace in the area immediately to the south of the Wall as to abandon the Vallum. That may, of course, contain a false assumption. The soldiers' families may have felt so insecure that they demanded to live under the walls of the forts and the authorities were now in no position to refuse such pressure. On the other hand, the answer could be that the area was now much better patrolled. It is at this time that new units known as *numeri* and *cunei* were being added to the regular garrisons of the northern forts, for example at Housesteads.[2] These were perhaps following the pattern of the older-established auxiliary cohorts and *alae* in becoming more or less regular units of the Roman army, but were probably still recognizable as semi-barbarian. There was little room to accommodate these extra troops in the forts if those were fully manned. It may be that these fairly rough troops were used to strengthen the

[1] The possibility that the post-Severan occupation in the fort at Cramond on the Firth of Forth is civilian is not relevant here, as that was in an area evacuated or being evacuated by the Roman army.
[2] e.g. *RIB* 1576, 1594.

patrols southwards as well as to the north. There is little doubt that the *exploratores*[1] and *Raeti gaesati*[2] who appear at outpost forts *north* of the Wall were intended for patrol duties, and there seems no reason why part of the duties of the enlarged garrisons on the Wall itself should not have been similar patrol work in the wild country to the south. The otherwise surprising reoccupation of Lanchester empty for some years somewhere between 238 and 244 *may* have been caused by some experience by these patrols, suggesting an even greater need for rearward control,[3] just as more than a century earlier the very creation of the Wall may have been one of the reasons that led the Romans to move the garrisons up on to it. On the other hand, the fact that the civil settlements now flourished may be due to the success of a policy of encouragement of better relations between troops and locals. Security and recruiting might benefit, and the third-century army needed all the goodwill it could get.

Readers will remember that Britain had recently been divided into two provinces. Despite the fact that Upper Britain ranked higher as a posting, information about the men who actually filled the governorships is, as we have noted, rather more satisfactory for the northern province. The first recorded governor of Britannia Inferior is C. Julius Marcus, known to have been in Britain in 213 and whose name seems to have been subject to deliberate erasure from inscriptions.[4] This is a sure sign of disgrace, but whether this was political or military is unknown, though the former is more likely. There may indeed be a clue in the appearance of a whole series of inscriptions set up in AD 213 recording public attestations of loyalty to Caracalla. These were erected by individual military units in the Lower province.[5] This sort of inscription always makes one suspect that it conceals trouble. It is possible that disturbances occurred after Caracalla had

---

[1] e.g. *RIB* 1262.

[2] e.g. *RIB* 1216. *RIB* 2117–18 suggest that both sorts of auxiliary units went on patrol and it may be that the parts of both left at base were housed within the fort. In cases where there was a substantial civil settlement, 'living-out' of troops probably released sufficient barrack space to allow for enlarged garrisons.

[3] For a possible wider reorganization at this time, see Frere, *Britannia,* 212 f.

[4] *RIB* 1235.

[5] *RIB* 905, 928, 1202, 1235, 1278, 1705, 1741, and perhaps 1018 and 1551 (R.P. Wright in note to 1202).

murdered his brother and co-emperor Geta early in 212. As Geta had been acting emperor, as it were, while his father and elder brother were campaigning in the north and had seemingly been based at York, he must have become quite unusually well known in Britain for a member of the imperial family, and in particular in Lower Britain. He could hardly have failed to be known personally at the military head-quarters and the rare spectacle of an imperial household in residence must have made a great impression locally. The fact that these inscriptions of loyalty to Caracalla are not dated till 213 may indicate that such discontent was not immediately quelled. C. Julius Marcus may have been impli-cated, but there is another possibility. It is risky practice to add another speculation to these conjectures. However, if Julius Marcus was the governor who issued the order for the display of loyalty—and backed it up by the savage punish-ment of ringleaders not that uncommon in the Roman world —then any excessive zeal could well have evoked the proce-dure of striking his name from the record (*damnatio memoriae*) as a subsequent official act of reconciliation.

The next governor of Lower Britain (there is some evi-dence for the year 216) may have been the elder Gordian, who was to be emperor for just under three weeks in AD 238.[1] This name, too, is erased. Unnecessary concern has long been caused to Romano-British specialists by the appear-ance of a famous name from the previous century on an un-dated inscription at Chesters: Ulpius Marcellus. While this *could* indicate that there was a second governor of that name in post around 217, it is extremely improbable and may be discounted.[2] At least for AD 219 we do know that one Modius Julius was governor, though nothing more, and after him in 220 it is a positive relief at last to find someone about whom one can say something. Tiberius Claudius Paulinus is known both in Gaul[3] and on an inscription in South Wales.[4] He had been at an earlier stage in his career commander of the Second legion stationed locally at Caerleon, and while he was subsequently serving as governor of one of the Gallic

---

[1] *RIB* 1279, cf. 1049.
[2] *RIB* 1463-4: cf. M.G. Jarrett, 'The Case of the Redundant Official', *Brit.* 9 (1978), 289 ff.
[3] *CIL* XIII, 3162.   [4] *RIB* 311.

provinces the *civitas* of the Silures (a people, the reader will recall, noted in the first century as exceptionally hostile to Rome) set up an official inscription recording their gratitude to him. It seems likely that he had done them some service, perhaps becoming their 'patron': the headquarters of the Second at Caerleon was not far from the administrative centre of their *civitas* at Caerwent. Maybe they had heard he was coming back to Britain (even if to the other British province) —or were just demonstrating their acquaintance with the great. The traditional connection between prominent Romans and the individual community was still operating. Such bonds mitigated some of the effects of distance on provincial communities and individuals. One may suspect that the need for friends at court was felt more keenly than ever in the troubled times of the third century, even if one could not always be sure at which court they ought to be.

From this point the record of governors becomes a mere catalogue. For three governorships the dating is reasonably close: Marius Valerianus (noted in 221 and 222), Claudius Xenophon or Xenephon in 223, and then one Maximus (recorded for 225). After Maximus the order and dating of the appointments become much less certain: Calvisius Rufus, Claudius Apellinus, and Valerius Crescens Fulvianus to be fitted in somewhere in the period 222 to 235 and, for the period of extreme confusion in the imperial government between the murder of Severus Alexander in 235 and the accession of Gallienus in 253, only Tuccianus, if that is his name, in 237, Maecilius Fuscus and Egnatius Lucilianus between 238 and 244, and Nonius Philippus in 242.

Considerably later, and he is included only out of convenience since we are listing governors of Britannia Inferior, we know of Octavius Sabinus, from an inscription at Lancaster apparently dating between 262 and 266.[1] There is a special interest in this particular piece of documentation. He is already called *praeses* (the later term which tended to replace *legatus Augusti* as the title of the governor of an imperial province) yet he is of senatorial rank. This is contrary to the politically significant third-century trend of putting equestrian rather than senatorial officers into important

[1] *RIB* 605.

military commands. Indeed this policy had been made the norm by Gallienus (emperor 253 to 268), and he was not loved by the senate for it, since it struck at their deepest traditions. It is perhaps relevant to note that Sabinus, though in office during the reign of Gallienus himself, is unlikely to have been appointed by him, since the usurpation of Postumus in Gaul occurred in 260. The adherence of Britain to his Imperium Galliarum meant that Britannia Inferior was already beyond the central emperor's control by the time that Sabinus' inscription was erected at Lancaster. Postumus may have been short of good equestrians: he may also have made this appointment quite deliberately with an eye to support from the senatorial class.

There is another interesting feature of the third-century governors. Professor Frere has pointed out that the governors on the British frontier were in general much less distinguished men in the third century than before and he has seen this as a measure of the success of the new frontier arrangements. The appearance of this particular appointment does not work against that view: Sabinus is hardly in the class of the men sent to Britain in the first and second centuries, nor were conditions normal when he was in post, even by third-century standards. One may also reasonably remember that whatever the pressures on Britain at this time may have been they are hardly likely to have loomed as large in the minds of Roman emperors as they might have done in more peaceful times for the empire at large. We ought not to forget, too, the simple fact that with Britain subdivided the individual governors no longer commanded armies on the scale they once had.

So far the history of the second and third centuries in Britain has been seen mainly in terms of the northern frontier, and this naturally has been chiefly military. To a considerable extent this is a circular process, since military events tend both to produce apparently recognizable archaeological evidence (for example destruction layers and rebuildings), and to be recorded verbally in official inscriptions commemorating victories and the construction or reconstruction of military buildings. This view of history would not, indeed, have seemed odd to Roman historians or their public, to whom military affairs were of major interest.

The comparative paucity of closely dated information from the more lightly garrisoned areas of Britain is not surprising The new southern province, Britannia Superior, however, though never dominated by military sites in the way the north was, possessed from its inception a substantial military establishment, including two of the three legions stationed in Britain, the Second and the Twentieth. In the course of the third century we shall see the governors of the new province reorganizing the forces under their command, doubtless taking account of the revised limits of their responsibility and the structure of their administration and reflecting altered military attitudes and thinking about security and defence. It is in this context that new military installations appear in what in the second century had been the almost exclusively 'civil' part of Britain and important historical information is gradually emerging about them. These developments included new and strong military bases, representing a major extension of the area in which it was felt a significant military presence was necessary and at least to some extent a shift in the weight of garrisons from the west towards the south and east. We may be confident that the reasons included both changes in the external threats to the island and also internal factors reflecting political instability, the demands of the troops for better conditions, and the worsening relationship between army and civilian population.

Who the governors were is a problem made difficult not only by the shortage of literary sources for the third century but also by the rarity of inscriptions surviving in the south. This is true of the whole Roman period, but exacerbated by the general falling-off in the number of inscriptions from Roman Britain as a whole from the third century onwards. It is significant that where we have had new discoveries of inscriptions recording otherwise unknown governors they should either have come from one of the new forts or from London. A particular stir was caused in archaeological circles by the discovery of a stone at the fort of Reculver on the Kent coast recording a certain Rufinus.[1] It was at first thought possible to identify him with one or other of two men of that name known elsewhere, but it now seems probable

---

[1] *JRS* 51 (1961), 191 f.

that he was neither. It is not impossible that he ought to be placed in the second century, but the pottery from the site is said to be assignable to around AD 220, and is therefore consistent with a date for Rufinus' term of office any time in the first half of the third century after Severus.[1] The names of two other governors are also known from this obscure period, T. Julius Pollienus Auspex and C. Junius Faustinus Postumianus, the latter having served previously in Britain as a staff officer under Septimius Severus. The former may have been in Britain around 223-6, the latter's dates are even more uncertain. It is just possible that all three served within the reign of Severus Alexander, between AD 222 and 235. An inscribed stone reused in the fourth-century riverside defences of London records another third-century governor, previously unknown.[2] Marcus Martiannius Pulcher puts on record, on this altar in honour of the imperial house, the repair of the temple of Isis 'collapsed through old age'. Unhappily it is impossible to be more precise in the dating of Martiannius Pulcher, but interesting to note active restoration work being undertaken in the provincial capital by a governor clearly not so preoccupied by events elsewhere as to neglect the routine of civil management.[3]

Troop movements and the occupation, evacuation, and re-occupation of specific military establishments do not of course necessarily tell us anything about the military situation in their immediate locality. However it is interesting that a series of maps of Wales presented by Professor Jarrett shows that the garrison there was gradually run down from the time of the first Antonine occupation of Scotland.[4] There now seems no real evidence for a major strengthening of the forces of Wales in the Severan period as was formerly believed. The governors of the new province of Upper Britain do not, therefore, seem to have had as a major military priority that part of their responsibility which is roughly represented by modern

[1] I.A. Richmond, *Ant. J.* 41 (1961), 224 ff.; A.R. Birley, 'The Roman Governors of Britain', *Epigraphische Studien*, 4 (1967), 63 ff.; J.C. Mann, in D.E. Johnston (ed.), *The Saxon Shore*, CBA Research Report 18 (1977), 15.

[2] *Brit.* 7 (1976), 378 f.

[3] Another inscription from the same wall records an imperial freedman named Aquilinus and three of his colleagues similarly repairing a decayed temple.

[4] M.G. Jarrett (ed.), V.E. Nash-Williams, *Roman Frontier*, figs. 4–11.

Wales, though of course their two legions still lay at Caerleon and Chester. It therefore seems likely that the extensive northern operations of the second half of the second century and the early third (and any temporary withdrawal of troops by Clodius Albinus) were not at the expense of internal security in Wales, which could now be garrisoned more economically.

There is one site that seems at first a remarkable exception to this picture. At Leintwardine, in western Hereford, a large fort of over eleven acres was built perhaps around AD 160 and continued to be occupied into the second half of the fourth century. However it would fit reasonably into a policy of reduction in the Welsh garrison. The site commands an important route into central Wales up the valley of the Teme and lies on the Roman road from Chester via the city of Wroxeter to Usk and Caerleon, therefore roughly midway between the fortresses of the two legions under the provincial governor's command. Those who know the Welsh Marches and Wales will know that even today Shrewsbury and Hereford are frequently used as venues for meetings of bodies concerned with the whole of Wales and can even be the seat of some parts of the Welsh administration. This has been a recurrent feature of the area for a very long time indeed.

At Leintwardine the fort must of course have had a local function in keeping guard on this tactically important position, but a powerful mobile force (perhaps a cavalry *ala milliaria*)[1] could have both patrolled the road far to the north and south and been ready to move into the hills at will. It foreshadows later military thinking, in which fairly static garrisons were supplemented by more mobile forces, not necessarily always in the shape of a permanent field-army. A fourth-century parallel could be the large new fort at Piercebridge on the Tees. It is not surprising that Leintwardine continued to be useful in the later period.

The postulated function at Leintwardine of making sure that the route between the two legionary bases was kept open gains support from the fact that almost to the end of the third century it is clear that the legions were still occupying Chester and Caerleon in strength. Building work is

---

[1] The *ala milliaria*, a squadron of 1,000 cavalry, was the largest and most prestigious type of unit in the *auxilia*.

recognizable in both, and at Caerleon reconstruction 213-22 suggests that the Second legion's base there played an important part in Caracalla's scheme of consolidation.[1] Occupation seems to have been normal. There may, as in the past, have been some posting of parts of the legion away from time to time. It has been suggested for example that the complete rebuilding of a barracks around 253-5 was to house its cohort on return from a lengthy spell on detached duty. The use of legionary detachments was a long-standing practice and should correct any notion of legionary fortresses as normally occupied by the whole legion, often with very little to do. The lesson that it was unwise to leave troops in idleness had been learnt long ago: moreover legionaries were becoming a more and more expensive commodity. In the third century the fairly regular use of large detachments as task forces away from their bases for long periods rather than a single campaign was becoming more common, and points the way towards the development of standing field armies and the reduction of the overwhelming predominance in the disposition of the Roman forces of the legion barracked together in its permanent fortress. Indeed, with Wales quiet, but for the increased use of detachments one might wonder whether the retention of two legionary fortresses on the Welsh border was a symptom of military inertia.

Thus far, then, we have seen the mid third-century governor of Britannia Superior with his main forces still based in the west, however many detachments he may have had elsewhere from time to time. Nevertheless there are signs that the needs of security were demanding attention in other parts of his province. Our own attention is in the first instance drawn to the new coastal forts of the south and east, structures both spectacular and for a very long time now the subject of speculation and argument. However it is clear that the Romans' awareness also took in the local security of individual urban centres. We shall have to look again at town defences.

---

[1] The possible Severan date for the rebuilding of the fort at Caerhun just inland from Conwy on the coast of North Wales (R.G. Livens, *Trans. Caern. Hist. Soc.* 35 (1974), 7 ff.) need not contradict the view that the garrison of Wales was not extensively restored under the Severi. Its forward position from Chester makes as much sense as Leintwardine as part of a scheme of holding just a few strategic points to ensure efficient control from the two legionary bases.

The probable dating of the new fort at Reculver (say between about 210 and 245) is not too far out of line with the gradual reconstruction of the defence installations in the north and reminds us not to separate the two provinces too firmly in our minds. Reculver is one of the series of forts known commonly as the 'Saxon Shore' forts.[1] This thoroughly unsatisfactory but completely entrenched term derives from the survival in the fifth-century document known as the *Notitia Dignitatum* of a list of those forts eventually established on the south and east coasts. This document, which seems to have reached its present form by the early fifth century, lists stations under the command of an officer called (in the traditional translation) the 'Count of the Saxon Shore'—*comes litoris Saxonici*. This officer's title, and almost certainly his command as well, have nothing to do with Britain before the *late* third century—at the very earliest. This list and title have also made it very difficult to break away from the idea that these forts were from the beginning a coherent series. Moreover, so firmly is the name Saxon Shore now ingrained that it is frequently applied also both to a style of architecture and to other forts of the third and fourth centuries irrespective of the part of the country in which they are found.

For a start we can detach from a late third- or fourth-century context two of the named series: Reculver itself, and Brancaster on the north Norfolk coast. They are both, as pieces of military architecture in Britain, stylistically in the convention of the second century. They have a broad earthen bank behind their stone walls and are without external towers or bastions. This is in direct line with the tradition of earth and timber forts and their immediate stone successors. It is necessary to be extremely cautious in dating by style but in these two cases there is no contrary dating evidence. They are both placed adjacent to major estuaries which allowed easy access by sea into Britain from the Continent. In the case of Reculver and the Thames, the access was to London, principal city and port of Britain and the hub of the British road system, as well as to a large part of the richest areas of southern England. Brancaster lies alongside the Wash, through which

[1] See Note, p. 320 below.

it would have been simple for a sea-borne enemy to penetrate deep into a region of dense occupation (which may have
been largely imperial estate) and to enter and disrupt the
system of waterways that was perhaps still of major importance for heavy transport for official purposes, including
crucial military supplies. It is perhaps a reasonable guess that
Brancaster was planned and probably built before the mid
third-century flood that wrecked much of the Fenland system for a long time.[1]

Whether or not the Lincolnshire and Cambridgeshire Car
Dyke artificial channels were used for transport (which now
seems increasingly unlikely), nevertheless as well as watching
for possible raids *from* the sea, Brancaster commanded a vital
exit *to* the sea and coastal shipping lanes. In other words this
fort, which it is reasonable to suppose lay within Britannia
Superior, could control one of the most convenient links for
heavy transport—possibly the only one—between one of the
greatest agricultural and industrial regions of the Upper province and major centres of Lower Britain, including its capital.
This has interesting implications for the dependence of one
province on another and may not, in the context of the
deliberate Severan policy of reducing the size of provincial
commands for security reasons, be accidental. It is interesting
too to note that there is a third site that may fit into this
period and context. This is at Caister-by-Yarmouth, which
commands two river mouths and the terminus of the Fen
Causeway, a road that also leads to the Fen waterways and,
furthermore, direct to the great industrial area around Peterborough (chiefly the Nene Valley potteries) which was
coming into full production in the third century.

How these forts operated remains uncertain, but the fact
that Reculver is obviously too large for its attested garrison,
the *cohors I Baetasiorum,* raises the possibility that it also
served units of the fleet, the *classis Britannica.* Are we justified in assuming these forts were intended to cope with sea-
borne raids by Saxons or other Germanic barbarians? It is
odd that the fort at Dover, which had been an active base of

---

[1] Anthony King draws my attention to the fact that Brancaster's civil settlement dates from the second century (see *Brit.* 6 (1975), 261). The new base may
therefore be the massive refortification of a site previously occupied by the army.

the *classis Britannica* in the second century, seems to have been run down and hardly occupied, if at all, in the first half of the third.[1] If true, this would suggest that the problems were now northward from the Thames to the Wash rather than in the Channel and on the south coast. Moreover, after Albinus, the Roman government may have been unenthusiastic about too strong a military control by any governor of Dover and the route from London to Gaul. These various possibilities ought to make us hesitate before assuming automatically, from the generally accepted theory concerning the function of the Saxon Shore and other coastal defences at a much later date (a theory itself largely based on circumstantial evidence), that the *prime* purpose of these new forts early in the third century was protection against barbarian raids from the sea. There really is no way yet of distinguishing this possibility from the hypothesis that the chief purpose was the control of internal routes within the empire and in particular between two of the major areas—Britain and Gaul—that had supported the last rival to Septimius' claim to the throne. Yet the fact that Reculver and Brancaster seem to be placed more to facilitate patrols out to sea than as garrisons for specific ports (as Dover could have been) does suggest at least half an eye was now on broader naval operations than simple control of the short crossing of a sea effectively within the empire. Possibilities must include not only coastal defence but also the protection of merchant shipping. In the middle of the fourth century it was possible to expand greatly the transport of grain to Germany as an emergency measure. Such protection, against piracy as much as serious sea-borne invasion, would make just as much sense in the third century, particularly in view of the Romans' military preoccupation from Caracalla onwards with the German frontier. The ease with which Constantius at the end of the third century seems to have disposed of the naval defences of the usurper Allectus and relieved London by sea perhaps supports the idea that these forts were not geared to dealing with a real invasion, at least not by a disciplined fleet.

---

[1] Current uncertainties about the dating of samian and the significance of coin finds of the early third century, however, may cast some doubt on the gap in occupation.

It was, after all, a very long time since the Romans had encountered a hostile navy in the west and they had no reason to expect one.

In view of these considerations, it is not unreasonable to guess that the role of these forts at this early stage was broadly one of security and policing, both external and internal. In this latter connection we ought to remember again that the attested garrison at Reculver is not a naval one but the first cohort of Baetasians, auxiliary infantry. In the previous century they had been stationed at Bar Hill, more or less in the middle of the Antonine Wall, but they were subsequently transferred to Maryport, one of the forts in the Cumbrian coast section of the Hadrianic frontier system, before coming to Kent. At Maryport they must have acquired experience of infantry operations in a coastal environment and it is not surprising to find them transferred to the new fort at Reculver, even if it now meant their being moved from the establishment of one province to that of another. On the other hand, the original garrison of Brancaster, *cohors I Aquitanorum*,[1] had been at Carrawburgh and then under Antoninus Pius at Brough-on-Noe, and on the face of it would seem to have no similar experience. On the other hand we have no evidence at all where this unit had been since the middle of the second century, and it may well have been at some other station since the general post that had occurred subsequently. We have here in the east the same picture as at Leintwardine: a few rather large forts, large enough in fact to allow the brigading together of more than one unit, perhaps more than one type of unit. There would be space for naval detachments to make use of these forts and perhaps share facilities and even be under the same command as the regular land force. As a general principle, this grouping of varied types of auxiliaries in a single fort would provide a very flexible system of mixed concentrations of troops with different capabilities. This is in some contrast to the general position in the previous century, where we are used to a large

[1] *Brit.* 6 (1975), 288, no. 25: a stamped tile or brick, undated but making most sense as representing the original garrison, preceding the *equites Dalmatae Branodunenses* (listed in the *Notitia* and probably originally raised by Gallienus and therefore most unlikely to have appeared in Britain before the end of the Imperium Galliarum in 274).

number of forts occupied by single, comparatively small units. A new pattern is being established, with the auxiliaries tending to be grouped into larger forces and the legions (from whom they were now no longer distinguished by lack of the Roman citizenship) being used more frequently as detachments. The broad differences between these two traditional branches of the Roman army were gradually being eroded.

In Britain we can also see a way in which another distinction was becoming blurred. For the late first century and most of the second there is *some* justification for seeing the province in terms of a 'military' and a 'civil' zone. In those days the army was largely concentrated in the highland areas of the north and Wales, or adjacent to them, and elsewhere the picture was almost entirely of open settlements of civil character. There were few regular military establishments in the latter part, and hardly any of the cities and towns were walled. This is not true in the third century. Now a governor of Britannia Superior not only had substantial military forces available readily in the south: he also had a growing number of urban centres with formidable defences.

Mr Wacher has recently summarized conveniently our knowledge of the development of town defences in Britain and, without necessarily accepting even his cautious attributions of their construction to particular events or closely dated periods, we ought here to take a further look at the pattern. Permission to build had to be sought from the emperor, and it is worth noting that it was not easy to obtain. Like the attitude of medieval English kings to applications for licence to build a castle, Roman emperors were unenthusiastic about the creation of strong-points not under the control of their own armies. Moreover, emperors had frequently had trouble over public works in provinces where cities and individuals vied with one another over impossibly expensive and often grandiose but ill-planned projects.

We saw the fearful havoc caused in the first century by the failure before the Boudiccan rebellion to provide proper defences for the new cities. After her defeat had been followed first by retribution and then by reconciliation, there probably seemed no urgent general need for wall-building. However the notion of a total lack of town defences at this time needs to be a little modified. Verulamium, Winchester, and Silchester at any rate provide evidence for first-century defences. Around the turn of the century the *coloniae* of Lincoln and Glouces- ter, recently founded in legionary fortresses evacuated by the army, seem to have had stone walls inserted into the front of the old military ramparts. Mr Wacher has drawn our attention to the fact that this could well have been a matter of status, since Roman colonies were highly prestigious and their foundation a direct act of personal imperial policy. Certainly Colchester, the senior colony, fairly soon followed, perhaps spurred into action by their example. Whichever Flavian emperor it was who founded Lincoln had perhaps wanted it to outdo in splendour the only existing colony in Britain. After him, Nerva is certainly not likely to have wished to see his colony at Gloucester fall short of what the Flavians had achieved. Nor should we entirely overlook what Tacitus said about the original purpose of Colchester—'as a precaution against rebellion'. There was only a limited period for which the original military veterans could serve this pur- pose, and in only slightly over a decade Colchester had proved singularly useless without defences in working-order. Half-trained rebels could take an unwalled city easily by virtue of sheer numbers, but without siegecraft or siege engines they were liable to find city walls impregnable, even when the defenders were comparatively few. Like a burglar faced by a burglar alarm, such enemies usually preferred to try elsewhere, unless they could rely upon friends within the city to betray it. This is a cardinal fact of ancient war- fare and an essential ingredient in the rationale for urban defences.

Paradoxically, it may be the existence of the earthworks at certain Romano-British towns that will provide the key to understanding this much-debated question, rather than the stone walls themselves. At some stage in the later second cen- tury, as we have noted, something happened to make a sub- stantial number of the larger unwalled urban centres and some of the smaller ones provide themselves with earthwork defences. Yet Cirencester and Verulamium were already building fine masonry gates and towers when this occurred and Caerwent and Silchester and perhaps others as well were apparently engaged in the same exercise. In the third century, as we shall see later, complete stone circuits became common and were still being built as late as the 270s.[1] It would be possible to argue that in the second century the masonry gates were not defensive in the military sense at all, but partly for show, partly to assist control of access to town markets and the general policing of the built-up area. The existence of the stone towers, however, precludes us from using this argument, for they must imply an intention to build continuous circuits. The grandeur of the gates themselves does not permit me to believe they were intended to be accompanied by earth ramparts and timber breast works, at least not permanently. The earthworks cannot be anything but a temporary expedient, an aberration in what now looks very much like a slow but continuous process of constructing permanent circuits in which the curtain as well as the gates and towers were intended to be in stone. It is perhaps not a coincidence that on Hadrian's Wall, too, the towers and mile-castles were built before the curtain wall: the pattern was there for the towns to follow.

In second- and third-century Britain towns clearly felt it worth starting on the construction of full circuits, thus committing themselves to large-scale expenditure over a long period. In Gaul they did not. The reasons are obscure, but the fact is important. It is, of course, entirely likely that among the *civitates* there was a strong element of emulating the prestigious *coloniae*. Yet, however idiotic local authorities often were, one would hope there was some more practical reason. Indeed, the development of town-houses in Britain has already pointed to an increasing interest in the towns by the Romano-British upper classes, an opposite movement to that in Gaul. However, for the moment we may confine ourselves to the observation that the construction of town defences had facilitated the running-down of garrisons in those areas of Britain where urbanization was developing actively.

If we now turn back to the situation in which a third-century governor would have found himself, then the over-all security picture may begin to make sense. He now has his regular forces concentrated into a number of units of

[1] See *Brit.* 9 (1978), 468, for recent excavation on the wall at Canterbury, built from scratch over existing urban occupation and complete with both stone curtain and earth backing.

medium size but big enough for fairly decisive action, these being distributed in a comparatively small number of strategically placed bases. His headquarters at London retained its unique garrison fort and was provided with a complete set of walls in stone from scratch. This had just been done (whether by Albinus or Severus). Having secured the safety of the provincial administration and ensured a tight grip on the principal city, there might have been good reason to demolish the defences of the other cities. This did not happen. Instead there is the spectacle of stone walls being provided for most of those towns as yet completely undefended or so far only supplied with earthworks.

If the political risk of leaving the towns and therefore the local aristocracies of a recently rebellious province with usable defences was overridden by recognition of a pressure on the towns sufficient to affect the interests of the Roman authorities, then that is of real importance to understanding third-century Britain. Nevertheless, if Roman appreciation of danger was based on a recent experience of invasion in which the emergency earthworks had saved the towns in general *and it was believed that this might recur at any time,* then we have to wonder why those towns that were still undefended were not encouraged to throw up earthworks as soon as possible. In fact we have a third-century process of walling in stone which seems to start in the earlier part of the century and run for perhaps fifty years. This is the same sort of rather leisurely progress we have already noted with the forts in the same period. Imminent danger therefore has to be ruled out and we are again brought face to face with the notion that perhaps the support for Albinus had not been all that great among the civilian population of Britain at large. This would allow us to assume that the third century imperial administration recognized that the second-century reasons for the walls were still valid and saw no special reason to stop the cities from continuing as they had begun in the previous era. Moreover, in sharp contrast to the walls eventually built in many of the cities of Gaul after the barbarian devastation of the second half of the third century, there is the very remarkable fact that these third-century stone defences are in the main long circuits enclosing all or a large area of the town, as in the second century. If one has argued that in the second century the towns were rich enough and living in sufficient freedom from fear of imminent dire emergency that they were able to embark on long-term wall-building programmes in stone and one has also argued that, except for one brief period, attack or disorder on a large scale was not reckoned an immediate possibility, then it is difficult to avoid the conclusion that for a very substantial part of the third century the same must again have seemed broadly true. It does however imply, as we have just seen, that the Roman authorities still believed there was reason in Britain to let communities build walls, and it also implies that those communities themselves still felt it worth doing and still had the resources to do it, even if architecturally these new walls tended to be more utilitarian in style. In the light of this argument it becomes extremely difficult to believe in a sharp decline in town life, nor do the wide circuits now being constructed suggest that we should expect to find large expanses of derelict land or abandoned property within the former built-up areas. Indeed, local magnates, powerful in their own communities, may have been able to ensure that land belonging to them which had 'development potential' was enclosed within the new circuits.[1] If there was any genuinely derelict property, then surely as in the City of London for very many years after the Second World War this was expected to be a temporary situation, in no way reflecting a loss of confidence in the towns as such.

For some considerable time now it has been realized that the small urban centres that developed, even in the frontier areas, round active military stations showed no general decline in the third century: indeed this was the period when they especially flourished. However it has been possible to argue that they were an exception, due to the deliberate courting by the Severans of the troops and in particular the official recognition of soldiers' marriages. More recently it has become clear that much building work within towns without a military presence went on as usual. It can also be

---

[1] Attention should be drawn to the inclusion of substantial areas of land within the walls of towns such as Canterbury and Cirencester which had not been built upon and where the decision must have been deliberate (cf. also Note, p. 411 below for further reasons for expecting significant quantities of land not given over to buildings within a normally functioning town).

contended, for example for Verulamium, that widespread replacement in stone in the second century of private buildings
constructed in timber in the first means that there was comparatively little requirement for total rebuilding because of
structural decay alone. It is understandable that in a period
of sharp inflation private citizens might not be inclined to rebuild when it was not strictly necessary. In the public sector
the same factor could well have inhibited the construction of
those major works that were commonly the product of private
generosity or came out of the collective purse of the members of the city council, frequently the same people. Moreover these same individuals are likely to have been heavily
committed to paying for the new walls, willingly or unwillingly. One may be sure that Agricola was not the last
Roman governor to apply pressure on the local gentry to
remember their public duty: it was, moreover, a duty central
to the social thinking of the ancient world, and inextricably
entwined with the fundamental feeling of the Roman upper
classes of the importance for the family honour of public
recognition of the worth and wealth of the individual. This
maintained a family tradition of public generosity, closely
identified in most cases with specific localities. Variations in
visible prosperity from town to town in the third century
may go back to the politics of particular cities and their leading citizens in the recent civil wars. There were doubtless
confiscations. Furthermore, conspicuous expenditure in the
recent past had traditionally attracted the more rapacious
emperors to discover improbable treasons. We ought not
necessarily to look in the more splendid cities of the second
century for signs of solid comfort in the third.

In many cases the owners of the more substantial properties in the Romano-British countryside are likely still to have
been numbered among the same people we have been discussing in their role as magnates in the cities. In fact, there
now seems little doubt that the picture of third-century decline has been overstated as much in relation to the villas as
to the towns.[1] As yet few villas have been excavated with
modern techniques on anything like large enough a scale to

[1] This was recognized at least as early as 1951 by Sir Ian Richmond in Salway,
(ed.) *Roman Archaeology and Art*, (1969), 60 f.

give a full picture of the history of the whole establishment (though we are now seeing a revival of interest in the villas, not before time). It is already certain that there were a few brand-new villas in the third century. But for the others a real difficulty exists in reinterpreting the publication of early large-scale excavations, where third-century phases are likely either to have been buried under grandiose constructions in the fourth century, and therefore often not reached by the excavators, or to have formed now unrecognizable alterations to the villa as it was in the second century. In the countryside as in the towns an urgent need for new buildings was probably not widely felt in the third century. Where it was, financial stringency probably prevented its being acted upon. Where an excavation report does isolate a third-century period, there has been a tendency to see a third-century decline. It would indeed be surprising if the political changes following the defeat of Albinus did not result in some country houses being abandoned. Confiscation is very likely to have resulted in the amalgamation of estates: abandonment of the main house need not imply any reduction in the working of the land. Few would suggest that this was an age of expansion, but this does not necessarily mean a catastrophic decline.

In one area of fairly dense rural population there was an undoubted decline in the third century, and we are here perhaps moving into the age of chaos after the murder of Severus Alexander. Nevertheless it was as a culmination of a *physical* process that had already started in the second century. The peak of farming activity in the Fenland was undoubtedly in the first half of the second century and the ambitious settlement of that period was fairly soon beset with drainage troubles. It is now clear that this became, in the southern Fenlands at least, acute in the middle of the third century, with many settlements abandoned. It is now probable that a slow process of worsening drainage culminated in a major flood with at least one river changing course. These events were probably mainly due to natural causes associated with river silting and changes in relative sea level, but may well have been aided by neglect of maintenance. It is possible that shortage of money compelled estate owners to neglect local drainage. On the other hand it is also more than possible that ignorance on the part of Roman engineers about the long-term effects of cutting certain channels was an important contributory factor in the disasters that now occurred.[1]

The skirtlands of the southern Fens were the worst hit by these troubles, and these are exactly the areas where private ownership of lands has been suggested.[2] The villas there were mainly on the high ground of the Fen margin, but many of the humbler settlements situated on low rises at the edge of the fen were severely affected. This, in its turn, is likely to have reduced the incomes of the landlords, whether as private owners or *conductores* (leaseholders from the Crown). A circular situation may have been created in which shortage of cash reduced maintenance, which led to diminished returns and thus more acute financial problems. Confiscation here too may have caused temporary disruption of estate routine.[3] It is equally clear that nothing serious was done to repair the damage for twenty-five years or more. In the chaos of the mid-third century neither time nor money are likely to have been available for large-scale public action. It is certain that there was no real revival in the Fenland till towards the end of the century. Some settlements indeed never recovered.

This evidence from the Fens is interesting and dramatic, but is it typical? When it was published in full in 1970 the research on this area stood alone as a detailed study of a region. Since the revelation of the quite unexpected density of ancient occupation in Britain brought about by aerial photography and by greatly accelerated change in the countryside in recent years, this was the first large tract of Roman landscape to be mapped and studied in Britain, and it was one with a high concentration of settlement. However, the Fenland has never been anything but a very atypical area of Britain. Now that other areas are coming under similar investigation we may be able gradually to approach through regional studies a much clearer picture of Roman Britain in general and to identify significant changes within the Roman

---

[1] The cutting of an artificial watercourse through a gravel spit north of Willingham, almost certainly in the Roman period, is the probable cause of a disastrous diversion of the Ouse.

[2] In Phillips (ed.) *Fenland*, 12 f.   [3] Ibid. 16.

period itself. We do not yet know if, in regions where the physical landscape did not require large-scale administration and resources to maintain it as productive farmland (as did the Fens, with its delicate balance of land and water), the middle of the third century shows the same widespread interruption of occupation.

We have seen that evidence for a dramatic decline in prosperity in Britain in the third century is not strong. On the contrary, it may have looked quite otherwise by the standards of the age. To understand why one of the British provinces may actually have been an attractive posting for a governor in the mid-third century, and to appreciate the background to the two periods of independence from the government at Rome, we need now to look in a little more detail at the state of the empire.

The accession of Valerian and his son Gallienus as joint emperors in AD 253 marks the end of nearly two decades of chaos at the centre, with usurper after usurper gaining and losing the imperial throne. Valerian and Gallienus gained power only just in time. Palace plot, mutiny, and murder had created a climate that elevated no less than seventeen would-be emperors to the purple between the assassination of the last Severan in 235 and the accession of Valerian, and as quickly disposed of them. The installation of Valerian and Gallienus halted this appalling procession—at least for the time being—and it never again reached quite that level of disorder over such a long period. On the other hand, their joint reign also marks the point at which pressure on the Roman frontiers in both west and east turned into a series of massive invasions. Up to this point, the third-century changes in administration and the deliberate fostering of professional leadership in the army by the Severan emperors had allowed the Roman military and civil machine to continue to function effectively despite lack of direction from the top. In the end, however, the concentration of attention on the internal struggles for power can only have opened the way to the external enemies of Rome. From the middle of the previous century there had been only temporary intermissions in the pressure on the western frontiers of the empire. Marcus Aurelius' reign was blighted, as we saw, by the desperate necessity to wage bitter campaigns to hold the Rhine–Danube

defences, and we have already noted that Caracalla's withdrawal from conquest in Scotland must be linked with the
need to mount a major campaign in Germany. In Germany,
as in Britain, Caracalla's energy seems to have won peace
for a substantial, though shorter, time. However, from the
230s the Roman territory east of the Rhine became again
subject to insecurity. The comparisons and contrasts with
Britain are important. In many ways life in Roman Britain
must have been very similar to that in the large areas of
Roman territory that lay between the Rhine, the Danube,
and the outer frontier, an area conquered and Romanized
by the Flavians in the last part of the first century like much
of Britain. This similarity must have been particularly true
for soldiers, soldiers' families, and that whole mass of officials
and private persons who were associated with the army and
the administration. Like Britain it was an area that not only
had its garrisons and its permanent frontier line: it also had
flourishing Roman towns and a Romanized countryside.
Troop movements between Britain and Germany had a long
history. A detachment from the Twentieth legion at Chester
(and probably from the other British legions as well) which
is known to have been on the Rhine at Mainz in AD 255 must
have actually seen what was happening there, and it is unlikely
that soldiers or civilians in Britain itself were unaware of the
situation that was developing in Roman Germany.

This situation became acute when Germanic barbarians,
the Alamanni, broke into the empire in strength, causing
widespread damage. With extraordinary effectiveness they
penetrated right down into Italy until they were halted at
last by Gallienus, who defeated them at Milan in 258. The
effect on the Roman public, particularly in those regions
hundreds of miles from the frontiers, can be imagined. Even
Milan, now increasingly becoming important as a centre of
government, was now within reach of the barbarians. The
psychological shock to the ordinary man is likely to have
been great. The northern barbarians were part of Roman
folk-history. The ancient threat from the north went back
in Roman consciousness to the sack of Rome in 387 BC by
Brunnus and the Celts, when only the Capitoline Hill stood
out. Most recently there had been a very alarming period in
the reign of Marcus Aurelius when the semi-subject peoples

across the Danube revolted and entered the north-east of Italy. Marcus, however, had forced them into a peace favourable to Rome and later carried war into their own lands with striking success, broken off only by his own death. This time, however, the struggle was to prove more desperate and more prolonged. Even under Marcus internal strife in the Roman empire had made it difficult for the government to deal with the northern barbarians once and for all, if that had indeed been possible. In the third century civil war was to weaken Roman attention to external defence so much that the whole system almost collapsed.

Once again, we have to remember the Romans' consciousness of their past, and the deliberate appeal made regularly by Roman administrations, however revolutionary their origins, to Roman tradition, particularly military tradition. Now in the third century AD the army was the open and unmistakable master of Roman politics: if it and its leaders were at least partially responsible for the barbarian invasions by concentrating on internal rivalry, at least the tradition was a long one. It is, of course, true that from the victory of Vespasian in the civil wars following the murder of Nero in 68 to the assassination of Commodus in 193 there had been no serious outbreak of civil war and only one assassinated emperor. Yet the army wasted little time in reverting to type. Nevertheless it would be very misleading to think even in the third century of a revolutionary proletariat in the ranks or a revolutionary officer class. The Roman soldier, however strict his discipline, was highly privileged in the ancient world by being paid a regular money wage, having secure employment, and being able to look forward to a comfortable retirement as a solid citizen even if he had not risen within the army to superior rank. Many retired soldiers had founded influential families. In times of civil war promotion was often extremely rapid, and the process of elevating their families to positions of wealth and influence consequently accelerated. The army had long been a powerful instrument of social mobility and produced men who expected to enjoy the fruits of the existing system of society, not to overthrow it. Very large numbers of non-Romans had passed through the auxiliary units and swelled the numbers of Roman citizens with a vested interest in the empire. In the third century, with the distinction between citizen and non-citizen largely swept away, and far more senior posts going to equestrian rather than senatorial officers, the limits of ambition among the ranks were correspondingly extended. It is a commonplace that the success of the Roman empire was largely due to its ability to Romanize and absorb very large numbers of people of very differing origins, at least in all but the lowest classes of society. It is often noted that the Roman aristocracy, despite its devotion to family, tended not to propagate itself. Moreover political revolutions such as the fall of the Republic eliminated many of the most prominent families, either entirely or at least from public life. Large gaps appeared at the top of the social scale and were immediately filled. The successors adopted their predecessors' attitudes and their way of life without doubt or delay. It is perhaps not perverse to suggest that Rome's enormous success in turning provincials into Romans was itself a major force in the eventual collapse of the Roman world. Perhaps, indeed, the most surprising fact is that there were such long periods when actual civil war was avoided. But by the middle of the third century disorder and military usurpation had become so frequent in recent experience that the Roman tradition must really have been militating against the chances of the empire surviving in its established form.

The reign of Gallienus was marked in yet another way by an event that in the context of Roman history must have seemed as striking as the invasion of Italy by the Alamanni. This time, however, the shock was not tempered by a subsequent victory. One of the worst blows ever suffered by Roman prestige had been the annihilation of an army under the politician Crassus by Rome's eastern enemy the Parthians in 53 BC at Carrhae. In AD 224 the Sassanians had overthrown the rulers of the Parthian empire, and their revived Persian empire, served by direct descendants of men who had led the army that destroyed Crassus, henceforth pursued a more or less consistently aggressive policy against Rome. This was to last for no less than four hundred years, with varying fortunes.

Coming to the throne in 253 the Roman emperor Valerian had left his son Gallienus to administer the west while he himself tackled the problem of the eastern frontier. From soon after the beginning of his reign Valerian had been struggling to deal with attacks on the eastern Roman territories from the north, in particular by the Goths, and from the east by the Parthians. In 260 his apparently not very successful attempts were crowned by his own defeat and capture by the Sassanian king Shapur I. The latter, not perhaps unpredictably, made the most of this extraordinary success. In a famous relief-carving the Roman emperor is shown kneeling in submission to the Persian king and, like Augustus himself, the latter recorded his victories in a monumental inscription, the *Res Gestae Divi Saporis*. Carrhae had been repeated in an even more dramatic fashion.

In the west Gallienus was at this moment successfully putting down a rebellion in the Danube frontier province of Pannonia, but perhaps while he was still attending to this problem his own lieutenant on the Rhine, Marcus Cassianus Latinius Postumus, murdered the praetorian prefect Silvanus and Gallienus' own son Saloninus who were at Cologne, the capital of Lower Germany. Under the weight of these family and national disasters Gallienus' run of success ceased. In Germany Postumus took the only possible step and made the by now traditional declaration of himself as emperor. The Roman provinces in Germany, Gaul, Spain, and Britain and their armies supported him. Thus began a curious phase of some thirteen years for which the whole of the north-western part of the empire was run as an independent but fully Roman state with its own series of emperors. Though it was called the 'Empire of the Gallic Provinces', it was once again a matter of internal Roman politics.

Even though it was an internal matter, however, it is vital to remember that the large military forces of the north-west now had to be paid for solely by the north west, not to mention the cost of supporting an imperial administration and an imperial court. It is uncertain how far the east had still been tapped as the traditional source of wealth for the Roman empire as a whole. However, the Imperium Galliarum had to exist on the revenues of what had never been a rich part of the Roman world. The provincials of the north-west now had to cope entirely alone with an army that, for the whole active life of almost every man, had been taught both to expect the best and to change its emperor if it did not get it.

This might not have been so bad if the military and civil situation from outside had not been so grave. The citizens of the new Gallic Empire had recently seen the Alamanni pour through a land of unwalled cities. Half a century earlier Caracalla's successful consolidation of the German frontier by military means and subsidies to the barbarians had secured two decades of peace. Under Severus Alexander the frontier garrison was gradually being run down. However in AD 233 a really significant point in the history of the west was marked with the first of the Alamannic invasions, foreshadowing that of 258 already described. The military situation had, indeed, been temporarily restored and there are signs of a recovery of civil life in the frontier region. In 258 Gallienus had stopped the Alamanni it Italy. But now, in 260, the frontier across the Rhine collapsed completely in the face of the same enemy. All that very large region of Roman provincial territory beyond the Rhine and the Danube, whose similarity to Roman Britain has already been remarked upon, was probably in chaos.

One might suppose the end must have seemed imminent. Indeed henceforth there seems to have been no permanent military presence across the rivers. Parts had probably already been severely damaged by the earlier German invasions. Yet despite all this there is no clear evidence of substantial German settlement till the following century and Roman life probably continued in a patchy and insecure way for at least forty or fifty years, foreshadowing conditions much later when the empire was disintegrating in the west. It is probable that neither the Roman provincials nor the barbarians really realized what was happening. It is a warning to us not to assume clear-cut dramas of victory and defeat between barbarian and Roman armies, paralleled by immediate and dramatic changes in settlement and way of life.

The first of the Gallic emperors Postumus deserves credit for preventing a much worse deterioration in the west, but his own rebellion must have weakened the empire very seriously. Gallienus, after an abortive attempt in 263, had to accept the loss of the north-western provinces to the Imperium Galliarum. This is therefore a point at which to reflect on the situation in Britain. We have noted that the British legionary troops at Mainz in 255 must have seen what was happening in Germany. As long ago as the first-century Roman legions had mutinied when told they were being transferred from a comfortable province in which they had built up strong local ties to service on a frontier regarded as dangerous and unpleasant. Now the local ties were much stronger and one may perhaps guess that there were troops in Britain who did not want to follow the detachments of 255 and obey a summons to join in the central empire's wars against distant barbarians. We have seen that there is reason to think Britain was considered free from imminent attack on any scale: this can scarcely have been thought true of many other parts of the empire. It is perhaps not surprising that Britain fell in with Postumus, influenced no doubt by the probable cutting of communications with Rome. When discussing the appointment of the senator Octavius Sabinus to the governorship of Britannia Inferior between 262 and 266, I suggested as another source of support for Postumus the members of the senatorial order being excluded from military command by the central emperor Gallienus. There were probably few of that class in Britain, but those that were will have been influential.

We may also note one other speculative point about Britain. If the wall-building programme was still being carried out by the cities (there has been a tendency to date a substantial number in the second half of the century), the determination to continue with it must have been reinforced by the fact that, both in the east and in Gaul, a major factor in the damage to the cities had been their lack of walls. Nor can the success of raids into provinces where the regular Roman forces were concentrated on the frontiers themselves have been ignored. Both of these considerations suggest we should look for *ad hoc* defensive works from this period. So far, however, there is still little sign of haste in Britain.[1] The British provinces must therefore have appeared secure. Across the Rhine there is some evidence that the Gallic emperors made attempts to restore the situation to normal, but the state of the land beyond the Rhine was perhaps only the most acute example of the contrasts between Britain and the Continent at this time.

---

[1] The rather crude renovation of the fort at the Lunt near Coventry is now dated later than 260-8 (excavation report *Trans. Birm. and Warwicks. Arch. Soc.* 87 (1975), 1 ff.) but might fit this general context.

To a Gallic emperor Britain must have appeared one of the healthiest parts of his dominions.

From AD 268 the gloom over the Roman world at large began to lift. A series of remarkable soldier–emperors commenced the process of reunifying and restoring the empire. After Postumus had been murdered in 269 while putting down an insurrection, the Imperium Galliarum fell successively into the hands of the Gallic emperors Victorinus and Tetricus. The central government, however, was recovering. In 269 itself, the accession of Aurelian brought to the throne an emperor both determined to restore the unity and security of the empire and capable of doing so.

By AD 274 he had defeated the barbarians who had crossed the Danube, crushed an attempt at another independent empire (in the east) and put an end to the military power of the Gallic Empire at the battle of Châlons. Like Julius Caesar, Aurelian was ruthless and merciful by turns as it suited him. Tetricus surrendered to him after Châlons, ceased to be an emperor and thereafter was permitted to pursue a useful and distinguished career in the public life of the reunited Roman empire. Britain was now back in the main stream of Roman affairs and one may suspect that Aurelian's treatment of their former emperor encouraged reconciliation and the continuance of normal life in the British provinces.

By the standards of the age, then, the third quarter of the century was not a particularly depressed period in Britain. Two examples taken at random should reinforce the point. The Witcombe villa in Gloucestershire developed from a small establishment to a large one: the first phase when it can be counted as really large appears to date from the period 250-70. Similarly, in the small town of Droitwich a very substantial urban house with painted plaster was started in this period, sometime after AD 250. Some property owners clearly had both money and confidence. On the other hand there is some sign that public works requiring major expenditure were liable to be put off—for example the restoration of the Fenland after its third-century inundation. Yet there is no reason to suppose that Britain lacked attention under the Gallic Empire. Indeed the presence of an imperial government in northern Gaul rather than Italy may have meant more interest rather than less, particularly from

a regime that was insecure and relied on the unwavering support of Britain and its neighbours to survive. It is interesting
to speculate on the fact that the *civitas* of the Carvetii,
apparently based on the city of Carlisle, is first recorded
under Postumus. Does this reflect administrative developments under the Gallic Empire? On the other hand, one might
argue that the new *civitas* recognized the importance of the
third-century expansion of the civil settlements directly dependent on the army in the frontier region. It would be a
logical development of the Severan policy of favouring the
troops above all else and recognizing legally the existence of
the soldier's family. It would make good sense to involve
soldiers and their families in a stable local community and to
give the retired soldier the opportunity to gain prestige in the
traditional way by being absorbed into a local municipal
ordo, but without having to move away from the Wall region.
One cannot imagine that it would have worried a third-century
emperor if he had had to take territory away from an existing
local authority in order to benefit the military class. On the
other hand, if a great deal of the north had been confiscated
by Antoninus Pius from the Brigantes, as I think is probable,
then it will already have been in the hands of the emperor.
Moreover the abolition of the military zone between Wall
proper and Vallum promoted the rapid growth of urban
settlements on land previously reserved for strictly military
purposes. With no local aristocracy long established in the
leading positions of a *civitas,* the military and their families
would have had immediate and absolute pre-eminence. Even
a Gallic emperor, forced to balance the demands of a third-
century army against the need to retain influential civilian
support, might have reckoned the Antonine action a century
earlier presented a peculiarly fortunate opportunity to reward the one without offending the other.

Turning now from the middle of the third century to its
last quarter, we can begin to estimate what happened in
Britain when the Gallic Empire finally collapsed in AD 274.
A substantial amount of new development in Britian is
being dated by archaeologists around 270/275. It is, as we
have noted, not always easy archaeologically to determine
whether such developments occurred now or around the end
of the century, and it is important not to assume that

changes *must* be attached to some known historical event. This time we have *two* such major events in the space of twenty-five years, the recovery of Britain by the central authorities in 274 and again in 296.

Taking the last quarter-century as a whole there are interesting signs of revived prosperity. In the private sector, for example, the villa at Witcombe mentioned above shows major alterations after 275; and at Frocester Court, another large villa not very far away, a formal walled garden was added around the same period. In the public domain, Brough-on-Humber, which had developed as a reasonably important centre between 125 and 200[1] and shows signs of military style after 200, is now being rebuilt in stone. If we really have a new wave of development from, say, 270/275, is the reason necessarily or solely the reunification of the empire in the west? Gaul was in a dreadful mess after 276, when the worst of the third-century invasions had included the capture by the barbarians of *fifty to sixty* towns and their subsequent recovery by Rome. It has interestingly been suggested that the great flowering of villas in Britain in the Late Roman period reflects a 'flight of capital' from Gaul. It might perhaps more likely reflect a flight of *owners*. This should show up in the archaeological record by an emergence of grand houses for the personal residence of the wealthy, balanced by a corresponding decline in Gaul. There is no reason to suppose that *land* in Britain may not already have belonged to rich men living elsewhere in the empire. It would be surprising if it did not. This does not, of course, rule out the further acquisition for improvement and personal occupation of fresh properties in Britain in 274 or 296, by purchase or through gift from the victor to his supporters after the customary round of confiscations.

Should, then, the strange failure of the Gallic cities to provide themselves with walls very soon after the recovery of the northern part of the empire by the central government be significant for the study of Roman Britain? Even the city of Rome itself was given a gigantic set of walls by Aurelian in the years 271–5, yet nothing happened in the most vulnerable part of Gaul. Certainly Aurelian proceeded to a vigorous

[1] It is not completely certain that Brough-on-Humber was a civilian settlement in the period 125–200.

restoration of the Rhine frontier, but it had been clearly demonstrated that linear frontiers were no longer enough. It is, of course, possible that the Gallo-Roman cities were under such deep suspicion after the Gallic Empire that the central government was adamantly set against allowing fortifications that might be used in a further revolt. It is also possible—though, I believe, less likely—that no one felt the cities worth walling because they had been so badly damaged in the invasions and civil war. I personally think it is much more probable that the primary reason was lack of funds. The emperor paid for forts, the local communities for town walls. Mr Michael Green demonstrated at Godmanchester how this worked in a small Romano-British town, and there is no cause to think that the same process did not apply elsewhere. At Godmanchester the town defences were completed where they ran at the back of a temple area, and left unfinished in a stretch clearly on private property. Responsibility therefore lay with the individual property owners. These may broadly be divided into three. The private individual, the semi-public organization (such as a temple guild), and the municipal authorities themselves. The sacking of cities will have been immediately ruinous for the first two groups (we may be certain that individual houses and businesses were looted and temple treasures—often built up from the gifts of the faithful over centuries—were carried off). The municipality, too, probably lost its immediate cash holdings; but more seriously, its fortunes could only be revived if the town notables—the councillors and any private patrons the town might be fortunate enough to have had—were on hand to replenish the coffers. If the local aristocracy had departed, despite the undoubted fact that they could not legally escape their duties to the *civitas*, the possibility of actually raising cash from them must have been infinitely less. Local taxation would certainly have been very difficult to collect—particularly if their lands in the district were in a poor way or even abandoned—and the chances of voluntary benefactions very low. The lack of response in the Gallic cities is therefore entirely consistent with a very substantial flight of their chief citizens abroad.

Professor Keith Branigan has taken the argument a stage

further.[1] Observing that in the region of Cirencester to Dorchester in Dorset there are apparently no villas datable earlier than the beginning of the third century and that around Bath, eventually the most densely occupied district, there seem to be none till the general flowering of villas from about 270, he suggests that former imperial estates may have been sold off to raise cash. Other changes about the same time include developments in villages and farms in the region, and it is possible that the appearance around this time of a small type of villa with a yard or large room at the centre well known in Gaul is further evidence for large-scale change and immigration from the Continent in this period. It will be suggested later in another context that an early third-century inscription from Combe Down outside Bath may relate to landed estates then in the hands of the emperor, perhaps after earlier confiscations.[2] All in all, the congruence of archaeological evidence makes the hypothesis a very attractive one. Nevertheless, we shall be wise to suspend firm judgement on this whole matter, since we have no single written reference to link it all together.

What now does seem to be established is that Britain was relatively untouched by the convulsions elsewhere in the empire in the mid-third century. While there was probably little money or inclination for new work at that time in Britain and projects may have been delayed or cancelled, nevertheless there was an underlying economic strength and stability on which the prosperity of the last quarter of the century could develop.[3] The 'immigration' theory is an attractive hypothesis and one which one may be inclined to accept, and the sale of imperial property a possible one, but we should beware of assuming a coherent 'policy'. Emperors frequently indulged in confiscation of property on the one

---

[1] His book, *The Roman Villa in South-West England*, Bradford-on-Avon (1977), appeared after this chapter was written and I have therefore not been able to take it fully into account.

[2] *RIB* 179 (Monkton Combe): reconstruction of *principia* (district headquarters?) that had fallen into ruin by an imperial freedman holding the post of *adiutor procuratorum*, dating from the reigns of Caracalla or Elagabalus (i.e. between 212 and 222). See also p. 531 below.

[3] Dr D.J. Smith has pointed to the development of a flourishing local school of mosaicists in the region of Cirencester, which probably responded to the new demands.

hand and gifts on the other—to supporters, favourites, or
with the rather more worthy motive of raising men they
needed in office to the necessary property qualifications—
but on an individual basis. Private owners, too, responded
to opportunity or not as fancy or financial pressures took
them; and if we detect general trends rather than deliberate
policies, we may well not simply be giving up hope of finding
the details of imperial planning but actually be closer to the
realities of the Roman world.

Whatever their origins and precise date, the British villas
are an archaeological fact and both their construction and
the implied presence of rich households must have injected
new vitality into the economy. There have been suggestions
that estates in Britain were changing from arable to sheep
farming or other large-scale ranching, with possible reduction
in farm labour and even evictions, but the sheer presence of
large upper-class households can only have stimulated many
branches of trade and the manufacturing and service industries. This ought also to have increased activity in the urban
centres, perhaps particularly in the market towns and at the
sites of major fairs, where in the ancient world markets were
often associated with religious complexes and pilgrimage
sites. Nor is there any reason to assume that any transference
of investment would only affect landed property: commercial
and industrial enterprise could also have benefited greatly.

A new interest in Britain by people of importance and influence could also help to explain the renewal of official
attention to the military security of Britain. The military
development of Brough-on-Humber may be one sign, the
next stages in the evolution of the 'Saxon Shore' chain
another. At Burgh Castle in Suffolk, for example, a new
stone fort was commenced in a rather archaic style with
rounded corners,[1] but incorporating the more recent trend
towards heavy stone walls without an earthen backing. Before these walls had reached their full height the plan was
radically altered by the addition of massive external bastions
fitted up for fixed artillery. At Richborough in Kent, again,
the venerable Claudian triumphal monument first began to
be converted into a small fort and then the whole site was

---

[1] Cf. Brancaster and Reculver.

remodelled to take a brand-new large stone fort on modern lines.

We have earlier recorded the need to remember internal security problems when looking at third-century military dispositions. It is certain that even after the breaking of the Gallic Empire political stability was not all it might have been in the north-eastern part of the empire. Of two risings in Gaul in the reign of Probus, who carried on Aurelian's work of military recovery, the second was that of Bonosus, a commander whose father had been British. Owing to his inefficiency, the Roman fleet based at Cologne was destroyed by the barbarians, and he rebelled to avoid the inevitable punishment. His revolt may have affected Britain. Certainly there were alarming disturbances in Britain about this time. It is not entirely clear whether Zosimus, writing at the beginning of the sixth century, refers to only one substantial revolt or several. It is at least certain that Probus was obliged to send a Moorish officer named Victorinus to put down a rebellion by a governor in Britain whom the latter had himself recommended;[1] and it is also recorded by the same historian that Probus settled Burgundian and Vandal prisoners of war in the island, whom he was subsequently able to employ whenever there were uprisings.[2] These barbarians were given new homes in Britain (it is not clear whether or not as organized units) after being defeated by him in AD 277. They were sent to Britain in 277 or 278, transferred in traditional Roman fashion away from their homelands. One may guess that they had as yet no personal ties with disaffected factions within the empire and it may have been for this reason that they were used for this purpose rather than the regular British garrison. Professor Frere has pointed to the archaeological evidence of burning on several sites in Sussex in this period as possible evidence for barbarian raids on the south coast.[3] However the internal situation in the reign of Probus could be another explanation.[4]

Do any of the developments of the period, then, reflect

---

[1] Zosimus, I.lxvi.2.   [2] Ibid. I.lxviii.3.
[3] Frere, *Britannia*, 216, n. 63.
[4] This cannot, however, be applied to the fire at Fishbourne, if Professor Cunliffe is right in dating the fire itself and the subsequent demolition and salvage work to the very end of the century.

hostile barbarian activity? Barbarians in the Channel in the late third century there certainly were.[1] Britain may have suffered actual or threatened raids, though our source refers to the coasts from Brittany northwards to Flanders. At the same time there was a serious outbreak of disorder in Gaul caused by the 'Bacaudae', a name that first appears in the literature in this period to describe bands of disaffected country people, refugees, deserters, and old soldiers who had been thrown into brigandage on a considerable scale by the barbarian invasions, civil wars, and financial chaos of the later third century. After a century of intermittent peasant disruption these elements broke into armed and organized rebellion in 284. Yet, interestingly enough, even these rebels could not escape from Roman tradition, but demanded their own 'empire'. The threat to authority and the current established order, however, was a real one, and it is likely that the provision of town walls in Gaul at last was as much a response to the growing disorder in the countryside as to the recurrent barbarian invasions, themselves an inevitable contributory cause in the upheaval in rural life. The Bacaudae therefore are likely to have been a further factor in any flight of the upper class across the Channel.

Ironically, vigorous action by the restored central authority to strengthen the Roman military presence in the north-west rebounded on its authors by producing the conditions for yet another army *coup*. The Roman problem was perhaps insoluble: Augustus had recognized that security from revolution required the smallest possible standing army; Severus refined this by combining a sharp reduction in the size of individual commands with maximum generosity towards the troops themselves. On the other hand increasing barbarian pressure and problems of political security inevitably required larger armies and were accompanied by the creation of a professional officer class at command level drawn from outside the traditional aristocratic circles. The need to create fairly permanent mobile field-armies further exacerbated the situation. The vicious circle was completed by the fact that the consequent increases in taxation and military recruitment, not to mention the unpopularity of an arrogant

[1] Eutropius, ix. 21.

11

THE TETRARCHY

'MEDIEVAL history' traditionally starts with the accession of Diocletian in AD 284. It has become conventional to accept the subsequent 'reforms', constitutional, political, military, social, and economic, including the so-called establishment of the 'Christian Empire' by Constantine (in particular the Edict of Milan in 313 conferring imperial favour on the Church and the foundation of Constantinople in 324), as marking a decisive break between the ancient and the medieval worlds.[1] Such landmarks are a great convenience, whether one is constructing a syllabus or trying to implant a framework of chronology in the minds of students. Nevertheless this particular landmark is of more convenience to the medieval historian and the Byzantinist than it is to those studying the ancient world. There it can be a positive barrier to understanding.

It will not have escaped the reader that we are already talking of a period of 40 years, AD 284 to 324. This is not a single event like the Battle of Hastings, nor a relatively short but decisive period such as 1939–45. It is, of course, extremely difficult to determine the limits of any 'period of change' when one tries to go beyond an impressionistic view. Nevertheless with hindsight a series of historical changes may, whether causally linked or not, seem to mark a major alteration in direction. In the case in question, perhaps Constantius II's establishment at Constantinople of a new constitutional apparatus for the Roman state, partly parallel to that at Rome and partly sharing with it, suggests AD 340 as a convenient limit for this period of change. Yet we have now gone over half a century in searching for some such point. In modern history we would have to take a very long view to regard the events of 56 years, say 1914–70, as those of a single moment in time. Even if the pace of technological

---

[1] AD 313 also marks the official abandonment of persecution of Christians in the last parts of the empire outside the territory controlled by Constantine where it had still been practised.

change makes this example a little unfair, the reader will recall the 'end' of medieval history in England, conventionally
1485. It is comparatively simple to point to the broad differences between England before Bosworth Field and after the
Dissolution of the Monasteries, but impossible to be more
precise unless one is examining one particular aspect of life.

Looking at Roman Britain one can apply these principles
and present a broad picture of 'third-century Britain' and
compare it with 'fourth-century Britain', but it can only be
impressionistic. Furthermore, we have already seen that the
older view of a province in calamitous decay in the third
century no longer can be supported with confidence, particularly after about AD 270. A contrast between the third
century and the striking prosperity of the first half of the
fourth is still with us but has become much less dramatic.
Moreover, the conventional line between ancient and medieval
history is of very little use indeed for Britain. Indeed, one only
has to think that the logical consequence of 'starting' medieval
history in AD 284 is to describe fourth-century Britain as part
of 'medieval England' to see the point. Whatever the changes,
Britain in the fourth century had immensely more in common
with its own history since the Claudian Conquest than its
condition after the middle of the fifth. Its way of life is
in broad terms that of the Classical world since Alexander
rather than that of Dark Age or Saxon England. With Diocletian we are entering not the Middle Ages but the 'Late
Roman' world, and for the purposes of this book that is the
term I propose to retain.

The study of Roman Britain has evolved its own individual
'landmark' date for the beginning of this period: AD 296. In
that year widespread destruction by barbarians has commonly
been held to have occurred in the island while the central
government was recovering Britain from yet another usurping
regime. But there is a curious paradox, whereby the general lack
of evidence for dramatic change has forced Romano-British
historians into a theory of insular conservatism in Romano-
British life, which indeed has some elements of real significance. Nevertheless the gradual changes that are apparent are
much more comprehensible if one looks at them in the context of a long period of change in the empire as a whole.

The *coup d'état* referred to at the end of the last chapter occurred approximately three years after Diocletian's sudden accession in 284. His elevation was the consequence of the mysterious death of the previous emperor, Numerian, whose personal guard Diocletian at the time commanded. After the murder of Probus by his own troops in 282 there had been another deplorable return to military insurrection and emperor-making by the army. This disorder produced four emperors, mostly of the same family, in the space of two years. Diocletian, however, originally named Diocles, was of humble provincial origin, from Dalmatia. His fate has been, as we have seen, to be marked as the arch-reformer, yet his work is notable for intense dedication to Roman tradition and conservatism. In himself he marks the total absorption of other peoples into the Roman way of life and in many ways his work has much in common with that of Augustus.

In 285 Diocletian appointed Marcus Aurelius Valerius Maximianus, one of his officers, as his chief lieutenant with the title of 'Caesar' and responsibility for the defence of Italy and the western provinces. In the same year Diocletian himself took the title of *Britannicus Maximus* and it seems reasonable to assume that a military success of some importance had been won in his name in Britain, which lay within Maximian's command. At this stage the latter was engaged in restoring order in the north-west of the empire, continuing the work of Aurelian and Probus, under both of whom he had served with merit. In particular, in Gaul, he had to contend with the Bacaudae. Maximian successfully dealt with these disturbances and in AD 286 was promoted to the rank of 'Augustus' to act as co-emperor, retaining his responsibility for the west.

There was nothing unusual in an emperor taking a colleague: Vespasian had thus elevated Titus, Marcus Aurelius chose L. Verus (insisting on full constitutional powers for his partner) and a number of subsequent emperors followed the same pattern. Nor was this out of line with Roman tradition in which many magistrates had colleagues, from the consuls downwards. It was conversely also within Republican tradition that, whatever the legal position, one magistrate should dominate his fellows through his own personal *auctoritas*. Diocletian thus had no difficulty in retaining the ultimate power, should he neet it.

This principle remains broadly valid throughout the fourth century and, despite the increasing polarization towards east and west, we shall only confuse ourselves if we think in terms of 'eastern' and 'western empires' in the sense of separate states. Except for periods when eastern and western colleagues were at loggerheads, this was not, even *de facto,* the position till after the death of Theodosius the Great in 395. Indeed, that the separation was not accepted everywhere even then as constitutionally valid is a key to much of what happened subsequently.

The elevation of Maximian to the rank of Augustus allowed Diocletian to delegate his formal functions in the west (such demands on an emperor's time had become more and more onerous as centralization increased) but it did not fundamentally alter the situation. Maximian now had greater authority in issuing commands but still faced the same military problems in the west and, because of Diocletian's *auctoritas,* was in practice answerable to him. The west was, indeed, no easy assignment and it was soon to become much worse. As well as internal disturbances, Maximian faced other serious military problems in the northern provinces. A little later he was to be obliged to put great efforts into the defence of the imperial frontier both on the lower Rhine and in Raetia. At this stage, he was tackling swarms of Saxon and Frankish raiders who were descending on the coasts of Brittany and Gallia Belgica. In charge of his counter-measures Maximian put an officer called M. Mausaeus Carausius, by origin a Menapian from the Low Countries. Carausius was said to have been of very low birth but to have acquired an impressive reputation as a soldier. Carausius was based at Boulogne, and seems to have had frequent successes, capturing many barbarians. Unfortunately a suspicion was growing that he had prior knowledge of raids. This he was alleged to use to his own advantage, letting the barbarians in and refraining from taking them till they were back at sea laden with plunder. It was said that he returned the stolen goods neither to the provincials who owned them nor to the emperors (it is unclear which was thought the worse crime) but converted them to his own use. Maximian ordered his execution. Carausius replied by proclaiming himself emperor and seizing the provinces of Britain. From late 286 or in 287 the island once again came under a Roman administration independent of the central government.

In Britain Carausius' safety from attack across the Channel was for the moment secured by the fleet he already commanded, but he clearly had substantial land forces in Gaul since he was able to deny access to the coast to Maximian. These forces perhaps included troops allocated to him for the defence of the coast itself, or they may have joined him subsequently. In Britain too he must have had some fairly solid support. One may assume at the least that there were survivors from among people who had found themselves on the wrong side in one or other of the upheavals of the previous decades. Here in Britain itself there had been at least two revolts by official Roman governors which were suppressed during the very recent reign of Probus. This must have affected a number of prominent people in the British provinces. We have noted above that the crucial role played in the second of these rebellions by the loyalty of Probus' recent Burgundian and Vandal settlers suggests very strongly that the mutinous governor had carried the regular garrisons with him. One needs to remember that at the proclamation of Carausius it was only sixteen or seventeen years since the fall of the Imperium Galliarum. Past independence from the central administration may by now have become an attractive memory: the people of the empire were faced with a central government dominated, in Diocletian, by a tough soldier obsessed by organization, determined to impose national discipline and to collect the resources for a vast overhaul of the defences of the empire behind which order could be restored and maintained. Moreover, since the Roman fleet in the Channel had bases in Britain as well as Gaul, it seems likely that there were officers in Britain who would be in immediate danger of execution if Carausius were defeated. Once he had successfully defied Maximian, there were doubtless excellent reasons for keeping him in power. Indeed, recent Roman politics did not give much reason to suppose that one claimant to the throne would be any more secure in the long run than any other. There must have been much to be said for submitting unobtrusively to the nearest would-be emperor who seemed to have solid support from his troops. Nevertheless it is interesting to note that there is some reason to suspect that support for Carausius in Britain was not unanimous, at least not continuously.

Diocletian's reputation as a reformer rests on the totality of his measures during his reign, some of which were introduced while Britain was cut off from the central empire. To us his most spectacular change was the introduction of the 'Tetrarchy' in AD 293 when the empire was again under serious strain. It was a development of his delegation of authority to Maximian. In outline this new scheme of government depended on the two senior emperors ('Augusti'), ruling respectively the eastern and western parts of the empire, each with a junior or 'Caesar'. This was on paper a fairly simple formalization of the devices from time to time employed by previous emperors. The system worked as a college of four emperors. They normally ruled their own sectors more or less independently, but the fact that they were regularly addressed as a group of four shows that Diocletian saw them as a team. It was a logical extension of his action in elevating Maximian. At its best the Tetrarchy could cope with the administrative and security problems caused by the sheer size of the empire in the context of the relative slowness of communications. It might also ensure a smooth succession to the throne: Diocletian added a touch of real imagination in proposing that both senior emperors should retire and be succeeded by their Caesars, who would in turn then have Caesars of their own.

This ingenious device was not to work, and proved no solution to the problem that had been a critical one for every Roman emperor from the beginning. Diocletian seems to have been trying to break away from the tradition of violent succession. His policy is often described as a revolutionary attempt to restore the second-century principle of nominated succession. Yet in fact, even in the second century, formal adoption into the family of the reigning emperor had been an essential part of the process, a device that had a very long history in Roman politics. It is important to remember that in private life adoption to provide an heir was a normal procedure; and that the urge to find an heir, when one was lacking, was not only a matter of the material possessions but the honour and continuity of the family. Adoption, whether imperial or purely private, had the advantage of a relatively rational choice: it broke down in the second century when Marcus Aurelius was faced with the possibility of preferring such a choice to nominating his own son. Nevertheless we should recognize that the two systems, in the light of Roman attitudes to adoption, are nothing like as separate as they appear to us today, when adoption rarely has such a purpose. Both essentially rely upon the Roman concept of the family. This becomes clear when one brings into account the additional principle on which Diocletian's Tetrarchy was based but which we have not yet examined. The two Caesars were linked to the Augusti by marriage alliances. Diocletian and Maximian had taken additional family names—Jovius and Herculius respectively, after the gods Jupiter and Hercules—emphasizing the exalted nature of their sovereignty. The two Augusti now adopted the Caesars and arranged the marriage alliances, so that the junior emperors became Iovii and Herculii as well. The line between this and hereditary dynasties is a thin one, and it is not surprising that in the next generation the troops (and the sons themselves) were not inclined to make anything of the distinction. In the first century it had been vital in retaining the loyalty of the armies to be a member of the Julian House: in the fourth the 'legitimate' imperial families established a similar advantage over their rivals. In truth the question of the succession was, in the context of the Roman tradition for personal reputation and family rivalry, quite insoluble. Nevertheless, though Diocletian's quadripartite scheme did not last at the top, it was a framework on to which could be hung major modifications of the administrative and military structure of the empire. These were to have far-reaching consequences in the future.

In the military field, too, it is doubtful whether Diocletian can be called a conscious reformer, in the sense of instituting major changes in the structure or methods of the Roman army. Rather he seems to have pursued with great vigour a policy of strengthening it more or less as it was. Zosimus, comparing Diocletian favourably with Constantine, says that

by the foresight of Diocletian the frontiers of the Roman empire were everywhere studded with cities and forts and towers, in the way I have already described, and the whole army was stationed along them, so that it was impossible for the barbarians to break through, as the attackers were everywhere withstood by an opposing force. But Constantine ruined this defensive system by withdrawing the majority of the troops from the frontiers, and stationing them in cities which did not require protection.[1]

We shall be returning to the Late Roman army more than once in the succeeding chapters. In the context of Roman Britain it is more usual to consider the features of the army in this period all together, and this is indeed the easier way. It makes clear the very marked differences between the army in the fourth century and preceding centuries, but it tends to mask from the reader the facts that it had evolved from the earlier army over a considerable length of time and that it went through a series of changes of major significance within the Late Roman period itself. We shall be chiefly concerned with the armed services in the western half of the Roman world. We shall see how, between the Tetrarchy and the time when they finally faded away among the barbarian successor states in the latter part of the fifth century, the Roman forces were more dramatically transformed than they had been in the whole period since Augustus. As always, the army was near the centre of affairs, and although the process by which it had changed and finally dissolved in the west is not fully understood, by noting the changes stage by stage against the social and political developments of the age we may be able the better to glimpse how the fragments of evidence we have from Britain fit into the pattern of the Late Roman world at large.

As we have seen, a standing field-army or armies had been emerging, more or less accidentally, from the system of *ad hoc* arrangements for specific campaigns. Diocletian split up the substantial mobile force of cavalry that had existed since the time of Gallienus, but this was counterbalanced on a more permanent basis by the facts that he raised new legions that came to be used in a more flexible way than the frontier garrisons—giving them the titles of *Ioviani* and *Heculiani* after himself and his chief colleague—and created certain élite mounted regiments intended to be deployed centrally.

---

[1] Zosimus, ii.34 (translation: A.H.M. Jones, *The Later Roman Empire*, Oxford (1964), 52). This passage may be more accurate on Diocletian than on Constantine. We shall look later at the innovations which have been attributed to the latter.

We know that by 295 the idea of troops permanently attached to the imperial court had become sufficiently entrenched to receive the description *comitatus*.[1] The late Professor A.H.M. Jones cited a proconsul of Africa referring to 'Christian soldiers serving in the sacred *comitatus* of our Lords Diocletian and Maximian, Constantius and Maximian (Galerius).'[2] This cannot be used as evidence for a single central field-army, since it was conventional to refer in formal documents to all four emperors together, nor is it certain that it records a structural change in the organization of the Roman army. That probably came with Constantine the Great. There had long been troops serving with the emperors in the guard units and in various headquarters or special posts. Nevertheless we gain the impression that the whole group had now acquired some appearance of permanency and we may be sure they profited from their presence near the emperors they served. It is not impossible that at this time there were also units normally stationed elsewhere that were designated as part of a reserve that could be assembled quickly for field service with the emperors. There is no reason, however, to think that as early as this they were regularly brigaded together or stationed away from the frontiers. Indeed, when a permanent field-army, formally constituted, does emerge clearly it seems at first to have been a fairly small force.

In the fourth century we shall observe the military *comitatus* becoming firmly established, and there are already at this time signs that its units were acquiring higher status from their privileged position, as the praetorians had long enjoyed over the legions. Yet there are also indications that in Diocletian's reign the old primary distinction between legions and auxiliaries remained: his arrangements for veterans still draw a line between the legions (now joined by the newer special cavalry units) and the old *cohortes* and *alae*. The distinctions of training, function, career structure, and pay had once reflected the difference between citizen and non-citizen, but the latter had long been eroded, first by individual cases and eventually by the wholesale extension of the citizenship under Caracalla. As the old auxiliary units of the army had

[1] See Note, p. 319 below, for a discussion of the term.
[2] A.H.M. Jones, op. cit. 52, where he also cites traces of an even earlier origin.

gradually become citizen they had, in the second and third centuries, been replaced as irregulars by newly raised *numeri* and *cunei* of native troops. Thus by the beginning of the fourth century the concept of an army that contained among its units numerous levels of status and emoluments was of long standing and thus capable of further development without offending tradition.

It is, however, probably in the matter of scale that we should look for Diocletian's own real contribution to army reform, if reform it should be called. It had been the aim of Augustus and on the whole that of his successors to keep the army as small and economical as was consistent with the security of the empire. Indeed the smallness of the army in the provinces could directly promote the security of the emperor at Rome. To work, the policy required the absence of simultaneous pressure on several frontiers at once, a reasonable degree of internal acceptance of imperial rule and abstention from large-scale military adventure on the part of the emperor. It also assumed that the advantage of the state and not the army itself was the prime consideration among the troops and their officers. All these conditions for success broke down. There is much debate on just how much Diocletian increased the actual size of the armed forces, but it seems clear that it was very substantially. The contemporary and hostile author Lactantius complained that he had quadrupled it. It has been reasonably conjectured that the total number of troops in the Diocletianic army was perhaps double what it was at the beginning of the third century. There are great problems in trying to be more precise. Even for the Severan period the total is elusive and it is extremely uncertain how much recruiting during the civil wars of the third century added overall, allowing for losses. It was once thought that though Diocletian raised many new legions their individual size was much smaller. This is now considered unlikely, at least during his reign. Fresh legions were certainly formed out of detachments drawn from existing legions and many other new legions seemed to have been raised from scratch. Indeed conscription had to be applied very severely to produce the recruits. As in administration (and other fields) Diocletian's prescription for recovery seems to have included coercion of the individual and a vast expansion of the numbers of persons in the direct service of the empire. The strain on the economy, which he was also attempting to put right by similar means, must have been enormous.

It is now clear that we can summarize Diocletian's genius in terms of the employment of organization as a cure for the ills of the state, adapting and expanding existing elements in the Roman scene on an enormous scale. Unlike Constantine the Great he was not a revolutionary, in the sense of admitting of a radically different political or social pattern—very much the reverse. Nevertheless, like the reforms of Augustus, his measures in effect created the conditions for a new framework for the Roman world. They were also at the cost of a vast increase in public expenditure—one feature we shall find repeated under Constantine. Of this period, for example, Lactantius complained that increasing the number of senior posts, probably unavoidable to cope with the expanding burden of administration, did not stop there. Referring to the division of provinces, he pointed out that every extra provincial governor meant an extra staff to go with him. When we are considering the appearance of four, and then five, provinces in Britain we shall do well to remember this—not to mention the fact that a new tier of provincial administration was added, the 'diocese' or group of provinces which had its own head (*vicarius*) and staff. And it was not very long before the armies in the provinces were to have their own quite separate command and headquarters establishments. The opportunities for extending the tradition of patronage and placemen increased enormously. One may indeed wonder how (or if) the empire could possibly stand it, especially after the ravages of the third century. Yet perhaps the answer to Diocletian's attitude lies in that last fact: the new formulation of government may at first have looked cheap compared to the prospect of renewed internal disorder, civil war, and barbarian invasion.

When one considers the possible detailed effects of Diocletian's reforms on Britain, it is worth remembering that the usurpation of Carausius occurred at a relatively early point in Diocletian's reign, and that the political break thus caused lasted a decade in which many of the changes in the empire as a whole touched upon above began to be implemented. At any period of Roman history it is unsafe to argue wholly from analogy, assuming uniformity of policy or practice throughout the empire. Analogy is a useful basis for hypothesis but an insecure foundation for belief. In this particular phase we have the interesting situation that, at a highly formative period for the Roman world as a whole (indeed for the Byzantine and medieval one as well), Britain was to the empire not unlike the Republic of Ireland to the United Kingdom. Complex factors sometimes induce parallel change in such a situation without the direct exercise of authority, sometimes not.

It is, however, important to use modern analogies solely to heighten one's consciousness of the situation. The Carausian episode has been romantically seen as the first occurrence of British national independence, even as the first British Empire based on a British Navy. This is not how Carausius portrayed himself. At the other extreme, archaeologists with their preoccupation with structures and stratigraphical phases are inclined to view the episode merely as providing, on the one hand, possible explanations in the long-standing debate over the dating and purpose of the Saxon Shore forts and, on the other, a destruction layer sufficiently frequently identified on Romano-British sites to provide a convenient end to the third century, just as that conventionally allocated to AD 197 had closed the second.

Looked at from the standpoint of the recently established Diocletianic regime, the revolt of Carausius was embarrassing and awkward, particularly to Maximian as newly elevated Augustus. Up to that point he had been generally successful in restoring order in the west, and Carausius' naval operations under his command had been a notable part of those victories. The suspicion that there was something wrong with the successes at sea and the fact that the senior officer in charge seemed to be implicated must have been a serious blow, compounded by the fact that Maximian's decision to take drastic action back-fired so seriously. Diocletian can hardly have been pleased at Maximian's bungled handling of the affair. Nor can he have enjoyed the consequent loss of provinces which were of considerable military importance and whose more or less undamaged economy contrasted strongly with the battered state of Gaul and Germany.

It is a measure of just how serious the situation remained

on the German frontier that Maximian seems to have delayed preparing for military action against Carausius till the latter part of 288. Maybe he also hoped to negotiate a settlement or to topple Carausius from his position by intrigue. Carausius for his part certainly tried to consolidate support for himself by playing on local interests. Something of his propaganda surely remains in the descriptions of himself on the coinage he began to issue as 'restorer of Britain' (*restitutor Britanniae*) and the like. Professor Frere rightly points to his originality in issuing the only Roman coin with an (adapted) quotation from Virgil: 'Come, O longed for and eagerly awaited one'.[1] Like much Roman propaganda it can be taken in more than one way and the background is complex. At one level it presents Carausius as the recently arrived political saviour, and implies, or tries to suggest, the existence of a general body of opinion that had awaited some such relief from unspecified troubles. The aura of divinity, too, that was becoming increasingly inseparable from the institution of emperorship is unlikely to have been absent from people's thoughts. It might not be entirely fanciful to detect in addition a touch of the messianic. Reference on other Carausian coins to the *genius Britanniae*, the half-personified spirit of the island, adds to the impression of an intelligent use of that blend of political and religious ideas that earlier emperors had used in the interests of themselves and the stability of the state. The historian Polybius had clearly identified this function of religion in the Roman state long before the emergence of the emperors; and its manipulation in the interest of the imperial system was hallowed by perhaps its greatest exponent, Virgil's own master, the first emperor.

Exactly where Carausius' support lay is entirely obscure. For that matter we do not even know the extent of his command under Maximian at the time of his revolt. The subsequent position can perhaps be inferred from a coin series of his that lists a number of legions, including not only two of the regular garrison of Britain but also various others. The inference is that he retained or managed to take command of legionary detachments present in northern Gaul, perhaps originally allocated to work with him in the campaign

---

[1] *Expectate veni*, cf. *Aeneid* ii. 282–3: *quibus Hector ab oris / exspectate venis?*

against the pirates. An intriguing feature of this coin series is the presence of II Augusta and XX Valeria Victrix but not the Sixth, whose fortress at York had been the pivot of the northern frontier since Trajan and the centre for the province of Lower Britain for the best part of a century. At some time during his reign Carausius' writ ran in at least part of the northern frontier area, since a milestone with his name was found at Carlisle[1] but this need not mean that the loyalty of VI Victrix to him was always beyond suspicion. The legions in Britain after all did not always support the same party in times of civil war.

There does not, however, seem any reason to doubt that Carausius was in a strong military position. The fact that the coin series mentioned includes the names of six legions normally stationed on the Continent suggests that even if he had only detachments from these, nevertheless he had substantial land forces available. Certainly Maximian made little headway in 289, not only apparently losing a naval battle but also being unable to dislodge Carausius' forces from the powerful land and sea base at Boulogne which he is still found holding in 293. It is an interesting reflection on the empire's inability to cope easily with Carausius that it was nearly five years more before any successful move was made against him. His repulse of Maximian in 289 must have immensely strengthened his position. Success against such an opponent was proof to his troops that he possessed to a high degree the divine gift of good fortune in war, enhancing his personal *auctoritas* and inspiring confidence in a military future that must otherwise have looked decidedly unpromising.

It was equally important—with civilians as well as soldiers—to establish the proper trappings of legitimacy. Carausius did not hesitate to follow tradition by proclaiming himself emperor. Indeed the administration both military and civil of his realm required an emperor as the fount of authority, to confirm appointments and to make its acts legal at every level. Anyhow, an usurper was only an usurper till he was firmly established. At some time Carausius took the imperial

---

[1] *RIB* 2291: found in a river bed at Gallows Hill, just south of the city of Carlisle, presumably displaced from the nearby Roman strategic trunk road that linked York to the garrisons at the western end of the frontier. Perhaps the city of Carlisle was more enthusiastic than the frontier army?

names M. Aurelius, and in the course of his reign adopted the neat device of portraying himself on his coinage as a third colleague on the throne with Diocletian and Maximian. Perhaps the best known of these coins is the issue picturing the three with the legend 'Carausius and his Brothers'. The others did not respond and, unlike Clodius Albinus a century earlier, there is no reason to suppose that Carausius himself thought he was genuinely accepted as a colleague. Yet the events of the past century need have given him no cause to feel himself less legitimate than them.

Carausius had taken care to issue a sound coinage, a sensible move in view of the disastrous state into which the Roman currency had fallen during the third century. It is particularly interesting to note that Carausius now aligned his coinage with the reformed system that Diocletian had introduced into the empire at large. It is probable that this too was partly to emphasize legitimacy and collegiality, but it may remind us of the introduction of decimal coinage in the Irish Republic as a matter of economic advantage and convenience of trade. With a sound currency there would have been every reason to encourage normality and the maximum flow of trade. Nor, with signs of returning stability and security on the Continent, would the commercial interests and those landowners with properties on both sides of the Channel have thanked him if he had not. These were the people who kept the Roman system going locally and (particularly the provincial gentry of less than senatorial rank) in this age supplied many of the administrators and some of the army officers on whom the emperors depended. Carausius may, too, have felt a fresh need to compete, now that the central government was showing clear signs of being there to stay and capable of beating back the barbarians. Conditioned by hindsight and the immense reputation of Diocletian in later ages it is difficult now to remember that at the time there had been little reason to expect any emperor to last more than a short while.

We touched earlier on the vexed question of the date of the Saxon Shore forts.[1] It is one of those historical controversies that have shed more light on the nature of historians than on the subject debated. I personally still favour

_____

[1] See also Note, p. 320 below.

the view that the series as we know it was the result of building and modification over a long period, probably serving different purposes at different times. This is not to say that there was not at least one moment when scattered elements already existing were not drawn together and combined with new forts and other features to form a coherent system for a specific purpose, and I agree with others that the reign of the emperor Probus is the most likely time. However it is not in the least likely that either the system as a whole or individual elements in it retained an identical purpose to the end of Roman Britain—or, for that matter, till their individual operational lives came to an end. We have seen that Reculver and Brancaster go back to the earlier part of the third century. Pevensey could have commenced well on into the fourth. Their ends, too, need not be contemporary. Nor is there any cause to think that defence against barbarian attack from outside the empire—generally assumed to be the purpose of these forts—excluded as a secondary function their maintaining a watch for signs of internal unrest and controlling, for both political and fiscal reasons, movement and communication within the empire. Civil war was a circumstance in which these secondary needs became particularly acute, and we may guess that some building or modification may be the work of Carausius and Allectus. However, in this field we are working without the precision of exact epigraphic or literary evidence, and trying to tie these structures down by archaeological means to a decade or less is a tricky enterprise particularly liable to rapid reassessment. It would be satisfying, too, if we could connect the radical modification in design at Burgh Castle (perhaps for artillery) with Carausius' need to protect Britain primarily against Roman military technology rather than barbarian raiders and to hold the island with much smaller forces than could eventually be mustered against him. But caution must remain.

As we have already noted, it was during this period of political break between the territory controlled by Carausius and the central government that important changes took place in the empire at large. The Tetrarchy, as we noted, dates from 293. It can be argued that the existence of Carausius as a putative third Augustus offended against this neat system of twin pairs of senior and junior emperor, east and west, and now required eradication. Yet Roman constitutional arrangements were rarely that neat and it was the Roman capacity for local modification that largely made the imperial system work in practice. It could conversely be that the presence of yet another separate and apparently workable empire uncomfortably soon after the suppression of the Imperium Galliarum itself underlined the need for a major attempt to tackle the structure of imperial government. One very important thing the new system did was to provide for the devolution of the supreme power in such a way as to make it geographically available where it was needed. Later we shall see how the same principle ran through the re-organization of the lower levels in the civil and military hierarchy. Concentrating however for the moment on the imperial power and its relation to Britain, the most important point to note is that it was felt necessary to establish one of the four holders in the north-west of the empire.

The appointment of Maximian's praetorian prefect, Flavius Julius Constantius (now renamed Flavius Valerius Constantius) to the post of 'Caesar' to Maximian served to inaugurate the new four-fold system in the west. Constantius had already put aside his unofficial wife Helena, the Christian mother of Constantine the Great, and married Maximian's daughter. In the east, Diocletian chose as his Caesar an officer of peasant origin, Gaius Galerius Valerius Maximianus, known to history as the Emperor Galerius. The latter now divorced his wife to take Diocletian's daughter Valeria. Each of the four emperors had his own staff and moved about his territory with much of it in attendance.[1] Like a medieval king, where the emperor was, there was the capital. This peripatetic tendency was of long standing: Hadrian's great tour of the provinces which kept him away from Rome for nearly seven years was an early example. It promoted the development of alternative centres of imperial administration which took on the character of capital cities. It also seriously widened the gap between the imperial house and the most prestigious section of the senatorial aristocracy, still centred on Italy and the city of Rome, which the third-century exclusion of senators from

---

[1] There can be little doubt that Diocletian and Maximian as Augusti each had a full imperial *comitatus*: the two Caesars may have had rather smaller staffs but these are still likely to have been substantial.

military commands and the governorships of 'imperial' provinces had done much to establish.

In the north-west Constantius followed Maximian in using the city of Trier frequently as his base. This great city had been badly damaged by the recent barbarian invasions, but took on a new lease of life as it became a regular imperial capital. It received over these years much grand imperial architecture itself, and its hinterland in the Moselle region witnessed the flowering of villa estates—including at least one probable imperial country residence.

Such centres as Trier must have taken on extra importance and extra dignity in consequence of Diocletian's deliberate cultivation of the remoteness of the emperor's person, accompanied by an elaboration of court ritual and court magnificence. In many ways this was contrary to earlier imperial tradition, where an emperor was praised for accessibility and often pretended to the part of *primus inter pares*. But it was in other ways a logical development of increasingly open autocracy, was supported by the long evolution of the religious cult of the imperial house, and had potential political advantages in making it psychologically less easy for any Roman officer to contemplate himself as a possible emperor. It doubtless widened the breach with the senatorial aristocracy even further and it was surely expensive, but it must have had a considerable local effect in stimulating prosperity in places like Trier and its region. One may reasonably surmise a direct effect on the building trades, the service industries, land values, and indeed the entire regional economy.

The contrast between Trier and the region a little further west is so striking as to be worth making here. It was only a short while since Maximian had defeated the Bacaudae, whose existence implied so much in the way of unemployment and destitution. Archaeology in northern France in recent years has revealed from the air a remarkable number of very large Roman villas, comparable to the development round Trier. Few of these villas in France have yet been excavated or closely dated, though they are strongly reminiscent of the largest of the fourth-century villas in Britain, though on an even larger scale. But before we leap to the conclusion that there was a uniform development of great

country houses at this time stretching from the Moselle to
Britain, we ought to look at a very interesting possibility. In
1972 the French archaeologist and air photographer M. Roger
Agache noted that since 1964 nearly 700 rural sites of the
Roman period had been discovered in the region of the
Somme: the plans of 270 Roman villas had been recorded.[1]
Such dating evidence as was available in 1972 suggested that
the villas were largely *early* and were destroyed in the first
major third-century invasions. M. Agache suggested that the
apparent replacement of these villas by villages is due to the
policies of Maximian and Constantius in using barbarians to
resettle abandoned lands.[2] It is particularly interesting that
M. Agache also thinks some villages had already existed alongside the villas. That is a situation which has been tentatively
recognized in Britain as well. The possibility of their survival
in Gaul after destruction of the villas is strongly reminiscent
of many places in France after the destruction or abandonment of châteaux in the Revolution. A similar development
may also have occurred in the fifth and sixth centuries. The
picture in northern France would therefore be quite different
from the Moselle, and represent a process starting well back
in the third century. It would be consistent with the theory
of landowners transferring themselves to Britain from the
later years of the third century, though it does not rule out
a similar movement *towards* the German frontier, where the
wealthy could feel safer in greater proximity to the legions,
not to mention the increasingly regular presence of an emperor
himself.

The appointment of Maximian's praetorian prefect Constantius as Caesar in the west put in charge of affairs, in that
region of the empire which is our prime concern, a man with
intimate knowledge of the situation. Carausius himself, after
all, had also been one of Maximian's senior officers. The praetorian prefects had for centuries been very important people.
From time to time they had gone beyond their strict duties
and become kingmakers and even emperors themselves. By
now they were in many respects regular deputy emperors,

[1] *Antiquity,* 46 (1972), 117 ff. See also R. Agache, *Détection aérienne de ves-
tiges protohistoriques gallo-romains et médiévaux dans le bassin de la Somme et
ses abords,* Amiens (1970).
[2] *Pan. Constant. Caes. (Pan Lat. Vet.* VIII (V)), 21.

including frequently holding the central command of the armies. Constantius' upgrading to Caesar both recognized his actual function, and put an emperor with title, powers, and an imperial staff permanently in the north-west who could give undivided attention to the restoration of order and prosperity there. For the former praetorian prefect this may have been a reduction in his responsibility in geographical terms but a very real increase in its level. He may no longer have had to keep the whole of the west under review, but now in almost all respects wielded final authority in his quarter of the empire.

It must have been a sobering realization for Carausius' units on the south coast of Britain that not only were the great legionary bases on the Rhine as close to them as the garrison of the British frontier in the north, but the hostile imperial capital at Trier was actually closer than Hadrian's Wall. To Constantius, looking at it from the other side, the elimination of Carausius' regime and the recovery of the lost provinces must have appeared a major item of unfinished business. It is difficult to see how the new Caesar could hope to maintain order in northern Gaul with Carausius in control of Boulogne, let alone tolerate the ever-present affront to his authority. A show of power was needed, particularly as Maximian had spoiled an excellent record in the north on the same hurdle. We are fortunate that for the taking of Britain by Constantius we have reasonably full contemporary and near-contemporary sources. The countervailing difficulty is that much of the detail comes from panegyric, specifically written to flatter the victor. Just as with Tacitus' *Agricola* one suspects the author of fitting the character and deeds of his hero to the ideal of the Roman officer and gentleman, so one has the uncomfortable feeling of *déjà vu* in reading of the exploits of Constantius. Indeed, it was presented to an audience that is likely to have read its Caesar and its Tacitus. If Carausius could expect his public to recognize a Virgilian quotation, there is no reason why Eumenius in writing his panegyric could not assume similar literacy. Nor would an audience educated on rhetoric and accustomed to the funeral oration and the set-piece honorific speech think such references, even modifications of the exact account, at all strange— the opposite, in fact. We must be very careful not to impose

modern approaches to historical writing on to the Romans.
In fact, once we have their attitudes clear, what they write reveals a great deal about what they felt *ought* to happen and
how great men *ought* to behave, and by implication how they
often did not.

With those reservations in mind, the account certainly records Constantius first proceeding to enforce his authority
in Gaul by taking Boulogne. Carausius had, it is said, won
over a legion to his side.[1] The suggestion that this was a Continental one, rather than one in Britain, is reasonable. This
would mean that he had on the mainland at least the bulk of
a legion—as well as the legionary detachments already deduced
—and makes it easier to understand how he could hold
Boulogne for so long. It seems clear that this position depended also on command of the sea and keeping the route
from Britain open. Constantius' capture of Boulogne by
building a mole to close the harbour is in the best tradition
of Roman military virtuosity and broke Carausius' foothold
in Gaul. He now no longer commanded both sides of the
Channel and had lost his access to the resources and recruiting
grounds of the Continent. It seems to have been a desperate
blow to his prestige. At any rate, his assassination by one of
his chief associates, named Allectus, followed promptly. Yet
even this did not lead to an immediate invasion of Britain by
the victorious Caesar. Instead, Carausius' place was taken by
his murderer, but, we presume, with an empire reduced to
the provinces of Britain alone. The final settlement of the
score with the regime in Britain was perhaps now less urgent,
since the pacification of Gaul could be carried out without
it. However for Constantius there was still the matter of a
hostile power just across the Channel and the authorities in
Gaul must have had to face the sort of problems that had
existed there before the Claudian invasion of Britain—a refuge
for dissidents across the water and the ever-present threat of
raids on the coast. In fact it was a worse problem, since the
hostile power was a Roman one, not a few barbarian tribes.
Constantius also had to tackle the pirates. The high praise
given him for dealing with marauding Franks who had penetrated the Low Countries shows how seriously these people,
who were ready to take to the sea, were still regarded. Having

[1] *Pan. Lat. Vet.* VII (V). xii, 1.

defeated them, he took an action of considerable significance
for the distant future, for he disarmed these Franks and quite
deliberately compelled them to settle within Roman territory,
'giving up their savagery.'[1] More immediately, with this
menace for the time being removed, the Roman navy—which
he augmented by constructing a new fleet in preparation for
the assault on Britain—had a new problem. With Boulogne
taken by Constantius, the naval units based on the opposite
sides of the Channel were under different commands and at
war with one another. It is a little difficult to imagine them
combining effectively against pirates: indeed Allectus' most
faithful supporters were to prove to be his own Frankish
mercenaries and one might wonder just how his fleet stood
in relation to the barbarians of the North Sea.

Allectus' position at the time of his assumption of power
is obscure. The contemporary author Eutropius simply
describes him as an associate or ally of Carausius.[2] A source
in the later fourth century uses a phrase which may mean
that Allectus had been appointed by Carausius as his finance
minister or *rationalis summae rei*.[3] Very little is known, even
in normal times, of the functions of the emperors' *rationales*,
but the office might suggest that Carausius fell victim to a
palace plot rather than a direct military coup. The inability
of Allectus subsequently to organize his regular troops into
an effective stand against Constantius' invasion may point in
the same direction.

Despite all this, it is still somewhat surprising that Constantius took another three years to launch an attack on
Britain. We should probably not underestimate the difficulties presented by the Channel. Caesar and Claudius had not
found it easy and Gaius had given it up. The lesson that
special ocean-going transports were required had perhaps
been learnt from reading the accounts of those expeditions.
To prepare them took time. One may wonder, too, whether
Constantius had failed to gain command of the sea. Moreover, ships and port facilities remaining on the Gallic side of

---

[1] *Pan. Lat. Vet.* VI (VII). v. 3.

[2] Eutropius, ix. 22: *socius eius.*

[3] Aurelius Victor, *Caesares,* xxxix. 41: *qui cum eius permissu summae rei praeesset.* It is interesting to note one interpretation of a mint mark on Carausian coinage—the letters RSR—is *R (ationalis) S (ummae) R (ei).*

the Channel may not have been in very good condition after the campaign of 293. The delay suggests, too, that Allectus was thought to have reasonably solid support from the substantial army stationed in Britain. Neither Caesar nor Claudius had had to contemplate a landing opposed by regular Roman troops, let alone in strength and on their own ground.

It is clear, also, that Gaul and Germany still presented problems. Maximian had been personally involved in heavy fighting on the lower Rhine and also on the upper Danube from 288 to 292, and it is worth noting that in order to release Constantius for the British campaign of 296 Maximian came back to take command in person on the Rhine once again. This is an interesting example of the Tetrarchy at work. It continued the old working partnership between the emperor and his former praetorian prefect. The same sort of relationship is reflected in the way in which Constantius delegated a major part in the expedition to his own praetorian prefect, Asclepiodotus.[1] As it turned out, the vagaries of navigation in the Channel were to leave the latter with most of the fighting. Given mutual trust, which Diocletian doubtless hoped he had secured by combining family ties with assured positions in a formal hierarchy carrying with them guaranteed eventual promotion to the top, the new system could provide both freedom for the exercise of initiative within defined areas of responsibility and a flexibility by which the necessary cover could be given by an imperial colleague when the emperor normally responsible for the area had to take the field in active command of operations. This seems a sounder idea than the frequent and dangerous practice where emperors had to take the field in person and leave behind subordinates in key positions in the empire. These could include some very powerful individuals—including ambitious members of their own families, whom the absence of any reliable tradition of loyalty to the emperor forced them to trust.

---

[1] There are some uncertainties as to whether the Caesars under the Tetrarchy had their own praetorian prefects or whether Asclepiodotus, for example, was seconded by Maximian. Later there are certainly some examples of praetorian prefects as part of a Caesar's staff but appointed by the Augustus. But there is at least no doubt that the praetorian prefect at this time still had operational military command.

It was fortunate that Constantius had a good lieutenant. The Channel weather managed to disrupt both armies. Constantius set out with one force from Boulogne, Asclepiodotus with another from the mouth of the Seine, presumably taking the crossing now followed by the Le Havre—Southampton ferries, which is longer but has the advantage of a choice of excellent landfalls in the Solent (where the defenders would have difficulty in watching every harbour in strength) and access directly into the heart of Britain. It is possible, too, that Constantius' own use of the short crossing was a deliberate feint, particularly sensible if a substantial part of the Second legion was now garrisoning the new fortress at Richborough.[1]

Whatever he had planned, Constantius himself did not land in the early phases of the operation. Irrespective of the tactical intentions of each side, the weather seems indeed to have played the major part. Allectus had stationed a naval force at the Isle of Wight in concealed positions to fall on the invasion force.[2] However Asclepiodotus' ships went straight past, unnoticed in the thick fog which had descended. It must have been a considerable piece of navigation on Asclepiodotus' part to make a landfall. Had it not been successful, it would surely have been judged foolhardy. Once ashore, he promptly had the ships burnt, the traditional gesture of confidence, no doubt, but perhaps also being unwilling to see them augment Allectus' untouched navy as soon as his back was turned and his main force had marched inland.

The panegyrist of Constantius says that Allectus promptly abandoned 'his fleet and port', and conjectures that having sighted Constantius' ships he preferred to face Constantius' generals rather than the Caesar himself. This is of course meant to flatter Constantius, but it also seems to indicate that Allectus had been somewhere in the south-east, perhaps at Dover or Richborough. Whatever the truth of this intended slur on Allectus' courage, it need not have been strategically foolish to head in the opposite direction. Allectus may or may not have assumed that his fleet and coastal forces now

---

[1] It appears there in the fourth century.
[2] One may perhaps assume warships lying in various creeks and inlets off the Solent.

alterted and perhaps including the Second legion could ward
off Constantius. The account seems to indicate that Allectus
had warships available here as well as those that had been bypassed in the Solent. He may even have suspected that Constantius was not going to land at all. In the event he was
right, the weather being given as a reason for that in the
Panegyric. Equally important for Allectus was the fact that
Asclepiodotus was now ashore—where, but for the fog, he
should not have been. He was heading into a wealthy part of
the province which was defenceless, as far as we know, once
the coastal screen was pierced. Moreover Asclepiodotus was
now apparently cut off. He had literally burnt his boats and
Allectus' undamaged fleet was across his line of communication with the Continent. It would make a lot of sense for
Allectus to concentrate all the units of the army of Britain
somewhere near London at the hub of the main road system,
except those keeping immediate watch on Constantius.

The panegyrist's account is worth quoting, since under the
rhetoric it seems to reveal what went wrong with this
movement:

Fleeing from you [Constantius], he ran straight into your forces: overcome by you, he was put down by your army. What happened was that
the turn of events, having seen you behind him, so overwhelmed Allectus that he rushed headlong to his death. He was, as it were, so deranged
with shock that he neither drew up his troops into a proper array for
battle nor in fact organised all the units he was collecting together into
an effective force. Instead, quite forgetting all this massive preparation,
he hurled himself into battle with only the old authors of the conspiracy
and some regiments of barbarian mercenaries. Thus, Caesar, your good
fortune[1] once again furthered the happiness of our nation, since while
the Roman empire triumphed hardly a Roman citizen was killed.

It is quite impossible to know how much of this is colouring.
Unless one is putting too much weight on the tense of one
verb, the wording does seem to indicate that the forces that
had been summoned had not all assembled at the time that
Allectus gave battle. It also may suggest that Allectus came
upon Asclepiodotus' army sooner than he expected. If not,
the decision to close with the enemy without waiting to
group his main army is reminiscent of Harold's disastrous

[1] *'Felicitas'*: this is that 'good fortune' of a military commander already referred to which was held to be of major importance and felt to have supernatural
overtones.

mistake at Hastings.[1] It has also been suggested that Allectus could not trust his regular Roman troops not to change sides. That was not uncommon in Roman civil wars. On the other hand it may have proved extremely difficult to organize the units that had actually arrived from their scattered garrisons into a field army fit to fight a battle straightaway. One may wonder how many of them had any experience of acting together in a large army, let alone fighting a pitched battle. Asclepiodotus, on the other hand, presumably had troops drawn from armies on the Continent which had fought one campaign after another in the past few years.

There has been speculation about the exact meaning of the phrase mentioning the 'old authors of the conspiracy.' It has been suggested that these were the soldiers from Carausius' original fleet. Yet unless these were mainly barbarian (which they might have been), it is difficult to account for the boast that hardly any Romans were killed in the battle. It is perhaps reasonable, while accepting that there really is insufficient evidence, to assume these merely to be whatever people were privy to the 'conspiracy' in the beginning. This may have been only a small group—and even then we do not know whether this conspiracy refers to Carausius' original actions or to Allectus' assumption of power. Whatever the truth, it gave Eumenius the opportunity to turn a neat compliment to his master, using a cliché of Roman panegyric, perhaps linking him in his audience's mind with another famous success in Britain: Agricola's triumph at Mons Graupius, 'the greater being the glory of the victory if it could be won without the shedding of Roman blood.'[2]

Despite the decisiveness of the defeat in battle of Allectus and his army, there was very nearly a major disaster at the hands of these same barbarians. The story is told by Eumenius and by an extraordinary chance dramatically illustrated by a superb gold medallion from the Trier mint found near Arras. The incident could not have been a better example of Constantius' *felicitas*. It was once again the fog that played the decisive part. Some of Constantius' troops, themselves

---

[1] It has been thought that some evidence of damage at Silchester should be attributed to the events of this campaign.

[2] Tacitus, *Agr.* xxxv: *ingens victoriae decus citra Romanum sanguinem bellandi.*

astray during the crossing and presumably part of Constantius'
division rather than Asclepiodotus', reached the city of
London. There they found that some of the Frankish warriors
who had escaped from the defeat of Allectus were on the
point of sacking and destroying London on their way, doubtless homewards across the North Sea. Constantius' soldiers
fell upon them and destroyed them. As Eumenius puts it
with evident relish, Constantius' troops 'not only rescued
your provincials but gave them the pleasure of witnessing the
slaughter, as if it were a public show (*in spectaculo volup-
tatem*)'. This is a nice insight into the feelings of the citizens
of Roman London and one of those touches of the real
world of the past that one so rarely experiences. The slaughter
was a bonus added to deliverance. Constantius had acted like
a properly behaved Roman magistrate, providing his loyal
people with, as it were, a fine gladiatorial show, complete
with the execution of criminals.

The Arras Medallion concentrates on the rescue. It shows
the personification of London kneeling before a city gate
which is being approached by a Roman warship. Larger than
the warship is portrayed the Caesar in the traditional mounted
guise of a triumphant emperor, with the words 'restorer of
the eternal light' (*redditor lucis aeternae*). There is no doubt
that Constantius regarded this as a great propaganda victory.
The details are important. Eumenius, in listing Constantius'
glories, makes particular play with the claimed 'almost complete extirpation' of the Franks, with the imposition of his
rule on 'many other people who had taken part in this
criminal conspiracy' and with the establishment of peace and
order at sea under Roman naval power. Although Allectus
had been defeated on land, it was clearly felt important to
emphasize the gaining of control of the sea. While the Franks
are considered the worst of those defeated, it is also clear
that various other barbarian peoples were involved. It is impossible to see through the victor's propaganda whether or
not there was really a general conspiracy. It was convenient
to represent Allectus' support as largely barbarian. Nevertheless a general concern about sea-borne barbarians does come
through. On the other hand, it also reveals that those barbarians would take service under Roman commanders if the
conditions were right. We are seeing here one foretaste of

the employment for pay in Late Roman armies of barbarians recruited from outside the empire. This stands in real distinction both from the enrolling of non-citizens from inside the empire or from adjacent regions under effective Roman control, and from the long-standing practice of incorporating in the Roman forces barbarian soldiers who had been taken as prisoners of war or extracted from a defeated foreign enemy as part of the price of peace.

Archaeology does not yet seem to have produced any military remains of Asclepiodotus' campaign and one may perhaps accept that it was over as swiftly as would appear from the written accounts.[1] Yet for Romano-British archaeologists the year 296 has had a rather different significance. Collingwood said of Allectus: 'It is evident that he had stripped the whole country of troops. For the first time since Clodius Albinus crossed to Gaul, the frontier was left undefended. The northern tribes took their opportunity: they broke in, and along the Wall we can trace the destruction they left behind them.' AD 296 has thus become another standard landmark like 197. Like it, indeed, this date too has been widely attached to archaeological signs of demolition, fire, and to reconstruction work in forts, sometimes dated by coins and pottery very broadly to this period. Yet it has been recognized on the one hand that the general phenomenon hardly extends outside the Wall region, and on the other than hardly a garrison on the Wall is different in the fourth century from the third. Professor Frere's account[2] deals with the evidence in some detail and points out that it is fairly thin—indeed that much of the dating evidence can be made to refer to no more precise period than the third century after about 270 or the early fourth. On balance he favours the 'traditional' interpretation, but makes it clear that the matter is uncertain. I personally agree with his caution. In particular there is the problem he underlines that 'in general, excavators have not been sufficiently careful to distinguish between demolition and destruction.' However, we may reasonably go further than just to accept that destruction 'can be assumed with any

---

[1] Could the crudely built late fort at the Lunt, near Coventry, be connected with this war?
[2] Frere, *Britannia*, 382 ff.

degree of confidence only where the reports speak of wide-spread signs of fire.' In the first place, hardly any of these sites have been excavated on a really large scale, at least to modern standards where one could be reasonably sure the same layers had been recognized throughout the site. In the second, there is not only the point that routine rebuilding and maintenance may well account for considerable traces of fire, with no hostile intervention, through the burning of rubbish, but the more important point that we very easily underestimate accidental fire as an everyday fact of life in the past.

There is, however, a circumstance which should increase our caution about 296 even further. It has been observed that there are very few coins of Carausius and Allectus from the northern frontier,[1] and that most of those come from Corbridge or South Shields where much of the activity was civilian. There are hardly any from the more normal Wall forts. Taken with a Carausian milestone—demonstrating (at least for the western end of the Wall region) that his administration was recognized here—the evidence is beginning to point towards a relatively lightly held frontier, entirely consistent with subsequent reconstruction of military establishments which had been abandoned or allowed to decay. The implication is that the frontier was regarded as safe, its garrisons removed or run-down for a fairly long period rather than withdrawn suddenly to repel invasion. If we do retain in our account a barbarian invasion in 296 we must probably regard it as little more than opportunist looting of sites that had relatively little worth the taking. We would certainly be unwise in the present state of knowledge to keep it as a major landmark in the chronology of Roman Britain.

The widespread occurrence of rebuilding in the military installations of the north around the beginning of the fourth century is, however, much more securely established. One should hesitate to use the word 'programme' in this context, as that implies that we know this represents a planned series of works by a single authority. It is reasonable to accept as an hypothesis—indeed it may well be the truth—Professor Frere's statement that 'the arrival of Constantius and the preparations

---

[1] Norman Shiel, *Arch. Ael.* 5th ser. 5 (1977), 75 ff.

for his northern campaign provide the required historical context for the initiation of the programme, which is confirmed
by building-inscriptions of the Tetrarchy from Birdoswald
and Housesteads, dating as they do before 305'. Yet these
two are the *only* such inscriptions. One of them records no
more than the names of Diocletian and Maximian, if that.[1]
The other specifically states that it refers to buildings 'collapsed and covered with earth'.[2] This gives no support at all
to the theory of a barbarian invasion from the north in 296.
So minor do the problems of the frontier seem to have been
at this time that in 297 Constantius returned to Gaul and it
was practically a decade before he came back to mount a
campaign in the north, in 306. Meanwhile he drew almost
immediately on Britain, in 297-8, for a large number of
skilled men (*artifices*) to restore the city of Autun, once
famous as a centre of learning, which had been severely
damaged after being besieged by the army of the Imperium
Galliarum in 269. These *artifices* were drawn from the
British provinces because 'those provinces had a surplus of
them'.[3] This tells against an urgent need to repair military
installations on the frontier or to take immediate action
against the northern neighbours of Rome. The Panegyric of
AD 297 mentions that following Constantius' recovery of
Britain the northernmost peoples of the island also were
obedient to his every wish. This is a nice traditional flourish:
yet there is no mention of invaders driven back or even forts
recovered. This is a little odd if the barbarians had just retreated after a destructive incursion on a large scale. Even a
diplomatic victory over them might have claimed a more
positive reference in a panegyric.

It is indeed quite likely that much of the rebuilding which
seems to have occurred around the beginning of the fourth
century was part of a Constantian policy for strengthening
the northern frontier. However, we should be very uneasy
about using 'required historical contexts' for archaeological
data, without unequivocal links to the written evidence. Nor,
for that matter, does one have to interpret the historical context the same way, even if the dating is agreed. One can

---

[1] *RIB* 1613 (Housesteads).   [2] *RIB* 1912 (Birdoswald).
[3] *Pan. Lat. Vet.* VIII (V). xxi. 2. We may wonder why there were so many, but
there seems no reason to doubt the statement.

reasonably accept Constantius' recovery of Britain as the starting-point for some restoration of military installations in the north without assuming an immediately previous barbarian invasion—or an intention yet on Constantius' part to campaign northwards. In fact it is just as reasonable as the 'traditional' view of 296 to take the Birdoswald inscription as suggesting that the authorities in Roman Britain had not really had to bother much about the northern frontier in recent years.[1]

One might speculate that subsequently the northern barbarians did not like renewed military interest in the north under Constantius, with the restoration of a strong barrier between themselves and the Roman province. A willingness to obey Roman wishes in 297 may have changed to quite a different attitude by 306. Apart from that, someone may now have suspected that Constantius was planning a campaign. Another panegyrist, addressing Constantius' son Constantine around AD 310, found it necessary to deny a 'popular belief' that the campaign of 306 was launched because Constantius wanted the laurels of a victory in Britain.[2] Instead, the panegyrist ingeniously declares that Constantius was summoned on by the gods to penetrate to the furthest limits of *terra firma*[3] — not that that is likely to have been much consolation to the tribes attacked.

This decade was the period when Britain was exposed to the full force of Diocletian's reorganization of the empire. At the end of it, on 1 May 305, after a severe illness, Diocletian felt he could retire and let the system take over. Maximian was required to abdicate at the same time. It was therefore as a full Augustus that Constantius returned to Britain to launch his campaign in 306, having succeeded Maximian as emperor in the west as intended, while the Caesar in the east, Galerius, succeeded Diocletian. Galerius looked like holding on to

---

[1] If we must find a comprehensive historical context for the signs of demolition and reconstruction in this period, perhaps we should refer back to the unknown cause of Diocletian's assumption of the title *Britannicus Maximus* in 285.

[2] *Pan. Constantino Aug. (Pan. Lat. Vet.* VI (VII). vii. 1-2). This may have seemed rather a different prospect than the victory already gained, which was in civil war, however much the part barbarian mercenaries played was emphasized.

[3] Ibid: *non Britannica trophaea, ut vulgo creditum est, expetivit, sed dis iam vocantibus ad intimum terrarum limen accessit.*

Diocletian's commanding influence throughout the empire, since not only was his nephew Maximian Daia appointed as his own Caesar in the east, but he managed to have a close friend appointed to the equivalent post in the west, Flavius Valerius Severus, another Illyrian soldier from a humble family. The latter was to prove an unfortunate error of choice.

It is uncertain how soon the fourth-century reform of the administrative structure of the empire came into effect in Britain, or to what extent local modifications were introduced. Overall the intention was to separate civil from military administration in a structural sense, though the army continued to have a very large influence and perhaps paradoxically purely civil offices and officials became much more military in form. The division was still only in an embryo stage by the end of Diocletian's reign, and only in a few instances does it seem that he had transferred the command of armies in those provinces that had them away from the governors to new, purely military, officers. As in other fields, the beginnings of great changes are discernible under Diocletian, but their development came under his successors and were probably not foreseen or intended by him. As far as the north-western group of provinces is concerned, as the system developed the administration came to be headed by a praetorian prefect, responsible in the first instance to the Caesar. As in the Severan period there was a multiplication of provinces by subdivision—Britain, for example, being split into four instead of two. The governors, often described as *praeses* or *rector*, were to become civil officers, mostly without function but with an increasing load of administration. However, despite the large number of provinces thus created, co-ordination was to be achieved by introducing a new level in the administration. The diocesan *vicarii* were, as their names imply, regarded as deputies of, and responsible to, the relevant praetorian prefect. Theoretically, since the praetorian prefect was himself a personal deputy to whatever Augustus or Caesar happened to be in control of a particular part of the empire at a particular time, this was a very changeable arrangement. Nevertheless, just as modern ministries tend to become static in their arrangements and responsibilities, irrespective of changes of Minister or even Government (unless there is a deliberate

Government-imposed modification), so, as the new system settled down, the 'Prefecture of the Gauls' (which included Britain) became a permanent part of the structure of the Roman state. The four new provinces of Britain constituted one of the dioceses of this prefecture, and were headed by the *vicarius Britanniarum*. The provinces are named not later than AD 314 as Britannia Prima, Britannia Secunda, Maxima Caesariensis, and Flavia Caesariensis.[1] Where the centre of the whole diocese originally lay is not recorded, but a later document places the station of a finance officer, apparently the diocesan treasurer, at London (*praepositus thesaurorum Augustensium*).[2] It seems reasonable to assume the *vicarius* was also normally based at London, though we should remember that it was the officer, not the place, that was of prime importance. This was true even of imperial capitals: Diocletian, for example, did not pay his first visit to Rome itself till the celebration of his tenth year as Augustus, despite the City's enormous constitutional and political prestige. This should make us pause to consider what we mean, when we speak of 'capitals', whether imperial or provincial.

In describing these reforms we have probably moved somewhat ahead of our narrative. It is likely that even those changes initiated by Diocletian himself were not introduced everywhere at the same time. Britain was furthermore in a special position of its own, having been beyond his control for a decade. It is clear that the division of military from civil commands was not implemented immediately after Constantius' recovery of Britain for the central government in 296, for an inscription of the period reveals a provincial governor, Aurelius Arpagius, in command of troops.[3]

The relationship between Constantius' Scottish campaign of 306 and the widespread reconstruction of the network of military installations already noted remains obscure. Professor Frere, writing of the period from Constantius' victory in 296 commented that:

We may be sure that the restoration of the frontier and its outpost system was effected under his own supervision, but the big programme of

[1] See Map VII. Cf. J.C. Mann, *Antiquity*, 35 (1961), 316 ff.
[2] *Not. Dig. Occ.* xi. 37: *praepositus thesaurorum Augustensium*—i.e. at London under its fourth-century title *Augusta*.
[3] *RIB* 1912 (Birdoswald), almost certainly to be dated between 296 and 305.

military reconstruction elsewhere in the north, and perhaps the completion of the system of coastal defence, may have been spread out over more than one subsequent decade. This is probably true too of the revival of building activity which has been recognised at *Verulamium*. Until the middle of the reign of Constantine the influx of new coins from continental mints was very small, and existing coins remained in circulation—a fact which has tended to result in the assignment of too early a date for buildings erected in the early fourth century.[1]

We may even go further and extend that opinion to the frontier works themselves, for it does not need to be assumed that they were all restored before rather than after the war of 306.

The abdication of Diocletian and Maximian in 305 had elevated Constantius to the rank of Augustus. It is perhaps not without significance that he decided to conduct this British campaign in person rather than leave it to his Caesar, that friend and supporter of the hostile eastern Augustus, Galerius. He was accompanied on the campaign by his own son Constantine, already a considerable figure. We do not know either the size of the forces involved or whether Constantius assembled an army from the troops already in Britain or brought in units from the Continent. It is not impossible that some such units had remained in Britain to assure loyalty after the defeat of Allectus.

The course of the campaign is unknown. The sources claim penetration to the far north of Scotland and a victory over the Picts. This is the period at which that name for the northern enemy of Rome first appears. It included the Caledones 'and others':[2] it was therefore a generic term that embraced the Highland tribes of Scotland beyond the Forth–Clyde isthmus and perhaps others as well. One cannot help feeling that some of the temporary camps identified from the air in north-east Scotland ought to be Constantian, where they are not Agricolan or Severan. A process of elimination may resolve this point, as the characteristics by which each of the earlier series of camps can be recognized from one another become more and more reliably isolated. In the literary accounts there are once again intriguing parallels between the story of the earlier campaigns and this one.[3] Constantius

---

[1] Frere, *Britannia*, 385 f.   [2] *Pan. Lat. Vet.* VI (VII). vii. 2.
[3] Dio, LXXVI. xiii. 1; Herodian, III. xiv. 5.

is, for example, reported making observations of the natural phenomena in the far north, just as Severus did. The crossing of marshes is similarly emphasized by the Panegyrist:[1] a feature that had given Severus considerable trouble before he overcame it with the loss of many men. Indeed, one begins to be sure that even if the fourth-century writer is not simply drawing on conventional material about such campaigns he is at least expecting his well-read public to draw the parallels and to credit Constantius with doing as well as, if not better than, the great generals of the past. To be fair, the parallels do go further than just the literary accounts. The occurrence of pottery of this period on the site of the old Severan legionary fortress at Carpow on the Tay and at Cramond on the Firth of Forth, one of the few Antonine frontier forts that also produces Severan pottery, perhaps suggests use of a fleet.[2] There is good reason to think Severus had done so, and in Agricola's case Tacitus reports simultaneous use of land and sea forces and the employment of ships to harry the elusive tribes of the Highlands into accepting battle.[3] It is, of course, likely that a similar enemy on much the same terrain forced successive Roman commanders to adopt the same tactics, even though there was a century or more between each of the wars. Nevertheless we have noted before that an important factor in these situations should have been that the generals or their staffs had read the historians. It was a proper part of Roman education.[4] We also may suspect that additional information was available in Roman military records deriving from earlier campaigns over the same terrain or accumulated over the centuries from innumerable sources, perhaps including many minor actions in Britain about which we are completely ignorant.

NOTES

Comitatus is a difficult term whose meaning both changed with time

[1] *Pan. Lat. Vet.* VI (VII). vii. 2: *Calidonum aliorumque Pictorum silvas et paludes.*

[2] It is not impossible that small units were maintained in these two forts throughout the third century.

[3] Tacitus, *Agr.* xxix.

[4] It was also felt worth publishing books of specifically military interest. The Flavian governor of Britain, Frontinus, for example wrote both a theoretical book *De Re Militari* and a compilation of examples of Greek and Roman tactics (*Strategemata*).

and had one sense in one context and another in another. Broadly it can be translated as 'escort' or 'retinue' or 'entourage'. It literally means 'companions', from *comes*. In one sense it came to mean the body of troops detached to accompany the emperor: this naturally conferred special status and soon special privileges. It was also used in connection with other posts in the emperor's entourage which were partially or wholly civil in character and encompassed the mixture of imperial household, personal staff, and ministers through which the earlier emperors had exercised direct power. For *comes* as a fourth-century *title*, see p. 351, n.1 below: it was to afford emperors at cross-purposes with the older senatorial aristocracy a means of creating a new aristocracy of their own.

The Saxon Shore. Since the narrative chapters of this book were first written considerable contributions have been made to the study of the 'Saxon Shore' by work, both published and as yet unpublished, which I have been able only partially to take into account during the final revision of my text. For our purposes the most important suggestion is that advanced by Stephen Johnson, in *The Roman Forts of the Saxon Shore* (1976), that most of the forts (except of course Brancaster and Reculver which were already in existence) were first built between 276 and 285 and were together with corresponding forts on the coast of Gaul and the fleet originally the basis of a co-ordinated system to trap pirates sailing from the north-east. This would have been initiated by the Emperor Probus. There is not yet enough dating evidence from the individual forts to confirm this generally attractive theory. It is possible that the main works at Richborough may be as early as Probus (*Brit.* 1 (1970), 240 ff.) and Lympne is currently being examined by Professor Barry Cunliffe and is likely to provide fresh evidence. The same excavator's series of campaigns at Portchester have been published, notably in *Excavations at Portchester Castle Vol. I: Roman* (1975), of which there is an important review by Professor Frere in *Antiquity*, 51 (1977), 163 f.). Both Frere and Cunliffe (review of Johnson, in *Antiquity*, 51 (1977), 72 ff.) agree that a gap in occupation at Portchester suggested by the archaeology for the end of the third century probably indicates that it was abandoned by Carausius when the unified command in the Channel collapsed with the capture of Boulogne by Constantius in 293. Frere argues that this was proved a disastrous mistake when Asclepiodotus' invasion force managed to avoid Allectus' defence in 296 and make a successful landing. The reoccupation is under this view attributed to the restoration of a single command in the Channel after Constantius' victory. Personally I find it difficult to believe that Allectus would have left Portchester ungarrisoned once it was obvious that Constantius was ready to invade, and think the reoccupation may be due to him. He certainly had ships lying off the Isle of Wight and was caught out only by the fog, in which Portchester would anyhow have been useless to prevent the actual landing. Further contributions to the whole subject on both sides of the Channel are contained in a collection of papers given at a conference in 1975 and published as CBA Research Report 18,

The Saxon Shore (1977), edited by D.E. Johnston. The late date of
Pevensey (330s or 340s) is still accepted. At a later date, perhaps in the
Theodosian reorganisation of 369 or under Magnus Maximus (383–8),
the unified Channel command was broken up and there are no naval
units stationed at any of the forts in the *Notitia*. The name of the
Litus Saxonicum remains a subject of dispute—whether it meant the
shore attacked *by* Saxons or settled *with* Saxons (as Germanic elements
in the Roman military system), or possibly both.

12

CONSTANTINE THE GREAT

SOME of the parallels between Constantius I in Britain and Septimius Severus were certainly not literary inventions. Constantius' last campaign was, like Severus', his war in northern Britain. And the parallels—or rather coincidences—went further. Both had their sons with them in Britain; both returned to York after a victorious campaign and there died. In the Severan case the succession was clear and the two sons, Caracalla and Geta, were proclaimed colleagues on the imperial throne. Nevertheless it was already inevitable that they would fall out. In 306, Diocletian's newly established constitutional system ought to have made the succession indisputable. Constantius' Caesar, Flavius Valerius Severus, should have become without question the western Augustus and a new Caesar been appointed to replace him. Unfortunately the old tradition reasserted itself: the army proclaimed Constantine as Augustus, apparently encouraged by a Germanic king, Crocus, who had been placed in command of a cohort of Alamanni serving in Britain, a fact that may have influenced him in his subsequent liking for German troops. Galerius had already been reluctant to release Constantine from service at his court in the east to accompany his father on the Scottish campaign. By remaining in the east, he could have served as a hostage. Now that Constantine was independent and had a victorious army behind him, the *de facto* control of the whole empire that Galerius might have expected to fall into his own hands upon the accession of his follower Severus as Augustus in the west was now impossible. For a while the matter was patched up, with Constantine accepting official appointment as Caesar. This made him formally responsible to Severus, a step down in rank. More important, however, it regularized his position. Legitimacy was still a very important element of power in the Roman world. The provinces of Britain, with the rest of the northwestern provinces, therefore now came on paper under the authority of Severus as senior in the west. However it is very difficult to imagine that he exercised any real power there. What had happened was the shipwreck of Diocletian's constitution on the same rock as previous reforms of the imperial system. In effect the Roman world was back to the mutually suspicious multiple emperors common in the century since the murder of Commodus, with the added element that they were now immensely strengthened by the emerging structures of separate and permanent civil services, armies, and courts to support each of them.

It took eighteen years of unstable arrangements, nominally respecting Diocletian's system—indeed bringing him once out of retirement to patch it up—punctuated by a series of tremendous civil wars, before Constantine finally emerged in AD 324 as sole emperor of an undivided empire. He had showed military and political ability of a high order and peace was at last established—for the rest of his reign. Immense changes were introduced under his rule, both before and after 324, but if Diocletian's great initiative to save the empire from its fatal flaw—the succession—had ever had a real chance it can hardly have had one now. Constantine certainly earns his own title of 'Great' in Roman terms: his military ability was matched by his imagination and originality in matters of state, by his considerable toleration and by his ruthless opportunism. He was also remarkably extravagant. This was not necessarily unpopular in the Roman world—indeed when lavished on the populace and public display rather than himself it was traditionally approved in a Roman magistrate. By the standards of the ancient world his rise to supreme power was not unreasonable. It can be argued that Galerius' attempt to bend the Diocletianic constitution to his own ends by endeavouring to undermine the authority of his western colleagues had already made its collapse unavoidable. Constantine's irregular acceptance of office at the hands of his father's army and his inexorable climb to unchallenged power were a reflection of clear-sighted political realism. He was certainly to prove that he could carry through fundamental changes in imperial policy and retain his position. We have often noted the devotion of Roman soldiers to the hereditary principle, and it has been argued that, even if the Diocletianic system had not been interfered with, this fact would have made it unworkable for any length of time. The death of Constantius I at the end of a victorious campaign, in a distant province in the presence of his troops and of a son who was already an officer with a creditable military record, had created the classic situation for the proclamation of an emperor by a Roman army in the field.

If it needed completing, this situation was completed by the other traditional element—the praetorian guard—who had on their doorstep at Rome the retired emperor Maximian's son Maxentius, who had been passed over in Diocletian's arrangements for the succession. Not surprisingly the praetorians proclaimed Maxentius, with the support of the senate which, not for the first time, must have been uncomfortably aware of the nearness of the praetorian barracks. The former western Caesar, Galerius' friend Severus, had of course by now been publicly proclaimed as Augustus. For a moment in 306 there were, then, no less than three Augusti in the west.

This situation is very relevant to our assessment of the evidence for what was happening in Britain. The tense situation in the empire created by Constantius I's death at York raises the question of whether much of the military restoration and reorganization which has been observed in Britain and loosely dated around AD 300 is, like that attributed to Caracalla a century earlier, the second choice of an emperor distracted by greater problems. Was it in lieu of further and final operations in Scotland which might lead to total conquest? Taking this a step further and before being too convinced that all or most of the reconstruction must be attributed to Constantius I himself, whether after a hypothetical barbarian invasion or not, we should remember that it is just as valid to argue that after his father's death the newly elevated Constantine was unable to spare the time, energy, and resources required to complete the reduction of Scotland and had to settle for consolidation of the frontier as it is to argue for Caracalla taking a similar decision to settle for strengthening the defences of Britain in the north under almost identical circumstances a century earlier. There is, however, one difference in the consequences. The work of Septimius and Caracalla may well have preserved Britain from the greater part of the horrors of the third century in neighbouring Gaul, but no one would argue that the third century was an exceptionally brilliant age in Roman Britain. The reconstruction carried out in the time of Constantius and Constantine, however, ushered in an era of spectacular prosperity, at least in so far as that can be judged by the private and public architecture of the age.

Among the signs of military reconstruction pride of place must surely go to York. The walls of the fortress were extensively rebuilt, and in particular the great river front was restored with a series of multi-angular bastions that make it arguably the grandest example in the west of the military architecture of its age. On some later Roman sites the provision of such bastions made it necessary to replace the old ditches close to the walls with a broad new ditch much further out: these are modifications typical of the fourth century and seem often to be consequent on developments in military thinking, particularly the greater use of fixed artillery on towers. At York this has not been proved.[1] Indeed at York this splendour, directly overlooking the *colonia* across the river, must primarily have been a demonstration of the power and deliberate magnificence of the new regime, whether the original order for the work was the responsibility of Diocletian, of Constantius I, or of Constantine. It accords well with Diocletian's enormous Baths, only one hall of which sufficed for conversion into one of the great Renaissance churches of Rome, with the fortified palace he built for his retirement at Split, or with the immensity of the 'Basilika' at Trier, which was probably the audience chamber of the imperial palace, centre of the new administration. At York we do not know the location of the palace, even for the Severan period for which it is actually attested, nor if the old one was still in use. However, magnificence was a political weapon deliberately used by Diocletian, his colleagues, and successors to elevate and protect the person of the emperor. The idea sank very deep: it is reasonable to see in it the origin of the style of life of the Byzantine emperors and their court.

Irregularly elevated emperors felt the need to use this psychological weapon as much as, if not more than, those more constitutionally appointed. Constantine's rival Maxentius, whose elevation was equally shaky, was responsible for the vast basilica in Rome which bore his name. He had an

---

[1] S. Coll. *Ant. J.* 54 (1974), 207; A.B. Sumpter and S. Coll. *The Archaeology of York*, 3 (1977), 57 ff.

added advantage: for the moment he held Rome itself and had been proclaimed with the support of the senate. He could make a gesture in the Roman Forum, the ancient heart of the Roman state itself. Once in possession of Rome himself Constantine created one ostentatious piece of architecture after another. His Arch at Rome is an exercise in the 'bigger and better' (if partly second-hand). The enormous Basilica of St. Peter (Old St. Peter's) honoured his new religion not only as a building but an earth-moving enterprise of huge proportions—incidentally demolishing a city cemetery in the process. He shared Hadrian's love of architectural gestures, but extraordinary though Hadrian's efforts in this direction were, they pale besides Constantine's deliberate conversion of provincial Byzantium into the vast imperial city of Constantinople, apparently intended from the first as a new and Christian Rome and decided upon within a year of his final triumph over his last serious rival. At Trier the exact date of the enormous monuments of this period cannot yet be determined, but I think that Dr Edith Wightman, in her study of that city, has probability on her side in pointing to Constantine, both on general grounds and with the support of a reference from the panegyric proclaimed in the presence of the emperor himself at Trier in 310.[1] At the slight risk of a circular argument, I feel that the refurbishing of York would not be out of place among the multitude of grand enterprises in the imagination of such a man.

It has, of course, to be admitted that at York, whether one wishes to attribute the new work to Constantius I or to Constantine himself, one still has to strike a note of caution, since the dating evidence is even more uncertain than at Trier. Despite the unambiguous labelling of all this construction as 'Constantian' in the Royal Commission report published in 1962, even the text of that publication cannot be more specific than 'later than AD 270, since coins of Claudius II and Tetricus Senior have been found sealed in the associated rampart, while pottery from the ditch . . . suggests that they were established by a date in the earlier 4th century'.[2] The

---

[1] E.M. Wightman, *Roman Trier and the Treveri* (1970), 108 f.; *Pan. Lat. Vet.* VI (VII). xxii. 5.
[2] RCHM *City of York: Vol. 1 — Eburacum: Roman York* (1962), 10.

most recent work does not take us much further.[1] Talking of
the military ditches on the south-west, that report says: 'In
the early fourth century, presumably dating the rebuilding
of the wall and towns of the fortress, the ditch was re-
excavated' on more or less the same lines and scale as its predecessor. 'It would seem that the excavation of a ditch in the
fourth century was necessitated, not by any major modification in defensive practice and Roman military engineering,
but simply because there was no ditch of reasonable proportions in evidence either due to neglect or other unknown
factors.' Even if it is a likely guess, it is a guess. We are still
left with a *terminus post quem* around the end of the
Imperium Galliarum.

This dating situation is parallel to that for a group of later
Roman town walls in Gallia Belgica. There it has been properly
pointed out that a *terminus post quem* for one element in a
set of walls does not date the whole circuit, since such a
project is likely to have taken some years to complete.[2] The
historical probability is placed on Probus as originator after
clearing the Germans out of Gaul. It is therefore just possible
that the remodelled York was the creation of Aurelian or
Probus. Indeed, Aurelian's vast fortification of the city of
Rome itself (defended by walls for the first time for many
centuries) shows the way his mind was working. But there is
another possibility. The argument about irregularly appointed
emperors applies *a fortiori* to Carausius and Allectus. Should
we perhaps see York as an achievement of their regime,
deliberately in competition with the rival emperors? It would
be just as consistent with what dating evidence we have and
entirely in accord with the spirit of the age. Nevertheless, in
the absence of evidence to the contrary, I am personally still
inclined to attribute York to Constantine, and not just on
grounds of general probability, strong though they are.
Various pieces of fragmentary evidence, when taken together,
are beginning to fit together to suggest a continuing interest
by the emperor in Britain. No fewer than nineteen milestones
have been found in Britain bearing his name, six of which
come from the short period 306–7 when he tolerated being a
Caesar rather than Augustus. Coins from the London mint of

---

[1] S. Coll, op. cit. 207.   [2] S. Johnson, *Brit.* 4 (1973), 210 ff.

the so-called 'arrival' (*adventus*) type have recently been conjectured to record actual visits by the emperor in 307, 312,
and 314.[1] At some point in his reign he took the title *Britannicus Maximus,* normally reflecting a victory gained by the
emperor himself or in his name—or something that could be
recorded as such. The date has been conjectured as between
315 and 318.[2] Finally, one may speculate that the changing
of the official name of London to Augusta, which Ammianus
writing after 378 puts some way back into the past, may have
been connected with Constantine's elevation or a subsequent
visit to the island.[3] Imprecise and inconclusive though this
evidence is, the impression of a close interest is strong. Indeed, the splendid walls of York make one wonder what else
may have been erected there.[4] What could be a more appropriate monument to the pious memory of his father and the
glory of his victorious army? How better to mark the site of
his elevation to the throne and celebrate the loyalty of troops
and provinces to his family? All the evidence I have mentioned
seems to date before AD 324 when Constantine finally eliminated his last rival. Till then, there was an immediate need to
maintain an absolute grip on the adherence of the west to
his cause. Constantine was acutely conscious both of his
divine mission and of the practical value of emphasizing by
every means the god-given pre-eminence of himself and his
imperial family.

York, nevertheless, was not just for show. In purely military
terms its refortification fits what is known of the pattern of
the early fourth century in Britain. The Wall was already being

---

[1] J. Casey, in *Collectanea Londiniensia: Studies in London Archaeology and
History presented to Ralph Merrifield* (1978), 180 ff.

[2] Professor John Mann has suggested 315 (*The Northern Frontier in Britain
from Hadrian to Honorius: Literary and Epigraphic Sources* (n.d.), under no. 189
= *CIL,* VIII 23116 = *ILS* 8942).

[3] Mann has also demonstrated what a complex, confusing, and natural affair
changes in city names constituted—and how unsafe it is to build theories on particular examples (*Latomus,* 22 (1963), 777 ff.). In the case of London some have
argued that the title of Augusta was conferred by Constantine's father, some even
that there was a stage between 296 and 305 when it would have been called
Caesarea.

[4] Or, for that matter, at London as well—and elsewhere in the province. If we
have repeated imperial visits, particularly from Constantine, we should be alert
for traces of imperial residences, accommodation for the *comitatus,* military and
civil, celebratory monuments, and perhaps (after 312) Christian evidence as well,
though some of these things may have been of a temporary nature.

refurbished and its garrison at least partially restored. The fortress at Chester was repaired at about this time. The completion of the main elements in the coastal system could date from this period, and forts inland were being reoccupied. It is therefore pertinent to ask what the widespread signs of revived activity observed archaeologically on a considerable variety of military sites in Britain may have reflected, other than imperial megalomania. We have seen that there is reasonable evidence for the view that the military, political, and economic crises of the third century had comparatively less effect in Britain than was general elsewhere; that it was thought worthwhile continuing the process of fortifying the cities and towns of Britain in the third century, an expensive process—at least for the provincials; and that there are substantial signs of renewed enthusiasm for building, including private construction, from the 270s onward. From around AD 300 there is a veritable epidemic of work in Britain on country houses—from improvements in the amenities of modest houses to vast extensions that convert relatively small country properties into grand mansions in the manner of the stately villas of Gaul.

It is perhaps significant that, unlike some in Gaul, villas in Britain do not seem to have fortified themselves.[1] Towns, on the other hand, received in many instances elaborate additions to their defences in the fourth century, or, in the case of some of the smaller ones, were fortified for the first time. The details of these works show great variety, suggesting strongly that the initiative was still largely local—probably both in applying for a licence to crenellate (to use a medieval term) and in carrying out the work. Indeed the fact that, for example, adjacent bastions can be quite different, as are the two visible in the north-eastern quarter of Roman Cirencester, supports the view that individuals could be responsible for different parts of the work. The provincials clearly felt in Britain that there was something worth defending in the towns. Moreover, since emperors would have needed convincing that local communities were not going to bankrupt themselves—they had after all to be able to pay the taxes for which they were responsible—we may assume the existence of substantial resources.

[1] With the probable exception of Gatcombe (Avon), where, however, the exact nature of the walled enclosure is at the time of writing still uncertain.

In this context we may remember Zosimus' criticism of
Constantine cited earlier,[1] alleging that he withdrew the
troops from the frontiers and stationed them in the cities
which did not need defending. That statement however is a
piece of evidence that needs handling with caution. The same
author also criticizes the Emperor Honorius for failing to de-
ploy all the forces available to him against the barbarians in
Italy. In 409, again, Zosimus claims troops (cavalry as well as
infantry) were dispersed throughout the cities.[2] These incidents took place nearly a century after Constantine, and it is
possible that Zosimus, writing after yet another century had
gone by, was either applying to Constantine, with no basis in
fact, a criticism of an emperor that had by his time become a
convention (a practice not unknown among the ancients) or
exaggerating the small beginnings in Constantine's time of a
feature that later became prominent. Nevertheless, Zosimus
is not inconsistent with the possibility that in the course of
the fourth century there was a significant transfer of troops
from the frontiers to cities. This was doubtless not only
popular with soldiers but, whatever its scale, may have made
emperors much more willing to allow towns to have modern
defences capable of withstanding anything short of full-scale
siege by an army equipped and trained to that end. If the
emperors had their own regular troops inside the walls on a
permanent basis, the political risk was obviously much less.
Moreover the garrisoning of well-fortified towns makes sense
if it were part of an official policy of defence in depth: it
would provide a network of strongpoints, each held by
relatively few professional soldiers, and would extend military protection to areas that had not been garrisoned for
centuries. It could be argued that this, not the stationing of
massive forces on the frontiers themselves, was in fact the
right way to deal with raids by large numbers of small bands
of men, looking for easy plunder, not conquest. The presence
of such troops locally in areas with a large civil population
might be a much better way of securing public confidence
than knowledge that the main fighting units of the Roman
army were a hundred miles away or even two. It is not difficult to imagine pressure for the presence of troops coming

---

[1] See p. 291 above.   [2] Zosimus, v. 35; v. 36; v. 45.

from the well-to-do and presumably influential people who owned the country estates of southern Britain in the fourth century. Indeed, those who were of senatorial rank, being exempt from service on the local councils, could probably have urged this without the prospect of having to contribute to the cost of the work on town walls themselves. We shall return later to the problem of narrowing down the dating of these fourth-century defences to a more precise period within the century.

The counterpart to the new pattern of civil government was the reorganization of the command structure of the army. Military and civil government had been so closely interlinked that radical alteration of the one must affect the other. Provincial governors had been commanders of any garrisons in their provinces: the cessation of this arrangement would automatically affect the whole system of command. The new military structure does not seem to have been the result of immediate reorganization by the Tetrarchy. Many of the army reforms seem to have been the work of Constantine, being either attested under him or known to us for the first time soon after his death. In this, as in other matters, Constantine was prepared to be much more radical than Diocletian and his colleagues.

Under the Tetrarchy and perhaps under Constantine as well the praetorian prefects continued to take the chief part in the supreme command of the armies, and under them their *vicarii*, the 'vicars' of the dioceses. In AD 312 the praetorian guard itself was dissolved after Constantine's final victory over Maxentius at the Milvian Bridge. Unfortunately for the praetorians as an institution the victor had, unlike Diocletian or for that matter Maxentius himself, little respect for Roman traditions as such. Under Constantine's sons new commanders-in-chief of the armies make their appearance: the *magistri militum*.[1] These were officers at the same sort of military level as the praetorian prefects had previously been, and like the praetorian prefects of the Later Empire themselves they tended to be rewarded with consulships. Constantine was accused subsequently of Germanizing the army and of raising barbarians to the consulship. A.H.M. Jones made a case for

---

[1] 'Master of Infantry' (*magister peditum*) and 'Master of Cavalry' (*magister equitum*).

these allegations referring specifically to Germans appointed as *magistri militum,* which would mean that the office was introduced under Constantine. Presumably the praetorian prefects were deprived of the operational command of the Roman army at the same time, though the office itself was not abolished.

Holding a position of crucial importance in the new civil administration, the prefects retained the vital areas of supply and recruitment to the army as part of the vast administrative responsibilities accruing to them. This was in fact a logical development, following from the massive increase in the size of the armed forces and the development of large-scale state manufacture of military equipment, including the personal equipment for which individual soldiers had once been themselves responsible. Supply became a major part of the machinery of imperial administration and one which was so vital as to justify a substantial part of the attention of an officer of state at the level of the praetorian prefects. Nor should we forget that this responsibility was exercised down the line by the diocesan administration and beneath them the provincial governors and their men on the spot. It is likely therefore that the removal from the prefects of their active command of the armies was as much due to the administrative load as to their long history of military usurpation. Diocletian's enormous increases in administration were probably making their jobs impossible. Nevertheless there must also have been much to be said from the political point of view for separating operational control of the armies from their supply.

The same change from military to civil seems to have come over the prefects' *vicarii* as their masters, and it is perhaps at this point that the divorce between the military and civil structures becomes decisive. In the fourth century the two services are recruited largely from different groups of people. The tendency in the army to favour promotion from the ranks is intensified and many more men of recent barbarian origin rise to the most senior commands. Yet it is an odd irony, and perhaps underlines the prestige of the Roman army, that in form civilian posts become more and more like military ones. In the civil service military titles are often used, military grade and pay structures are applied and even the wearing of uniform insignia by holders of civil office is increasingly adopted.[1]

A further consequence of the division was that it became unnecessary to base the organization of the army on the arrangement of provinces (and *vice versa*), since provincial governors no longer commanded the troops in their territories. This doubtless had considerable advantages. The division and redivision of provinces must previously often have made areas that were highly inconvenient for military purposes. By setting up a formal military structure spanning provinces Rome recognized and regularized on a more rational basis a situation that had often been necessary as a military expedient. The new area commands were headed by generals with the title of *dux*. At what point of time these became directly responsible to the new *magistri militum* is not known: this was certainly the arrangement in the later fourth century.

The territorial responsibilities of the new generals (if they were always appointed on a geographical basis, which is not certain) can be observed running through several provinces. Thus we have for Britain a *dux Britanniarum* and a *comes litoris Saxonici*, for example, both of whose commands clearly included units based in more than one of the fourth-century provinces. These commands seem to make good sense operationally, though one may guess that the problems of dealing with more than one provincial governor on matters of supply must have been tiresome. A central administration for the whole of Britain had, of course, been restored with the setting-up of the diocese. On the other hand, the introduction of a new tier in the structure is hardly in the nature of things likely to have assisted the commander in the field, nor the fact that his supplies were now coming from a department with no operational responsibilities.

It is now thought that Diocletian's legions had remained up to the traditional size, at least on paper, though the practice of employing substantial detachments on duty away from their parent units was continued. Under Diocletian himself these seem normally to have returned to garrison

---

[1] This fact ought to act as a warning to us when we are tempted to assume automatically the presence of the Late Roman army when items of uniform or similar equipment are found in archaeological contexts.

duty when the special tasks were eventually completed, but in the course of the Late Roman period it appears many such legionary detachments were formally constituted as legions in their own right. Constantine can probably be credited with making these detachments permanent. We have noted that in the troubles of the third century the old practice of using such detachments to construct field-armies for campaigns had already pointed in the direction of fairly permanent mobile field-armies. Constantine built on this practice by setting up, as a *formal* structural division of the Roman army, the distinction between the soldiers of the *comitatus*[1] and the garrison troops of the frontier provinces (*limitanei*). It is, of course, important not to associate these titles too closely with function at any particular point in time, as Roman conservatism tended to retain titles for very long periods (or re-use them) even where functions had changed. The *comitatenses*, as they came to be called, acquired higher status than the *limitanei,* but this should not mislead us into assuming that the latter were necessarily just border-guards or even a militia. It is only necessary to note that *all* the units under the command of the *dux Britanniarum* were so classi-fied to see that this is too simple a notion. It may also have been under Constantine that the new military post of *comes* was introduced, a commanding general of higher rank than the *dux,* though actual examples of *comites rei militaris* are lacking till the reigns of his sons.

There was nothing startlingly new in the idea of a central military force as it emerged between Diocletian and Con-stantine. From the time of Augustus there had been elements of a standing army regularly stationed in or near Rome. In the early days this had been the City troops—praetorian guard, urban cohorts, and *vigiles.* Severus had made it into a substantially larger force, reforming and possibly doubling the size of the praetorian cohorts and stationing his own favourite legion, II *Parthica,* close by. Indeed he adopted the

---

[1] The name might erroneously suggest their prime function was as personal guard to the emperor. Their position became more like the Guards regiments in the modern British Army. The disbanded praetorian cohorts were in fact re-placed by the so-called *scholae domesticorum.* Even the praetorians had not al-ways supplied the emperor's own bodyguard: a number of emperors had had a specially chosen body of men for this purpose.

practice of moving this special legion around the empire as he needed it. The events of the later third century meant that not only the emperors and their courts became much more mobile, as we have seen, but they spent a great deal of their time actually in command of troops on the move. In line with Severus' adage to look after the troops above all else and the experiences of the past century these new developments made good political as well as strategic sense.

There were now also changes in the relative importance given to cavalry as against infantry. Indeed, in the old *auxilia*, cavalry had been more highly rated than infantry and commands of mounted units went to more senior men. But in the prestigious legions the infantry had been the major arm. Vexillations of legionary cavalry, however, had as we have noted become important in the third century. In the fourth century the old frontier legions remained in being, but were classed among the *limitanei*. Among the new *comitatenses* there were cavalry units of 500 men which were called, interestingly, *vexillationes*, and *legiones* of infantry, which may have been of 1,000 men like the cohorts of the old praetorian guard. It is perhaps in this connection that Diocletian's full-strength frontier legions were permanently reduced in size by being drawn upon for the new units. There were also new infantry formations known as *auxilia*, apparently first recruited from Germans living within and outside the empire. It seems almost certain that these *auxilia* were introduced by Constantine and, along with units raised from the Germanic settlers or *laeti* introduced under agreements providing for military service, formed the core of Constantine's new mobile striking-force in the west. Despite their name, these *auxilia* were among the best troops at Constantine's disposal, and their inclusion among the *comitatenses* in the army lists demonstrates their superior status in the Late Roman army. Later on, we shall examine a further development of the fourth-century army, the separation of 'palatine' troops from the rest of the military *comitatus*.

This outline of the reorganized army is necessarily simplified, and probably presents an appearance of neatness that is spurious. Much of the evidence is contradictory and we have to remember that we are dealing with a long period and one in which from time to time some pretty desperate expedients must have been necessary. Much of the difficulty lies with the document known as the *Notitia Dignitatum,* a detailed but now incomplete list of military and civil commands in the eastern and western parts of the empire. Its date and purpose are hotly disputed; though it does seem reasonably clear that it was compiled from documents which were not all very recent at the time when the list reached the form in which it has come down to us, for the western list perhaps around AD 425. It is possible that it did come originally from the official registry of the *primicerius notariorum*, or one of the other central government departments. However it has been conjectured that what we have is an unofficial version which someone had attempted to correct with insufficient recent information.[1]

We have already noted that Diocletian's reforms were not confined to strengthening the constitutional and military institutions of the state. His immense concern over the ravages of inflation and the terrible condition of the central currency led him to take initiatives that were the beginning of radical changes in the economic and social pattern of the empire within which fourth-century Britain must be viewed. It will come as no surprise that Diocletian's propensity for seeing solutions in terms of close regulation by law and elaborate administrative structures appear as much in the economic field as elsewhere. It is also to be noted that his financial systems involved a much wider use of payment in kind than in the past, both from the state and to the state. It should not surprise us today that after a long period of disastrous inflation, allowances and benefits in kind could seem much more attractive to the holders of public offices than in times of a more stable currency, when a high money salary allowed accumulation of capital essential to acquire or retain personal and family social status.

Payments in kind to the state now far outstripped those dues that continued to be paid in cash. Great extensions

---

[1] Professor Eric Birley once suggested that this 'will allow us to suppose that there were rational men in the Roman Record Offices.' However, the presence of rational men in such positions does not necessarily rule out official 'establishment' records in this sort of condition. Anyone who has wrestled with personnel print-outs in a large modern organization is likely to be overtaken by a powerful sense of *déjà vu* on first reading the *Notitia*.

were made to the old system of direct victualling of the army as a levy on the taxpayer, abuses of which we saw Agricola stamping out in Britain two centuries earlier. Though assessments are thought to have become much fairer under Diocletian's reforms, the sheer handling of the material implies the need for a larger administrative machine. The army supply system was also vastly augmented by the development of a substantial number of state-owned industrial concerns manufacturing items of equipment, including those we noted that soldiers had previously purchased for themselves rather as a modern craftsman or mechanic buys his own tools. As with his frontier policy, Diocletian did not shrink at the manning implications of these reforms. We shall find that it is quite a long time before the trend towards greater complexity in structures—not to mention their duplication—and therefore in the number of men employed by the state is given any check.

We have already mentioned how in the fourth century the provincial governors' posts and those of the praetorian prefects and their *vicarii* became purely civilian. Looking back to the middle of the third century we may recall that, at least from Gallienus onwards, governors were increasingly appointed from among the equestrians. By the end of the third century the job of a provincial governor had been extended in scope and largely taken over the functions of the equestrian provincial procurators who previously ran the financial secretariat in each province and had had a separate responsibility direct to the emperor. These provincial procurators disappear. In the fourth century the new system of taxation and controls required a refashioning of the imperial financial service.

The old main branch of the central financial administration of the empire remained in being, but was reduced by circumstances in importance. The central offices of the chief secretaries who made up that branch—one in charge of taxation collected in cash, the other of imperial estates—were reorganized to take account of the new provincial structure. The *rationalis rei summae* still controlled the money taxes, and to him new diocesan *rationales vicarii* were responsible. To the *rationalis* of the diocese the individual provincial governor was now responsible for the tax collection in his province. The same *rationalis* was also charged with the official issue of coinage and with the administration of mines throughout the diocese. The imperial estates were now controlled by the emperor's *magister rei privatae* who similarly had diocesan *magistri* under him with procurators responsible to them. There is evidence that these two financial departments often worked closely together at the diocesan level, even to the extent of sometimes carrying out tasks strictly in the remit of the other department. Their work remained of substantial importance. Nevertheless the greatest financial responsibility now fell to the praetorian prefect, who was in charge both of the assessments for and the collection of the tremendous new system of exactions in kind. This became the major finance department of the Roman state.

The government was attempting to deal with crises seriously threatening collapse of the imperial system, on the one hand by means of much greater control of everyday affairs by imperial edicts and rulings and on the other by replacing the older administrative systems that left much to the provincials with new ones requiring far more direct intervention. We have noted the obvious reason why the military and civil administration had to be separated, that the load would have been impossibly great. However there was a further reason— the type of men now commanding the troops. From the earlier Principate there had been a strong tradition of giving the provinces in which major armies lay to imperial legates who had been deliberately selected early in their careers by the emperor and then directed into successive posts designed to give them serious military training as well as expertise in civil administration. Nevertheless their background had been the senatorial class, whose education was in rhetoric and law, whose social world was that of Rome, the senate, the courts, and the City administration. The third-century exclusion of senatorial governors must have struck a heavy blow at the civil administration of the empire and the standard of justice in the provinces. Since this happened at the same time as the more and more common rise of able but unlettered men through the army to senior military commands (and the throne itself), the need for a separate class of civil administrators must have become pressing. It is this latter class, men with a background of classical education and experience in law and administration but not military affairs, that we find holding the important posts in the fourth-century civil administration.

From where the governor of a fourth-century province in Britain sat the next level of authority above him was almost certainly all centred on London, and much of his attention must have been directed there. For the bulk of his duties that authority lay in the person of the *vicarius,* whose own job, even though it lacked the old total responsibility for the security of Britain, must have been of a scale and complexity comparable to that of the first- and second-century governors of the undivided British province. The fourth-century governor's other duties included assistance to the diocesan *rationalis* and *magister*—perhaps not always separate departments—also in London. Beyond London his perspective is likely for most of the period to have been to Trier, to the praetorian prefect in the main but also the financial secretaries of the current Caesar or Augustus, as appropriate. The task of keeping all those more senior officials happy must have been formidable, particularly when they were themselves in conflict.

The knowledge that the fountainhead of authority for the senior administrators of Britain now lay for practical purposes in Gaul was something they came increasingly to share with their military colleagues (we shall trace how the military command of the empire became regionalized). Though we shall see that the civil officers themselves were by no means necessarily from the region, the very fact that the organization itself was evolving something of a unity in the north-western provinces of the empire implies a profound political and cultural effect on the British scene. More and more we have to see Britain in the light of its immediate Continental neighbours, its fellow dioceses of the Gallic prefecture.

Apart from the army, there was one further power structure that a fourth-century governor had to take into account. This was the bishops of the Christian Church. For a considerable span of time before the Tetrarchy there seems to have been little real persecution of Christians in the empire. Christians had become increasingly accepted and in places were even ostentatious. The not wholly explained outbreak of persecution under Diocletian in AD 303, nearly twenty years after his accession, found Britain and Gaul unusually well protected. The Caesar Constantius, whose unofficial first wife Helena was later canonized, was not anti-Christian and apparently went no further to comply with the imperial edicts than to demolish existing churches.[1] While it seems that the full fury was only let loose in Egypt, for a short while it was clearly a great deal more unpleasant in most other parts of the empire for Christians than in Gaul or Britain. The possibility of Christian refugees in these provinces is thus not to be discounted, even if it was only a few people unobtrusively transferring their residences or getting themselves posted on duty to the north-west.

The usurpation of Helena's son Constantine assured the continuation of Constantius' policy of toleration. However it was his tremendous victory at the Milvian Bridge in 312 over Maxentius that gained him recognition as the senior Augustus, and it was the fact that he seems genuinely to have believed this victory was due to the intervention of the Christian God that turned him from mere toleration to enthusiastic support. From AD 313 and the 'Peace of the Church' the Christian religion was legal in the empire and the western Church in high favour. From 324 Constantine's total supremacy extended this to the whole empire. It is clear that he believed it was of paramount importance for the Roman state to retain the approval of the Christian God that had been made manifest at the Milvian Bridge, though his *personal* beliefs remained for many years ambivalent.[2]

There were immediate and immense political, social, and economic consequences. Constantine's own enthusiasms tended to make things happen fast and on a large scale. Even from Britain, which does not seem to have been very deeply penetrated by Christianity so far, three bishops appear at the Council of Arles, only two years after the Milvian Bridge,[3] together with a priest and a deacon who may be representing

---

[1] See A.H.M. Jones, *Later Roman Empire*, 1079 (= 1964 edn. III, 9), n.67 for references. Frere (*Britannia*, 375, n.26) also cites Augustine, *Letters*, lxxxviii. 2.

The hoard of plate from a Christian church, dated stylistically to the late third century or early fourth and found concealed in the Roman town at Water Newton (Chesterton, *Durobrivae*) without stratigraphical association, was possibly buried at this moment though there are many other possibilities.

[2] For a considerable time he combined Christianity with continued devotion to the Unconquered Sun.

[3] Eborius of York, Restitutus of London, and Adelphius of Lincoln or possibly Colchester (see Mann, *Antiquity*, 35 (1961), 317).

•a fourth bishop. This Council was itself called to settle a dispute within the Christian Church and, when it failed, the emperor himself arbitrated. It is a change of the first magnitude that, from 312, doctrine, schism, and the politics of the Church become matters of major concern to the emperors. This adds a new dimension to Roman politics.

One important consequence was to sharpen the developing antagonism between the largely pagan and conservative senatorial class at Rome and the imperial house and its great officers who were mostly recruited outside the senate. However it ought to be mentioned briefly here in Constantine's favour that he did try to reverse the trend of excluding senators from major offices. Moreover many of those of lesser birth successful in the imperial service were eventually absorbed into the senatorial order. The Church too suddenly began to find itself rich—and wealth was the prerequisite to respectability and influence in the Roman world. Not only did Constantine immediately begin to restore to the churches property that had been confiscated from them but also to add to this very large sums from his treasury. Throughout the eastern part of the empire Constantine was to make available funds from the public purse for the rebuilding of churches that had been destroyed. In addition the future of the churches was put on a sound footing by massive grants of estates as endowments. At the same time individuals were encouraged to make gifts and bequests to the same end. Substantial rights and privileges (some quite surprising) were also granted to men in Christian orders.

While Constantine seems to have destroyed or closed few temples, he did carry out a comprehensive programme of stripping them of their wealth. It has to be remembered that public and private donations to the innumerable temples of the Graeco-Roman world had been going on for many centuries.[1] While the barbarian raids and the civil wars of the previous century had doubtless reduced the amount of portable treasures and cash, the total must still have been immense. Moreover many of the more famous pagan religious centres had become great property owners. Constantine's acquisition of this enormous wealth and his great gifts to the

---

[1] In fact many had also doubled as public treasuries.

Christian churches represent a shift in wealth and power throughout the empire comparable to the Dissolution of the Monasteries in sixteenth-century England.

If individual churches became rich almost overnight, one may wonder what happened to individual churchmen and secular Christians. Many a fortune in Tudor England was based on the spoils of the religious houses and the favour of the king. Respectability fell naturally on to the new Tudor landowner and monastic estates and buildings formed the foundation of the rising gentry and new aristocracy. Many older-established families did not hold back from the process and merged with the others to become the Protestant upper classes of Elizabethan England. It should, therefore, not surprise us in Roman Britain when we find Christian motifs displayed on the mosaics of the reception rooms in fine villas such as Frampton in Gloucestershire or Hinton St. Mary in Dorset. After 312 (and perhaps from 306) there was only one period when it was likely to be disadvantageous to be well-off and demonstratively Christian in Roman Britain—under Julian as Augustus—and that was only an interlude of three and a half years in the course of a century or more. Not all the wealth taken from the temples went to the Church: large funds were retained by the emperor to finance other projects. Overall, one can hardly imagine that in such a large operation a good deal did not stick to various fingers. When we consider the remarkable prosperity of Britain in the fourth century compared with Gaul we may perhaps reflect on the fact that its temples had not suffered the third-century ravages of Gaul. We shall see later a good deal of evidence for the continuance of pagan cults in Britain right on through the fourth century, particularly the local ones, and even some new temples built, but we have no way of knowing what financial losses they suffered. However we may suspect that their treasures had survived till Constantine relatively undisturbed and their lands and other property now lay unpillaged and tempting.

Such wealth in private hands could confer status and influence. Equally, imperial favour must have meant that many Christians were now promoted or preferred in public office, especially since the enormous increase in the imperial service since 284 meant a vast new range of appointments in a world where the exercise of patronage by the influential was expected. This would have occasioned little surprise. What must really have shocked traditional Romans was Constantine's transfer to the Church of certain powers that had always been the prerogative of Roman magistrates. Even Constantine's own praetorian prefect, himself a Christian, was not sure he had understood the emperor aright when Constantine decided that in any legal action either party could have the case transferred out of the ordinary courts to the local bishop for verdict[1] —and that if it were necessary the secular authorities were required to enforce the judgement. While we have yet to come on evidence for grand churches in fourth-century Britain and while the fact that three of the bishops who went to Italy in 359 for the Council of Ariminum had to accept assistance with their travel may suggest that as institutions the churches in Britain were not well-off, nevertheless this sort of temporal power given to the Church, compounded with the presence of well-to-do Christian landowners and backed by the known favour of the imperial house, meant that a Roman governor had to take the wishes of the Church and its officers, however few in number, very seriously— indeed, in certain matters, to carry out their decisions. This was a real revolution.

It was not, of course, revolutionary to find religious authority entwined with that of the Roman state or to have it inextricably political. For Augustus the restoration of traditional Roman religion, particularly the ancient institutions and rituals of the Roman state, was integral to his restored Republic. Observance of the official sacrifices was held an essential display of loyalty both in the army and in civilian public life and election to membership of the various priesthoods played an important part in binding together the provincial upper classes in the service of the empire. Such loyalty mattered more and more in the upheavals of the third century. At the same time those troubles had led to an increase in religion in the modern sense of personal belief and its consolations. A further powerful force in the rise of Christianity was paradoxically that public misfortunes could be attributed to the anger of the state gods at the rise of Christianity, for

---

[1] This extraordinary ecclesiastical privilege was subsequently withdrawn.

when the persecutions failed the belief could be exactly reversed. The persecution of Christians had from the first had much of the perennial fear of the Roman state about secret societies and conspiracy. If so clear-headed an emperor as Trajan could refuse permission for a volunteer fire-brigade on these grounds, it is not surprising that the Christians had so much trouble, particularly as they were long confused with some of the extreme Jewish terrorist groups. However, by the beginning of the fourth century the idea that religious *belief* really mattered to people—enough to force them to refuse the normal gestures of loyalty to the emperor *without* intending any political disrespect—was becoming generally intelligible. As far as the Imperial Cult is concerned Constantine largely incorporated it: it was too important to do otherwise. What was new was to find a cult whose members had just been persecuted as dangerous revolutionaries and an offence to the gods of the state suddenly become the basis of the new state religion and adherence to it a symbol of loyalty. Moreover it was a real change that actual *belief* in a religion (or the pretence of it) had become politically and socially important—and in a religion that was exclusive of all other religions. To be a Christian was now like being a member of the Party in certain modern states.

We have seen that Constantine's religious policy did much to alienate the Roman upper classes, but also that he made real efforts to bring them back into public life. Some offices that had become equestrian in the third century were now upgraded again: for example certain provincial governorships given the title *consularis* and reserved for senators.[1] Constantine was, it is true, extending the pool of experienced men who could be drawn on in this way by substantially increasing the number of successful members of the imperial service admitted as members of the senate. The enormous funds at his disposal as the result of confiscations in the Civil Wars, new taxation and the confiscation of temple property enabled him the more easily to raise the private fortunes of these men to the necessary level of capital to make them eligible to be proposed for senatorial rank. Both ancient and

---

[1] Under the Late Empire the *consulares* became the lowest grade in the hierarchy of rank that qualified for senatorial status.

modern critics have accused Constantine of financial prof-
ligacy. In this instance he was perhaps directing imperial
generosity in a very sensible way.

Constantine's redistribution of the temple treasures (to
use a contemporary euphemism) allowed him with the mass
of precious metal acquired to establish a new currency based
on a new gold coin, the famous *solidus*. It also, as we have
seen, permitted unparalleled imperial expenditure. In addition
the vast increase in the numbers of officials must have brought
much employment among all the trades that looked after
them. The beneficial results in the short run, particularly in
a group of provinces that had not been so badly damaged as
to be unable to take advantage of the opportunities, must
have been very considerable. Professor Haverfield was surely
right in seeing fourth-century Britain as coming into an age
of prosperity such as she had never had before.

There could of course be problems from too much prosperity, not all of them obvious. For example, the new aristocracy of office, secular and ecclesiastical, gained not only
wealth but privileges, and these did not necessarily work to
the advantage of the state. Like those attaining senatorial
rank, a member of the municipal gentry ordained in the
Church became exempt from the extremely heavy financial
burdens placed on *curiales*. Indeed, the situation in respect of
taxation and local administration became so serious that
strict laws had to be enacted to avoid the worst financial
consequences of the privileges attached to a growing number
of offices.

About the actual holders of the major offices in the reorganized structure of Roman Britain we know very little.
From Constantine's period as western Augustus we have the
name of Pacatianus in the post of *vicarius* in the year 319 [1]
and under Constantius II there is the case of the suicide of
the *vicarius* Martinus who tried to stop the excesses of the
reprisals after the defeat of the usurper Magnentius in 353.
Subsequently, still under Constantius II, one Alypius from
Antioch is recorded as *vicarius* by Ammianus.[2] The same
author, in his account of the reconstruction of the British
provinces after the barbarian incursions of AD 367, mentions

[1] *Cod. Theod.* XI. vii. 2.   [2] Ammianus, XXIII. i. 2; XXIX.i, 44.

the appointment in 368 of one Civilis to what is surely the vicariate of the Britains.[1] References to two further *vicarii*, Chrysanthus[2] and Victorinus,[3] both probably under the Emperor Honorius, and the occurrence of the office in the *Notitia Dignitatum* let us reasonably presume that there were still *vicarii* at the end of the fourth century and most likely into the fifth.

Hardly anything is known of the governors who presided over the individual provinces within the diocese of Britain. The reopening of provincial posts to members of the senatorial order by Constantine would lead one to expect the appearance of such people regularly in office in Britain once more. The *Notitia* does record one of the provinces that originated in the Diocletianic reorganization as *consularis*—the province of *Maxima Caesariensis*—but we do not know how early that happened. It was probably normal that such upgrading within a particular diocese was first applied to the province that also contained the diocesan capital itself. If indeed the whole British diocese was administered from London, then it seems very probable that London housed a *consularis* as governor of the local province and his staff in addition to the superior establishment of the *vicarius*, not to mention the one, and possibly two, departments dealing with money revenues at diocesan level that were independent of the rest of the civil administration. The social and economic implications for London as a city of such a concentration of the new aristrocracy of office provoke interesting reflections. If nothing else, there are not likely to have been many offices standing empty in fourth-century London.

At least one governor of a British province in the mid-fourth century possessed the attribute of good connections, which became increasingly vital as the emperor became more remote and the bureaucracy more impenetrable. This was one Flavius Sanctus, who was associated with the remarkable Gallo-Roman poet and professor Ausonius, whose appointment as tutor at the imperial court to the young Gratian, subsequently emperor, led to provincial governorships and eventually a consulship.[4] Another British governor who was probably in

---

[1] Ammianus, XXVII. viii. 10.   [2] Socrates, *Eccl. Hist.* vii. 12 and 17.
[3] Rutilius Namatianus, *De reditu,* i. 493–510.[4] Ausonius, *Parentalia*, xviii. 7–8.

office around the same general period as Flavius Sanctus is the equestrian Lucius Septimius (the rest of his name is lost), *praeses* of Britannia Prima. Unlike Sanctus, however, Lucius Septimius' contacts are not likely to have been with the strongly Christian circle of Gratian and his father, for he made an almost aggressively pagan dedication at Cirencester.[1] This is more likely to have occurred under the pagan emperor Julian (360–3) than at other periods, but we cannot be sure of the date. Its importance here is that it reminds us of the continuing strength of pagan feeling among people in positions of authority and influence. This is particularly true among that class of men educated in the classical tradition, whom we have seen occupying the senior positions in the fourth-century magistracy and increasingly separated in terms of career from the professional soldiers. The latter were not necessarily unlettered but had different traditions and attitudes to life. The topmost level of Roman society was certainly tending to polarize into two groups, one based on senatorial families, often pagan and with an essentially civilian background, the other centred around the army, the emperor, and the court, largely Christian and military in its attitudes to life. The professional civilian administrators, such as many of the *vicarii* and governors now were, helped to bridge the cultural gap between senatorial aristocracy and court.

[1] *RIB* 103.

13

THE MIDDLE OF THE FOURTH CENTURY

THE immense personality and prestige of Constantine held the whole empire firm in his grip while he lived. His death in 337 changed all that. A chain of events which was to prove very serious for Britain began with the new outbreak of murderous squabbling in the imperial family immediately Constantine died. I shall later be suggesting that Britain's early fourth-century age of peace and prosperity began to vanish in the 340s. For a brief moment the island seems to have escaped the consequences of Constantine's death. They were momentous. For three months there was no Augustus at all: a major army revolt at Constantinople refused to accept any of the appointments to imperial rank that were proposed other than the sons of Constantine themselves. His ghost would not have been surprised. The troops proceeded to dispose summarily of various other members of the imperial family and a number of appointees left by the late emperor. His second son Constantine II had formally held the rank of Caesar since he was a month old. This itself demonstrates how far imperial attitudes to the succession had reverted to former practices. Out of the chaos this Constantine emerged as senior Augustus, personally controlling Britain, Gaul, and Spain (which is almost beginning to show the characteristics of an hereditary fief). Another brother, Constans, controlled Italy, Africa, and the Illyrian provinces and a third, Constantius II, held Constantinople and most of the east. All three assumed the rank of Augustus.

The arrangement in the west did not work. Constantine II objected to the attitude of Constans and launched an invasion of Italy in 340. It was a disaster: he was defeated and killed at Aquileia. The shock must have been immense in Gaul and Britain, which had not had a violent change of regime since the death of Allectus now 44 years ago. Unlike much of the rest of the empire, leading civilians in the north-west had not been much disturbed for political reasons (other than those connected with the establishment of the Church) for a generation or more. Even the first shock of Constantine's great assault on the ancient religion and the endowments of its institutions was by now a quarter of a century in the past. Among military men, the armies of the north-west had suffered no defeats. Indeed Constantine the Great's own rise to power had been from the beginning in the hands of these troops and he had finally been made supreme by the massive victories they won under his command over his rivals. Now the north-western armies had been defeated in battle and their emperor killed.

What were the immediate effects on the army in Britain we do not know. We do not have details of the military units making up the army that Constantine II had with him in Italy in 340 or what he lost at Aquileia. This means we have no evidence to indicate which troops were drawn from Britain for this campaign, if any. Constantine's single field-army had after his death been replaced by three separate *comitatus* (each of the Augusti had his own *comitatenses*). This had given Constantine II a permanent field army of first-rate troops of his own and may have meant relatively slight with-drawals from the static garrisons of Britain where few *comitatenses* are found at any period in their history. Nevertheless, something happened here in 342 which brought Constans in person to Britain at the beginning of 343 in mid-winter, a very unusual time to cross the Channel. Like Agricola, he probably took people in Britain by surprise. His actions were certainly represented as daring.[1] It would be very interesting to know why he came. It has been widely conjectured that the refortification of cities in Britain in the fourth century was undertaken as the result of decisions taken by Constans during this visit; and that this might have been in consequence of an inability of the army in Britain to cope with barbarian attacks after being weakened by postulated troop with-drawals by Constantine II two years earlier. This is a theory that should not be discounted but still rests on too many assumptions. We shall be examining later a much more likely period for the refortification. In place of—or perhaps as well

[1] Julius Firmicus Maternus, *De errore profanarum religionum,* xxviii. 6 = Mann, *Northern Frontier,* 192.

as—barbarian attack we should be remembering the possibility of political and military unrest in a relatively inaccessible part of the defeated emperor's former domain as a reason for Constans' visit, particularly in winter when conspirators might feel safe. This explanation would make permission to fortify cities most unlikely.

Turning for a moment to the broader military picture, two of the important developments appear in the Roman army around this time which we need to note if we are to examine with greater understanding what we can glean of the military situation in Britain in the middle of the fourth century and later. We have noticed how the *comitatus* (formalized and developed by Constantine I as the emperor's own powerful field-army normally operating directly with him under the immediate command of his *magistri militum*) had recently been divided into three, the consequence of reverting to multiple emperors. It now proceeds to divide again, into armies that operated separately from one another as required, though responsible to the *same* emperor. The way the Roman army was developing is conveniently summarized for us by A.H.M. Jones, in the course of discussing how the post of *comes* was used:

The title [of *comes*] seems to have been given to officers commanding groups of *comitatenses*, ranging from substantial army corps to a couple of regiments, allocated to a special task or assigned to a particular area.

The field army thus tended to split into an increasing number of local groups, some larger under *magistri*, some smaller under *comites*. When Constantius reunited the empire under his rule [AD 353] this practice continued. There was a substantial part of the army which was attached to the emperor's person, and was commanded by a *magister peditum* and a *magister equitum*, who to distinguish them from the regional commanders were styled *in praesenti* or *praesentales*. But wherever the emperor might be there was a large body of the field army permanently stationed on the Eastern frontier under a *magister equitum*, and another large body in Gaul under another *magister equitum*. There were also substantial groups in Illyricum and Thrace; their commanders normally bore the lower title of *comes*. And there were smaller groups in Africa and elsewhere, also under *comites*. The system was still at this date flexible. The ranks of the various group commanders were not rigidly fixed . . . A temporary need might demand the dispatch of field army units to some province, and a *comes* might replace the local *dux* for the time being but the troops and their commander later be withdrawn.[1]

[1] A.H.M. Jones, *Later Roman Empire*, 124 f.

There is a particularly interesting early example of the latter situation which relates to Britain. At some time before 350 the elder Gratian, father of the emperor Valentinian I, held a command in Britain with the rank of *comes*.[1] He had previously held the same rank in Africa where the post became an established one. In Britain, since we find a *dux Britanniarum* in office subsequently, the arrangement was almost certainly temporary, and we may presume units of *comitatenses* posted in for a specific task and probably then withdrawn. It has been suggested that Gratian's appointment was connected with Constans' surprise visit in 343, a not unreasonable theory.

The elder Gratian is moreover an instructive example of the sort of men we noted earlier who were rising to senior commands and whom one might expect to find among the *comites* and *duces* encountered in Britain. He started in the ranks, was selected for the *protectores,* troops of the Guard who seem to have had a secondary function as a proving ground for potential officers, appointed *tribunus* and then given two tours of duty as *comes rei militaris.* Under him in Africa served his son Valentinian, who was subsequently an officer in Gaul with Julian and later rose to be emperor. When we consider the decisions and actions of fourth-century commanders—and of most of the emperors themselves—it is important we do not forget the sort of men they were nor their personal and family experience of service as professionals in the ranks and in command. Valentinian himself demonstrates they were not necessarily uncultured, but they have a background very different from the *vicarii* and provincial governors and in the main from the senatorial aristocracy itself.

There are a few slight clues as to what Constans actually did during his winter visit. The relevant text of Ammianus is lost, but he later speaks of 'the *areani,* a category established by our forefathers, certain affairs relating to which I mentioned

---

[1] The fact that Ammianus refers to Gratian as *comes* does not automatically mean that he had a military command. Professor J.C. Mann very properly emphasizes that *comes* was introduced as a *rank,* not an office (in fact it had three grades) (J.C. Mann, in Johnston (ed.), *The Saxon Shore,* 13). However, it seems likely that, as will appear later, there was a whole series of *ad hoc* commands of expeditionary forces in Britain in the fourth century, and that Gratian's was one of them.

earlier in connection with the actions of Constans.'[1] By 367
these men had the job of collecting information about tribes
bordering on the Roman territories in Britain by moving
about among them.[2] This, or a similar patrol system, may go
back to the point (whenever that was) when the Antonine
garrisons in Scotland were withdrawn. Constans may, therefore, have had to react to events on the northern frontier
which may be reflected in signs of severe fire damage at three
of the outpost forts of the Wall (Risingham, High Rochester,
and Bewcastle) at some stage between the restoration at the
beginning of the century and the barbarian war of 367 which
I shall describe later. Of these three, the furthest forward,
High Rochester, was not restored after its fire. Constans may
have decided on a treaty arrangement with the northern barbarians, monitored by the *areani*. However, there is no evidence that the *areani* themselves were established now for
the first time.

Constans may also have strengthened the defences of the
south. The fort of Pevensey could have been added to the
coastal chain at this time (a coin sealed beneath a bastion
dates the construction of the fort after 334-5) and an increase in the number of coins from Richborough and Portchester suggests substantial activity there in this part of the
century. One theory would attribute the establishment of
the post of *comes litoris Saxonici* itself to Constans, but it is
not at all sure, as we shall discuss later, that this was so.
There is certainly no reason to connect the elder Gratian with
it. Whatever his precise function, it was most probably an *ad
hoc* appointment. It is true that in the same period the use of
units of *comitatenses* to reinforce *limitanei* begins to appear
elsewhere, and a general reorganization and modernization of
the military set-up (which we have noted could have significance for internal as well as external security) would be a
suitable context for the employment of some *comitatenses* in
Britain. Nevertheless the appointment of a *comes* is likely to
have been only on a temporary basis to carry out the emperor's
decisions. We have to be aware of what we are doing if we try

---

[1] Ammianus, XXVIII. iii. 8.
[2] Ibid. Their function is described: *id enim illis erat officium, ut ultro citroque,
per longa spatia discurrentes, vicinarum gentium strepitus nostris ducibus inti-
marent.*

to construct an archaeological picture of Constans' actions and attach it to the brief literary references for the visit. We do *not* know that the reason for his journey was military nor what business he had with the *areani,* nor for certain what the latter were. Even for 367 the evidence is only just enough to associate the *areani* positively with the northern frontier, but it does refer to 367 and not 343 and does not prove that *areani* acted in the north only. We do not know at all closely the date of the damage to the three outpost forts—and certainly not of the fourth-century work on the town walls. We do not even know the precise dates of the elder Gratian's service in Britain. The accumulation of possibilities does give some support to a general proposition. Further we should not go.

The struggle between Constantine II and Constans had a further result of considerable importance for Britain. The military consequences of dividing the imperial *comitatus* on a fairly permanent basis have been discussed. But each of the three Augusti also had his own praetorian prefect and the associated civil administration. Despite the defeat of Constantine II in 340, the separate praetorian prefect for Britain, Gaul and Spain continued to be appointed, even though there was no locally based Augustus or Caesar. In other words, this north-western governmental structure was no longer seen essentially as attached to the person of an emperor and at least theoretically following him around. Constans' action in the north-west, even if largely recognizing facts, is highly significant in that it formally implies a regional government for 'the Gauls' (Britain, France, Germany west of the Rhine, and Spain) with a regional praetorian prefect not immediately attached to the retinue of the emperor, independent from the praetorian prefect of Italy and the rest of the west, and not dependent on the way in which the empire as a whole was divided between emperors at any specific time. This Gallic prefecture, on the other hand, continued till the early fifth century to be filled by men sent out in the ancient fashion from Italy.

It is interesting to find that the senatorial aristocracy is reappearing regularly in the imperial administration of the west now that civil and military have been formally separated. We have noted that in Britain the province of Maxima Caesariensis was consular, and we have imagined senatorial *vicarii* of the diocese stationed in London. Administratively their responsibility was to the prefect of the Gauls in Trier, but socially many of these men were of the class that looked more to the City of Rome for its style of life than to the imperial court, wherever that might currently be.[1]

The Emperor Constans' sole rule in the west lasted ten years, with his brother Constantius II firmly established as eastern colleague. We can therefore assume that the Gallic prefecture was well established as a permanent institution before a new upheaval struck the north-west. In 350 Constans fell victim to a palace plot. The conspirators proclaimed at Autun the elevation to the throne of one of themselves, Magnentius, commander of two units of the field-army. Almost immediately two further Augusti were proclaimed by other groups—a nephew of Constantine in Rome and in Illyricum Vetranio, *magister militum* to the late Constans. The first of these was promptly put down by Magnentius. The second, though much more formidable, retired from the field and let Constantius II take over what may have been a substantial part of the main western field-army.

Britain was now under the rule of Magnentius, *de facto* Augustus of most of the west. We cannot estimate the amount of support for him in Britain. However, we have to remember that it was only ten years since Constans had defeated the north-western armies and killed his brother Constantine II, who had ruled the region as successor to Constantine the Great, put on the throne by the army in Britain. The savagery with which supporters of Magnentius were hunted down in Britain after his defeat suggests that sympathy for him was by no means negligible. The assertively Christian design of his coinage was doubtless intended to reassure the Christian party and underline his claim to legitimacy, while at the same time his toleration of the pagans was well known. He doubtless collected many former supporters of Constantine II and others offended by the fratricidal struggle. This is conjecture: however it may be, he set about organizing his realm, appointed his brother Decentius as Caesar in Gaul, and collected forces for the war that was clearly coming.

[1] Now, when in Italy, normally at Milan, which was geographically more convenient than Rome.

It is worth looking at the personal background of Magnentius and Decentius, for it is particularly significant in the
context of the age. Their family origin seems to have lain
among the so-called *laeti* whom we noted earlier, once
Germanic barbarians who had been deliberately settled within
the empire. This term, *laeti,* appears in the panegyric addressed to Constantius I as Caesar—in other words before AD
305—and there refers to Franks settled by Maximian on land
in Gaul which was not in cultivation at the time. Similar
settlements were made by Constantius I himself. It is thought
that the object was to restore the productivity and prosperity
of districts whose agriculture had been abandoned during
the barbarian invasions of the second half of the third century.
Imperial interest in the problem of *agri deserti* was no new
thing. Hadrian had paid particular attention to bringing back
such lands into cultivation long before, and it was a problem
Rome faced at various times. Barbarian settlements became
an important part of Roman military and diplomatic policy—
and as the grip of Roman government declined the initiative
in making these arrangements passed more and more to the
barbarians. In this period, however, we are dealing with an
act of Roman statesmanship in the interests of Rome. As we
noted earlier, many of the great villas which studded this
part of Gaul seem to have been replaced by simple farming
settlements, and it has been conjectured that these farms
represent the arrival of the *laeti*. However by the time of
Magnentius' elevation to the throne this settlement of *laeti*
was itself half a century old. While it looks forward to further
settlement of groups of barbarians within the empire which
became more and more frequent in the fourth and fifth
centuries, it is by no means the first, as we have seen. The
appearance of the Emperor Magnentius from such a background (if indeed it was so) also looks back to the long tradition of absorption of foreigners into the Roman way of life.
These *laeti* were by now second- or third-generation Romans.
Much more recent Germanic immigrants were to dominate
Roman politics later in the century.

Magnentius had just over two years' rule in the west before
he met Constantius II for the first time in battle, near Mursa
in modern Yugoslavia. One may presume that most of those
troops of the western army that Vetranio had commanded

were now incorporated on Constantius' side. However, there were now *two* field armies in the west, and Magnentius had the other. We may guess that with only part of Constans' former *comitatus* available to him, Magnentius reinforced it for the campaign with frontier troops, possibly including detachments from Britain. The battle of Mursa was a tremendous one and the casualties large. Magnentius retreated, and in 353 was brought to battle again at Mons Seleucus in Gaul, was defeated, and driven to commit suicide. After a long period of confident success, the Roman armies of the northwest had now been defeated three times in major battles—under Constantine II at Aquileia in 340, and now Mursa in 351 and Mons Seleucus in 353.

Britain had been part of Magnentius' dominions for three and a half years. The civil war had been a bitter one. Moreover the fact that Magnentius had permitted pagan worship added a very nasty element to the situation, for both Constans and Constantius II were aggressive Christians. Magnentius' reign must have given a respite to pagans in Britain and may have encouraged them to come out into the open. If so, it was probably disastrous for them. Constantius' hatred of paganism was very real. He ordered the closing of all remaining temples but he also went much further. He deeply shocked and offended traditional Roman sentiment by removing the ancient altar of Victory from the Senate House in Rome, which neither Constantine the Great nor his other sons had touched. This was coming close to what many felt was at the heart of centuries of Roman success. He compounded this by reaffirming the death penalty for individuals offering pagan sacrifice, or worshipping the images of the gods, acts that had been central to the concepts of loyalty to the state and the home and strongest among the great aristocratic families.

It was, however, not only pagans that were in danger for their religion. In Constantine the Great's reign it had been clearly established that the emperor had both the authority and the duty to suppress heresy and promote the unity of the Church. This is a development of major historical importance, whose effects have not yet ceased to be felt. When Constantius defeated Magnentius and restored the unity of the empire under a single Augustus, the western and eastern churches were in a state of major schism over the Creed. The bishops in the west (now men of importance as we have seen) largely adhered to the Athanasian version (the Nicene Creed), believing the Father and the Son to be of *one substance*. The eastern bishops were various shades of Arian, mostly believing in broad terms that the Father and the Son were not the same but *similar*. Constantius felt it necessary to call a series of Councils of the Church and, unfortunately for the western bishops, to put on them irresistible pressure for the acceptance of the Arian view. By AD 360 this was universal. It is ironic that Constantius both managed to make Christianity the only permitted religion throughout the whole empire and forced the Church to agree officially on fundamental doctrine, but that the Church itself was subsequently to declare Constantius' Councils irregular and the Arian doctrine a major heresy. However, compulsory Christianity and the regulation of doctrine by the state were now here to stay.

In the meantime, however, many people in Britain must have faced the prospect of serious trouble for recent acts or expressions of sympathy when Constantius gained control of Britain in 353. Any such apprehension was well justified. The emperor sent to Britain one of his senior civil servants, the *notarius* or 'imperial notary' Paulus, to deal with disaffection. These 'notaries' were a class of official who became of considerable importance in the government of the empire. The head of the branch, the *primicerius notariorum*, controlled the *notitia* or establishment records of all official posts both civil and military and was responsible for the issue of their commissions to all the senior officers on both sides of the public service. The branch is first attested at a fairly humdrum level in Constantine's day but later rose so far that, in the reign of Valentinian I (364-75), the *primicerius notariorum* is found with a higher status than the *vicarii* of dioceses and subsequently all notaries became eligible for senatorial rank.

Paulus' fearful reputation for ruthless and devious cunning in the hunting down of opponents of the regime earned him the nickname of 'The Chain' (*Catena*). His original brief in Britain was to arrest certain military men who had supported Magnentius. Meeting no resistance, he extended his operations without warning, trapping some who had been implicated but also imprisoning many on trumped-up evidence. Though it appears that he exceeded his orders, the emperor subsequently approved of his actions and did nothing to prevent the conviction and punishment of those Paulus had seized. The methods employed were so extreme and the injustice so blatant that the *vicarius* of Britain Flavius Martinus, who seems to have been a loyal supporter of the emperor, attempted to persuade Paulus to release those who were not guilty, and, failing, threatened resignation. This only resulted in false accusations against himself and other senior officers in Britain. As a final desperate act, Martinus was driven to attack Paulus in person with a sword. Unsuccessful, he committed suicide. His name deserves to be remembered in Britain.

Ammianus' account suggests the arrests and confiscations were most acute among the richer classes, as one might expect.[1] Moreover, in this atmosphere it must have been difficult for anyone of any prominence not to be accused of treason, since political, military, or religious evidence could all provide grounds for condemnation. Even those who changed sides were not safe. In Gaul an army officer named Silvanus had deserted Magnentius and been appointed by Constantine II to command the troops in the Gallic provinces. Almost immediately he fell victim to a false accusation of treason and was forced, in attempted self-defence, into an unsuccessful proclamation of himself as Augustus. Suspicion became endemic, and no one against whom an allegation was made escaped. Constantius seems to have accepted the slightest rumour of guilt, and the appointment of a man from Antioch, Alypius, as *vicarius* of the British diocese soon after the death of Martinus probably reflects imperial concern to avoid men with western associations in this sensitive post. It must have been a very unhappy time indeed. It may be in this context that we should place the strange appearance in Britain, at some point between AD 354 and 358, of local coins bearing the name of one 'Carausius II', for whom we have no other evidence.[2] Nevertheless, in this miserable time,

---

[1] Ammianus, XIV. v. 6–9.

[2] Another interesting piece of numismatic information is that two of the four burials of soldiers in the late Roman Lankhills cemetery at Winchester are dated by coins to the middle of the century. One had coins of Constans and Magnentius issued between 350 and 353, the other a single coin of 330–40. The possibility that these soldiers, buried outside a city, had something to do with emergency

further pretenders are hardly unlikely. Many people can have had nothing to lose.

In 355 Constantius made a decision that perhaps took some of the heat out of the situation. He put his young cousin Julian in charge of Gaul and Britain, with the rank of Caesar. This was a remarkable appointment. Julian's father had been murdered by the troops during the debate about the succession to Constantine the Great, his brother executed the previous year for incompetence. He had been brought up in deliberate obscurity in the east, partly in a remote fortress. This exclusion from public affairs (which probably saved his life) had the same effect as on the Emperor Claudius. He acquired a passionate interest in the past, in Classical literature, Roman religion, and Roman tradition. He was to show originality, not to say eccentricity, and proved a man of great talents and integrity. Summoned out of obscurity by an unenthusiastic emperor, he immediately won the allegiance of the troops in the west (if not the affection of his senior staff) by insisting on sharing their hardships in the field and by displaying brilliant generalship. He fought a series of campaigns against the barbarians who had taken the opportunities offered by the recent troubles to break into Gaul. He drove them out and proceeded to campaign beyond the Rhine, inflicting considerable damage by the use of speed and surprise. His tactics, as befits someone devoted to reading Roman history, are strongly reminiscent of those of Julius Caesar on the same ground four centuries earlier. They prove that with inspired leadership the Roman army could still perform feats equal to those of the past, feats significantly of the type where training, organization, and discipline gave it superiority over the barbarians.

The continuing importance of Britain to Roman power in the north-west of the empire is illustrated by one action taken by Julian. It was probably in connection with one of his operations against the barbarians, the lower Rhine expedition of AD 359, that he organised a fleet of 600 ships (400 built specifically for the purpose, in the fashion typical of him) to transport corn from Britain. Just as his grandfather Constantius I had drawn on Britain for skilled men to re-

dispositions by Magnentius or with the hunting of dissidents by Paulus is worth noting.

construct the devastated cities of Gaul, so Julian used Britain to supply large quantities of stores needed for his military efforts to restore the effectiveness of the Rhine frontier. Britain, relatively undamaged, was clearly still regarded as a major reserve of resources, and it is apparent that Julian was consciously reopening a supply-route that had for a time ceased to function, probably because of barbarian activity at sea. This makes it easier to understand the recurrent imperial concern for peace in Britain throughout the fourth century, when there were plenty of acute problems in areas much less geographically peripheral, and account for the elaborate nature of its defences. Britain, however, may have been physically relatively undamaged but that does not mean it was happy. Within a year the morale of the British provinces is described as very low 'because of past calamities'.[1]

Julian did not hesitate to exploit the resources of Britain to supply the hard-pressed Rhine frontier. Yet, given a longer reign, he might also have done much to raise the spirit of Britain by lightening the load government was increasingly piling on to the empire. Constantius had appointed a praetorian prefect, one of his own men, to head Julian's civil administration. When this official provoked Julian by demanding the raising of taxes to meet government expenditure, the latter characteristically took over in person to demonstrate that efficient and honest operation of the existing system could not only bring in sufficient revenue but enough of a surplus to allow substantial reductions in the level of taxation. On other occasions irritation at waste caused him to cut public spending on inessentials and to reduce the number of persons in state employment. To do this was to attempt reversing the trend of three-quarters of a century or more. In Britain, however, reform can hardly have begun before fresh military problems fell upon the unhappy diocese.

At the beginning of 360 Julian was wintering at Paris when he was informed that the Scots and the Picts had broken an agreement and were plundering lands close to the frontier. We do not know what this agreement was, but it may have been part of arrangements made by Constans in 343. This

---

[1] Ammianus, XX. i. 1: *provincias praeteritarum cladium congerie fessas*—though it is not clear if this includes *all* the British provinces.

was the final blow on top of the 'past calamities' and was spreading great alarm among the British provinces. Julian decided against emulating Constans by a personal visit, considering the problems facing him in his Continental provinces too menacing and in particular expecting that the Alamanni, understood to be in a state of ferment, would attack again. He therefore sent his *magister militum,* Lupicinus, with four units of the field army—the *Heruli,* the *Batavi,* and two *numeri Moesiacorum.* It is interesting that this is an officer of much higher rank than the *comes* Theodosius whom Valentinian was to send to Britain to tackle the great *barbarica conspiratio* of 367. It suggests a very serious situation in the island in 360. Nevertheless Julian also had immediate problems with his senior staff in Gaul which may have affected his choice. What Lupicinus actually managed to do we do not know, except that he halted at London as it was now fully into winter. This, we are told, was in order the more quickly to move into battle when he had exact intelligence of how affairs stood. The facts that London was the centre of the road system and almost certainly of the main departments of the civil administration, whose agents must constantly have been bringing in reports from all over the diocese, were doubtless major factors in this decision. In the event, there can have been not much time before imperial politics again took a hand in changing the immediate priorities.

During the same winter Constantius, uneasy at Julian's successes and popularity, sent orders to Julian that he should detach for duty with the emperor four of his best units, the pick of the men in his two Guards regiments and a further 300 from each of his other units. Two of the élite units specifically mentioned in this list are the Heruli and Batavi, who were currently with Lupicinus in Britain. Perhaps Julian or his staff had received advance intelligence of Constantius' demands and deliberately chosen them for service across the Channel. At any rate, the reaction of Julian's troops was unequivocal: they proclaimed him Augustus. If the sources are right, Julian does not seem to have provoked this revolt or hurried to accept the elevation. His original inclination, in fact, seems to have been not to resist Constantius' order. However he did accede to his army's demand. There were some nasty moments. As we have noted, his relations with his senior officers were shaky.[1] The future emperor Valentinian, for example, son of that Gratian who had served in Britain as a *comes rei militaris*, was dismissed from his staff in Gaul on what appears to have been no real evidence. Now Lupicinus was across the Channel with some of the best units in the field army and the whole garrison of Britain, and Julian was not at all sure of his probable attitude when he heard the news. Like Domitian recalling Agricola,[2] Julian resorted to an elaborate subterfuge to get the *magister militum* back to Gaul before he discovered what had happened. This was successful and Lupicinus was duly arrested. At the same time Julian was still trying to come to an arrangement with Constantius. The latter refused any accommodation. In the end Julian decided he had to march east against his cousin, but before he reached Constantinople Constantius was dead, This time the Roman world had been spared another great civil war. The empire was once again united under one government and Julian was sole Augustus.

Julian was now able to come out into the open as a devoted pagan, set on restoring traditional Roman religious observances. These he not only permitted but enthusiastically encouraged. The pagan cults had indeed survived and between 360 and 380 enjoyed something of a real revival, not by any means due to Julian alone, of which the impressive new sacred complex of the healing god Nodens at Lydney on the Severn is one example. Not all Christian emperors, to be sure, made pagan observances impossible, even after Julian had demonstrated that an official revival was something that could actually happen rather than a romantic traditionalist dream. For more than two decades after the reign of Julian there was a degree of toleration for pagan cults. Under Valentinian I, for example, we find a most distinguished prefect of the City at Rome restoring some of the most hallowed images of the gods in the ancient Forum itself.[3] Indeed, the fact that Julian took his powerful prejudice against the Church further than just favouring pagans and the old religion may partly explain why he succeeded in producing little more than a temporary aberration in imperial

---

[1] See also Note, p. 373 below.
[2] Tacitus, *Agr.* xxxix: *nam etiam tum Agricola Britanniam obtinebat.*
[3] *ILS* 4003 (AD 367–8).

policy. He not only abolished the penalties on pagan worship but also extended religious toleration to Christian heretics, abandoning the position established by Constantine that it was an imperial duty to promote unity in the Church. Indeed he seems to have enjoyed the spectacle of Christians in bitter disarray. He went even further, not only cancelling the extensive privileges that had been granted to churchmen but also requiring the return of temple property that had fallen into other hands under Constantine and his Christian successors. It is perhaps not surprising that his pagan revival did not generally outlive his early death, despite the survival of pagan practices in relatively unchristianized areas like Britain and the strength of pagan sentiment among the senatorial class. The redistribution of wealth and the granting of privileges had by now been a fact for fifty years. If I may return to my earlier analogy, to reverse this is about as likely to have been successful as to demand the return of the possessions of the monasteries at the end of the reign of Elizabeth I.

Julian took his tendency to draw inspiration from the past to a point that led him to his death. His rule as sole emperor lasted only three years. His campaigns in Germany had demonstrated that it was still possible to use active and aggressive campaigning in the field and beyond the frontier to beat back the barbarians, rather than a policy of ever more elaborate static fortification to resist barbarian attack. Arrived in the east and now in supreme power, Julian resolved on a great campaign to settle the problem of the Persians and other neighbours threatening the eastern frontier. He had the illustrious example of Trajan, if not Alexander. This had been a recurrent dream of ambitious Roman generals for centuries, from Crassus, Julius Caesar, and Mark Antony to Trajan himself, Caracalla, and others. The Roman dream was only partially fulfilled, the conquests made never long-lasting and the campaigns, if actually started, sometimes ending in terrible disasters. This is not likely to have made the spur to later ambitions any the less. At the opposite end of the Roman world we have seen how the conquest of Britain exercised the same sort of fascination over the Roman mind. One emperor had set his face against these traditional ambitions and he applied the same policy in both areas. That was

Hadrian, who had promptly abandoned Trajan's conquests in the east and made it quite clear in Britain with the Wall that he did not envisage that there would ever be permanent military occupation in Scotland. His views, as we saw, were not acceptable to subsequent Roman opinion. Julian was in line with Roman tradition in launching a major invasion of Persia and we may be sure that, being the person he was, he was fully aware of it. As with so many of his predecessors his eastern ambitions were cut short by his own death, and like some of the most distinguished of them this occurred after he had proved the seriousness of his intentions by commencing his campaign. We do not need to judge whether he was right, either from our own very different perspectives or in the terms in which Romans habitually thought.

The fascination which the idea of conquest in the east exercised on Roman minds cannot entirely be divorced from the fact that ever since the Republic the eastern part of the Roman world had both been regarded as the largest source of revenue and also had a much higher density of cultivated and rich urban culture, which was true civilization in Graeco-Roman eyes. Like the west, the eastern part of the Roman world had suffered heavily from invasions in the third century, not only from the new Sassanian empire and some dissident part-Roman regimes on the borders but also from completely unhellenized barbarians such as the Goths, who raided not only the frontier provinces of the Danube, but also deep into Asia Minor and Greece. Nevertheless the eastern provinces still held a high position in Roman esteem, including the intellectual world, despite the fact that even Athens had been temporarily occupied by the barbarian Heruli in 267. The flourishing intellectual tradition of the Greek-speaking provinces is an essential element in the doctrinal debates in the Christian Church in the fourth century. These were at their most intense, bitter, and often violent in the eastern provinces and occupied much of the attention of the emperors.

The domination of Roman attention by eastern affairs had become of greater importance to the balance of the empire when Constantine the Great founded Constantinople in 324 and lavished resources and attention upon it on an enormous scale. From the beginning it was different from previous imperial foundations, however large and splendid, because it included privileges parallel to those of the City of Rome itself. To us one of the more extraordinary is that Constantinople was provided with a free corn-dole (like Rome), in this case for 80,000 people. This certainly ensured a rapid build-up of the urban population: it also created a second publicly subsidized metropolitan mob which became of great political importance. It must have made those senatorial families whom Constantine induced to emigrate from Rome feel quite at home.

There can be no doubt what Constantine was doing, but in formal terms the status of the new city relied in his day on his personal *auctoritas* and the presence of the imperial court. It was not yet the undisputed hub of the empire. Indeed the reappearance of multiple Augusti and separate imperial courts after Constantine's death ought to have checked its climb to pre-eminence. The seat of the senate and the ancient apparatus of the Roman state remained at Rome. However, it is in the period we are now considering, the middle of the fourth century, that two crucial developments in the status of Constantinople were instituted, both by Constantius II. To understand them we have to remember again that the City of Rome, and in particular the senatorial element, was still substantially pagan. From the beginning Constantinople had been by design overwhelmingly Christian. In 340 Constantius formalized the establishment of a parallel senate at Constantinople, with the accompanying apparatus of traditional magistracies, and arranged that henceforth one of each pair of consuls should normally be inaugurated there. In 359 he introduced a prefect of the City for the eastern capital with a full City administration. This is highly significant in its fourth-century context, for the office of *praefectus urbi* was becoming of first importance and was held in the greatest respect in the City of Rome.

Three points of major importance for the whole empire need to be made. Firstly there was now a full constitutional apparatus for the Roman state established at Constantinople in parallel to that in the west; secondly it was entirely Roman in form but, unlike that seated at Rome, purely Christian; and thirdly, again entirely unlike the west, this senate, City prefecture, and the Roman nobility whose life they dominated, were *located in the same city and alongside the imperial court and the imperial administration*. The prerequisites for a permanent shift in the centre of gravity of the Roman empire from west to east were now complete. Further, the main structures for running two separate empires were now on a permanent footing, unlike the *ad hoc* arrangements made by imperial colleagues many times in the past. The differences between the eastern and western situations meant potentially very different political development; and the prestige of Constantine the Great and his Christian foundation provided an impetus for the eastern structure (perhaps at first sight so artificial as to be unlikely to survive) that gave it a probability of separate development and a good chance of separate survival, whatever happened in the west. Thus, by the time Constantius II was dead in 360, the view from Britain of the larger Roman world had fundamentally changed, whether or not people noticed its full significance at the time.

There were, however, changes of a more detailed kind that doubtless were noticed. New developments in the organization of the Roman army mark another stage in the fourth-century evolution of its structure we have previously followed. We have already noted how the military *comitatus,* originally comparatively small, had by now evolved into several quite large separate field armies serving separate emperors. Some of these no longer normally served their emperor as his own mobile force in attendance wherever he might be but were becoming regional field armies. This was now marked by a formal distinction between those élite *comitatenses* who formed part of the force actually attendant on the emperor and those that were regionally based. The former are first recorded with the new title of *palatini* in AD 365, two years after Julian's death, and it seems reasonably certain that their creation was part of army reforms carried out by the new senior emperor, Valentinian I. Valentinian had stationed himself in the west and sent his brother Valens to govern the east. He seems quite deliberately to have made a more formal division of the army between east and west by subdividing a large number of the units in the mobile *comitatus*, naming the sections that he kept with him 'seniors' (*seniores*) and those allocated to Valens 'juniors' (*iuniores*). Further regiments of *auxilia* were also raised and all in this category included in the 'palatine' forces. Those *magistri militum* who commanded the *palatini* received a change of title parallel to that already noted for the praetorian prefects, becoming *magistri praesentales* or *in praesenti*, recognizing that their service was in the imperial presence.

Also from 365, we find another new title in the army— *pseudocomitatenses*, literally 'false' *comitatenses*. These seem to be regular units drawn from the frontier garrisons, *limitanei*, who had been transferred to the field-army but not upgraded. Somebody had probably realized that the more the size of the field forces was increased by transfer from the static garrisons the greater the total expenditure on military salaries and allowances, even though it was without any increase in the total number of soldiers, if units so transferred were to be given the higher pay and privileges accorded to the *comitatenses*. In later sources one also finds *comitatenses* transferred into the palatine armies retaining their former status. Conversely, one can find palatine units in course of time stationed in the regions but still entitled palatine: clearly it was felt impossible to downgrade troops when military convenience dictated their redeployment away from the most prestigious postings. Whatever their actual job, the personal grade of a unit and presumably of its individual soldiers had to be maintained. There was doubtless no point in provoking a mutiny: one may suspect that soldiers could easily feel aggrieved by apparent demotion but be mollified by retaining status and a formal, if fictional, appearance of the situation being merely temporary. Sometimes detachment from the main field armies clearly was still temporary, as it had regularly been in the past. The field units that Julian sent to Britain in 360 with Lupicinus could be regarded as an expeditionary force detached by the Caesar resident in Gaul, under the direct command of a *magister militum*.

In discussing the army reforms of Valentinian we have moved of necessity a little ahead of our narrative. Renewed mention of the expedition of Lupicinus should lead us to reflect on how critical a moment this was in the history of Roman Britain, indeed to look both forward in time and backward. What, one wonders, might have been the effect if politics and imminent civil war had not forced the almost immediate recall of Lupicinus. We have already noted that there is evidence for very low morale in Britain at that time and suggested that it may at least date back to the events surrounding the fall of Magnentius. But now that we have followed the narrative of the fourth century through to this point, we may be able to take a broader view in assessing the situation facing Julian. There is, as we have noted, some reason to think that the army stationed in Britain had been unable to cope with barbarian harassment since the time of whatever emergency it was that brought Constans over in winter in 343. Yet, with hindsight, we may be able to go even further, and suggest that the army and the diocese had been in a poor way more or less continuously since the forces of the north-western empire had been defeated at Aquileia in 340. One cannot help suspecting that AD 340 marks the true beginning of Britain's troubles. A strong Britain, with its reserves of military supplies and troops, must have seemed of major importance to Julian, both in his task of restoring the north-western frontier of the empire and in view of his own extremely precarious position, mistrusted by the emperor. Julian could not afford either a weak Britain or one which, neglected, might produce an usurper to stab him in the back. The orders carried with him to Britain by Lupicinus were not, I suspect, just to do with a sudden crisis but the combined effect of fresh barbarian troubles and twenty years of military and civil decline. Julian's intention, one may reasonably conjecture, was not merely to win a quick victory over the current batch of intruders but to set in train a more thorough restoration of the diocese. Had this indeed happened now, rather than a decade later after the great barbarian invasion of 367, it is not only obvious that the restoration would have been much easier and probably more complete but more than possible that the defences and population of Britain would have been in much better state to resist that onslaught.

In the event, of course, the exigencies of imperial politics forced the recall of Lupicinus. Julian's survival was at stake in the immediate present, and considerations of a longer-term nature would have to wait. Certainly, for Britain, if Lupicinus' force did achieve anything, it did not prevent the barbarians continuing to simmer ominously. For AD 364, the year after Julian's death on the Persian expedition, Ammianus paints a dramatic picture of the empire assaulted by barbarians from all sides: 'the most savage tribes being aroused and each bursting through the frontier nearest to it.'[1] Britain, we are told, was constantly being harassed by 'Picts, Saxons, Scots and Atacotti'. Raids, it would seem, were coming from Scotland, Ireland, and across the North Sea from north Holland and Germany. In 360 itself the Scotti had apparently been operating in the north of Roman Britain, perhaps attacking by sea via south-west Scotland. The origins of the Atocotti are unknown: Professor Frere points to a probable origin either in Ireland like the Scots or in the Western Isles and refers to their cannibalism as seen by St. Jerome in Gaul in this same period.[2] We are left without any clear impression of where the attacks hit Britain at this time or how deeply they penetrated.

Roman response to these attacks is likely to have been minimal, since considerable confusion had been caused by the death of Julian. This abruptly brought to an end the House of Constantine (and therefore any obvious candidature for the succession) and reopened the religious question. The fact that there was not another vast internal upheaval is perhaps to be explained by the perilous military situation: Julian's main army was in mid-campaign in the east and the barbarians were erupting on all sides. A young Christian officer from the Danube named Jovian was appointed Augustus, and managed to extricate the army from its immediate predicament, ceding substantial Roman territories in the process, but himself died at Constantinople in 364. With the issue again reopened, a quite extraordinary conference of the holders of the senior military and civil imperial posts chose Valentinian, who had previously served in Gaul under Julian. He had been another of the officers with whom Julian could not apparently get on. He was son of the elder Gratian, and despite his ability had been retired by Julian, to be recalled by the short-lived emperor Jovian. His strong Christian faith was probably an element in the antipathy he had set up in Julian, though we shall see that he himself made unfortunate judgements in his appointments. It was perhaps his service in Gaul and his father's record that

---

[1] Ammianus, XXVI. iv. 5.   [2] Frere, *Britannia*, 391.

made him choose to stay in the west, an interesting decision in view of the eastward trend of Roman interest. He was a great practical soldier, possibly the last to make a major contribution to the strengthening of the whole western defence system. As an administrator he was able and efficient, but as a judge of subordinates he was bad. As a devoted Christian he had objected to taking part in pagan sacrifices under Julian. Most unfortunately he accompanied this with strong prejudices against traditional education and the upper classes, even if he tried to help the lower who were certainly in need of imperial favour.

Valentinian's own knowledge of Gaul under Julian must have made him keenly aware of problems and current priorities on the western frontiers. In fact he spent the next ten years largely in fighting the Alamanni on the Rhine, mostly based on Trier, which was once more a long-term imperial residence. Being at Trier, still capital of the Gallic prefecture and seat of the most senior departments responsible for the administration of Britain, the emperor must have had constantly the most up-to-date intelligence of affairs in Britain that was then available. One may assume therefore that during this period Britain had such military attention as was possible, but that it had to be seen in the greater context of a constant struggle along the Rhine frontier, not to mention threats elsewhere. Unfortunately this conscientious attention may have been counterbalanced for Valentinian's subjects by his habit of promoting brutal and uncivilized men to high office, despite his own quick intelligence and literary tastes. For some members of the upper classes, already faced with sudden reversion from pagan to Christian rule, the outlook must have been unpleasing, not to say bleak. Under such circumstances, the preservation of firm imperial rule did not necessarily look as attractive a prospect as we might now with hindsight imagine. They were not to know the chaos that was to come with the slow disintegration of the emperors' rule in the west. Indeed, during the fifth and even in the sixth century rule by the imperial government did not seem better than the alternatives to all Romans: as late as the middle of the sixth century, for example, there were great Roman landowners in Italy to whom the reappearance of central Roman authority in the shape of Justinian's armies

was anything but welcome in exchange for their recent Ostrogothic kings. Further down the social scale, where the balance
of advantage lay is much less clear.

We ought not to leave the mid-fourth century without
touching on a recent hypothesis which argues that by AD 350
the towns of Britain had declined to no more than villages
and that they did not recover.[1] This theory has at the time of
writing been too little tested yet to discuss at length, but if
true could have so important a bearing on the idea of a
general collapse of Britain in the middle of the fourth century
that it demands mention here and a few words of discussion.
We are immediately faced with major problems. The first is
whether it is possible to demonstrate decisively that the towns
had lost all distinctively 'urban' function, the second whether
what might be true of 350 or thereabouts is necessarily true
of the sites' subsequent history within the Roman period or
immediately thereafter.

On the first point, much turns on how we view 'urban' life
in the context of the fourth-century western provinces. There
is a little evidence suggesting that Constantine appropriated
city revenues as well as temple treasures and endowments.
Indeed, the sequestration of pagan religious funds will automatically have reduced to a very considerable degree a major
element in the public life of the cities, since secular and
religious ceremonial and the activities of the colleges of priests
had been largely interlocked in the world of local government. But probably quite as important in depressing the
position of the cities as centres of a vigorous public life was
the vast increase in imperial administration, when both public
business and private interest must have been deflected away
from the old institutions towards the new centres of government and influence created by the multiplication of provinces and administrative departments. Nor can we be sure
that these new centres of power were as static as the old
civitas capitals. Fourth-century governors, though they were
no longer the great commanders-in-chief of the Early Empire,
nevertheless were often men of considerable social standing.
In the new, small civil provinces, one may assume they
naturally formed a centre for the administrative and social

---

[1] See detailed Note, p. 411 below.

world that must have detracted from the importance of the old city councils in the eyes of the local upper classes, and they may also be presumed to have spent a proportion of their time travelling about their provinces with their staffs, unlike the static council of the old-style local government. There will now have been less incentive for the provincial upper classes to make their mark by showy benefactions to their local city, except out of sentiment or ancestral piety. Moreover it was precisely the municipal aristocracy that was worst hit by the exactions of fourth-century government. Greater men, whether senators or imperial officers, more easily avoided the burdens or profited from the new order.

There does indeed seem to be much less archaeological evidence for expenditure on public buildings such as the forum or basilica in the fourth century. Financial stringency is suggested by lower standards in the municipal services, illustrated by the blocking of street-gutters or the accumulation of rubbish on such sites as the theatre at Verulamium. However, as we know from the present day, this by no means proves that the towns were less populous or active than before, only that their appearance, standards, and perhaps organization and functions were changing. We should certainly not be surprised when we find, as at Carmarthen in west Wales,[1] large residential development continuing, since more and more property generally in the empire was falling into the hands of institutions and individuals exempt from municipal obligations—the state itself in various guises, the Church and individual clergy, civilians of senatorial status, and members of the armed forces. All these classes were expanding as the curial class contracted—a situation emperor after emperor in the fourth century deplored but which was fostered by their own policies. Businesses in the town may also have tended to fall into the same hands. There was certainly a decline in long-distance bulk trade under the Late Empire and we shall later observe how Britain became increasingly self-sufficient in many products. This is likely to have affected the prosperity of the great emporia more than the smaller towns. However while there was factory-based industry and factory products to be distributed, trading

[1] *Brit.* 1 (1970), 270.

centres were still required and the towns provided them. Moreover the landed estates still required markets nearby so long as there were manufactured goods to be bought and a population able to buy their surpluses. While there was a money economy, the economic necessity for urban centres remained. Without wishing to quibble about words, these are urban, not village functions, even if all important official transactions may now have taken place elsewhere. This is very different from the Mediterranean urban role that may once have been envisaged for the towns of Britain, even if rarely achieved in any real sense. One may certainly expect future research to show much more variation from town to town than in the earlier periods, when illusions of civic independence and dignity were perhaps more universal. Yet somewhere in the mid-fourth century imperial authority thought it worthwhile allowing major expenditure on the re-fortification of British towns at large—and I shall indicate below that I think this was later rather than earlier in the period. Someone, too, was able to raise the resources and carry this work out, and it looks to have been done locally rather than centrally. By the 360s, I suspect, the towns were by and large much poorer, politically inactive, and socially weak, but by no means dead. If they were temporarily in disarray, I believe it was as part of the general malaise of Britain, not something peculiar to themselves. To go further on present evidence is to risk creating yet another myth in the world of Romano-British studies.

NOTE

Julian and his senior officers. Julian seems to have had a lack of rapport with a number of his senior officers, some of whom, like his praetorian prefect Florentius, were entirely Constantius' men. It is possible that Julian sent Lupicinus to Britain to get him out of the way. He was a solid Christian, and Julian's own account of the affair written the following year (*Letter to the Athenians*, 281–2) alleges that Lupicinus had orders from Constantius to act with other officers in arresting him for attempted usurpation.

The occurrence of the name Eutherius as a graffito on the Mildenhall Treasure, now in the British Museum, is insufficient evidence to link that great hoard of plate with the Eutherius who was grand chamberlain (*praepositus sacri cubiculi*) to Julian. We do not therefore need to postulate any explanation in the context of the expedition of Lupicinus for its presence in Britain (cf. K.S. Painter, *The Mildenhall Treasure*, British Museum (1977), 22 f.)

14

THE RESTORATION OF ORDER

THE state of Britain continued to deteriorate in the early part of Valentinian's reign, till he was at last able to give the province some of the attention that had been concentrated on the Rhine. Whether he had intended to turn to Britain at some stage we do not know: in the event it was forced on him by a spectacular and apparently unforeseen climax in the harassment by barbarians which had been developing for a long time. Struck by a serious illness in 367, Valentinian discovered that various names of possible successors to himself were being bandied about. His answer was to appoint his eight-year-old son Gratian as co-emperor. The sequel suggests that some very shrewd and well-informed minds were at work among the enemies of Rome. We should not ignore the fact that in recent times a substantial number of Germans had been appointed alongside Romans at the top levels in the military hierarchy. This was continuing to be the practice. Thus in the middle of the fourth century a profound knowledge of Roman military affairs must have built up in professional Germanic military circles, in a class of men not all of whom may have taken service under the empire. It is not necessary to postulate treachery to account for a capacity among the barbarians for estimating accurately the effects on military readiness of political events within the empire, though this was indeed suspected in 354.[1] As long ago as the first century some of the most dangerous enemies of Rome had been men like Arminius and Civilis who had previously commanded auxiliary units in the Roman army. The situation in the fourth, however, was of a different order of magnitude: a succession of Germans rising to appointments as *comes rei militaris* and even *magister militum*, men at army commander level with an intimate knowledge of the Roman forces, men who handled the most confidential information on a routine basis and, in some cases, served close

---

[1] Ammianus, XIV. x. 8.

to the emperor, observing how he dealt with the broad strategic issues and what affected his judgement. This adds up to a body of experience of tremendous potential importance to the enemies of Rome. Professor A.H.M. Jones argued that there is very little evidence this was a serious threat to Roman security, and quite rightly pointed to the fact that the ancient Germans were so fragmented into hostile tribes that German patriotism is most unlikely to have played a part. Indeed he also demonstrated that such German officers normally became completely Romanized, a process that had been going on since the beginning of the Empire. These were the Prince Alberts or von Brauns of the Roman world. Nevertheless German soldiers did sometimes visit their homes and leakages of information must have occurred, whether inadvertently or under pressure on themselves or their families.[1] There can have been few remaining mysteries about how the empire and its armies worked. It is not therefore improbable that, whatever the means by which they received intelligence of the emperor's difficulties in 367, the barbarians should have known both of them and their significance. What is impressive is the remarkable way in which they exploited the opportunity.

Valentinian was on the road back to Trier from Autun, when news was brought to him of disaster in Britain. The various barbarian peoples that had been harassing both Britain and the Channel coast of Gaul had suddenly combined to organize a concerted attack, the Picts (described as divided into two main peoples, the Dicalydonae and the Verturiones), the Attacotti and the Scots assaulting Britain, the Franks and Saxons descending on the coast of Gaul.[2] Such a 'barbarian

---

[1] A case of careless talk by such a visitor home is recorded by Ammianus (XXXI. x. 3) for the year 377. Professor Malcom Todd has drawn our attention to the fact that material from graves that may possibly be associated with Germanic officers retiring to their home areas tends, interestingly enough, to occur predominantly in the Anglo-Saxon areas outside the empire rather than the Frankish (Todd, in R. Reece (ed.), *Burial in the Roman World*, CBA Research Report 22 (1977), 42 f.). There had also, of course, always been deserters from the Roman armies, who took refuge outside the empire, not to mention prisoners taken by the barbarians.

[2] I have accepted the interpretation 'coasts of Gaul' for *Gallicanos tractus* in Ammianus, XXVII. viii. 5, rather than assuming that it must refer to the parts of Britain 'facing Gaul.'

conspiracy'[1] was very rare. This was fortunate for the Romans, since it had always been extremely difficult for their defences to cope with simultaneous attacks. Diocletian's strengthening of the frontier garrisons and doubling of the size of the army and the development and elaboration of mobile field-armies were doubtless intended to mitigate the dangers of this situation. In origin the situation itself stemmed from Augustus' determination to keep the size of the armed forces to the minimum, stationing the bulk on the frontiers and relying upon the possibility of moving units from one frontier to another as pressures changed. However, since Diocletian's reforms there had been one damaging civil war after another to weaken his dispositions, not to mention frequent fighting on a large scale against external enemies in many of the frontier areas. Barbarians acting in concert were a very alarming prospect. As we have surmised, the events of 367 imply at least one very capable and well-informed military mind on the barbarian side. But they imply more: a leader with the personal reputation and persuasiveness to weld such disparate peoples into a league to take common action, if only for one operation, and, perhaps even more remarkable, to keep news of such a plan secret from the Romans. We are moving into the age when great figures such as Alaric begin to appear on the barbarian side in the west, men who treat with Roman emperors at their own level. This had long been the case in the east with such figures as the Persian King of Kings. In the west, as we have noted, inside the empire Germans were already appearing as generals in the Roman armies on equal terms with Romans. The day was not far off when they would hold certain of the great offices of the Roman state. Their position could indeed be equivocal: in the next century such figures as Theodoric could at one time hold high rank under the Empire, at another be carving out vast kingdoms to be dominated by their barbarian followers.

In 367, however, while these elements were already present

---

[1] *Barbarica conspiratio* (Ammianus, XXVII. viii which with Ammianus, XXVIII. iii, contains the account of the war of 367–8 and the subsequent reconstruction). I have assumed that Ammianus' account is reliable, and that he neither misunderstood a coincidental set of raids by unconnected barbarian tribes nor deliberately fabricated a conspiracy to excuse the disaster and magnify the scale of the subsequent Roman successes.

in the Roman world, the attack was still unequivocally from without. Not that there had been no element of treason within the Roman system: the *areani* had gradually abandoned their duty. Ammianus tells us this in words that suggest a process that had been going on for some time, adding strength to our picture of deepening disorder in Britain.[1] Under promises of booty to come they had treacherously allied themselves in secret with the barbarians. Just what they did, we do not know. It may well have been passing information to the enemy and giving misleading intelligence to the Romans. One fact particularly supports this possibility: Valentinian heard that his *dux* Fullofaudes had been put out of action 'by the wiles of the enemy', either killed or pinned down somewhere.[2]

This was very serious. Fullofaudes was probably holding the post later attested as *dux Britanniarum,* in command of the bulk of the static garrisons of Britain. We may guess that this defeat occurred somewhere in the region of the northern frontier. None of the outpost forts in front of the Wall seems to have been held after this date and, though these may already have been abandoned, it may be that part of the treachery of the *areani* was to betray any units that were still beyond the Wall in 367, in other words in the region where the *areani* seem most likely to have operated. Signs of later reconstruction on the Wall itself may support the same hypothesis, possibly being repair of damage caused by enemy action.[3] Perhaps this should be taken with the subsequent abolition of the *areani* by Valentinian's victorious general Theodosius[4] as evidence that the mid-fourth century frontier arrangements had proved disastrously inadequate.

However, before we can consider how Theodosius recovered

---

[1] Ammianus, XXVIII. iii. 8: *paulatim prolapsos in vitia a stationibus suis removit.* Constans' business with them in 343 could have been an earlier attempt to improve their performance.

[2] The wording is ambiguous: *hostilibus insidiis circumventum* (Ammianus, XXVII. viii. 1.)

[3] At the fort of Birdoswald on the Wall a stratified coin of Valentinian I places the restoration as certainly after the war of 367. Comparison of pottery and types of building-construction have linked with this phase repairs noted in other installations on the Wall. The story hangs together, but this is the type of archaeological deduction that is particularly subject to revision, and may need reassessing site by site.

[4] Ammianus, XXVIII. iii. 8 (above).

and reconstructed Britain, there are further details of 367. The elimination of the *dux* was only part of the calamity reported to Valentinian. Another of his generals had certainly been killed, this time an officer bearing the rank of *comes*. This commander, Nectaridus, is described as '*comes* of the maritime region'.[1] While it is likely that his command included the 'Saxon Shore' forts—in other words the forts of the east and south coasts of Britain later listed in the *Notitia* under the officer then known as the *comes litoris Saxonici*— it is perfectly possible that he also commanded the forts on the west coast, notably Cardiff and Lancaster. The fact that the subsequent restoration of order included naval warfare against Saxons reminds us that the primary role of the Saxons and Franks in this enterprise was to attack Gaul rather than Britain.[2] The war was to be carried on by both sea and land. This may cause us to recall that Carausius' original command eighty years earlier against the same peoples had apparently been based in Gaul, not Britain. Nectaridus' authority in 367 may well have included both sides of the Channel and its scope been large enough to require an officer of the rank of *comes*, as understood in Valentinian's day.[3] The command may still have been an *ad hoc* one. It is possible, in fact, that Nectaridus had been appointed to lead a task force specifically to clear out pirates, either by Valentinian or even by Julian at some time after the hasty recall of Lupicinus in the winter of 360–1, perhaps in response to the raids recorded for 364. Whatever the precise reason for his appointment, however, the loss of an officer of this rank would have been a most serious blow to imperial prestige.

After their initial successes the barbarians expected no further serious resistance in Britain. They split up into small bands, collected booty as they went, and destroyed whatever they liked. Whatever central command existed among them could probably not have held them together beyond this point, even if it had wished to do so. Indeed it was for the moment hardly necessary. Ammianus reports desertions

---

[1] *Comes maritimi tractus.*

[2] *Saxo consumptus bellis navalibus: Pan. Theod. Aug. (Pan. Lat. Vet.* II (XII). v. 2).

[3] Even if this rank has become of lesser significance by the time it appears in the *Notitia.*

from the Roman forces and emphasizes that when Theodosius recovered Britain for Valentinian he had to restore forts and provide frontier garrisons. The army in Britain was in a demoralized state and its installations in a serious condition. From the fact that Valentinian also had to restore at least some of the cities of Britain (which Ammianus mentions in the same phrase as the forts), we may presume that even town walls and any military garrisons within them had not everywhere sufficed to keep the barbarians out. In the countryside Ammianus paints the picture of a fearful mess, with bands of raiders wandering about unchecked, taking prisoners and loot where they fancied, and destroying and killing at will. In unprotected rural areas and on the roads everywhere it is likely that deserters from the Roman army were a real menace as well. The number of armed men on the loose was swelled by soldiers who, we are told, claimed to be on long leave, a story that in the circumstances must have been difficult to check even if anyone cared to enquire too closely. For the civilian population there was doubtless little to choose between them all.[1]

This whole episode is one of the very few instances in the history of Roman Britain where we can set against the archaeological record clear written evidence of major destruction due to invasion by enemies from without. We are doubly fortunate that in Ammianus Marcellinus we have a fine historian who was not only contemporary with the period of which he was writing but was himself an army officer with a creditable record who had actually served in Gaul under one of Valentinian's prominent supporters. On the archaeological side, widespread evidence of change has been noted in forts along the Wall and in the Pennine area to the south.[2] As for the civil settlements outside the northern frontier forts (except for Piercebridge, in the south of the frontier region

---

[1] For the depredations of Roman troops in frontier provinces being accepted as a normal feature of life in the later Roman Empire see P. Salway, *Classical Review*, n.s. 19 (1969), 3, 273 f. discussing *OGIS* 519. The reference to leave also reminds us that in normal times it was a rare privilege in the Roman army and required elaborate authorization. Venial officers were sometimes known to sell leave-passes to soldiers. Indeed the troops themselves sometimes had plenty to complain of in the imperial system: see A.H.M. Jones, *LRE*, 646, for examples from the later fourth century of scandalous neglect of the men by corrupt officers.

[2] It is however extremely difficult to date these repairs: the problem is summarized by Breeze and Dobson, *Hadrian's Wall*, 221 ff.

and otherwise a special case), where these have produced any evidence there is little sign of reoccupation after this war.[1] In the walled town of Corbridge, lying just behind the Wall itself, there are signs of destruction at this time. In military establishments in the southern Pennines, other signs of reconstruction and change have been noted. Nevertheless a word of warning must be sounded. Professor Frere rightly put us on our guard against automatically assigning to the war of 367 any signs of destruction or rebuilding we may find on later fourth-century sites in Britain.[2] This needed saying when Professor Frere first said it in 1967 and still needs repeating now. Indeed, it can be taken a stage further in the light of the view I have taken of the years between 340 and the war of 367. An over-all decline in both the military and civil fields, coupled with sporadic but persistent attack, is likely to have left archaeological traces, partly caused by neglect and abandonment, partly by actual destruction, that have hitherto tended to be lumped together as the product of 367. Nevertheless, the testimony of Ammianus does put us in quite a different position for 367 than for the hypothetical barbarian invasions of 197 or 296. This time, we do actually know a major incursion took place and widespread chaos ensued.

Valentinian reacted to the news from Britain in 367 in much the same way as Julian in 360. He did not set sail himself, for as we saw earlier he already had a host of extremely pressing problems on his hands before reports of the defeats in Britain arrived. Moreover we know that the presence of Franks and Saxons on the coast of Gaul was believed by Ammianus to be part of the *barbarica conspiratio,* and it may have been deliberately designed to delay news from Britain as well as to tie down the emperor and his *comitatus* in Gaul, thus doubly hindering the dispatch of relief to Britain. Valentinian's first reaction was to send the commander of his guard, the *comes domesticorum* Severus, to see what could be done. Severus was almost immediately recalled and another officer, Jovinus, sent in his place. Finally

---

[1] Salway, *Frontier People,* 14 f. Nevertheless Chesterholm *vicus* is said now to show occupation after 367 and excavation elsewhere has been scanty.

[2] Frere, *Britannia,* 353.

Valentinian took the decision to dispatch a task force very similar to that Julian had sent under Lupicinus. He selected four first-class units from the field army, the Batavi, Heruli, Jovii, and Victores. Of these, the first two had actually served in Lupicinus' expedition. In command Valentinian placed Theodosius, the father of Theodosius the Great who was to reign as emperor from 379 to 395. At this time the elder Theodosius held the post of *comes rei militaris,* rather lower than Lupicinus' rank had been but at the same level as Valentinian's own father when he was in Britain.

Theodosius established himself first at Richborough, once the main base for the Claudian invasion and now a major fortress in the coastal system. As soon as his four units were assembled he advanced to London, eliminating bands of barbarians which he found scattered widely and laden down with captives, loot, and stolen herds. Ammianus tells us that he returned all but a small fraction of the booty to its rightful owners (in contrast—perhaps intended—to the alleged behaviour of Carausius), giving the balance to his troops as a reward. His unexpected arrival at London was met with scenes of great rejoicing from its inhabitants, who had been in despair. Theodosius entered the city like a Roman general enjoying the honours of victory at Rome. At London he proceeded to take measures to restore the army of Britain as a fighting force, by issuing a general pardon to those who had deserted and recalling to the colours those who had claimed to be on leave. He also put the administration back into action by arranging for an official named Civilis to take over as *vicarius*—it is not recorded what had happened to the previous *vicarius*, who had presumably been caught up in the events of 367. It is a very interesting rarity in the *Notitia* that the *vicarius* of Britain is shown with military insignia, indicating some command of troops, though of course we do not know how far back this situation goes.[1] Nevertheless Civilis

---

[1] It is perhaps worth remembering that the fort incorporated in the city of London is a great rarity in the empire—though Anthony King draws my attention to the interesting possibility that the headquarters of the *comes litoris Saxonici* might have been in London. There are plenty of reasons why the *vicarius* might have needed special powers in the late fourth century and the early fifth, particularly if the main military commands were in the north and on the coast, a long way from London. His exposed and remote island diocese was exceptional. Speculation on the subject is unpromising without any further evidence on which to base it.

had an unusually difficult job to do in his group of provinces. Theodosius also brought in a general named Dulcitius, to whom Ammianus, who should know, gives a mark of approval for military ability. Dulcitius was presumably intended to replace Fullofaudes and take command of the main garrison in Britain. A replacement for Nectaridus is not mentioned: it is possible that at least while Theodosius was in the island there was no need for a second *comes*. This may strengthen the argument for regarding Nectaridus' post as a special commission and not in fact the regular Saxon Shore appointment tnat is recorded later.

Theodosius himself took the field. With energy, intelligence, and a fine army (as Ammianus tells us) he took every opportunity to trap what raiders he could and to put to flight the varied barbarian peoples who had become confident and careless with success. These operations included the naval warfare against the Saxons to which I have already alluded.[1] In the latter context we may reasonably imagine Theodosius directly exercising the command which had formerly been in the hands of Nectaridus. This warfare should have relieved the pressure on the northern coast of Gaul as well as on Britain. This harrying of Gaul was, as we have seen, a significant part of the total *barbarica conspiratio* and perhaps nearer to threatening imperial security than the assault on Britain, since it was not only closer to the administrative nerve-centre but also in a region where peasant revolt had historically been a serious problem.

There is some debate on how long an interval there was between the first news of the *barbarica conspiratio* reaching Valentinian and Theodosius' clearing the invaders out of the Roman part of Britain. Nevertheless it seems that by 369 Theodosius was able to get under way the general programme of restoration, apparently on a large scale, to put the diocese back on its feet. Even discounting a strong element of panegyric in the account, the military achievement was a great one. This was not just success in the field but ranged from the initial and accurate analysis of the situation, through the

---

[1] The poet Claudian, writing in the period 396–8, also refers to Theodosius' naval exploits, though one hesitates to push the interpretation of his exact words too far: he was attempting a literary conceit.

rebuilding of a demoralized and disintegrating army into part
of a force that went on to victory, and was rounded off by
the replanning and physical reconstruction of the defensive
system of Britain.

We have already referred to the signs of reconstruction,
particularly in the forts of the north, since it was necessary
to see if that provided any evidence for destruction during
the barbarian attack in 367. We saw that the evidence is thin.
We cannot ignore Ammianus' statement that Theodosius
restored cities and forts 'which had suffered manifold harm'[1]
but it is easier to see the repair of forts and the 'protecting of
the borders with sentinels and frontier garrisons' as an over-all
programme of re-equipping and remanning than a physical reconstruction piece by piece of a system of fortifications that
had everywhere been razed to the ground. There is indeed
one small area where we have evidence for a brand-new series
of constructions, providing a new sort of sentinel. The north-
east coast of England was now provided with a set of well-
fortified watch-towers extending from Filey to Huntcliff and
possibly beyond. These may have been linked to the eastern
end of the Wall system and provided this flank with the sort
of warning system that had been available on the west in the
second century. In the early days of the Wall the need for a
coastal screen seems only to have been felt there, and was
probably aimed chiefly at preventing that flank of the Wall
being turned by enemies ferried across the shallow waters of
the Solway Firth from south-west Scotland. The western system, despite some Antonine refurbishing, seems to have gone
largely out of commission by the end of the second century.
In the fourth, however, evidence is beginning to accumulate
that certain of the forts and milefortlets were put back
into operation and a military presence maintained at some
points on the coast for a great part of the century.[2] In the
east, especially since the extension at an early date of the
Wall to Wallsend, attack by British tribes across the mouth of
the Tyne had presumably not been anticipated, though one
may presume that the river entrance itself was closely watched
in view of its importance for military shipping. Now, however, deep-water seaborne attack from outside Britain was a

---

[1] Ammianus, XXVIII. iii. 2.   [2] *Brit.* 8 (1977), 183.

reality of life, and the need to provide the command at York and the garrisons of the north with coastal warning-systems had clearly become apparent. Indeed, with raiders who were professional sea-pirates, it may have been Roman shipping itself that was the most vulnerable target, with all that implied in terms of disruption of military communications and supplies. These north-eastern signal stations may have come under a maritime command. They do not appear anywhere in the *Notitia* and the only relevant inscription is very difficult to interpret.[1] They may however equally well have been directly under the land forces probably still centred at York, or possibly controlled from the fort at Malton.

Theodosius' attention to naval defence may be reflected in two pieces of evidence relating to the western coasts of Britain. A dedication at the important temple at Lydney on the Severn made soon after 367 by T. Flavius Senilis, who describes himself as *praefectus reliquationis*, may indicate a navy-yard somewhere on the Bristol Channel and it is likely that the waterside fortifications at Holyhead and possibly Caernarvon as well should be attributed to this period. For fleets protecting the south and east coasts we have surprisingly little evidence. No naval units are recorded in the *Notitia* for the Saxon Shore forts. Professor Frere has suggested that the transfer of a naval contingent from Pevensey to Paris which may have taken place in 368 could have been part of a wider reorganization of the southern coasts by Theodosius. The establishment of a new base at Bitterne near Southampton may indicate a change to coastal defence by land-based forces defending river-mouths and anchorages.[2] The attacks on the Gallic coast and the need to control the crossing may have suggested that a quicker response could be made by the imperial command in Gaul if the entire Channel fleet was concentrated on the French side.

The Theodosian reconstruction is a good point at which to

---

[1] *RIB* 721 (Ravenscar): it appears to read 'Justinianus *praepositus*; Vindicianus *magister* built this tower and fort from the ground up.' Among other uncertainties it is quite unclear whether this refers to the original construction or a much later major rebuilding: see the notes in *RIB* for the possibility that this is the Justinian who served under Constantine III (Zosimus, VI. ii. 2).

[2] The coin dating which gives a *terminus post quem* of Constans for Bitterne according to S. Johnson (*The Roman Forts of the Saxon Shore*, 142) has been corrected to Valens by Professor Cunliffe (*Antiquity*, 51 (1977), 73).

consider some general features of the Late Roman military scene in Britain, since they are of such wide-ranging significance that our view of them must colour our general picture of late fourth-century Britain. All have given rise to much literature and debate, some of it heated. This includes Roman relations with the tribes north of the Wall, the nature of the garrisoning of the Wall itself and—a matter that takes us away from the Wall to the island as a whole—the evidence for the widespread presence of Germanic 'mercenaries'.

On the northern frontier it was long thought that the presence of Roman names in the earliest generations of the well-known genealogies of the kings of the four kingdoms that were forming beyond the frontier in Scotland indicated that the northern tribes were now friendly to Rome. Indeed, the occurrence of the Celtic epithet *pesrut* (red cloak) had suggested a transfer of imperial authority, perhaps to semi-autonomous *praefecti*. Such a creation of client kingdoms was, of course, one of the oldest traditions of Roman frontier policy, and would accord with Theodosius' abolition of the *areani*, whom the new arrangements would suitably replace—indeed make superfluous. With this, we were asked to see Hadrian's Wall now occupied by a peasant militia, with the civil settlements (*vici*) in ruins and the soldiers' families now living for safety inside the forts.

This picture did present some difficulties. It was hard to understand why, if the neighbouring barbarians were now friendly, the civilians should need to abandon the civil settlements. In fact there is no unequivocal evidence for such a movement into the forts, nor is it certain that all the *vici* ceased occupation in 367. The notion of peasant militia in the empire (once indeed thought to stem from origins early in the first half of the third century) is now also fading. The very institution itself seems to belong primarily to the fifth-century imperial system, after the end of official Roman rule in Britain. The alterations in forts in the north once thought to reflect such an arrangement are themselves no longer regularly interpreted in this way.[1] Such evidence as there is points to the Wall being garrisoned with regular troops till the end of imperial administration in the early fifth century.

---

[1] See Breeze and Dobson, op. cit. 221 ff.

Moreover, doubt being thrown on the long-established view that there were now friendly relations with the northern British barbarians provides a reason why these garrisons were still needed. It has now been suggested that the adoption of Roman names in the northern tribes has nothing to do with political friendship but with the spread of Christianity.[1] It is certainly extremely odd that none of the characteristic east Yorkshire pottery of the period after the war of 367 seems to have been found in the region north of the Wall. The most obvious explanation is that there were no further peaceful communications between the northern barbarians and the provincials once the invaders had been driven out by Theodosius. Traprain Law, the old hill-fort capital of the Votadini of the Lowlands of Scotland, shows extensive quantities of ordinary Roman material from earlier periods. Now all it has to show is a great treasure of stolen Roman plate.

Where do the 'German mercenaries' fit into our picture of fourth-century Britain? This question brings us to a particularly interesting example of how theories can grow and then change. For a number of years the view has been developing that the presence of German 'mercenaries' is indicated by the fairly widely scattered occurrence in Britain of items of metalwork stylistically under strong German influence, identified as pieces of military uniform of Late Roman date, particularly belt-buckles and other strap-fittings.[2] These mercenaries, variously called by modern writers *laeti* or *foederati*, are assumed to be in Roman pay but essentially irregulars. The finds have a further interest, in that they occur chiefly in the Midlands or the south, often in cities or in rural contexts. Since these pieces were at first thought to be exclusively military, this led to the idea of barbarian troops being used to garrison the cities, and possibly some being employed to guard individual estates. The occurrence of coins as early as the period 330–53 with this type of material in burials in a city cemetery at Winchester even encouraged the idea of barbarians being associated with the hypothetical reorganization of British defences by Constans

---

[1] J.C. Mann, *Glasgow Archaeological Journal,* 3 (1974), 34 ff.
[2] S.C. Hawkes and G.C. Dunning, *Medieval Archaeology,* 5 (1961), 1 ff.; S.C. Hawkes, *Brit.* 5 (1974), 386 ff.

on his visit in 343 that we discussed earlier.[1] The 'mercenary' theory has been elaborated in two ways. German barbarians have been associated with the adding of catapult-towers to town walls, which some specialists as we saw attribute to Constans. The mercenaries have also been seen as part of a field-army, billeted in towns and even given allotments of parts of Roman estates. Indeed, we referred earlier to the possibility that city garrisons go back to Constantine the Great, and the practice of land-sharing certainly became established in the Germanic kingdoms that formed in the next two centuries in Roman Gaul.[2] This all adds up to a formidable picture and would if true suggest major changes in the way of life of Roman Britain.

There are, nevertheless, serious weaknesses in the argument. In the first place it is not certain that all these pieces of equipment were necessarily worn by soldiers. One is of course always uneasily aware of the dangers of assuming the presence of troops from the archaeological occurrence of stray pieces of equipment that may be 'army surplus'. But in this case there are further difficulties. We have already noted the adoption of military systems of grading and insignia in the new civil administration.[3] Another is the inherent difficulty of assuming nationality from style. Assemblages of finds from the Late Roman Rhineland give one the strongest impression that Germanic styles of ornamentation were very much in fashion, often made in Roman provincial workshops. It is often entirely uncertain whether they were first sold to barbarians or to Romans with 'ethnic' tastes. Indeed the ancestry of many of the latter was itself Germanic.

A further consideration has now emerged. It has recently been shown as highly probable that certain categories of uniform equipment of so-called 'Germanic' type formed part of the official issue to regular troops in the Late Empire, some very likely being made in the state ordnance factories of the Danubian provinces.[4] This is not of course in the least inconsistent with the fact that, as we have seen, there were many Germans serving in the regular Roman army alongside provincials and indeed rising with them to the highest ranks;

[1] Nothing certain is known about the purpose or outcome of this visit.
[2] See also note on *foederati*, p. 410 below.
[3] See also Note, p. 410 below.   [4] C.J. Simpson, *Brit.* 7 (1976), 192 ff.

but as has been pointed out recently, it really is most unlikely that such fourth-century regular soldiers wore different
uniforms according to their national origins.[1]

The history of the 'German mercenaries' theory is an instructive one. Once this metalwork had been recognized as a
distinctive and potentially significant group of material—in
itself a distinguished piece of archaeology—an hypothesis was
required to cover it. The theory that emerged was excellent
and imaginative, breaking new ground as many of the best
do. Now it seems an unnecessary one, since with further
work it has become clear that the data can be more easily
explained by a simpler hypothesis. This is the way archaeology progresses.[2]

If the idea of irregulars to explain this material is abandoned, do we on the other hand have to accept the alternative theory that has been advanced, the presence of regular
Roman troops in the cities and on the estates? As far as substantial garrisons are concerned this is a much more open
question. We have referred to Constantine and the cities and
we shall look at Theodosius' work in the towns of Britain
shortly. There is, for example, evidence for one (but perhaps only one) Late Roman soldier in the city of Wroxeter,
which has also produced a piece of the metalwork we have
been considering. It is perhaps reasonable to assume that
some of the objects were worn by soldiers and *some* of
those from basically civil sites were (with rather less certainty) deposited at the places where these soldiers were
serving. Yet the use of individual soldiers—and small detachments—on official business which was not strictly military
in character is a practice that goes back to the earliest days
of the Empire. It would be entirely unsafe to assume a new
role for the army on this evidence alone.

There is, however, another line of inquiry. The possible
implications of Ammianus' twice-repeated assertion that

---

[1] Ibid. 205. They are quite unlike the auxiliaries of the Early Empire, raised
as units from particular communities.

[2] The purpose of this argument is to indicate that this group of archaeological
data probably cannot tell us anything about the use or distribution of barbarian
mercenaries, if there were any in the fourth century. It does *not* disprove the idea
that bodies of barbarian troops in Roman pay were employed in Britain but only
indicates that this material does not necessarily have anything to do with them.

Theodosius restored cities as well as forts have recently been drawn out very effectively by Mr John Wacher.[1] He reminds us that by the fourth century all the cities and most of the smaller towns and substantial villages in Britain had been given linear defences.[2] Most of these were subsequently modified by the adding of external towers to the curtain wall.[3] Such dating evidence as there is makes it unlikely that these external bastions date before about 360.[4] It is, of course, still impossible to be sure all the modified walls represent a single programme, but Ammianus does at least give us one date at which a general restoration of towns is attested and Mr Wacher plumps for Theodosius as the probable instigator. However he points out that the design, frequency, and placing of these towers is very inconsistent, and comments that 'this very lack of consistency might point towards careless supervision over the task of strengthening defences, and to an indifferent understanding of the tactics involved'. This observation certainly makes one wonder how great a part the Roman army actually played in this programme, and reminds us again of the evidence from Godmanchester suggesting that the various owners of land in the town were separately responsible for sections of the defences. Overall, local responsibility for and execution of the work with a minimum of professional supervision seems by far the most probable explanation.

The attribution of the town programme to this date is consistent with the scope and thoroughness of Valentinian's approach to strengthening the imperial defences. If in Britain the remodelling of the town walls took place concurrently

[1] Ammianus, XXVIII. iii. 2; XXVIII. iii. 7. Wacher, *The Towns of Roman Britain*, 75 ff.

[2] This is perhaps an over-confident statement: Dr Graham Webster has since pointed out (*Brit.* 6 (1975), 299) that 'there are a dozen or more such settlements, some a hundred acres in extent without any signs of defences'. However it is perhaps going too far on negative evidence to argue that 'the provision of town defences, except for the main urban centres, appears to be the result of military considerations based on a road network rather than on the provision of general protection', though it would accord with my earlier suggestion of the use of walled towns as a form of defence in depth.

[3] This usually necessitated the filling of any existing ditch that ran close to the wall and replacement by a new ditch further out. These new ditches were often wider than the old.

[4] Frere, op. cit. 256.

with Theodosius' reconstruction of forts, then it seems a reasonable guess that the bulk of the programme on the civil sites fell on the civil administration, in other words on the *vicarius* and his provincial governors and on the local councils.[1] The army supply and secretariat function of the praetorian prefects' organization has already been mentioned, as has the rare occurrence of military insignia among the badges of the *vicarius* of Britain in the *Notitia*; but perhaps when it came to the planning of modern military works, their adaptation to the individual site, and their actual construction, these civilian staff were rather inadequate, particularly if the usual experts in military architecture were temporarily engaged elsewhere. It was unfortunate, perhaps, that current thinking had moved away from the old tradition of using stereotyped plans for military installations and these men were dealing, too, with specialized architectural problems, arising from the wider use of fixed catapults. It would not be surprising if they made mistakes.

Mr Wacher also points out another implication, which brings us back to the actual role of the army:[2]

The provision of bastions for the use of artillery must imply the deployment of personnel trained in its use. We know nothing of either the strength or compositions of garrisons provided for this purpose; nor do we know anything of the way in which such defences were manned before bastions were constructed. No town in Britain has yet produced evidence for buildings which might be interpreted as the quarters of a garrison. Before trained garrisons were required for artillery it may be that townspeople themselves provided the guardians for their fortifications. Moreover it would appear likely that all would have been billeted among householders in the town, and not in special barracks.[3]

The suggested existence of specialist garrisons for artillery might explain why some towns do not appear to have been given bastions, while others are deficient in numbers. Given the known shortage of trained manpower in the army towards

---

[1] It will be remembered that Ammianus goes out of his way to mention Theodosius' move to have Civilis appointed *vicarius,* taking some of the burden of recovering the island for the empire.

[2] Wacher, op. cit. 77 f.

[3] Except of course the regular fort at London. Mr Wacher points to *Cod. Theod.* VII. viii–xi for fourth-century regulations on the billeting of toops in towns. We noted earlier how Constantine was criticized for allegedly transferring troops from the frontier works to cities.

the end of the fourth century, it is likely that there were just not enough men to go round, and that they would have been distributed wherever the need was greatest'.[1]

The provision of artillery was itself an economical use of manpower, as opposed to less sophisticated methods of defence requiring much larger numbers of men. If town garrisons were of this sort, we must be thinking in terms of troops numbered probably in dozens at most rather than hundreds to man one town. Taken along with the other possible reasons we have already explored it may help to explain the presence of the occasional piece of Late Roman military equipment in towns. If any of the towns did survive well into the period when there were no longer any imperial troops in the island —and, as I shall show, I think the balance of the evidence is at present in this direction—then it must have been immensely assisted by the fact that small numbers of men could hold great stretches of wall. Theodosius may well have foreseen a situation where towns had to hold out alone till another expeditionary force could reach them.[2] I do not believe that Theodosius intended to station the main Roman forces in Britain permanently in the cities. His emperor, against the trend of the times, reverted to the traditional policy of strengthening the frontier defences of the empire themselves. But what Theodosius had done in Britain—incidentally, as it were—was to create the conditions in which different forms of defence could be adopted with comparative ease when circumstances again changed.

The repair of towns and forts and the restoration of the civil and military hierarchies in Britain, along with his victories over the barbarian enemy, were not all that Theodosius did to restore the island to the empire. We have already noted the restoration of morale in the army that had been stationed in Britain. However there was another extremely serious area of concern, affecting the stability and security of the diocese as part of Valentinian's domains. Ammianus

---

[1] We ought to be able to learn something from this about which places were thought most seriously threatened (and/or worth protecting).

[2] Barbarians seem to have found town walls very formidable. See A.H.M. Jones, op. cit. 154, for the failure of the Goths to take Constantinople in 378, quoting a remark of the Gothic commander Fritigern after being unable to take the city of Adrianople: 'we are at peace with walls'.

gives an account of two matters not yet described, in each of which he is able to give Theodosius credit for success, but where reading of what he has to say suggests that all is not necessarily quite what it appears to be on the surface.

Of these two matters, one has given rise to great debate among Romano-British historians, but not necessarily for the most interesting reason. The problem lies in Ammianus' statement that Theodosius regained a lost province—and this seems to be a success regarded as something rather separate from his recovery of Britain as a whole. We are told[1] that he had

> restored to its former state a province which was recovered that he had previously abandoned to enemy rule. This he did to the extent that it had a properly appointed governor (*rectorem haberet legitimum*), and it was from that time onwards called 'Valentia' by decision of the emperor.

There is general agreement that the new name is meant to refer jointly to Valentinian himself and his brother Valens, but the location of this province is in dispute: indeed this is the aspect of the affair that has attracted particular attention. The *Notitia* has frequently been scanned in this context. There the list of units under the *dux Britanniarum* is divided into two. The first records a group of garrisons from Doncaster to the Tyne, all on the eastern side of the country except for a series along the Stainmore Pass route to the west as far as Kirkby Thore. The second part is labelled '*per lineam valli*',[2] conventionally translated as 'along the line of the Wall' but in fact representing sites running as far south on the west as Ribchester on the Ribble. The first half of this *per lineam valli* set is apparently in strict geographical order, east to west, from Wallsend to Stanwix (Carlisle). The second is not.[3] There *are* differences between the garrisons listed in the

---

[1] Ammianus, XXVIII. iii: I have attempted a literal translation.

[2] *Vallum* in this context seems to mean the whole linear system, not just the artificial barrier.

[3] Except for the fact that some forts neighbouring on the ground do come next to one another in this second part, neither here, nor in the list of the *comes litoris Saxonici* which is similarly disordered geographically, does it seem to me possible to see any very convincing principle. Indeed, though the sources for parts of the *Notitia* as we have it may have been arranged in geographical order, as a record of establishment that order may have been irrelevant to those officials who had to use it.

north-east and those in the north-west. For example more changes of unit seem to have occurred in the west than in the east; and there are forts inland in the west that archaeologically seem to have been occupied after 369 but are not listed under the *dux*. These differences have been used to argue that the area now roughly represented by Cumbria was more thoroughly devastated by the enemy in 367. The argument then suggests that this region was reorganized and turned into a fifth British province named Valentia by Theodosius, perhaps with its own separate military command.[1] Now, it is perfectly possible to accept that this evidence does indicate that the north-west had been more disrupted than the rest of the north and had had to be more thoroughly reorganized, perhaps even with a military command separate from that of the *dux* to take care of a special situation, but none of that provides us with any evidence for locating the *civil* province of Valentia.[2]

A more profitable line of inquiry may be to consider what Ammianus' words can imply politically. He seems to say unequivocally that part of Britain was at first abandoned by Theodosius and only later recovered and given a 'properly appointed governor'. This must indicate a change of circumstances or of policy in the course of Theodosius' time in charge of Britain. Secondly, Ammianus actually describes the territory abandoned and later regained as 'a province'. The naming of this as Valentia ought therefore to be a renaming of an existing province, not the creation of a new one. Since Valentia appears in the *Notitia* (with a *consularis* as governor) together with the other four known provinces of the British diocese, it cannot be a renaming of one of the latter. It therefore looks as if there were five provinces in Britain *before* the expedition of Theodosius.[3] One of these he did not at first expect to recover for the emperor.

We have noted that Valentia seems to have received its new

[1] The identification of this area with Valentia has for example recently been argued by Miss Ann Dornier. (Birley, Dobson, and Jarrett (eds.), *Roman Frontier Studies,* Cardiff (1974), 102 ff.)

[2] See also Note, p. 411 below.

[3] The four are, after all, otherwise known primarily from the Verona List, which seems to describe the empire in about AD 312–14, more than half a century earlier. There is ample time between that period and the expedition of Theodosius for a reorganization.

name as a compliment by Valentinian to himself and his brother. Yet Ammianus does make the slightly odd remark that the emperor named it *velut ovans,* 'as if celebrating a "minor triumph"'. Such 'minor triumphs' ('ovations') were a formal honour that had traditionally been awarded in Republican times where the victory had either been unspectacular or over a slave revolt. The last actual 'ovation' with a full public processional entry into Rome recorded is that of Aulus Plautius, when he arrived back from Britain in AD 47. By that time even major victories only got an ovation if the general was not a member of the imperial family. Full 'triumphs' were reserved for the imperial house. After Aulus Plautius other generals no longer received even a public ovation, but were granted them in title only. But there was one area in which full triumphs had always been avoided, even under the Republic. That was for victories over Romans, whether in civil war or otherwise. For true glory to be garnered, the enemy had to be foreign. The question that now occurs is, if Valentinian's general had recovered a Roman province from invading barbarians, why was the emperor's celebration of the event so restrained? There was nothing new in an emperor taking the full glory for a victory gained in his name but not by himself: anyhow, Ammianus is referring to Valentinian's action, not Theodosius'.

The occurrence of the term *ovans* is not the only curious feature in Ammianus' account. The immediately preceding section, which he gives considerable prominence, records an extraordinary episode. A Pannonian named Valentinus was in exile in Britain for a serious crime. He was the brother-in-law of Maximinus, one of the more sinister figures of the period. The latter was a barrister who was currently making a name for himself in prosecuting members of the aristocracy at Rome, most notoriously for magical practices. Valentinian's own Christian rigour and his class prejudice against the Roman nobility are as well known as are his misjudgements of men. Maximinus not unexpectedly made himself thoroughly hated—Ammianus does not spare the epithets—and the following year was promoted to be *vicarius* of the City, subsequently serving with Valentinian as prefect of the Gauls. In the latter part of Valentinian's reign and for a little while after, therefore, it was through him that the civil administration

of Britain was responsible to the emperor.[1] In 369, however, Maximinus was still on his way up, though he had
doubtless already attracted the attention of Valentinian.
Several of the family fell foul of the emperor, but it is interesting that, though we are told that Valentinus' crime was
a very serious one, he was punished with exile rather than
anything worse. This was a political mistake, due perhaps to
influence brought to bear on the emperor by Maximinus,
interceding on behalf of his relative. At the time it was made,
the mitigation of sentence may not have seemed out of the
ordinary, since exile was not uncommon as a punishment for
upper-class offenders, and there were other exiles in Britain
at the time.[2] However, it was the presence of these exiles
that made the error dangerous. Valentinus approached his
fellow exiles, as well as troops to whom he offered enough
prospect of booty to persuade them to support him. He
seems to have gathered together a substantial party. We are
told, however, that Theodosius was too quick for him and
crushed the conspiracy. Valentinus and his closest associates
were handed over to the *dux* Dulcitius for execution. However the number condemned was deliberately kept small and
Theodosius forbade further investigations lest fear should
spread widely and 'rouse again tempests lying dormant in
the provinces', presumably the provinces of Britain.

With this affair in mind, it may be worth looking again at
the matter of Valentia. The emperor is, we have seen, remarkably restrained about regaining a province. Our source
emphasizes that it has been recovered after being initially
abandoned by Theodosius to the rule of enemies (*in dicionem
concesserat hostium*) and makes a special point of the fact
that it now has 'a legitimate governor'. Is this necessarily a
province recovered from the barbarians? So far our over-all
picture of the state of Britain on the arrival of Theodosius
has perhaps wrongly been one of Roman organization in

---

[1] He was dismissed by Gratian after Valentinian's death in 375, but not immediately. Gratian subsequently appointed to this post his old tutor Ausonius.

[2] This is not without parallel in the fourth century: Ammianus records two
others by name: Palladius, *magister* (XXII. iii. 3); Frontinus (XXVIII. i. 21).
It does not mean that Britain was a Roman Devil's Island: *relegatio in insulam*
was a particularly common form of judicial exile, but the essential element was
remoteness, not unpleasant surroundings.

disarray and the countryside roamed by barbarian war-parties, but not of a land firmly under barbarian rule. We have not seen Theodosius' operations as reconquest of an island under foreign rule but the sweeping out of barbarian war-parties. What, then, of this seemingly special case of a province regained for the legitimate government? *Hostis* does not automatically mean a foreign enemy: it simply means an enemy of the state. Traditionally, Roman traitors had formally been declared *hostis,* including for example, the Republican revolutionary Catiline and at one stage even Julius Caesar himself. Had Valentia had an 'illegitimate' Roman regime? I do not think it is possible to associate this possibility specifically with the conspiracy of Valentinus, since Ammianus makes it clear that Theodosius' speed prevented that one from developing into actual revolt. But that does not rule out the possibility that other dissident Romans had taken advantage of the confused situation in 367–9 to seize power in part of Britain. The conspiracy of Valentinus proves that there were men ready to try, even after Theodosius had arrived, and we have seen that there is good reason to suspect for a long time the presence in Britain of malcontents of various political and religious factions. Valentinian I has been described in modern times as the last of the great Roman emperors in the west, and Theodosius' work of restoration in Britain was only part of the vast programme of reconstruction of the defences of the western provinces carried out under his direction. However in some ways he may have worsened the instability of society in the west by further alienating the traditional upper classes from the emperors and the army that upheld them. Theodosius' unwillingness to pursue the ramifications of Valentinus' conspiracy suggests that discontent was uncomfortably widespread, and there is that interesting reference in the context of the punishment of Valentinus to the 'tempests that lay dormant'. Was it in the newly named province of Valentia that a storm had been calmed? If in fact a whole province that had successfully seceded could be brought back without more ostentation than was necessary to underline the re-establishment of the emperor's authority, it would accord well with the remarkable blend of resolution and moderation that marks the rest of Theodosius' restoration of Roman Britain.[1]

---

[1] The fact that Theodosius was, unlike very many of the army commanders,

Even if the army was unpopular with important sections of the public, there is good reason to think that the beneficial effects of Theodosius' work in Britain lasted long after the Roman army had ceased to be present. Professor Frere has again summarized the situation in words that should cause some common notions to be reconsidered:

> though the actions of usurpers and the deterioration of Roman military power on the Continent in due course led to the evacuation of almost all the armed forces in Britain, the work of Theodosius in the towns of the island enabled them to hold out far into the following century. Evidence is accruing that in towns as well as villas the last quarter of the fourth century was in general a period of great prosperity.[1]

The restoration of order by Theodosius certainly marks a new phase in Roman Britain and, particularly in contrast to the miserable quarter of a century or more that preceded it, we are probably right to see it as a much brighter age from the viewpoint of the inhabitants of Britain. The jolt to pre-conceptions of a rapid decline in the late fourth century and a dramatic 'end' to Roman Britain at the beginning of the fifth suggests we should perhaps take a brief look at our impressions both of Britain and of the western empire in general before we go on to consider the narrative of events following the completion of Theodosius' work in Britain.

One general historical observation seems in place here. It is important that we should not fall into the common trap of equating 'late' with 'decadent', a version of the anthropomorphic idea that cultures always and inevitably rise, flourish, and decline, rather than change. In Romano-British archaeological circles this has been curiously encouraged by two accidents. The first is that fourth- and fifth-century levels on Roman sites normally lie closest to the surface and are thus most easily damaged or more readily missed by excavators than the earlier periods.[2] Moreover, while they themselves by

---

himself a member of the wealthy provincial landowning class (in his case in Spain) may have assisted the work of reconstruction and reconciliation.

[1] Frere, op. cit. 399. The question of evacuation or disintegration of the army in Britain (or a combination of factors) will be discussed later: that particular problem does not affect the force of the view of Britain here stated.

[2] Recent work at Wroxeter and elsewhere has made excavators much more sensitive to this, but the physical problems of excavation are acute—and on many sites previously excavated it is now too late.

sealing the remains of the earlier Roman periods have protected them, the absence of substantial reconstruction on
many sites in the immediately succeeding period has left the
late layers much more exposed to accidental damage or
robbing in later ages. The second factor is that on Hadrian's
Wall, where the Theodosian reconstruction was first recognized, the workmanship then attributed to him (without
direct evidence) tends to be crude compared with earlier
phases of construction. It is advisable to be alert to the
existence of the largely unconscious assumptions about Late
Roman Britain to which these factors have given rise.

It is intriguing, to say the least, to note the terms in which
Valentinian issued a directive in the year 369 to the praetorian prefects in the west concerning the duties of provincial
governors.[1] He instructs the prefects to remind their subordinate provincial governors of the duty to reside at their
official stations and to keep their official residences in good
repair and properly furnished. This is so far consistent with
a picture of hopeless decline in morale in face of overwhelming barbarian pressure. But what are we to make of the
rest of the imperial instructions? The governor is not to go
'frequenting delightful retreats'[2] nor to spend his time being
entertained on the estates of local landowners. The latter
practice was apparently so common as to need the introduction of the drastic penalty of confiscation of the hosts'
estates. It does in fact help to illuminate a very important
feature in the political behaviour of the age to which we shall
very shortly return, but in the context of contemporary
feelings about security and the stability of life it also says
quite a lot. Two years earlier, in the critical year 367 itself,
the emperor wrote to the prefect of Egypt ordering him to
use his legal powers to prevent decurions, the members of
the town councils, from transferring their whole households
permanently from the cities to the country, 'an action which
has repeatedly been prohibited by law.'[3] It was clearly not an
age when the well-off, the class most likely to fear for the
safety of themselves and their possessions and the most likely
to be able to move house and home if they wished, felt that

---

[1] *Cod. Theod.* I. xvi. 12.   [2] *Non deverticula deliciosa sectetur.*
[3] *Cod. Theod.* XII. xviii. 1 (cf. ibid. XII. xviii. 2, of AD 396 or 397).

they had to shelter together in the defended cities. It implies that serious barbarian attack was not considered likely, at least in some parts of the empire, and that a good deal of internal order now prevailed.

The fact that Roman civilians were forbidden to carry arms—except when on a dangerous journey—implies a great deal about life in the empire and deserves to be reflected upon. Even under the Late Empire there was no relaxation of this rule: express permission was required before arms could be worn. The chaos in Britain when Theodosius arrived has to be seen through Roman eyes. It is something extraordinary from which he rescued the diocese, not the normal state of affairs. Of course, in 367 itself there were doubtless very few Britons who contemplated moving to a new villa in the country, and in 369 one cannot imagine the governors of the British provinces finding they could take many days off for hunting or house-parties, but these are the norms of life, with which the archaeological evidence from late fourth-century Britain to which Professor Frere alludes is entirely consistent.

There is another side to this, as I have hinted above, for it recalls an important feature of upper-class life in the fourth century—a distaste, or at least an affectation of distaste, for *negotium,* public life, and in particular the burden of office. By the middle of the fourth century it had become a polite commonplace to commiserate with someone on receiving an appointment and to hope he would soon be able to lay it down, though recognizing the honour. Indeed it was still felt very necessary for the family dignity to attain to the most prestigious offices, but there are signs that they were often held for as short a time as possible, and sometimes avoided altogether. On the other hand, when the fourth-century aristocrats did occupy public appointments, there is no sign they did not carry out their duties conscientiously.[1]

The death of Valentinian I in 375, caused characteristically by a fit of apoplexy at the behaviour of some barbarian envoys, ends an era of government that was competent,

---

[1] For an important discussion of this whole subject see John Matthews, *Western Aristocracies and Imperial Court, AD 364–425*, Oxford (1975), 9 ff.

See p. 727 below for the relationship of Christianity to the concept of retirement from the world in the Late Roman period.

energetic and tough, unpopular in influential circles but by succeeding standards tolerant in the religious matters which were now so important. Valentinian's elder son Gratian, in control at Trier, accepted his young brother Valentinian II as a nominal co-Augustus in the west, but proceeded to rid himself of his father's associates. For Britain one happy result was the early fall of the dreadful Maximinus, now praetorian prefect of Gaul. The replacement of him and his friends as a major influence at court by the cultivated Ausonius and his Gallic circle is of considerable importance, for it signifies the beginning of the drawing-together of the aristocratic classes and the imperial court. Though in public life they still had largely separate careers, there were increasing contacts and interchanges, and Christianity began to take a real hold in some of the principal aristocratic families.

The disgrace of the anti-aristocratic party among the late emperor's supporters was one thing: but in Britain it must have been with sadness that news was received of another event, the execution at Carthage of Theodosius, now risen to the rank of *magister militum,* immediately after another victory over enemies of Rome. Nothing is known of the reason for this execution, but successful *magistri militum* could be felt a serious threat to a new emperor.

The family of Theodosius did not, however, long remain in obscurity. In 378 the empire received a most dreadful blow, largely through its own fault. The brutal mishandling of the Goths on the Danube frontier by the eastern Augustus, Valentinian's unstable brother Valens, ended in a tremendous defeat for the Roman army at the battle of Adrianople. Both a great part of the Roman forces and the emperor himself were lost. Gratian turned to Theodosius' son, also called Theodosius, whom he first appointed *magister militum* to drive back the Goths and in the following year had proclaimed in the east as Augustus, co-ruler with himself.

This younger Theodosius, known to history as Theodosius the Great, is the central figure for the rest of the century, dominating the period down to his death in 395. His Christian fervour matched that of Gratian. The history of the western part of the empire in the late fourth century in many ways reflects the fact that the prime concern of the dominant Augustus was with the east. Seen from Britain, this means a

period of persistent instability in the proximate imperial
government, in contrast to the relatively stable but distant
authority in Constantinople.[1] For Britain this situation was
not necessarily improved by occasional but powerful interventions from the east. Britain itself was to be twice out of
the control of the central imperial regime, for five years
under Magnus Maximus (383-8) and for two under Eugenius
(392-4), which together represent nearly half of Theodosius'
reign. Also running as a thread through the period is the
growing political power of the magnates of the Church, including such figures as Ambrosius, the great Catholic bishop
of Milan. Elevated to office by popular acclamation from
being consular governor of that part of Italy, Ambrose became a most powerful influence on Gratian, on Valentinian
II, and on Theodosius the Great himself.

It was a mixture of religion and politics that weakened
Gratian's reign. He fell out with the pagan aristocracy in
religious matters even more decisively than his father, for
he replaced tolerance by a policy of sweeping away what
remained of Julian's pagan revival. He ordered confiscation
of the endowments of the Vestal Virgins and other venerable
priestly colleges and went so far as to eject the Altar of
Victory from the Senate House at Rome. The latter was
particularly resented by the senatorial party, now led by
Ambrose's anti-Christian opponent, Symmachus, one of the
leading orators and public men of the age. Nevertheless,
though Gratian may have struck at the political heart of the
old religion, there is relatively little evidence for repression
in Britain and paganism survived long after Julian, in both
humble shrines and public places. Where we are most likely
to find positive action against pagan religion is where troops
were stationed and could be used to carry out imperial orders.

We do not know if pagan discontent in Britain may have
weakened loyalty to Gratian, and it is perhaps ironic that
though he was in fact brought down by an army revolt that

---

[1] It is perhaps worth noting however that Theodosius the Great may be presumed to have known a great deal about Britain, since he was in his twenties when
his father was restoring the British diocese. He should, too, have been particularly
well equipped to appreciate his father's military achievement, since he had himself
already commanded a frontier army (as *dux* of Upper Moesia on the Danube)
before the elder Theodosius was killed.

started in Britain in 383, it was by means of the elevation to the throne by the troops of an officer who was quite as rigorous a Christian as Gratian himself.[1] Magnus Maximus had served with the elder Theodosius in the British expedition and like him came from Spain. He will previously have been acquainted with officers in the reconstituted army in Britain and was perhaps well known to the younger Theodosius, now emperor in the east. It is quite likely, too, that he was personally known at the western imperial court. We do not know exactly what post he currently held in Britain. Our only evidence is the report of a victory by him over invading Picts and Scots in the previous year, 382.[2] This both preserves a record of an attack otherwise unknown, and indicates that he probably held a major command. It has been conjectured that he was *dux Britanniarum,* but the possibility of his holding an appointment as *comes* like the elder Theodosius cannot be ruled out. At any rate, he was in the characteristically dangerous position of a general who had just won a victory in Britain.[3] The affair developed as a military usurpation in the traditional Roman style. Maximus invaded Gaul from Britain, Gratian's army began to desert and the emperor himself was caught and killed by one of Maximus' generals. Maximus set up his court at Trier and was baptized as a Catholic, securing administration and Church at the same time. He now controlled the prefecture of the Gauls, holding Britain, Gaul, and Spain. Maximus therefore replaced Gratian *de facto* as senior Augustus in the west (there were uneasy diplomatic relations with Gratian's young brother Valentinian II in Italy[4]) and was so recognized for the time being by Theodosius, heavily committed in the east. Indeed there were, as has been pointed out, a lot of reasons why joint rule by Theodosius and Maximus might have been a well-balanced long-term arrangement.[5] And for the present it meant

---

[1] See Note, p. 411 below.

[2] Chronicle of 452 (*Chron. Grat.* iv. 7: *Chron. Gall.* AD 382): *incursantes Pictos et Scottos Maximus strenue superavit.*

[3] We have no direct evidence of his motives: see Frere, *Britannia,* 361; but also Matthews, op. cit. 165 and 175. Orosius (VII. xxxiv. 9) implies that he had not been anxious to assume imperial power.

[4] Bishop Ambrose played a large part in these negotiations.

[5] Matthews, op. cit. 175 f.

firm government from Trier by an emperor who had been elevated by the army in Britain.

There is no certain evidence that the rule of Maximus had so far been deleterious to the security of Britain. It is generally conjectured that Maximus' need for troops on the Continent drastically depleted the garrison of Britain, to such an extent that it never fully recovered. However, like alleged withdrawals by earlier usurpers, the evidence is extremely thin. The sixth-century British writer Gildas,[1] the reliability of whose sources is uncertain, lists three Pictish wars before the middle of the fifth century and states that the first of these started after Maximus had invaded Gaul, continuing 'for many years' (*multos per annos*). A recent study has suggested that it did not come to an end till 389/90.[2] If so, it does not appear to have worried Maximus overmuch. He had previously defeated the Picts and Scots and his army had not had to fight Gratian's. Of course his main preoccupation must have been with Theodosius. Civil war was perhaps inevitable and there are sure signs that Theodosius at least was expecting it, but it was not till Maximus decided to cross the Alps four years later, in 387, to occupy the imperial city of Milan from which Valentinian II and his court fled ahead of him, that it became real. Maximus had now obviously decided that the time had come to put an end to the rival western government in Italy which was a permanent threat to his claim to equality with Theodosius. Though not impossible, this does not look like the action of a leader with a serious and unresolved war raging in his rear, particularly in the homeland of an important part of his army, but on the contrary of one who, having failed to secure satisfactory recognition of his position by diplomacy, now felt his military position strong enough to risk the certain war with Theodosius that expelling Valentinian by force would mean. Maximus' move failed, but he seems to have been defeated by superior generalship rather than any weakness caused by distractions behind. After careful preparations, Theodosius moved westwards in 388 with remarkable speed. His naval forces, bringing Valentinian II back with them, slipped past

---

[1] Gildas, *De excidio Britanniae*, 14.
[2] M. Miller, *Brit.* 6 (1975), 141 ff.

Maximus' fleet, while his land armies first defeated Maximus twice in Pannonia and finally caught and killed him at Aquileia.

It would certainly not be surprising if some of the troops normally in Britain were lost in Pannonia, or deployed elsewhere than in their province of origin in the course of arrangements Theodosius must have had to make after his victory. However we know so little about the disposition of troops in late fourth-century Britain that we cannot be sure that the evacuation of specific forts, where it can be demonstrated, represents a reduction in the total forces rather than a transferring elsewhere in the island. Theories that the Wall was abandoned with the northern barbarian tribes now friendly have been already discarded, and a once strongly held notion of the transfer of a northern chieftain named Cunedda with his people to North Wales by Maximus to replace Roman garrisons withdrawn has fallen out of favour.[1]

It does however look as if some of the Pennine and Welsh forts were abandoned at this time and the Twentieth legion withdrawn from Chester. There is also the inconclusive appearance of a unit called Seguntienses among the *auxilia palatina* in Illyricum in the *Notitia,* possibly garrison troops from Caernarvon promoted by Maximus to the palatine army and transferred permanently out of Britain. It is indeed interesting that early Welsh tradition seems to preserve memories of Maximus, and his occurrence in Welsh genealogies suggests that he may have been responsible for establishing loyal men in posts of authority in Wales that later became hereditary, possibly to counter the Irish raiding which seems to have been going on in remote Welsh coastal areas and by the end of the century developed into settlement. On the south coast Portchester may have lost what remained of its main garrison around this time. But we should not think of the defence of Britain solely in terms of troops stationed in the island. Maximus himself told Ambrose that he had large numbers of barbarians among his fighting forces, and this may mean he had avoided withdrawing too many regular units from their stations by recruiting widely outside the empire for his campaigns. His military policy was

---

[1] Frere, *Britannia*, 406. Cf. D.N. Dumville, *History*, 62 (1977), 181 ff.

certainly very costly and may have led him to unjust confiscations of property as well as high taxation.[1] But there were those who praised his rule, and as far as Britain is concerned the tenuous nature of the evidence for a dramatic and dangerous reduction in garrison leaves the question very much open.

It does not look as if Britain fell into Theodosius' hands straightaway, at least if Gildas' account of the end of his first Pictish war preserves an echo of a report of what actually happened. Gildas states that messages were sent from Britain promising submission, and that when this had been accepted a *legio* was sent by sea and drove out the enemy.[2] This suggests that the Pictish problem had now grown serious— perhaps after the outbreak of the civil war or even not till Maximus had actually been defeated—and that the sending of a force from the Continent was part of a bargain involving the surrender of Britain to Theodosius which he might not otherwise have gained easily. As to the details, we should probably not try to put too close an interpretation of the word *legio* in so late a writer.[3] It would fit fourth-century precedent if this were another of those task forces which we have seen before and which seem almost to be becoming the standard imperial response to military problems in Britain. At any rate, whatever the means, Gildas' account would indicate, if true, a successful operation, probably accompanied by some overhauling of defences.[4]

[1] See A.H.M. Jones, op. cit. 159 and references for his military and fiscal policies and the opinions of contemporaries.

[2] M. Miller (op. cit. 144) points out that this cannot have been before 389 at the earliest or 390, since Maximus was not killed till August 388. *Multos annos* (p. 403 above) will therefore refer to the period 383-9/90, but that does not prove that the Pictish troubles were acute without intermission.

[3] In passing, however, we may note that the poet Claudian uses the same word to describe the troops withdrawn from Britain to form part of the army that defeated the Goths in North Italy in 402.

[4] Gildas says that after the first war the *legio* established a frontier at a turf wall, and just before the second was instructing the Britons on how to build a stone one. Despite the temptation to dismiss this entirely, picking and choosing from Gildas what one feels believable, and to assume this an attempt to explain the Antonine and Hadrianic Walls that must still have been prominent landmarks in Gildas' day (or even to record tales about the replacement of the Turf Wall by the Stone Wall in Hadrian's day), Gildas may be reflecting some genuine information, however garbled, about Roman attention to the northern frontier at the end of the fourth century. This is easier to accept now it seems clear that Hadrian's Wall was still held around 400, rather than abandoned by Maximus as was formerly thought.

Maximus' remark to Ambrose about the barbarians in his forces is, of course, in line with the traditional care to avoid Roman casualties, especially in civil war. However it ought to alert us to note a momentous change taking place at that time. The reign of Theodosius the Great was conspicuously marked by a much greater employment of barbarian allies alongside Roman troops. In the east Theodosius had to cope with the consequences of the massive loss of regular soldiers at Adrianople. In the west he fought two civil wars and we must assume casualties in the opposing Roman forces. The barbarian allies now brought in must not be confused with those barbarians recruited into the regular army and who, as we have seen, cannot be distinguished from their colleagues of Roman origin. These allied barbarians, *foederati,* have also to be distinguished clearly from those communities of *laeti* we noted earlier. The latter were settled under Roman officers, in comparatively small numbers. The new 'federates' varied in size and composition but the common characteristic which set them in a new category altogether was that they were independent barbarians, under their own rulers and following their own customs.[1] The largest groups were nothing less than barbarian kingdoms on the move, and even where they were given land within the empire as payment for their services they retained their status as free allies.[2] We shall note later the extremely uneasy and sometimes bloody relationship between the regular army and these new allies, and the Roman reluctance to allow them into the cities. But at this point it is important to note that a change had occurred that was to assume immense significance in the future.

We should also observe another trend in other frontier provinces under the Late Empire that runs counter to the policy that had been in force under Valentinian I but incorporates elements we have recognized before. The attempt to hold the whole frontier in great force was replaced by an elaborated employment of the principle of defence in depth. Many forts were abandoned or lightly held, others, notably legionary fortresses, were given more powerful defences but occupied by units reduced in size. Fortified granaries also

[1] On *foederati* see also Note, p. 410 below.
[2] The prototype seems to be the Gothic treaty of 382, between Theodosius and King Fritigern.

make their appearance, presumably so that an invader could be prevented from seizing military supplies or living off the land. Towns were remodelled to act as impregnable strongholds during an invasion and as springboards from which the main Roman striking forces could launch a counterattack after an enemy thrust had exhausted itself.[1]

We should therefore not be surprised if reliable evidence one day appears for the presence in Roman Britain of organized barbarian allies around the end of the fourth century (more probably outside the cities than within), for regular frontier garrisons undergoing reduction but not total elimination, for the provision of fortified stores (perhaps in old forts), and for mobile field-units based in towns or other strongpoints.[2] This was, of course, a pattern to which the earlier refortification of the towns and repair of frontier forts, which we accepted as most likely the work of the elder Theodosius (under a different strategy), could easily be accommodated. It must however be emphasized that for Britain this is as yet no more than a theoretical model and that it is much less likely, indeed very unlikely, to be encountered here before AD 380/90.[3]

Having defeated Maximus in 388, Theodosius reinstated Valentinian II, now sole Augustus in the west. However, perhaps rightly, he was less than confident of the unfortunate young man's capacity to rule, and made sure that a number of major offices including the praetorian prefecture of the Gauls were held by men of his own, many of whom he had brought with him from the east. One at least of these men should not go unrecorded here. Chrysanthus, who was one of Theodosius' *vicarii* of Britain, was the son of a bishop of Constantinople and had been consular governor of one of the Italian provinces before being posted to the senior job in Britain. Later he himself became a sectarian bishop in Constantinople, at a time when he was regarded as a likely prefect

[1] Cf. G.D.B. Jones, *John Rylands Bulletin*, (1978), 141 (after E. Luttwak).

[2] See Note, p. 412 below.

[3] In 408 and 409 the fact that Roman troops were dispersed among the cities made it extremely difficult for the central imperial government in the west to assemble an army to repulse invasion (Zosimus, v. 35; v. 36; v. 45); but by that time Britain was out of central control, and we cannot assume that units in Britain had been similarly dispersed. On the other hand it may reflect something more general.

of the eastern city.[1] Theodosius clearly felt he needed first-rate administrators to keep Britain loyal once it had been recovered. Britain was still reckoned important, even viewed from Constantinople.

This time the defeat of a north-western emperor in whose control Britain had lain did not mean a change in religious policy. Theodosius was as determined a Christian and Catholic as Maximus, and the growth in the power of the Church was unchecked. Indeed there is a remarkable continuity, in terms of actual personalities wielding influence and only incidentally affected by violent changes of regime (and this applies to many secular notables as well, both Christian and pagan), right through from the court of Gratian to the death of Theodosius and beyond. Theodosius himself, not without signs of irritation, adopted as one of his major advisers the irrepressible bishop of Milan, and it is probably under Ambrose's influence that the campaign against paganism was eventually intensified, despite the emperor's considerable tolerance of leading pagans.

By 391 Ambrose had won and Theodosius issued an order making all sacrifices illegal, whether in public or private, and closing permanently all temples. In addition and perhaps most effective of all, he imposed large fines on officials who did not carry out the law.[2] This order was followed by a much more extreme one in the following year, prohibiting the ancient domestic worship of the *lares* and *penates*, the household gods. No one was now allowed to honour them in his own home with the traditional garlands, lamps, or incense, and the property in which they were found was to be confiscated.[3]

This outlawing of pagan worship was intended to apply to the whole empire. However the second decree was issued by Theodosius on his return to Constantinople, and in the meantime the west had again rebelled. The young emperor Valentinian was left in the charge of Flavius Arbogastes, Theodosius' general of Frankish origin, who had previously been employed

---

[1] See the mid-fifth century church historian Socrates (vii. 12).

[2] *Cod. Theod.* XVI. x. 10.

[3] The chilling atmosphere is unmistakable, but there is evidence that enforcement was inefficient and it was pagan practices, not the expression of pagan belief, that was illegal.

to hunt down and kill the son of Magnus Maximus. The discovery of Valentinian's body hanging in his apartments put
both Arbogast and Theodosius into impossible positions.
Even if it was suicide—which is not improbable—the accusation of murder was inevitable. It was apparently with reluctance that Arbogast was forced into rebellion, declaring an
administrator named Eugenius as emperor. Like Carausius a
century earlier Arbogast and Eugenius are found proclaiming
the legitimacy of their own regime by implication in continuing to recognize the imperial authority in the east, deliberately recording the titles of Theodosius and his elder son
Arcadius in public as Augusti. There was, however, in fact no
joint rule of the empire. The west, including Britain, had for
the present once again slipped from Theodosius' grasp. It
was now effectively in the hands of three men, Arbogast himself, Eugenius, and Nichomachus Flavianus, praetorian prefect
of Italy. The direct effect of their rule on Britain is unknown,
but two features are worth noting. Firstly, Arbogast conducted
a successful campaign against the barbarians across the Rhine
and seems to have carried out restoration work at Cologne.[1]
Secondly, both he and Flavianus were enthusiastic pagans—and
Eugenius a Christian who could be persuaded (under pressure)
to permit a pagan revival. Temples could now be rebuilt,
that great symbol, the Altar of Victory, was restored to the
Senate House and the major public festivals again celebrated.
The Christian party was extremely worried, and though some
leading aristocratic pagans, including Symmachus, kept fairly
aloof from the official enthusiasm, there is good reason to
suppose real support.

The pagan regime however did not last. In 394 Theodosius
invaded Italy for the second time to put down a rival emperor.
At the battle of the Frigidus, not far from where Maximus
had been killed, the army of Eugenius was defeated, Eugenius
himself was executed, and Arbogast and Flavianus both committed suicide. The empire was reunited under Theodosius.

By the end of the following January he too was dead, but
the pagan revival was at an end. Speaking of the Christian
apologists of Theodosius, John Matthews incidentally summarizes his reign:[2] 'Theodosius, the most Christian emperor,

---

[1] *ILS* 790   [2] Matthews, op. cit. 262.

had given them what they, as members of a particular group in the empire, most wanted. Christian piety, deference to bishops, Catholic legislation, the suppression of paganism— these, for them, were the virtues and achievements of Theodosius.' It might also be said that whatever his motives—or one's opinions of his outlook—he had striven with considerable success to maintain or restore firm government and a unity of policy and purpose throughout the whole empire. And in his time, partly by his efforts and partly under regimes hostile to him, the Roman army was still winning substantial successes against the pressures on the frontiers, however precarious the situation was on some sectors of the imperial perimeter. His death is in many ways the end of an age.

NOTES

Military uniform and civilians. The adoption of uniforms by civil officials under the Late Empire (A.H.M. Jones, op. cit. 566) is neatly illustrated by the painting showing a fourth-century civilian being dressed in his uniform reproduced by Professor Peter Brown (*The World of Late Antiquity*, 28–9). We may compare the disapproval shown by the late fourth-century Pope Siricius for the election as bishops of men who had 'once gloried in the belt of secular office' (*qui cingulo militiae saecularis adstricti olim gloriati sunt*): Siricius, *Letters*, VI. 1. He even prohibited the ordination of anyone who had held public office after being baptized, using similar words: *si quis post remissionem peccatorum cingulum militiae habuerit ad clerum admitti non decet* (*Letters*, V. 2). A ruling by the Council of Toledo in AD 401 forbidding the bestowing of the diaconate or any higher Christian orders employs another such phrase: *si quis post baptismum militaverit et chlamydem sumpserit vel cingulum* . . . ('. . . the cloak or belt of office . . .'). Some confusion has perhaps been caused by the fact that *militia* had by this period come to mean civil as much as military public service.

Foederati. Professor Frere has pointed out that we cannot use the transfer of an Alamannic king, Fraomar, to Britain in 372 recorded by Ammianus (XXIX. iv. 7) as evidence for the institution of *foederati* (Frere, op. cit. 270, n.5). Fraomar was in fact sent to Britain as a deliberate act of imperial favour by Valentinian I as a military tribune to command a normal Roman unit of Alamanni already stationed in the island. (See also A.H.M. Jones, op. cit. 621 and 642). We may recall the presence in Britain earlier of another Alamannic leader close to the imperial house, that Crocus who played a prominent part in the usurpation of the throne by Constantine the Great (Aurelius Victor, *Epitome de Caesaribus*, xli. 3).

The province of Valentia. The fact that Valentia was one of the only two British provinces out of the five to rank a *consularis* as governor indicates the importance attached to the post, whatever the reason. There is still no certainty on the geographical location of Valentia: it has been conjectured that it included York, and contained Hadrian's Wall and most of the *dux Britanniarum*'s command. The lack of evidence for destruction on the Wall leads Drs Breeze and Dobson to suggest that 'the Wall was probably the safest place in the province' (op. cit. 221). If they are also right to accept that 'it was the north of England where control had been lost completely for a while and there that Theodosius with judicious flattery created a new province of Valentia out of a pre-existing one' (ibid. 229) then the notion that Theodosius was dealing with an area that had been under dissident Roman rule, rather than lost to the barbarians, becomes much stronger. It is, of course, just possible that like the Roman troops at Neuss on the Rhine during the revolt of Civilis and Classicus in AD 69-70, the northern garrisons had felt the situation hopeless and transferred their allegiance to the enemy. This might explain the odd description in Ammianus of the *dux* Fullofaudes as *hostilibus insidiis circumventum* (XXVII.viii.1.).

Maximus and heresy. As emperor Magnus Maximus personally took a leading part in the trial of heretics and would have used troops to hunt them down if not dissuaded. The use of the death penalty caused concern even among Catholic opponents of heretics. St. Martin, bishop of Tours, who had formerly served in the imperial guard and is himself known on occasion to have borrowed troops to demolish pagan shrines, intervened in the case of the Priscillianist heretics to persuade Maximus not to use the army to search for them. These heretics were probably condemned technically for offences against the state. The old fear of conspiracy which had formerly inspired imperial persecution of the Christians was now reappearing in the attitude of Christian emperors to nonconforming Christian sects.

The towns in the second half of the fourth century. Mr Richard Reece has suggested[1] that there is no archaeological evidence for urban life in Britain after about AD 350: that all the evidence adduced for urban survival in the later fourth and fifth centuries could on the contrary be interpreted as either military or traces of life at no higher level than an agricultural village. I agree with him that it would be worth excavating some Roman town sites with this hypothesis in mind, and it would be consistent with my view that the consequences of the troubles of the mid-fourth century, particularly the defeat of Magnentius, were catastrophic for the prosperity of the towns, if we redate all or most of the defences before 350 or assume the town walls were strengthened to provide places of refuge for a large population from the countryside, even though the towns themselves were normally empty. The theory does *not* fit Ammianus' description of the relief of the city of London

[1] A short report of the paper delivered by Mr Reece at a conference in Durham in March 1978 was published in *The Times* for 7 April 1978.

by Theodosius or of his subsequent restoration of the cities of Britain (*in integrum restituit civitates et castra . . . instaurabat urbes et praesidaria* (*ut diximus*) *castra . . .*). It is difficult to imagine Theodosius going to the trouble of refortifying the lengthy circuits of the British cities if the purpose was *solely* military: it would have been much simpler to build a series of the small but very strong forts that are a feature of new military work of the period on the Continent. The work is surely too permanent in character and occurs on too many sites to represent temporary refurbishing of the walls of empty cities to provide camps for a large expeditionary force. I am sure difficulties only arise if we insist on imagining the towns as the same sort of animal as in the second century. Ammianus' own term of reference was almost certainly the weakened cities of Gaul of his own day, not the *civitates* of the Early Empire. But that does not carry with it the implication that the towns were depopulated and no longer fulfilled any urban purposes. That is to fall into the old trap of assuming that a town cannot be a town without the trappings of civic dignity, however hollow.

Late frontier defence. In the north it is interesting to note that none of the three walled towns of Carlisle, Corbridge, and Catterick are included in stations listed in the *Notitia* under the *dux Britanniarum*, commanding *limitanei*. We ought perhaps to be watching these for signs of the presence of mobile *comitatenses* or other field units. On the other hand, his list does include the Sixth legion, though without a station named. Though it is easiest to assume it remained at York, this is not proven. Hadrian's Wall was unusual among Roman linear frontiers in never having had a legionary fortress on it, and although the great fourth-century fortifications of York could have served the legion till the end, it may have been moved elsewhere, perhaps reduced in size.

For a note of caution regarding the interpretation of finds of one category of Late Roman military equipment (*plumbatae* or weighted darts), see my note in a review in *Classical Review*, n.s. 21 (1971), 263 ff.

IV

ROMAN BRITAIN AND THE FIFTH CENTURY WORLD

15

THE COLLAPSE OF IMPERIAL RULE

THE death of Theodosius left the empire to his two sons Arcadius and Honorius, both already invested with the rank of Augustus. This is often taken as the point at which the division into eastern and western empires became final. To consider the division as absolute from this date is in fact a simplification that makes much subsequent history more difficult to comprehend than is necessary, but in the context of the reign of Honorius and the collapse of imperial control in the west it has sufficient truth to be a vital factor in the events which concern this book.[1] Honorius' reign, from 395 to 423, is one of those rare periods in which the cumulative effect of changes we have observed occurring over a long period combine with a series of crises to create a genuine turning-point in western history, nowhere more dramatically than in Britain. At the death of Theodosius the frontiers of the empire were still maintained and within them the vast structure of Roman society and the Roman way of life stood largely intact. Both within and without the empire Rome's prestige and position in the world were not seriously doubted. By the time Honorius died, the western Roman world had been shattered into fragments to which unity would not be restored. Though much of Rome's culture, way of life and even prestige survived, the change is dramatic, and its effects on the north-western provinces immense in scale and very varied in character. In 395 Britain was a stable and particularly prosperous part of the prefecture of the Gauls. Its administration and its army were firmly answerable through the established chains of command to the imperial government in Italy. Its culture, in common with its Gallic neighbours, was a

---

[1] It is an interesting corrective to the simple view to note that coinage continued to be valid and laws to be issued throughout the whole empire in the names of both emperors. (The Museum of London for example has a silver ingot and three gold coins of Arcadius and Honorius of 395–408, found at the Tower of London, which look like the sort of bonus still paid to individual troops at the beginning of a new reign, in this case of joint emperors.)

mixture of local and cosmopolitan. Despite all the upheavals that had occurred in the previous two centuries, these were facts of life that no one would have had good reason to doubt were permanent. Yet by the time Honorius was dead, Britain had ceased forever to be part of the empire. The task of this chapter is to examine how this happened and what it meant for Britain and her inhabitants.

The accession of Honorius and Arcadius was marked by a basic change in the role of the emperor. It affected east and west differently, and what happened is of major importance in comprehending what occurred subsequently in the two halves of the empire. By and large, Roman emperors after Theodosius the Great were heads of state but no longer held effective power. This now fell into the hands of their chief ministers. The change was almost complete in the west, less so in the east where emperors still emerged from time to time in absolute command of their realms. A crucial factor in this difference—not the only one but perhaps the most important —was that while in the east these chief ministers generally held one of the civilian offices of state, in the west they were almost without exception the professional soldiers who commanded the army. An historical accident helped this process on its way. At the death of Theodosius most of the field army of the entire empire was in the west, reunited after the defeat of Arbogast and Eugenius. In command was a figure whose name is well known to students of Roman Britain and whom this accident put into the position to dominate the history of the first part of Honorius' reign and fundamentally affect the future of the west. This was the remarkable Flavius Stilicho, Vandal by birth, but married to Theodosius the Great's formidable niece Serena. He had long been close to Theodosius and in the later years of his reign had become the emperor's chief lieutenant. The fact that Serena was also Theodosius' adopted daughter emphasized the connection, and since while Theodosius lived the real centre of authority lay at Constantinople, Stilicho's claim to continued influence throughout the empire after the emperor's death is an understandable one. He was now *de facto* regent in the west, basing his authority on a claim that the dying emperor had secretly asked him to oversee both his sons. If this was indeed Theodosius' wish, his failure to make it public was calamitous. While Stilicho's rule was for a decade more or less unchallengeable in the west, where it had open support from Ambrose and powerful groups in both court and senate, it was never effective in the east. The dynastic connection of Stilicho and the imperial house was cemented by the marriage of Stilicho's daughter Maria to the youth Honorius.[1] The attention of the western government was dominated by attempts to assert authority in the east, and the west was chronically impoverished by being cut off from the sources of money, military supplies, and recruits that lay in the provinces under eastern control. The struggle for the Danubian provinces plays a particularly crucial part in the story, and Rome's disastrous involvement with the Visigothic king Alaric, sometimes as enemy and sometimes as ally, is intimately connected with these issues.

Barbarian allies were coming to play an increasingly large part in Roman policy. We observed that during Theodosius' reign the make-up of Roman armies had significantly changed. We noted Magnus Maximus claiming to have large numbers of barbarians in his pay—though that may have been an emergency measure—and in the war between Arbogast and Theodosius there were great contingents of Franks and Alamanni on the western side and Goths in the army of the east. It was now much more common for Roman generals to command forces that contained major contingents of barbarian troops under their own leaders, free *foederati*, and others.[2] Some of the independent barbarian peoples co-operated with Rome on a strictly temporary, often purely cash basis. They could amount to large armies on their own account, and getting them to combine for a campaign or to act on Rome's behalf was an important part of the imperial government's preoccupations. Diplomacy of this sort was at least in part forced on Rome by shortage of manpower in her own regular army, yet was very difficult to carry out

[1] Her splendid burial, with elaborate grave deposits including wedding gifts, was discovered in Rome in 1544 (see J.M.C. Toynee in M.W. Barley and R.P.C. Hanson (eds.), *Christianity in Britain, 300–700*, 191). Arcadius also married the daughter of a German general, the Frank Bauto who had been *magister militum praesentalis* in the west. She too was to play an active role in imperial politics.

[2] In addition, the old practice of enrolling defeated barbarians continued when opportunity arose, as, for example, after Stilicho's victory over the Ostrogoths in 405.

successfully with the limited financial resources at the command of the western imperial government. It was made worse by extreme reluctance on the part of the Roman nobility to provide either cash or recruits from their own properties.

For the historian, the fact that the western *Notitia* gives no help in estimating the size and distribution of these purely barbarian troops in the Roman forces of the period makes it very much more difficult to assess the size of Roman armies. It is now, at the end of the fourth century and in the fifth, not earlier, that the likelihood of substantial groups of 'barbarian federates' needs to be taken into account in trying to understand Roman Britain, but our lack of knowledge about their location and numbers makes what we know about the movements of regular units, unlike earlier days, of comparatively little utility in calculating the total forces available to Roman commanders in Britain.

Whatever their numbers, the existence of these new barbarians within the empire was socially and politically important as well as militarily. Various unpleasant incidents in this period make it clear that the barbarian soldiers themselves were felt to differ fundamentally from the regular army, and their families not to be part of the ordinary population. In 408, for example, we find Stilicho at one moment intending to use the barbarian part of his army to suppress a mutiny among his Roman units, at another he is warning the towns of northern Italy in which the barbarians' families were housed not to let the barbarian soldiers themselves within the walls.[1] Stilicho's own fall in the same year was followed by a terrible massacre by the Roman troops of those families that did not escape to take refuge with Alaric, himself currently an ally of Rome.

The constraints on Stilicho's policy were thus crippling: indeed by 408 we have the extraordinary sight of Stilicho and the emperor Honorius attending the senate in person to try to argue it into voting for diplomacy rather than war with Alaric. Not only does this reveal how the prestige of the imperial government itself had declined at home and how the senate had become after centuries once again vitally

---

[1] Zosimus, V. xxxiv. 2.

involved in foreign policy, but also that Stilicho had a much clearer sight of changed realities than the senators.

John Matthews has pointed out how, both in the senate and at the imperial court, old-fashioned Roman patriotism prevented a realistic appreciation of what was now possible, nor was this problem confined to the west. He points to the influence of upper-class opinion 'which maintained a deep-rooted faith in the effectiveness of conservative army reform and traditional military methods—that is, the suppression of the barbarians on the battlefield and their elimination from the Roman armies—and was only too ready to be disillusioned as to the effectiveness of diplomacy'.[1] This is, of course, closely allied to the equally deep tradition that the highest glory for a Roman statesman was success in war. Roman opinion was largely wedded to attitudes it could no longer afford.

It is not therefore surprising that when the only contemporary source for Stilicho's policy towards Britain, the eulogizing court poet Claudian, mentions these provinces it is in connection with claims of military success. It is not easy to deduce from his poetic language what actually happened. However it looks as if the Roman forces were able to assert control over the sea approaches to the north-western provinces in 398,[2] including the defeat of both Saxons and Irish Scots. It is not clear whether the Picts, also mentioned as beaten, are included as sea-borne enemies or are intended to refer to a purely land campaign. With this remark of Claudian has been linked the second of Gildas' 'Pictish wars'.[3] The latter reports an appeal for help from Britain to which the Roman government again responded by sending an army against the enemy, this time 'against expectation'.[4] If there is anything behind that phrase, it may suggest that the barbarians, as in 367, were taking advantage of knowledge that the imperial government was distracted by other affairs. In the first half of 398 Stilicho had been involved in suppressing the potentially

---

[1] Matthews, *Western Aristocracies*, 270.
[2] Claudian, xvii, 50 f.; xviii, 391 ff.; xxii, 247 ff.
[3] M. Miller, *Brit.* 6 (1975), 145.
[4] Gildas says this attack (if he is indeed talking of this particular war) came as the *legio* which had won the previous Pictish war (?389/90) was returning to the Continent (*domum repedante*). This seems a long time for a temporary expeditionary force, but see 421 f. below.

extremely damaging revolt, if that is the right word, of Gildo, *comes Africae,* who had decided to assert allegiance to Arcadius and the eastern government on the issue of legitimacy. If anything was 'against expectation' it was the ease and speed with which Gildo was suppressed, leaving the western government free to turn to other problems such as Britain.

We do not know whether Stilicho took charge himself in the British war. However by the beginning of AD 400 the claims made in his honour are considerable. It is worth looking at Claudian's account in detail.[1] After an introduction depicting Britannia with the trappings of a Caledonian savage, she is made to declare:

> When I too was about to succumb to the attack of neighbouring peoples —for the Scots had raised all Ireland against me and the sea foamed under hostile oars—you Stilicho fortified me. This was to such effect that I no longer fear the weapons of the Scots nor tremble at the Pict, nor along all my shore do I look for the approaching Saxon on each uncertain wind.[2]

Earlier the previous year Claudian seems to have been expecting news of naval successes, waiting to hear of 'the Saxon conquered, the Ocean calmed, the Pict broken and Britain secure'.[3] Yet only a month after the detailed eulogy of January 400 the trumpeted claims of major success disappear, and they do not reappear. In mid 402 Claudian gives us news of troop withdrawals from Britain[4] (to which we shall return) but this seems too late to explain the change of tone in 400. It is perhaps first worth noting that the eulogy of 400 does *not* clearly confirm victory in battle, but concentrates on defence. Archaeologically we ought to be on the look-out for signs of restoration in the coastal forts[5] and probably the Wall as well, or at least regarrisoning. Perhaps the answer is that there was no actual victory and it was becoming obvious that Stilicho was in fact having to run down

---

[1] Claudian, xxii, 247 ff.: it is a piece in honour of Stilicho's consulship, given at the court at Milan in January 400.

[2] Ibid. (the key word *munivit* = 'fortified, put into a state of defence' is a disputed reading, but seems the most probable).

[3] Claudian, xviii, 391 ff.

[4] Claudian, xxvi, 416 ff.

[5] Unfortunately the one apparent piece of epigraphical evidence, two stamped bricks from Pevensey, has recently been proved to be forged (*Brit.* 6 (1975), 293).

the garrison of Britain. Professor Frere[1] has suggested that Stilicho was already abandoning forts at an early stage of his regency. Gildas may help us to develop this idea. We have already seen that it would fit the general situation to have troops being withdrawn in 398. He goes on to state that just before the Romans left (after defeating the Picts in this second war), they helped the Britons to build the stone wall, constructed watch-towers on the south coast and provided patterns of weapons for the Britons (*exemplaria armorum*). They then left, and the Picts and Scots occupied British territory as far as the Wall (*muro tenus*).[2]

If we really can put the accounts of Gildas and Claudian together, then perhaps we may conjecture the following course of events. The force sent out in 389 or 390 had become semi-permanent (whether intended to be or not:[3] at this time there was a strong tendency for armies of *comitatenses* to become fairly permanently localized, each under a *comes* as before but acquiring territorial titles). In 398 it was being recalled, perhaps with consequent adjustments in the stationing of the garrison units in Britain, including evacuation of some less vital forts. The barbarians took the opportunity to attack but were thrown off-balance by the unexpected collapse of Gildo in Africa and did not press home their attack. Finally, though the planned withdrawal was resumed, the warning was heeded and measures were taken to strengthen the defences of Britain. We do not have to assume the large-scale removal of garrison *limitanei*: the new work on coastal defences and the fact that the barbarians stopped at the Wall suggests the frontiers for the moment held. The provision of *exemplaria armorum* and the instruction in the building of the stone wall is interesting: the first suggests the provision of patterns for local manufacture of equipment up to now normally supplied by the state ordnance factories, especially in the disputed Danubian provinces.[4] The latter, while in itself probably an attempt to explain Hadrian's Wall

---

[1] Frere, *Britannia*, 268.   [2] Gildas, *De Excidio*, 19.

[3] There may have been internal problems of loyalty—not to mention the upset of plans by the revolt of Arbogast and Eugenius.

[4] Simpson, *Brit.* 7 (1976), 204 f. If any examples of the Late Roman military equipment do eventually prove to have been manufactured in Britain, such deliberate official action could be the origin.

when the truth about its construction was lost, may preserve a tradition of deliberate instruction of civilian builders in the techniques of military construction. We have already seen that they probably had need of it. We also ought to note the *possibility* that permission was given to disregard the *lex Julia de vi publica,* the ancient general prohibition on the carrying of arms by civilians. Yet we do not know how much of all this applies to the arming of civilians and how much to the making of arrangements for the surviving garrisons of the regular army in Britain, whether in forts or in detachments in towns. Indeed, the withdrawal of *comitatenses,* whether from a previous task force or upgraded from among the regular units of the *limitanei,* may have led to the remaining regular units taking on new duties, including mobile ones with temporary billeting in towns. It is fascinating, too, to note that as early as AD 395 Stilicho's government had been attempting to divert municipal funds in the west to pay for local defence.[1]

If what Gildas describes as the *legio* being withdrawn when the second Pictish war happened was indeed the same force as had been sent by Theodosius the Great to deal with the first Pictish war in 389 or 390, it may have been in Britain much longer than was intended.[2] If it was, then, a task force becoming almost a fixture, it provides one possible answer for that presence of a *comes Britanniarum* in the *Notitia Dignitatum* over which much ink has been spilt. The *Notitia* army, nine units of *comitatenses,* looks just like a task force. I cannot help suspecting that this might be the period when this post became a fixture in the army lists, even if (like others of its kind) it was from time to time being held in abeyance.[3]

If there was, therefore, a campaign in 398 (after the defeat of Gildo) by the Romans against the barbarians threatening Britain, it is likely it was a sudden decision to seize an unforeseen opportunity. Yet Stilicho may have harboured longterm ambitions for a major offensive in Britain, but the moment was in general inauspicious. A withdrawal of as many

[1] Matthews, op cit., 276, n. 5.
[2] However, in the exact form described in the *Notitia,* the force must date from 395 or later, since it includes a unit named after Honorius (*equites Honoriani seniores*).
[3] See also p. 476, n. 2.

troops as possible in about 399, intended to be temporary, seems likely, coupled with a reorganization of the coastal command. Such a policy is particularly convincing if an unexpected success had sapped barbarian confidence. Even so, we shall see that Stilicho's withdrawals may not have been as drastic as has often been thought. But for the moment he needed all the troops he could obtain. We ourselves do not know precisely what Alaric had been doing since he retreated into Epirus with his Visigoths in 397, but there is no reason to think the western Romans were so ignorant. However there was one factor that must have been quite enough to worry Stilicho. In 397 the eastern government had forbidden him to pursue Alaric, being very unwilling to see his power increase to the extent victory over the Visigoths would mean. Now they had gone much further by granting Alaric the rank of *magister militum per Illyricum*, which, as Professor A.H.M. Jones pointed out, gave him the opportunity to draw on the Roman military ordnance factories of the Balkan provinces to equip his men.[1] It would therefore make sense if Stilicho still saw Alaric in these years as the principal threat and decided to collect such forces as he could before tackling him again. Nor, for that matter, had Stilicho given up his claims on Constantinople. The appointment of Alaric in Illyricum by the government of Arcadius was especially pointed, since the provinces of eastern Illyricum were themselves a matter in dispute between east and west. There was a double reason, therefore, for dealing with Alaric, one way or another.

Towards the end of the summer of 401 the Visigothic threat to the west became acute once more. Alaric came down through the Alps and wintered in northern Italy. Stilicho spent that winter raising recruits on the Danube and had the walls of Rome itself put into order (it was not just the provincials that were being urged into repairing their defences). Among the troops collected by Stilicho Claudian describes a *legio* (the same word) 'protector of the furthest Britons, which curbs the ferocious Scot and has watched the tattooed life draining from the dying Picts'.[2] If Claudian

---

[1] A.H.M. Jones, op. cit. 183: this adds another complication to the task of trying to use archaeological finds of Late Roman military equipment to determine the identity of their wearers.   [2] Claudian, xxvi, 416 ff.

could be trusted not just to be using literary convention —which we may legitimately doubt—this ought to mean part of the static garrison of northern Britain, but it is just as likely that this is the same force we have being withdrawn at the time of Gildas' second Pictish war. One may perhaps guess that if this meant leaving the post of *comes Britanniarum* without a substantial body of troops, then there was occasion for a reorganization of the coastal defences of Britain which fixed the Saxon Shore in the form in which it stands in the *Notitia*. It is not impossible that the title *comes litoris Saxonici* (which does not appear anywhere earlier) is itself due to Stilicho.

The fact that the *Notitia* lists a number of British units serving elsewhere in the empire might be evidence that Stilicho's withdrawal of troops from Britain was substantial and that they did not come back.[1] On the other hand we do not know for certain that these units were not transferred in some previous phase. Indeed, for earlier periods when we have more details about the recruiting of troops, it seems that very few units raised in Britain were actually stationed there. The fact that these particular troops are found in the eastern as well as the western sections of the *Notitia* makes a date substantially after 395 difficult to accept. Moreover we have already noted that our lack of knowledge about the barbarians in the western Roman service at the end of the fourth century makes it unsafe to assume that any removal of regular units necessarily reduced the total garrison of Britain. On the other hand, there is another piece of evidence that *could* support the idea that Stilicho's withdrawal of troops, not for the general purposes of the economy. There by the emperors was always primarily for the purposes of government expenditure, pre-eminently for the payment of troops, not for the general purposes of the economy. There had been no mint in Britain since the time of Magnus Maximus, and the last Roman coins that occur in large numbers are those issues Arcadius and Honorius struck down

---

[1] Frere, op. cit. 407. A.H.M. Jones, op. cit. 1417 (= 1964 edn. iii, 347) argues that the *eastern* army list represents the situation there soon after 395 and was hardly altered thereafter. It is also a problem that from 395 to his death in 408 Stilicho was at odds with the east and it is difficult to imagine Stilicho withdrawing troops from Britain and subsequently transferring them to the eastern army.

to AD 402.[1] Coins were normally shipped in bulk to the provinces; and struck in the name of both emperors. The cessation in Britain from 402 may imply there were no longer enough Roman troops in Britain to be reflected by significant finds of coins. This would certainly support the common view that Stilicho stripped Britain of most of what remained of its garrison. Yet it could reflect a replacement of regular troops by barbarians paid with grants of provincial land in return for military obligations. Equally—perhaps more probable—it may mean that Honorius' government, desperately short of cash and having extreme difficulty in raising the money for war and diplomacy with the Goths in Italy, simply stopped paying the garrison and the civil service in Britain. Nor is it impossible that disorder in Italy and Gaul made the job of ensuring the transhipment of cash safely to Britain extremely difficult. Any or all of these explanations would have the same effect in Britain, and might well help to explain the extreme mood of discontent there that was to lead to three successive revolts in 406-7.

However, on the larger imperial scene, Stilicho's moves were rewarded with limited but for the moment effective military success. Alaric suffered sufficient losses in battle in 402 that he accepted an agreement with Stilicho that he should withdraw from Italy. The immediate threat was thus removed, but there were important long-term political consequences in the permanent retreat of Honorius and the imperial court from Milan to the remote Adriatic coastal city of Ravenna, breaking the long-established communication links with Rome on the one hand and Gaul and Spain on the other. This change established the centre of government close to the great naval base that looked to the Mediterranean and the eastern empire. The 'Milan–Trier axis' from which the north-western provinces had been governed was now broken.

It is difficult to blame Honorius. Nor was it any time to be moving troops back to the outlying provinces. In 404 an Ostrogothic army followed the Visigoths, and it was not till 405 that Stilicho was able to bring their king Radagaisus

---

[1] A convenient recent summary of coinage in Roman Britain is A. Burnett, *The Coins of Roman Britain*, British Museum Publications (1977).

to battle and defeat him at Fiesole near Florence in old Roman style, subsequently enrolling a large number of his men in the Roman army. For the moment western military prestige was restored, but the success was short-lived. On the very last day of 406 a horde of Suebi, Vandals, and Alans crossed the Rhine, defeated the Frankish federate forces opposed to them and drove on into Gaul. Major invasions of this kind had, of course, happened before, but this time the consequences were irreversible. At just about the same moment (the exact chronology is uncertain) a mutiny in Britain against Stilicho detached the British diocese from the western imperial government. What followed from these two events was to prove fatal for Britain as part of the Roman world—but not immediately.

There is some sign that the situation in Britain was already tense. Reports from Irish sources of attacks on the south coast of Britain by the 'high king' of Ireland, Niall of the Nine Hostages, are perhaps to be associated with the year 405. It looks as if Stilicho's work on the coastal system in 399 I have conjectured above was based on an accurate assessment of returning danger. Barbarian confidence was coming back. However the Gothic wars of 402–3 and 404–5 meant the concentration of western troops and Stilicho's personal attention on Italy, not to mention the eastern empire. There is argument about whether the first of the German invaders were already penetrating the Rhine frontier when elements in Britain took an opportunity for another military revolt. E.A. Thompson has argued persuasively for dating this mutiny before the barbarian crossing of the Rhine on 31 December 406.[1] The army first elevated a soldier named Marcus, but very shortly murdered him as was the wont of mutinous troops who did not get quite what they had expected. The second was a Briton named Gratian, who appears to have been a civilian and probably a member of the local Romano-British upper class.[2] By this time, since Gratian was proclaimed in 407, the barbarians were certainly across the Rhine. Gratian's reign was brief: he was deposed and murdered after four months. Professor Thompson argues

---

[1] See Note, p. 444 below.
[2] *municeps eiusdem insulae* (Orosius, VII. xl. 4).

that by now, which must be at least the beginning of May 407 if not later, the barbarians' move across northern Gaul was enough to provoke the forces in Britain to replace their emperor. Certainly Zosimus alleges that the British army feared a barbarian crossing of the Channel,[1] and they may well have believed they would receive little help from the imperial government. Indeed, before the German invasion and while basking in the success of defeating Radagaisus in Italy in 405, Stilicho had revived a project that may seem extraordinarily dubious to us but underlines the way Roman foreign policy now worked. His scheme was to co-operate with Alaric in detaching the provinces of eastern Illyricum from the government of Arcadius at Constantinople. There were thus not likely to be many Roman troops available for strengthening remote western provinces. Indeed in 406 we find Honorius urging the *provinciales* of the west to take up arms in their own defence and offering freedom to slaves who volunteered to join them. Nor were deals with the Goths likely to be cheap—at one stage Alaric asked for the whole province of Noricum as land for his followers.

The army of Britain may have believed that Britain should not stand alone, for having deposed Gratian they elevated a soldier with wide ambitions. The fact that an attempt of the traditional sort from Britain on the empire was even contemplated—the sort of action undertaken by Clodius Albinus or Constantine or Magnus Maximus—suggests the army in Britain felt its own strength still sufficiently great to overawe and win the support of the surviving Roman and allied forces in Gaul and Germany, or to defeat them if they remained loyal to the government at Ravenna, and sufficient too to risk a major war against the German invaders. This does not really support the view that Stilicho had largely drained Britain of troops in 401 (or, if so, that they had not been replaced). Indeed, the initiative is assumed to have come from the army itself. It is, I suppose, just possible that there were still Continental *comitatenses* in Britain who did not want to see their home provinces devastated nor to be stationed permanently across the dreaded Ocean. Moreover, for troops whose homes were in Britain or the neighbouring

---

[1] Zosimus, VI. iii. 1.

provinces it was probably preferable to be part of a stable north-western army than under threat of an eastern campaign, in company with a doubtful ally, against the power and prestige of the senior Augustus. Moreover there were the old attractions of booty and rapid promotion as the rewards of successful civil war, and the confused situation in Gaul may have looked most promising. Certainly one ancient source thought the British army had probably elevated all three of their pretenders in order to gain the empire,[1] and he believed this Constantine III was chosen because the connotations of the great name he bore suggested that he would succeed in grasping the imperial throne.

Whatever the army's motives, Constantine moved swiftly from Britain into Gaul before the Germans could occupy the Channel coast, sending his own officers ahead to take command of the surviving Roman units where they could. In the event the barbarians did not move in that direction but turned southwards. By the end of 407, but only after stiff fighting, apparently against loyalist forces, he had taken over the administration of Gaul and was both repairing the defences of the Rhine and closing the Alpine passes into Italy. He did not manage to bring under control all the barbarian invaders who still moved about Gaul; but in the following year his son Constans as Caesar and his British general Gerontius took Spain in a swift campaign, rooting out opposition by relatives of the Theodosian imperial family. The latter, it will be remembered, had emerged to national prominence from its Spanish estates at the time of the recovery of Britain by the elder Theodosius, grandfather of Honorius and Arcadius. In 408 Stilicho seems to have incited some unspecified barbarian tribes to spread further havoc in Gaul,[2] presumably in an attempt to dislodge Constantine. However in 409 Honorius was forced by the successes won by the rival regime to recognize Constantine as Augustus and to hold the consulship jointly with him in the same year.

It looked for the moment as if the army of Britain had made the right decision. Apart from the bands of barbarians still loose in Gaul (and from the purely British point of view

---

[1] Sozomen, IX. xi. 2: see E.A. Thompson, *Brit.* 8 (1977), 318 (appendix).
[2] Chronicle of 452, *Chron. Min.* I, 652.55.

they were at least heading for Spain), Britain was once again part of a united Gallic prefecture under firm Roman control. In Constantine III they had a properly legitimized emperor who owed his elevation to them and whose Continental forces contained senior officers from their own number. He was resident in the prefecture and one of his major concerns was to be the security of the northern frontiers. We have no evidence that any temporary depletion of the garrison of Britain to provide troops for the Continental invasion of 407 was not made up after the initial successes of Constantine's regime. In fact, the notion that Constantine removed the remaining garrison of Britain in 407 for a Continental adventure from which it was never to return is one of those apparently unshakeable ideas about Roman Britain for which there is no hard evidence either way.

For Britain there was a disquieting feature in the situation of quite a different kind. I have already referred to the retreat of the western government from Milan to Ravenna, and mentioned how this weakened the traditional axis of administration. We have also previously noted how Trier had been the effective centre of government as far as Britain and the neighbouring provinces were concerned for more than a century. Now Constantine found the capital of the prefecture had been moved very far south, to Arles, a transfer that had very probably only just happened as a direct consequence of the barbarian invasion of 406. Indeed one might perhaps hazard a guess that the flight of the administration from Trier was a contributory cause of the moves in Britain.[1] At any rate the change was a permanent one, and the hub of Constantine III's government was in consequence much more distant from the affairs of Britain than it would otherwise have been. The centre of gravity of the Gallic prefecture was now inevitably a Mediterranean rather than a northern one.

In the meantime, however, the actions of the army of Britain had had much greater consequences for the history of the Roman world as a whole than anyone had anticipated. Constantine's neutralization of the remaining loyalist forces in Gaul by the end of 407 put an end to Stilicho's plan for a

---

[1] Nevertheless the transfer does not seem yet to have been total: the important mint at Trier went on striking coins for Constantine III and even for Jovinus, his successor.

joint operation with Alaric against the eastern government, but it was too late to prevent Alaric from marching into Italy on his way to join forces with the Romans. The task then facing Honorius and Stilicho was to assemble an army to dislodge Constantine and his British supporters from Gaul. Unfortunately Alaric considered he had the right to be paid for his march into Italy, and a series of immensely complicated and extraordinary events followed, disastrous for the empire.

The year 409 demonstrated at an early stage the fragility of the alliance between Stilicho, Honorius and the senate, and within the imperial court itself. This had depended on success. The same year witnessed at one stage a temporary alliance between Alaric and the senate against Honorius, including the elevation of a puppet emperor by the Visigothic king. It was also marked by the death of the eastern emperor Arcadius and a new plan by Stilicho and Honorius to exploit the situation and take control of the government at Constantinople, reuniting the empire. This plan foundered: Stilicho discovered Honorius changing sides under the domination of a rival court party that favoured peace with the east. He was too late. These enemies at court out-manœuvred Stilicho and swiftly engineered his arrest and death. Stilicho, for whatever motives, had attempted to continue the tradition of a Roman world dominated by a single strong man, but the unforeseen consequences of his actions in many ways contributed substantially to the approaching break-up of the empire in the west. In the short run his overthrow simply added to the confusion reigning in Ravenna and Rome.

The following year, 410, was the most traumatic of all, for the breakdown of relations between the senate and Alaric led to the devastating sack of the city of Rome itself by the latter's Gothic troops. The effect of this almost accidental incident, largely brought about by Roman diplomatic incompetence, factional strife, and unwillingness to dip into their own pockets for the public good has to be seen in the context of the eight centuries of security from foreign enemies since northern barbarians had last sacked the City and the belief both of Romans and probably most contemporary barbarians as well that in the last event the empire could not be defeated.

This is perhaps one reason why senators who could quite

easily have paid what Alaric at one stage asked, for services rendered, would not co-operate. But the imperial government, too, cannot be absolved of being bemused by the traditional success of Roman arms. John Matthews summarizes the situation:

It is perhaps too much to expect such governing classes to have accepted the humbling realities of a situation, where not merely the security of distant frontiers, but the position and survival of the court in Italy itself were in jeopardy. But the Roman government could not afford to pay for its pride; and it was precisely, and only, this intransigence and obstinacy of the government that made its failure inevitable. On numerous occasions, after as before the death of Stilicho, the court of Ravenna could have chosen to negotiate with Alaric on reasonable and constructive terms, upon which in its impoverished state it was in no position to improve, and it can only be blamed for refusing to do so.[1]

Alaric's sack of Rome has left him in history with the reputation of a monster, but the behaviour of both Romans and other barbarians towards him and his people was certainly no better than his towards them, and sometimes worse. This, too, is consistent with Roman tradition, since their attitude towards peoples outside the empire had almost always been strictly pragmatic, untouched by feelings of moral obligation of any kind.

The sack was to be Alaric's last major act before his death in the same year. However, a new Gothic figure had entered the scene, Alaric's brother Athaulf, whose career was to bring further the fusing of Roman and barbarian worlds. In 409 he had brought another Gothic army to reinforce Alaric's in Italy. Honorius was in a desperate state. He had sought, as we have seen, to neutralize the rival Roman empire to the north by recognizing Constantine III. The cities of North Italy were ordered to raise their own troops and the court at Ravenna was in a state of chaos after the execution of Stilicho.

---

[1] Matthews, op. cit. 301. He does, however, point out that it would not have been easy to realize capital tied up in land; and that the huge sums recorded as having been spent on ostentatious celebration of public office were savings put aside from years of income. Nevertheless the resources were there; and the discovery, for example, of the Esquiline Treasure (J.P.C. Kent and K.S. Painter (eds.), *Wealth of the Roman World*, British Museum, exhibition catalogue (1977), 44 ff.) shows the sort of wealth in plate and precious objects being concealed by the aristocracy in the period—perhaps as much against forced levies for this sort of purpose (or as the equivalent of numbered bank accounts in case of a *coup d'état*) as under threat of actual barbarian raids.

This chaos was not really resolved till one *coup d'état* after another finally established another general, Flavius Constantius, in a position similar to that formerly held by Stilicho. With some stability restored to the western government at Ravenna there was now a prospect of being able to deal with Constantine. Honorius' hand was further strengthened by the changed situation brought about by the restoration of good relations between Ravenna and Constantinople, extending even from time to time to practical assistance. Our prime interest in Britain tends to make us concentrate on Stilicho: A.H.M. Jones' general summary of the position since the division of the empire in 395 is an important corrective:

During most of the period when the sons and grandsons of Theodosius [*the Great*] ruled the two halves of the empire relations between East and West were as close as they had hitherto normally been, and on several occasions the Eastern government gave military support to the Western. Anthemius sent 4000 men to aid Honorius against Alaric in 409; Theodosius II's government sent a large expedition to crush the usurper John [*after the death of Honorius*] and install Valentinian III in 425; and on two occasions, in 431 and 441, it sent important forces against the Vandals in Africa. But for the first thirteen years after Theodosius' death, while Stilicho ruled the West, there was friction between the two governments which had serious results.[1]

Circumstances were changing in the north-west, too. Constantine III's empire was disintegrating, partly no doubt due to external pressures but also to a great extent from internal causes. Gerontius and Constans, having taken Spain, seem to have made a serious mistake by handing the defence of the Pyrenean passes over to barbarian federate troops. In 409 these failed to resist the Germans who had crossed Gaul, taken all they could, and were now intent on starting on a similar process in Spain. Constans sent orders dismissing Gerontius from his post as *magister militum*, but it was no moment for heeding such a command. Gerontius instead proclaimed a rival emperor, one Maximus. John Matthews has suggested that this was because it was essential to be able to treat with the Germans at imperial level.[2] Whatever the reason, the Spanish part of Constantine's empire and the army under Gerontius' command were now out

[1] A.H.M. Jones, op. cit. 182.   [2] Matthews, op. cit. 311.

of his control, and about to become dangerously hostile. Gerontius and Maximus were shortly to invade Gaul, bringing barbarian allies with them. Yet in the same year Constantine himself was attempting to take advantage of the chaos in Italy itself by advancing into the northern part of the country. There is even the possibility that he had ideas of rounding off his conquests by expelling Honorius from the western throne, or it may have been that he was to cement his nominal alliance by supporting Honorius against Alaric. Whatever his precise intention, it was not to work. Despite Honorius' desperate plight, Constantine's own realm was disintegrating. Gerontius and Maximus raised a German revolt, defeated Constans in battle and slew him. Constantine, withdrawn from Italy, was himself besieged in the city of Arles. The empire set up by the British army was now in a very serious state of civil war. In addition, a substantial part of the Burgundian nation took this chance to settle inside the Roman frontier on the Rhine. Constantine III had proved unable to control his own armies. Gaul—which he might have been expected to clear of the German invaders—had been looted from one end to the other and now Spain was laid open to the same treatment. The Burgundians looked like setting up a permanent kingdom inside the Rhine frontier he had been trying to repair. He was now besieged in his capital, which implies not only that he could not enforce his will elsewhere in his empire, but that normal administrative communications (including the collection of taxes and payment of troops)[1] were abruptly severed between Arles and his provinces, including the diocese of Britain.

In the meantime, probably in 408 while the Germans were still ravaging Gaul and while the attention of Constantine's government had been on its campaign in Spain,[2] barbarians launched a serious and destructive attack on Britain. Constantine probably did not have the troops to spare to deal with this emergency: it is at least clear that when Gerontius

---

[1] Constantine had operated an active mint of his own. Some Constantinian officers in the neighbourhood of Trier may have been able, it is true, to draw on that mint, still open: it is interesting that the Rhineland did not surrender immediately after the fall of Constantine.

[2] E.A. Thompson's defence of J.B. Bury's date of 408 is strongly argued (*Brit.* 8 (1977), 307 f.; cf. Bury, *A History of the Later Roman Empire* (1923), i. 200).

revolted against him the bulk of his army was in Spain. Moreover in 409 the situation became even worse, for this was the point when Gerontius tried the same trick on Constantine as Stilicho, inciting a barbarian attack in Gaul. Zosimus describes the situation and its consequences:

Gerontius . . . gaining the support of the troops [*in Spain*] caused the barbarians in Gaul to make war on Constantine. Since Constantine failed to resist this attack (the larger part of his army being in Spain), the barbarians across the Rhine attacked everywhere with all their strength and brought the people of Britain and some of the nations of Gaul to the point where they revolted from Roman rule and lived by themselves, no longer obeying Roman laws. The Britons took up arms and, fighting for themselves, freed the cities from the barbarian pressure; and all of Armorica and other provinces of Gaul, in imitation of the Britons, freed themselves in the same manner, expelling the Roman officials and setting up their own administration as well as they could.[1]

The year 409, therefore, saw Constantine III as Augustus but with his British provinces already hard pressed by a barbarian attack which had started in the previous year. The Gallic Chronicle confirms that the enemy was Saxon.[2] Before the end of the year he had lost both Spain and Britain. In Britain the revolt implies that those of his administration who had remained loyal were now ejected. If we must have an 'End' for Roman Britain this would be a convenient one.

Despite the convenience of having an end at this point, as we shall see there is no reason to suppose that anyone believed it to be so at the time and good cause to think the opposite. It is worth looking at the civil and military aspects separately. And it is worth, too, considering for a moment what sort of men staffed the senior posts in the imperial administration in the early fifth century, because it helps us to see the context of the expulsion. In ordinary times, when there was no rival regime preventing the central government from acting normally, the *vicarius* of the diocese and the

---

[1] Zosimus, vi. 5. Zosimus finished his book soon after 498 and must have understood the legal and administrative implications of what he described: he himself served as a senior official in the eastern imperial administration and rose to the rank of *comes*, and despite the passage of time and differences between eastern and western systems it seems unreasonable not to assume a fairly close understanding of what the events meant.

[2] *Chron. Gall.* iv. 62: this, however, does not exclude the possibility that Britain was also at the same time threatened by other barbarians.

governors of his provinces would still have been appointed by the government in Italy and quite likely but not always be by origin from one of the western provinces of the empire. We have at least one *vicarius* from the city of Constantinople itself, though after 395 the jobs are more likely to have gone to loyal adherents of the western court. Indeed, in the west, unlike the east, the great landowning families once again in the fifth century dominated the civil offices. In 417 we find the distinguished Gallic landowner Rutilius Namatianus stopping off on a journey home to visit another Gaul, Victorinus, an Aquitanian who had served at court like so many of his Aquitanian compatriots since the days of Ausonius' friendship with Gratian. Before his time at court this Victorinus had been *vicarius* of Britain. It is reasonably certain that he headed the British diocese before the usurpation of Marcus in Britain in 406. He had retired to Aquitania after serving in Britain and Italy, but had retreated before the barbarian disruption of his Gallic homeland in 409 or 414 to other property belonging to him in Italy, which promised more security.[1] The world was shrinking for the western provincial aristocrats, but they were to display an astonishing capacity for survival. Victorinus had sought a more tranquil retirement. Others were, as we shall see, to retain considerable property and influence in their home provinces in spite of the profound changes in their world.

One notes that Victorinus was a provincial, but not a Romano-Briton. There had been a convention that governors should not head their home provinces. Army officers, as we have seen, are as likely to be German as Roman by descent, but that does not say anything about their personal place of origin, and they too would receive their commands from Italy and have a varied career. If we assume, as we have, that some of the men appointed to Britain by Stilicho changed sides in 406, the usurpers will have still had to fill vacant posts. Constantine III almost immediately had the whole of the Gallic prefecture to draw upon. Yet it is not surprising to find a Briton, Gerontius, in his most senior military post. The British army had put Constantine into power and needed to be rewarded: moreover Britain had had a much larger

---

[1] Matthews, op. cit. 326.

garrison than Spain and Gaul, and the Rhine army had just been involved in defeat. On the other hand we find the civil office of praetorian prefect under Constantine being occupied first by a Gallo-Roman noble, Apollinaris. He was grandfather of the famous statesman and author Sidonius Apollinaris, and is typical of that group of Gallo-Romans who had been supplying many of the leading personalities of the imperial court and administration. He was followed by another such man, Decimius Rusticus, and it is very notable that the political traditions of their families were not seriously interrupted even when Constantine's empire fell. The sons of both had distinguished careers in the imperial service and Apollinaris' son actually came back later from Italy to hold the praetorian prefecture in Gaul under the restored legitimist regime.

Romano-British nobles do not seem to have been playing the same sort of part in the imperial government, and it is therefore perhaps unlikely that Constantine could draw on a similar pool of experience from among them to fill his senior civilian posts, either in Gaul and Spain or in Britain itself. Doubtless some of the men who did hold the posts under him owned property in the island even if they were not resident, but their local involvement was probably minimal. It is also worth remembering that the tenure of senior posts was tending to be comparatively short. All this adds up to the likelihood that the Constantinian civil administration ejected by the Britons was largely staffed, at least at the senior levels, by men who were strangers. These are the 'Romans' who were expelled. That it could be done at all is perhaps an argument supporting the notion that only relatively few regular military units were left—or at least only a few that bothered to remain loyal.

On the military side, it is difficult to imagine that, whatever troop withdrawals may have been made by Constantine, the whole military apparatus had been dismantled by him. The skeleton, at least of a command and maintenance structure, must have remained. We may reasonably ask both what happened to it during the ejection of the Constantian officers and how the remaining troops had been reacting to events on the Continent. I cannot help suspecting that the phase between the revolt of Gerontius and the expulsion of the officials from Britain was the moment when large bodies of troops left Britain, whether in response to orders or of their own volition to seek their fortunes in the renewed troubles on the Continent. Many of the troops who were up to this point still in Britain may have felt their sympathies with their colleagues supporting Gerontius in Spain rather than Constantine at Arles; others may well have been barbarian allies who had no particular reason to stay loyal to anyone unless he paid and paid well. However, none of this carries with it the implication that anyone at the time thought the whole elaborate structure of the army in Britain had come to an end for ever. Indeed, the retention of lists of units and arrangement of commands in the *Notitia* probably argues the opposite. Certainly, till the expulsion of Constantine's men by the Britons, we may reasonably assume at least a core of officers and men remaining at their posts in the island. Indeed the army was so central to Roman administration that it is difficult to see what the expulsion could mean if it did not involve the holders of military as well as civil office.

We are greatly hampered by the total lack of direct information on what happened to the army in Britain after 409. We have very largely to rely on analogy drawn from the collapse of better-documented provinces and the general dissolution of the Roman forces in the west. Much of that can only be grasped in the wider context of fifth-century western history, and we shall therefore defer considering the general picture till the next chapter. However, it is worth looking briefly here at what may have happened with the warning that much of the argument is from analogy from other parts of the west much later in the century.

If the *Notitia* as we have it reflects the state of the official records around AD 420/425, as some students of the document think, then the lists for Britain can hardly have been other than a paper establishment. There is no evidence for an imperial reoccupation after the break with Rome that will stand up to serious scrutiny. It is, of course, perfectly possible that the old British establishment remained in the files from nothing more than administrative inertia. On the other hand, there is no cause to think the Roman authorities would have assumed Britain permanently lost. Provinces, including those of Britain, had been lost and regained many times before. There was probably no reason to delete the British section, and a positive advantage in having a reference list that would act as a contingency plan for the day when the restoration of Britain to its normal form of government became a reality. Nevertheless, I do not think the military establishment described in the *Notitia* records, even in part, anything that was actually in being in Britain after the break with Roman rule. If, as I believe, the British rejection of Roman government—first that of Constantine III and thereafter, in all probability, of the restored legitimist regime in Gaul—was substantially fuelled by a desire to rid themselves once and for all of the burden of the imperial establishment, the likelihood of their being able or wanting to maintain in being the very expensive Late Roman military system seems extremely low. We are, after all, told that the Britons themselves successfully organized their own defence at that time.

We have a little guidance on what could happen to regular units when the link with the central command was broken. One of the most quoted and graphic sources is Eugippius' *Life of St. Severinus* which describes the situation in Noricum in the 470s, half a century or so later. There were still many regular units stationed at various cities in that province, but when their pay ceased to arrive they were disbanded, and the frontier was abandoned with them.[1] One last unit despatched a deputation to Italy to collect what was due: when this failed to return, this unit too disbanded itself. That enabled the neighbouring barbarian king to cross the Danube and take over military control of the Roman towns and their populations.[2] This is, of course, long after Britain became separated from the empire, but in the absence of contrary evidence, it is perhaps fair to guess that something similar may have happened after 409 with the regular troops that had not left Britain. While we may be certain that Constantine III would have had to pay his troops generously when they elevated him, as was the invariable custom, it is extremely unlikely that after the revolt of Britain any cash would have

---

[1] Eugippius, *Life of St. Severinus* (*V. Sev.*), 20.
[2] It is interesting to note that this particular king was in touch with the eastern emperor and was encouraged by him to make war on the western regime, now dominated by the Ostrogoth Odoacer.

come through for troops remaining, even if, as is improbable, Constantine had been able to keep up payments once Gerontius had intervened in Gaul. A rapid dissolution of regular units in Britain at this point is therefore indicated. A hint of what this process might have been at its most orderly is given by a reference to the inclusion in the Roman forces at the Battle of the Catalaunian Plains, which took place in Gaul in 451, of the Olibriones 'who had once been Roman soliders'. This description suggests a regular unit that had been settled on the land like *laeti*, with an obligation to military service when required, kept together but presumably not paid.[1] Even this degree of organization was probably a rare exception, but is a great deal more likely than that local initiative took over responsibility in Britain for regular wages and provision in kind.

The latter, as we have noted, had in the fourth century reached a high level and involved state factories on a large scale. To control it required the intricate bureaucracy of praetorian prefects, *vicarii* and provincial governors, the very officialdom we assume the Britons expelled. It would, moreover have required the active support of the Romano-British landowners to maintain the regular army in being. Yet that system was extremely unpopular with the Roman landowning class elsewhere. Not only was it very expensive in cash terms: it also imposed what was felt as an intolerable burden on the manpower required for agricultural estates—conscription. The Late Empire is marked by a continuous struggle by the propertied class against the imperial government over recruiting,[2] and in the fifth century, as we have noted, this landowning aristocracy was in control of the civilian offices within whose remit recruiting lay. One must, indeed, wonder with what enthusiasm the civil service now responded to the demands of the emperor and his generals. It was not as if the regular army had proved politically reliable. For centuries it had been tolerated at best and often hated by the civilian population at large, bringing disaster on more than one noble family by its emperor-making and civil wars. It was not even popular under the Late Empire with those

---

[1] Jordanes, *Getica,* 191: *quondam milites Romani, tunc vero iam in numero auxiliarium exquisisti.*
[2] See A.H.M. Jones, op. cit. 198 f.

actually compelled to serve in the ranks, if the savage penalties laid down for evasion are a guide. Settlement on the land would have avoided the probability of another coup by unpaid and disaffected troops, been a much cheaper method of retaining a reserve than by keeping them as a standing army, and added to the agricultural labour force.[1] Indeed, the last advantage could probably have been gained very simply and with little risk by allowing the last units to dissolve of their own accord, if they were by now very few. Some such move to the land, organized, disorganized, or a mixture of the two, may indeed explain some of the finds of Late Roman military equipment on villa sites and help to fill in our picture of society immediately after the break with Rome.

By 409 the practice of relying upon barbarian soldiers employed on contract was becoming common in other parts of the Roman world. The dangers inherent in Britain becoming totally dependent upon them are therefore not likely to have been widely appreciated—or, if appreciated, been strong enough to overcome the realities of contemporary practice. In the face of the widespread resistance in the western world to the burdens of the army, it would hardly have been practical politics for British rulers in the years after 409 to win the necessary support among the civilian population to maintain regular units in being, even if they wished to do so. This was not just a matter of a central authority with the will to issue the orders and command the loyalty of troops: it was also paying for a network of officials physically to collect and account for both taxes and actual recruits. That network formed a major part of the system the Britons had just rejected; and, while there is no positive evidence that the Britons did not replace these officials with their own nominees, there is no reason why they should have done so unless a new usurper commanded the overwhelming military support necessary to force it upon them. In this general context, eventual British employment of barbarian federates wholesale takes on a certain inevitability.[2]

---

[1] Later in the fifth century the aristocracy that remained within the empire won the remarkable concession that sons of *laeti* who had married women from among the *coloni*, the tied work-force of the great estates, should serve on the land and not in the army.

[2] It is interesting to note that the imperial commander Aetius had Saxons in his army at the Catalaunian Plains (Jordanes, op. cit. 191).

We do not know what form of administration emerged after the break from Roman rule, but we can set one very important limit to the possibilities. The Romano-British upper classes had not shared in that burst of activity in the latter part of the fourth century and the early fifth which had put their Gallo-Roman counterparts into leading positions in the imperial hierarchy. This must have meant that, apart from any senior officials previously posted into Britain who had turned their coats rather than be ejected or murdered, Britain was now very short of men with experience of senior office. It would therefore have been extremely difficult— even if they had wished to do so—to organize the sort of centralized system that Constantine III and the many predecessors who had set up north-western empires, able to draw on a wide area of the west for the men to run the machinery of government, had achieved. There is no reason to suppose the traditions and attitudes of the Romano-British were any different from those of the Gallo-Romans, but the fortunes of recent politics had not given them the same opportunities. The purge of Constantine's administrators seems to have been thorough: the gap to be filled was large. The late Dr John Morris drew our attention to a Christian tract known as the *De Vita Christiana*, dating from about AD 411. This may very likely have emanated from Britain, and while there is no direct evidence for the context, it is not improbable that it refers to the overthrow of Constantine III's men in Britain:[1]

We see before us plenty of examples of wicked men, the sum of their sins complete, who are at this present moment being judged, and denied this present life no less than the life to come . . . Those who have freely shed the blood of others are now being forced to spill their own . . . Some lie unburied, food for the beasts and birds of the air. Others . . . have been individually torn limb from limb . . . Their judgements killed many husbands, widowed many women, orphaned many children. They made them beggars and left them bare . . . for they plundered the children of the men they killed. Now it is their wives who are widows, their sons who are orphans, begging their daily bread from others.

It is, of course, likely that there were some people at all

[1] John Morris, 'Dark Age Dates', in M.G. Jarrett and B. Dobson (eds.), *Britain and Rome: Essays presented to Eric Birley*, Kendal (1966), 148.

levels in Constantine's service who did in fact successfully change sides when they saw how the wind was blowing: such changes of regime were too common an occurrence to cause a wholesale flight from Britain of the entire corps of military and civil office-holders, faithful to the last. But even they, strengthened by local appointments, could hardly have kept the whole administrative machine working, including surviving sections of the regular army, when cash remittances from central funds to the diocesan treasuries stopped. Salaries and running costs were enormous, and we have to reckon with an extreme lack of enthusiasm on the part of the provincial aristocracy to take office in a new diocesan administration—besides being unwilling to pay the necessary central taxes or supply recruits from their estates when imperial pressure could no longer be applied, either from Arles or Ravenna. When Zosimus tells us that the Britons were living on their own, no longer obedient to Roman laws, and that other provinces copied their example, establishing their own administration as best they could, I think we have to expect in Britain not a new central administration in London or even in the separate provinces that made up the British diocese, but a whole series of local arrangements, probably differing greatly from place to place.

Much has been made of a 'rescript' from Honorius at this time alleged to have been addressed to the cities of Britain, instructing them to organize their own defence. This has been interpreted as an answer to a loyalist appeal to Ravenna.[1] Rescripts were one of the normal ways in which the emperors laid down law and issued instructions: they were in the form of answers to queries addressed to them. It would imply an appeal for help or at least a request for instruction but it is not really possible to build a picture of a loyalist party in Britain on this basis. At the most, it may be no more than a readiness to barter submission to imperial authority in return for assistance (as in 389). But even if it were certain that it was a formal rescript, which is not so, it is not even possible now to be sure that Britain is the province concerned—it has recently been suggested the text may mean Brettia,

---

[1] Zosimus, VI. x. 2—letter of 410 to the πόλεις (*civitates* or local authorities): Ὀνωρίου δὲ γράμμασι πρὸς τὰς ἐν Βρεττανίᾳ χρησαμένου πόλεις φυλάττεσθαι παραγγέλλουσι.

(Bruttium, in Italy).[1] The troubles were so acute it would not be surprising if the provincials had appealed to all and sundry. Dr J.N.L. Myres has certainly made a convincing case for a struggle in the early fifth century between Pelagian heretics and a Catholic party in Britain (Pelagius himself had originally come from Britain)[2] and it would be an interesting implication that the prime issue now was heresy rather than paganism (despite a short-lived pagan revival in Alaric's time in the western senate itself). But though religion remained extremely important in politics it is not necessary to invoke it as a major reason for the actions of the British. Weight has also been put on the fact that the letter is addressed to the cities, not to a *vicarius* of Britain (or, for that matter, a *comes* or *dux*). Yet Honorius could hardly have done otherwise. Constantine's officers were out—and anyhow Honorius is unlikely to have wished to recognize them even if they had not been. We have just seen there is every reason to think it improbable the Britons had re-staffed the central administration. With Constantine III himself still at Arles and barbarians in Gaul and Italy, Honorius could have had no chance of getting men out from Italy to take over the British diocese in the normal way, even if there was a loyalist party asking for it. In fact if it really is Britain that was addressed, he was simply giving the same instructions in time of emergency that he had already given to cities much closer to home and where there was every chance of restoring normal conditions in due course. I see no cause to assume Honorius was deliberately abandoning Britain for ever. If this point does mark the 'End of Roman Britain' it is only with hindsight. It may indeed be the point when the Romano-Britons lost confidence in their last candidate for the imperial throne and decided to try doing without another, not to mention all the expensive trapping that went with imperial administration, but that does not mean that they no longer believed in the credibility of the western imperial government itself, even if some of them hoped to keep themselves out of its clutches.

Professor Thomas has neatly summarized our position as

---

[1] Rivet and Smith (below, p. 761), 102; cf. Matthews, op. cit. 320, n. 7.
[2] J.N.L. Myres, *JRS* 50 (1960), 21 ff.

historians, often obsessed with defined dates when 'periods' end:

> There is no single year in which we can claim, with confidence, that the Roman occupation of Britain ended—suddenly, definitely and for ever. In T.S. Eliot's words, the end was marked, not with a bang, but a whimper. The process now appears to have covered a good half-century, and the selection of some such horizon as A.D. 400 (or 410, or 425) to mark off Late Roman from sub-Roman times is an aspect of convenience rather than of reality.[1]

For the purposes of this Oxford History of England we have a formal line we could draw for the end of our period, yet the Roman world goes on, in Britain and on the Continent, as do our Classical sources. This is true both of Greek and Roman authors, many still working within the empire, and of certain archaeological material of Roman or mixed Roman-barbarian origin. Indeed, 'a good half-century' may prove to be an underestimate. We shall therefore try to pursue, at least in outline and broadly from the Roman side, what seems to have been the slow run-down of the Romano-British way of life—punctuated by occasional violent incidents of the sort that more often get recorded by contemporaries—in its setting as part of the Late Roman world. Indeed it is probably not fanciful to think many Britons would have seen their world themselves in this light. There are times when the imperial government itself seems to regain real credibility; and, as we shall see, even when the empire itself was dead as an institution in the west, the Roman world had by no means come to an end.

NOTE

Britain, AD 406-10. Since the chapter above was first written an article by E.A. Thompson appeared with this title (*Brit.* 8 (1977), 303 ff.). The first part is a convincing reassessment of the chronology of 406-9, and where possible this has been taken into account in revising this chapter. The second re-examines the nature of the British revolt against the officials. By assuming that the revolt of Armorica and other Gallic provinces was of exactly the same nature as that in Britain and that the Armorican revolt was a rising of *bacaudae*, he is able to argue that the British cities were rescued from the barbarian invaders by separatist

[1] Charles Thomas, *Britain and Ireland in Early Christian Times, A. D. 400-800* (n.d.), 13.

lower-class revolutionaries. The argument then proceeds to explain the context of Honorius' letter to the British cities (which E.A. Thompson accepts, rejecting Matthews' doubt) as the upper-class leaders of the *civitates*, having been rescued by the rebels, now appealing for military assistance against them.

There are extreme difficulties in this interpretation. It depends on certain inferences. One is that the Armorican revolt of 409 continued into that reported in 417 (when Rutilius Namatianus mentions that the order of society there was being turned upside down) and if so that no change occurred in its nature. There is no proof of continuity, but such a revolutionary movement in Armorica is perfectly believable: north-west Gaul was chronically affected by this sort of disturbance. It had been so in the third century and was for long into the fifth. But there is no reason at all to import this characteristic into Britain: there is no other evidence to support such a theory and the general level of stability and prosperity in Britain in the third and fourth centuries was quite different from that in north-western Gaul. Secondly, Zosimus is assumed to mean that the nature of the rebellion was the same in Britain, in Armorica, and 'other Gallic provinces'. Yet he merely says that the Armoricans and some other Gauls imitated the Britons in expelling Roman officials and living according to their own rules. We cannot assume that the rebels were of the same social class or set up a similar way of life in all three cases. Furthermore we have to explain what had happened to the putative British *bacaudae* by the time of Germanus' visit in 429 (see Thompson, op. cit. 318, who himself raises just this question). Thompson has attributed the repulse of the barbarians in 409 to peasant rebels, as an achievement not paralleled by the aristocracy of the *civitates* elsewhere in the western provinces; and interpreted the response of Honorius as to an appeal from the British upper-classes for rescue. Must we then assume that the British aristocrats overestimated the abilities of the rebels when appealing to Honorius and subsequently defeated them (though previously unable to cope with the barbarians)—or should we take the troops listed under the *comes Britanniarum* in the *Notitia* as representing an unrecorded and improbable imperial expedition at this time? In fact the introduction of British *bacaudae* into the equation creates a completely unnecessary complication and may be discounted.

16

BRITAIN, THE END OF THE WESTERN EMPIRE, AND THE SUCCESSOR STATES

As early as 411, the government of Honorius was regaining the initiative over its enemies. Honorius' generals Flavius Constantius and Ulfila marched on Arles, where Constantine III was being besieged by Gerontius. The latter fled at the approach of the imperial army and shortly after committed suicide. It is interesting that many of his Roman troops, as opposed to his barbarians, deserted to Honorius' army.[1] Gerontius' emperor Maximus took refuge with his barbarian friends in Spain. Honorius' army next defeated Frankish and Alamannic reinforcements coming to join Constantine and was rewarded by the surrender of Constantine himself, who was soon executed. There must have been many in Britain who now expected the immediate return of imperial officials.

There was however one further act of rebellion before the rival western empire that had been set up by the army of Britain finally disintegrated. The former Constantinian praetorian prefect Decimius Rusticus assisted in the proclamation of yet another emperor, Jovinus, on the Rhine. He was supported by Burgundians, Alans, and others who were now settled inside the frontier and perhaps had been accepted by Constantine as federate defenders of it. However the main Visigothic force was now in Gaul, and after briefly flirting with this new usurpation its leader Athaulf took the opportunity to negotiate peace with Honorius, promising the heads of Jovinus and his brother, an offer readily accepted. Jovinus was executed by Honorius' praetorian prefect of Gaul, and the empire of Constantine III finally came to an end.[2] This execution was followed by a ruthless purge of

[1] One wonders how many of them were, like Gerontius, British, or at least serving in units drawn from Britain.

[2] The fact that the mint at Arles as well as that at Trier issued coins for Jovinus and his brother suggests that at least for a short while they were able to gain fairly wide acceptance.

officers who had served Constantine or Jovinus, including
Rusticus, and a large number of aristocrats (*multique
nobiles*),[1] presumably in the main notables from the various
provinces of the Constantinian realm.

In this context it is perhaps not surprising that now, in
413, Britain seems to have made no move to bring itself
back under Honorius' rule, even if some Romano-Britons
might earlier have been prepared to accept the financial
burden of Roman rule again. Procopius, the sixth-century
historian who became prefect of the City at Constantinople
under Justinian and knew the west, having served with
Belisarius in the reconquest of Italy, describes how, though
Constantine had been defeated, 'the Romans were never
able to recover Britain, but from that time it remained on its
own under local usurpers.'[2] Why the western imperial government could not (or perhaps would not) extend its successes
to Britain is worth considering, for it illuminates important
features of the setting in which 'post-Roman' Britain
developed.

In theory, the rule of Honorius was now re-established
throughout Gaul and Spain. In fact he was still in a very weak
position. It is fashionable to play down the influence of
individuals on large movements in history, but one reason
that nothing decisive was done about the Goths—and without
that Gaul could not be properly brought under control—was
that they still had in their hands Honorius' half-sister Galla
Placidia, whom Alaric had captured during the sack of Rome
in 410. The Visigothic army which had suppressed Jovinus
was now moving southwards from the Rhineland, accompanied by an important group of Alans. It was to have a very
chequered history in the next year or two and several times
tried to do deals with the Romans. Athaulf actually married
Galla Placidia and seems to have had a genuine desire to unite
the Roman and Gothic nations. It was not till after his death
and the return of Galla Placidia[3] to Honorius that the Visigoths

---

[1] Frigeridus: text in Matthews, *Western Aristocracies,* 315, n. 6. Perhaps
we may guess that there were a fair number of Britons serving at the court at
Arles or elsewhere outside Britain.

[2] Procopius, *De Bello Vandalico*, I. ii. 38.

[3] She married Flavius Constantius in AD 417, without enthusiasm, but this
marriage made it easier for Honorius to give him the title of Augustus in 421.

were turned out of Spain, now pacified, and in return for an obligation of military support for Rome were firmly settled in a permanent kingdom by Flavius Constantius. This new kingdom comprised the lands of Aquitania, a large and rich region stretching from the lower Loire to the Garonne and the homeland of many of the most distinguished men that Roman Gaul had produced, particularly in the past half-century.

This date of 418 does unquestionably mark a new era in the history of the west. The Rhineland was by now Burgundian, the Suebi and Franks had much of north-eastern Gaul, and even in parts of north-western and central Gaul which were still Roman the writ of the prefecture of Arles could only be enforced spasmodically. There are signs that central Gaul was taxed, but Armorica was persistently the seat of peasant revolts. By the time one reached the Loire disorder was clearly felt to reign, at least judged by the standards of southern Gaul. Roman intervention tended to be in terms of punitive expeditions. In 417, the first time we hear of Roman armies operating in northern Gaul since the fall of Constantine's empire, Rutilius Namatianus' relation Exuperantius crushed a slave revolt, 'restoring law and liberty', in other words bringing back the normal way of life, the settled order of things.[1] But this does not seem to have been permanent. Later interventions were necessary but more and more through the agency of barbarian federates rather than the direct use of Roman troops. Disorder in the region seems to have been endemic, and it was regarded as a haven for those who could not bear the level of taxation of the south. A number of names and features relevant to Britain enter the story here. The city of Auxerre on the Yonne, east of the great bend of the central Loire, seems to have been inside the sphere of Roman control. Its remarkable bishop, St. Germanus, appointed in the same fateful year 418, had been a barrister and a provincial governor—a background rather frowned upon by the Church, but his experience doubtless stood him in good stead.[2] At one point we find him appealing on behalf of locals to the praetorian prefect for tax reductions. On another occasion (as late as 448) he

---

[1] Rutilius Namatianus, *De Reditu,* I. 215 f.

[2] Constantius, *Life of St. Germanus* (*Vita Germ.*) is an important source both for Gaul and Britain in the fifth century.

travelled to Ravenna to intercede on behalf of the Armoricans against a planned attack by federate Alan barbarians under the orders of the Roman general Aetius.

Perhaps the most interesting area of Gaul is the northern region that was eventually centred politically on Soissons, where a Roman government successfully held out till 486: it will be worth coming back to this in a little detail later, since it has interesting analogies and connections with Britain and lay not far from it. But to return south to Arles for a moment, it is clear that great efforts were made to emphasize this city as a seat of imperial splendour. Roman propaganda meant it to rival and obliterate the memory of the old capital at Trier; but it was not easy to disguise its much shrunken territorial authority and its military weakness, depending on barbarian alliances and occasional direct assistance from Italy. There was a further important change, too, away from the old concept of the prefecture of the Gauls as a form of devolution of imperial authority, albeit a very limited one with all the major appointments and final decisions lying at the imperial court. It is symbolic that in 418, the same year again, the Council of the Gauls was revived and sited at Arles, it is said at the instigation of Agricola, the praetorian prefect of the day. It was described as a congress of the leading citizens (*optimorum conventus*), a forum for debate of public and private issues, especially those affecting the propertied classes. It was, in fact, a barons' parliament, if one may use a phrase with overtones not entirely inappropriately medieval.

Many Gallo-Roman nobles (and this may have included Britons who had been at Constantine's court or governing his provinces) had suffered from the terror following the fall of the regime set up by the British army. In Britain they were out of reach of Honorius' officers. In Gaul others had come to a reasonable accommodation with the new, generally friendly, and Christian (if often Arian) barbarian kingdoms, which allowed them to carry on a fairly high style of life, the greatest of them continuing to style themselves senators and living a country life still essentially that of the great Roman villa-owner, even if in many cases embattled like some Renaissance Italian nobleman. Thus, to quote John Matthews' description of the villa occupied by Pontius

Leontius, a member of what had been one of the great old families of Roman Bordeaux:

Leontius resided in spectacular security in his family seat, a fortified stronghold overlooking the Garonne, which was known as 'Burgus' (hence identified as Bourg-sur-Gironde). It was equipped with walls and towers, and possessed granaries and storehouses adequate to receive the huge harvests accruing from Leontius' estates in the region. At the entrance to the establishment was an inscription bearing the names of its founders. In the dining-room was a fish-pool; in the porticoes, wall paintings of legendary scenes, Classical and Christian. For this great establishment also, like Consentius' villa near Narbonee [*within the Roman prefecture*], possessed its chapel of the Christian faith.[1]

The rich, therefore, if they were politically adroit—and lucky—could survive.[2] The much greater impact must have been on the middle and skilled lower classes. While the barbarian kingdoms in Gaul preserved to a varying degree what suited them of the Roman civil administration, the career opportunities formerly offered by an empire-wide bureaucracy had largely disappeared. Perhaps even more important was the loss of the chance of improving one's position in life through promotion in the Roman army, a traditional channel of advancement of the greatest social importance. Similarly the civilian trades that depended on that military and civil machine for their market must have been severely disrupted, even if their new Gothic masters still needed supplies. But most of all, the wealth and security for lesser men that flowed from the system of patronage and favour (which a few emperors had tried to stem) was largely gone. It is not, therefore, surprising to find Romans who lived in the Visigothic kingdom taking every opportunity for office and advancement in the Church. This was one area the Visigoths themselves avoided, since the historical accident of their involvement in Alaric's time and before with the eastern empire had made their conversion to Christianity an Arian one. They were thus not competing with Romans for positions in the Catholic Church of the west.

[1] Ibid. 342 f.
[2] Some stories have interesting implications for the flavour of upper-class life in those times. One Gallo-Roman nobleman had his house ransacked because he did not have a Gothic 'guest' living with him. Another finally had to *sell* his last property to a Goth to raise money to support himself in old age.

In career terms this was of major importance for the Roman part of the population and it made the bishops natural leaders of the Roman community.

In the Roman-controlled territories of the Arles prefecture the private style of life of the rich was not dissimilar: indeed they were in close contact on a personal level with their peers in the allied Visigothic kingdom. In political terms, however, things were very different; and different too from the days before Constantine III. Before the barbarian invasions of 406 and Constantine's seizure of power, the praetorian prefects of Gaul had been sent out in the traditional way from Italy, usually after a career including posts in other parts of the empire than Gaul. Moreover, as we have seen, there had been much movement the other way, with Aquitanians in particular dominating the imperial court and penetrating the senatorial aristocracy. Now Aquitania itself was Gothic, while not one praetorian prefect of Gaul from this time on can be shown to have been other than a Gallo-Roman noble. This new regime at Arles, therefore, while not in rebellion from Ravenna, did not necessarily always share common interests with it. Relations were in general cordial, and there was sometimes military support from Italy for the government in Arles, occasionally direct intervention. On several of these occasions the objective was the crushing of rebellion, particularly where the old spectre of peasant revolt was raised.

One wonders how much of the civil administration of this surviving group of provinces remained intact. The capacity of bureaucracy to survive and the depth to which it was embedded in Roman life are such that one suspects it was still mainly in being. This is perhaps one reason for lack of enthusiasm in Britain for returning to the imperial fold. Opportunities in the army, however, may have been more limited, with the increasing use of barbarian federates and the reluctance of landowners in the west to allow local recruiting. However, survival of an administrative machine as an integral part of the imperial system should indeed have meant better opportunities for the middle classes than in the barbarian kingdoms. It certainly gave greater scope for public life to the upper levels of society, but the constant pressure on landowners to supply recruits and the demands of imperial taxation upon them makes it a question whether it was that much better to be an estate-owner under Roman rather than Visigothic rule. Politically, it could be just as uncomfortable. An interesting, if extreme, example is Claudius Postumus Dardanus, the loyalist praetorian prefect of Gaul who had executed Jovinus, finally restoring imperial authority in Gaul, and justly hated by the Gallo-Roman nobility for the bloody purge that followed. He was well known for his Christian piety (and so addressed by both St. Augustine and St. Jerome) and in the name of holiness had withdrawn with his family into a remote valley of the Alpes Maritimes near Sisteron. This was accessible only by a gorge through which he built a special road fortified with walls and gates, to protect, as he put it, the local inhabitants, creating a fortress community named 'Theopolis'.[1] One cannot help feeling however that barbarians or even Roman peasants were not the only enemies against whom a rich man might feel it necessary to prepare physical defences, backed up where appropriate by hope of divine assistance.

The fortified or semi-fortified villa has, of course, plenty of parallels. At the grandest end of the scale we can go back to the house Diocletian prepared for his carefully planned retirement in 305, the enormous fortress-palace of Split on the Dalmatian coast, or the extraordinary castle-like villa of the mid-fourth century at Pfalzel near Trier, with which Edith Wightman has rightly compared the comment on Leontius' house: 'ostentation and protection in one'.[2]

It has become customary to refer to the corner-towers present on a famous mosaic picture of a villa in Africa[3] in terms of fortification. They appear quite frequently also in the villas of the Danubian provinces, but one wonders whether they are meant to be anything more than reasonable pre-cautions for the security of property, normal in settled society, or perhaps simply an architectural fashion for corner-towers

---

[1] *ILS* 1279: see Matthews, op. cit. 323 f.

[2] *pompa vel auxilium.* See Sidonius, *Carmina,* xxii, 114 ff. Wightman, *Roman Trier* (1970), 169 f.

[3] From a villa at Tabarka near Tunis (now in the Bardo Museum, Tunis)—illustrated in K.D. White, *Country Life in Classical Times* (1977), pl. 10 and elsewhere.

and pavilions.[1] We ought perhaps more appropriately to be looking at the increasing evidence in Britain for the reuse and even refortification of Iron Age hill-forts.[2] It is fascinating to note that a hill-fort like Cadbury Congresbury in Somerset is producing substantial quantities of Mediterranean pottery of the fifth century, which also occurs in smaller quantities at the more famous South Cadbury hill-fort, which was itself refortified in the late fifth century. In this context one may note Sidonius Apollinaris, himself a Gallo-Roman noble, son-in-law of a short-lived emperor, and politician and public servant both in Gaul and at Rome, writing in the second half of the fifth century about the many '*montana castella*' of his friend Aper in central Gaul.[3] Aper, it would seem, is still a landowner with a number of different estates to his name (others were less lucky and had seen their holdings gradually dwindle).[4]

Aper has simply adapted to circumstances by providing his properties with suitable hill-fortresses instead of villas—or perhaps as well as them. This is, of course, a little later than the period we are now considering and by Sidonius' day matters had progressed further down the road to the final Roman collapse in the west. Yet in Britain this may already have been a feature of the daily scene. Even in Gaul there is no disguising the fact that already the prefecture meant essentially the rule of the rump[5] of Roman Gaul by the Gallo-Roman upper classes in their own interest and no longer by an Italian government acting primarily for the benefit of the western emperor and his entourage. At least in this sense Constantine III's creation lived on. Britain was a

---

[1] There are also Roman walled parks on the Continent, and we should note the villa wall at Gatcombe. But are they fortifications?

[2] But see also p. 738 below.

[3] Sidonius, *Letters* V. xiv. 1.

[4] See Matthews, op. cit. 324.

[5] This rump was further contracted very substantially by another agreed settlement of barbarians, that of the rest of the Burgundians in Savoy in AD 443. Other smaller settlements, some by encroachment, others by treaty, also occurred. In 475, to the horror of Sidonius, who had followed a term as prefect of the City at Rome by accepting a bishopric in the Auvergne and was acting strongly on behalf of the Gauls against Gothic pressure, Rome handed his region over to the barbarians. It will be remembered that his was precisely the area (*apud Arvernos*) in which Dardanus had carried out his purge of the former supporters of Jovinus and the last remnants of Constantine III's empire.

stage further along the same road: we shall see what looks like the survival of the provincial Roman upper class in a similar fashion, but without even a nominally legitimate Roman government. It might, indeed, have been politically advantageous for some of these Romano-Britons if the prefecture—in its new form—had been able to regain the diocese of Britain. In practical terms, however, this could not be, for at this time there seems to have been no prospect of imperial forces gaining permanent military control in northern Gaul. Nor did the Romano-Britons apparently have another alternative open to the Gallo-Romans—rule by comparatively civilized barbarian kings. But we shall see later that a third way of life evolved in Gaul that may be much closer to the situation in Britain.

What in the meantime was happening to the economy of Britain? We have already seen the official import of new coinage in large quantities coming to an end in 402. To what extent that implies extensive reductions in the salaried classes, civil and military, we do not know, but we have already speculated that failure to pay salaries regularly may have had important political repercussions. However, whether it was a matter of a hitherto salaried class not being paid or in fact no longer existing at all, the economic effect on the trades and services does not need much imagination to comprehend. By the period 420–30 the use in Britain of coinage—at least of silver, the normal means of substantial payment—seems to have died out more or less altogether.[1] We must not, of course, forget that for a century allowances in kind had become very important elements in the income of persons in the public service. Troops, too, had no longer had to pay for their own personal equipment. It is also true that Leontius' estate in Gaul and others demonstrate how a large degree of self-sufficiency not only was possible but could support a high level of comfort. It has been suggested that the probably fifth-century corn-drying equipment found in a late town mansion at Verulamium—and even more what may be a major storehouse that succeeded it—demonstrates that the same could be true in the towns of Roman Britain. Indeed

[1] Recent work on coin hoards suggests the use of coinage ended a few years after 420. (R.A.G. Carson, *Brit. Mus. Yearbook,* 1 (1976), 67 ff.)

that a general trend toward provincial self-sufficiency was a feature of the Later Roman Empire has been generally accepted by historians and seems to have been developing for a long time. It was at least partially caused by inflation and insecurity in the third century, including the increased cost and risk of long-distance shipping due to piracy. However, one would expect Britain to be hard-hit by its insular situation. Roads, too, were in a bad state in parts of the western empire. In 417 in Italy bridges were still down and the staging-posts in ruins, nothing having been done since the Visigoths had left shortly after the sack of Rome in 410.[1] Yet Italy had been less badly damaged than Gaul and by 417 there was clearly a feeling there that life was returning to normal.[2] It is difficult to know how Britain may have fared compared to these two regions. It had escaped both the Germans and the Visigoths, but we are ignorant of the exact nature of the barbarian threat to Britain that the British warded off by themselves in 409 or what sort of damage inland the Irish raids of five years or so earlier may have done. One may perhaps fairly guess that travel by sea was very dangerous, now that there was no Roman navy in the northern seas. Road may have been a shade better. Brigandage (common elsewhere) must have been discouraging to transport, but had not prevented travel in the past. But we seem to be contemplating a much more local form of self-sufficiency than just the ability of Britain as a whole to look after itself. The collapse of the money economy is perhaps both a symptom and a cause of the breakdown of large-scale trade in factory-made objects. It is really very difficult to imagine how a barter system could have operated to pay for mass-produced low-priced items that depended on reasonably wide distribution in large quantities to keep their manufacturers in business. It is very noticeable, for example, that the large 'Alice Holt' Hampshire pottery industry had apparently been operating into the early fifth century.[3] Its confidence indeed was such that it was introducing new

---

[1] Rutilius Namatianus, op. cit. i. 41.
[2] Matthews, op. cit. 352.
[3] *Current Archaeology*, 54 (1976), 212 ff. (Full report, M.A.B. Lyne and R.S. Jefferies, *The Alice Holt/Farnham Roman pottery industry*, CBA Research Report No. 30, published at the end of 1979).

wares at the end of the fourth century or the beginning of the fifth. Yet a decade or so later, except for the very occasional sherd of imported Mediterranean pottery, all Roman factory-made pottery has disappeared and we have nothing except a little locally-made material. This commercial collapse is a remarkable contrast to, for example, the huge Rhenish glass industry that continued largely unchanged from Roman into Frankish times. It could of course be a matter of what appealed to the new market, though the source of 'Romano-Saxon' pottery and other products of indeterminate ethnic origin and to some extent date remain a matter of intense debate. The Rhenish factories were certainly already producing glass drinking-horns in the fourth century.[1] We have discussed the hideous difficulties of equating style in this period with race or politics. But it may perhaps be more relevant to note that the barbarians in Gaul used Roman coinage or struck their own deliberately on Roman lines (even to the extend of acknowledging the current Roman emperor on their issues). Of course a lot of glass products were intended for the well-off, Roman or barbarian, so the parallel with the domestic pottery industry of Britain is not quite fair; but the survival of Rhenish glass as a factory industry is important and the circulation of coinage must have been vital to it. Perhaps we ought also to note that of the major cities of the region Trier had several times been sacked since it lost its capital status and was in a depressed state, and that Mainz had been largely destroyed in the great invasion of 406. Cologne at the heart of the Rhineland on the contrary was not lost to the Franks till 463, and there is some evidence that the Frankish king proceeded to set up his royal court in the former Roman governor's palace there. Thus there was at the very centre of this industry still a great city to provide both the market and the commerical organization to promote its survival.

To set against the archaeological evidence for a cessation of a broadly based commercial economy in Britain, we have Gildas' assertion of a long period of high prosperity after the break with Rome. Perhaps we can best interpret this as

---

[1] It is interesting that it was *Frankish* federate troops that were defending the Rhine in 406.

an account based on an aristocratic point of view. The lifting of the enormous burden of taxation and of conscription of labour from the estates and the disappearance of the officials and most of, perhaps all, the army are likely to have been felt as a vast material benefit by the provincial nobility. We have already seen how well they could live, even under direct barbarian rule. The great mass of the lower-class population that worked on the land was also probably not adversely affected by the end of Roman control. The damage to the professional and mercantile classes and the loss of employment among Romano-British artisans may have touched neither class seriously.

Even among the former merchant classes of the empire, life in the midst of fifth-century barbarians was not necessarily worse than a return to Roman rule. A.H.M. Jones draws our attention to a story recounted by the contemporary historian Priscus of Panium, who was sent to Attila in 448 as an ambassador:

He was surprised to be greeted in Greek by a man dressed as a Hun. It turned out that he was a Greek who had settled at Viminacium on the Danube and prospered as a merchant.[1] When the city was sacked by the Huns he had been taken prisoner; his Hunnish master had later set him free, and he had decided not to return to the empire but to live among the Huns. When Priscus reproached him as a renegade, he justified his conduct on two grounds, the exorbitant taxation which Roman citizens had to pay, and the abuses of the Roman courts of justice. 'The laws are not the same for all,' he declared. 'If a rich man breaks the law he can avoid paying the penalty for his wrongdoing. But if it is a poor man, who does not know how to pull strings, he suffers the penalty of the law—unless he departs this life before the trial, while proceedings drag on interminably and vast expenses are incurred. That is the most monstrous thing of all, to have to pay for justice. An injured party cannot get a hearing unless he pays money to the judge and to his officials.'[2]

The cessation of easily recognizable pottery and closely datable coinage is as inconvenient for the archaeologist as it must have been for the Romano-Britons. However,

---

[1] He had also married a rich wife and clearly had become a well-off member of the provincial middle class, before his city was taken by the Huns.

[2] A.H.M. Jones, *Later Roman Empire*, 516, citing Priscus, viii. Juvenal had been complaining of the interminable delays of the law for civilians at the beginning of the second century and of how a soldier could be sure of getting his case heard first (Juvenal, xvi. 35–50).

stratigraphical evidence is now accumulating from excavations in Britain, particularly in the towns, that confirms that Romano-British life by no means stopped in 409, and even then it is easy to underestimate both the duration and extent that this new evidence represents. It is often very difficult indeed to know what period of time is represented by layers which clearly indicate continued occupation after the latest level containing datable Late Roman objects. There is also the problem that upper layers themselves are very subject to destruction or damage (as we saw earlier) and also often represent structures built in archaeologically fragile materials. The latter point is well demonstrated at Wroxeter, where meticulous excavation of the topmost layers by the latest techniques has revealed large fifth-century timber buildings constructed after the demolition of what had previously been thought to be the last Roman structures. It is also clear archaeologically, as we have already suspected on general political grounds and as can be supported by analogy from Gaul where the written evidence is much more abundant, that conditions varied greatly from place to place. An example of the character of the data now appearing from excavation comes from Lincoln. A coin, probably to be dated to the period 388–92, was found in the material of a Roman street— not, as one might have expected, in the top surface but in the third layer down.[1] It was clear that this street had there-fore been made up again twice after the resurfacing in which this particular coin was lost.

At Verulamium there is a truly remarkable sequence. First of all, two large town houses with good mosaics were built near the end of the fourth century. On top of one of these mosaics a corn-drying plant was subsequently constructed: Professor Frere has argued that the absence of coins or pottery in this phase suggests a date after about 430—not absolute evidence, but a fair inference. This drying plant was in use long enough for it to need repair, before the whole structure was demolished to make way for a large stone barn or public hall. Both may imply the need in troubled times to bring the harvest into the city swiftly and store it there in safety. However, for the moment it is the continuity

[1] *Ant. J.* 55 (1975), 245.

that is our affair. That last building had itself come down before a brand-new water-main was laid across the site, constructed in normal Roman fashion. There can therefore be no doubt of the presence of a substantial population, some form of civic organization with control of the actual source of the water supply, and enough public confidence in the future to make the work seem worthwhile. This whole stratigraphic sequence is so lengthy that it is very difficult to compress it into the first fifty years of the fifth century. A date of around 450 for the water-main cannot be too late: it could easily be too early and there is every chance that urban life continued in Verulamium in some form into the second half of the century. In London[1] a large house that had been first built at the end of the second century or the beginning of the third was reconstructed several times before the early fifth century.[2] The stoke-hole for the heating system of the residential part of the house still contained ash when excavated. In this was the handle of a large amphora or transport-jar of east-Mediterranean manufacture that was probably imported in the fifth century rather than the fourth.[3] At this stage the house was still in normal use. A hoard of coins ending certainly not earlier than 395 seems to have fallen from its hiding-place into the debris of this part of the house after it had collapsed. This supports the idea that the house continued into the early fifth century. We have no clear indication of when it finally went out of use. In the separate bath-block a Saxon brooch of a type thought to have been made around AD 450 was found on top of the fallen remains of its roof, but the furnace of these baths was not in use in the final phase of occupation of the main house itself and the length of time an object of personal adornment of this kind might remain in someone's possession

---

[1] A hoard of coins from Bermondsey now in the Museum of London, with issues dating between 380 and 400 but well-worn, suggests that coinage was circulating locally well into the fifth century.

[2] Lower Thames Street, excavated 1968.

[3] These amphorae have been variously dated (see for example *JRS* 59 (1969), 224; *Brit.* 1 (1970), 292; 7 (1976), 350) from the fourth century to the seventh. Mr Ralph Merrifield (to whom I am grateful for putting me right on details of this site) has suggested to me that such amphorae may not have reached London till the much more convenient wine-trade with Spain was disrupted by the barbarians in the early fifth century. A fair amount of the same pottery had by 1978 been found in London, but not in stratified contexts.

must be quite uncertain. Overall it looks as if the Roman building may have become derelict somewhere in the fifth century, but not necessarily very early. From these examples it is obvious we are dealing with very imprecise limits within which to locate our physical evidence, but the impression is of town life continuing at a reasonable level of sophistication well after AD 409. Cirencester is another town where life went on in some style after coinage ceased to be in general use: the forum was certainly maintained after that stage.[1] There is no sign of a calamity sweeping the cities of Britain at any one date. Gildas does talk of plague in Britain before Vortigern (to whom I shall come shortly) invited in his Saxon allies. If it has any truth, this ought to indicate a period somewhere in the first half of the fifth century, but the evidence seems to be against an outbreak sufficient to destroy town life in the island.[2]

We must continue to suspect that the picture was very varied. Some cities or whole regions may have been deliberately evacuated at one point in time, others actually abandoned after sack or local epidemic and not reoccupied by anyone, Roman or barbarian. In others, again, it may never have been clear at what point one might say they had passed from Romano-British to barbarian control. Some Continental evidence on the uncertainty that can surround the most famous and well-documented cities will be considered shortly. But for deliberate evacuation we have the case attested in Noricum. There barbarians had taken over military control of the Roman towns whose garrisons had dissolved when, as we noted above, they were no longer paid. These barbarians were subsequently defeated, and the Goth Odoacer, who dominated what was left of the western empire, ordered the evacuation of the whole Roman population. This was organized by St. Severinus, who became in effect the national leader in their new home.[3] It is not impossible that some such orderly evacuation formed part of the attested migration of Romano-Britons to Gaul around 460 and there may have been other examples as well, but all evidence is lacking.

It is only recently that stratigraphical data from Romano-

---

[1] Frere, *Britannia*, 422.
[2] Malcom Todd's argument (*Brit.* 8 (1977), 319 ff.) is convincing.
[3] Eugippius, *V. Sev.* xliv. 4–5.

British cities has begun to add up to something tangible.
It is still rare in the countryside, but there are interesting
pointers. We have observed that many older villas were
certainly still occupied late in the fourth century and that
some new ones were being built after 369. The archaeological
evidence no longer suggests a general cessation of villa life
any earlier than the point when Roman coinage and factory-
made pottery fade out. Pieces of the same Late Roman
military equipment that we noted in connection with the
towns are also being discovered at villa sites,[1] though the
exact significance is subject to all manner of speculation.
Cemeteries of late type also occur in association with villas.
It used to be asserted that the Saxons shunned both Roman
town-sites and Roman villas, either because they were too
overgrown to be useful or because the newcomers were
afraid of ghosts. It was also believed that Saxon agriculture,
having allegedly superior equipment, chose heavier and
therefore different soils from Roman settlement. We ought
therefore to take note of the fact that the *earliest* Saxon
settlements, in other words those of the fifth century, even
of the fourth, do *not* seem to avoid proximity to Roman
sites in the countryside. It is the later Saxons who are often
to be found on new sites well away from earlier occupation.[2]
There seems to be nothing exclusive between Roman and the
earliest Saxon settlement, and it may well be that the later
Saxon incomers found the most desirable land already
occupied, either by the descendants of their own predecessors
alone or by a population of Roman and Saxon, mixed or
side by side.

Returning now to the literary sources to see what we can
deduce about the regimes in Britain that followed the revolt
against Constantine III, it is notable that Procopius stated
that the Britons lived henceforth under usurpers. This may
indeed mean that there were more would-be emperors:
Gildas remarks that the parents of Ambrosius Aurelianus,

---

[1] e.g. Ducklington (Oxfordshire).
[2] Though by no means always: at Barton Court Farm, Abingdon, for example,
sixth-century Saxon graves have been found in the ruins of the villa (which was
certainly in use in the late fourth century), much Saxon material has come from
the fill of the villa ditch and a Saxon sunken hut has been discovered alongside
the Roman site (*Brit.* 5 (1974), 456; 6 (1975), 279; 7 (1976), 372).

who appears to have been a British leader later on in the
fifth century, had 'worn the purple',[1] though this may merely
mean a claim to family connection with one of the many
families that had produced Roman emperors of varying
shades of legitimacy in the past. There is no reason to think
that the political and private importance of claiming holders
of great office among one's ancestors had died out. Indeed
the Celtic dynasts subsequently seem to have been positively
obsessed with genealogy, a trait they shared with their
Roman predecessors. But on the whole these *tyranni* were
perhaps more local, whatever their pretensions.

One incident, in which the indisputably historical St.
Germanus of Auxerre appears in person, gives us a glimpse of
influential Britons of the time. Already, possibly in 403,
Victricius, bishop of Rouen, had visited Britain at the request
of his fellow bishops in Gaul to restore peace among the
clergy here: it has been suggested that this may have been
due to controversy over the Pelagian heresy.[2] Dr J.N.L.
Myres has pointed out the possible political overtones in this
heresy (itself the creation of a Briton), which turned on the
doctrine of Grace. Unfortunately the term *gratia* was only
too well known in the context of the immense web of
patronage and favour. Certainly by 429 Pelagianism was a
real issue in Britain, whether religious or political or both.
In that year Germanus and his colleague, Lupus, bishop of
the neighbouring see of Troyes, were chosen, at a meeting
of the bishops of Gaul which was influenced by the Pope,
to visit Britain to combat the heresy. One may perhaps
speculate that both these bishops had had experience of dealing
with difficult situations in regions on the fringe of direct
Roman power. Their chief clerical opponent in Britain was a
leading Pelagian named Agricola, himself the son of a bishop
and clearly backed by a powerful party of local magnates.

In support of the survival of the traditional landowning
upper class of Britain is often adduced the story of the early
life of St. Patrick. Dates, details, and interpretation are all
hotly disputed, but something of use for our immediate

---

[1] Gildas (*De excidio*, xxv). It is an odd coincidence that Clovis is described
as doing literally that and Theodoric requested some similar honour (see p. 497,
n. 2 below).

[2] J.N.L. Myres, *JRS* 50 (1960), 21 ff. (for Victricius see ibid. 23 f.).

purpose may perhaps be extracted. His grandfather Potitus and his father Calpornius seem to have belonged to the local decurionate or class from which the members of the municipal council were drawn.[1] The fact that both took Christian orders has been cited as designed to preserve their fortunes from the heavy burdens which the compulsory acceptance of the honour of local office (*munera*) laid upon this class. Patrick's youth was (as he later confessed) spent in idleness and luxury—almost the traditional requirement for someone to be converted to sainthood, but presumably only convincing if indeed it fitted his known background. It looks as if he lived the life of many a young gentleman. At the age of sixteen he was captured in an Irish raid, and spent the next six years a slave in Ireland. He then escaped back to Britain, but, turned to religion by his experiences, refused entreaties to accept *munera* and stay at home. Whether or not this implies the *munera* of office or in the opposite sense of personal inducements is now unclear:[2] it cannot be used as an argument to demonstrate continuation of normal civic life in Britain. Whatever the nature of the pleas, he refused them and went to study theology, almost certainly under Germanus at Auxerre.[3] That ought therefore to mean after AD 418, when Germanus was appointed. It certainly looks as if he was at home with his family in Britain as late as 418 and possibly later, though, depending on how long it took him to make up his mind, he could have arrived home after his escape from Ireland quite some time earlier, which in its turn would put his captivity and, before that, his unruly boyhood, back a number of years. It is not out of the question that he was captured in the days when the Irish king Niall was raiding Britain around 405 or when the Britons were attacked by barbarians in 408-9. His whole youth may well therefore have been spent while Britain was still a Roman diocese and the opportunity for an idle young man to enjoy an irresponsible good time may have nothing to do with continued security of life in an independent Britain.

[1] The locality is much disputed: recent evidence for Carlisle as a city and the centre of a *civitas* make identification with the north-west more plausible but it remains very uncertain.

[2] L. Bieler, in Barley and Hanson, *Christianity in Britain,* 129, n. 4.

[3] Ibid. 125 and references.

That all being said, however, the story is not inconsistent with the continuance in influence and affluence of the upper class after the break with Roman rule. John Matthews has emphasized the great importance of the 'provincial clarissimate', those families that had achieved senatorial rank[1] (though often taking little or no part in senatorial life and society at Rome), in continuing Gallo-Roman life and culture as the power of the western court itself declined; a role closely paralleled in Italy by the senatorial class of Rome itself. Both, as we have seen, had increasingly been augmented from the ranks of those who had come through the imperial service; and their political experience and tastes in culture and fashion had much in common. For Britain we have little specific evidence for the presence of this 'provincial clarissimate' but one may reasonably assume some members whose families had been ennobled in the normal ways,[2] plus at least some who had received recent honours at the hands of one or other of the locally-elevated emperors. And whatever the fate of supporters of usurpers themselves, we have seen that under the Late Empire *families* could continue at the same political and social level once it was attained, irrespective of change of regime. Nor should we ignore the tendency of the lesser gentry to adopt similar fashions and tastes, particularly in the classical world where both authority and taste tended to come from the centre. The visit of Germanus and Lupus in 429 gives us a fascinating glimpse of the sort of men one might meet in Britain two decades after the break with Roman authority. It also suggests how much interest could be aroused in independent Britain by a formal visit from persons of high standing within the empire—and

---

[1] By 398 all provincial governorships were of this rank: emperors made various attempts to cut down the flow of decurions into the senatorial order, including in that year forbidding them to hold provincial governorships (A.H.M. Jones, op. cit. 180).

[2] The ancestors of Ambrosius Aurelianus are perhaps an example (see J.N.L. Myres, *JRS* 50 (1960), 35, n. 98; and p. 461 above). John Morris drew attention to a letter from a young Briton writing home around 410 or so to an elderly relative who acted as a judge, which includes the greeting *'opto te semper Deo vivere et perpetuii consulatus honore gaudere.'* (Morris, 'Dark Age Dates', in Jarrett and Dobson, *Britain and Rome*, 148). I do not myself think it necessary to assume this is connected with an effort on the part of the Britons after the break with Rome to set up some sort of a senatorial republic: the reference is more interesting in the context of the 'clarissimate'.

perhaps what sort of a show it was felt worthwhile to put on to impress them.

The confrontation between the Roman bishops and the Pelagians took place at a public meeting. The religious and political importance that was clearly attached locally to the issue is underlined by the huge crowd (*immensa multitudo*) who came to hear the episcopal visitors. The Pelagian party at the meeting is described in words that make one think immediately of the proud, elegant Gallo-Roman nobility we have earlier noted. We are told that they were 'conspicuous for riches, brilliant in dress, and surrounded by a fawning multitude'.[1] That fawning multitude puts one in mind of the ancient Roman aristocratic tradition of the *clientela*. The conspicuous wealth is characteristic of the Roman world, perhaps particularly so in the fourth and fifth centuries. The brilliant costume reminds us of that period's taste for splendid multicoloured dress, as seen for example on the fourth-century wall-paintings of the Lullingstone villa in Kent, and at its height in the imperial splendour of Justinian's court portrayed in mosaic in San Vitale at Ravenna. We have already seen in the Gallic context how luxury and display among the Roman provincial nobility in the fifth century cannot be equated with the political system under which they were at any particular moment living. It is at least clear that here in Britain in 429 we are observing not a ruined class living in bondage to savage barbarian masters, nor even a few fortunate survivors, but a substantial body of men of influence who carry weight both with their personal following and the community at large. The pride of the Pelagian party, moreover, is underlined by a rescript from Honorius in 418 which, while it applies to the heretics of this persuasion at large, fits well with this picture from Britain. The emperor there accuses the Pelagians of 'considering it a mark of common vulgarity to agree with opinions that everyone else holds'. The superciliousness and magnificence, to which the Latin word *superbus* was applied, will be met with again in examining the ruling elements of post-Roman Britain.

---

[1] Constantius, *V. Germ.* xiv: *conspicui divitiis, veste fulgentes, circumdati assentatione multorum.*

The strength of the opposition at that meeting is, of course, played up by the biographer of Germanus, but the description rings true even if probably coloured by the author's own experience of wealthy Romans. The fact that Germanus and Lupus succeeded in bringing the crowd over to the official doctrine against such opposition is an interesting testimony to the still-effective powers of public debate, the art of rhetoric in which any Roman gentleman was trained. It displays the diplomatic powers Germanus showed elsewhere in his career and which we have seen were becoming of prime importance in this new world where the final sanction of Roman military power was no longer easily available. It may, too, have owed more than a little to the surviving prestige of Rome itself: the mission from Gaul did after all represent both the official Catholic faith of the western court and the full weight of imperial law, while the choice of these spokesmen had the backing of the Pope himself.

What happened just after the meeting is also very interesting. The Gallic bishops paid a visit to the shrine of St. Alban. This reminds us of the growing importance of Christian shrines, particularly the graves of the martyrs.[1] They are a particularly memorable example of continuity in some of the Roman cities of the Continent such as Cologne. It almost certainly places the scene of the great debate at Verulamium, which would fit very neatly indeed with the archaeology described above. Furthermore, we are also told of the miraculous healing of the child of 'a man with tribunician power' (*vir tribuniciae potestatis*) whom the bishops met there.[2] At first sight it looks as if on top of all the other evidence for a surviving Roman city at Verulamium we have proof of a city garrison of Roman type still in being. Unfortunately the word *tribunus* as a military rank seems to be extremely loosely used in the Later Empire, but as specifically applying to the commander of a city garrison appears to have come in only at the time emergency measures were taken in north Italy during the Lombard invasions of the later sixth century. In the period we are now considering it could apply to almost

[1] In this context, it is an irony that it was a practice of which the Pelagians disapproved as being the religious equivalent of the search for an earthly patron.

[2] Constantius, op. cit. 15.

any sort of unit commander, including (like 'prefect') the command of a band of 'native' troops, even barbarian federates,[1] or, which is even more inconvenient for us, to an officer on detached official duty (*vacans*). If he currently held a proper imperial commission of any kind it would be extremely interesting to know what he was doing at Verulamium in 429. Since Germanus had once practised at the Bar and was apparently a former provincial governor he would certainly know a legitimate officer when he met one, and if he came back from Britain saying that he had met such a person we ought, if his biographer has not distorted his account, to be able to believe him. It is, of course, possible that the man held some locally granted appointment, which for a number of reasons may not have been recorded in the *Vita*. However there is another possibility, that this tribune had in fact commanded a unit of the Roman army in Britain which had disbanded after the break with Rome: A.H.M. Jones conjectured that a military tribune at Favianae in Raetia who had become a cleric, and whom St. Severinus persuaded to organize military action after the province had been abandoned by Rome, had in fact stayed on after his unit faded away.[2] Within the empire we find the rank of military tribune granted to a category of civil servants not long after this date, an act of a piece with that blurring of rank and insignia between civil and military which we noted as a paradoxical accompaniment to the functional division introduced in the fourth century. It is very disappointing that the possibilities are so wide that we have no way of knowing the truth in the case in point. It is at least very clear that we cannot assume the presence of regular troops of any kind on the basis of this man's existence, either at Verulamium or elsewhere in Britain.

Whoever he was, one is probably justified in assuming that this man did not represent the topmost level in local society. That seems to be represented by the Pelagian notables already described. The status of the real military leaders of the day is a very difficult matter and their relationship to the old provincial nobility obscure. The most prominent of

---

[1] For AD 417 see Jones, op. cit. 965.
[2] A.H.M. Jones, op. cit., 924, where it is pointed out that this is the only officer known to have taken clerical orders (*V. Sev.* iv).

these in modern literature on the period is undoubtedly
Vortigern. His place in historical demonology has been
assured by Gildas,[1] who alleges that as a *superbus tyrannus,*
outflanked in internal British politics, he imported Saxons
to fight on his side. The latter subsequently rebelled and
were the chief cause of the downfall of Britain and its being
overrun by barbarians. The fact that later authors describe
him as 'reigning' is no evidence that he followed the practice
of some of the Continental barbarian rulers of the day
who described themselves as *rex* while nominally professing
allied or client status *vis-à-vis* the Roman emperor. Indeed
the word *tyrannus* is perhaps more apt, in that it implies
the opposite—a denial of allegiance to Ravenna. Vortigern,
in being called a 'tyrant', has bestowed upon him the term
that Procopius used for the rulers of Britain after the break
with Rome, a word commonly used for usurpers. Yet I
am sure we cannot safely infer either from the adjective
superbus[2] or the fact that the name Vortigern means something like 'high king' that one man, or succession of men,
actually held supreme power throughout the former diocese—
or claimed it. Leaders in Britain may have been chary of
taking the title Augustus after recent experiences of Marcus,
Gratian, and Constantine III, even if they had any hope
of exerting more than regional power. Did any of them
come from the old upper class? We know nothing of
Vortigern, but some sources give him an opponent named
Ambrosius (to whom I shall return), who may or may not
be the same as the Ambrosius Aurelianus whose family
we have already seen conjectured as senatorial or imperial.
A reasonable and fascinating conjecture about the latter
is that he was a member of the same family as Ambrose
of Milan, whom we saw dominating the imperial court
at the end of the fourth century.[3] St. Ambrose himself was

---

[1] I am convinced by David Dumville's judicious examination of the evidence
both that Vortigern did exist and that his name almost certainly should be read
in the text of Gildas. (See Note p. 501 below and Dumville, *History*, 62 (1977),
183 ff.)

[2] One ought to compare Virgil's use of the word *superbus* in a political context: see p. 66 above.

[3] J.N.L. Myres, *JRS* 50 (1960), 35, n. 98. S. Applebaum, who accepts the
identification of Ambrosius Aurelianus with Vortigern's enemy, argues that a
series of place-names in the south of England such as Amberley and Ambersham

the son of a praetorian prefect and, as I mentioned earlier, had served as a *consularis* before his episcopal election. It is characteristic of the fifth century to find descendants of those who had played roles on the imperial scene in the fourth century taking a leading part in individual fragments of the empire. Certainly the magnates whom Germanus encountered at Verulamium did not hesitate to employ the traditional weapon of the Roman upper classes, the outward show of wealth and patronage to try to overawe opponents and influence opinion. If any Britons did assume imperial or quasi-imperial titles, it should be remembered that in Britain after it had rebelled from Constantine, expelled his office-holders, and received no help from Honorius, there may have been a real need for someone to treat diplomatically with the barbarians at the most exalted level. It has been suggested that Gerontius needed such an Augustus in Spain in 409 for the same purpose.

The oddity about Britain is perhaps not that it produced *tyranni* when out of imperial control, but that this phase did not come to an early end. As A.H.M. Jones summarized the general situation:

In the west, the military disasters which overwhelmed the empire, and the inability of the legitimate government to cope with the situation, produced a crop of 'tyrants' between 407 and 413, but they all proved ephemeral. As soon as Honorius' armies appeared on the scene they were quickly subdued and their troops returned to their lawful sovereign's command.[1]

It will be noted that this view of the 'tyrants' sees them as commanding the temporary allegiance of Roman troops (with or without barbarian allies). I have already suggested that one reason for the failure to regain Britain was the probable difficulty Honorius' army would have had in campaigning so far north with so much else to deal with in

---

are derived from estates owned by Ambrosius, including Bignor which has two names of this type in its immediate vicinity. (H.P.R. Finberg (ed.) *The Agrarian History of England and Wales*, Cambridge (1972), I, pt. 2, 24; *Brit.* 6 (1975) 131 f.) This would support the notion of the British leaders still being the land-owning gentry, in this case on a wide scale. Dr Morris argued that the names might indicate garrisons placed by Ambrosius, and identified many more such names throughout the southern part of England (J. Morris, *The Age of Arthur* (1973), 100).

[1] A.H.M. Jones, op. cit. 174.

Gaul and Spain; but another possibility—or contributory cause—is the very strong probability that there were now no longer any regular Roman troops in Britain who might be induced to change sides again. The apparent failure to elevate an Augustus after 409 in Britain may at least in part be due to the absence of regular Roman troops demanding one. And without them, Honorius' army (particularly if, as I have suggested, those Romano-Britons who had expelled Constantine's administration had subsequently been alienated by the behaviour of the imperial victors in Gaul against their own class) would have faced a more more difficult situation than Constantius I in 297. At that time, the dubious loyalty of the regular Roman garrison in Britain to the rebel regime had been, it seems likely, a great help to Constantius in defeating Allectus and his faithful barbarian allies.

It is worth reflecting on why it was Germanus that proceeded to organize and lead the Britons in a war against a combined army of Picts and Saxons.[1] The tale is that he baptized his men and taught them to shout 'Alleluia' as their battle-cry, this causing the enemy to flee in dismay. We do not know where this battle was fought, though the description of the ground, as lying in mountainous country near a large river is circumstantial enough to suggest both that the battle actually happened[2] and that it was a good march away from Verulamium. The mass baptism implies it was a largely pagan force and therefore perhaps in these latter days mostly made up of rural Romano-Britons.[3] That Germanus had to take the lead at all may suggest either that the bulk of the Romano-British upper class was in the now discredited Pelagian party or that the Pelagians, worsted in argument, were enlisting the help of barbarian allies, the very Picts and Saxons whom Germanus now defeated in battle. The 'tyrants' we encounter in Britain in the fifth century do indeed appear with military backing, but there does not seem to be any hint that this

---

[1] The notion that Germanus had once been a *dux* in the Roman army may stem from the less probable interpretation of a passage in *V. Germ.* i. 2: see A.H.M. Jones, op. cit. 923, n. 135.

[2] John Morris has pointed out that Germanus' biographer knew Lupus of Troyes personally and could easily have verified the story.

[3] See p. 737 below: the inference is not certain. Moreover there may have been barbarian allies on this side as well.

contained surviving units of the old regular army. Vortigern, in the tradition, is Germanus' greatest enemy in Britain.[1] He is, therefore, not likely to have come to the aid of Germanus' Catholic converts and is noted for his belief in Saxon alliances. We have to remember that there is nothing in the least unlikely in such a combination. It was becoming the common political currency of the age.

There is one more British leader of whom we should take brief note before we turn in more detail to Vortigern and the so-called *'Adventus Saxonum'* or arrival of the Saxons. It is interesting that the traditional genealogy of Vortigern himself seems to preserve the name of a Vitalis or Vitalinus of Gloucester.[2] These genealogies are of such doubtful historical value—usually constructed retrospectively to buttress a claim to territory or power—that one would not normally take a great deal of notice. However there are two intriguing pieces of information that may or may not be connected and help to build up the picture of the age. The first is that recent excavation at a site at Gloucester has produced an early fifth-century secondary burial in a Roman funerary building. The body was accompanied by equipment indicating a man of high rank but who David Brown has suggested was neither a Late Roman officer nor a Saxon, but a Briton.[3] We do not know whether the Vitalis or Vitalinus associated with Vortigern is the same as the Vitalinus who we are told[4] fought a battle against the forces of a man named Ambrosius at 'Guolloppum', supposedly just before 440. Despite one's extreme lack of confidence in the details, it does look as if one fact emerges, that in the second quarter of the fifth century warfare had broken out between Romano-British factions who were now producing military leaders of their own.

Vortigern's status and role in this world remain uncertain,[5] though the English tradition makes them important. The action for which he is best known and by the British sources

---

[1] J.N.L. Myres, *JRS* 50 (1960), 35.
[2] Morris, 'Dark Age Dates', in Jarrett and Dobson, op. cit. 164.
[3] *Ant. J.* 55 (1975), 294.
[4] Morris, op. cit. 165.
[5] See Note, p. 501 below.

most abused is the importation of the Saxon allies who
subsequently turned on the Romano-Britons. The abuse
from the Britons is intelligible: the preservation of his memory
by posterity equally so. The actual course of events is obscure. He may not even date from this century but be part
of the Saxon expansion in the next. However the various
scraps of evidence seem to suggest that Vortigern brought in
Saxon allies around 430, that with order restored the Britons
became unwilling to continue paying them, and that Vortigern
then strengthened his barbarian forces very considerably
to consolidate his position. There is a story that he married
the daughter of the barbarian commander and handed over
part of eastern Britain to him:[1] this would fit the archaeological material for Saxon settlement in Kent and near
London, where a series of sites has suggested deliberate
posting of federates to protect the city. All these features
are entirely in line with what was happening under imperial
authority in Gaul and elsewhere. And it does seem as if at
least in the early stages Vortigern's policy was successful:
Gildas claims that the long period of great prosperity after
the break with Rome had been broken by plague and new
attacks from without, but that the *superbus tyrannus* had
successfully brought in Saxons to drive off the Picts, by
this means restoring peace. A passage in the *Historia Brittonum*
summarizes the pressures on Vortigern and it contains a
real surprise: 'Vortigern ruled in Britain, and during his reign
he was driven by fear of the Picts and Scots *and by Roman
assault*, and not least by apprehension of Ambrosius'.[2]
Ambrosius we have already met fighting Vortigern's apparent
associate Vitalinus. But the fact that a *Roman* attack was
seen as a real possibility is new and important. This brings us
right back into imperial affairs: it is easy to forget the empire
and treat fifth-century Britain as if it were a world apart.
As to date, the entry in the *Gallic Chronicle* composed in 452
was long thought to give 441/2 as the year in which Britain,
long disturbed, 'passed under the dominion of the Saxons'.

---

[1] The story itself has the ring of a genealogy invented to justify a Saxon
dynasty.

[2] Nennius, *Hist. Britt.* xxxiii: *Guorthigirnus regnavit in Britannia et dum ipse
regnabat urgebatur a metu Pictorum Scottorumque et a Romanico impetu necnon
et a timore Ambrosii.*

One fact is obvious from the Romano-British archaeology, that 442 is much too early for Britain to have passed finally under the control of the Saxons (at least any very large part of it). Now even the manuscript date is in doubt. One possibility is that it ought to be a little later but only a little, another that the date as such is a ninth-century gloss. One may reasonably feel that the Gallic Chronicler knew *something* drastic had just happened in Britain connected with Saxon victory, but it may only have been that the Saxons had gained control of the part of Britain with which the Chronicler was in touch. I do not think we can extract anything geographically exact from the Chronicle. On the other hand, he is the one contemporary source, and Mr Patrick Wormald has pointed out to me that the Chronicler is making exactly the same point as was made about the emperor's lamentable arrangement with Gaiseric and the Vandals in Africa. It falls into place as a terrible warning to contemporaries of what could happen if Roman authorities placed themselves in the power of barbarians. What we can therefore say is that in 452 someone writing on the Continent believed that the Saxons, after causing trouble for some time and given their opportunity by being invited into a key position by the native authorities for their own ends, had quite recently seized their chance and gained a decisive victory over their employers. The important feature for our immediate purpose is not whether it was true of a very large part of Britain but that it was believed to be so at the time. The passage certainly cannot be stood on its head and used to prove 441/2 or 455/6 was the *beginning* of Saxon expansion in Britain.[1] The wider and much more important point is the contemporary realization of the acute danger of such arrangements with the barbarians. It puts Vortigern and Britain clearly into the context of contemporary western Roman practice. Moreover it emphasizes a recognition of the desperate dangers of such a policy well before it actually proved fatal in Gaul. To a large extent Romans now had little option but to make such use of the barbarians, with all the risks attached to a situation where the barbarian components

---

[1] I am grateful to Dr Myres for emphasizing this point, with which I thoroughly agree, and for making me aware of the recent work of M. Miller at Glasgow on the manuscript problems.

of Roman forces were in the large majority, but when it was done in the furtherance of civil war it was indefensible.

The report that Vortigern had been stationing Saxons 'in the eastern part'[1] of Britain and the stories about his bringing in of more Saxons under 'Hengist and Horsa' and of handing over Kent for barbarian settlement suggest that he was deliberately blocking the route across the Channel. This is completely consistent with fear of attack by Roman forces from the Continent. However from the moment that the Saxon allies revolted and, as Gildas describes, destroyed cities, committed massacres, enslaved some Britons and drove others to flee abroad, no one on the Romano-British side is likely to have had much time to worry about a hypothetical Roman invasion. Thus, if the Gallic Chronicle's date is about right and has been correctly associated with Gildas' Saxon revolt, then we must look to the period from about 425 to 450 for a time when the imperial government might have been able to make a serious attempt to retake Britain from without. We can, with almost complete certainty, make the assumption that by now there were no loyalist forces anywhere in Britain. A contemporary belief that Vortigern's enemy Ambrosius might have a real chance of bringing in Roman military support from the Continent is, however, quite a different matter, particularly if he was in fact related to St. Ambrose and therefore had family connections with the imperial and Catholic Roman court.

On the Continent the death of Honorius in 423 had produced another crop of usurpers, control of the west passing temporarily to Johannes, *primicerius notariorum*, till decisive military intervention from the east in 425 put the infant son of Constantius III, Valentinian III, on to the throne with his mother Galla Placidia as effective regent. But the situation was seriously complicated by the fact that John had sent the remarkable Roman general Aetius to ask for help for his usurping regime from the Huns. This brings the Huns for the first time into the story, though it is believed that their gradual movement westwards had been the pressure that caused many of the problems the Roman empire had experienced from the barbarians on its frontiers, who were

---

[1] *In orientali parte.*

being driven on by others behind them. Aetius' own relations with the Huns play a very important part in the history of the fifth century. He is best known as the Roman who stopped Attila and the Huns by fighting them to a standstill in the crucial battle of the 'Catalaunian Plains', but his involvement with them was much more personal. He himself had been a hostage of the Huns as a young man and had close connections with their royal court. It was for this reason that he was sent by John to solicit Hunnish assistance against Constantinople, and it was because he arrived back with a large Hunnish army at his command that Galla Placidia and her legitimist regime were never able to do anything effective about him.

For the next few years Aetius was *magister militum* in Gaul, and following a lengthy internal struggle, sometimes amounting to civil war, finally established himself with the offices of 'patrician' and *magister utriusque militae* as effective ruler in the west, after the style of Stilicho. This mastery was still his in the period of the Saxon rebellion in Britain. Ever since the death of Theodosius the Great the empire in the west had, as we noted earlier, been characterized by weak emperors dominated for long periods by strong advisers, usually soldiers, who *de facto* ruled it. This was to continue to the end of the imperial throne in the west, but for half a century after the fall of Stilicho there were no more men of German ancestry in the dominant office. The now established nature of the position was emphasized by the introduction of the new title: 'patrician'. The first holder had been Flavius Constantius who become emperor as Constantius III for a very short while before his death. Aetius' political climb to supreme power in the west was completed by attaining this office, with absolute command of the western armies, by 433. However, for four years from 425 Aetius' position was as *magister militum* of Gaul—and the reason he retained this post was the 60,000 Huns we are told had accompanied him. Even if that figure has to be taken 'with a grain of salt',[1] they were obviously taken very seriously indeed by his enemies in Ravenna. Aetius was in a tricky position: a slight change

---

[1] A.H.M. Jones, op. cit. 176.

in the balance of power and he would have been condemned for supporting John. He certainly had plenty to occupy him restoring order in Gaul: John's praetorian prefect at Arles had been murdered in a mutiny[1] and that city itself was being besieged by the Visigoths, who had broken their treaty with Rome. Indeed in 430, just after forcing his way to more senior rank in Italy, Aetius had to return to defeat the Visigoths and relieve the capital of the prefecture. However, in 428 we find Aetius already successfully campaigning against Franks on the Rhine. A quick victory in Britain sometime in these five years 425–9 would have suited him very well. Apart from the immense prestige traditionally to be gained from such a triumph, it would also have given him added resources and a bolt-hole if it were ever needed. Even if he lost his stranglehold over the politics of Ravenna, he would at least have the traditional northern empire that so many would-be masters of the whole empire had held.

This situation gives an added piquancy to the diplomatic victory of the episcopal envoys at Verulamium in 429, and even more to their subsequent military success against the barbarians in Britain. The possibility that Vortigern was facing not only local rivals in the person of Ambrosius and a Catholic party but also behind them Aetius with 60,000 Huns and the legitimate command of all the regular Roman troops in Gaul makes the original employment of Saxon allies by Vortigern and the Britons the act of a sensible man in the face of tremendous odds.[2] It gives added point to Germanus' otherwise rather strange decision to turn general and fight the Saxon and Pictish forces himself.

If this speculation is anywhere near the truth, then one may ask why full Roman invasion did not follow on after Germanus' success. The likely explanation is that from the time Aetius moved to Italy till he gained supreme power

[1] Prosper Tiro, 1285. This is the same Exuperantius who had led the first Roman army in northern Gaul we know of after 411.

[2] In passing, if the western part of the *Notitia* really does originate in some sort of a copy of around 425 of the lists in the office of the *primicerius notariorum* then those lists, in preserving an establishment for garrisoning Britain, might have been extremely useful military information if Aetius had a conquest and rapid occupation in mind. One almost hesitates to point to the coincidence that John himself had actually been the *primicerius notariorum* when he was proclaimed emperor.

he was engaged in a vicious political and military battle with Galla Placidia and her party which he nearly lost. Moreover, in Gaul and neighbouring areas there were problems more or less continuously down to 443, including further peasant insurgency from the middle of the 430s and outbreaks of warfare with the Visigoths, Franks, and Burgundians. Aetius' Huns were, with characteristic ferocity, to the forefront in these campaigns but still on the Roman side. From 440 Aetius seems to be pursuing a policy of extending the settlement of friendly (or defeated) barbarians within Gaul under treaty, rather than Roman reconquest. Two groups of Alans were settled thus, sharing the land with the Gallo-Roman inhabitants. One of these, in 442, possibly on the Loire, led to a major clash, in which the Alans had to eject the Gallo-Roman owners.[1] In 443 Aetius followed this by creating, as I have already mentioned, the second great barbarian kingdom in Gaul, that of the Burgundians in Savoy. It is ironic that Vortigern's policy of large increases in federate settlement was in the 440s in line with Aetius' actions in Gaul. Imperial methods were now similar to Vortigern's. It was the results that were different. Aetius was able, for example, to keep his Alans loyal—at least as a military force at the bidding of Rome, though the local provincial landowners fared very badly out of the deal.

I think that on the present reading of the evidence we have to accept something like an *apparent* final barbarian mastery of Britain around 450, at least as viewed from the Continent, due to British failure to achieve the same success in controlling their allies as Aetius. If we want to make a case for a long period of fluctuating fortunes in which Roman Britain was effectively destroyed as it was fought over, I think we have to assume it is due to revived British resistance

[1] It would be very interesting indeed to know whether the expulsion of Roman landlords by the Alans in 442 was in fact on the Loire, since that region had close ties with Britain in the fifth century (as we shall see again) and the date accords so well with that for the Saxon rising in Britain. John Matthews speculates that it may have been in the region of Orleans: the texts are *Chron. Gall.* iv. 124: *deserta Valentinae urbis rura ... partienda*; ibid. iv. 127: *terrae Galliae ulterioris cum incolis dividendae*. There were Alans in Orleans in 451 (Jordanes, *Getica*, 195 f.). It is another curious coincidence that Germanus is found interceding with Galla Placidia subsequently to prevent Aetius using the Alans against the Armoricans (*V. Germ.* 28 ff.).

after the latest information available to the Gallic Chronicler, in other words effectively after 445/450 or thereabouts. This perhaps took the form of a counter-attack from parts of Britain not yet in Saxon hands or a revolt of Romano-Britons against their new masters. The longer the period we can accept for any establishment of settled Saxon life in the parts conquered in the fifth century and the longer the period of extreme disturbance to the Roman community,[1] the easier it becomes to understand why what little we know of British life in the lengthy period of peace alleged for the first half of the *sixth* century seems so far away from the Roman Britain we know till 409. As we have seen much of that Britain still seems recognizable archaeologically till at least the middle of the fifth century. Recent work in Wessex has suggested that the reason why the early Anglo-Saxon immigrants there are so difficult to identify from the finds is that culturally they were being more changed by the Romans with whom they came into contact than the reverse.[2] This makes more acute the key question we have to put to the historians specializing in the earlier part of Anglo-Saxon England, the question why the general picture A.H.M. Jones painted of the Germanic take-over in the west does not seem to fit Britain:

The German kings not unnaturally maintained more or less unchanged the civil administration of the provinces which they ruled. Some, like Theoderic the Ostrogoth, had a genuine respect and admiration for the Roman way of life, and sedulously preserved ancient institutions. Most probably maintained the existing system merely through inertia. They had to preserve law and order in their dominions and to collect the revenues, and they knew of no other way of doing so than to apply the ancient law and make use of the administrative machinery which they found in being. Naturally also they employed Romans to fill the civil offices, for they alone knew the law and could operate the complicated fiscal system. In most things the provincials must have felt little change when for the imperial government there was substituted the rule of a barbarian king. They took their mutual disputes to the same courts, were judged by the same law, and paid the same fees that they had always done. They paid the same taxes to the same collectors, and suffered the traditional exactions—the use of false weights and measures, the arbitrary fixing of prices in compulsory purchase, the extraction of perquisites by the officials.[3]

[1] Morris, 'Dark Age Dates', in Jarrett and Dobson, op. cit. 165.
[2] See M. Biddle, in G. de G. Sieveking, and others (eds.), *Problems in Economic and Social Archaeology* (1976), 323 ff.
[3] A.H.M. Jones, op. cit. 248.

Jones goes on, of course, to point out that 'in one respect, however, they suffered a drastic change for the worse, in the settlement of the barbarians on their lands'. As he says, 'this was effected in different ways in the several kingdoms', ways which varied greatly in method and severity, in places reaching the extreme of arbitrary dispossession on a vast scale. But the essential point is that on the Continent the structure of Roman civil life remained, changing gradually but as a living part of the new world. In Britain it did not.

Without attempting to answer that question, but with a view of what was to come, we can now return to the 'Arrival of the Saxons'. Into a picture of a lengthy period of chaos and fluctuating fortunes following after what had appeared to be irreversible Saxon conquest around 445/450, it becomes possible to fit two incidents that are reasonably well attested and dated. The first is the famous appeal from the Britons reported by Gildas, the *gemitus Britannorum Agitio ter consuli*[1] or 'lamentations of the Britons to "Agitius", thrice consul'. Agitius is usually and probably rightly assumed to be Aetius,[2] and the date must therefore be between his third consulship in 446 and his death in 454. The other incident is the second visit to Britain of St. Germanus of Auxerre, perhaps in 446–7. There is no evidence that Aetius sent any direct military support. The Britons lamented that 'the barbarians drive us to the sea and the sea drives us back to the barbarians; death comes by one means or the other: we are either slain or drowned'. Though the neatness of the phrasing makes one hesitate to attempt extracting too much meaning, it suggests the Britons were being squeezed between the revolted Saxons on land and other enemies from the sea. But Germanus had led them to victory over Saxons and Picts before, and it is interesting that he should be sent back to Britain at about this time. And once again he came with a second bishop, this time Severus of Trier. The choice of the latter makes sense. In 446 the writer Merobaudes could describe the Rhine frontier as having been restored under Aetius, and the famous imperial mint of Trier struck its last coins under his control.[3] Edith Wightman

[1] Gildas, op. cit. xx.
[2] Anthony King has suggested to me that it might refer to Aegidius (see p. 491).
[3] E.M. Wightman, op. cit. 69.

has pointed out how the city had survived, citing Salvian who wrote sometime between 400 and 450:

He tells how Trier had four times been sacked, and gives an eye-witness account of its state after the third destruction. While dead and dying were to be seen untended in the streets, the survivors turned to eating, drinking and merry-making, and called for circuses. Salvianus, a native of the Rhineland and well acquainted with Trier, was convinced that the destruction of that and other cities was a judgement of God on the immorality of the inhabitants, and his account is correspondingly slanted. He does however betray the fact that in between the horrors of destruction, some kind of civilized life was still possible in Trier: he mentions *nobiles* and *honorati* among the inhabitants.[1]

The visit of the two bishops may indeed have been primarily, like the first, to deal with the remnants of the Pelagian heresy, but they also carried between them a remarkable combination of experience that was very relevant to the situation probably then pertaining in Britain. It may have been the best response Aetius could give to the British: if so, they were being offered military, civil, and spiritual leadership of proven quality from men who must have had access to the latest information on the situation in the wider world outside Britain. What the immediate effect of their visit was, we do not know, though the Pelagian heresy is not henceforth heard of. In Church terms close contact was clearly maintained with Rome, since the modification of the date when Easter was to be celebrated which was introduced in 455 was adopted in Britain. On the secular side the visitors are recorded as having made contact with a named personality, one Elafius, described as *regionis illius primus*,[2] whose status is unclear but whom one may perhaps assume to be another local 'tyrant'.[3] However, whatever the precise details of the visit, British life continued, and there is a little more evidence to consider.

If the second visit of Germanus in fact took place in lieu of military assistance from Aetius, it would be consistent with the preoccupations of the Roman commander on the Continent. In 446 the Rhine frontier may have been stabilized,

---

[1] Ibid. 70.

[2] As a Roman name, an official named Aelafius is recorded in Africa under Constantine the Great (A.H.M. Jones, op. cit. 82).

[3] Frere points out the similarity of the description to that of a πρῶτος τῆς πόλεως mentioned in the south-west in the early sixth century (*Britannia*, 370).

but by 448 there was serious internal trouble again with the Armoricans. This is the context of Germanus' journey to Ravenna to plead for Galla Placidia's intervention to prevent a Roman-directed attack on them by the Alans at Aetius' instigation (Germanus himself had presumably failed to deflect Aetius from his purpose). The situation was a complex one, which had been developing over a number of years, and involved both the Vandals and the Huns. In 431 the government in Constantinople had sent a force to assist the west in dealing with Vandal invasion. The defeat of this eastern Roman army seriously weakened the prestige of the Romans with their allies the Huns. However, it was shortly after this, in 433, that Aetius, whose survival had originally depended on Hunnish support, won complete control of the western imperial government. He now unequivocally led the empire in the west, and real trouble was brewing with the Huns, though the alliance was not yet broken. From 434—and shortly after that under their new king Attila—they become more and more demanding. In 441 the eastern government again sent a large force to help against the Vandals in the west: in the confused situation that followed Attila took the chance to allege Roman failure to keep faith with him and between 441 and 443 invaded the Danube provinces, moving eastwards. After inflicting a massive defeat on the eastern Roman army, he extracted a much larger subsidy in exchange for peace. In 447 the same happened all over again and between then and 450 he extracted further advantages. So far the west had escaped, but he then decided to try his luck in their territories, taking as his excuse a dispute between the Emperor Valentinian and the latter's sister, in which she had foolishly appealed to Attilia.

In 451 Attila entered Gaul with a great horde of Huns and allies. Aetius collected all the regular Roman troops and federates he could muster. This joint force, of which the Visigoths of the Aquitanian kingdom established in 418 formed a very important part, met Attila and so wore him down in the battle of the Catalaunian Plains[1] that he could no longer continue his advance into the empire. This action had both been described as the greatest single act of

[1] An unknown site somewhere between Troyes and Paris, possible Châlons.

co-operation between the Romans and the Germans against a common enemy and also the last great Roman military victory in the west. It is ironic that it should have been Aetius that stopped the Huns. It is also revealing that the army commanded by the leading Roman general of the day should have depended so much on barbarian troops supplied under treaty from a kingdom which, though nominally within the boundaries of the empire, was in practice independent. In fact it is quite likely that regular Roman troops were in a minority in Aetius' army.[1] In truth, the Germans were fighting for the new world in which both Roman and German shared the old empire in the west. The new wave of barbarians represented by the Huns was the common enemy to the form of co-existence that was gradually emerging.

The Catalaunian Plains was not a complete victory, and for us as concerned with Britain this is important. Attila was not beaten in 451. His advance was halted, but Aetius' vigilance could not be relaxed and Roman forces had to be kept on the alert. In the following year Attila moved his forces into Italy, but in 453 he died. Thereafter the Huns were unable to control their German subjects, and the great horde dissolved into fragments.[2] The Hunnish threat to the west was now over, but Roman attention had been diverted from matters such as Roman Britain.

It is probably fair to assume that Aetius, with his close contacts with the Hunnish court and his use of Hunnish allies as part of the Roman forces at least till 439, knew for a long time what was happening among them. One may guess that he expected some eventual move against the empire, though whether he was able to use any influence to delay it we do not know. Certainly from the point that Attila declared his hand in 441 and was clearly prepared to resort to large-scale war against Rome, Aetius must have had the probability of a Hunnish attack very much on his mind. The Visigoths, despite the terms of their settlement in 418, had proved in subsequent years to be unreliable, and he may well not have been sure of their support. If the 440s was the period when the Saxons in Britain first chose to revolt, it

---

[1] A.H.M. Jones, op. cit. 201. It is important to note, as Jones does, that the Armoricans in this army seem by now to have become more or less independent.

[2] Some Huns were even to serve again subsequently under Roman command.

is not surprising that Aetius dispatched no expedition. Indeed, if Myres and others are right in seeing the regime of Vortigern as anti-imperial, such a Saxon revolt may even have been welcome to Ravenna. Certainly after Attila's second great attack on the eastern empire in 447 it is even less likely that Aetius would have been prepared to send troops from the Continent to Britain, even if the appeal came from a pro-imperial faction. The Anglo-Saxon Chronicle indicates a series of victories by 'Hengist and Horsa' over the Britons in the course of a few years, but Britain must have seemed relatively unimportant. The Huns were becoming very dangerous indeed. Nor, as I have just mentioned, did the Battle of the Catalaunian Plains end the problem. It is therefore not true, as has often been said, that Aetius would now have been free to send military aid to Britain. He could hardly have taken his attention from the Hunnish invaders until Attila was dead in 453, in fact till it was clear that the horde was finally breaking up in the subsequent period. In 454 Aetius himself was murdered by Valentinian III: six months later the emperor too was assassinated, by a group of Aetius' friends. The western empire was plunged into another struggle for the throne and for supremacy in the imperial government. It was no time for peripheral matters.

In Britain we know very little of what happened after the Saxon revolt. Some British resistance does seem to be a reality, and we are given to understand that it was led in the latter part of the fifth century at first by the Ambrosius Aurelianus we have already noted. It is not clear whether this is the same man as Vortigern's opponent at an earlier stage in the century. If the internal struggle between Vortigern and that 'Ambrosius' was really at the same time as the threat of a Roman invasion, and I have correctly put that before about 430, then it is perhaps more likely that we are now dealing with a later Ambrosius. However, we do not have to assume that the threats to Vortigern from Rome and from Ambrosius were exactly contemporary, nor is it impossible that Vortigern's enemy had a long career. Ambrosius Aurelianus certainly appears in Gildas and the view that he represents an attempt by a pro-imperial party to gather together the pieces of Roman Britain after the discrediting of Vortigern's policy by the Saxon revolt is a credible one.

Professor Frere summarized the position as he saw it in 1967:

A long period of fluctuating warfare culminated at some date rather before 500 in a British victory at Mount Badon, an unidentified site perhaps in the south-west; after it there was peace for two generations. Gildas, writing soon after 540, is able to speak of 'our present security' and of a generation which had no experience of the great struggle. Soon after 550, however, the Saxon conquest was renewed. In 571 an area from Buckinghamshire to the upper Thames was overrun, and six years later came the fall of Gloucester, Cirencester and Bath. About 590 the Britons in the north suffered a serious defeat at Catterick, and by 600 most of Britain had fallen to the Saxon kingdoms with the exception of the Dumnonian peninsula, Wales and parts of the Pennines and the north-west.[1]

It has long been recognized that there is an apparent contradiction between this literary account of the conquest and the abundance of early Saxon material in certain areas, for example the Upper Thames Valley.[2] Yet this need only worry us if we suppose all these early arrivals to be conquerors. Just who was master and who subject is much more likely to have varied greatly from place to place, and in some districts there were doubtless still arrangements by which Germanic tribesmen served as warriors under contract to Britons. There is no reason at all to assume a uniformity based on national consciousness, certainly not on the barbarian side and probably not on the British side either. Since Frere wrote, the date of Mount Badon has been further examined, appearing now to fall somewhere between 491 and 516.[3] The half-century before it seems to have been the period when the old patterns broke up; the half-century after, the breathing-space in which Britain had a chance to consolidate the new 'Celtic' society which had emerged from the period of conflict. Nor should we omit to note that Irish settlement probably contributed as much as Saxon to the transforming of Britain, but has received relatively less attention. Indeed, as Professor Charles Thomas has pointed out, Irish settlers may well have been numerically as great in the fifth and sixth

[1] Frere, *Britannia*, (1967), 382 f. (= 1978, 427 f.)
[2] For the conflict see David Brown, *Anglo-Saxon England*, (1978), 18 ff. For unbroken settlement from Romano-British to Anglo-Saxon in Wessex see Martin Biddle in G. de G. Sieveking and others (eds.), *Problems in economic and social archaeology* (1976), 323 ff.
[3] Mount Badon (*Mons Badonicus*): see M. Miller, *Bull. Board of Celtic Studies*, 26 (1974–6), 169 ff., on Gildas.

centuries in western Britain as the Germanic peoples in the south and east.[1]

There is, however, one element that has so overshadowed attempts to reconstruct the story of Britain in the second half of the century that it demands to be considered at this point and a decision made whether to attempt to incorporate it in our picture of the period, reject it or put it firmly aside, pending further evidence. I refer to the possible identification as a real historical person of 'King Arthur' and the notion that he was the British leader who won the war that ended at Mount Badon. Over recent years there has been a growing movement to believe in the historicity of Arthur, and to go much further, identifying him with actual places, even to the extent of recognizing in the Dark Age refortification of the hill-fort at South Cadbury in Somerset the site of 'Camelot'. It should be said that the archaeology is extremely interesting but very difficult to interpret. But so much doubt has now been thrown on the state of knowledge about the Celtic written sources for Arthur[2] that both his connection with the archaeology and his very existence are matters that need to be held in abeyance by historians till the value of the texts is re-examined by those specialists qualified to do so. I personally am not prepared to say whether Arthur was a real figure or not—least of all that he was a national British leader who fought battles at identifiable places and had a capital that can be placed on the map—till a new and convincing case has been made one way or the other.

This state of affairs over Arthur, however, does not mean that it is not worth looking a little further at the Continental background in the second half of the fifth century, for this, from the point of view of the Romano-British historian, is the Late Roman world in which the final stages of his subject are set. Indeed, in the light of what is happening on the Continent, we may occasionally have insights into what conditions in Britain may have been like. We have to start with the deeper and deeper confusion into which the west fell after the successive murders of Aetius and Valentinian. Though the pattern of weak emperors with strong military advisers continued for some while, the latter role was now being taken once more by men of barbarian origin who had

[1] Thomas, *Britain and Ireland*, 66.   [2] See Note, p. 501 below.

at last recovered the position they lost with the disgrace of Stilicho. The western emperor had less and less of an effective role to play, and finally in 476, when the Emperor Romulus was deposed, the Roman senate went so far as to send an embassy to the eastern court with the imperial regalia, announcing that they felt no need for a new emperor at Ravenna and were happy to accept a single imperial throne at Constantinople. Although the immediate response from the east was the reappointment of a previously removed holder of the western throne, Julius Nepos, whose earlier short reign had not been without some success, this emperor's authority was now nominal and he was himself killed four years later.[1] Though this did not mean the formal end of the Roman state in the west, it was the end of the western emperors.[2] The German military advisers or commanders-in-chief were now kings and called themselves *rex* like the barbarian leaders in the west, even if they maintained the structure of Roman civil government, appointed praetorian prefects and saw that the western senate was still provided with a consular appointment to match the consul in the east. Nevertheless the western empire was in effect now one kingdom among several, in which the participation by Romans varied as greatly as did the degree to which the different societies achieved a fusion of Classical and barbarian culture and the amount by which they professed fealty to the emperor at Constantinople.

Closely associated, of course, with the western imperial throne was the western section of the Roman army, and it is relevant to what was happening in Britain to look at what we can make of its history in the fifth century, both in relation to the Roman military position on the Continent and to see what analogies one may draw when estimating the probable military effect in Britain of severance from the empire. We have already seen above what could happen when regular units were no longer paid. It is now worth looking a little more closely at the

---

[1] It perhaps reveals the equivocal nature of Roman relations with the barbarians, even the Huns, that Nepos, in his earlier period as emperor, appointed as his commander-in-chief (patrician) a Roman named Orestes who had formerly been secretary to Attila.

[2] An equally bizarre but pleasing footnote to history is that Romulus himself lived for the rest of his life in southern Italy on a substantial pension, not dying till 510.

Roman forces in general and their history in the fifth century.

The massive reliance on barbarian federates and the dissolution of the regular army, which were essentially a fifth-century and not a fourth-century process, may have happened very quickly in Britain but not very different in kind from the wider rundown of the western army. Theodosius I is, as we noted, criticized for admitting barbarians on easy conditions into the regular army, but this is by critics with hindsight of what was to come in the next century. Jones points out that it is the reign of Honorius which shows very heavy losses in the regular field-army, especially in the Gallic commands, and that these were made up not only by a heavy programme of recruiting new formations but also by withdrawing and upgrading units from the *limitanei*. The Roman generals were now forced to rely more and more on barbarians, to such an extent as radically to alter the balance and character of Roman armies. Regular soldiers were becoming harder and harder to obtain. They were also, if conscripts, likely to be the rawest material straight off the land who had to be trained from scratch in all the complicated methods of the Roman army. On the other hand many of the barbarians were warriors and had known no other life. There are signs that Roman generals regarded barbarians as more expendable than the former.[1] This had always tended to be a Roman attitude to the non-citizen, but the military reason that they were more easy to replace was perhaps even more pressing now than it had ever been. There were always more barbarians ready to serve for pay, but Roman recruits were difficult to come by.

These developments continued under Valentinian III, but even if Aetius' Roman troops were in a minority among his forces at the Catalaunian Plains they were still substantial in numbers. The actual nature of the Roman units of this late period is difficult to discover. As A.H.M. Jones put it:

The final stages of the disintegration of the Roman army in the West are most obscure. The *comitatenses* seem to have been allowed to run down, partly through lack of recruits, and partly through lack of funds, which were absorbed by the maintenance of the federates. What re-

---

[1] A.H.M. Jones, op. cit. 199: there seems to have been a tendency to employ purely barbarian groups when a fight to the finish was likely; and a hesitation to commit regular units in the same way.

mained was progressively more barbarised, federate bands being taken *en bloc* on to the establishment and graded as *auxilia*.[1]

This was a process that seems to have been happening as early as the reign of Honorius,[2] and was in addition to the upgrading of *limitanei* into the field armies already mentioned. Now we move into yet another stage. In the period after the murders of Aetius and Valentinian the regular army in the west seems to have run down to nothing. Under Valentinian III the government had been in extreme financial straits and hardly able to pay the troops they had. Then, as Jones points out 'As the government lost control of Africa, Spain, Dalmatia and all but the south-western corner of Gaul, its recruiting grounds shrank to Italy itself, and there is no record of the conscription being applied here after the death of Aetius.'[3] The senatorial aristocracy was still in control of the administration, and it preferred paying barbarian federates to conscription off its own lands. Even as early as Aetius, there is that curious appearance of the Olibriones 'who had once been Roman soldiers'. After the last western emperors had gone, the Gothic king Theodoric, who had taken over the imperial court in Italy with, in effect, eastern acquiescence, finally pensioned off the western palace guards, the *protectores domestici*, and the *scholares*.[4] However already by 475–80 there was probably no longer any real western army in being.[5]

The murder of Valentinian III had precipitated a period of anarchy that was brief but marked by extraordinary events. The worst was perhaps a lengthy sack of Rome itself by the Vandals against whom there was for the present no effective Roman leader; the oddest was the appearance of a Gallo-Roman senator proclaimed emperor with the support of the Visigothic king, ratified by a conference of other Gallic senators, and attempting to secure permanency on the throne by marching on Rome at the head of an army of Roman troops drawn from Gaul supported by Visigoths. But by 456 a new man had effectively taken Aetius' place as patrician and commander-in-chief of the western empire, this time a

[1] A.H.M. Jones, op. cit. 612.   [2] Orosius, VII. xl. 7.
[3] A.H.M. Jones, op. cit. 244.   [4] A.H.M. Jones, op. cit. 256.
[5] The eastern section of the Roman army, of course, remained, weathering the storms of the fifth century to provide the basis for Justinian's western conquests in Africa, Spain, and Italy in the sixth.

Suevian German named Ricimer, who was an Arian and not a Catholic. Like Stilicho and Aetius he was to be the real ruler, for sixteen years indeed, but unlike them plagued by being quite unable to find a suitable figurehead as emperor: as an Arian he would have had extreme difficulty in taking on the post himself.

We are gradually approaching the position where the now regularly barbarian commander-in-chief is discovering common ground with the senate in finding the emperor an unnecessary embarrassment. This was a situation which was not paralleled in the east. We earlier noted that at Constantinople the dominant ministers, at times when there were such, were civilian. No eastern post of patrician as commander-in-chief had been created. Instead there were two *magistri militum praesentales* rather than one and a corresponding division of the army. A determined emperor was thus able to exercise that crucial leadership of the Roman forces that was, except for the briefest interludes, absent in the west in the fifth century. Moreover the eastern army could be kept in better shape not only because of greater potential financial resources and recruiting grounds, but because the imperial government had a much closer control of the upper classes. Since the foundation of Constantinople the upper class in the east had been an aristocracy closely associated with the court in the capital. Like Louis XIV, the eastern emperors preferred to have their aristocracy at court, not dispersed on distant estates where they could become entrenched as great provincial magnates. The eastern government was not without extremely serious frontier problems, and we have seen how they suffered from the extortions of Attila until he turned westwards when there seemed no more to be gained from pressure on Constantinople. However, it is perhaps significant that despite some successes in the field against the Roman army in the east Attila did not attempt conquest. The survival of the Roman army in the eastern half of the empire is, of course, of major importance for the course of medieval history. Yet the domination of the eastern administration by the great civil officers, in contrast to the west, and its fundamentally Christian basis since the deliberate foundation of Constantinople as a Christian Rome by Constantine have given rise to the odd notion among some historians that the eastern empire had broken with Roman tradition and was essentially pacific, preferring diplomacy to war. For the fifth and sixth centuries at least this is anachronistic, whatever may have happened later. If anything, we have seen that the western government was even more dependent than the east on diplomacy, as it became weaker; and it is difficult to see pacifism in either Justinian's great ambitions for the reconquest of the west or Heraclius' amazing destruction of the Persians in 622–9 after so many centuries of more or less equally balanced struggle on the eastern frontier. These depended on both the will to wage war and certainly in Justinian's case the traditional Roman attitudes towards it. We have to remember both the survival of Roman imperial attitudes and the gradually reviving Roman military and economic strength in the east, while we contemplate the final fading-away of Roman Britain.

Indeed, even among the last emperors in the west there were occasions when the old spirit of leadership reasserted itself. In Britain Vortigern seems to have been quite discredited after the Saxon revolt and lost his following.[1] In the absence of other information we have to assume that Britain remained still locked in struggle with the Saxons, as yet, it would appear, more interested in loot than settlement[2] and therefore one may presume particularly destructive, unlike the major barbarian kingdoms forming in Gaul. On the British side, the leadership of Ambrosius Aurelianus played some part, perhaps taking over a more united British resistance since the fall of Vortigern. On the Continent Ricimer's first emperor, Majorian, proved unexpectedly vigorous. There had, indeed, been considerable difficulties in getting a candidate properly recognized by the east, but at the very end of 457 Majorian was formally settled on the throne. He proceeded to act as a real emperor. Taking the field in person he had a series of substantial military successes. These included expelling the Visigoths and Burgundians from Roman cities in Gaul which they had occupied in the chaos following the failure of the recent Gallo-Roman attempt on the throne, and restoring order in Spain, which had become an apparently intractable problem. It appears he was showing much too much sign of becoming an emperor in the old style, for,

[1] Nennius, op. cit. xlv–xlviii.   [2] Gildas, op. cit. xxiv–xxv.

caught without his army, he was deposed and executed by Ricimer in 461. But for a short while the possibility of firm Roman authority being restored in the Gallic prefecture must have seemed real, and it is unlikely this went unnoticed in Britain. Indeed, one act by Majorian not only shows that Roman military authority was now again present in northern Gaul, but started a train of events that has direct links with Britain. To the post of *magister militum per Gallias* he had appointed a Roman officer named Aegidius. Ricimer prevented Aegidius from marching on Italy when news of the emperor's murder arrived in Gaul by suborning the Visigoths and Burgundians to oppose him, and to reward them he formally deposed Aegidius from his command. Once again, the exigencies of Roman internal politics had intervened. However, Ricimer found himself unable to enforce his order: Aegidius' troops remained loyal to him and part of northern Gaul thus fell once again under an independent Roman authority.

After Aegidius' death there must have been some sort of a reconciliation, for later we find them under the command of a *comes* named Paulus acting in concert with Ravenna. In 466 the Visigoths had a new king and the Visigothic kingdom now turned determinedly anti-imperial after playing an equivocal part for so long. In 467 the west, without any enthusiasm on the part of Ricimer, received a new emperor, a highly distinguished officer from the eastern empire named Anthemius. Like Majorian, Anthemius was determined to restore order in Gaul. Though eventually unsuccessful, his operations had important consequences. Against the Visigoths he organized a combined army which included Paulus' Roman troops, Burgundian federates, and—an entirely new element in the situation as far as our knowledge goes—a joint federate force under a King Riothamus of Armoricans (who had never been permanently pacified since they had followed Britain in revolting in 409) and of Britons. Important migrations of Romano-Britons in the period from the Saxon wars of the 440s and subsequent troubles seem to have established a substantial British presence in the Loire region by the 460s, though the details are extremely obscure. Gildas mentions survivors of the Saxon revolt emigrating and by 461 we find a British bishop from among the Britons resident in Gaul attending a conference at Tours. It seems quite probable that the movement from Britain to Gaul took place over a number of years and for more than one reason, rather than as a single event. The long-term consequence was the fusing of these British immigrants with the Armoricans to form the Breton nation. Their numbers seem to have been substantial and themselves to some extent organized. Their immediate settlement was apparently in the region of eastern Brittany and Normandy. The position in Britain itself at this time probably appeared to many to be hopeless and that in Gaul not without promise of a better life. Indeed, from Majorian's accession at the end of 457 the prospects of improved order in Gaul may have made emigration particularly attractive. The various peoples on the Continent, Roman and barbarian, may now have appeared much more pleasing as neighbours than the Saxons at home; and the confused situation in the Loire region a prime opportunity for a fresh start. The immediate advantage to the Romans was an added element on their side in the containment of Visigothic expansion. The organized presence of Britons in the Roman army gathered for the campaign of Anthemius against the Visigoths indeed suggests that at least some of the Britons now arrived in Gaul had been deliberately recruited and invited over by the Roman authorities. St. Germanus had, after all, demonstrated their effectiveness in action against heretics and pagans when properly organized, and they had more recently spent years of hard fighting against barbarians. Moreover, a settlement of Romano-Britons as *foederati* may well have seemed a useful counterbalance to the unstable Armoricans. Armorica, as we have observed from time to time, had been an intractable problem since the third century. One recalls, for example, Germanus pleading with Galla Placidia for a moderate approach by the Romans to Armorica, after being appealed to by an Armorican delegation attempting to ward off a punitive attack by Alans in the service of Aetius. This plea had failed, the Armoricans having again risen in the meantime and been duly subdued. John Matthews reminds us that:

For an upper-class audience in the south of Gaul, the regions by the Loire were those in which men lived according to the 'law of nations', where everything was allowed. Peasants were advocates, private men passed sentence, in those same forests to which they took the fruits of their 'brigandage'.[1]

To introduce a settlement of people from outside the empire to control such a situation was, of course, regular Roman imperial policy. The Armoricans may well have been weakened by the Alan attack, so making the subsequent establishment of Britons in the region comparatively easy. However, the results seem not to have been quite what was expected. In the event, British immigrants acquired a tough reputation in Gaul, not wholly to the liking of their neighbours, and soon became the dominant element in their region. The adoption of the name *Britanni* for the whole population of the area is no accident; and it is an irony of history that the Bretons were to become such a thorn in the flesh of central authority in medieval and modern France.

The campaign against the Visigoths and Burgundians in which the Britons took part had other interesting and important consequences. Riothamus occupied and then lost Bourges. Anthemius' initiative misfired, resulting in the general loss of the cities of that region by the empire. A curious and important consequence of this was the permanent cutting-off of the Roman forces in northern Gaul from the rest.[2] As the remainder of the western empire dissolved in the next decade, this Roman enclave survived. It evolved into a kingdom centred on Soissons, ruled by Aegidius' son Syagrius, known later to the Franks as *rex Romanorum*.[3] This was neighboured on one side by the combined Armoricans and Romano-Britons and on another by the relatively friendly Franks. The Franks themselves were as yet still fragmented. One king, as I have already mentioned, had recently taken Cologne and seems to have installed his court in the Roman governor's palace. Another kingdom was centred on Cambrai, to the north of the Roman enclave and perhaps ruled by King Childeric. This Childeric was a close ally of the Romans of Soissons, where Aegidius and his

---

[1] Matthews, op. cit. 337. The Robin Hood touch is an intriguing one, not likely to appeal to local Gallo-Roman magnates.

[2] It is an interesting question why they did not disintegrate, as elsewhere, if they were regular Roman troops. In Childeric and his men Aegidius certainly had effective barbarian support, probably as federates.

[3] One would not be surprised to find Romano-British leaders in Britain now calling themselves 'kings'.

Roman successors seem to have played on a small scale the same complicated game of barbarian alliances as the empire at large. This was very much the policy Vortigern had disastrously employed in Britain. Further south the empire was losing ground to the Visigoths—for example the surrender of Clermont-Ferrand despite Sidonius Apollinaris' defence— and there was certainly fighting in the Loire region with Visigoths and now Saxons as well. But Childeric seems to have remained a trustworthy ally right down to his death in 481. He was succeeded by his son Clovis, who had greater ambitions.[1] In 486 he overthrew Syagrius, annexed his kingdom, and brought Roman rule in northern Gaul to its final end. By 496 the rest of Syagrius' allies seem to have submitted and Clovis was at the Loire. In 507, conveniently converted to Catholicism and apparently now recognized by the Roman emperor in Constantinople, he was ready, in alliance with the related royal house of Cologne, to start the campaign that drove the Arian Visigoths out of Gaul and established the great kingdom of the Franks. At this point there can be no doubt we have entered the early Middle Ages.

The collapse of the Roman empire in the west in the second half of the fifth century is generally recognized as an important but perhaps rather distant background to the beginnings of Anglo-Saxon England. However this narrative brings out something much more directly relevant: the fact that from Majorian's restoration of order in Gaul until the overthrow of Syagrius there was a Roman regime in continuous existence in northern Gaul. It is perhaps significant that the migrations from Britain seem to have taken place just about the time of Majorian's Gallic operations. At any rate, from around 460 to perhaps as late as 496 this Romano-British settlement in Gaul remained independent. To the north, Childeric's magnificent burial at Tournai indicates that his kingdom stretched into modern Belgium.[2] Thus, though we know nothing of possible political difficulties, the background to Britain for most of the second half of the fifth century is at the least a potentially friendly group

[1] Childeric's father was 'Merovech', from whom the Merovingian dynasty takes its name.

[2] His burial was discovered in 1653 and described in detail: the grave-goods have since been lost.

of states occupying the whole of Gaul opposite the south coast of England.

It would be pleasing to have some definite evidence of relations between the surviving Roman population in Britain and this group of states in Gaul. It is perhaps worth noting the discovery in the Thames near Battersea of eight ingots of pewter, stamped with Christian symbols and the name Syagrius.[1] He is not necessarily the Syagrius of this period: it was a distinguished Gallic name, held for example by one of those Gauls who rose to power under Gratian a century earlier.[2] Nor do we know how this batch of ingots came to be in the Thames. However, if the original dating of the amphora-handle from the Lower Thames Street house to the late fifth century was in fact correct, then a connection between the Roman realm in northern Gaul and a still-functioning city at London would have been more than possible. Gildas says nothing that betrays a knowledge of villa-life in Britain, and this has been interpreted to mean that by his time the villa had disappeared completely from the island. This is quite possibly true—though it could mean the opposite, that country estates were still the unremarkable norm in his day, at least in the parts ruled by British princes that he knew well. He does, however, emphasize the desertion of the cities in the course of the Saxon troubles. Yet this desertion itself need by no means have been complete, even where the Saxon problem had been most acute, in the south-east. There is an apparent absence of late fifth-century Saxon material from the area immediately north of London, and Roman occupation of the city itself may have been continuing in some form.[3]

For an idea of what this life may have been like, it is worth looking at Trier in the same period, for which we have

[1] Now in the Museum of London.

[2] See A.H.M. Jones, op. cit. 160; also Matthews, op. cit. 338. It is not certain that Syagrius of Soissons was related to the well-known fourth- and fifth-century family.

[3] At Exeter a major Roman public building was apparently still occupied into the seventh century (*Brit.* 4 (1973), 313) and Professor Frere has pointed out that a colony of Britons seems to have occupied its own quarter of the same city till expelled by Athelstan in the tenth century (*Britannia*, 422). But it would be stretching the point ludicrously to consider this *Roman* town life: it is one element in settled Anglo-Saxon England.

both literary and archaeological evidence. It is a highly interesting feature of the countryside surrounding Trier that Frankish graves with fifth-century material seem to be conspicuously absent from it, in contrast to Belgium (where we have seen a Merovingian kingdom established) and the area round Cologne (where we saw a related dynasty established in the 460s).[1] Even though Trier had been sacked several times and possibly attacked by plague, the former capital still survived. Edith Wightman describes it before it fell, as it did prior to the end of the century, to the kingdom of Clovis:

For a time, however, it was in the hands of one Arbogast, descendant of the Arbogast of the late 4th century. Though Frankish, he bore the title of *comes*, a title which shows that he claimed to represent Roman authority, and he may have worked in conjunction with Syagrius . . . Moreover, we know that he was a man of Roman education, for Sidonius Apollinaris . . . corresponded with him, and addressed him as an orator and man of letters. Bishop Auspicius of Toul wrote for him an epistle in verse, congratulating Trier on its ruler, addressing Arbogast in the most flattering terms and declaring that his Christian faith made him superior even to his famous ancestor. It has been suggested that on his mother's side he may have been descended from one of the high-ranking families of 4th century Trier: in any case, he stands as the last known representative of Roman rule in the Mosel valley.[2]

She goes on to point out that it is not easy to determine an exact date when Roman rule may be said to have ended:

This does not of course mean that life in the city was continuing as before. There must have been an enormous drop in living standards, and a fall in population resulting from not only the actual victims of war but also from an exodus of all people who had, or thought they could find, a means of livelihood elsewhere. This exodus had started at the end of the fourth century, when Trier ceased to house the *praefectus praetorio Galliarum* and his entourage, and there is every reason to suppose it continued. Arbogast himself may eventually have left, for it is probable that he is the same man as the like-named bishop of Chartres attested for the 480s. The middle classes, and all who relied on trade and commerce for a living must also have suffered badly, and it will have become increasingly difficult to finance, administer or police the city. Disease may have added to the troubles: Salvianus' description of the corpses lying in the streets suits a disease- or even plague-ridden

[1] Edith Wightman, op. cit. 251.

[2] Ibid. 70. The narrowing of the horizons of such a magnate since the days of the first Arbogast is perhaps as revealing of the times as the fact of the survival of the man and the city.

city as much as a sacked one, and the continued demand for entertainment would also be psychologically appropriate.[1]

Mutatis mutandis, this might perhaps be a description of fifth, even late fifth-century London, also once a capital. But less in the realms of speculation, this information about Trier adds one more piece to our political map of the age. A possible link with the realm of Syagrius to the west brings connections with the new Breton kingdom and with Childeric's Franks, and through them with those of Cologne. We may therefore perhaps extend our concept of a group of relatively friendly states from the Channel coast inwards all the way to the Rhine. This may well have remained true at least till Clovis started on his career of conquest in 486.

It is not surprising that these Gallo-Roman states all fell comparatively easily to Clovis. The tradition of Romano-German rulers was now extremely well established in the west, and Clovis, despite brutality and treachery worthy of many Romans in the past, proved ready to incorporate Roman traditions and Roman personalities into his new realm. Gregory of Tours describes his reception of what are described as 'consular tablets' from Anastasius and his proud wearing of a purple cloak and a diadem.[2] It was perhaps precisely this degree of recognition from the eastern emperor that helped encourage a substantial group of Gallo-Romans to support the other side to the extent of joining the Visigothic army when Clovis in the same year made his final attack on the Visigothic kingdom. They may not have been entirely unaware of the vast reforms the Emperor Anastasius was carrying out in the east which was restoring its economic and military strength, though they are hardly likely to have foreseen that this was to bring Justinian's resurgent Roman army westward only a few years later. Nevertheless, a considerable unease at renewed imperial pretensions is not impossible. The Gallo-Roman contingent in the Visigothic army that was defeated by Clovis was in

---

[1] Ibid. 250.
[2] Theodoric had asked the eastern emperor for permission to wear the purple in 490: this was refused at the time, but after he had seized Ravenna and been proclaimed king of the Goths in 493 the position changed. In 497 Anastasius sent back to Ravenna the western imperial regalia. Theodoric nevertheless continued officially to be entitled *rex*.

fact commanded by Sidonius Apollinaris' own son. Even more significant, perhaps, is that this younger Apollinaris was, after the defeat, appointed by the Franks to his father's old bishopric of Clermont-Ferrand. Thus the great-grandson of Constantine III's praetorian prefect continued the tradition of this eminent provincial Roman family through into the Frankish kingdom of the early Middle Ages.

It is therefore against a background of independent Roman states with Frankish support from around 460 to 486, followed by an aggressive Frankish kingdom with a strong Romanizing element, that we have to set the position of Saxons and Romano-Britons in the second half of the fifth century. While there is clearly little likelihood there was ever any real possibility of intervention from the Continent on the Roman side, the Saxons were in no very good position either. Probably their best moment was in the very few years after the murder of Aetius in 454 before Majorian restored order in the Roman part of Gaul, and one can well imagine that Saxon confidence at that time accentuated the desire for emigration on the part of many Romano-Britons. Nor should we be surprised to find renewed Saxon activity *in Gaul* around 460: reviving British spirit and the conflict between Rome and the Visigoths may have suggested that prospects were now more promising in Gaul for Saxon soldiers of fortune than in Britain. However obscure, the scene is now set for the eventual British victory that at the end of the century was to set back further Saxon aggression in Britain for fifty years or more.[1] But Gildas, writing from the British, or 'Celtic', side of the fence, complains that after the generation of peace that followed the victory of his compatriots at Mount Badon 'our cities are still not occupied as they were; even today they are dismal and deserted ruins.'[2]

Alongside this is the fascinating problem I have already touched upon—why Britain did not evolve along the same lines as those taken by Gaul as it turned into early medieval France. Part of the answer lies in much later periods of history and much must fall into the province of my Dark Age colleagues. But there are one or two further observations

[1] For signs of Saxon migration back to the Continent from settlements in Britain in the first half of the sixth century see Dixon, *Barbarian Europe*, 53.
[2] Translation: Dixon, ibid. 56.

with which to end this narrative. Gaul had the best part of a century longer than Britain to adapt itself to barbarian rule. This came in stages, and for a long period Gaul was partitioned between barbarian kingdoms, served by Roman officials and containing a strong Gallo-Roman upper class, and Roman territories under the control of an army extensively manned by barbarians and in fluctuating alliance with barbarian powers. When the final conquest of Gaul came it was by barbarians, chiefly Franks, but also Burgundians and others, who had served Rome or been closely associated with her and were taking over a country already divided between Roman and barbarian. It has been often asserted that the prime reason for the differences between post-Roman Britain and post-Roman Gaul was that Roman culture had sunk much deeper into Gaul than Britain. This is an argument it is most difficult to find unequivocal evidence to support: the survival of vernacular Latin to become French is a relatively weak point, particularly as we have the example of the Rhineland and the Moselle, where Roman culture certainly went as deep as anywhere in northern France, yet German became the dominant tongue.

Among the many factors, some perhaps as yet quite undetected, we have to take into account differences between the barbarians themselves, perhaps most of all between the Saxons in Britain and the (mostly Christian) barbarians who formed the new kingdoms in Gaul. This may in its turn have caused fundamental divergence between the responses of the Gallo-Romans and of the Britons to the replacement of Roman rule by barbarian. I suspect that the Saxons were a very different proposition from the Visigoths or even the Franks, but this needs qualification. It will be remembered that in the fourth century Saxons and Franks are often grouped together as a scourge that descends from time to time on the northern provinces of the empire. Yet by 406 it is Frankish allies that are defending the Rhine against the invading Germans, and thereafter till Clovis turns against Syagrius eighty years alter they are powerful allies of Rome in the north, becoming more and more part of the Late Roman world. In Britain, too, of course, we have the spectacle of many Germans in the Roman army from an early date and Saxons as allies perhaps in the fourth century and certainly in the fifth. These Saxons one might expect to have followed the same pattern as the barbarians in Gaul. Indeed, we have seen that fifth-century Saxon settlement in Britain seems often to be alongside Roman. Yet one possibility is that the Saxons brought in by Vortigern were radically different in character from those already serving or settled in Britain. We may therefore have two quite separate types of Saxon, the latter maritime pirates largely untouched by previous peaceful contact with Rome. Another important possibility is that the revolt of the 440s and the apparent involvement of the issue of employing Saxon mercenaries in the internal British politics of the time may have changed Romano-British attitudes to the barbarians in Britain in much the same way as relations between Romans and barbarians in Mediterranean Europe and the Danube had been embittered by the awful events of AD 376–8: the invitation to the Goths to settle inside the empire that went out of control, the destruction of Valens and his army at Adrianople, the massacre of Goths serving in the eastern section of the Roman army. Such events had opened the way to later atrocities on both sides. On the Continent, however, time and self-interest were on the side of reconciliation and fusion. This was powerfully assisted by two factors: the need of the barbarians for a mechanism to administer their new kingdoms and the fact that both sides were jointly threatened by other, very powerful enemies.

In Britain these two factors do not seem to have operated. On the one hand, by the time Britain erupted into the wars that were to occupy it for half a century there was, I feel we can say with certainty, no centralizing Roman administration and no uniform political and social structure for the barbarians to take over, nor had there been for a generation. On the other hand—though the effects of Irish immigration remain imperfectly understood—there was no organized, unmistakable common foe to temper the savagery of the struggle between Briton and Saxon that culminated at Mount Badon.

Paradoxically, that victory itself may have finally made sure there would not be the same fusion of Roman and barbarian cultures here that occurred on the Continent.

However, what Britain was like after AD 500 and how the Saxons who renewed the attack in the second half of the sixth century compared with those that took part in the events of the fifth are matters for the Anglo-Saxon and Celtic archaeologists and historians, not the student of Roman Britain. There are few clean breaks in history, but the very different but broadly contemporaneous changes marked by Mount Badon in Britain and Clovis in Gaul are such that somewhere around 500 is a point at which we can end the narrative part of this book.

NOTES

Sources for fifth-century Britain. David N. Dumville's radical reappraisal of the value of the sources commonly used for the history of the fifth century in Britain—at least in our present state of knowledge about them—appeared in June 1977 ('Sub-Roman Britain: History and Legend', *History*, 62 (1977), 173 ff.), and I am very grateful to Patrick Wormald for drawing my attention to it. At the time of revising this chapter it is too early to judge how it will affect the thinking of specialists on this period, but I personally find it sufficiently striking to be even less confident about the course of events in fifth-century Britain than before. I have made some minor revisions in this chapter in the light of Mr Dumville's article, but think a much wider reassessment of the whole period will be required when the highly pertinent questions Mr Dumville raises have been thoroughly debated, particularly those relating to the Celtic sources.

Vortigern and the 'Concilium Britanniarum'. We should be very wary of accepting the late John Morris' concept of Vortigern ruling all of Roman Britain, and in particular his idea that Vortigern acted 'with his "seniores" or "concilium", plainly the *Concilium Britanniarum'* (Morris, 'Dark Age Dates', Jarrett and Dobson, op. cit. 164). It does not in fact look as if Vortigern had all the notables on his side (e.g. Ambrosius) and there is no direct evidence for a *concilium Britanniarum* at any time as a descendant of the old provincial council. Even for the earlier provincial council itself there is only a very little clear evidence (see p. 532 below) and the council of the provinces of the Gauls of the fifth century seems to have been created between 403 and 408 and then fallen out of use till 418 'because of the laxness of the times and the indifference of the usurpers.' The creation of the Gallic council, indeed, is attributed to one particular praetorian prefect of Gaul and its revival to another (Matthews, op. cit. 334 etc.), both under Honorius, and it is not suggested that it is a descendant of the provincial councils of earlier times, or that it was a general policy. Indeed, if at all, the British before the break ought to have been attending the council of the Gallic prefecture to which they belonged, not one of their own.

V

BRITAIN UNDER ROMAN RULE

17

THE ASSIMILATION OF BRITAIN

THE INSTRUMENTS OF ROMANIZATION

To understand how the provinces came to be Romanized we have to abandon some of our common conceptions. There is little evidence that the Romans had any general racial prejudice in the modern sense. Hence they assumed anyone, or almost anyone, could absorb Roman culture and manners, even as they themselves (despite the protests of moralists and conservatives) borrowed extensively from other cultures, especially in the fields of art and religion. They had a keen sense of class and an enormous pride in their family histories, but on the whole treated a man as he was now rather than the background from which he had come, though they were not above making fun of the *nouveaux riches*. Moreover, while privileges attached to class and legal status—slave, freedman, citizen or non-citizen, equestrian, senator—there was nothing immutable about a man's position. This is a real difference between Rome and the Classical Greek world before it and in many senses the medieval to come. In the letters of that Italian aristocrat the Younger Pliny we have the cautionary tale of the senator Macedo.[1] Macedo was an ex-praetor and therefore only one stage from the highest of all social levels, those who had held the consulship. He was murdered by his slaves, and Pliny draws the lesson that no master can feel secure because he is kind to his slaves: slaves are naturally savage and given the chance will murder out of sheer love of violence, not because they have thought out the advantages by use of reason (indeed, the penalties were so awful that it is difficult to see how any could have so reasoned[2]). But Pliny goes on to say that of course Macedo was a pretty unpleasant master *only too inclined to forget that his own father had been a slave—or perhaps because of it.*

---

[1] Pliny, *Letters*, iii. 14.
[2] They included a legal provision for the execution of the whole slave household.

We also have to avoid confusing culture and politics. To quote myself in another place:[1]

We have already seen British tribes before the Conquest producing coins modelled on Classical patterns. It is perhaps odder to us today to find at Colchester, the very centre of anti-Roman resistance, much evidence of an avid taste for Roman products. But the Greeks had happily traded with the Persian Empire through the Persian Wars, and ladies in England sought eagerly for news of Paris fashions during the Napoleonic period. It is important not to confuse politics with taste or to assume that the influx of Roman culture into Britain was either imposed or automatically resisted on nationalistic grounds. We may feel that the imported art was often inferior to the native, but it is no business of ours to project this feeling on to the Britons.

It is highly significant that Tacitus singles out, in his account of how Agricola fostered Roman culture among the Britons, the teaching of the children of their leading men the liberal arts. 'The result was that those who had once shunned the Latin language now sought fluency in it'. The key to participation in the Roman way of life was Latin. A gentleman with pretensions to culture was expected to read Greek, but the language of law and public administration was Latin and it was essential to speak it to get on in the complex world of the empire. There is some evidence that in Britain it remained a second language, but like English in India it was not only indispensable for public affairs but the only practical *lingua franca* in what was becoming a very mixed population. We should have quite the wrong impression if we thought of Roman Britain as Romans from Italy or long-Romanized Mediterranean provinces on the one side facing native Britons on the other. Juvenal the satirist complained bitterly that the city of Rome was being polluted by the influx of easterners. Britain was remote and peripheral, but inscriptions here record a fair sprinking of Greeks, even Syrians, numbers of Gauls, and above all Germans. In the eastern provinces of the empire they eventually used Greek as their means of overcoming the innumerable problems of language:[2] in the west it had to be Latin.

The rather archaic type of spoken Latin which appears

---

[1] *Britain and the Early Roman Empire*, (Open University, 1974), 40.
[2] Nevertheless even in the east the official language of government and law was Latin till after the time of Justinian.

to have been more common in Britain than in other western provinces has suggested it was at least in the early days largely learnt at school and maintained in this form by the educated speech of the island.[1] This incidentally underlines the rather isolated nature of the Romano-British upper classes, who seem to play little part in the empire as a whole. Celtic certainly survived, as is obvious not only from the existence of Welsh and Cornish, which are linguistically separate from the Irish languages and therefore not re-imported after the Roman period, but also in the adoption into Celtic of many words from Latin to describe concepts and articles not previously available.[2] These essentially describe the sort of ideas that would be needed in urban or villa society, and correspond with the distribution of graffiti in Latin, which occur on military, town, and villa sites but very rarely in the 'native' farms and villages. At the bottom end of the scale the industrial worker could clearly use Latin. From London comes a tile inscribed before firing 'Austalis has been wandering off on his own every day for a fortnight', relic of a shop-floor grievance; and there is even one from Silchester with a couple of words echoing the opening of the second book of the Aeneid.[3] It has been pointed out that this should cause no surprise: if one wanted to write, one had to write in Latin as Celtic had no script. This is not entirely true, but any written Celtic in Britain was probably confined to the priestly and possibly princely classes. It is probably reasonable to suppose that in remote settlements little Latin was spoken and possibly relatively little understood (though we shall look at the role of army service in the spread of the Latin tongue). Villa-owners, traders, and officials had to communicate with native peasants, whatever their own origins. But one may suspect that such contact was often through the slave bailiff or clerk,

[1] Cf. Agricola's action in having the sons of the leading Britons *taught* the *liberales artes* (Tacitus, *Agr.* xxi.). This in itself suggests a rather slow start among the upper classes.

[2] Cf. J.P. Wild, 'Borrowed Names for Borrowed Things?', *Antiquity*, 44 (1970), 125 ff.

[3] *Pertacus perfidus Campester Lucilianus Campanus conticuere omnes.* A study of possible social and regional implications in what is recorded of British Latin is contained in E.P. Hamp, *Brit.* 6 (1975), 150 ff. For the literary classics in Britain see A.A. Barrett, *Brit.* 9 (1978), 307 ff.

and it was the latter, who as slaves and freedmen often rose into the lower middle class and beyond, who are most likely to have been bilingual. Once the local aristocracy had adopted Latin with enthusiasm they will certainly have demanded good spoken and written Latin from upper servants, secretaries, and the tutors they provided for their children, if, as Tacitus says, they were swept with the fashion for all things Roman. They could hardly let themselves down with their neighbours or the Roman upper classes with whom they mixed by having half-barbarian homes.[1]

Despite the deliberate education of young British aristocrats, probably by far the greatest reason for the spread of practical Latin was the army. Not only did a soldier need to speak Latin, he also needed to be able to read it. He might enter the auxilia of the Early Empire as a raw barbarian provincial: he left it with two decades' experience of literacy and numeracy in Latin,[2] an extensive knowledge of Roman skills in a very wide range of trades and, perhaps most valued of all, the Roman citizenship. It is true that only in time of extreme emergency were the legions themselves recruited from men who were not already Roman citizens, though grants of citizenship for this purpose to individuals were apparently fairly freely made. Except for the raising of entirely new legions recruitment seems by the second and third centuries to have been in the hands of the governors of the provinces in which they were stationed. Indeed, as early as the beginning of the second century Italians seem no longer to have been entering the legions as individual volunteers, but preferred service in the more prestigious and much more lucrative praetorian guard and other special units. Henceforth legionary recruits tended to come from wherever citizens were found, particularly the civil settlements around the legionary bases where sons frequently followed family tradition. Before the civil wars of 68–69 auxiliary units were normally stationed in or near the areas where they were raised: after that upheaval they were usually

---

[1] Graffiti on pots suggests there was kitchen and market-place Latin as well.

[2] Cf. the wooden writing-tablets containing accounts and private letters from Chesterholm (Vindolanda), Northumberland, mostly from the pre-Hadrianic fort (see A.K. Bowman and J.D. Thomas, *The Vindolanda Writing Tablets,* Newcastle-upon-Tyne (1974), for a convenient summary).

posted elsewhere and rarely continued to draw recruits from their original provinces, except for certain units with highly specialized equipment. By the second century, therefore, both legions and auxilia were largely made up of men locally recruited. As the number of provincials with Roman citizenship grew, the type of recruit each category attracted differed less and less, though there were still important differences both in the entry standards required and in pay and status during service. The direct evidence for Britain is thin, but Dr Dobson and Professor Mann have made an important contribution to the study of this vital element in the life of Roman Britain.[1] In their words:

Our conclusion must be that in the present state of the evidence there is nothing to prevent us, with due reservation, postulating in Britain local recruitment of the auxilia and legions stationed there, from the 80's for the auxilia, by the mid-second century for the legions; but in each case it must have taken some time before most of the needs of the army, the largest provincial army in the empire, were met from the island itself.

Again, except in times of emergency or in the special case of auxiliary units compulsorily raised from newly conquered regions or exacted from enemies as part of a peace settlement, conscription was largely avoided till the fourth century. Its unpopularity with landowners who saw their workers being drained away when it had to be brought in perhaps best explains the unwillingness of earlier emperors to impose it. It may also have been considered that much better material was obtainable by offering a secure and attractive career to volunteers. Hence the importance of the gradual build-up in provincial families of the tradition of joining the army. Ironically this probably made easier the imposition of a hereditary obligation to military service on such families in the fourth century, when the much larger army of the period had to be kept supplied. These hereditary military families in the frontier provinces must have lightened the total burden on the rural estates imposed by the forced levy of men. In Britain where the establishment changed comparatively little, things probably went on much as before. The growth of field-armies required different methods, and this

---

[1] B. Dobson and J.C. Mann, *Brit.* 4 (1973), 191 ff.

is where we should chiefly seek the newer types of recruit: those barbarians more recently settled and Romanized within the empire with an obligation to service, free barbarians from outside the frontiers as volunteers, and conscripts from Roman estates.

Until the reign of Septimius Severus, soldiers, other than officers, were not permitted to marry,[1] but there is a very large body of evidence that many had wives, though not legally recognized as such. Under Roman law illegitimate children followed the condition of their mother, so before Severus the children of serving soldiers were citizen or non-citizen depending on their mother's status. However, there is the extremely important qualification that the grant of citizenship to time-expired auxiliaries also included the right to full legal marriage with wives they had at the time of their discharge from the army or that they took thereafter. There is no evidence that the wives themselves became citizen, but the children, now being legitimate sons of Roman fathers were Romans. This latter right was partially abrogated in the second century, when in order to encourage recruiting the sons had to wait for their own citizenship till they themselves enrolled in the army. Even this became largely a dead letter by the late Antonine period, as by then few recruits even into the auxilia were not Roman citizens on entry since in a very large number of cases both their parents had achieved the citizenship by one means or another. The total effect was to set up a machine that passed large numbers of provincials through a long training process that turned them into complete Romans.

We have seen that, as under Claudius at Colchester, legionary veterans were seen as in some sense a military reserve, though they did not prove in that case very effective. But veterans were very important in a province, particularly where there was a large garrison. This was not confined to the deliberately founded *coloniae,* nor to ex-legionaries alone. Compulsory savings schemes (and grants of land in some cases) made them men of substance in their communities. If one takes as an example T. Flavius Longinus, who had held commissioned rank in the auxiliary cavalry unit *ala II*

---

[1] See Salway, *Frontier People,* 31 f.; Brian Campbell, *JRS* 68 (1978), 153 ff.

Pannoniorum, we find him elected to the councils of a colony, a *municipium,* and the *canabae* or civil settlement surrounding a legionary fortress.[1] Even during his service a soldier might have a slave or two of his own,[2] or a freedman like the young Moor Victor who worked for Numerianus,[3] a trooper of *ala I Asturum* stationed at the military port at the mouth of the Tyne. Soldiers could engage in business (other than farming)[4] in the provinces where they were stationed, and it is likely that such slaves and freedmen often acted as their agents in such matters, since their masters were not granted leave by the army for personal affairs (*negotia privata*).[5] It is clear that as early as the first century soldiers in some provinces had their *familiae* resident near them.[6] We have seen that the extra-mural settlements in which we may suppose many of them to have lived grew into active centres of trade and in these one may suspect soldiers and their establishments played a very considerable part and greatly accelerated the merging of Roman and native. As we have noted, soldiers were in the early third century granted the legal right to set up a home (*domum comparare*), including without doubt not only wife and children but also the slaves and freedmen that made up a Roman household. The third-century emperors were very ready to follow Severus' precept in favouring the soldiers above all else, but in this matter the state was probably doing no more than recognizing fact while making it appear a favour. On Hadrian's Wall the fact that the civil settlements were now allowed to cross the Vallum and crowd up to the walls of the forts is a different matter. This was a real concession to the troops and their families. Soldiers, sons, and indeed the whole of these communities, must have been very well acquainted with the ways of the Roman army, so that by the time young men came to enter the local unit from these settlements they

---

[1] *CIL* III, 1100: his civic career was probably under Trajan.

[2] In the fourth century St. Martin was praised for the austerity with which as a young guardsman he restricted himself to a personal servant.

[3] *RIB* 1064 (South Shields).

[4] They were not allowed to hold land in the provinces where they were serving lest they lose their military preparedness, according to the jurist Aemilius Macer writing after AD 217 (*Dig* XLIX. xvi. 13), and they were specifically prohibited from trying to avoid this regulation by using a nominee.

[5] Vegetius, ii. 19.   [6] Tacitus, *Hist.* ii. 80.

were already well prepared for service. Moreover we may reasonably assume that such communities became thoroughly imbued not only with the Roman way of doing things but also the mood of the army of the time. This cannot be without considerable social and political importance. In the final event it was the support of the troops that so often made or unmade emperors, and in these settlements must have lain one of the main seed-beds in which the attitudes of ordinary soldiers were formed. The third century provides us with a particularly clear indication of the status of the Roman soldier in his world. By that time, as we have observed, the old distinction within the empire between citizen and non-citizen was disappearing and very soon was to be almost entirely abolished by law. In its place a new legal concept had appeared, a distinction between the upper category of society (*honestiores*) and the lower (*humiliores*). Both were free, not slave, but in many respects were now treated differently before the law. In particular, the punishments for criminal offences were much more physcially degrading for *humiliores* than *honestiores*. The former might, for example, be sent to forced labour in the mines for a crime where the latter would be banished to an island. The cruellest forms of execution such as being thrown to the beasts in the amphitheatre were also reserved for the lower class. The line between them was not strictly defined, but in general it appears that military veterans were clearly accepted as members of the *honestiores*. It is not therefore surprising to find them rising to positions of eminence in civic life, and their progeny climbing to greater heights. It has been observed that relatively few veterans are recorded on the inscriptions of the northern frontier of Britain, and at one time I surmised that either the climate drove them south on retirement or few lived that long. But it may be the much greater density of cities further south and the attractions of villa properties which were very few in the north that led them to retire away from their stations. Veterans do appear in Britain more noticeably settled outside the legionary fortresses,[1] and the fact that these were much larger and

---

[1] e.g. *RIB* 478, 495, 500, 517, 526, 534 (Chester); 358, 359, 361, 363 (Caerleon); 679, 685 (York).

more urban and situated in more pleasant places than many of the *vici* of the smaller forts perhaps supports a preference for civic amenities and prospects, but may only reflect the general thinness of our knowledge about the recruiting and subsequent lives of soldiers specifically in the army in Britain. We are however sure that Roman troops often developed strong affinities with the peoples and localities where they served. This process could go so far as to include legionaries even in the early days of the Empire when they were likely to have been recruited far away. In the Year of the Four Emperors, one of the main reasons that caused the legions stationed in Syria to declare for Vespasian was this inter-mingling:[1]

What most of all inflamed opinion in the province and army alike was that Mucianus declared that Vitellius intended to transfer the legions on the German frontier to the quiet and lucrative life of service in Syria and send the Syrian garrison to the fortresses in Germany where they would endure hard work and a bitter climate. It was also a matter of the provincials preferring to deal with soldiers with whom they had long been on terms of familiarity (indeed there were ties of marriage and property in many cases) as much as the fact that the troops had served so long in those bases that they had grown fond of them as if they were their own family homes.

Sometimes soldiers actually returned on retirement to a province in which they had been stationed. There is the third-century case of Tiberius Flavius Virilis, who held four jobs in the centurionate in legions in Britain, acquiring a wife who from her name was almost certainly a Briton. Her husband also had other postings, including one in Algeria, and on retirement seems to have gone back to settle alongside the station of that unit, his former unit there.[2] Intermarriage and movement of this sort around the empire contributed considerably to making the provinces what they were.

Veterans occasionally engaged in commerce[3] and are recorded in one case living in a settlement together with traders.[4] It is however probably much more important

---

[1] Tacitus, *Hist.* ii. 80.
[2] *CIL* VIII, 2877 (Lambaesis). Lollia Bodicca's first name suggests that she came from a native family that first received the Roman citizenship during Lollius Urbicus' governorship.
[3] *CIL* XIII, 6677.   [4] Arrian, *Periplus,* xii.

that the army attracted merchants from other parts of the empire. One of the best-known British examples is Barates of Palmyra, who appears to have been a dealer in military standards or banners. He himself was buried at Corbridge with a comparatively humble tombstone.[1] His wife, however, has a much more remarkable monument at South Shields.[2] It has many noteworthy features, not least the facts that it seems to have been carved by an eastern craftsman and the inscription is bilingual, in Latin and Palmyrene. From it we learn that Regina had been Barates' slave before he freed her and married her, and that she was Catuvellaunian, a member of what had once been the proudest nation in Britain. These personal changes of fortune and the mixture of races in this marriage demonstrate how varied and colourful society could be, even in so remote a province as Britain. It underlines our earlier point, as to why the working language had to be Latin and how the common culture, however peculiarly it might sometimes be interpreted, was Roman.

Nearly all the people we have so far been considering have been long-term residents in the particular province. We should not, however, forget the impact of the large number of Romans, from many parts of the empire but predominantly Italy and the most Romanized regions of the west, who came on short-term appointments at every level of military and civil government. These ranged from the governor and the procurator to legionary legates, military tribunes, centurions, commanders of auxiliary units, and a host of lesser men in public posts. Most could bring their households with them and many had official accommodation provided with the job. This meant an ever-changing social scene and constant employment in all the service industries that provided them with the standard of life they expected. It is not surprising that, to take just one example of such a creation of employment, we find a mason from the region of Chartres working at the Roman spa of Bath.[3]

Romans were used to public bathing establishments, often on a huge scale, as major establishments for relaxation and social intercourse. Any substantial Romano-British town—and many small ones—would expect to build one as a matter

---

[1] *RIB* 1171.   [2] *RIB* 1065.   [3] *RIB* 149.

of course. Bath is, of course, exceptional, in that it was the centre of a major healing-cult, as were many of the great shrines of the Middle Ages, but its social function should not be overlooked. Romans seem to have gone there in substantial numbers, mostly, to judge from the inscriptions found there, from the middle ranks of official society and including many army officers taking the cure,[1] with whom the local gentry might easily mix.

Later in this book we shall look in some detail at the extraordinary variety of race and culture in the religious side of Roman Britain, but in the context raised by the subject of Romanization and the function of such centres as Bath it is worth making briefly one or two points. It helped the process of Romanization greatly that the Romans were deeply devoted to the notion that every place had its guardian spirit and it was thus relatively easy for them to respect local deities, such as Sulis at Bath, and to identify them with their own, as, for example, 'Sulis Minerva'. The grandest manifestations of Roman religion were, of course, the great festivals of the 'Capitoline Triad'—Jupiter, Juno, and Minerva—and the cult of Rome and the imperial house in which the highest Roman officials and the leading provincials took part. The latter, of course, had had a disastrous start at Colchester, but the gradual social and political fusing of the varied elements in the society of the province, permanent and temporary, made religion more and more of a bond. Like the military ceremonies and sacrifices to the Imperial Cult carried out by every unit of the Roman army, this form of religion was essentially about loyalty to the state. Indeed, the very fact that more and more provincials had served in the Roman army meant that the local element that took part in the public observances of the state religion was increasingly one that had been exposed for years to the daily ritual of Rome and the public expression of allegiance. For the first three centuries of the Christian era the Roman authorities had extreme difficulty in understanding that Christian refusal to take part in such worship was not a sign of disloyalty. When the situation

[1] For example *RIB* 143, 144, 146, etc. (Many of these were put up by their freedmen, and one does wonder if sometimes the latter were sent by their masters as proxies to set up a dedication at the healing shrine.)

was reversed and Christianity became the state religion, emperors considered refusal to accept it, indeed the particular brand of orthodoxy they happened to support at the time, to be equally treasonable. State religion was an essential part of government, and government in the Roman empire was as much a matter of ensuring loyalty to the emperor as it was of administration. The Roman genius for organization was essentially employed by government in the interests of power and security. Government in practice often failed to secure those ends, but, as we have noted, the side-effect of their efforts was long periods of peace and internal order in which vast numbers of ordinary people were able to go about their everyday business, relatively undisturbed.

THE MACHINERY OF GOVERNMENT

In the narrative chapters of this book we have seen the Roman government of Britain proceed from the *ad hoc* arrangements of the Conquest period to the regular form under the Early Empire, whereby the *legatus Augusti* and *procurator provinciae*, each with elaborate administrative substructures, controlled the whole of the conquered territories. In the third century the island is divided into two provinces, with a slowly changing but essentially unmodified structure, now in duplicate. In the fourth the changes are much more drastic: two provinces become four and then five, but much more important the division is no longer between general administration (including command of the army in Britain) and finance but between military and civil. In his civil role the old *legatus Augusti* of the undivided province reappears in the person of the *vicarius,* to whom the governors of the individual fourth-century provinces are responsible. However, unlike the *legatus Augusti* he does not have a direct relationship with the emperor, but is himself responsible to the praetorian prefect of the Gauls, in which Britain is included. The praetorian prefect becomes a civil official, and from time to time is responsible to a Caesar rather than the emperor himself or to one of two or more *Augusti.* The army now has its own separate organization independent of provincial boundaries, with *comites* and *duces,* similarly responsible to a *magister militum* in Gaul or elsewhere and like the praetorian prefect also with varying degrees of closeness to the dominant emperor.

These changes have important consequences for the location of the centres of power, as they affected people in Britain in practical terms. Apart from occasional incidents such as imperial visits, for example by Claudius or Hadrian or Constans, or the island happening to be involved in a claim to the throne, as with Clodius Albinus or Constantine the Great, the pattern remains constant for long periods. With an initial period at Colchester, from Flavian times to the early third century there is the seat of a single *legatus Augusti* at London, who has direct access to the emperor. In the first half of the third century there are two such centres, London and York, but soon after the middle of the century, though this remains the formal position, the real centre of power has shifted to northern Gaul, most frequently Cologne or Trier. At the end of the century this becomes formalized with the Tetrarchy, followed in the fourth century by the establishment of the prefecture of the Gauls. The multiplication of layers in the government structure and the deliberate withdrawal of emperors from ready accessibility meant that individual provincial governors were now relatively far from the fount of authority. Nevertheless, the establishment of the provinces of Britain as a complete diocese within the prefecture meant that the *vicarius* himself was only one step away from the proximate emperor, at least on paper, through the praetorian prefect. London thus regained its position as the centre of government. But it was now more limited in that not only did the praetorian prefect himself become more distant from the court as his post became a fixed one in Gaul and another praetorian prefect accompanied the emperor, but also because the greatest influence on the emperors in the west was coming to be the *magistri militum,* to whom the military commanders in Britain were largely responsible. Access to anyone who could speak with imperial authority was becoming more and more remote. This was compounded by the long periods when the senior Augustus was resident in Constantinople. It is hardly surprising that there was a rash of usurpers in Britain at the beginning of the fifth century or that the case seemed hopeless when the last, Constantine III, was forced to set up his court not in London or Trier but far away at Arles, with barbarians at large in between.

If we have seemed to harp on this matter of accessibility, it is with reason. Pliny's correspondence with Trajan[1] shows that in his day the emperor was closely involved in what seem to us minor details of provincial administration. Though Pliny himself was rather a timid administrator, even the most independent-minded governor is likely to have hesitated before taking decisions of importance without referring back to the emperor. Thus a negligent emperor or slow communication could paralyse the system. Moreover all important appointments were made by the emperor, and a conscientious emperor could take a great deal of interest in the career and performance of individuals at every level. This sort of 'performance appraisal' from the top doubtless kept officials up to the mark, but Pliny's letters also show the other side, that since everyone's job (and sometimes his fortune and even his life) depended on the emperor, it was extremely important to have the emperor's ear, both for one's own advancement and that of one's friends and clients.[2] Under the Early Empire, while the provincial governors came from the same class as the emperor and were well-known to him socially, in action in the senate and law courts and as his generals in war, their personal status in the province was enormous and their own accessibility crucial to the provincials. They, too, had important patronage at their command, and we find Pliny writing to his friends asking them to take protégés of his own onto their staffs, though the emperor usually reserved entirely to himself the choice of men for senior positions such as the command of legions.

This situation inevitably led to great uncertainty. It is easy to become so absorbed in the career of the hundreds of individuals whose appointments are known in great detail from the thousands of inscriptions surviving throughout the empire, that we assume 'standard careers' and forget that there was little to stop a capricious emperor from interfering with the system. In some ways the death or fall of an

[1] Pliny, *Letters*, x.
[2] In the jargon of modern business management this process is known as 'career development review'.

emperor or his favourite adviser was not unlike a change of president in the United States, where vastly more appointments are a matter of party and indeed of one man and his personal advisers than in Britain today. Similarly, the disgrace of an individual Roman senator could bring the ruin of the many careers that depended on his influence. Patronage ran through the Roman system from top to bottom, and Rome cannot be understood without grasping that fact. Nor was it felt to be dishonourable, rather a matter of pride and obligation to do the best for those who depended upon it. And a good emperor was expected to be the greatest and best patron of all.

The third-century trend towards excluding senators from military commands and provincial governorships, replacing them with equestrians including many who had risen from the ranks, changed the personnel and doubtless the social character of the relationships, but it remained just as important to have the ear of the provincial governor. But with the great changes that came under the Tetrarchy there was no longer a governor with both military and civil power or one who was likely to be well-known personally to the emperor. It was now extremely difficult to approach the emperor at all, his associates were likely to be the professional soldiers who commanded the field-armies—not even the frontier garrisons—and he was surrounded by a massive screen of protocol operated by an elaborate hierarchy of court functionaries, notably the notorious if unfortunate eunuch chamberlains. It is ironic that to a great extent an emperor's job had been an impossible one in the first and second centuries because he was too accessible, and in the fourth and fifth because he was too out of touch. In the third, he was too busy trying to keep alive to be much bothered about provincial administration.

The growing evidence for London's role as the capital of Roman Britain gives us some interesting insights into life at the centre of a Roman province. The early second-century statue of a military clerk now in the Museum of London is particularly telling. It depicts him in uniform, with his writing materials in one hand making his function clear, but his military cloak is deliberately arranged to reveal the short sword worn on his right side, the characteristic mark of a legionary and one of which he is obviously proud. We have the text of one letter which we know came from the secretariat of a British governor, and a remarkably high standard it displays, as Professor Frere has commented.[1] It is an interesting fact that of the 20 Londoners from the Roman period whose names we know, eight are soldiers, including representatives of the Sixth, the Twentieth, and the Second Augusta. One member of the last records his legion with the additional title *Antoniniana,* which probably puts him in the reign of Caracalla. This has an additional interest for us, for it is in the third century that there is an important change in military careers.[2] Up to then, soldiers had normally carried out the full range of duties within their careers. Now there was a strong tendency for some to spend their whole careers as fighting soldiers, others to be kept permanently in administrative postings. This in a curious way foreshadows the Late Empire, when civil officials were nominally enrolled in military units and adopted the trappings of the army but continued to perform purely civilian tasks. A governor's headquarters had always been run by a staff of officers drawn from the army. His chief administrative officer was a centurion of senior rank, the *princeps praetorii,* who had six heads of department beneath him, three *commentarienses* on the legal side, and three *corniculardii* or adjutants. Each of these had their own assistants. It is interesting to speculate whether any noticeable change came over the character of the headquarters when it became more common for some soldiers to spend their entire careers in administration.

There is no particular reason to doubt that most, probably all, of the soldiers mentioned at London were men detached from their units for service on the governor's staff. The Cripplegate fort is quite large enough at 5 hectares (12½ acres) to have accommodated men employed on a wide number of duties—its possible function as a military headquarters for the whole province has already been mentioned. But a governor also had two other major bodies of troops

---

[1] CIL XIII, 3162 (cf. Frere, *Britannia,* 226). It is, in fact, from Lower Britain and therefore probably third century and not from London, but it can stand for the thousands that must have issued from London as well as elsewhere.

[2] Probably after the end of the Severi: see D.J. Breeze, *Bonner Jahrb.* 174 (1974), 245 ff.

attached directly to him, his personal guard, generally assumed to be 500 cavalry and 500 infantry (the *numeri* of *singulares consularis*) and the *beneficiarii consularis* who acted as police and administrative officers. It is, as we noted earlier, very unlikely that Cripplegate also accommodated an urban cohort. Trajan is on record refusing a request to send an eastern city even a single centurion to aid its magistrates.[1] He explains that he has decided to follow the practice of his predecessors in supplying Byzantium with a garrison commanded by a legionary centurion to support the city authorities, because it is exceptional in being a focal point for large numbers of travellers from all directions. That case therefore does not set a precedent, but to agree to the present request would open the floodgates. London was certainly also a great centre of traffic, but hardly on the scale of Byzantium.[2] Moreover, as the capital, as I am assuming it was, it will have had the governor and his head-quarters troops on hand to suppress any trouble. Trajan, in whose reign the Cripplegate fort was almost certainly established, is therefore most unlikely to have authorized a special city garrison. Yet even the troops we can be reason-ably certain were at the governor's immediate disposal might be thought a tight fit at Cripplegate, if it were not known that individuals were often stationed elsewhere for specific purposes. In the third century it has been assumed that there was a second guard unit when the island was divided between two governors, and it is even more difficult to see where they could have been accommodated at York if it were not for outstations. All five *singulares* recorded in Britain appear at forts in the north[3] and R.W. Davies, who has drawn attention to the way in which these men were probably used,[4] points out that the Catterick inscription is dated to AD 192 and the rest are all probably of the third century. Dr Davies comments on the man recorded at Chesterholm (Vindolanda):

[1] Pliny, *Letters,* x. 78.
[2] A.N. Sherwin-White (*The Letters of Pliny*, Oxford (1966)) points out that Trajan's Dacian wars may have added substantially to the difficulties of the city magistrates of Byzantium, by increasing even more the traffic through the city and the motley throng of people attracted to it.
[3] Maryport (*RIB* 865), Chesterholm (1713), Ribchester (594), High Rochester (1266), and Catterick (725).
[4] R.W. Davies, '*Singulares* and Roman Britain', *Brit.* 7 (1976), 134 ff.

Victor was aged fifty-five when he died, while still serving as a soldier with no less than twenty-six years' service. Moreover, he was by birth a Pannonian and it is most strange to see an auxiliary soldier from such a recruiting area in Britain at this time; it would be easiest to suppose that while serving on his staff he had caught the attention of a governor, who brought Victor with him when he was transferred to Lower Britain; his father, Saturninus, had been a *primus pilus*, and so would be in an excellent position 'to pull strings' for his son.[1]

He goes on to produce evidence that the *singulares* as a whole were regarded as a mobile reserve, that could be moved to other provinces when need arose, and makes the interesting social point that Victor's wife may not have accompanied him to Chesterholm but stayed living near the provincial headquarters. We thus have a picture of a body of troops who might be expected to move about a good deal more than most (which is rather what one might expect of a governor's own guard, since he must have travelled a good deal in his own province) and separated frequently from their families. The British evidence suggests that men of the guard were often scattered on individual assignments about the Lower province. At Catterick and perhaps here at Chesterholm as well they are associated with *beneficiarii*. Since the latter do not seem to have been provided with staffs of their own, Dr Davies has suggested that some *singulares* had the duty of operating communications between the governor and such agents in the field.[2] We may perhaps imagine them as travelling fairly frequently between the headquarters and the stations of the *beneficiarii* with orders and reports, and doubtless they had to catch up with the governor if he was on campaign or on a progress round his province.[3]

The governor's *beneficiarii* were also normally based at headquarters, but like the *singulares* are found from time to time stationed by themselves at distant points, for example at Chesterholm as just mentioned,[4] Greta Bridge,[5] Binchester,[6]

---

[1] Ibid. 137: see also Note, p. 537 below.
[2] There were also officers entitled *frumentarii* attached to governors' staffs. They were originally employed in the collection of the corn supplies for the army. Their frequent travelling made them a useful source of information, and Hadrian allocated to them an official role as intelligence agents.
[3] A *strator consularis* was buried at Irchester (*RIB* 233): *stratores* were also on the governor's staff, but their function is uncertain, though perhaps related to the supply of transport for the governor.
[4] *RIB* 1696.   [5] *RIB* 745.   [6] *RIB* 1030, 1031.

Risingham[1] and Dorchester-on-Thames.[2] They seem from the inscriptions to have proliferated in the north in the third century, and it has been suggested[3] that one of their functions was to provide surveillance for the civil settlement that burgeoned outside the forts in the region at that period. The fact that the Severan House deliberately increased the privileges of the troops did not mean they were unmindful of the need for discipline and even more for political security. By such means the governor could keep a sharp eye on areas that were nominally the responsibility of the local authorities and, as Dr Davies points out, also keep watch on key points in the road system. The first two inscriptions mentioned above also bring another very interesting feature of third-century organization in Britain to our attention. On both it is specifically spelled out that the officers serve the governor of *Upper* Britain and the others imply the same—though all except the last were found at sites in *Lower* Britain. In other words, the consular governor in London was not only superior in status to his praetorian colleague at York, he also maintained some officers in the northern province directly responsible to himself.[4] This may have a straightforward administrative explanation, though one may suspect that, like the dividing of large provinces under the Severi, it was another manifestation of the desire to tighten political security.

These examples of the intervention of the governor of one province in another should alert us to the danger of assuming too readily that modern ideas of boundaries and frontiers can be transferred to Roman times. It is of course true that the Romans were careful to define the limits of authority and where it ran: the basic meaning of the word *territorium* is lands or territory under a particular authority[5] and a particular officer was left in no doubt what were the boundaries within which his writ ran. Even in Republican times a proconsul could only act within his province and automatically forfeited his commission when he crossed the city limits of Rome itself. Yet there are two points to remember that complicate the issue. The first is that officers

---

[1] *RIB* 1225.   [2] *RIB* 235.
[3] Salway, *Frontier People*, 187.   [4] See also Frere, *Britannia*, 205.
[5] *Dig.* L. xvi. 239. 8.

and bodies had different powers and different limits. These limits might be geographical or of some other kind. For example, magistrates of a local *civitas,* depending on their status and detailed local powers, might have power to try cases that occurred within their geographical boundaries, but only certain types of case and certain types of person. A governor could try a much wider range of cases, had greater powers of sentencing, and his limits were those of the whole province. Secondly, when it comes to the frontiers of the empire itself these principles become much extended. The long dominance of Roman frontier studies, primarily military, over the study of Roman Britain gave rise to a widespread assumption that a fortified line was the 'frontier of the empire'. It is of course clear that a governor of a frontier province must have known how far geographically he could go, since he was forbidden to make war outside his province without authority from Rome. Yet that may not mean he could not take other action and it certainly does not mean that his forward line of posts was necessarily the limit of the empire.[1] If the imperial estate in Upper Germany could extend on both sides of the *limes,* then the procurator at any rate must have been able to issue valid orders beyond the military *limes.*

The emperor himself was proconsul or governor of all the frontier provinces—indeed fairly early in the Principate of all provinces with any substantial army and many others. The actual governor of such a province was *legatus Augusti,* a deputy carrying out within defined geographical and functional limits the duties and powers of the emperor as proconsul.[2] Thus the governor was limited by whatever restrictions the emperor chose; but the emperor himself as

[1] Even the military line was often illogical on purely military criteria, being the accidental consequence of the Roman army ceasing to be employed for continuous and unlimited expansion. (cf. J.C. Mann, in H. Temporini (ed.), *Aufstieg und Niedergang der römischen Welt, II: Principat,* I (1974), 508 ff.)

[2] Some provinces were left in the gift of the senate, and these might have a *proconsul*—in other words an ex-consul who went out with consular powers. But in the 'imperial' provinces, part of the emperor's own total provincial command, the governor was titled *pro praetore,* in other words junior in rank to the emperor, the actual proconsul, even in those provinces which were regularly commanded by a former consul. In practice these were often the provinces with large armies and great opportunities, and thus were much sought-after by men of consular standing despite the theoretically lower rank.

proconsular representative or embodiment of Rome had no such limits, and to him and to Rome the 'frontier' had no reality except as the limit beyond which power or influence could not for the time being be exercised. Rome might indeed voluntarily bind herself by agreements with neighbouring states, but these were matters of temporary expediency and did not abrogate her right in her own eyes to act arbitrarily and unilaterally if she felt it desirable. By the early second century the concept had shifted slightly, and we find the historian Appian[1] explaining that certain areas Rome did not choose to incorporate within her realm, even when begged by the inhabitants, because they would bring her no benefit. Other poor regions Rome was even good-hearted enough to subsidize. But there is still no sign that Rome doubted her right to make the decisions: she gives to foreign states kings of her choosing if there is no point in conquest. Thus the absolute concept of Roman right to rule is still paramount. Whether it is Trajan choosing expansion or Hadrian consolidation and defence, the basic assumption remains unaltered.

At the level of the local community or the individual, Rome similarly reserved to herself the right to make the rules. There were elaborate provisions in Roman law regulating private legal relationships between citizens and non-citizens, or *'peregrini'*, for example over marriage and litigation, and between *peregrini* themselves when they made use of the Roman courts. The position of communities and individuals with full or partial citizenship ('Latin' cities, for example, or freedmen) and Roman and non-Roman authorities was laid down, but this did not reduce the final authority of the Senate and People of Rome—in practical terms generally the emperor—inside or outside the current boundaries of Roman occupation. It is not, therefore, surprising that a Roman governor needed to have a keen understanding both of the theoretical and actual limits of his power, and a thorough grounding in law and practical politics was as important as military aptitude and experience.

The governor was the chief justice of his province and had the *ius gladii*, the power to sentence to death, though Roman

---

[1] Appian, Preface, 7.

citizens could demand to be tried at Rome. His duties included not only heading the judicial service but hearing petitions and presiding at trials in his capital and at assizes elsewhere in his province. From to time, as we have noted previously, his other duties, military and civil, or the sheer volume of legal work were such that a special judicial officer was appointed to act as the governor's deputy in the administration of justice, the *legatus iuridicus* who had full praetorian rank. This post was introduced by Vespasian. I have so far referred to three by name for Britain—C. Salvius Liberalis and Javolenus Priscus, both probably in the governorship of Agricola, when the load on the governor must have been extreme, and M. Antius Crescens Calpurnianus, who was acting governor for a short while under Septimius Severus. We also know of C. Sabucius Maior Caecilianus,[1] who served late in the reign of Marcus Aurelius and of M. Vettius Valens,[2] to whom we shall return shortly. There is also from London a handsome fragmentary inscription on green slate apparently celebrating one of Trajan's Dacian victories, either 102 or 106, which was set up by a *legatus iuridicus provinciae Britanniae*.[3]

The *commentarienses*, who included the heads of the legal departments in the governor's headquarters under his chief administrator, have already been mentioned. Also attached to the staff was the corps of *speculatores*, consisting of ten men from each of the legions in the province, whose main functions were in connection with the law, including the holding of prisoners and the carrying out of executions. The tombstone of one of these men was found in Blackfriars and was set up by two of his fellow *speculatores* from the same legion.[4]

We have heard much of corruption, injustice, disorder, and civil war in the empire, but the fact remains that the imposition of Roman rule meant the substitution of a world based on recognized, written civil and criminal law for one in which tribal custom and the ever-present threat of local warfare dominated relationships between individuals and

---

[1] *ILS* 1123. [2] *CIL* XI, 383. [3] *RIB* 8.
[4] *RIB* 19. The high proportion of skulls among human bones from the ditch of the early legionary fortress at Colchester has been interpreted as representing executions (*Brit.* 8 (1977), 74).

between communities. It is a fact of the highest significance that throughout the period of imperial rule it was forbidden for civilians to carry arms, except in certain carefully defined circumstances. While this had the primary purpose of preventing internal disorder, nevertheless the mere fact that it was possible to maintain it as a general law for this long period implies that everyday life enjoyed a state of peace and stability that, seen in the perspective of history, is quite exceptional. Similarly, while individual instances of maladministration and uneven application of the law abound in the record, it is likely as always that the exceptional and sensational were most reported. It is not unreasonable to assume that in his everyday affairs the ordinary inhabitant of the empire enjoyed such protection as the law afforded his particular class and circumstance and, perhaps in day-to-day matters more important, that his transactions with his neighbours were governed by rules that had the backing of a developed legal system. The very fact of the existence of such a system must of itself have transformed the relationships between individuals and often made the settlement of business, even disputes, a matter of discussion and agreed settlement where it might once have led to armed conflict. But it also, particularly if the individual had a patron, meant access to legal arbitration. The more Romanized a province became, the more this must have improved internal stability as provincials became used to legal redress as the normal means for settling disagreements. On the other hand, it must also have meant an enormous increase in routine cases, either for hearing in the courts, for arbitration or for presentation as petitions for decision by the governor. What the governor gained in time previously taken up by problems of public order and security within the province as the rule of law became generally accepted he must have lost by the increase in volume of legal business falling on the system for which he held responsibility and upon himself.

Nevertheless, when we reflect on what opportunities afforded by his job must most have appealed to an ambitious Roman governor, we still have to remember what Cicero has told us, that, despite the immense importance the conduct of legal business had in Roman public life, military affairs commanded the higher prestige. The command of the army of Britain must have remained uppermost in the minds of the governors under the Early Empire. Responsible directly to them were the legionary commanding officers, each an ex-praetor with the title *legatus Augusti*, but without the suffix *pro praetore* which was reserved for the governor himself. They took their orders from the governor, whether he was an ex-consul, as for the whole of Britain in the first and second centuries or the Upper province in the third; or a former praetor, in the case of the Lower province. In fact the latter officer also commanded the Sixth legion, and we may assume a combined headquarters at York. It is likely, though not proven, that each legionary commander controlled the auxiliary forces in his area. Similarly it is sometimes argued that the senior auxiliary commander, in other words the commander of the auxiliary unit with the highest status, might exercise delegated command over other auxiliary units in a particular district. Thus it is possible that the commander of the famous *ala Petriana*, one of the rare 1,000-strong units of auxiliary cavalry, which was stationed fairly certainly at Stanwix at the centre of the Hadrianic system under Hadrian himself and possibly continuously till the end, exercised immediate command of the Wall garrisons. Through him they would then be responsible to York. Nevertheless the way the structure worked both in theory and practice remains subject to some debate.

The fleet under the Early Empire, the *classis Britannica*, presents greater problems. The latest study, by Henry Cleere, is brief but extremely helpful in bringing together the scattered evidence and pointing to the serious gaps in our knowledge.[1] He points out that its *normal* role was as a 'support command', transporting troops and supplies, though on occasion used during a campaign, as by Agricola, in a raiding and scouting role closely integrated with the land forces. Its command is interesting. Individual ships had separate sailing and fighting commanders and crewmen both worked the ship and fought if occasion required. At least in the first and second centuries its bases all seem to be in the south, perhaps first at Richborough and then from

---

[1] Henry Cleere, in Johnston (ed.), *The Saxon Shore*, 16 f.

about AD 85 in a major fort at Dover.[1] The fleet commander was, unlike the legionary legates, an equestrian procurator. The post was one of those that occur in careers that included other procuratorships. It ranked high as such, only the command of the *classis Germanica* equalling it among the provincial fleets. The most interesting holder is M. Maenius Agrippa, who was possibly simultaneously *praefectus classis Britannicae* and *procurator provinciae Britanniae* under Antoninus Pius.[2] This raises acutely the unanswered question of the relationship of the fleet to the governor of Britain. Since provincial procurators were normally responsible directly to the emperor, was this also true of the fleet commander? Or was this an exceptional instance? A further complication is the known presence of the *classis Britannica* at Boulogne. We do not know if this was simply a small detachment supervising transhipment of goods to Britain, or whether it implies that the fleet procurator had at least one regular base in Gaul. It may in fact be an example where different geographical limits are laid down for this officer than for the governor of Britain or his cross-Channel counterpart. A particularly attractive idea is that the fine mid-second century villa at Folkestone, which incorporates officially stamped *classis Britannica* tiles and looks out over the Channel, was the residence of its commander. We have previously noted the political importance of controlling the Channel crossing, and I believe an independent procurator might have suited the ever-suspicious imperial government quite well.

It now seems certain that there were radical alterations in the dispositions of the fleet in the middle of the third century. The base at Dover was dismantled, iron-making establishments inland that it had apparently operated were closed down and the last reference to it as *classis Britannica* is from an inscription of the reign of Philip (244-9).[3] The dating evidence is too imprecise to suggest any direct connection, but it is worth noting that by this time South Shields fort at the mouth of the Tyne had been converted into a military supply base in connection with the

---

[1] Rescue excavations by B. Philp: see references in article above, also *Brit.* 7 (1976), 376 and earlier issues.
[2] See note to *CIL* VII, 379.   [3] *CIL* XII, 686.

port.[1] Moreover the first of the new southern coastal forts, Brancaster and Reculver, came into commission sometime in the third century, probably before or around the middle of the century, and had regular land units as their main garrisons. It is reasonable to assume that these forts came under the governors in the normal way.[2]

It is possible that the financial administration of Britain under the *procurator provinciae* himself had already moved to London before the governor's headquarters left Colchester. It was almost certainly at London when Classicianus' wife erected the great monument to her husband very shortly after the Boudiccan revolt had been put down. Among the evidence are the discovery of gold-smelting activity on the site of the later Flavian governor's palace and therefore dating to early Flavian times or before, and the find of an official iron punch which was probably used for marking gold.[3] Taxes paid in gold were regularly melted down into bars and impressed with the official stamp. The provincial procurators, of course, also moved from time to time about the province and we have noted a number of instances when they are recorded elsewhere. Under them were public enterprises of various kinds and crown estates, and it is likely that those imperial freedmen of whom we have records were in their service, or assisted the local procurators or agents who operated enterprises direct or supervised the letting out of crown property to tenants.[4] One such *libertus Augusti*, in collaboration with three men whose status is unknown, restored the temple of Jupiter Optimus Maximus in London—

---

[1] Twenty granaries had been added at South Shields to the normal two under Severus, probably in connection with his Scottish campaigning. However some at least were converted to barracks after Carpow was evacuated and there were subsequent demolitions. Nevertheless the *Notitia* records the *numerus barcariorum Tigrisiensium* there, apparently Tigris river bargees. Thus it clearly had from time to time important functions in connection with supply and transport by water, but it is not certain that this was continuous, and the middle and later third century is one of the gaps in the record. (For *barcarii* having other possible duties see *Brit.* 4 (1973), 206 ff.)

[2] In this context it is also interesting to remember that from the middle of the century the duties of the governorships themselves too were being exercised more and more by equestrian officers (except perhaps under the Imperium Galliarum).

[3] See Marsden, *The Excavation of a Roman Palace Site*, 69.

[4] Rich private landowners had their own land agents (*procuratores*) administering large estates with a staff of assistants (*actores*) (cf. Pliny, *Letters*, iii. 19).

the stone was reused in the fourth-century river wall,[1]
another erected an altar to the personified goddess *Britannia*
at York,[2] and a further imperial freedman is found at Combe
Down in Somerset under Caracalla or Elagabalus reconstructing the *principia* or headquarters building which was
totally in ruins.[3] Taken with a lead seal from the same
building it seems highly likely that this was a district office
from which local imperial estates or industries were run.
We have to remember that imperial property was increasing
more or less all the time. Certain industries, for example
probably salt-production, had always been a state monopoly,
but the personal property of each emperor was absorbed
into the crown estates. Huge wealth was acquired by confiscations,[4] particularly after civil wars and during deliberate
campaigns against opposition to the throne, as under Domitian.
Other acquisitions came from legacies to the emperor
(particularly under the very common practice of leaving the
emperor a share in one's will)[5] and by the provision of
Roman law that in the case of intestacy the deceased's
estate went to the state. Hence the administration of the
personal property of the reigning emperor and the general
crown property (in practice hardly distinguishable) became
a larger and larger operation and its manipulation an
important part of financial and political control.

The workings of the government departments in London
are brought vividly to life by the discovery of a writing-
tablet branded with the mark of the provincial procurator[6]
and perhaps even more by three small seal-boxes bearing
the eagle and the portraits of Vespasian and Domitian, the
first from Aldgate and the two of Domitian from the
Walbrook stream, close to the governor's palace.[7] It is
unlikely that such seals could be used without the authority
of the most senior officers in the province.

The financial administration was still at London in the
fourth century, as the *Notitia* records the *praepositus*

---

[1] *Brit.* 7 (1976), 378, no. 1. [2] *RIB* 643. [3] *RIB* 179.

[4] An outstanding example of this in Britain may be the 'greater part of the
territory of the Brigantes' under Antoninus Pius.

[5] For example, the case of King Prasutagus of the Iceni.

[6] See Marsden, op. cit. 69, with references.

[7] *JRS* 26 (1936), 265, no. 5.

thesaurorum Augustensium.[1] The safe-keeping and administration of large sums of money in bullion and cash
for the payment of troops and remittance of taxation was
always important, but became particularly so under the
Late Empire. Mr Kenneth Painter has pointed to the reason:

Officially stamped ingots, whether of gold or silver, occur comparatively
frequently at the end of the fourth century. They were probably
made because in the later Empire, unlike earlier times, the Treasury
required large sums in gold and silver for payment to its soldiers and
officials. In the development of the financial system the *comes sacrarum
largitionum*, 'Count in charge of the sacred distributions', became
the principal officer because payments took place on the Emperor's
birthday, with supplementary payments on the occasion of imperial
accessions and five-yearly celebrations. The five-yearly donative consisted of five gold solidi per man; but the accession donative, at least
between AD 361 and AD 518, is known to have been five gold solidi
and one pound of silver. The practice of presenting pounds of silver
is known to be earlier than AD 361, and it is closely related to the
official distribution of plate, both in silver and also perhaps in other
expensive materials, such as figured cut glass.[2]

The presentation of plate on such occasions to senior officials
certainly goes back as far as AD 317, and it is perhaps significant that it should be first recorded when Diocletian's system
of the orderly sharing of imperial power was breaking down.
These distributions certainly came to be expected and were
important elements in the struggle to retain loyalty. It is
interesting for us that one of the best known of the silver
ingots bears the stamp of Magnentius and was part of the
largest of all the Late Roman hoards yet found. This came
from the fourth-century fort at Kaiseraugst on the Rhine
in Switzerland, and it seems extremely likely that it had
been in the hands of the emperor or one of his most senior
officials and was buried between Magnentius' defeat at
Mursa in 351 and his suicide in 353. This was followed, it
will be remembered, by the purging from Britain of alleged
dissidents by Paul 'The Chain'. Treasures of this sort were
doubtless one of his prime targets.

A political body for whose existence in Britain we have
only two pieces of certain evidence is the provincial council,

---

[1] *Not. Dign. Occ.* xi. 37. There was also a mint at London from the time of
Carausius to 325/326 and again under Magnus Maximus.

[2] Kent and Painter (eds.), in *Wealth of the Roman World*, 26.

a formal assembly which brought together the leading members of the provincial community and whose official function was chiefly to display loyalty to Rome and the emperor. However, failure to pass the customary vote of thanks to an outgoing governor could cause an imperial investigation into that officer's conduct, potentially a check of considerable importance. In 1806 an impressive hexagonal statue base was discovered in London on Ludgate Hill, bearing an inscription erected by Anencletus, a slave in the service of the province (*provincialis*), to the memory of his nineteen-year-old wife Claudia Martina.[1] It is probably of late-first century date, and suggests that there was an office in London to arrange the business and meetings of the council at that time. Another inscription, found near Cannon Street, is a dedication to the *numen* of the emperor by the province of Britain (*provincia Britannia*), and it seems likely that this was put up as an act of the provincial council, probably voted at a meeting in the capital.

We earlier noted M. Vettius Valens, *iuridicus Britanniae*, who had been in office around the middle of the second century. He seems to have been both trusted by the provincials and thought to have influence at Rome, for he was invited to become patron of the province. This type of association was common and went back to the Republic. With friends at Rome it was possible to bypass the governor or procurator and appeal for help against maladministration.

The power which aggrieved provincial communities could sometimes exercise is illustrated by a case in which both Pliny and Tacitus were involved as advocates.[2] Early in the reign of Trajan the provinces of Africa and of Baetica in Spain suffered successively from the same two disreputable governors. In the case of Priscus, governor of Africa, the case was brought by a single city, but Classicus, governor of Baetica, was accused by the whole province, presumably acting through the provincial council. In AD 93 the senate had appointed Pliny to act for Baetica in another case;[3] now the provincials asked the senate to appoint Pliny again, as they had been very satisfied with his previous conduct

[1] *RIB* 21. [2] Pliny, *Letters*, iii. 4; iii. 9; cf. ii. 11; ii. 12.
[3] Ibid. vi. 29; vii. 33.

on their behalf. He claims to have been persuaded into it against his will, but is clearly proud of the affair. The case was obviously taken very seriously, since it was heard in the senate with both Pliny and Tacitus appearing for the prosecution and in the presence of Trajan himself. Classicus had in fact committed suicide, but the case continued, as the provincials were entitled to insist. They won their case, and all the possessions in Classicus' estate that had been acquired since his appointment to Baetica were confiscated and divided among the people he had defrauded, and at the same time a number of lesser officials and accomplices were similarly found guilty. The case illustrates how, though a governor had virtually unlimited power while within his province, it was possible for him to be brought very effectively to account. This might be done by direct appeal to Rome, but there is no doubt that it helped a great deal to have influential friends in the capital. What a whole province might do alone was much more difficult for a small community or a single individual, and to them the possession of a patron was of even greater importance. We noted earlier how the decurions of the *respublica Silurum* marked their respect for just such a man by a notable inscription in their city at Caerwent, though we do not know whether he had actually accepted an invitation to be their patron.[1]

The Silures had once been so savage that, as will be remembered, Ostorius Scapula had intended to exterminate them. They had fortunately survived, to become one of those essential bastions of Roman stability, a Romanized community organized and running itself on Roman lines derived eventually from the formal structure of Rome itself. The various forms these local authorities might take have been mentioned from time to time—from deliberately planted citizen *coloniae* (the title was sometimes bestowed as an honour in later times on existing communities), through grades of *municipia* where in certain types in early times only those who had been elected to principal office received the Roman citizenship if they did not already possess it, down to peregrine *civitates*. Within any of these authorities might occur subdivisions,

---

[1] *RIB* 311. For a recent note on this inscription see M.G. Jarrett, *Bull. Board Celt. Stud.* 26 (1974-6), 513 ff.

generally *vici*, wards or villages, with their own minor officers or *magistri*. In some areas it seems likely the Gallic *pagus* or rural district survived as part of the subordinate system.

The Roman objective, of course, was not to confer local autonomy as a political principle but to transfer as much as possible of the burden of government, the administration of justice, and the collection of taxes on to the locals as soon as possible. Without such delegation the imperial machine either became so stretched as to be impossible to run efficiently or needed ever-increasing resources. The abandonment of client-kingdoms as a normal method of indirect government in the course of the first century was largely due to their unreliability. Replacing them with communities organized on Roman lines administering their districts within clear terms of reference became obviously preferable. It should—and in many parts of the empire surely did—relieve the pressure on the Roman provincial government to a very significant extent. One detects a distinct note of irritation when Trajan and subsequent emperors were forced to introduce imperial commissioners to regulate the affairs of communities who had proved incapable of sound management of their affairs. The trend towards ever-increasing centralization and growing imperial bureaucracy cannot be blamed solely on emperors bent on consolidating their power and increasing their control of the wealth of the empire. It has to be shared by provincials who could, or would, not order their own affairs sensibly. Yet centralization was a very slow process that was never complete, and the contribution of local effort, fuelled by the ambition of local families and urged on by government pressure, was for centuries crucial in running the empire. There were, however, areas where the governor and procurator were not so fortunate in having much of the routine administration taken off their hands by unpaid local worthies. There is, of course, the special case of land directly needed for army purposes, but there were also civil districts where the imposition of direct rule was felt necessary. Elsewhere in the empire it is not unusual to find centurions detached to act as district commissioners in charge of such areas. In Britain we do not so far have any examples of the *praefectus civitatis*, but it is likely that they occurred, especially in the early days when proper local

authorities were being formed out of the old tribal organization, and one might expect them—or their equivalents—at a
later date in some of the most difficult areas.[1] One special
case is the appointment of a legionary centurion as commander of the Sarmatian cavalry unit at Ribchester who also
has the title *praepositus regionis.* Two holders of this post
are known, one at some point between 222 and 235,[2] the
other 238 or later.[3] It has been argued that on discharge
those of the Sarmatians that had been compulsorily enrolled
and sent to Britain by Marcus Aurelius in 175 and not
subsequently posted elsewhere were settled together on land
in the neighbourhood of Ribchester.[4] However these appointments are a quarter of a century or more after the last of the
Sarmatians is likely to have left the army, and it is difficult
to believe they still needed special surveillance. Unless the
post (or title alone) remained because of administrative
inertia, it is likely that this district required direct control
for some other reason than a need to control an unusual
group of veteran settlements. One suggestion has been that
the area had developed as a consequence of the Sarmatian
settlement into an important breeding centre for cavalry
horses. However it is difficult to see why the commander
of the local unit has a special title, since other auxiliary
forts are known to have had *territoria* and if necessary the
district could have formed part of the *prata legionis* if it
was felt desirable to have it directly under legionary control.
The instance is not yet to my mind completely explained,
and others may well be found. Nevertheless, there is little
doubt that most of what was not imperial estate or directly
in army possession came to be administered by the normal
civil local authorities.[5] Moreover, whether it is lack of
evidence, or a compliment to the integrity of the British,
there are no known instances of the *correctores* and other
officials put in by emperors in other more sophisticated
provinces to disentangle the finances and administration
of cities. Britain seems in general to have been peacefully
and quietly governed under her local gentry. And if at
times it was not, then ordinary *civitates* could be overruled

---

[1] Cf. the *centuriones regionarii* found even in Italy.
[2] *RIB* 587.   [3] *RIB* 583.   [4] *JRS* 35 (1945), 25.
[5] See e.g. Salway, op. cit. 177 ff., for a fuller discussion.

immediately by a Roman officer with delegated *imperium*: the powers of the local authorities were limited and were granted for the convenience of the Roman administration, not to stand in its way.[1]

NOTES

The municipal aristocracy. Professor John Wilkes has drawn attention in an article that appeared after I had written this chapter (reviewing A. Mócsy, *Pannonia and Upper Moesia*, (1974), in *JRS* 67 (1977), 232 ff.) to the fact that in Pannonia there seems to have been an important weakness in the municipal organization that became increasingly worse rather than better. That weakness was a lack of local recruits to the *ordo* of the local communities, so that they were always dominated by the official town clerk and by foreigners. He suggests that some similar weakness may have affected British local authorities, perhaps reflected in the absence of any mention of local magistrates on the Hadrianic forum dedication inscription at Wroxeter[2] and perhaps on the fragmentary Flavian forum dedication at Verulamium.[3] One could make a case for both of these being out-of-the-ordinary instances, but the point is worth noting.

Chesterholm (Vindolanda). See Robin Birley, *Vindolanda: A Roman frontier post on Hadrian's Wall* (1977), 31 ff., for a convenient summary of the excavations outside the fort. The first buildings outside the fort, 'Vicus I' (occupied, it would appear, in broad terms from the middle of the second century to the middle of the third and then abandoned) form a group quite unlike 'Vicus II' which follows the normal pattern for civil settlements outside forts in the Wall region. Vicus I, besides the usual military bath-house, has a *mansio*, a corridor-house and three structures identified by the excavator (I believe erroneously) as 'married-quarters' for troops posted to the fort (there is no independent evidence for the official provision of married quarters for common soldiers). Except for one example the characteristic strip-houses are absent. The whole is very unusually surrounded by a rampart, reminiscent of the annexes attached to forts on the Antonine Wall.

The well-known civilian dedication by the *vicani Vindolandesses* to Vulcan (*RIB* 1700) more appropriately belongs to Vicus II, where there is substantial evidence of metal-working, than to Vicus I, where there is not. However the *beneficiarius consularis* (*RIB* 1696) and the *singularis consularis* (*RIB* 1713) mentioned in the chapter above would be wholly consistent with an official function for the group of buildings making up Vicus I. Its position on the Stanegate highway between

---

[1] Cf. Plutarch (*fl.* AD 50–120), warning the municipal magistrate: 'You who hold office are a subject, ruling a state controlled by proconsuls and by the procurators of the emperor ... Do not have great pride or confidence in your crown [of office], for you see soldiers' boots just above your head ...' (See Lewis and Reinhold, *Roman Civilization: Sourcebook*, II, no. 82, quoting Loeb translation).

[2] *RIB* 288.   [3] *JRS* 46 (1956), 146.

Corbridge and Carlisle is where we might expect to find such officers. The dedication *RIB* 1695 found at nearby Beltingham seems to record some form of tribal assembly, the *curia Textoverdorum*, which may be another reason for the presence of government officers. One recalls the confiscation of territory from the Brigantes by Antoninus Pius, and the possibility that it returned to more normal civilian administration in the course of the third century.

In short, I suspect that Vindolanda Vicus I is not a *vicus* at all: its exact nature is by no means proven, but I think is related to functions carried out by central government. It seems to have been no longer required after the middle of the third century.

18

THE HISTORICAL GEOGRAPHY OF ROMAN BRITAIN

W RITING under Trajan Tacitus displays sublime confidence in his geographical knowledge:[1]

Many previous writers have spoken of the situation and peoples of Britain. I am proposing to do so again, not to compete with them in ingenuity and diligence of research but because the conquest was only completed at the time of which I am writing. My predecessors had to fill out their lack of information with tricks of style: I can offer facts. Britain is the largest island known to us Romans. Its shape and location cause it to face Germany to the east, Spain to the west and its southern shore is in sight of Gaul. The northern coasts are pounded by the vastness of the open sea, for no land faces them. Livy and Fabius Rusticus, the best of the older and more recent writers, have compared the shape of the island to an elongated triangle or an axe. This is indeed the shape as far as Caledonia, hence the usual description. But going further one finds a very large tract of country extending to the furthest point of land and tapering into a wedge-shape. The coastline of that remote sea was explored then [under Agricola] and Britain proved by circumnavigation to be an island. At the same time the Orkneys were discovered and taken.[2] Shetland was seen in the distance, but orders and the onset of winter prevented the fleet from approaching nearer . . . [3]

Tacitus then goes on to look at the composition of the population:

Who were the original inhabitants of Britain is impossible to be certain, as is common with barbarians: we do not know whether they were aboriginal or immigrant. Nevertheless their physical characteristics vary a good deal, and that in itself is evidence. The people of Caledonia have large limbs and reddish hair which indicates a Germanic origin; the Silures have darker skins and tend to have curly hair, and the fact

---

[1] Tacitus, *Agr.* x.
[2] See Ogilvie and Richmond, *De Vita Agricolae*, 168 ff., for a discussion of the probable meaning (and text) of this sentence.
[3] In fact the Orkneys were already known, and Claudius claimed to have conquered them (Eutropius, VII. xiii. 2-3). Juvenal, ii. 160-1, however, seems to put the actual seizing of the islands at about the same time as Tacitus.

that their land lies opposite Spain makes it probable that they originated from the Iberian peninsula. Those closest to the Gauls resemble them, whether because original characteristics of race persist or because lands that come close together have similar climates. On the whole, however, we may assume that it was Gauls who occupied the island opposite them . . .[1]

After a consideration of the language of Britain and some pointed comparisons of the manners and virtues of the Britons and Gauls which remind us that his primary purpose is edification, not geography or history, he gives us some notes on the environment:

The climate is unpleasant, with frequent rain and mist, but it does not suffer from extreme cold. The day is longer than elsewhere in the empire and the night is clear and in the north short, with only a brief interval between nightfall and first light. If there is no cloud it is said you can see the glow of the sun all night . . . The soil is fertile and is suitable for all crops except the vine, olive and other plants requiring warmer climates. Crops grow quickly but ripen slowly. This is due to the high rainfall and dampness of the soil. Britain contains deposits of gold, silver and other metals, wages of victory. There are also pearls in the surrounding seas, though they are dark and uneven in colour. Some think the locals unskilled at finding them . . . I prefer to believe that the quality is too low to make them worth while than that we are not sufficiently avaricious to insist on it.[2]

What Tacitus does not give us—and there is no reason why he should—is figures, and without figures it is extremely difficult to employ the approaches of a modern geographer or economist. Yet much modern work on Roman Britain has been written as if we had such figures, and what in another field would be dismissed as merely anecdotal evidence is taken as highly significant. Professor M.I. Finley has attacked this approach to the study of the economics of the ancient world:[3] 'This is all too vague: such generalizations cry out for a more sophisticated effort to approach quantification and pattern-construction' and the same is as true of ancient geography, a closely allied subject, indeed one from which it cannot be divorced. Yet it is also very necessary to remember that we are dealing with an *historical* period, even if the amount and character of the written evidence is

---

[1] Tacitus, *Agr.* xi.   [2] Ibid. xii.
[3] M.I. Finley, *The Ancient Economy* (1973; paperback, 1975), 33.

often very thin indeed. It is entirely possible to become so obsessed with the mathematical models which are sometimes applied to prehistory as to believe they are the only, or necessarily the best, way of looking at a problem in Roman Britain. It is perhaps in the exercise of 'pattern-construction' that we need to tread most warily. We may be able to discover a pattern, but that only tells us where to look next, not why it happened. Professor Finley points us in the direction of 'modern central-place theory' with an example from Roman Britain:

Thus, although the road-building in the Romanized southeast of Britain stimulated the growth of villages, the average distance from the small local market to the edge of its 'tributary area' remained at the standard maximum distance to a market preferred wherever means of transport are primitive, namely, four to five miles. Peasants (and not only peasants) are ruled by what economic geographers have called the 'law of minimum effort' or the 'principle of least effort'.[1]

What this is doing, of course, is to assume that when we find the same pattern in two societies at roughly the same level of development the same explanation can be applied. It assumes, too, that the Romano-Briton's behaviour was conditioned by economic forces beyond his control and perhaps unrealized by him. In this context, David Hinton's recent account of the establishment of medieval markets in the south of England (where the same pattern ought theoretically to appear) reads as a cautionary tale:

It was thought that the growth of prosperity of one place must be at the expense of another, not that the volume of trade was expanding and that growth could be general ... To avoid clashes, rival markets were supposed to be six and two-thirds miles apart; in practice very few in the south were. Markets did not 'grow' where there were gaps in the system, for they depended on a landlord's initiative. It is an amusing game to decide where a good place for a town would have been; one of my own choices is Lewknor, where traffic using the Icknield Way crosses one of the main London—Oxford—Gloucester routes. But the Abbot of Abingdon, the main landowner in Lewknor, was not a founder of towns. In his own town he had the problem that the prosperity of its market led to violent attempts to achieve independence from him by the townsmen. This may have biased him against

---

[1] Ibid. 127, citing I. Hodder and M. Hassall, 'The Non-Random Spacing of Romano-British Walled Towns', *Man*, n.s. 6 (1971), 39 ff.

the town-founding activities of the bishops of Lincoln or Winchester. Villagers did not necessarily go to the nearest market: Abingdon was the market to which men are recorded as going from Cuxham long before 1416, although Wallingford was closer, and many of them had to go much further afield on carting services. The nearest market was not the limit of a man's horizons.[1]

Formalized model-building exercises are recent developments in the study of ancient history; but an area where the pattern of Roman Britain has long been considered to have been determined by relatively immutable forces has been the influence of the physical geography of the island. Tacitus is in fact setting the fashion by starting with the map and discussing the soil and the climate. But it can be more illuminating to put it the other way round, for until we have some idea whether there was one person or a hundred to the square mile, we can form no sensible idea of how they might have been affected, for the whole balance of man and nature (and man and fellow man) are quite different depending on scale.

POPULATION

For medieval England historians have expended a great deal of effort on the size of the population at different periods. Their conclusions are very varied, since the evidence is subject to different interpretations, but they are right to place so much importance on the subject. It is extremely difficult to approach many aspects of life in the past without an idea not only of the size but also of the density and distribution of its people. In 1929 Collingwood doubted that it was possible to conceive of figures that 'could allow to Britain more than half a million or at most a million inhabitants.'[2] In 1930 Sir Mortimer Wheeler calculated a million and a half,[3] and in 1976 W.G. Hoskins, writing a new introduction to a reprint of his 1955 classic *The Making of the English Landscape* commented:[4] 'All our previous estimates

---

[1] D.A. Hinton, *Alfred's Kingdom* (1977), 178 f.
[2] R.G. Collingwood, 'Town and Country in Roman Britain', *Antiquity*, 3 (1929), 261.   [3] *Antiquity*, 4 (1930), 95.
[4] W.G. Hoskins, *The Making of the English Landscape* (1977), 12. His earlier estimate for Britain just before the Roman conquest had been not more than 400,000; for 1086 (Domesday Book) possibly 1¼ million and the medieval peak nearly 4 million.

of population in Romano-British times, and possibly even in the prehistoric period, have been far too low'. The reader is entitled to ask why the estimates have changed, and changed dramatically upwards. In 1974 I tried to summarize the problem and suggest one possible line of research:

The real problem . . . is the lack of national census figures before 1801. The only general document even faintly approaching the requirement is Domesday Book and for 1086 this can produce estimates anywhere between one million and two million. The Ordnance Survey Map of Roman Britain,[1] in particular, provoked attempts to estimate the total population, but this really confused the issue since not even the latest edition has been able to distinguish between sites occupied at different periods and it ranges over more than 350 years . . . There is one laborious way forward which shows promise. Where we can be reasonably sure of being able to make an estimate of the total number of Roman sites occupied *at a particular period* within a given area and, averaging the probable number of households and people in a household,[2] can compare this with Domesday figures for similar types of occupation in the same area, we may begin to break through the fog. But the leap to using this for a general comparison with the Domesday 1–2 million for England alone (perhaps nearer 2 million) is a real leap in the dark. The local comparison has been made by Mrs. Sylvia Hallam (with all the snags admitted) for some northern Fenland parishes,[3] and her conclusion is that at its second-century peak the Roman population was around or above two-thirds of the Domesday figure. I do not believe it is safe to transfer this to the national level. For a start there is a suspicion that in the Fens there was a deliberate Roman introduction of an alien population; but apart from that there is no evidence one way or the other to support a guess that local variations would even out over the country.[4] Nor does Domesday include the then unconquered Welsh.[5] There really is no alternative to local study after local study; and even then we shall only approach an order of magnitude . . . What has

---

[1] Collingwood's 1929 figure was based on the second edition.

[2] This involves various assumptions: a particular complication is that the relationship of occupants to floor area varies greatly from culture to culture and period to period. For the sort of difficulties that are encountered in such studies in estimating the number of inhabitants in a given house or how many houses within a settlement can be assumed to be occupied simultaneously see George Jobey, 'Notes on some population problems in the area between the two Roman Walls', Part I, *Arch. Ael.* 5th ser., 2 (1974), especially p. 21.

[3] In Phillips (ed.), *Fenland*, 71 ff.

[4] Moreover the system only begins to work if the type of settlement is relatively homogeneous, which does appear to be the case for the Fens but probably rare elsewhere.

[5] Thought to be about 100,000 and therefore not substantially affecting the total.

become quite clear, first from aerial photography and now every day from motorway and other large-scale clearance, is that all previous ideas of the density of settlements were very much on the low side.[1]

Another approach was used by Professor Frere, employing —among other factors—the size of city amphitheatres in Britain, Tacitus' figures for the losses during the Boudiccan rebellion, medieval populations of towns that remained within the circuit of their Roman walls, the calculable size of the army and approximations for its dependents, and so on. His conclusion for the end of the second century was a total population 'rather over two million.'[2]

The pace of discovery, however, has proceeded at great speed, only moderately affected by the slowing-down of discoveries through construction work in the economic crisis of 1973 and thereafter, and accelerated by aerial photography in the extraordinary conditions of the drought of 1976. Regional studies are also appearing in numbers, pushing the number of sites up with each new publication. A study of the valleys of the Tame and Middle Trent rivers published in 1977 produced so many new sites that it was suggested that 'if these increases reflect a national trend it may be necessary to revise the estimate of the Romano-British population to 5 or 6 millions.'[3] Other localized studies are producing figures that, if extrapolated for the whole country, produce totals of the same order of magnitude, say 4 to 6 millions.[4]

If other regional and local studies confirm these calculations, we should no longer be comparing Roman Britain with 1086 (recent work on Domesday Book suggests 1.75 to 2.25 million) but with England in the middle of the fourteenth century shortly before the Black Death, when a figure towards the upper end of the range 4.5 to 6 million is

[1] *Britain and the Early Roman Empire*, Open University A291 Unit 12 (1974), 37.

[2] Frere, *Britannia*, 296 f.; 349 f.

[3] Christopher Smith, in John Collis (ed.), *The Iron Age in Britain*, Sheffield (1977), 55.

[4] For example, Barry Cunliffe, in Cunliffe and Trevor Rowley (eds.), *Lowland Iron Age communities in Europe*, British Archaeological Reports, Oxford (1978), 3 ff.

currently thought likely.[1] Allowing for the fact that Roman
Britain covered a rather larger area than England alone, and
that the medieval peak may have been a little earlier than
AD 1300 (a rather larger figure has been hazarded to around
1300), nevertheless it is clear we are facing a very different
picture from Collingwood's or even Frere's. Indeed, some
historians have conjectured that the fourteenth-century
population was about as large as the country could support
agriculturally before the technical improvements of the
early modern period. We may reflect with interest, too,
on the comparison between the proposed figures for Roman
Britain and those currently suggested for the middle of the
reign of Henry VIII, somewhere in the region of 2.25 and
2.75 million. But such musings apart, the Romano-British
estimate does pose very acute problems for the student of
the centuries between Roman Britain and the Norman
Conquest, for it is necessary to take into account a fall to
around 2 million—indeed, to presumably something well
below that figure, since it is very unlikely that there was no
growth in the relatively settled conditions of Late Saxon
England. Our immediate concern, however, is to inquire
whether any changes can be detected within the Roman
period itself and in particular after AD 200.

It should be said straightaway that the direct evidence
for Britain is so thin as to be practically non-existent. All
we have is a few pieces of information to interpret by
analogy from elsewhere, and the interpretation itself largely
depends on general theories similarly derived. It has indeed
been generally held that the population of the empire declined
from about 200 onwards: A.H.M. Jones summarizes a
position typical of the moderates in this historical debate:

Depopulation has been regarded as a major factor in the decline of the
empire. Unfortunately our information is so vague, and facts and figures
are so sparse that it is impossible to calculate what the population of
the empire was at any date, or how much it declined, if, as is very
probable if not certain, it did decline. All we can do is to note certain
demographic trends, and speculate about their causes.[2]

[1] John Hatcher, *Plague, Population and the English Economy, 1348 — 1530*
(1977), 68. His graph (p. 71) showing the range between plausible estimates of
the population curve from 1086 to 1525 is particularly useful. See also E. Miller
and J. Hatcher, *Medieval England: Rural Society and Economic Change 1086 —
1348* (1978), and the bibliography in M. Postan, *The Medieval Economy and
Society* (1972).   [2] A.H.M. Jones, *Later Roman Empire*, 1040.

Very briefly, the usual argument for decline depends on two main elements: evidence for abandoned land (*agri deserti*) and for a severe shortage of labour. Laws about *agri deserti* show the emperors attempting to deal with a problem from the third century to the sixth. The first part of the argument then runs:

As we have seen progressively less land was cultivated, and less food must therefore have been produced. The empire never either imported foodstuffs or produced a surplus for export. Since consumption per head could hardly sink for the mass of the population, who were already near subsistence level, the population must have grown smaller. There was moreover an increasing maldistribution of the diminishing quantity of food which was produced. Soldiers enjoyed ample rations—their consumption was perhaps twice as much as that of poor peasants—and civil servants and most of the clergy were at least as well fed. As the army, the civil service and the clergy increased in numbers, the proportion of the total amount which was left for the mass of the population sank, and their numbers must have sunk correspondingly.[1]

The other half of the argument is manpower:

There are many indications that there was a chronic shortage of manpower in the later empire. It must have been for this reason that the government forbade workers in essential industries—miners, armourers, weavers and dyers in the state factories, and above all agricultural workers—to leave their occupations, reclaimed them when they strayed from them, and compelled their children to follow their fathers' occupation. The labour shortage is most manifest on the land. It is plain that landlords are perennially short of tenants to cultivate their land. They were always ready to accept barbarian prisoners of war as *coloni*. They would rather pay 25 or 30 solidi, more than the normal price of a slave, than give up a *colonus* as a recruit to the army. They hunted down their *coloni* when they escaped, and despite all penalties they welcomed fugitive *coloni* from other estates . . . The shortage of labour on the land was not, so far as we can see, due to a movement from the country to the towns: the movement was rather in the opposite direction. *Coloni* normally, the laws imply, moved to another farm if they left their own. Miners and urban craftsmen often had to be reclaimed from the land.[2]

Acceptance of this general theory has led to a search for causes, many of them medical or socio-medical—malnutrition, infant mortality, low adult life-expectation, infanticide, plague, an alleged deliberate unwillingness of the upper classes to have children, and even lead-poisoning from the

[1] Ibid. 1042 f. [2] Ibid. 1041 f.

piped water-system. Yet at bottom the theory itself depends on such thin material that there is no need to produce an explanation for it. We simply do not know whether there was a substantial over-all change in the size of the population or not. Just how thin that material is, we ought briefly to note, if only to avoid wasting more time on impossible calculations.

The actual figures for *agri deserti* are extremely few. As Jones says, it is true that there were some areas of the empire in which conditions were particularly difficult where the loss, as in Africa, was up to 50 per cent by the fifth century and 'in others which there is no reason to think exceptional it amounted to some 10 per cent or 15 per cent.'[1] Yet the latter is in itself a small figure and would only be of great importance if all the cultivable land in the empire had once been under agriculture. But any estimates of the entire population of the empire at its peak show so small a number of people—of the order of 50–60 million—spread over so vast an area that it is difficult to believe that proposition can ever have been true, even if, at least for Britain, the older population figures ought to be increased several-fold. Nor do we know enough about the other side of the picture—new land brought into cultivation. In fact, if agricultural land was becoming less and less attractive, then it ought to have been reflected in the value put upon it. Yet Jones points out: 'It must be emphasised that there was no general agricultural decline; land of good and medium quality continued to pay high taxes, yield high rents and command high prices.'[2] Why, then, the imperial concern about abandoned land? I have already mentioned Hadrian's interest in the problem—which puts it well before the generally accepted beginning of decline in population—in connection with the Fens. The story of the Fens is instructive. The large-scale exploitation seems to be Hadrianic and a great deal of it short-lived—partly due to deterioration of drainage probably caused by changes in the relative land and sea level, and partly to errors of Roman water-engineers. In Britain, at any rate, we have to take into account the possibilities of ill-judged expansion on to land which was easy to work initially (and being previously uncultivated was simple to take over) but

---

presented long-term difficulties; and we also have to consider the changes in climate and other environmental factors which we shall examine later. We have to take into account the possibility that the *location* and perhaps the *type* of agriculture changed, rather than its total output of food, even if methods and yields altered little. Is there, then, a reason other than the food supply why emperors should have been so concerned? If Jones and other writers are right in thinking that more and more land fell into the hands of the emperor, of great senatorial families whom the later emperors proved increasingly unable to tax effectively and, from the fourth century, of the privileged Church and individual churchmen, then less and less good land is likely to have been held by the smaller gentry who were the *curiales* of the provincial cities or free farmers, whether as owners or tenants. This would have left much less land and people to tax when the need to raise money was increasingly pressing. Thus any abandonment of land would become a more and more serious matter for the imperial government, even if the total amount uncultivated remained the same.

The same sort of reasoning can be applied to the manpower shortage. The Tetrarchy, by doubling the army and very substantially increasing the administration, must have created a vast magnet to draw men away from increasingly grim prospects on the land to secure and regularly paid employment and a privileged position in society by joining the government service. In the course of the fourth century these advantages were also offered by the Church, where salaried posts and opportunities for advancement multiplied, despite the honourable if eccentric exception of the ascetics. It is not surprising that the labour problem was worst in agriculture, nor that many of the disputes were about conscription—in other words forcing landowners to give up their men. Nor is it surprising to find the miners and the workers in the state factories in the fourth century among those compelled to stay at their jobs, for these were essential to the contemporary system of military supply.

The need for all this extra money and men caused by the huge increase in the army and administration was due partly to obsesssion with internal security but partly to the pressure from the barbarians outside the frontier. And it is the barbarians *within* the frontiers that are the element that we have so far left out of the calculation. As early as Marcus Aurelius we have seen them being settled deliberately inside the empire, most notably in the Danube region on abandoned land but even, in the persons of the Sarmatians, in Britain. Under Probus there are Burgundians, too, in Britain, and towards the end of the third century we have had German *laeti* brought into northern Gaul to re-establish cultivation where estates had been devastated by recent invasions. People such as these became settled inhabitants of the empire, and in the fourth century—even more in the fifth—the presence of families with such origins must have become a regular feature of daily life in many parts of the Roman world. Where they came in as prisoners of war and were not drafted straight into the army they probably can fairly be included in the category of agricultural *coloni* on the large estates whom we are told were in short supply; but those who arrived as free settlers cannot be thus treated and we have no way of estimating their numbers. We have already seen how our lack of knowledge about the size of the barbarian allied contingents in the late army makes estimates of military manpower fruitless. It is now obvious that the barbarian element makes calculation of the *total* population of the empire equally hopeless. We can reasonably argue for a redistribution of wealth away from the indigenous peasants and smaller landowners which may have led to an actual decline in their numbers; but we certainly have wholly insufficient evidence to say whether there was a net decrease or increase in the population of the empire at large after AD 200, let alone that of Britain.

Turning now from the size of the ancient population to its physical condition, it is symptomatic of how once again we rely on shaky and anecdotal evidence that when we try to look at the population at large we find Galen's study of malnutrition in the countryfolk, which we considered earlier, comes from the middle of the second century when general theory would put the prosperity of the empire at its highest. Yet there are some things we can say about the medical condition of people in the Roman world that are worth noting, as they add greatly to our understanding of their lives and the atmosphere in which they lived. One source of information is the enormous number of tombstones with detailed inscriptions. These indicate a high rate of mortality among infants and small children and that men as a whole lived rather longer than women. We are accustomed to thinking of a high incidence of death in childbirth as a major feature of all periods up to living memory, but it has recently been pointed out that we are conditioned by the Victorian period, the maternal death-rate being exceptionally high in the nineteenth century.[1] Of those who survived childhood in the Roman world inscriptions in some areas suggest an expectation of surviving to around 30 for women and 45 for men: some more detailed figures for Africa give only 28 per cent of women and 38 per cent of men reaching the age of 62.[2] The over-all expectation of life under the Empire is a subject of some controversy,[3] but since the very poorest people (particularly in the countryside where there were not the same opportunities of belonging to a burial club that would record their deaths)[4] could probably rarely afford a regular tombstone, the general impression is unlikely to be optimistic. For the frontier areas the higher expectation for men is perhaps to be explained by better hygiene, diet, and medical care among the troops and the civilian population. If not actually killed or wounded in action a soldier doubtless had a much healthier life, and for very long periods many units probably saw no fighting. Even men whose role was officially front-line may have gone through their entire army careers without ever being involved in action.

Most of that information is derived from inscriptions. This information is extremely patchy and coverage suspect even though their numbers are large. More recently archaeologists have begun to build up a fund of more reliable information from the large-scale excavation of Roman cemeteries. For the Early Empire the study of skeletal remains is made very difficult by the fact that the prevalent burial rite was cremation, though by no means universal. However, as inhumation became more common and eventually normal, it becomes much easier. One of the earliest publications of

[1] Calvin Wells, *Bull. New York Acad. Med.* 51 (1975), 1235 ff.
[2] A.H.M. Jones, op. cit. 1041; cf. Salway, *Frontier People*, 23.
[3] See K. Hopkins, *Population Studies*, 20 (1966), 245 ff. on pitfalls in using tombstones.   [4] See p. 696 below.

such a cemetery excavated under modern conditions is that
of the Trentholme Drive cemetery at York.[1] This has particularly interesting possibilities, as it is thought to have been
mainly used by the lower classes. Comparison of bones from
this sort of cemetery with those associated with funerary
inscriptions may, when enough of them have been studied,
provide fresh insight into the physical condition of the
poorest people, at least in urban society. Further burials are
now being published from the same city,[2] and other important
reports describe the latest work on, for example, the great
Poundbury cemetery at Dorchester in Dorset with a substantial
Christian element, and the fourth-century Lankhills burials
at Winchester. It is too early yet to make generalizations, but
there is no doubt that there is a real chance of building up
significant medical statistics. We are beginning to form some
idea of the wide mixture of physical types, of diet, of disease
and of expectation of life.[3] We still need a wider range of
sites, and are particularly hampered by the fact that rural
cemeteries, when they occur at all, tend to be small. A
parallel line of enquiry is human parasitology, the study of
vermin, and possibly bacteriology. York,[4] again, is giving us
new information from the sewers about parasites, and from a
granary about problems of infestation in grain and how the
Romans dealt with it. At Chesterholm the excavator claims
to have recovered living bacteriological material from a
Roman deposit. If we can resist the temptation to draw
sensational general conclusions from the first few samples
and allow the evidence to accumulate gradually, we may well

[1] L.P. Wenham and others, *The Romano-British Cemetery at Trentholme
Drive, York* (1968). The site was excavated in 1951–2. See also *Eburacum:
Roman York. An Inventory of the Historical Monuments in the City of York*,
Royal Commission on Historical Monuments (1962), 79; 95; 101 ff.
[2] These will appear in Vol. 5 of *The Archaeology of York* series being issued
by the York Archaeological Trust.
[3] See, for example, *Archaeometry*, 18 (1976), 221 ff. (lead content in bones);
Medical History, 18 (1974), 365 ff. (bone disease among agricultural workers);
Caries Research, 7 (1973), 139 ff. (dental caries). For military medicine see
among others *Saalburg Jahrbuch*, 27 (1970), 84 ff.; *Arch. Cambr.* 118 (1969),
86 ff.; *Chester Arch. Soc.* 55 (1968), 7 ff. and Sir Ian Richmond's classic article,
Univ. of Durham Medical Gazette, 46, pt. 3 (1952), 2 ff. For trephining as a
surgical technique observed at York see *Journ. Arch. Science*, 1 (1974) 209 ff.
[4] See *The Archaeology of York* series, vol. 14, *The Past Environment of
York*, for example fasc. 1 (P.C. Buckland, *The Environmental Evidence from the
Church Street Roman Sewer System*).

be on the way to gaining a whole new source of evidence on the Roman past, complementing but not superseding other means of inquiry.

It now seems possible that we shall be able to identify at least some of the prevalent diseases and causes of death in Roman Britain, but, since some leave no trace, we are unlikely ever to have a comprehensive picture. One of the most difficult problems is that of epidemics or plagues. It is rarely possible to identify those described by ancient writers in modern terms—partly because the organisms causing them tend to mutate and partly because resistance and the build-up of natural immunization are so variable in different populations at different times that the symptoms described are not sufficiently clear. But the literary references cannot be ignored. The plague which went through Europe in 166–7, brought back by Lucius Verus' troops from his eastern campaign, is unlikely to have missed Britain. One of the penalties of the immense network of communications and the constant movement of soldiers, officials, and merchants about the Roman world and beyond must have been a much greater exposure of Britain to epidemics; and one may reasonably assume that at least in the earlier days there were serious consequences even from otherwise mild infections that were new to the island. After the plague in Marcus' reign there was another that appeared at least three times between 251 and 271,[1] during the worst period of disorder in the empire and probably assisted by it. Mr Wacher has made out a detailed case for thinking that the incidence of plague in the fifth century was one major reason for the abandonment of towns in Britain.[2] We may hesitate to follow Mr Wacher's identification of particular cities in Britain probably affected by plague,[3] but consider it a reasonable supposition that a town in Britain that had survived to the middle of the fifth century which was severely hit by disease is much less likely to have recovered or been reoccupied than when there was still a Roman government in control of the island.

---

[1] A.H.M. Jones, op. cit. 1043.
[2] Wacher, *Towns*, 414 ff.; but see p. 460, n. 2, above.
[3] Cirencester; Wroxeter; Caerwent.

LANDSCAPE

In the first chapter we saw how the broad division of Britain into highland and lowland zones had dominated thinking about the later prehistoric and Roman periods; how it partially held good but needed to be extensively qualified; how we have to take into account the fact that man's capacity for tackling and intentionally or unintentionally altering his environment has varied greatly at different periods in the past. The geographical 'zone' concept had unfortunately been adopted by Romano-British archaeologists from the prehistorians and geographers at a time when Roman Britain was seen very clearly as divided politically and socially into a civil zone in the south and east of the island and a military zone in Wales and the north. Hence the two concepts had become conflated and there was a strong tendency to assume that the character of the Roman occupation was determined by the terrain and was both inevitable and permanent. We have seen this approach breaking down. Today, we have to be much more cautious, and in particular need to take care in defining periods within Roman times for we now recognize extensive change in the five centuries that are our chief concern.

Few would now accept Sir Cyril Fox's poetic vision of the ancient condition of southern Britain dominated by 'an illimitable forest of "damp" oakwood, ash and thorn and bramble, largely untrodden. This forest was in a sense unbroken, for without emerging from its canopy a squirrel could traverse the country from end to end . . .'[1] Even for the beginning of the Iron Age, about which he was then writing, this picture no longer holds good, and by the Roman Conquest the land was more open and settled than not long ago was believed. The question to which we have to address ourselves is whether a further transformation occurred in Roman times. Prehistorians often take a negative view:

Rather surprisingly, the Roman occupation of Britain appears to have had little impact on the rural economy, the pattern established during the Iron Age continuing right through. This, at any rate, is the picture presented by the pollen evidence. The main impact of Rome was in the

[1] Sir Cyril Fox, *The Personality of Britain*, 4th edn., Cardiff (1952), 90.

military sphere—the construction of roads and various types of fortification. The Romans brought with them no innovations in agricultural
technology. On the contrary, they exploited Britain to the extent of
exporting her cereal crops to the Continent.[1]

The first part of that quotation raises the possibility that
agriculture was already of the same general character and
occupying much the same area of land when the Romans
arrived as throughout the period of Roman rule itself. In its
turn, that forces us back to population size, for it raises the
question of whether the Iron Age population was already
approaching the size we have tentatively postulated for
Roman Britain. In making such a hypothetical calculation
we might reasonably subtract the Roman army and administration, though we may perhaps allow for a few British
aristocrats who spent more time on war and hunting than
speeding the plough. The hypothesis we can then put to the
prehistorians is a pre-Roman Iron Age population substantially
larger than at the time of Domesday Book.

Experimental work done at the reconstruction of an Iron
Age farm at Butser in Hampshire has produced figures for the
amount of farm-land required to fill a single grain-storage pit
of the type present in very large number on Iron Age sites.
The area is so large—in round figures something between a
half and three-quarters of a hectare—that it has led Mr P.J.
Reynolds, the Director of the Butser project, to observe that
'the major implication is that in the Iron Age there was
virtually total domination of the landscape and a proportion-
ally large population.'[2] This, as he observes, is supported by
the initial analysis of the 1976 aerial photographs, suggesting
that 'our problem in the future will be to isolate the areas
where prehistoric man was not active.' Prehistorians who do
not accept such a large Iron Age density of settlement will
have to postulate a very substantial population growth
during the Roman period, say in the first and second
centuries, with either more agricultural land cleared or higher
production. Either way, Roman rule would mean real change.
The truth probably lies in a moderate increase in population
under Roman rule and a sharp decline sometime after the

[1] J.G. Evans, *The Environment of Early Man in the British Isles* (1975), 154
(but see Note, p. 571 below).
[2] Peter J. Reynolds, *Iron-Age Farm: The Butser Experiment* (1979), 77.

end of it. We do know of land opened up by the Romans (which we shall consider later in this chapter) and can reasonably conjecture an increase in productivity (which we shall examine in the next).

It is difficult to believe that Roman activity had no real effect on the ecology of Britain. In relation to 'roads and various types of fortification' alone one cannot help recalling Sir Ian Richmond's comment that the stripping of a wide belt of land to provide the materials for the original Turf Wall phase of the western end of Hadrian's Wall must have devastated the landscape through which it passed. Nor can one forget the more recent demonstration from pollen in lake deposits in Italy that the driving of a Roman highway through the Ciminian Forest extensively altered the ecology of the area. We have a great deal to learn about how the creation of cities, of new types of rural centre, and of deliberate Roman interference with the natural pattern (for example the digging of canals and diverting watercourses) affected the environment. We have previously noted how it became clear in the Fens that there had been no Iron Age occupation to speak of and that it looked as if the Romans took advantage of a natural change in the balance of sea and land, but that in the course of the second century and certainly by the mid-third the water level was again rising. At the time of that research it was not possible to tell whether it was a matter of world-wide climatic change, actually increasing the total amount of water in the oceans, or of 'crustal change', differential movements in the earth's crust leading to local variations in the relation of land and sea.[1] Nor did we know to what extent Roman intervention had affected the situation, though we had strong suspicions that the digging of waterways had serious consequences that were not apparent till a period of exceptional flood pressure. Most of all, we did not know whether or not the relative rise in sea-level in the Wash region was a purely local phenomenon,

[1] Since the writing of this section, an important symposium was held in October 1977 organized by the Society of Antiquaries of London on 'Archaeology and Coastal Change in Southern Britain.' The difficulty of interpreting the data was particularly emphasized by a paper by C.E. Everard on 'Southern Britain: an Unstable Crust and a Changing Sea-level.' It is clear that we have to proceed to generalizations with extreme caution.

though there were hints of similar happenings elsewhere in Britain[1] and across the North Sea in Holland. Now the report published on one of his Fenland excavations by Dr Timothy Potter, who has also worked extensively in Italy, has made it clear that we have to reckon with a very significant change indeed:

What, however, has not received emphasis is the ubiquity of flooding on low-lying sites in the later Roman period. At the large Roman valley-bottom site at Braughing, Hertfordshire, for example, excavations by the writer revealed evidence both for 1st century flood levels and for a thick level of alluvium which overlay the 4th century deposits. More-over, as a recent study by Vita-Finzi (1969) has clearly demonstrated, the same pattern occurs widely in the Mediterranean: valley-bottom Roman sites are invariably covered by upwards of six feet of alluvium, which began to form in the later Roman period. In Central Italy, this sequence has been demonstrated by excavation of a Roman mausoleum at the Fosso della Crescenza, where the main phase of alluviation began after AD 209 (Judson 1963; Ward-Perkins 1964, 14–15), and the writer has recently obtained similar results from a valley-bottom section at Narce, near Rome . . . Sufficient has been said to suggest that many low-lying Roman sites, both in Britain and abroad, were troubled by flooding, particularly from the 3rd century . . . Causatory factors are however extremely hard to identify. Deforestation has sometimes been cited but, as Vita-Finzi (1969, 105–11) has convincingly argued, this is not an adequate explanation. Much more likely is a hypothesis which would involve the notion of some degree of climatic change, which, in combination with the neglect of drainage systems, might account both for the Fenland alluviation and the heavy silting over valley-bottom sites (Vita-Finzi 1969, 112–15). Much more work will be required to test this hypothesis and there are many obvious objections. Meanwhile, it brings into focus the importance of environmental studies for even so well-documented a period as the later centuries of the Roman Empire.[2]

In some areas, however, it looks as if local movement of the land surface may have counteracted a more general rise in sea-level. There has long been a suspicion that the problem was much more acute on the east and south coasts of Britain

---

[1] See particularly Barry Cunliffe, 'The Somerset Levels in the Roman Period', in C. Thomas (ed.), *Rural Settlement in Roman Britain*, CBA Research Report no. 7, 1966, 68 ff.; but also see p. 557 below.

[2] T.W.J. Potter, *Proc. Camb. Ant. Soc.* 66 (1976), 49 f. His references are to C. Vita-Finzi, *The Mediterranean Valleys*, Cambridge (1969); S. Judson, 'Erosion and deposition of Italian stream valleys during historic time', *Science*, 140, no. 3569 (1963), 898 f.; J.B. Ward-Perkins, *Landscape and History in Central Italy* (J.L. Myres Memorial Lecture), Oxford (1964), wherein see p. 11 f. for the Ciminian Forest.

than in the west. Recent work on the Severn estuary has produced no evidence for a general marine transgression in the Roman period and it becomes clear that we have to take the evidence of each stretch of coast on its merits, while bearing in mind the general trend. Here, too, we ought perhaps to reflect that reactions are likely to have been different locally and centrally. To local people, what mattered was what affected their own land and homes. But the Roman government, observing the empire as a whole, may well have detected a general phenomenon that could only increase their worries about abandoned land.[1]

Excavation on the waterfront of the Roman city of London has disclosed successive timber wharves and proved that in the fourth century the city wall was continued along the Thames to complete the circuit, probably after about 330[2] and in parts perhaps not completed till around 390. For our present purpose it is very important that the early wharves have already shown that in the first century AD the level of the river opposite the City was around 4 metres below present high-tide level.[3] There is not yet the evidence for what happened within the Roman period, though work on the fourth-century wall may reveal it, but 'the Saxon waterfronts, where they exist, may be located above and further north of those of Roman date'.[4] London seems to have been an extreme case, and it is probable that so great a change is not to be expected elsewhere, even in other parts of the south-east. Yet it is interesting to note that the evidence from the Fens far to the north of the Thames estuary is joined by other evidence far to the west off the

[1] Recent work on the Severn includes J.W. Murray and A.B. Hawkins, *Journ. Geol. Soc. Lond.* 132 (1976), 385 ff., and research by G.C. Boon that has suggested that the Second legion at Caerleon was exploiting the farming potential of the alluvium till it was transferred at the end of the third century. Similarly, on the other side of the Severn, the villa at Kingsweston, rebuilt about AD 300, and other settlements on the edge of the alluvium seem to have been placed to make use of the alluvium. The siting is very similar to the Fen Edge situation, but at least before the end of the third century seems unaffected by the flooding that caused disruption in the Wash region.

[2] Based on radiocarbon and tree-ring dating (*Current Archaeology*, 57 (1977), 310).

[3] G.H. Willcox, 'Problems and Possible Conclusions related to the History and Archaeology of the Thames in the London Region', *Trans. Lond. and Middx. Arch. Soc.* 26 (1975), 285 ff. (reprinted as *Archaeology in the City of London*, No. 5).   [4] Ibid. 289.

Dorset coast, where material from the end of the third century or the beginning of the fourth has come from a site about 1.25 m (4 feet) below present high-tide level.[1] Such variations from present and medieval relative sea levels imply that the appearance of rivers must have been very different from today. There are great implications for the reach of the tides, depth, width, and navigability and the natural and artificial drainage of the river valleys themselves. The biggest question of all, perhaps, is the implications for the coastline. In fact the Royal Geographical Society's Roman Fenland survey started from a proposal to map the coastline of Roman Britain, and was intended to be a modest start to what was recognized in 1960 as an enormous task. Only the most tentative conclusions were in the end reached on the coastline of the Wash. Subsequent to the completion of that survey further work in Lincolnshire has suggested not only that the Roman coastline was much further inland than was previously thought[2] but also that some of the dense settlement then thought to lie behind the Roman coastline was probably on large offshore islands.[3] There is, however, no guarantee that the situation was static throughout the Roman period, and the effect on the coast of the radical changes in the courses of rivers observed further south in the Fenland basin within Roman times is likely to have been considerable.

It is clear that in the Wash area subsequent to the Roman period the land has actually been *encroaching* on the sea despite higher relative sea level, at least partly due to the intervention of man since early medieval times. The construction of successive seaward dykes has led to the natural creation of silt marshland in front of each of them, so that the land has advanced in stages. Elsewhere severe erosion has meant a *loss* of land—for example at some of the Saxon Shore sites. There is no simple equation between sea level and coastline. It is therefore exceptionally difficult to envisage

---

[1] H.C. Bowen, *National Trust Yearbook* (1975-6), 42 f.: Brownsea Island, compared with Hamworthy.

[2] See *Current Archaeology*, 53 (1975), 177.

[3] B.B. Simmons, 'Ancient Coastlines around the Wash', *South Lincolnshire Archaeology*, 1 (1977), 6 ff. (also his paper read at the October 1977 symposium, p. 555 n. 1 above: 'Iron Age and Roman Coastlines round the Wash'). This work is based on further survey and the availability of much more detailed contour-maps than previously.

the actual coastal appearance of Britain in Roman times or how much it altered between the first century BC and the fifth century AD. Like the population problem, I believe it can only be solved by both the testing of general hypotheses by means of a very large number of local studies in great detail[1] and a readiness to accept that local conditions almost certainly often ran quite contrary to general trends. What we need most of all to appreciate is that we cannot rely on modern or medieval coastal conditions as an indication of Roman, and to recognize the magnitude of the changes that have in many places clearly taken place.

What happened to the landscape of Britain in the fifth century in the years after the end of Roman rule is even more difficult to determine. I know of no evidence to suggest an early return to a drier climate, and one may assume that problems connected with or worsened by administrative failures in the third century are likely to have been even greater in the fifth. On a more local scale, man's effects on the environment are likely to have been much more varied as central government broke down. It is important for the study of the landscape that early Saxon settlement has been observed on or near Roman sites, while mid Saxons seem to have founded new settlements on different sites. This suggests that the physical conditions were broadly the same in the fifth century as in the fourth. It also implies that no large-scale dereliction of agricultural land had taken place, at least not of such an order as to require more work to restore than the opening up of fresh lands. While the early Saxons were settling alongside, and perhaps intermingling with, the Romano-British population under Roman rule or its immediate 'sub-Roman' successors, or taking over Roman lands just vacated, the Late Roman landscape pattern is likely to have persisted.

Much has been made in the past of the notion that the Saxons were forced into cultivating virgin land because it was impossible to reclaim Romano-British fields that had been abandoned and run to ruin. Mr Frank Noble has shown

[1] e.g. work at Lympne by Professor Barry Cunliffe, which suggests the existence of a major inlet where part of Romney Marsh now lies and which would have important implications both for the siting of the Saxon Shore fort and the *classis Britannica* operations in the Weald (see p. 637 below).

from observation of land near Monmouth in the Welsh border country that the process is much more complex. Agricultural land there that was abandoned in the nineteenth century became a tangled jungle for fifty years, but thereafter as trees matured the undergrowth died back for lack of light, the sodden ground was naturally dried out by the trees and the whole area became easily penetrable again. At that point forest husbandry or clearance becomes once more relatively simple. Where there has been a real gap in occupation one may therefore expect something like half a century before resettlement is likely and in these circumstances changes of settlement site and land division are probable. But where there was no substantial break, then continuity of pattern is perhaps more likely to occur than not (provided that methods of farming are not radically different) *even if the population has completely changed.* We may be left with the strongest suspicion that where substantial changes of land use can be discerned in the Saxon period it occurred either where Roman agriculture was abandoned for a relatively long period or where radical alteration in political organization and social structure was imposed. Thus it is not surprising to find some early Saxons adopting Roman patterns, while after the great disturbances of the second half of the fifth century and the Saxon conquests of the later sixth quite new patterns emerge in many places. This tells us practically nothing about break or continuity in population but much about the presence or absence of substantial gaps in farming. And we have, therefore, to reckon with the survival of some agricultural units from Roman times to the recent past or even the present. Professor Hoskins, the great proponent of English landscape studies, wrote in 1976 a most significant retraction of some of his highly influential earlier thinking:[1]

I have said above that everything in the landscape is older than we think ... In many parts of England more or less massive boundary banks survive, some of them still awaiting explanation. In Oxfordshire, the boundaries of the Roman villa estate of Ditchley have been traced with considerable certainty, enclosing an area of about 875 acres.[2]

---

[1] Hoskins, op. cit. (1977 edition), 13 f.
[2] In round figures, 355 hectares.

A good deal of these boundaries consist of earthen banks thrown up about the middle of the first century A.D., known in parts as Grim's Dyke. There are gaps where dense woodland afforded sufficient protection. Even to this day a nearly complete periphery of ancient woodland can be traced around the villa estate. The other remarkable thing is that most of this extensive boundary dating from the first century is followed by parish boundaries of Saxon origin: in other words there was still a farming unit here which was recognisable in Saxon times, . . . Villas may have been destroyed or even decayed like many a modern house, but the tenant farmers go on from year to year and generation to generation.

Across in Suffolk . . . a parish named Mickfield which means literally 'the great field'. What did the Old English colonists see when they moved in here? I think they saw a large area already cleared for farming, part of the old villa estate, and that they took over the boundary ready-made . . . So I believe in general that *boundaries* are one of the most ancient features in the English landscape.

In all probability we are faced with real change in the landscape of Britain caused, during the Roman period, by worsening natural conditions that may have continued right through the Saxon period, and by man's behaviour during the often disorderly replacement of Roman rule by the sub-Roman kingdoms and by the full Saxon conquest of the sixth century. On the other hand we are also faced with the strong likelihood of continuity of activity on the land where none of these factors was overwhelming. We might therefore appropriately end this review of the landscape with one tentative comment on the effects of political change on it between the Roman period and the Saxon and early medieval periods. The comment is that such change may have had much less effect on the ways of organizing and working the land than we have been accustomed to think. Indeed it provokes the question of whether for a given locality there was much difference in practice, as far as the working of the land went, between the relationship of the Roman gentleman to his agricultural slaves or tied *coloni* and the Saxon noble to his slaves and dependent farmers, or for that matter the Norman knight to his serfs. Perhaps we might even project the pattern back, and suggest that some of the Iron Age aristocrats who were to become the *curiales* of Roman Britain already had a very similar relationship to the people who worked the same land in their time. If the population really was of much the same order of magnitude before the

Roman conquest as shortly after the Norman, then Professor Hoskins' suspicion of substantial continuity in land use may well be right. This would lead us to two conclusions. One is that it was often the *people* who changed rather than the man-made landscape—perhaps only the actual landowning class. Secondly this approach implies that the *residence* of the owner of the land, or even the settlement from which it was worked, is of less importance for this purpose than the unit of land itself. This in its turn strongly suggests that it is worth extending the practice of trying to isolate such traditional units as still exist or have done so in the recent past and tracing them back as far as possible, alongside the study of the distribution of *settlements* of different periods which is now so well and successfully established.

COMMUNICATIONS

Where Roman Britain differs most sharply in its historical geography from the periods before and after is in its provision of communications by land and by water.[1] Yet the amount to which this affected the lives of the people of the Classical world is a matter on which there is a strong division of opinion, as will be seen by comparing two modern writers on the subject. Professor Frere writes:

A striking fact about trade and industry in Roman Britain is the ease with which the problems of transport were overcome. Wherever manufactured or produced, goods were easily distributed throughout the province, and the long distances over which exceptionally heavy objects such as stone sarcophagi, large altars and other massive pieces of masonry were moved from their source is most remarkable. These facts point to the skilled development of carts and wagons equal to these demanding purposes, and to the efficient maintenance of the road system ... Subsidiary to the roads in Britain, but not negligible for transport purposes, were her navigable rivers and the canals[2] which in Cambridgeshire and Lincolnshire linked some of the most useful of them. Finally, there was the coastal shipping, whose influence can be seen in trade with the barbarian North, or in the transport of pottery from the kilns of Colchester to the Antonine Wall, but which was also active between ports in southern Britain, as is suggested, for instance, by the distribution

---

[1] For the road network, see Map VI.
[2] But see p. 564: not all of those artificial watercourses formerly considered canals are now thought to have been used for transport.

of pewter goods made in the south-west . . . All the sea routes which had linked Britain to the Continent in prehistoric times were still used . . .[1]

However, if we turn to Professor Finley on the ancient economy, we find a different emphasis:

There were also certain constants, the ox to begin with. The ox was the chief traction animal of antiquity, the mule and the donkey his near rivals, the horse hardly at all. All three are slow and hungry. The transport figures in Diocletian's edict of maximum prices imply that a 1200-pound wagon-load of wheat would double in price in 300 miles, that a shipment of grain by sea from one end of the Mediterranean to the other would cost less (ignoring the risks) than carting it seventy-five miles. A state could afford to engage ox-teams for the extraordinary purpose of shifting marble column-drums for temples, employing on an average thirty yoke for each drum, and it could perform other extraordinary feats, especially if the army required them. But individuals could not move bulky merchandise long distances by land as a normal activity, nor could any but the wealthiest and most powerful communities. Most necessities are bulky—cereals, pottery, metals and timber—and so towns could not safely outgrow the food production of their own immediate hinterlands unless they had direct access to waterways.

Not even the famed Roman roads, built for military and political, not commercial reasons, made any significant difference, since the means of traction remained the same. It was the many rivers of Gaul, not the roads, that elicited comment from Roman writers and facilitated the growth of inland cities.[2]

The ease with which heavy loads could be transported by water as opposed to land is of cardinal importance in the ancient world.[3] For shipping between Britain and the Continent it is clear that Dover and Richborough served as ports for the Channel crossing to Boulogne and it is probable that the Tyne communicated directly with the Rhine.[4] Exeter and the ports of Southampton Water were almost certainly heavily used and we have conjectured that the Wash and the Norfolk and Suffolk estuaries further south were also busy. The greatest traffic, however, was through London, the hub of the road system and the centre of government. In Roman times the Thames at London had a crucial advantage:

[1] Frere, op. cit. 338 f.   [2] M.I. Finley, op. cit. 126 f.
[3] Compare, for example, the fact that in the eighteenth century new canals serving the Staffordshire pottery trade were able to charge as little as 15 per cent of the former cost by road.   [4] See Frere, op. cit. 339.

it was then beyond the reach of the tide.[1] This enormously extended its usefulness as a port and must have been extremely attractive to Mediterranean seamen used to a practically tideless sea. It greatly simplified, too, the design and construction of the necessary quays, and lengths of the massive timber wharves that stretched in the second century continuously for about a kilometre along the waterfront of the Roman city have been excavated in recent years.[2] Remains of river craft and coastal ships have also been found in the Thames at London, the most notable being that found at Blackfriars and whose date of launching or refit is established by a coin of Domitian deliberately placed in the socket into which the mast was stepped.

The importance of canals in Roman Britain is more problematic. It is reasonably certain that the Foss Dyke between the Trent and the Ouse is a canal, probably associated with military supplies to York. However it is now very doubtful whether the Lincolnshire Car Dyke or even the Cambridgeshire watercourse of that name was used for transport. The former, with a recently discovered parallel artificial cut in front of it, was almost certainly a catchwater drain between the high ground of the Fen Edge and the new lands beyond. Other cuts, particularly those of the south-eastern Fens, may have had a dual function, serving both water control and as transport routes, particularly where they link rivers together. In the transport field, the most important function of waterways, both natural and artificial, must always have been the provision for inland areas of access to the sea.

It stretches credibility too far to believe that Professor Finley's transport analysis holds good for Britain. Even if we leave out of account military sites and major public works where official policy might often override purely economic considerations, there is still an enormous amount of archaeological material that proves the mass distribution of goods over long distances, and a high proportion of these must have

---

[1] My attention was drawn to the significance of this discovery by Dr John Fletcher.

[2] At New Fresh Wharf and Seal House they appear to date from the second half of the second century (*Brit.* 6 (1975), 265; 7 (1976), 345 f.). Dating by tree-rings has indicated somewhere around AD 155 for timber used. See also G. and C. Milne, *Current Archaeology*, 66 (1979), 198 ff. for an account of work on the Roman and subsequent history of the London waterfront.

gone to private individuals. Pottery is the most obvious category, and the one which has been subject to the most sophisticated and detailed analysis. Samian pottery from Gaul, for example, or the British Nene Valley wares, appear all over the country, both in the towns and in the villas of the well-to-do and in the humblest 'native' sites, not always in large quantities but still present and clearly available to the ordinary inhabitants. Another example is oysters. Their shells appear on almost every Roman site. They imply an efficient and fairly rapid use of road transport, for if they were carried in tanks of water they were very heavy; if without water, then they required reasonable speed of delivery before they were dead and dangerous. These are only two out of many items that are so common as to be almost an embarrassment to the excavator of Romano-British sites. They cannot be ignored as occasional finds inflated to support a general theory—on the contrary it is their sheer quantity and ubiquity that hinder proper quantification and analysis.

We have so far concentrated on communications as they relate to the commerical distribution of goods. Both scholars quoted above have emphasized the military and political purpose of the road system. In fact, their point could be extended to say that in the conveyance of people and messages it was vital. In passing it ought to be said that that factor in itself was of economic importance, even if it was only an incidental one. We have, for example, writing-tablets from Roman Britain bearing business messages that indicate the sort of purely civil information that was carried, and most of it must at some stage have travelled by road. There is, for example, a letter found at London between an owner and his steward about the sale of a slave-girl and other business matters, and correspondence concerned with private business has come from the Vindolanda excavations. But the prime reason why the Roman state took such an interest in protecting the flow of information was administrative and political.

The roads served not only to facilitate the passage of troops and their supplies but also to carry imperial messengers and duly authorized officials. Speed was a vitally important feature of the *cursus publicus* or Imperial Post: without it the extreme difficulties the emperors had in knowing what was going on in the empire and maintaining control over it would have become overwhelming. A normal rate of travel by the Post was in the region of fifty miles a day, but faster journeys are known, Tiberius once managing the feat of two hundred miles in the space of twenty-four hours. Governors were responsible for seeing that the main highways required for official purposes were maintained and the system of stations for changing horses (*mutationes*) and posting-houses (*mansiones*) was kept up and strictly regulated. Individuals could only travel by means of the Imperial Post if issued with a permit, and these permits were sent out to governors by the emperor. The seriousness with which this was regarded is illustrated by an exchange of letters between Trajan and Pliny. Pliny wrote from Bithynia enquiring if out-of-date permits could be used, as he was anxious not to hold up important dispatches. Trajan was short and sharp in reply: 'Permits must not be used after they are out of date. It is my invariable rule to have fresh permits sent to each province before the dates they can be required.'[1] Trajan himself could be generous, for when Pliny later wrote to apologize most profusely for giving his wife a permit to travel in connection with a family bereavement, the emperor replied kindly and excused him. There is implied in this latter correspondence that governors or equivalent officers were in the habit sometimes of issuing permits for private travel, but an inscription from Burdur in Turkey[2] suggests that Pliny is emphasizing his own otherwise impeccable adherence to regulations rather than nervousness about use of a discretion he officially possessed. This inscription, dated to the time of Tiberius, shows that as early as Augustus' reign the official system was in being and was already abused.

The financial responsibility for providing this transport was laid on the local communities and the bitter complaints about cost and misuse run continuously throughout the Roman period. The Burdur inscription defines who was entitled to use the service—broadly speaking only people on

---

[1] Pliny, *Letters*, x. 46. The reserving of the right to the emperor to issue permits seems to have been introduced under the Flavians (*JRS* 66 (1976), 126).

[2] S. Mitchell, 'Requisitioned Transport in the Roman Empire: a New Inscription from Pisidia', *JRS* 66 (1976), 106 ff.

official business carrying a permit allowed by the provincial governor or the governor of another province[1]—and how much transport each grade could command and with what priority. Theoretically many of these travellers had to pay for what they used and could not demand extra services, but this was where the complaints chiefly originated. The inscription lays down that goods for sale must not be carried by such transport (which suggests they often were). It also limits those persons entitled to free transport and free lodging. These included the members of the governor's staff, persons on military business from other provinces, imperial freedmen, and imperial slaves and their beasts. The cost fell on the local authorities, but by the third century the actual provision was regularly organized by the provincial administration. In the third and fourth centuries the word *mansio* regularly describes the actual station, but in the Tiberian inscription we have been considering it seems to be used in the abstract sense of the service itself. In the first century the actual system of stations may not yet have been set up, only the obligation to provide the service laid on the local communities. Buildings for this purpose appear in Britain as early, for example, as that reasonably identified at Chelmsford which was put up in the late first century and, with some alterations in the middle of the second, continued substantially unaltered till the end of the Roman period.[2] This is perhaps an early example of official provision or may have first been erected by the local authority as a less troublesome way of meeting its obligations than an *ad hoc* search for accommodation and transport every time someone arrived with a permit. It is not impossible that the state took over establishments that had been started in this way. Some may even have originated as privately owned inns. Varro, writing in the late first century BC before the establishment of the Principate, suggested owning an inn as a profitable sideline for a villa estate that lay near a road.[3] Eventually the state may have reorganized and extended the provision of staffs and buildings, particularly where the services that the law laid down in imperial times were not being efficiently provided.

---

[1] It appears that at this early stage governors could authorize other officials to issue permits, including municipal magistrates.

[2] *Brit.* 7 (1976), 343.   [3] Varro, *Rerum Rusticarum*, I. ii. 23.

The detailed entitlements to services continued to be regulated by the grade of the traveller, and we find that a *vicarius* could claim a set provision just as his predecessors had been able to do for three hundred years or more.[1]

It is likely that many of the small towns that grew up on the main routes of Britain, for example those spaced along Watling Street, either originated as post-houses or were kept going as settlements in the period immediately after the army moved on by the presence of such an establishment. The post system was kept up conscientiously, as the history of the *mansio* at Chelmsford would illustrate. Another of these urban examples excavated in recent years is at the small walled town of Godmanchester.[2] Continuing excavation on the site at Wall in Staffordshire will, it may be hoped, give us more detail for one of the great highways of the province.[3] It is likely, too, that the buildings identified as *mansiones* outside such forts as Benwell or Chesterholm on Hadrian's Wall were used by people travelling officially. They are usually the only reasonably spacious and comfortable residential accommodation other than the commandant's house capable of housing a person of consequence and a few servants, and sharply differentiated from the ordinary run of private houses and shops outside the fort. They must have been particularly welcome to those persons obliged to travel in outlandish parts of the empire who, in more civilized regions, would have scorned public inns and moved from hospitality at one friend's villa to another, by far the preferred method of travel among the aristocracy.

We need have little doubt that the imperial government attached great importance to the maintenance of administrative and military communications throughout the whole period of the Empire. Inscribed milestones certainly record road maintenance down to the middle of the fourth century, and though the British series (which anyhow is not large) gives out then, the survival of the roads as important features into subsequent periods is circumstantial evidence that repair

---

[1] *Cod. Theod.* VIII. v. 38.   [2] *Brit.* 1 (1970), 287.
[3] The 'villa' at Wall may have a continuous history from the Neronian period (*Brit.* 7 (1976), 328). If it is in fact a *mansio* this would be very interesting. The problem there is not only to demonstrate that the successive buildings on the site are on the same lines but also that they had a similar use.

continued on a substantial scale in the open country, just as more direct evidence from towns shows us streets being maintained and resurfaced into the fifth century. The fact that Rutilius Namatianus[1] noted as worthy of special comment that bridges were still down and posting-inns deserted after the sack of Rome by Alaric suggests that to his Gallic correspondent such a failure in the system would still have seemed unusual in 417. We may perhaps assume that the regular maintenance of main roads in Britain continued at least till 409, and lesser roads, which were the responsibility of the local authorities, were perhaps kept up longer still but with wide variations in standard and persistence.

Rutilius clearly also felt that to travel by sea required an explanation, and I have noted how it was feared[2] and the normal season limited by the design of ships and navigational aids. Yet the case should not be overstated.[3] All travel to Britain had to be by sea, many private individuals made the journey,[4] and in our consideration of official travel the importance of the sea routes must not be overlooked. Indeed, even when there was the alternative of travel by land, official journeys were not automatically made by land. Pliny the Younger, travelling in company with his entire staff out to his appointment in Bithynia, writes to Trajan of his decision to travel partly by carriage and partly by coastal boat 'for the great heat makes it too difficult to go all the way by road and the prevailing wind prevents me from travelling entirely by sea'.[5] Indeed, he had originally intended to go the whole way by ship—but, it will be noted, that was in summer. All the remains of ships of the Roman period so far discovered in Britain have been merchant in character, but there is no reason to think that official passengers may not have travelled by civilian transport. However, it may also be assumed that the fleet played an important part in the carrying of official travellers, especially when there were security problems involved.

[1] See p. 435 above.
[2] See also C. Caplan, *Arch. Ael.* 5th ser. 4 (1976), 171 ff. (a most useful note on *RIB* 1319 and 1320).
[3] There do for example seem to have been merchant ships designed to cope with winter sailing (A.S. Toby, *Int. Journ. Naut. Arch. and Underwater Exploration,* 3 (1974, 205 ff.).
[4] Aristides, *Orat. Aegypt.* xxxvi, 19.   [5] Pliny, *Letters,* x. 15.

We have so far considered official communications largely in terms of official travellers. However there were two other aspects of major importance. One was the carriage of official goods, whether it be a small package or the shipment of military stores and the output of publicly controlled industries such as the iron-working of the Weald, in which, thanks to the research of Mr Cleere, we now know the British fleet was closely involved. An important source of information on such freight traffic is provided by official lead sealings. Those from the Pennines that probably represent official control of the lead-workings around Alston have long been known and were studied by Sir Ian Richmond. Others from the fort at Brough-under-Stainmore suggested a collecting point for traffic from other military stations, and yet others, where private seals occur along with those of military units, may well have been attached to packets and letters dispatched by duly authorized officers.[1] These examples seems to be of the third century. Tags of the Neronian period giving the weight and value of parcels have been found in Wales at Usk[2] and a second-century military seal has come from Wallsend on the Tyne[3] and others perhaps of the same date from Leicester.[4] Procedures doubtless changed, but the traffic clearly was frequent and long-standing.

The other form of official traffic was of equal or perhaps even greater importance, the passing of official messages. Frequent use was of course made of messengers travelling by the Imperial Post, and we saw Domitian's courier meeting Agricola's ship in the Channel on the way home from his province.[5] But on land use could also be made of signal stations, though we do not know how sophisticated the messages sent by them could be. The reliefs on Trajan's Column in Rome show towers with flares and piles of material for beacons, and platforms that were probably for this purpose have been found on the Stainmore Pass[6] and towers on the Gask Ridge in Scotland.[7] Some other

---

[1] See Richmond (ed. Salway), *Roman Archaeology and Art*, 29; *Trans. Cumb. and Westm. Arch. and Ant. Soc.* 2nd ser. 36 (1936), 104 ff.

[2] *Brit.* 6 (1975), 291 ff.   [3] *Brit.* 7 (1976), 388.

[4] Ibid. 386 f.   [5] Tacitus, *Agr.* xl.

[6] I.A. Richmond, in W.F. Grimes (ed.), *Aspects of Archaeology*, 293 ff.

[7] A.S. Robertson, *Trans. Perthsh. Soc. Nat. Sci.* special issue (1973), 14 ff., indicating a possible Flavian date.

British examples are a tower at Pike Hill incorporated into the structure of Hadrian's Wall but apparently of earlier origin and two more now known on the Roman road from Annandale into Clydesdale.[1] These could largely be explained as having a fairly local tactical purpose.[2] A fourth-century signal station found at Wapping just to the east of the Roman city of London,[3] which was presumably part of a system for passing messages to the capital, may have had no more than a purely defensive role, providing early warning of danger to the city, but on the other hand raises interesting but unanswered questions of a possible function in transmitting urgent signals to and from the military and civil government of the British diocese. In the final analysis, information was the most vital commodity that passed along all these routes, because intelligence meant power, and without it the whole apparatus by which the empire was controlled could not have worked.[4] In this context, the unique position of Britain among the heavily garrisoned areas of the empire in being an island separated from the Continent by the often-difficult waters of the Channel takes on a new significance. This, we need not doubt, was well appreciated on those not inconsiderable occasions when she took a leading role in proclaiming emperors or arousing suspicions of conspiracy in the minds of the imperial government of the day.

NOTE

Palaeobotany and the ancient environment. Generalizations are extremely risky. Against the data that suggest no change between the Iron Age and the Roman period, pollen can also be used to suggest there were sometimes changes in use of particular pieces of land, perhaps indicating a shift in the location of cultivation, a different type of land exploitation or even abandonment (see, for example, D.D. Bartley, *New Phytol.* 74 (1975), 375 ff. studying a moorland area in Yorkshire where Iron Age pasture and arable seems to have reverted to woodland in the early Roman period). On the other hand, initial botanical results from a Stainmore site in Cumbria suggest clearance of woodland in the 'late prehistoric/early Roman period' supporting an impression of farming expansion onto the fells (*CBA Newsletter and Calendar*,

[1] *Brit.* 7 (1976), 33 ff.
[2] For further information on British examples see also Graham Webster, *The Roman Imperial Army* (1969), 246 ff.
[3] *Brit.* 6 (1975), 269; 7 (1976), 351.
[4] Cf. p. 522 above on intelligence officers.

January 1978, 107). The Stainmore palaeobotany was in association with a 'native' settlement: it will be interesting to see whether further work will suggest an undeviating process running from the prehistoric into the Roman period or any form of change coinciding with Roman occupation of the area. The site itself certainly had new construction in the third century and possibly again in the fourth.

19

TOWN AND COUNTRY

THE relationship between town and country in Roman Britain is a subject on which opinion has veered from Collingwood's view that the towns were mere parasites on the country to J.S. Wacher's opinion that they were the vital catalyst between new ideas from the Classical world and those of Celtic society that transformed Iron Age Britain into a land fully integrated into the empire. Some have seen the Roman towns as a largely superficial imposition on a way of life that was hardly changed by the Roman conquest and in many areas lasted long after the end of Roman rule and the decay of the cities themselves. Others have argued that towns survived well into the fifth century because of their own strength, while the characteristic society of the Romano-British countryside broke down. One question we must ask is whether there is not behind the discussion an assumption in many people's minds that the two modes of settlement, urban and rural, were totally distinct, even opposed, forms of existence.

CITIES AND THEIR REGIONS

The modern reader needs first and foremost to understand that, to the Roman, indeed to the Classical world as a whole, the proper mode of life was that of the city-state. In one sense the empire was the City of Rome and her conquered territories, in another a vast patchwork of *civitates*, city-states of varying status but all striving towards the character and condition of assemblies of Romans, with their own local constitutions and customs based more or less closely on that of Rome herself and subject to the overriding control of Roman magistrates. Since the emperor held an overwhelming and unique combination of those magistracies, allowing him to speak for Senate and People, every *civitas* naturally recognized his supreme power, both *imperium* and *auctoritas*.

For the same reason they were also subject to his deputies: the provincial governors, legionary legates, procurators, and others who derived their authority from him in varying degrees and in differing circumstances. But as city-states they had their own functions and duties and could not be written-off as formal luxuries. I have already mentioned some of the ways in which they played their part. In 1958 Professor A.L.F. Rivet made a necessary point:

> The evidence for the political geography of the province is inadequate and inconclusive, but it does not follow that the subject itself is a mere historical detail of little interest to the archaeologist. On the contrary, it is central to our understanding of Roman Britain. In this period we are dealing not with primitive 'cultures' but with a highly organised state, not with prehistory but with history. Human dispositions, deliberately made, influenced the course of events as much as the blind forces of nature, and it was the very artificiality of the Roman organisation that made its final collapse so complete.[1]

The word 'artificiality' need have no pejorative sense. A system of local government that lasted largely unchanged in structure for three or four hundred years needs no defence of its stability or the soundness of its original planning. It was artificial in the sense that it introduced new forms of organization not seen before in Britain, and in that, while largely basing its territorial organization on existing tribal areas, it sometimes combined, split, or otherwise altered them to form the new authorities, indeed sometimes even inventing new ones where there was no convenient unit to hand. The Local Government Reorganization of 1974 may similarly be described as 'artificial', but whether it is in a pejorative sense or not depends on one's politics, one's degree of emotional attachment to the familiar, and one's experience of the new. If it lasts as long as the Roman, it will have become a part of traditional England.

To recapitulate briefly on what has been said before about local authorities, the broad divisions are *coloniae, municipia,* and ordinary *civitates*. There are four known examples of *coloniae* in Britain, three deliberately founded as veteran settlements—Colchester, Lincoln, and Gloucester—and one,

---

[1] A.L.F. Rivet, *Town and Country in Roman Britain* (1958), 137. It may now be debated how complete or quick the collapse was, but the general observation stands.

York, raised to that status from humble origins, probably at the time of the residence of Severus and the other members of the imperial family there. The large settlements or *canabae* that grew outside the other permanent legionary bases at Caerleon and Chester may however not have received the same rank, but London, as the metropolis of Britain, ought to have received a title. Certainly its fourth-century name, *Augusta*, indicates a high status. Verulamium is the only reasonably certain example of a *municipium*, but there is some evidence pointing in that direction elsewhere, for example for Leicester. It is highly likely that other major cities that had grown from native settlements or been formed as urban centres for the new local authorities based on the native aristocracy and had flourished as such were granted this status. The main difference between these and the other *civitates* was that they were chartered Roman cities and all, or most, of their governing class were Roman citizens. This distinction more or less disappeared with the rapid growth of the citizenship in the second century and quite went with the *Constitutio Antoniniana* in the third, but the titles were still sought. The core of the organization was the *ordo* of decurions or members of the council (more commonly known under the Late Empire as *curiales*, after the *curia* or council-chamber). The minimum age limit was normally thirty, and their character is immediately recognizable by the facts that from the second century, at least, popular election was replaced by co-option and that the members were required to have a certain level of property (an almost universal feature of qualification for rank or office through-out the empire at both national and local level). The member-ship of the *ordo* was commonly set at one hundred. A councillor's availability for duty and his stake in the well-being of the community was assured, at least in law, by a rule requiring him to maintain a house of a specific minimum size within it. In this respect, as in most others, the constitutions of the local authorities copied, in appropriately scaled-down form, the pattern of Rome herself: senators were expected to own property in Italy, whatever their origin. In formal terms, the local councillor's house was to be in the relevant city or within a mile of it, but—as Mr Mark Hassall has pointed out—some of the places in Britain that were certainly the centres of their *civitates*, for example Silchester, were physically too small for this to have been enforced. It is therefore probable that, particularly in the earlier days of a province such as this, the requirement was interpreted as residence within the boundaries of the *civitas*, an interpretation which would have caused little legal difficulty. Under the Late Empire this theoretical problem was overtaken by more serious ones, as the *ordo* can rarely have been up to strength in that period due to deliberate avoidance of office. In the heyday of the local administrations, however, there must have been, as Mr Wacher has demonstrated, a total of around 2,000 decurions in Britain at any one time. It is an interesting corrective to the notion that they were a tiny oligarchy that, if our population figures are right, then something approaching one person in every two or three thousand was a decurion. When one subtracts women, children, slaves, freedmen, most soldiers, and an increasing number of people exempt from service on the councils (such as senators and, in the fourth century, Christian priests) the proportion is quite impressive.

The cities were run by two senior and two junior magistrates elected by the councils, who had responsibility for a wide range of local services, including such matters as water supplies, and presided in the local courts. Gradually the attractions of office became less. It could be very expensive. Many municipal dues were levied in the form of services to be provided free by the wealthier citizens and a newly elected magistrate, as at Rome, was expected to become a local benefactor as well. New decurions paid an entrance fee and the expenses of actually holding a local magistracy were likely to be heavy. Perhaps the most crucial function of the councils in the eyes of government was their responsibility for the collection of taxes. This was not just the levying of local taxes for local purposes, but national taxes as well. Diocletian made the individual councillors personally responsible. This act must have ben highly unpopular though it probably codified a practice that governors and procurators had already been carrying out. The councils' actual freedom of action had also been severely curtailed. The reader will recall the commissioners whom Trajan introduced in many cities to prevent mishandling of municipal funds and needless extravagance. We find the emperor allowing the city of Sinope in Bithynia an aqueduct, provided that Pliny is satisfied that his own engineers approve the line and that the town bears the whole cost.[1] Prusa, in the same province, has to ask for permission to rebuild its public baths, which are old and in poor repair, and is told it can use its own money to do so, provided that essential services are not thus starved of funds.[2] Bithynia had certainly come under special scrutiny, and so may be rather exceptional for the beginning of the second century, but commissioners gradually became common and turned into permanent paid officials. It is not surprising that we find so many fourth-century imperial laws to prevent those qualified for service as *curiales* from avoiding it.

The burdens on the *curiales* were in fact vastly increased by direct acts of government in the first half of the fourth century and only partially alleviated thereafter. Constantine, as we have seen, confiscated the treasures and endowments of the pagan temples. This immediately affected the finances of the cities, since they had had the managing of the funds of many of them and was only partly alleviated later in the century when the public religious observances for which they had been responsible were formally prohibited. Moreover Constantine had not stopped at the temples. He also deprived the local authorities of the revenue raised from local taxes, which were henceforth paid into central funds. This was compounded by a further massive blow, probably under Constantius II, when the cities suffered the transfer to the emperor of the lands and endowments which as corporations they had acquired over the centuries. By the middle of the century, therefore, all the expense on public works, which had formerly been defrayed at least partly from municipal funds, now had to come out of the pockets of the *curiales*. This reason alone would be sufficient to explain the sharp decline in civic standards. The Emperor Julian returned some of their financial independence to the cities, but this was rapidly reversed by his successors. The situation had become so serious by 374 that one-third of the income from the properties they had once owned was allowed to the

---

[1] Pliny, *Letters*, x. 91.   [2] Ibid. x. 24.

cities, as well as the same proportion of the local taxes. There are signs that by the beginning of the fifth century they were building up some accumulation of capital again from bequests and other sources and regained certain powers of local taxation. There is thus reason to believe that the cities of Britain are likely to have been in a better state under Honorius than that to which they must have sunk in the middle of the fourth century.

The public services provided were on the whole worthwhile. Mr Wacher has shown for example that almost every town of consequence had an engineered water-supply. It went to public installations, such as the public baths and, as at Lincoln, to fountains in the streets, and private individuals could be connected to it on payment of charges. The surplus flushed the sewers and waste water was normally channelled into a proper system of drains. Not all of these features have been proved at every town, but where a supply has been discovered an outfall must be implied and vice versa. But things could go wrong with municipal engineering, sometimes through ambition outstripping financial resources[1] and sometimes through incompetent architects. At Cirencester the forum subsided into an old military ditch, and we find Pliny writing to Trajan to say that the city of Nicaea has spent an enormous amount of money on a theatre which it cannot finish because the foundations have been badly designed and the building is sinking.[2] In another city a huge set of public baths have been started on an unsuitable site.[3] In both cases the question is whether to make the best of a bad job and finish the building as well as may be, or to start afresh on a new site. Pliny asks the emperor to send out an architect to investigate and advise. Trajan replies that *every province* has architects that can tackle such inquiries, and that it is a problem for Pliny to settle on the spot.[4]

[1] This is one possible explanation for the unfinished baths at Wroxeter.

[2] Pliny, *Letters*, x. 39; x. 40.

[3] In this case the resources are available from the fees of new members whom the emperor has permitted the town to recruit to its council, but money for capital expenditure must often have been difficult to find, since local taxes tended to be services to be supplied rather than cash. Hence the dependence on benefactors.

[4] Trajan also points out that it is a fallacy for Pliny to think an architect can most quickly be obtained from Rome, since they generally go there from Greece, the chief source of the profession.

As well as baths and theatres,[1] the cities also provided the highly popular entertainment of the 'games'. There is no evidence in Britain so far either for the aristocratic and at least theoretically amateur athletics known elsewhere in the empire, or for the construction of 'circuses' for horse and chariot racing,[2] though Procopius tells us that by the sixth century every part of the empire as it then was suffered from the polarization of the population, even in individual families and between husband and wife, into fanatical and often violent supporters of the two teams or 'factions', the Blues and the Greens. However the existence of civil[3] amphitheatres is certain at five Romano-British towns[4] and probable at several others. Beast shows were always popular and gladiators were not finally banned in the west by the Christian emperors till the reign of Honorius. Both were extremely expensive forms of entertainment, sometimes provided by the council or other official bodies, often by rich private individuals. Entry was usually free and under the Republic these games had been a popular means of winning votes. Even during the Empire they were felt to be politically sensitive, for they drew spectacular attention to the wealth and influence of an individual. Gladiatorial shows, in particular, always required official permission and in Italy their presentation was restricted to the imperial family from Domitian's time. In the provinces this absolute restriction did not apply, and it was possible for immense sums to be expended on this side of provincial life. Unattractive though it is to us today, it nevertheless must have performed an important function in providing mass relaxation for all classes of the population and in establishing the city as a regional centre of amusement and pleasure, as well as of commerce and administration. On the other hand, the violence associated with the Blues and the Greens is unlikely to have been the only disorder caused by supporters at public events. Indeed, we know that riots were not uncommon under the Late

[1] For example Canterbury and Verulamium.
[2] There are representations in art but no examples of the circus itself.
[3] This excludes the military amphitheatres at legionary bases such as Caerleon and Chester or the auxiliary fort of Tomen-y-Mur since their prime purpose was probably for weapon training and drill, though they were doubtless also used on occasion for entertainment, executions, or other public occasions.
[4] Dorchester, Silchester, Chichester, Cirencester, Carmarthen.

Empire in connection with the election of bishops, and this aspect of urban life suggests cities may often have been more attractive to visit than live in.

The cities were responsible for the upkeep of public temples and the provision of official religious ceremonial. This was supervised by city priests, of which there were several grades, the best known being the *seviri Augustales* whose exact subdivisions and functions have been the subject of much study. Their function in the celebration of the Imperial Cult was important and the group had a special social role in that its members, unlike the decurions and magistrates, did not have to be of free birth. This provided a route by which well-to-do freedmen could enter the higher ranks of local society and their own sons aspire to municipal office and beyond. Since many of these families were of foreign origin or had originally been taken prisoner in the wars of conquest, the local upper classes were thus enriched by fresh blood. M. Aurelius Lunaris, who was certainly a Roman citizen, describes himself as *sevir Augustalis* of the colonies of Lincoln and of York 'in the Province of Lower Britain' on a dedication he erected in 237 at Bordeaux.[1] His family's citizen status was, from his name, relatively recent and he is presumed to have been shipping wine from the Gironde to Britain. Another *sevir Augustalis* of York was M. Verecundius Diogenes, whose Greek name may indicate slave ancestry. He himself came from the *civitas* centred on Bourges in the Loire region where his family had clearly been absorbed into the Gallo-Roman community, and his wife was Sardinian. Lesser colleges of priests widened even further the net which drew people into public or semi-public affairs.

In theory at least there was a distinction between the chartered towns, the *coloniae* and *municipia*, and the urban centres of the other *civitates* in their relationship to the lands that surrounded them. The actual relationship in each case was detailed in the charter of the particular authority. Broadly speaking a chartered town was itself an official Roman unit of government, the land around was its *territorium* and subject to it, and citizens born there gave the city as their

---

[1] *JRS* 11 (1921), 101.

official place of birth, their *origo*, where they had civic rights and duties. In the other cases the *civitas* or tribal area was the unit and the city had no separate formal existence, though in both groups the concept is the same, the city-state. There are occasional variations, even cases such as Avenches in Switzerland where the *civitas* of the people from the surrounding countryside seems to have had a separate formal existence alongside the city itself.[1]

Before the spread of the citizenship that culminated in the *Constitutio Antoniniana* a citizen's *origo* mattered a good deal, and this is why auxiliary veterans carried with them the diploma that recorded their grant of Roman citizenship. Legionary soldiers' children, being sons of citizens, required an *origo* but were often born in the *canabae* outside the fortress. They were given the origin 'at the camp' (*castris*). This is not wholly a legal fiction, since a legion was a citizen body, commanded by a Roman magistrate—or rather the deputy (*legatus*) of the most powerful of magistrates, the emperor. It could therefore possess a *territorium* of its own and probably be regarded as the equivalent of a chartered town. But all these distinctions became blurred, and it is likely that even while they still retained practical import-ance many people did not understand their niceties. Hence we can place little reliance on the phrases used on private inscriptions such as tombstones to prove the constitutional position of cities given there as origins, unless the inscription is very clearly giving a precise definition of legal status. Of more immediate importance to the individual—unless he became seriously entangled with the criminal law and needed to prove his citizenship—was the distinction between a *civis* of the local authority within whose boundaries a person was living, usually someone born there, and who could not escape certain local obligations, and an *incola*, or incomer from elsewhere, for whom there were different rules.

The two third-century provincial capitals, London and York, provide illuminating examples of how such cities could reach the same point in quite different ways. In neither

---

[1] One may wonder what the future will make of those modern English cities like Birmingham that now house both a city council and a county council, the former being much more prestigiously housed and recorded by public monuments yet being constitutionally much the inferior authority.

case is the evidence absolutely firm, but the details we have hang together reasonably well and can for this purpose be filled out with analogy from elsewhere. Tacitus tells us that at the time of the Boudiccan rebellion London was 'not indeed graced with the title of *colonia* but thronged with merchants and a famous centre of commerce'.[1] We know that groups of Roman citizens, often merchants, resident in a particular place abroad sometimes formed an expatriate organization (*conventus*). An interesting Danubian example is provided by the *cives Romani ex Italia et aliis provinciis in Raetia consistentes* which illustrates that such people were not necessarily all from the same part of the empire.[2] Another inscription gives us 'retired soldiers and local people (*pagani*)[3] living together within the same walls'[4] and we have already seen how the German and Roman inhabitants of Cologne felt themselves as one people in time of crisis. However in the case of London it is possible that the large number of *incolae* from other places may have stunted the growth of a local *ordo* at the same time as it boosted the size and splendour of the city. Even its giant basilica may originally have had a provincial rather than local purpose; but in the end I am sure the absorption of a great variety of people into the citizen body that may have started with a simple if prosperous *conventus* of merchants justified the elevation of the chief city of Britain to full Roman status.

At York we have a different form of growth. Prior to the early third century there was no provincial capital here, but a major legionary fortress, the hub of the army in the north. *Canabae* developed outside its walls in the usual way, and a further civil settlement grew up just across the river to the south. Again we have a Danubian inscription to help. We find the *cives Agrippinenses Transalpini* from the great colony of Cologne on the Rhine settled far away in the legionary *canabae* of Aquincum.[5] This inscription shows us such expatriates mingling with the local population, since they

---

[1] Tacitus, *Ann.* xiv. 33: *cognomento quidem coloniae non insigne, sed copia negotiatorum et commeatuum maxime celebre.*

[2] *ILS* 1362a.

[3] The word comes to mean a countryman, i.e. someone living in a *pagus* or rural district. The survival of non-Christian practices in the Late Roman countryside is reflected in the modern word 'pagan'.

[4] *ILS* 6885.   [5] *CIL* III, 10548.

join with a Roman citizen who was born in the *canabae* there in erecting a memorial to his wife. Gradually a new communiy could form out of such a society and hope for elevation to chartered status.

It is, however, notable that in most of the known cases it was not the *canabae* themselves that were made into cities, but a new foundation created a short distance away or making use of an adjacent settlement. This may have been to avoid problems that would arise if an independent *colonia* existed right up to the walls of the legionary fortress, particularly as there were often military installations such as bathhouses outside the perimeter itself.[1] At York it is virtually certain that the *colonia* consisted of the settlement across the river, raised to that status, certainly by 237[2] and probably either at the time of Severus' residence there (we have noted the reference to a *domus palatina*)[3] or when York became the capital of the new province of Britannia Inferior. It has been noted that the fourth-century description of Severus' death at York in 211 describes it as a *municipium*.[4] If there is any chance of this being accurate, it suggests an intermediate stage. Either or both grants may well have been a reward for loyalty to the Severan House.

As to the ordinary *civitates*, the rate of development is likely to have been very variable as between one and another. At Silchester there is an intriguing fragment of an inscription that seems to record a *collegium peregrinorum*, suggesting that in what one assumes was still a peregrine *civitas* in formal terms the non-citizens were now in such a minority that they had formed their own association.[5] In the case of a *civitas* like the Atrebates, with Silchester in the centre of a peaceful and well-Romanized countryside, one may guess there was comparatively little difference in level of Romanization and spread of citizenship between the town-dwellers and the country people. The distinction, anyhow, would have been

[1] It is interesting that there is a boundary wall between the civil settlement and the fortress at Caerleon. [2] *JRS* 11 (1921), 101.
[3] SHA, *Severus*, xxii. 7. [4] Aurelius Victor, xx. 27.
[5] *RIB* 69: an alternative explanation is that they were *peregrini* because they had an *origo* elsewhere, not that they were non-citizen. I feel this the less likely use of the word; and it would anyhow only increase the reasons for thinking that the *civitas* had become largely citizen without formal action, just as had the *auxilia* of the army by the later second century.

an unreal one to the upper classes, particularly where the countryside with its villas was well developed and the town relatively unsophisticated. A rather different situation may have obtained in the *civitas Cornoviorum*, with its centre at Wroxeter, *Viroconium.* The origin of the town may have lain in the *canabae* of the early legionary base, but they had only a relatively short time to develop before the army moved on, and we have seen the *civitas*-centre suffering a distinctly shaky start in the Flavian period. It looks as if they needed a determined push from Hadrian to sort out their affairs and build themselves a proper civic centre. Their hinterland to the west had still been close to the scene of serious fighting as late as Agricola's war with the Ordovices. Forts were retained for much of the first century throughout their district and for far longer they lay under the shadow of the tribes of the Welsh hills that continued to need some military supervision. This is perhaps the reason for the comparatively small number of villas in the surrounding countryside and the exceptionally large and numerous private houses of the city itself. There is nothing that indicates a difference of status here between town and country, but in practice the contrast must have been marked.

Cirencester and Gloucester are neighbouring cities whose development and that of their countryside are worth comparing. *Corinium Dobunnorum*, too, probably started as a civil settlement outside the early fort, though here as usual it is very difficult to demonstrate actual continuity between such a *vicus* and the subsequent town. Nevertheless its extremely favourable position in the highway system may well have encouraged traders to stay who would otherwise have followed the troops. It is very likely that a general market had grown up, even if unofficially, and one would expect a posting-station to have been retained after the army had gone. Indeed the importance of the site as a centre of commerce is underlined by the fact that in the Hadrianic period it became one of the towns to build a regular market-hall (*macellum*).[1] But there were other reasons for its prosperity as well. In the fourth century it was almost

---

[1] Other examples in Britain are Verulamium, Leicester, and probably Wroxeter, all major cities.

certainly the seat of the governor of a province, and this will have given an additional fillip to the second largest city in Britain. Here not only were the city and its private houses of a high standard but it became the centre of the richest area of villa estates, for which the terrain was particularly attractive. We have, though, no evidence for Cirencester itself having any special status, but one might expect the whole community to have acquired at least an honorific title. In apparent contrast, Gloucester started as a full Roman colony, *Glevum colonia* or *colonia Glevensis*, founded as a settlement of legionary veterans at the end of the first century when it should have been able to take advantage of the Flavian impetus to Romanization in Britain. It ought, too, to have benefited from its position on the Severn, though navigation is not easy and the port seems eventually to have developed, as did the later one, on the Avon at Bristol.[1] Whatever the exact reason, Gloucester does not seem to have attracted the merchants and other foreigners one might have expected. Nor does it seem to have the same rich hinterland as Cirencester, even though we do not know where the boundary ran between the colony and the *civitas Dobunnorum* to the east. To the west were the Silures, who had had such a savage reputation in the fairly recent past, and the lesson of Colchester had perhaps taught Roman colonists to tread warily where their British neighbours were concerned. Sir Ian Richmond suggested that both Lincoln and Gloucester were, unlike Colchester, settled in previously sparsely inhabited territory for just that reason.[2] The riverside lands, too, may have been unattractive to the ex-legionaries as sites for villas and they may have preferred the comfort and security of the city, farming their lands at a distance or through tenants. Though they had a flourishing municipal organization,[3] their housing closely followed the lines of the preceding legionary phase, and on the fringe of the Roman world they may have felt little inclination at first

[1] In fact at Sea Mills, between Clifton Gorge and Avonmouth. We also do not know the effect of the lower relative sea level on the strange tidal flow of the Severn which is still the subject of much research.

[2] However, recent work on the river valleys may change our view of the Iron Age occupation around both Lincoln and Gloucester.

[3] Tiles with the stamp of the *res publica Glevensium* suggest the possession of a municipal tilery, an enterprise paralleled by many legionary tileries.

to move out into the countryside and set themselves up as an essentially villa-dwelling gentry, unlike their British counterparts—or, indeed, their Roman ones in more settled parts of the island.[1] Later, as the area became more peaceful, the colony faced competition from the now-flourishing *civitas Silurum* centred on Caerwent, just possibly a *municipium* or *colonia* at Caerleon, as well as from Cirencester itself. Whatever the reason, it never regained the supremacy among the cities of the south-west it ought to have had nor did it raise the standard of its *territorium* to equal its splendid neighbour. It is not therefore surprising that the fourth-century government brushed aside old distinctions and acknowledged reality if it settled on Cirencester and its region as the centre of a new province.

However, we are justified in enquiring whether the ways of life in Cirencester and Gloucester were really so different. Was the former solely the residence of the rich and the place of business of officials, merchants, and master craftsmen? Was the latter in contrast a close-knit community of veterans and their descendants, owning allocations of land outside the city? The excavation of what appears to be a very comfortable and prosperous fourth-century farmhouse and associated buildings *inside* the walls of Cirencester[2] ought to make us think twice about our conception of Romano-British cities. A purely 'urban' concept is anachronistic. It is also insular, as a cursory exploration of the back-streets of many a modern French or German town of moderate size will reveal.[3] We have to expect a proportion of the inhabitants of most ancient cities to be farming land outside the town or, like the Mayor of Casterbridge, closely involved with agriculture. Similarly we may expect to find farms or 'suburban' villas directly adjacent to the town, as at Kenchester,[4] where

---

[1] It is also a question whether a substantial amount of land may not have been held back for subsequent allotment in anticipation of the release of later batches of veterans from the army, thus inhibiting the rapid growth of private ownership, at least on a large scale by the assembling of small units into large estates by purchase or inheritance.

[2] *Current Archaeology*, 42 (1974), 216 ff.

[3] The difference in this respect between English and Continental towns goes back at least to the seventeenth century.

[4] Under excavation at the time of writing by Professor P. Rahtz (personal communication and *CBA Newsletter and Calendar*, January 1978: 'Summaries 1977', 111).

many of the advantages of both worlds might best be obtained. With the cost of transport high, land for horticulture and pasture, too, was a valuable asset for a city to have in its immediate neighbourhood, to supply it with vegetables, fruit, and other produce for the table. Nor should the presence of farm buildings or even cultivated ground[1] within city walls be taken to prove the decline or abandonment of urban life. Surviving records of medieval walled towns show many examples of orchards, kitchen gardens, and closes for animals.

Another line of approach to the relationship of towns with their surrounding country has been taken by Dr Warwick Rodwell.[2] He has used apparent discrepancies in the distances between towns in the *Antonine Itinerary* to suggest that the *coloniae*, ordinary *civitas* capitals, and some lesser towns had 'town-zones' around them. These were most likely the area within which the city had responsibility for the roads and quite possibly represents the land which it directly owned, though the relationship with the concepts of *prata* and *territorium* need, I think, direct confirmation. It is particularly interesting that by far the largest such zone seems to be round London, which would strengthen the case for its having had a high status. This is a line of research which will make us look with fresh eyes on any new evidence relevant to the setting of towns in their countryside, but, since it also implies that such lands were farmed from within the town, it gives no support at all to any notion that Romano-British cities were divorced from agriculture.[3]

There were hardly any cities in the ancient world that were sharply divided from the country as are the industrial centres

[1] For example, as surmised in London for the third century onwards (*London Archaeologist*, 3 (1978), 227 ff.; CBA *Archaeology in Britain 1978* (1979), 72).

[2] Warwick Rodwell, 'Milestones, Civic territories and the Antonine Itinerary', *Brit.* 6 (1975), 76 ff. In 1967 Dr Irwin Scollar remarked to me in the context of his air surveys in Roman Germany that at that time no villas were known round Cologne or Bonn, that only one had been found near Xanten and one near Neuss and that around Koblenz they did not occur till one was outside a radius of about 10–15 km (6–9 miles).

[3] Much the same conclusion was reached by Professor A.L.F. Rivet (in Rivet (ed.), *The Roman Villa in Britain* (1969), 180 f.) who pointed to the lower Rhône valley where the normality in Roman terms of working land from the city is emphasized by the large number of *coloniae* and the relative infrequency of villas. More recent work on Late Iron Age Britain suggests that the idea was perhaps not as foreign to native Britons at the Conquest as then appeared.

of today. Rome, Constantinople, Alexandria, and perhaps one or two others were large enough to have had a life largely divorced from the country, and the first two of these had a state-organized, free or heavily subsidized food supply that allowed their urban proletariat to exist without being supported either by work on the land or by the employment now given in cities by modern industry. Virgil's awe-struck peasant exclaims:[1]

I was ignorant enough to think the city they call Rome . . . would be like our local town where we often drive our young lambs. I assumed one could imagine the large from the small, as the dog is to the puppy or the kid to the goat. But Rome stands out from all other cities as the cypress towers above the lowly shrubs.

The rest of the free town-dwelling world, if it was not of private means or in public employ, either had to work in trade or in the craft and service industries of the city or was employed in the suburbs and surrounding countryside in agriculture or rurally-based industry.

RURAL PATTERNS

In this section we shall look at the network of country towns and villages, villas and farms of rural Britain. Two aspects that were of great importance to the countryman, religion and industry, will be touched upon only briefly as each needs also to be seen in the context of Roman Britain as a whole, and taken a little later. For the moment, let us continue to hunt down the mistaken notions which have grown up about the contrast between 'town' on the one hand and 'country' on the other. Two further misconceptions have been generally prevalent on this subject until quite recently. One is that there were no villages in Roman Britain, only isolated farms and villas, or at the most a hamlet of two or three homesteads —and even those were on occasion explained away as the product of the 'extended family' or the practice (known from Welsh law) of subdividing the property among all the sons instead of inheritance by primogeniture. This was

[1] Virgil, *Eclogues*, i. 19–25.

believed to be the Celtic pattern, and to have persisted unchanged throughout the Roman period and beyond. The second is that a 'town' in Roman Britain can only be called such if it is demonstrated by written evidence to have been a *colonia, municipium*, or the centre of an ordinary *civitas*, or can be shown archaeologically to possess the main public buildings of a local authority (forum and basilica)—with a strong presumption in cases where those buildings have not yet been found but other suggestive features exist, such as exceptional size or the possession of a regular grid of streets.

The assumption that there were no villages had been viewed with growing mistrust by many and was finally dissolved by Mrs Sylvia Hallam's demonstration that there were large numbers of 'nucleated settlements' in Britain,[1] ranging from tiny hamlets to large villages or small towns, depending on one's preference for an English term to describe them. Since then the idea has been widely accepted. It is much strengthened by the work of Iron Age specialists, for example Professor Barry Cunliffe at Danebury hill-fort in Hampshire, who has shown that permanent settlements on a very substantial scale were well-established in the pre-Roman period. Furthermore, we no longer have to treat the centres of the Catuvellauni and their like, such as Cassivellaunus' hidden stronghold (Wheathampstead?) or Cunobelinus' seat at Colchester, as rarities imported from the Continent at the last moment before the Roman occupation and essentially un-British. Nor do we have to find convoluted reasons for explaining the Roman period 'nucleated' settlements of the north, especially those long known on the fells of Cumbria, or the 'minor settlements' that occur on many of the roads of the south.

However the idea that a 'town' has to be the centre of a local authority still gives trouble. In that it is based on common usage in modern England, this should gradually die out, since we have now reduced large numbers of our own towns, including many boroughs and cities of great antiquity or impressive size, to the level of parish councils. Since 1974

---

[1] S.J. Hallam, 'Villages in Roman Britain: some evidence', *Ant. J.* 44 (1964), 19 ff. This was followed up in greater detail in Phillips (ed.), *Fenland*, 22 ff.

it is not difficult in England to conceive of a town that
performs all the functions of an urban centre except administration. In that the problem derives from difficulties in
understanding the Roman structure, it can best be dispelled
by adding briefly to what has already been said about the
organization of local government. The Romans themselves
seem in practice often to have been not very precise in their
use of terms, and it is clear that in ordinary parlance the city
frequently became identified with the *civitas* itself. This is
particularly clear from the place-names of Gaul, where,
for example, *Lutetia Parisiorum* has survived as Paris and
Augusta Treverorum as Trier, the name of the people, not the
city, having predominated in the Later Roman period. This
process is certainly less pronounced in Britain, but
Durovernum Cantiacorum has become Canterbury and the
process was under way within the Roman period elsewhere
in the province. But there were occasions when the Romans
had to be precise, chiefly in matters to do with a man's
official birthplace and the law. When in earlier research I was
attempting to discover the formal position of the *vici* outside
the forts I was obliged to consider how the Romans treated
vici in general. Fortunately there is an admirable authority,
the jurist Ulpian who wrote under Caracalla and was held
in high regard for his knowledge and handling of earlier
legal writings and precedents. Roman law was a practical
subject and the jurists wrote for the men who were responsible for applying it. Ulpian clearly felt it was necessary to
define the position of a man born in a *vicus*, any *vicus*. The
problem was, we may therefore presume, one that faced
magistrates and on which they needed guidance. 'The man
who was born in a *vicus*', he says 'is considered a citizen of
that authority (*res publica*) to which his *vicus* answers'.[1]
In Roman eyes, then, there was a *res publica* and a *vicus*.
We have already seen that the *res publica* was a unit of
government that could be a civil organization like a *colonia*
or a *municipium* or an ordinary *civitas*. We have seen the
Silures actually using the term when referring to their *civitas*
on an inscription contemporary with Ulpian himself.[2] The

---

[1] *Dig.* L. i. 30: *qui ex vico ortus est, eam patriam intelligitur habere, cui rei
publicae vicus ille respondet.*

[2] *RIB* 311 (Caerwent): . . . *ex decreto ordinis respublica civitatis Silurum.*

unit could also be a military one like a legion; and there were *vici* on imperial estates where the immediate authority was the *procurator saltus*, responsible to the procurator of the province. The *res publica* is therefore in legal terms not a place but something in which authority resides.

Once we realize that a *colonia* or *municipium* is for this purpose the *ordo* and citizens (like the 'Senate and People of Rome'), not the actual city, we should have no difficulty in seeing how in an ordinary *civitas* it is the *ordo* and *cives* that are relevant, not the city where the administrative functions may chiefly be carried out. Conversely, absence of a *forum* and *basilica* in a town does not tell us anything about the status of that town, just that the *res publica* did not use that place to carry out certain administrative functions. This is why '*vicus*' can be used indiscriminately of a village, a settlement outside a fort, a ward of a city, even a sub-division of the *canabae* of a legion. Ulpian was dealing with a universal problem. An individual or an administrator needed to know how someone was to be classified. The case of someone born inside the walls of a colony was the easiest, and the problems became increasingly more difficult as one came to the man born, say, in the *canabae* of a legion or on an imperial estate. Ulpian is saying—find the *res publica* and you will classify the man. This is advice of immediate value to the harassed official trying to determine who has jurisdiction in a particular case or to assess liability for taxation or public service. In common usage the *civitas* did often come to be identified with the city at its centre. I have mentioned how the Classical world thought in terms of the city state, of which the clearest symbol was the actual city. But armed with his Ulpian the local magistrate or administrator could determine the situation of someone born in the neighbouring countryside. The *normal* presumption would be that there was no difficulty: he was in exactly the same position as someone born in one of the *vici* of the city itself. But supposing the man claimed that he was not subject to the jurisdiction of the *civitas*. Then the simple rule was to find whether his *vicus* was in fact subject to some other *res publica*. What matters is not the physical location of the *res publica* but of the *vicus*. Does it lie within or without the boundaries inside which the magistrate's authority is valid? If within, there is no problem. The crucial matter is not difference in status between the city and other towns or villages within the boundaries of the *civitas* but determining the limits of jurisdiction.

As to the *res publica* itself, if the *ordo* chose to meet in the middle of nowhere within its own boundaries, that is where the embodiment of the *res publica*, in other words its magistrates and *ordo*, would for that moment reside. It follows therefore that the possession of a forum and basilica does not by itself prove that a town had a special status apart from other settlements within the *civitas*, only that it was found convenient for the *ordo* to meet there. The provision of buildings for the *ordo* and magistrates and the usual accretion of permanent staff and records would follow naturally from such a decision, but it also follows from the argument that the absence of these buildings from a particular Romano-British urban site cannot be used to prove that it had a lower *legal* status. The country town might have less prestige than the 'civitas-capital' (though, as we shall see it might be no smaller), but it could still be a town in the common sense of the word. Indeed, the archaeologist's term 'civitas-capital' may itself be confusing us, since it is perfectly possible to conceive of a *civitas* that had no one principal town, yet functioned normally with a rural network of small towns and villages within its boundaries.

We have also to remember that the government of the *civitas* by its *ordo* and magistrates was only one of the activities a town could house, and even in the case of a fairly extensive town there is no need to assume that local government was its chief fuction—or even that it was one of its functions at all. This reminds us again of the modern analogy. A 'town' or even a 'city' today can have many roles —economic, social, and even administrative—without being the seat of a substantial unit of local government, and this continues all the way down the scale of 'urban' or 'nucleated' settlement. If we can now accept that there is a continuous spectrum from hamlet to city we can turn—without being bothered further by definitions of status—to the very significant part the country towns played in the landscape of Roman Britain. We noted earlier the importance of the substantial *vici* outside the forts and their relationship to their hinterland. In the parts of the province where no or very few garrisons remained the 'small town' is equally important. Professor Malcolm Todd performed a valuable service in 1970 by reminding us of how little work had been done on them.[1] He collected together what was then known and posed a series of pertinent and difficult questions.

Among the many points Professor Todd made was the matter of size, and he pointed out that to calculate the area enclosed by walls can be misleading, as the extent of extra-mural occupation—or of occupation before the walls were built—is not thereby taken into account. Moreover it does not tell one anything of the *density* of occupation. In addition, some small towns seem to have remained unwalled. Nevertheless their size *relative* to the large towns and the range within their own group is determinable in general terms by looking at walled areas. The administrative capitals, for want of a better term, range from Caistor-by-Norwich (*Venta Icenorum*) at 35 acres (14 hectares) within the walls to Cirencester at 240 acres (97 ha.), with London far outstripping all at 330 (134 ha.). The walled small towns run from Ancaster at 10 acres (4 ha.) to Chesterton (Water Newton) with 45 acres (18 ha.), though the last is about 10 acres bigger than any of the others. Yet Hockwold on the edge of the Norfolk Fens which is unwalled and whose edges are very difficult to define is at least as large as Chesterton and probably larger. Professor Frere has pointed out that the large towns average around 100 acres (40 ha.), and that Gloucester (46 acres, 19 ha.) and the first stage of Lincoln (41 acres, 17 ha.) are misleading because they represent densely packed veteran settlement inside old legionary sites.[2] Nevertheless, the small towns do overlap in size the undoubted administrative capitals and as a group represent the lower end of a fairly continuous scale.

Where these small towns do, however, seem to show a real difference from the large is in their lack of planning, given that our knowledge of their interior layouts is still very sketchy. In certain cases, for example Catterick or Alchester,

[1] M. Todd, 'The Small Towns of Roman Britain', *Brit.* 1 (1970), 114 ff. The proceedings of a subsequent conference in 1975 were published as W. Rodwell and T. Rowley (eds.), 'The "Small Towns" of Roman Britain', *Brit. Arch. Reports*, 15, Oxford (1975).   [2] Frere, *Britannia*, 292.

there is something approaching a grid of streets, but it seems partial and blocks (or *insulae*) are irregularly subdivided by lanes. In others the main street is the only dominant feature, as at Kenchester. To quote Professor Todd:

In general, then, the picture at the larger sites under review is one of limited planning in the main streets, followed, presumably, by haphazard growth as the settlement developed in size. The humbler villages do not appear to have attained even this modest level of planning. In many cases, their elongated character will not have lent itself to such a development, even supposing the idea was ever mooted.[1]

This description might equally well have been written of the civil settlements outside the forts of the northern frontier, and it would also describe the *vicus* recently discovered alongside the fort at Brancaster.[2] The area of cropmarks so far noted at this latter site is 57 acres (23 ha.), and finds have been noted on the ground even further afield. Looking at the published aerial photographs,[3] one cannot help being struck by the resemblance both to Hockwold (and a number of lesser Fenland sites) and to the internal appearance of the small walled towns. At Brancaster there is some attempt at over-all rectilinear planning, with a main crossroads visible east of the fort and another to the west, but there is much irregular subdivision and the ends of the principal thoroughfares divide and wander off. Returning to the north, much the same pattern can be seen at Corbridge, where a walled town developed around the military base.[4] The overall pattern, therefore, is very similar, whether in the south or the north, whether walled or unwalled and whether the civilian settlement is associated with active military stations or is without any known military connection. In summary, what we are saying is that there is a very substantial number of nucleated civil settlements that occur with broadly similar characteristics and cannot be distinguished clearly on archaeological or historical grounds from the administrative capitals at one end of the scale or the smaller villages and hamlets at the other. This means that quite a lot of civilians

[1] *Brit.* 1 (1970), 118.
[2] See particularly Johnston (ed.), *The Saxon Shore*, 21 ff.
[3] Ibid. 23 ff., with plan, fig. 7.
[4] Salway, *Frontier People*, fig. 5. For an unwalled *vicus* outside a fort on Hadrian's Wall see fig. 8 in the same book.

in Roman Britain were living in settlements that were neither large towns nor single farms. Allowing for differences of a regional nature and in the circumstances in which individual settlements originated and developed, there is a broad similarity which not only makes us further revise our older notions of the division between town and country but has important implications both for the transmission of ideas and the general way of life in Roman Britain.

If we look at some of the activities that have been detected in these small towns and their environs we should see better how they relate to the countryside. For this purpose it is fair to exclude the settlements outside the forts, since it is clear that so many of their inhabitants were soldiers' families or civilians otherwise dependent on the army for a living, though their probable function as a market and point of contact with the local farming population is not doubted. For the other small towns, their connections seem to be predominantly agricultural. There are indeed signs of industry, for example at Camerton in Somerset which has produced an important range of pewter moulds, doubtless connected with the lead-production of the nearby Mendip mines and the tin deposits of the south-west. Inside the small towns the ubiquitous 'strip-house' appears, well known in both the settlements outside the forts and in cities such as Verulamium. This type of building is in fact almost inevitable where street-frontage is limited, and while as at Housesteads it is clear it was sometimes an open-fronted shop or workshop with storage and living accommodation behind or above, it is probable that it was also used for other purposes and frequently as a dwelling without commercial activity. Professor Todd has pointed to the presence of the 'aisled-building' in one or two small towns.[1] This is common in the countryside as a farm-house or barn, often as part of a larger villa-complex where it may have been used to house workers as well as animals and farm-equipment, but does not seem to be a normal city type. We may reasonably imagine all small towns to have had some shop-keepers and small craftsmen, but, to quote Professor Todd in 1970: 'Chesterton, Mancetter and possibly Weston-under-Penyard are the only places yet

[1] *Brit.* 1 (1970), 120 ff.

known to have depended upon industry as a mainspring of their economic life.'[1] I am not sure that this list is now exhaustive, but the general point stands. Temples seem to be relatively common, as normal both in ancient cities and countryside, and we ought not to forget their effect on the economic life of a town or their role in bringing people together, with results not all connected with religion. A place like Springhead, in Kent, which has a large group of religious buildings reminiscent of the 'temple region' of the city of Trier, may well have become prosperous as a pagan pilgrimage centre. But in the end we have to come back to agriculture. Professor Todd rightly emphasizes this point: 'Some of the evidence available to us suggests further that a number of the component buildings of these minor settlements were themselves the homes of farmers. While this might in any case appear inherently likely, conclusive evidence can hardly be said to exist'.[2] Yet despite the shortage of direct evidence from these settlements this accords with what we have already said about the cities. It is likely to have applied equally, probably much more, to the small towns.

The grouping of the villas themselves is also worth further exploration in this context.[3] On another occasion Professor Rivet observed that hardly any villas were more than half a day's ride from a town,[4] yet it is the smaller towns of which this is true, not the main cities. This suggests to me that villas had a good deal of day-to-day business with the country towns, and only on infrequent occasions with the cities.[5] It is not difficult to imagine why. It must surely be that the lesser towns provided the essential services, shops, and marketing facilities, but had nothing that would encourage the upper classes to move into them, a point supported by the apparently sparse provision of such amenities as public baths. The cities, however, did have the facilities for civilized living and also an active public life. Thus we may imagine the upper-class Romano-Briton either moving into a city or living part of his time on his country property, part in the city. Indeed, he might even prefer the provincial capital itself to

[1] Ibid. 129.   [2] Ibid. 129.
[3] See Note, p. 614 below, for discussion of the term 'villa'.
[4] Archaeological News Letter, 6, 2 (1955), 32.
[5] Cf. Salway, Proc. Camb. Phil. Soc. n.s. 13 (1967), 35 f.

his own local city, when public duties did not compel him to spend his time in the local courts and council-chamber.

The small town, therefore, is essentially dependent on the countryside, either because it largely houses people who work the land or because it serves the daily needs of the estates and peasant farmers of the district, probably both. Even where there is industry on any scale this is still true, since in Roman times industry was by and large located in the country, not the big cities. The distribution of villas, however, points to one other function the country town may commonly have had. We earlier noted the development of small towns on the main highways, particularly in connection with the Imperial Post, and cited some examples of *mansiones*, as at Godmanchester. Various modern writers have noted the interesting phenomenon that towns in Roman Britain, especially small towns, often have just one villa close to them, for example Great Casterton. These have been named 'satellite villas', and may in some cases in fact have been *mansiones*. Thus the *strator* who was buried at the small town of Irchester may have been stationed there to provide horses for the governor and his staff. But if these satellites do have an official purpose, there may well have been other officials who used them. One thinks of the *beneficiarius consularis* at Dorchester-on-Thames, for example, or the imperial freedman Naevius in the employ of the procurator's department whose reused inscription was found near the villa at Combe Down just outside Bath.[1] Where the occasional villa occurs just outside a city, as at Cirencester, one is tempted to think of a more exalted official, such as the *correctores* who, as we have noted, are known to have been appointed in other provinces to supervise the running of local government on behalf of the emperor.

In the case of a major city such as Cirencester, one may expect sometimes to find further out the luxurious villa, for example Woodchester, to which a prominent gentleman might ride out for the night after a day's work in public affairs, as Pliny liked to do from Rome to his place at Laurentum.[2] In the fourth century, to which Woodchester

---

[1] It is possible that the villa itself was the headquarters (*principia*) he restored, or the residence of the local procurator of an imperial property.

[2] Pliny, *Letters*, ii. 17.

and its like in Britain chiefly belong, Ausonius describes his country house as being not far from the city, yet not close up to it, so that he may exchange one for the other, as the fancy takes him.[1] It is not clear to what extent this was considered acceptable behaviour by the authorities. Probably people of the highest senatorial rank could do much as they pleased, in Ausonius' day as much as in Pliny's. However in the fourth century the emperors seem to have made strenuous efforts to prevent decurions from moving home completely into the countryside. Laws of 367 and 396 or 397 specifically prohibit the practice, the latter laying down confiscation of the country property as the penalty for so 'impiously abandoning one's native town'[2] and the former emphasizing that there had been many previous edicts on the subject.[3] The laws can hardly have been to prevent tax evasion, since *curiales* who moved house would still have remained responsible for their public duties and taxes. A more likely motive on their part was avoidance of the unofficial burdens placed upon them by custom rather than law. What this could mean to a Roman gentleman is illustrated by the case of Apuleius. His marriage took place at the suburban villa which belonged to the widow who was to be his bride in order to avoid the distribution of largesse to the urban populace that had taken place at the marriage of her son.[4] The emperors seem to have been more troubled by a threatened decay of the cities,[5] perhaps motivated by the greater difficulty of political surveillance. It is ironic that the moralists of the Republic had deplored the opposite movement. Varro laments the fact that in the good old days people only attended to business in town one day in eight, while in his day, the late first century BC, practically all heads of families[6] have moved into the city. But we have to remember that he is speaking from

---

[1] Ausonius, *De Herediolo*, 29–32: this passage was kindly brought to my attention by Professor A.L.F. Rivet.

[2] *Cod. Theod.* XII. xviii. 2.   [3] Ibid. XII. xviii. 1.

[4] Apuleius, *Apologia*, lxxxvii.

[5] *Cod. Theod.* XII. xviii. 1: *ne vacuatis urbibus ad agros magis, quod frequenti lege prohibetur, larem curiales transferant familiarem.*

[6] Referring, of course, to the landowning class. Nevertheless we have also to remember the anxiety under the later Republic over the flight to the City of the small farmer who could no longer make ends meet, both swelling the idle urban mob and reducing the traditional recruiting ground of the citizen army.

the traditionalist standpoint that believed country life and country people infinitely preferable to the city.[1] Moreover when he was writing there was no threat to urban prosperity or the political organization that depended on it and his preoccupations were quite different from those of the Late Roman emperors, though his ideals were the same as many fourth- and fifth-century Romans. But emperors had to deal with immediate problems facing them, and their edicts reflect what was actually happening. The frequency with which edicts had apparently been issued indicates that little headway was made. Whatever the full reasons for the legislation, the practice was clearly common, and in Britain fits with the evidence for construction and refurbishing of villas late in the fourth century to indicate that the Roman pleasure in the countryside was still unabated. There is no sign here of a wealthy class taking shelter behind the city walls, retreating from a countryside no longer safe.

I have so far in this chapter assumed that the inhabitants of the Romano-British villas were local gentry,[2] apart from the few officials about whom I have speculated. However it is certain that even in Britain the pattern was much more complicated. Some of the grandest villas such as Fishbourne or Folkestone were indeed probably official residences, yet many, both large and small, must have belonged privately to individuals other than the *curiales* of the cities of Britain. We have seen the possibility that much land was owned by rich men who lived elsewhere in the empire. Even British land-owners need not have been local. A.H.M. Jones summarizes the overall picture:

Landlords, both great and small, rarely owned a single consolidated estate. Their possessions were usually scattered and consisted of a number of farms, some larger, some smaller. The greatest landlord of

[1] Varro, *Rer. Rust.* II. Intro. 3; II. Intro. 1.

[2] Dr and Mrs Rodwell have suggested that the first Roman phase at Rivenhall (Essex) which dates from *c.* AD 60–75 represents the residence of a Trinovantian aristocrat rather than a colonist from Colchester, even though it is exceptionally early. It was preceded in the early first century AD by a 'native' site with unusally rich material, including two Celtic mirrors (*Brit.* 4 (1973), 116 ff.). This villa continued in use till the end of the Roman period, and its 'aisled barn' appears to have been occupied by people using Germanic pottery and glass in the fifth century, in effect becoming a Germanic hall. This would suggest the possibility of continuous occupation by native British aristocracy until replaced directly by Germanic successors.

the empire, the *res privata*, owned besides some large blocks of territory, mostly ancient royal lands, countless estates which had accrued to it by bequest, escheat or confiscation in every province and almost every city. The great churches, as a result of donations and bequests from emperors and other great benefactors, acquired very far-flung estates ... The estates of great private landlords were often scattered over many provinces. Symmachus in his letters mentions twelve villas which he owned in various parts of Italy, and speaks of his lands in Samnium, Apulia, Sicily and Mauretania. The biographer of Melania draws a vivid picture of her making a leisurely progress from Rome to Carthage, systematically selling her estates in Campania, Apulia, Sicily, Africa, Numidia and Mauretania: she also owned lands in Spain, which were at the moment unsaleable owing to the barbarian invasions, and even, we are told, in Britain. Senators had many opportunities of acquiring lands in distant provinces. Though they were forbidden to exploit their authority in this way, they married rich heiresses in the provinces which they governed ...[1]

Land was not only attractive because it was the basis of high social respectability: unlike the present age it was also extremely profitable to be the owner of landed property on a large scale. Melania drew a huge income, yet she was financially only in the middle rank of the fourth-century senatorial class in the west.[2] This, of course, was also the century of the greatest development of the villa in Britain, and we saw earlier the suspicion that some owners may have transferred themselves, or at least their investments, from Gaul to Britain at that time. We have no way of knowing how often a particular villa might see its owner, if ever. We must very often be dealing with tenants or bailiffs, the latter, the *vilicus*, frequently being a freedman or trusted slave. Yet some great owners did care much about their property and travelled to visit it. Pliny complains frequently about the labour of looking after his own and his mother's estates, yet conveys the impression that he rather enjoyed it. The relationship between such a landlord and the country people, both his own tenants and the people of the local town, is brought out in a letter he wrote to the emperor:[3]

Your late father, Sir, the deified emperor Nerva, encouraged public benefactions both in his speeches and by his example. I asked him if I might transfer to the town of Tifernum statues of earlier emperors I

---

[1] A.H.M. Jones, *Later Roman Empire*, 781 f.
[2] Ibid. 554.   [3] Pliny, *Letters*, x. 8.

had acquired as the result of legacies and which, as they came, I had
housed on my estate some way from the town. I further asked if I
might add one of himself. He gave his permission and I wrote immediately to the town council asking them to designate a site on which
I could erect a temple at my own cost. Their answer did me the honour
of allowing me to choose the site myself . . . I should therefore be very
grateful if you would let me add a statue of yourself to the others that
will be housed at the temple I am intending to build and also give
me leave of absence from my duties so that I can have the work done
as soon as possible. However I should be lacking in candour if I exploited
your kindness by not mentioning the benefit to my own private affairs.
The farms I possess in that area produce an income of over 400,000
sesterces, and I cannot put off letting them, particularly as the new
tenants should be in to take care of the pruning of the vines, and this
has to be carried out more or less immediately. Also a series of bad
harvests have made me think that I must consider reducing rents, and
to estimate the amounts I must be there myself. If you will allow me
thirty days leave I shall be most grateful at being able to complete my
demonstration of loyalty to you and settle my own affairs there.
I am afraid I cannot manage in less time, as the town and the farms are
more than 150 miles from Rome.

It will readily be appreciated from the foregoing that it is
generally impossible to know from archaeological evidence
alone whether on a particular villa site we are dealing with a
resident owner or the property of someone who rarely
appeared in person, if ever. Cato urged owners to build a
villa urbana[1] on their properties, for it would give them an
incentive to visit them and a farm that was frequently seen
by its proprietor was one that flourished.[2] However, whether
the incentive always worked is another matter. Nevertheless
an occasional villa like Lullingstone in Kent where a pair of
Antonine family busts were apparently venerated and later
sealed in a basement room prior to the establishment of a
private Christian chapel or possibly a 'house-church',[3] allows
one to guess at personal occupation. This still seems true
there in the fourth century, when the full-length figures
painted on the walls seem to be family portraits. On the
other side of the coin it is equally rare that one has sufficient
evidence to postulate imperial estate or, in the late period,
Church property. The ninety-seven infant burials at the
Hambleden villa near Marlow point strongly to a rural industry

[1] See Note, p. 614 below.   [2] Cato, *De Agri Cultura*, iv. 1.
[3] Cf. p. 724 below.

employing female slaves. The fact that the villa was a modest one, facing away from the compound, has suggested the enterprise was an imperial weaving-mill or similar state concern supervised by an official, though it could equally have been under the resident agent of a great property owner. In the case of the very simple villas we shall not know whether they were in the hands of free owners of modest means, or tenants (in the fourth century probably tied to the land), or of bailiffs.

Proceeding down the scale from these simple villas there is a gradual progression to the more or less untouched native farm, and I am not convinced that any clear line can be drawn between them. Differences in prosperity, in the availability and price of materials, and in local taste make it extremely likely that what was acceptable in one part of the country was not in another at the same level in society, and that these standards changed with time within a locality. In the Fens, for example, there is very little large timber and no stone to be had locally: the building materials to hand are clay and reeds. Yet comfortable and long-lasting houses are still made of these materials in East Anglia, and both the size of the house-plots and the amount of Roman portable objects, including plate and coin hoards, that have been found in the region suggest a good standard of life. I think that future advanced research has to concentrate on defining the standards within a particular area at a particular time, comparing sites with their neighbours and establishing local definitions, before it will be possible to label any one example with confidence. We now have to recognize that when we use 'villa' as a technical term in Romano-British studies we have to use it with different emphasis and different degrees of precision depending on circumstances. We also have to recognize that when we use it as a technical term, we may not be employing it in quite the way a Roman would have done. It is quite obvious that we should follow Roman practice and confine it to houses in the country.[1] But our problem is a special one: we need some criteria by which to distinguish the *archaeological* remains of villas. Thus for our purposes we may need to be more exclusive

---

[1] See Note p. 614 below.

in our use of the word than a Roman. Just where he would
have drawn the line between a 'native' house and a villa at the
lower end of the scale we do not know, and the probability
is that he would not have needed to worry about it. Even
remembering the proviso above about establishing standards
for particular times and places it is, for example, impossible
to know whether the large farmhouses of the fourth century
northern Fenlands would have been villas or not to a Roman
observer. But, without being too pedantic, we do need both
local definitions (as we have observed) and on the level of
generalization we must tackle in a book of this kind a broader
definition that is not too far from the concept of a 'Roman
villa' which has an accepted, if in detail inaccurate, meaning
to the informed layman. Probably the nearest we can
approach such a description is to apply the word to any
house in the countryside that has clear signs of the inhabitants
having both accepted to a significant degree the Roman style
of life and achieved the prosperity to put this into practice
in more than a very minor way. Archaeologically this is
likely to require signs of Roman forms of building
construction and decoration to a certain level—for example
tiles, dressed stone, painted plaster, hypocausts, or mosaics.
An abundance of pottery or small finds of little intrinsic
value will not do for this purpose, as there is ample evidence
for these being acquired by communities that otherwise
changed their style of life very little. On the other hand, we
shall certainly miss some villas by using these purely archaeological criteria, since there must have been examples
(particularly where building materials were expensive or
relatively impermanent) which do not show up archaeologically but whose inhabitants had adopted personal fashions and
a Roman outlook on life to a considerable degree. Such are
the limitations of archaeology.

Admitting the uncertainties inherent in the nature of the
evidence, it is nevertheless worth looking at the distribution
of Romano-British villas as defined in one or two stretches
of countryside, for something of social significance may
emerge. We may start by taking the very example of the
Fenland, for there is a major difference between the seaward
and inland parts of it. I know of not one unmistakably
Romanized house on the silt lands towards the Wash (if we

can omit the large fourth-century farms whose status is uncertain). In that part it appears that, once the district to be occupied was defined by higher authority, a large number of peasant cultivators were allowed to develop the land in the early second century as best they could, probably, but not certainly, as tenants of imperial property. Thus the overall pattern is built-up of hundreds of small single farms and nucleated settlements, surrounded by their stockyards and other small enclosures, some probably tilled, and tending to cluster in groups with large open areas between, not unlike much of the medieval English landscape. But of the Fed Edge inland I wrote in 1970:[1]

The skirtlands present a rather different pattern of settlement. The small single farms or minor village settlements still appear, but there is a fair sprinkling of sites on which there are known or probable villas (e.g. at Exning, Swaffham Prior and Feltwell). These occur even as near the silts as the island of Stonea and Denver. It might be thought that some of these represent the estates of private persons, perhaps the *conductores* who farmed the rents of the imperial properties. At any rate it is impossible to argue for an imperial estate in the peat fens and their skirtlands as a whole on the grounds of a uniform lack of villas, though of course this cannot rule out the possibility that the Emperors acquired these villa properties piecemeal . . . Indeed there is a little evidence for the presence of one of the Severan political party on one of the sites at Mildenhall, which suggests that the process of confiscation which was so drastic in Spain was being carried out also in the province which had produced Severus' most formidable rival. It also does not rule out the presence of substantial blocks of imperial domain land in between these private estates—part of Mr. Bromwich's area,[2] for instance, has this appearance and significantly seems to have traces of planned layout. Nevertheless, remains in the skirtland seem to suggest the individual *fundus* (farm or estate) as the unit rather than vast tracts of imperial *saltus* let out to small tenants. This is, indeed, likely, since most of it was not virgin land, unlike the silts, but had had Iron Age occupation even if this was sometimes sparse. Similarly in the area immediately adjoining the fen edge proper, around Maxey and Tallington, pre-Roman boundaries were retained in use. It seems very likely that some properties passed into Roman hands intact, or remained in those of Romanized descendants of the pre-Roman owners. Such people, moreover, are the most likely to have become decurions and *conductores*.

---

[1] Salway, in Phillips (ed.), *Fenland*, 12.
[2] Mr J.l'a. Bromwich, one of the co-authors of the RGS Roman Fenland survey, carried out a very extensive programme of research on an area of the south-eastern Fenland.

Other types of evidence from different parts of the country point in the same direction. It may well have been Romanized gentry of this sort who erected the great barrows or burial mounds known as the Bartlow Hills, on the Essex border not many miles south of the Fen Edge. There is a little evidence for a modest villa alongside these striking family monuments, one of which produced, among the rich collection of grave goods of Roman manufacture, an iron folding-stool such as a slave would carry for his master's use. As Agricola realized, it was not too difficult for tribal aristocrats to adopt Roman ways. The villa at Park Street in Hertfordshire was preceded by a native farm, and it is the earlier phase that produced a slave chain and a manacle. Similarly the great Iron Age hoard of metalwork found in the ancient lake of Llyn Cerrig on Anglesey represents a collection of objects from many parts of Britain and seems to have been thrown in as votive deposits in the first century BC. It includes a gang chain, which must have been made for slaves or prisoners well before the Roman conquest. There is no direct evidence in Roman Britain for the great slave-run estates or *latifundia* of Republican Italy, with their barracks reminiscent of the American South. By imperial times Roman writers were doubting their economic efficiency and preferring tenant farmers;[1] and by the second century AD there was a move towards rents paid as a percentage of the crop rather than as a fixed annual sum, as being more flexible in terms of good years and bad and overcoming the sort of management problem we have seen worrying Pliny. Two long seasons of excavation on the second-century small town or village site at Hockwold produced vast quantities of coarse pottery (though very little fine) but not a single coin, and there was a suspicion that the settlement was attached to a

[1] Indeed Varro (op. cit. I. xvii. 3) writing in the late first century BC prefers free hired labourers to slaves as bringing a better return. Cato, a century earlier, does mention the rations to be allowed for chain-gangs, but is already also talking about the rules for tenancies in which free men worked the land in return for a small proportion of the crop (Cato, op. cit. lvi; cxxxvi–vii). Under the Empire, as conquests became less frequent and the demands of the army for recruits from captured barbarians rose, the availability of new slaves must have become less. Home-born slaves were indeed barred from joining the army under severe penalties (an enactment much in the interest of the slave-owners) but prisoners of war were a different case if the state decided to enrole them.

villa. It looked like a settlement where money was hardly used, and suggested either slaves or tenants paying in kind.[1]

Security for the tenant on a Roman estate was theoretically very poor: tenancies were re-let at regular intervals, normally five years or less, and the system is reminiscent of the 'hiring-fairs' for servants that existed in rural England till recent times. Nevertheless in practice a good tenant was a great asset, and one may imagine that the re-letting of the tenancies on an estate was often more like the stages in a modern lease where the rent may be revised. Moreover emperors anxious to encourage the cultivation of marginal lands improved security of tenure, in some cases making it (like modern agricultural tenancy reform) hereditary, and granting remission of rent for those prepared to take on poor land. In some cases those who wanted good land had also to take a proportion of bad. The movement over the centuries was away from slave-worked direct labour estates towards a system of long-term tenancies, passing from generation to generation and paying their rent as a percentage of the product in money or kind. Diocletian's act in making these *coloni* into a tied occupation, like so many of his reforms, took an existing trend, enlarged upon it, and gave it the force of law. In the fourth century, the villa-system was indeed beginning to look very like the medieval relationship of lord and peasant.

Returning to the southern Fenlands, we find that the occupation clustered thickly in a band along the slopes leading down towards the peat fen proper, with practically no finds actually from the peat itself, yet soon becoming scarce as one proceeds uphill beyond the twenty-five foot contour. There was intense utilization of the gravel terraces by farms of simple native type, and such villas as there were had pleasant sites on the slopes. It seems clear that the fen was being intensively exploited, and that Roman settlement and field systems came as close as possible to (and clearly occasionally below) the flood line. As far as can be judged the villas themselves were comparatively modest, probably in the main representing the homes of native farmers who had managed to achieve a reasonable degree of

---

[1] See *Proc. Camb. Ant. Soc.* 60 (1967), 39 ff.

Roman comfort. But there were a few rather grander establishments (for example the probable villa at Fenhouse Farm,
Brandon) and we have to remember the discovery of the
Mildenhall Treasure, which appears, apart from some slight
uncertainty, to have come from another site in that neighbourhood. Indeed the south-eastern corner of the Fenland
does seem to have been a sector where there was some
concentration of larger villas, and perhaps rather fewer of the
native farms. Nevertheless, we may be reasonably certain that
all these villas were making the maximum possible use of the
fen, without being uncomfortably close to it.

A very similar pattern, with villa settlement relatively high
on the slope and native farms further down, is emerging on
the northern edge of the Somerset levels. A more extreme
example of this tendency of villa and native types of
establishment to occupy separate but adjacent areas appears
in yet another part of the country. Publication by the
Oxfordshire Archaeological Unit of the survey of the Oxford
Upper Thames gravels (confirmed by subsequent excavation) has shown that the riverine gravel terraces were
intensively settled and farmed in Iron Age and Roman
times.[1] The general appearance of the native settlements is
very similar to those in the Fens. Here, however, the
important extra dimension has been added to our knowledge.
In the Fenland the waterlogged nature of the land in the
immediate pre-Roman period had prevented Late Iron Age
occupation. In the Upper Thames Valley, on the other hand,
Iron Age farmers had been active, and it is clear that the
decisive change to a settled form of agriculture with regular
boundaries had already taken place before the area fell into
Roman hands. Yet there is very little trace of villas on the
river plain itself—a marginal site being the probable villa at
Ducklington, near Witney.[2] Yet once the slopes of the
Cotswolds are reached the narrow valleys of the tributaries
of the Thames, particularly the Windrush, Evenlode, and
Glyme, are thick with one villa after another. They were
presumably served by side-roads (*diverticula*) off Akeman

---

[1] D. Benson and D. Miles, *The Upper Thames Valley*, Oxford (1974).
[2] The site is at Red Lodge on the Ducklington by-pass (*Brit.* 7 (1976), 336,
but see *Brit.* 8 (1977), 400 for corrected location). Finds extend into the fifth
century.

Street, which crosses these valleys on its way from Alchester
to Cirencester. Today this is still a district of large country
houses, and like theirs the home-farm boundaries of the villas
must often have come close to one another or marched
together, making a continuous landscape. These villas fall
into the eastern sector of the great spread of villas round
Cirencester, and number amongst them such celebrated
examples as North Leigh, Stonesfield, and Ditchley.[1] I should
like to hazard a guess that the villas belonged to landowners
who deliberately chose to site their country houses and parks
in these very pleasing upland valleys, each close to the
congenial company of his neighbours, in good sporting
country[2] and conveniently sited adjacent to the fast road
to the small town at Alchester which was ten miles or so in
one direction and the city of Cirencester around twenty-five
in the other.[3] At the same time, we may surmise, their
tenants were farming other properties belonging to them on
the less picturesque but easily worked flat lands along the
Thames itself. There, with boundaries already fixed and a
settled pattern of agriculture already in operation, the
landowners (Roman or Romano-Briton) will have been
obliged to make few changes in the physical layout of the
landscape or in methods of working, but, one suspects, many
in organization and management.[4]

We are still hampered in any attempt to reconstruct life
in a villa by the strange fact that after two centuries of

[1] See p. 560 above for Professor Hoskins's discussion of the probable size and
boundaries of the Ditchley villa estate. The excavations of the Shakenoak villa
have been appearing in a series of privately published reports over the past few
years, and represent at the time of writing the most recent detailed information
from any of this group of villas.

[2] Cf. Varro (op. cit. III. xii. 2) which mentions the four square miles of
chasse gardée owned in Transalpine Gaul by Titus Pompeius. One wonders if the
palaeobotanists will be able to tell us how far back Wychwood forest goes.

[3] Alchester is one of the small towns that may have had a market-building
(*Brit.* 1 (1970) 123): cf. p. 584 above. As a small town it seems to have been a
rather superior example: there is an approximation to a street-grid (ibid. 118)
and it was probably walled early (the *terminus post quem* for the rampart-backing
to the stone wall, which are all of a period, is the late second century (*Brit.*
6 (1975), 256). In lawless times it could be a disadvantage for a town (or a villa)
to be on or near a main road.

[4] Excavation at Odell in Bedfordshire (see Brian Dix, *Current Archaeology*,
66 (1979), 215 ff.) similarly suggests that the Roman Conquest hastened, rather
than originated, 'the development of an ordered society and countryside'.

digging on villa sites we still have hardly one in which both the main house and the subsidiary buildings have been excavated. The second problem is the impossibility of being sure to what use many of the rooms in any particular villa were put.[1] Nevertheless we can say that the diversity of plan is wide. At one end there is the simple single range, often quite small, only differentiated in our definition from the native house by the use of some Roman materials—tiles, perhaps, or cut stone, or wall-plaster or concrete floors—and a rectangular plan (though rectangular, rather than round, houses are not entirely unknown in Iron Age Britain). To this was sometimes added a corridor, and then short wings between which the corridor might make a veranda. In some instances a second corridor is found at the back. Some such structure tends to form the core of the larger villas. In them it is not unusual to find much longer wings, which are then joined at their ends by a wall and gate, making an enclosed front yard or garden. It is relatively rare to find a court completely enclosed on all sides by buildings, though Fishbourne does display this feature and has minor courts of the same type also incorporated in the wings. Beyond the gate is sometimes a second courtyard and a second wall and gate or gatehouse, this lower court seeming to have more humble buildings. It is not uncommon for one of the wings or lesser buildings to be in the form of the aisled building I mentioned earlier, which also occurs by itself as a small villa. The main house is generally supplied with at least one bath-suite, usually in a wing and sometimes more or less self-contained. The centre is frequently occupied by a large room, often with a recess at the back and small passage-like rooms at the side. This room may possess the best mosaics in the house and be one of those heated by means of under-floor and wall ducts, the latter also serving as flues to draw off the smoke from the furnace which supplies heat to the hypocaust below the floor. It is reasonable to assume that this main room is the principal reception room, often serving as the *triclinium* or main dining-room, the top table being placed in the alcove. The side-rooms may well be pantries and

---

[1] The final result is also often the result of many alterations, reconstructions and additions over the years which are not always easy to disentangle. It is indeed often not even possible to be sure which parts were in use at the same time.

serveries. Kitchens are found in the wings, and water-supply by well, spring, or pipe is to be expected, and drains were provided for baths, kitchen, and latrines.

The outer court is most likely to show signs of use for service and agricultural purposes, but this is where our knowledge from excavations fails us most, primary concentration having been till very recently on the mosaics, wall-plaster, and more elaborate architecture of the principal blocks. We should, however, expect at the least to find stables, coach house, accommodation for domestic and perhaps farm staff, and storage of every kind, including barns and granaries. While it is reasonably certain that almost every villa will have been in some sense a working establishment (mostly agricultural but a few running rural industries),[1] we know far too little about the actual examples, and there may have been one or two that were purely residential, perhaps for very occasional use. In all these things the pattern is very close to the country houses of England from the fifteenth or sixteenth century to recent times.

Further development of our picture of the life of the Romano-British villa may be possible from another observation made in the Fenland:

A further interesting feature appears in connection with a number of the probable sites of villas in the southern Fen area. This is the apparent association of a villa with a village. Examples of this are at Hockwold, Brandon, Denver, Stonea and Somersham/Colne. There are other possible instances, and it is likely that this conjunction of manor house with village, common in Gaul, was more often met with in Roman Britain than has been usually supposed.[2]

Since that observation was made it has been suggested that the village could in Gaul often outlive the villa,[3] and we

[1] It is important not to glorify all signs of crafts or manufacture with the misleading term 'industry'. The needs of a large house and estate have always been likely to make it economical and sensible to employ a substantial number of craftsmen to make and repair objects and to carry out quite elaborate processes such as brewing or smithing.

[2] Salway, in Phillips (ed.), *Fenland*, 12 (where references to the particular sites will be found). At Hockwold in particular I would not like to press the villa identification too far, but since writing that passage possible examples have begun to emerge in other parts of the country—including Lockington and Cromwell in the Trent Valley, and Whitminster (Gloucestershire).

[3] R. Agache, *Détection aérienne*, 207 ff. Possible implications, for a breakdown of the relationship between lord and dependants within the Roman period, of a similar phenomenon noted in Bulgaria are raised in a review in *JRS* 67 (1977), 229.

should perhaps be more on the lookout in Britain for the
remains of villas close to Saxon settlements or to medieval
villages. Deserted medieval villages and excavations in
churches and churchyards would perhaps be a particularly
rewarding field in this context. The observations that the
barn at Rivenhall became a ready-made Saxon hall in the
fifth century and that finds from the churchyard point to
continued occupation of the site throughout Anglo-Saxon
times suggest at the least that suitable parts of villa out-
buildings could be used in apparently peaceful continuity.
The same is perhaps much more likely to have been true on a
wide scale of the associated villages, where Germanic people
may already have been settled or where a purely British
peasant population simply passed from one master to another.

We can study peasant settlement in the Roman period in
two ways. The Fenland survey allowed us to look at a large
area where there had been very little Iron Age occupation,
so that it was possible to study a pattern of peasant occupation without it having been predetermined by existing
settlement. Another large-scale project in the south seeks to
look at the problem the other way round—the total history
of a landscape where there has been more or less continuous
farming before, during, and after the Roman period and on up
to the present day. Differences and similarities between the
two landscapes should, for the purposes of the Romano-
British historian, be extremely illuminating. This project is
the Society of Antiquaries' research into the evolution of the
landscape launched in 1973, which has chosen three areas
in Hampshire. To quote the *Antiquaries Journal*:

Wessex has been chosen for the first sponsored investigation because it
has such an extent and variety of prehistoric and Roman remains that a
large number of visible connections or relationships are available for
investigation. In general this means that there are innumerable ditched
enclosures, boundaries, burial mounds, ritual monuments, field systems
and so on—sufficient to demonstrate a high degree of integration of
religious and secular features and also to present a series of determinable
links and sequences.[1]

Both of these studies are of course in the south. In the

[1] Collin Bowen and Barry Cunliffe, *Ant. J.* 53 (1973), 10: the areas are
approximately Windmill Hill, Crawley, to Brockley Warren; around Danebury;
and about 6 sq. miles near Chalton (around 15 sq. km).

areas of Britain permanently garrisoned the impact of Rome
is likely to have been different from that where an almost
totally civilian Roman way of life developed, but it was not
necessarily any the less. The communities perhaps the least
likely to have been culturally affected are those that dwelt
beyond Hadrian's Wall. I consider it probably outside my
brief and certainly beyond my competence to deal with the
peoples of the Highlands of Scotland and the northern isles
that were never thoroughly conquered and only momentarily
even in name within the empire. But for the sites between
the Antonine and Hadrianic Walls we are fortunate that many
years of fieldwork and excavation have given us a considerable amount of detailed information.[1] Mr Jobey's study of
the problems of estimating population size incidentally gives
us much to think about in the broader context of rural life
under Roman rule:

A now well-known phenomenon in the eastern Border counties is the
manner in which non-defensive stone-built settlements of the Roman
period can be seen to overlie earlier hillforts and related settlements,
providing thereby not only a general context for the stone-built settlements but also what has been claimed as an eloquent reflection of the
pax Romana at work in parts of the Tyne-Forth Province.[2] What is
perhaps not generally realized is the extent to which this may occur.
There are seventy-one possible instances in the four counties under
consideration, not including other occasions where later stone-built
settlements lie in such close proximity to earlier defensive works
that there could be little to quibble about in attributing to them the
same location. Further excavation on less well-preserved sites in the
more low-lying areas could also reveal more examples, as the recent
excavations at Hartburn illustrate ... some nineteen per cent of the
surviving hillforts and related settlements in the four counties would
at the moment appear to have later stone-built huts either within them,
overlying their defences, or immediately adjacent to them. It is of
course not known if these later huts represent settlement on the same
site without any significant break in occupation, and excavated
examples do not always give an unequivocal answer ... In terms of
size it may be noted that many of these later settlements ... remain

[1] See particularly G. Jobey, 'Notes on some population problems in the area
between the two Roman Walls', *Arch. Ael.* 5th ser. 2 (1974), 17 ff.; and excavation
reports in other issues of *Archaeologia Aeliana*. Much mapping work has also been
done on the Scottish side of the Border by the Royal Commission on the Ancient
and Historical Monuments of Scotland. An earlier summary by Mr Jobey was
published in C. Thomas (ed.) *Rural Settlement*, 1 ff.

[2] K.A. Steer, 'The Severan Reorganisation', in Richmond, (ed.), *Roman and
Native*, 103 ff.

small, the average number of huts per settlement being of the order of six. On the other hand, fifty per cent of the settlements with ten or more huts occupy the sites of earlier defensive works, including three of the four largest settlements, presumably in situations which still had much to commend them even though defensive requirements had gone. Morover, even a cursory glance at the published plans will indicate that some of these larger settlements, if all stone huts were in contemporary use, are greater than could be accommodated within the earlier defences.[1]

This work on the Roman 'intra-mural zone' is now being joined by much needed reappraisal of the native communities that dwelt in the north-west *behind* Hadrian's Wall. I have earlier mentioned the recent aerial photography of farms in the Cumbrian Plain by Professor G.D.B. Jones that has added new sites to the many already known from earlier work on the ground and from the air. These sites are perhaps the most likely of the native sites of the south to show signs of close contact with the Roman military and the mixed civilian population settled outside the forts, and probably formed the core of the farming population of the *civitas Carvetiorum* which was eventually organized with its centre almost certainly in the city of Carlisle. Long-term survey work now in progress on the more remote and often wilder western fells in Cumbria and Lancashire promises insight into an intermediate situation.[2] There the communities were continuously ringed by Roman garrisons for over three hundred years. It is true that many of the settlements lay in countryside extremely difficult to police and, as in the early days, the network of forts doubtless continued to perform the essential function of control. Nevertheless, recent work suggests that the environment was not as harsh as would appear from the modern landscape, since the woodland cover was apparently much greater.[3] There is good evidence for forest pastoralism and some arable, raising the possibility that troops continued to be stationed here in large numbers because they could be fed easily from a population less able to complain effectively than the villa-owners of the south.

[1] Jobey, op. cit. 21 ff.
[2] See *Current Archaeology*, 53 (1975), 183 ff. for a note on research programmes in the valleys of the Lune and the Kent.
[3] Pollen and food bone evidence: see forthcoming article by Anthony King in *Bull. Inst. Arch.*

Either way, any economic or cultural advantages gained by the locals from Roman rule are likely to have been won against decidedly adverse circumstances.

NOTE

The Roman villa. There has been a great deal of dispute over the correct use of the term *villa*, much of it unnecessary. The villa was a house in the country (see A.L.F. Rivet's rightly uncompromising note, *Brit.* 5 (1974), 284). A *villa urbana* was a country house with pretensions to dignified living; a *villa rustica* purely functional. There is no reason why both should not exist on one estate or in the same complex. Varro makes it perfectly clear that 'villa' is properly applied to both categories (*Rer. Rust.* III. ii. 10: *nihilo minus esse villam eam quae esset simplex rustica, quam eam quae esset utrumque, et ea et urbana*). Many have argued that a villa was always a farm. Varro indeed thought it ought to imply husbandry (op. cit. III. ii. 5-6) but he was writing against a background of traditional belief in the moral worth of country life and work, and as a hard-headed Roman: property ought to pay. We do not have to take his definition too seriously: he was prepared to allow chickens, bees, a commercial aviary, a fishpond, a warren, or even the rearing of dormice to qualify (op. cit. III. ii. 11 etc.). Pliny the Younger, discussing a small country property in which Suetonius was interested, remarks that a literary man needs only a modest house and enough land to go with it to provide pleasure (*Letters*, i. 24). Under the umbrella of the term villa, the range from the seaside villas of the very rich near Rome to the smallholder's farmhouse is enormous. It is equally clear that as between one owner and another the importance of the 'economic' activity of villas varied very greatly.

20

THE ECONOMY

T HE 'economics' of the ancient world is an area in which we are more in danger of anachronism than perhaps any other. Though emperors intervened from time to time in one 'economic' field or another—debasing or reforming currency, trying to control prices or the movement of labour, imposing or altering taxes—few if any of their measures had an economic motive in the sense employed in modern government. It was in terms of revenue and politics that emperors considered the economy of provinces, not in the context of any general economic theory aimed at a common good. No one attempted to co-ordinate the economic life of the Roman world. If we are to avoid being unhistorical it can only be viewed as the separate activities of enormous numbers of individuals pursuing their own activities, some of their own free will, some under compulsion. This chapter might, indeed, better have been entitled 'Wealth and Work' than 'The Economy', though nowadays a section on economics is expected from historians of any culture. The sum of all this activity does add up to a whole, however incoherent and constantly changing, but that whole must be recognized as the undirected and largely accidental thing it was.

Archaeologists under pressure to account for the distribution of particular categories of artefacts are peculiarly prone to fall into the temptation of employing whatever fashionable economic theory seems to fit their observations, however distant in place or time the society on which it was originally erected. I am not here referring to those mathematical hypotheses or 'models' constructed by observation of patterns apparently discernible in material from the same period of history, though those may individually be subject to objections of their own. The question is one of analogies taken from primitive or early peoples irrespective of date or location, and these are particularly dangerous where there is little or no written evidence against which they can be tested. In general they can be dismissed. However there is one theory derived from economic anthropology which cannot be ignored, since its influence is strong on modern archaeological thought. It divides 'trade' or the exchange of material objects into two. In primitive societies the objects exchanged, the value set upon them, and the methods of exchange are largely determined by social factors. In sophisticated economies trade is on the contrary an activity in itself, with the objective of making profits for the trader or entrepreneur. The theory as applied to Britain sees the Iron Age down to the Roman Conquest as almost entirely in the former condition. Valued objects are exchanged as gifts, often as part of an elaborate ritual relating to kinship or political relationships, and chiefly among the élite. The Roman empire appears in contrast as an advanced commercial society. The Conquest is seen in economic terms as the imposition of a fundamentally alien system, rooted in completely different attitudes to society and exchange. Further elaboration of the theory seeks to explain features of coin-usage before and in the early years after the Conquest, and to attribute to difficulties on the part of the Britons in assimilating the new ways the relative slowness of urbanization. Only comparatively late does Britain accept the commercial approach to life sufficiently to become wholly integrated into a system of long-distance trade between centres of manufacture based on a fully monetary system.

The original theory, however, has a fundamental flaw. In simplistic form in which it is applied to Roman Britain it assumes an almost complete antithesis between one system and the other. This is false. Both can exist within a single society. In modern Japan a highly developed ritual of giving is embedded in social relationships, where favours must be balanced in honour by gifts and gift by gift. Yet we can hardly ignore the fact that Japan today demonstrates an exceptionally high level of aggressive commercial enterprise. But we do not have to look for modern analogies to illustrate the point. The Roman world itself, through the all-pervasive institution of the *clientela* and the mutual obligations of patronage as practised at many levels of society, displayed immensely strong bonds of social duty, marked by exchanges of favours and gifts, by the public recognition of indebtedness, and by the honour that was obtained from acquiring, through the use of influence, advantages for others where social ties dictated. At the same time the Romans were exploiting every means of making money through industry and commerce, with the senatorial class making the gesture of recognizing ancient taboos against such traditionally degrading activity by putting up the thin pretence of working through nominees. Commercial activity was, we may confidently assert, much more important in Roman society than it had been in Britain, but, whatever the truth about individual artefacts found here, we cannot use a supposed violent antithesis between the attitudes of the British élites towards money and exchange and those of the Roman invaders to explain political tensions after the Conquest or to invent economic ones.

As with the population (a subject with which it is of course linked), the Romano-British economy has left us almost totally deficient in reliable statistics. That alone would make most modern methods of studying economic life inapplicable.[1] We are, moreover, dealing with a world that, though highly sophisticated, worked in such a different way from our own that many of the commonplaces of modern economics are largely irrelevant. Take, for example, the concept of the balance of trade. In terms of the financial relationship of the Roman empire with the outside world, this may make some limited sense, since many of the most expensive imports had to be paid for in the only acceptable way, in precious metals whether in the form of coin, when not debased, or bullion, and the Roman state could only lay its hands on a certain amount of those metals. Whether the imports were paid for by the state or individuals, there was probably a net outflow of wealth in that sense. But one may suspect that since this was largely a matter of the luxury trades the effect was small. On some frontiers the empire was exporting manufactured goods and may well have gained more than it lost. But figures for volume, indeed even order of magnitude, are so lacking as to make estimates entirely vain.

If one attempts to consider the balance of trade of a single province such as Britain, the concept is almost meaningless,

---

[1] See M.I. Finley, *The Ancient Economy* (1973), for a modern attempt to define the limitations and possibilities of the subject as a whole, and R. Duncan-Jones, *The Economy of the Roman Empire: Quantitative Studies*, Cambridge (1974), for a detailed and critical study of the figures we have or appear to have.

since the empire had a single currency and no internal tariff barriers. There were, certainly, frontier duties of a sort (*portoria*) but these were a form of tax and not intended to manipulate trade for economic purposes. It is revealing that the writer Strabo, working in the last days of the Roman Republic and the early years of the Principate, remarked that if Britain were to be conquered there would be an actual loss of revenue to Rome. It is known that provinces were grouped together for the purposes of the *portoria* and it is quite likely that a higher rate was levied on trade at the frontiers of the empire itself. This therefore implies either that Britain would be included with Gaul and no border taxes be collected, or that the rate would be much reduced. The actual percentage, however, at which this border tax was levied never seems to have been high, and the changes can have had little effect on the flow of trade or on prices when Britain was incorporated in the empire. Strabo was thinking purely in fiscal terms.

While it is probably fruitless to seek to understand the underlying working of the ancient economy, we can look at the surface and perhaps gain some idea of how ordinary people were affected by economic activity. In terms of employment, at least three-quarters of the people in Roman Britain, probably more, were in agriculture. By the fourth century the country was apparently more than self-sufficient in grain, since in an emergency Julian was able to increase regular shipments to the Rhine by 600 extra loads. In the first century Agricola had dealt with abuses in the levying of corn supplies from the provincials for the army, but there is no hint that it was even at that early date in short supply, merely that the system was being deliberately mishandled for dishonest purposes by Roman officials. Corn was supposed to be delivered to a convenient point and paid for by the authorities: under proper management this ought to have meant a guaranteed market and a cash income for the producers, something they can never have had on any scale before. This by itself represents a revolution in agricultural economics even if the price offered by the army was not generous. The Roman army consumed enormous quantities of grain. One modern estimate put the need of a legion at 500 bushels a week. In addition we now have ample evidence that the army had a much more mixed diet than was once believed. Substantial quantities of meat, vegetables, and fruit had to be found for the troops as well as cereals.[1] The supply operation was enormous.[2] The government set a fixed price and decided how much was to be purchased in any particular region, leaving the local authorities with the responsibility of collecting the supplies. Sometimes the army itself handled the operation, sometimes the procurator or other officials, and food was also acquired by this method for civilian staff and for the Imperial Post. There was, of course, ample opportunity under lax emperors or local officers for fraud on the one side and extortion on the other. Some scholars consider that the system of purchase was replaced by a direct tax in kind (*annona militaris*), but the evidence is disputed. But whether bought or collected direct, the food still had to be forthcoming in huge quantities.

This brings sharply into focus the crucial problem of how Britain can have produced enough to feed the army over and above the civilian population unless overall production was increased very substantially beyond what it had been before the Roman conquest.[3] Without any allowance for supplies to the cities or exports, something in the region of 100,000 acres (40,000 hectares) of corn land was needed to supply the military alone.[4] Moreover, in this matter of grain production there is a further puzzle. Where the typical small rectangular 'Celtic' fields are preserved, they often do not look like arable on a scale to achieve this result. For the Fenlands, where a whole landscape is revealed (and where it was once assumed that the enclosures were largely arable fields) the evidence points away from grain production. To quote the Fenland survey:

[1] See in particular R.W. Davies, 'The Roman Military Diet', *Brit.* 2 (1971), 122 ff.

[2] Cf. W.H. Manning, 'Economic influences on land use in the military areas of the Highland Zone during the Roman period', in J.G. Evans, S. Limbrey, H. Cleere (eds.), *The effect of man on the landscape: the Highland Zone*, CBA Research Report 11 (1975), 112 ff. citing among others S. Applebaum, 'Roman Britain', in Finberg (ed.) *Agrarian History*, I, pt. 2, 203 ff.; G.R. Watson, *The Roman Soldier* (1969), 126; A.H.M. Jones, *Later Roman Empire*, 628 f.; G. Rickman, *Roman Granaries and Store Buildings*, Cambridge (1971), 271 and 278, on various aspects of diet and supply.

[3] Some corn was exported before the Conquest as we noted (Strabo, IV. v. 2), but it is unlikely to have been on the scale of the surplus now required.

[4] See Note, p. 663 below.

The total area covered by fields is rather low. The majority of the field-like enclosures tend to be rather small and to cluster around the nucleus of the settlement. They are more like gardens and stockyards than the fields of arable farms. Such extensive systems as that at Christchurch are rare . . . We also have to remember that ancient crop yields were much lower than they are now. The significant feature of the landscape seems to be the large open spaces between the settlements . . . which are sometimes delineated by long boundary ditches. In conjunction with the large number of animal bones found in the settlements these open spaces suggest animal husbandry on commons or ranches as the principal occupation. Cattle, sheep and horses were of major military importance. The Roman army used hides in vast quantities—for the leather tents which appear on Trajan's Column, for shields and protective clothing, for harness and for many of the purposes for which webbing is now used. Gut was probably also a requirement for the works of Roman artillery. Wool was needed in quantity for military uniforms. Statistics of animal bones from neighbouring fen-edge sites may suggest that farmers were at least as interested in keeping beasts for wool and milk as for young meat . . . on the other hand such bone statistics could be misleading if there was much transport of animals away from the region to market—and it appears that one specifically official activity was the conveying of beasts on the hoof and as salt meat over long distances to supply the army. This would be particularly suitable in a region with extensive imperial estates adjacent to good water communications,[1] especially if Mrs Hallam is right in suggesting that the numerous industrial sites in the Fenland were in fact producing salt. Nevertheless the number of older animals recorded does support the notion of a degree of wool and dairy farming. In addition we have to take into account that horses became more and more important as the use of cavalry increased. Moreover, at Hockwold there is some evidence that horses were a source of meat, for Mr. Leslie Cram's analysis of the distribution of bones shows horse bones mixed indiscriminately with those from cattle and sheep or goats . . . I am now fairly convinced that the major agricultural products of the Fenland were animal (and perhaps fish) rather than cereal. Some cereals were probably grown in the little enclosures around the settlements and other crops are likely as well, but there is no evidence for the market gardening which is today so prosperous in parts of the region. Slow transport in the ancient world made market gardening a local affair profitable only near great centres of population: it seems, on the contrary, that the Fenlands throve on those products which would not perish in transit . . .[2]

This not only seems to eliminate the Fenland but also warns us to be cautious of assuming any relatively small area of 'Celtic fields' associated with settlements to represent

[1] Even if the Lincolnshire Car Dyke is no longer accepted as a canal, this remains substantially true.

[2] Salway, in Phillips (ed.), *Fenland*, 13 f., with further references.

arable on any scale without closer examination. It leaves us
with the awkward question of where the grain surplus was
produced. It is, of course, true that there are places where
there are really substantial areas covered with rectangular
Celtic fields, for example Bathampton Down in Somerset or
Grassington in North Yorkshire, which were indeed in all
probability arable, but one cannot help noticing that this is
distinctly hilly country and not particularly attractive to
more recent arable farmers. One may perhaps hope that the
Society of Antiquaries' landscape project in Wessex will give
us more precise information on the use of land for arable,
particularly where ancient field-patterns and land usage are
less obvious but may still be in the end recoverable. In the
meantime Dr Manning's analysis of the supply of the troops
has brought out two factors of major importance:[1]

In the past, British archaeological opinion has generally held that most
of this grain came from the Lowland Zone . . . The reasons for this are
twofold. Firstly there is a generally unstated, but none the less widely
held, opinion that few areas within the Highland Zone were suitable
for cereal production, an opinion which is clearly incorrect. Within the
general area of the Highland Zone there are quite large stretches of
excellent arable land, as is shown by the farming regions of Wales, for
example, in the Tudor period, when agricultural techniques were not
vastly improved in comparison with classical ones . . . Even in the hills
there are still many places where cereals could be and were grown.
Often, it is true, these areas are quite small, lying in valleys or on the
more sheltered slopes, but in total they can be considerable . . . The
second argument is based on the assumption that there was no tradition
of cereal cultivation in the Highland Zone. It has been suggested that
the absence of storage pits and Celtic fields, together with the heavy
emphasis on cattle in the Celtic literary sources, indicated a society
based on stock raising, with arable farming playing at most a very
minor part . . . The relevance of storage pits and Celtic fields can be
much exaggerated. Storage pits are only one way of storing grain,
and one which was not universal even in the Iron Age of southern
England, as their absence from large parts of the south-east shows . . .
Celtic fields are not completely absent from the Highland Zone, of
course . . .; quite large areas are known and others are being discovered.
What is too often forgotten is that they represent only those parts of
the Iron Age and Romano-British arable lands that have escaped
medieval and later ploughing. The great bulk even within the Lowland

[1] Manning, op. cit. 113, citing Sir Mortimer Wheeler, *The Stanwick Fortifications* (1954), 27 f.; S. Piggott, 'Native Economies and the Roman Occupation
of North Britain', in Richmond (ed.), *Roman and Native*, 1 ff.; A.L.F. Rivet,
Roman Villa, 189.

Zone was destroyed centuries ago, as the distribution of settlements shows. Within the Highland Zone, areas of good agricultural land have always been at a premium and therefore liable to ploughing. If an absence of Celtic fields today is taken to mean an absence of arable land, we must cease to regard Roman villas as farms, for scarcely any can now be shown to have an associated field system.

Dr Manning goes on to produce other evidence that the highland zone was capable of arable production and was in fact so used, and moreover draws our attention to the substantial evidence for the employment of the military *territorium* for the direct production of food for the army.[1] It does, of course, make strategic and financial sense for garrisons not to have to rely on supplies of food from far away if there was any closer source of supply, and Dr Manning points out that this view was taken by the Roman authorities:[2]

There is a considerable body of evidence from documentary sources and from other provinces showing that it was the aim of the Roman government to avoid moving supplies over long distances wherever possible. This is stated most clearly and authoritatively in an instruction of the Emperors Valentinian and Valens to the praetorian prefect in 369 which is preserved in the Theodosian Code: 'Just as We, by Our beneficial foresight, have commanded to be done throughout all frontiers, you shall order supplies of subsistence allowances to be brought to the camps by the provincials nearest to the borders' (7.4.15).

This still leaves us with questions as to how the increased production was achieved, a problem the more acute if the garrisons were entirely supplied by the highlands rather than the villas of the lowlands, though it is unnecessary to press the argument that far. The question of improved agricultural technology under the Romans has from time to time been raised and generally dismissed. At one time it was thought that the 'Belgic' people introduced a wheeled plough, enabling them to farm heavier soils previously unworkable, but that theory is currently out of fashion. However recent re-examination of the famous Piercebridge bronze model of a Roman ploughman and his team has suggested a fairly advanced version of the prehistoric 'ard', which has had a flange added to the share, earth-boards, and a coulter or cutting tool, which would be capable of working fairly heavy

[1] Manning, op. cit. 113 ff.   [2] Ibid. 114.

soils behind a pair of oxen or cows.[1] Indeed, Mr Reynolds'
experiments have indicated that even the simple ard
(provided that the tip of the wooden spike is protected with
metal to prevent rapid wear) can cope effectively with heavy
soils.[2] It is very important that we should not imagine the
Roman farmer as being restricted by his tools to cultivating
only the easiest land and excluded from soils worked extensively in later ages. In some respects, in fact, the Roman may
have had more advanced technology at his command than
his Iron Age predecessor. The multiple reaping-machine,
known from the Buzenol relief sculpture in Belgium, has not
yet been found in Britain, but some of the enormous scythes
or reed-cutting blades found on the Fen Edge prove the
capacity for producing large hand or semi-mechanical tools.
But, overall, the farming techniques required for large-scale
production were probably already here in Britain before the
Conquest.

What, then, was the critical element that allowed the
production of the quantity of grain required under Roman
rule? Mr Jobey, speaking of the upland settlements, surely
points us in the right direction when he produces evidence
suggesting that these settlements themselves increased in
size in conditions of peace. Professor Rivet must be right
when he says:[3] 'Rome did not increase the fertility of the
land, but by her system of roads and the enforcement of
peace she made more of it accessible and allowed it to be
more intensively worked . . . by organized production and
marketing she made it more widely available.'

It is quite possible that the existing Iron Age agricultural
system could have produced more than it did if the incentives
had been there. With the arrival of the Romans came a ready
availability of consumer goods to encourage the farmer to
produce a surplus that could be sold, and officials to back
this up with compulsion if need be. It is also possible that
widespread adoption of more efficient methods of processing and storage of food in bulk in the Roman period
also encouraged the farmer to produce more. Recent
experiments have shown that Iron Age grain-storage pits

[1] W.H. Manning, in G. de G. Sieveking (ed.), *Prehistoric and Roman Studies*
(1971), 125 ff.
[2] Reynolds, *Iron Age Farm*, 51.   [3] Rivet, *Town and Country*, 100.

worked well if properly made,[1] but it is difficult to see why a farmer should store more than he—and perhaps his lord—required for immediate use and a modest reserve, except in areas where grain was being produced for export. But with military and civil granaries ready to take what he could grow an entirely new dimension entered the economics of farming.

Despite the potential of the native farm, however, I suspect that it was the advent of the Roman or Romanized estate-owner that actually changed the scale of agricultural output, taken over the whole country. This new system we can broadly call the villa-economy, remembering however that it is highly likely that many of the old native farms now became part of the organization without necessarily being adjacent to a villa or being directly run from a villa. The agricultural surplus to feed the urban population had to come from somewhere, and if we can now see the army as being largely supplied from its highland hinterland, then the main production of the lowland farms can have gone to the cities. In that market prices could not be fixed by the private consumer to the extent that the army could achieve, and a much better return to the producer can be imagined. A small proportion of the surplus from the farms was doubtless earmarked for the governor and other official purposes—and this must have increased in the south with the re-establishment of garrisons in the third and fourth centuries—but most of it was presumably available on the open market for the highest price it could fetch. Nor should we assume that imperial estates were outside this system, for in areas where the immediate priority was not keeping the army supplied the emperor will surely have expected his lands to produce the maximum profit. In organizational terms, no clear line can be drawn between estates belonging to the emperor and to private owners, and the economics are broadly the same for both categories, except in so far as the private owner may often have consumed a larger proportion of the products of the estate himself and spent more of the profits on non-utilitarian projects, such as villas and other beautification, than on the actual estate itself. The real change in the system

[1] P.J. Reynolds, 'Experiment in Iron Age agriculture', *Trans. Bristol and Glos. Arch. Soc.* 86 (1967), 60 ff.; 88 (1969), 29 ff.; also *Iron Age Farm*, 71 ff.

from prehistoric to Roman times is a matter of character of ownership, direction, and philosophy. The direction may come from a private owner working his estate direct or through tenants, or it may be an imperial procurator letting the land out to small farmers or large.[1] But the essential concept common to all is the landed estate *existing in a world with money economy, urban markets, and the availability of organized transport.*[2] Someone now not only had to think about making the crops grow but also had to keep accounts, calculate profit and loss, and take heed of the requirements of officialdom. We have passed from a comparatively primitive world to one in which conscious estate management is not only practised but also, it must be remembered, studied and written about. Some owners were doubtless willing just to allow their stewards to collect rent off the peasants or drive the slaves but many must have read their Columella or Varro. Though the precepts of those authors might in detail be more applicable to Mediterranean agriculture, the reader must have been fully aware that the management of country estates was a proper subject for a Roman gentleman and been prepared to think about ways of extracting more profit from the land. They were often now in the position of having bigger and much more varied over-all holdings of land, with parcels and whole farms in different districts or even different provinces. Large landowners will have had wider information and substantial resources at their command. In estate management this means the ability to take decisions (including investment and the buying and selling of land as well as how to farm particular properties) within a broader context—though doubtless often with results not much to the liking of individual tenants or other local people.

The economy of one large villa in Britain has been studied in detail. At Bignor in Sussex a full range of domestic and agricultural buildings has been revealed on the ground.[3]

[1] There is, of course, no reason to think that the approach was any different even where the army was in fact the landlord and native farmers working under its direction, since senior military officers were themselves drawn from the landed gentry or had aspirations in that direction.

[2] Cato (*De Agr. Cult.* I, i. 3) emphasizes the importance of access to a flourishing town and nearness to good water or road communications.

[3] For the results of aerial photography on our knowledge of villa layouts see D.R. Wilson, 'Romano-British Villas from the Air', *Brit.* 5 (1974), 251 ff.

Unfortunately the main excavations were conducted in the eighteenth century. There is both a strong probability that timber structures were missed and also far too little of the internal detail known to permit more than intelligent guesses at the use of the individual agricultural buildings recorded. That S. Applebaum's analysis of Bignor has produced so much by way of reasonably convincing figures, even though he has had to make a large number of assumptions of basic matters, makes more urgent the completion of the total excavation of entire villa complexes by modern methods, incorporating the scientific analysis of organic remains that is working so successfully on other types of site such as York, and is now a commonplace of medieval urban archaeology.[1]

What potential such a complete programme of research holds may be judged by noting some of the conclusions that Applebaum was able to draw despite the severe limitations under which he was working. His study was based both on examination of the surrounding countryside and on the villa itself, which is the type with an inner and outer court described briefly above. There is good reason to think that the farm buildings studied were associated with the fourth-century residence and some evidence that at that stage the owner himself lived elsewhere. A lane, as often, connected the villa to a main road. As Applebaum says, his conclusions are not proven but highly probable:

At this time, following an access of prosperity, well-planned farm buildings are laid out in a new farmyard, reflecting a peak in cereal production and the maximum extension of the estate, part of which seems to have been leased to tenants. In the granary, if fodder is considered, there is hardly sufficient provision for storage of the whole annual crop, which suggests a rapid turn-over by sale. We are in the presence of a prosperous supplier of the market . . . The Bignor proprietor farmed between 700 and 800 acres of cereals, possibly on a three-course system. It does not follow that his cultivations were limited to the two winter and one spring ploughings imposed by his teams and evidenced in late Roman Gaul; he may have been able to

---

[1] Bignor was originally excavated by Lysons, with some re-excavation in 1957–62 by Professor Frere. S. Applebaum's analysis was published in H.P.R. Finberg (ed.), op. cit. 212 ff. and expanded in *Brit.* 6 (1975), 118 ff., but originally written in 1950. Winterton in Lincolnshire is a site where total excavation is being gradually accomplished.

call on the tenants in the western part of the estate to send additional ploughs and labourers, as was the habit in the ninth-century Frankish villa and earlier on the *saltus Augusti* in north Africa . . . If we are right in believing that the enclosed grazing land on Burton Down served the villa, this has an interesting social and economic implication; it suggests that there was a continuity of the grazing economy from the pre-Roman to the Roman period, and that the size of the flock did not vary a great deal from one period to another. It must either have been the flock of the Belgic chief whose family developed the Bignor estate, or alternatively this was the communal grazing area of an Early Iron Age community, taken over by the owners of the estate in the course of the Roman occupation.[1]

This grazing was probably important to the working of the estate and the study of the farm-buildings itself suggested that this was a mixed-farming property: 'Bignor, then, would seem to have possessed accommodation for a flock of some 197 sheep, 12 teams of oxen, and 55 other cattle. The latter was quite possibly only that part of the herd which was maintained throughout the winter after the rest had been sold or slaughtered.'[2] In this context it is interesting that bone evidence from Hockwold indicated that Romano-British farmers were not obliged to slaughter most of their livestock through inability to feed them through the winter, as was once believed normal in early farming, and other subsequent studies have supported this conclusion. Applebaum says that though there is no direct evidence for root crops as cattle feed at Bignor it is likely, both on evidence from Gaul and because:

By Roman scales the proprietor's stock was adequate to manure his arable, but the number of cattle wintered suggests that roots were available and that part of the stall dung was employed to grow them. There is here a co-ordination of marsh-grazing (by the Arun), downland pasture (sheep) and arable, and of grain-production for the market.[3]

The probable sale of livestock to other farms wishing to increase or replenish their herds or to military and civilian butchers as meat for the army and the towns is important in widening our appreciation of the output of such an estate.

[1] Applebaum, *Brit.* 6 (1975), 130 f.
[2] Ibid. 121: autumn killing of stock, however, does not seem to have been the normal practice in the Roman world (see E. Higgs and J. White, 'Autumn Killing', *Antiquity* 37 (1963), 282 ff.   [3] Ibid. 130.

For a long time it was thought that in the fourth century there was a widespread change from arable to grazing, representing large-scale ranching on the part of selfish villa-owners in place of labour-intensive arable. This was seen as depressing the lot of the peasant farmer—even dispossessing him. Indeed, long ago Varro had deplored the turning over of arable to pasture.[1] Yet we have to remember that Roman writers of the first century BC were living in the recent shadow of the social and political upheavals associated in their minds with the drift of the Italian small farmer to Rome; and we ourselves are conditioned by tales of the complaints of late medieval peasants against sheep and the historical legacy of the Highland clearances. We have to dismiss these influences and see Romano-British villa agriculture in terms of a much more mixed production at all periods than previously imagined. Against an increasing pressure on agricultural labour in the Later Empire any movement towards increased animal husbandry that might be detected in particular districts must be recognized as a sign of prudent management of the land.

The picture of a farming system that could both support the larger non-agricultural population of the Roman period and bring a handsome return to its owners begins to build up. On the scale and character of estates I feel that both Hoskins on Ditchley and Applebaum on Bignor have tended to assume too readily what we might call a 'unitary' estate when they have traced the boundaries on the ground. Few large country landowners today are lucky enough to possess all their land in one piece, even on a single estate, and great efforts are frequently made to tidy up the holding and increase efficiency by purchase of adjacent fields or whole farms. Pliny the Younger rehearsed the arguments for and against this practice.[2] On the one hand there were the obvious economies: only one house need be kept and furnished (including single sets of hunting gear and the like). One bailiff could supervise the whole property and the owner need no more than a single foreman. On the other hand there was the risk of putting all one's eggs in one basket. It might be better to spread the risk from weather and the other

---

[1] Varro, *Rer. Rust.* II. Intro. 4.   [2] Pliny, *Letters*, iii. 19.

hazards of farming to have land in different places. But in the end the choice came down to the quality of the land and buildings, how much money would need to be put into the property and whether the purchase price was right.

Other factors also affected the size and character of estates. Losses occurred through forced sale of parcels of land in time of hardship. On the other hand there were accretions through inheritance or marriage, not necessarily resulting in a tidy overall holding. Ditchley and Bignor may not, therefore, have owned all the land within the boundaries that have been deduced nor their total estates been contained therein. It may perhaps have been comparatively easy to establish a neat estate at the time of the Conquest, but three hundred years later it is extremely unlikely that this was still the case. We earlier suggested that villa-owners were leasing out land away from the villa and its immediate surroundings to peasant farmers. This means that a single villa might have as part of its economy not only its home farm and tenants adjacent to it but other tenants well away from its boundaries. This would considerably increase the size of the financial and management unit a single villa represents; and we have to remember that we are talking in terms of 600–800 known villas. If we add to that the probability that many were backed by the resources of very large landowners including the emperor himself, then the hypothesis of a large overall rise in production from the land under Roman rule becomes feasible. This could be true with minimal change in technology and perhaps without any substantial increase in the rural population.

Anyone who has excavated on Romano-British sites will know that by and large they indicate a population which was a heavy consumer of manufactured goods; and in the south at least this extends even to the humblest peasant settlements. The finds imply a large volume of trade, both of items produced in Britain and in imports from other provinces. This in its turn implies industry, and we shall see that Britain was not only a manufacturing province but also a primary producer of raw materials. We also have to take account of important commercial activities that fall under none of these heads, notably the building industry and all its associated trades, which in itself was an importer of materials and an important stimulus to home production.

There is no doubt that the Romans regarded Britain as a valuable producer. Before the Conquest, Strabo listed agricultural exports (cattle, hides, and corn), hunting dogs, slaves, and metals—gold, silver, and iron. Tacitus confirmed the richness of the crops and the importance of the mineral deposits of the island. At the end of the third century the author of the panegyric to Constantius as Caesar still sees Britain in the same terms: the abundance of the crops, the great amount of pasture, and the large quantities of metal ores. But the panegyrist also goes on to talk not only of Britain 'with ports on every side' but also of its enormous profitability in terms of financial revenue.[1] Throughout its contact with Britain the Roman view has little reference to any idyllic vision of bountiful plenty and a great deal to do with profit, the prize of victory.

As this book is a historical rather than archaeological study of Roman Britain we are concerned more to see what we can deduce about the way of life from the remains and records of trade and industry than with the objects themselves or the processes by which they were made. We have seen that the Romans set a high store on the prospects of a good return from the extractive industries, principally metals. Britain was to supply gold, silver, lead, iron, copper, and tin. Both Caesar and Tacitus also clearly put pearls under the extractive heading, though the output is likely to have been tiny. Not so, as we have seen, the oysters themselves! Stone was very extensively quarried, and only in a small number of cases as at Fishbourne do we have evidence for imports of special stone from far away, except in small pieces such as are from time to time found in mosaics. The wholesale transporting of large blocks or part-finished architectural sections by sea as the ancients were accustomed to do in the Mediterranean does not seem a feature of importance. Nevertheless the large-scale moving of stone around Britain was regular. The great slabs of the monument of Classicianus, for example, were brought from one of the limestone areas to London. This emphasizes the mechanical efficiency of Roman transport, whatever its financial cost. Timber was perhaps the

---

[1] *Pan. Lat. Vet.* IV (VIII). xi.

largest of the industries supplying the building trade,
particularly in the first and early second centuries when most
military as well as private buildings were in timber or half-
timber. It must always have been in great demand, not only
for the minor trades such as door and furniture-making but
to supply major items such as beams and joists for roofs and
floors. Moreover it was widely used for many heavy
constructions like bridges and wharves, even for cranes and
other pieces of machinery where we would now use metal.
Lumbering can properly be considered an extractive industry,
though there seems to be some evidence for replacement
forestry as part of Romano-British agriculture.

Fuel and power in the ancient world are subjects on which
much has been said and still relatively little known, as figures
are again lacking. It is reasonably clear that the main source
of fuel was timber. The charcoal-burner is a traditional part
of the ancient scene, gaining literary immortality in
Aristophanes' political comedy *The Acharnians*. Since the
charcoal industry must have added greatly to the ancient
consumption of natural forest its impact on the environment
needs reinvestigation. In Britain open-cast coal mining also
provided what may have been more than a minor percentage
of the energy requirements both for industry and domestic
use. Coal appears for example on the Heronbridge site near
Chester, where a Roman dock was excavated, from a level
dated to the end of the first century or the early second.
This dock was within easy reach of both the legionary
fortress at Chester and the military tile-factory at Holt.
Similarly coal is found in very substantial quantities in forts
in the north and there is little doubt that the army made
considerable use of it in metal-working and probably for
domestic purposes as well. It appears too in the Flintshire
(Clwyd) lead-processing works and was used by villas in the
south-west for operating their central heating systems. The
wonder expressed by the geographical writer Solinus at
the strange glowing coals on the altar of Sulis at Bath[1] must
have caused considerable amusement to those local gentry
who had it shovelled into their hypocausts.

For water-power there is perhaps more evidence to be

---

[1] Solinus, *Collectanea rer. memor.* xxii. 10.

found than has yet been identified. Leats and fragments of the works of water-mills at Chesters and Birdoswald indicate that the garrison of the Wall was operating mills and there are traces in the south at Great Chesterford and Silchester. On the other hand donkey-power has been implied from fragments of mills at Cirencester and London and this seems very likely. The ubiquity and efficiency to this day of donkey and other animal power in the Mediterranean for grinding and water-lifting suggests that this source of power was common in the Roman provinces. However I cannot but suspect that fragments of large millstones found here and there in Roman Britain sometimes came from water-mills, and I think it would be worth re-examining many water-channels previously interpreted as drains or aqueducts for possible operation of such mills. The Romans were capable of constructing extremely elaborate systems to exploit the power of water. In the great complex of mills at Barbegal near Arles the designeers made the maximum use of the energy available by arranging the wheels in series down a hillside. Moreover water-mills could apparently be built quite quickly. As late as the sixth century we find Justinian's general Belisarius building mills on the Tiber during the siege of Rome to provide emergency food supplies for the City, which suggests not only that experienced designers, craftsmen, and the necessary materials were still to hand but also that the machinery could be built and installed in a reasonably short time.

The series principle is also seen in the reverse situation in the enormous water-wheels that drained the galleries at different levels, upwards one to the other, in mines of Roman Spain.[1] Similar wheels operated in the Roman gold-mines at Dolaucothi in Wales. Such availability of new mining technology must have given Roman miners an advantage over their Iron Age predecessors not unlike the revolution in the Cornish mining industry made possible by the beam-engine. But it is noticeable that where we have such evidence in Roman Britain it is in an industry where the product is exceptionally valuable and where the imperial government

[1] Part of one of these wheels is preserved in the British Museum. Being largely of wood their remains are likely to be rarely found even if they were common at the time.

was directly interested. The implication is that such installations needed very substantial resources and that the ancient
world's real lack was not knowledge of how to build some
types of large machinery or carry out complex civil engineering works associated with them, but methods of harness-
ing and applying energy that were relatively cheap to install
and maintain and whose profitability once running was
much higher than the use of human and animal power. It is
often alleged that the availability of slaves inhibited the
ancient world from developing technologically, yet Roman
authors compare the productivity of slaves unfavourably to
that of free workers. We have already noted the decline in the
supply of slaves during the Roman period, and although
criminals were often condemned to the mines, surviving
legislation indicates that mining in particular was frequently
in the hands of concessionaires.[1] I see no reason to suppose
that the Romans would not have used cheap mechanical
power if it had been available nor any evidence to suggest
that the failure to put to practical use the power of steam, of
which the ancient world was aware, was due to anything
more than the lack of those crucial inventions in the eighteenth century that made commercial steam engines a viable
proposition.

Professor Frere has pointed out the revealing fact that
exploitation of the main metal deposits in Britain seems to
have started as soon as the army had won control of the
district. This underlines the acute Roman appreciation of
the *pretium victoriae*. The clearest example of how the
organization then developed is the lead-mining industry. The
attraction of this product, of course, was not only the lead
itself which was extensively used by plumbers but also the
prospect of extracting silver from it.

Gold and silver were, of course, vitally important to the
imperial government, both for coinage and, under the Late
Empire, for official payments in plate and ingots. Wherever
there is a lead-mining district in Britain, there I think we
should be looking for a military presence, however small.
Sir Ian Richmond was sure that the fort at Whitley Castle

---

[1] The key document is the *Lex Metalli Vipascensis*. (Text: R.M. Pidal (ed.),
Historia de España, Madrid (1935), II, 336 f.)

near Alston supervised the Northumberland lead mines, but so far evidence is lacking elsewhere on the ground. However for the Welsh gold mine at Dolaucothi we do now have the fort situated alongside at Pumpsaint, with a series of construction periods between AD 75 and 150.[1] In the course of its life this fort was halved in size, suggesting that though the district in general was pacified the mines still needing guarding, partly perhaps due to the intrinsic value of the product but possibly also because of convict labour. For the relatively much larger lead and silver industry we have better evidence from the discovery of stamped ingots or 'pigs' of lead. It seems reasonably certain that the earliest area to be exploited was the Mendips, since two pigs were lost in transit towards Southampton Water and bear inscriptions that show they were cast in AD 49. Another was found on the Somme stamped by the Second legion under Nero. It may be assumed that a primary task of Vespasian's force in the invasion was to secure the rich metal-bearing areas of the west, and while the Second consolidated its hold on the population it clearly supervised the development of the mines.

The army may well have continued to provide security and transport, but at an early stage the government followed its usual course in shedding the immediate administration of the workings to concessionaires (*conductores*). Claims were probably let out by a procurator of mines,[2] and we find both individuals and companies.[3] C. Nipius Ascanius was acquiring lead from the Clwyd deposits as early as AD 60, at or beyond the limit of actual military occupation. We may imagine that the responsible procurator, like the *procurator saltus* in Upper Germany cited earlier, was not bound by the area actually garrisoned, but controlled operations in regions beyond where Roman bases lay, either under treaty with the natives or by the threat of force. It is, of course, possible that Nipius Ascanius was obtaining the metal by trading with the Deceangli, but it is interesting to speculate whether the activities of such operators may not have fanned the unrest that made the conquest of North Wales eventually necessary.

---

[1] *Brit.* 4 (1973), 272.   [2] See p. 531 above (on *RIB* 179).
[3] e.g. the *socii Lutudarenses* operating in Derbyshire.

By Flavian times the much greater ease with which the surface deposits of Britain could be worked than the mines of Spain and Gaul had proved a serious embarrassment to the imperial government and production was limited by law,[1] presumably for political reasons, such as the protection of interests in the other provinces. But there was clearly still an important local demand for lead for official purposes, as is indicated by the water-pipe stamped with the name of Julius Agricola as governor from Chester and the plates of lead with which the Great Bath is lined at Aquae Sulis. This official interest probably explains an apparent change of policy under Hadrian, when the appearance of the emperor's name on pigs from the Derbyshire field and the absence of private stamps elsewhere suggests closer control of the industry. This may well have been due to the requirements of the vast new military works initiated by Hadrian.[2]

It is not unreasonable to suspect that at this point the limit on production was lifted and exploitation under imperial management probably continued at a fairly high level throughout the half-century of the construction and modification of the Hadrianic and Antonine Walls. It is perhaps not coincidence that the last dated pigs are of the period AD 164-9, suggesting that, when whatever reconstruction was carried out under Julius Verus and Calpurnius Agricola, whether based on the Hadrianic or the Antonine line, had been completed, then demand dropped sharply and it was no longer necessary to keep the direct administration in being. Without a large requirement for lead as construction material the relatively low silver yield from the British ore, particularly the Derby, Shropshire, and Yorkshire deposits, may well have rendered the system unprofitable. However, mining continued, but in the south probably in private hands. Nevertheless, as Professor Frere has pointed out, since mine-owners had to surrender half their production to the state for the use of the mints, the industry remained of interest to the Roman government while costing it nothing to run.

In the third and fourth century there was fresh demand for lead from the British pewter manufacturers, as they filled

---

[1] Pliny the Elder, *Nat. Hist.* XXXIV. xvii (xlix). 164.
[2] See Frere, *Britannia*, 323.

the gap in the domestic market caused by the decline we shall observe in the import of fine pottery, and from undertakers as a fashion for lead coffins spread. From this demand we should probably not divorce the increased production that has been noted in the British tin mines. These indeed seem to have been under some degree of state control under the Late Empire, as a stamped ingot from Cornwall attests. Both the Spanish tin mines and the Gallic pottery industries were in decline in this age of barbarian invasions and civil war and British industry clearly benefited by the opportunity to exploit the market for good quality table ware.[1] There are special difficulties in dating the usage of pewter, since individual pieces not only had a long working life but could, unlike pottery, be reused as raw material in the factories. It is certain that fine pottery was often treasured and therefore can appear apparently out of context alongside later coarse wares in the same excavation level,[2] and much late 'samian'[3] has been repaired by rivetting. Pewter could be even longer-lived, and though fine pottery is sometimes found repaired, pewter is much more easily mended. Nevertheless the Camerton pewter works in the Mendips have not been shown in operation before the middle of the third century, and, to quote Mr P.D.C. Brown:[4]

... it is to the last part of the third and fourth centuries that most of the surviving vessels seem to belong. At this time it must have been usual for every reasonably stocked household to have a dresser stacked with six or a dozen or even twenty or more, assorted plates, bowls and jugs.

Ancient industrial growth was, it would then seem, due to the response of commercially minded individuals to an

[1] In the fourth century Britain was actually exporting fine pottery to northern Gaul. (M. Fulford, in D.P.S. Peacock (ed.), *Pottery and Early Commerce* (1977), 35 ff.)

[2] For example at Hockwold (*Proc. Camb. Ant. Soc.* 60 (1967), 51). Most of the samian was found together in one spot on a site where there was very little overall (and almost no decorated pieces) but a very large quantity of coarse pottery.

[3] Fine red-gloss ware: see below, p. 642.

[4] P.D.C. Brown, 'A Roman Pewter Mould from St. Just in Penwith, Cornwall', *Cornish Archaeology*, 9 (1970), 108 f. For an important general study of the pewter industry see C.A. Peal, 'Romano-British Pewter Plates and Dishes', *Proc. Camb. Ant. Soc.* 60 (1967), 19 ff.

opening, sometimes to direct imperial intervention to secure military supplies or increase revenue, but never, as far as we can see, to acts of official policy to promote local economic prosperity as an end in itself. Work by Mr Henry Cleere on the Roman iron industry gives us the clearest picture yet of a major British industry whose rise and fall seems directly linked to central government requirements. It is an industry, too, for which we now have glimmerings of those real statistics whose overwhelming absence stultifies, as we have noted, most study of ancient economic life.[1] To start with the distribution, iron-production in Roman Britain was dominated from the late first century to the early fourth by three main areas—the Weald, stretching down to the south coast, the Forest of Dean and, to a lesser extent, a string of settlements along the 'Jurassic Ridge', the limestone hills that run from Somerset to Northamptonshire and Lincoln. Both in the Weald and the Forest of Dean there is reason to suspect imperial estates, but the Weald has an important subtlety. While the western part appears to have been worked by free miners, the eastern can convincingly be associated with direct involvement of the Roman fleet in Britain, the *classis Britannica.* Mr Cleere has argued that state involvement on a substantial scale started there under Agricola, when major new requirements for iron were created by the large programme of public and private works initiated by him, and that the fleet may first have become involved when it moved from its original base at Richborough to its new headquarters at Dover around AD 85. It seems very likely that a major role of the fleet was the provision of supplies and technical expertise to the industry and the exporting of its products. On the other hand, there is a little evidence that the works were under a procurator.[2] It is remarkably interesting that under Antoninus Pius we find a commander of the *classis Britannica* who seems also to hold the provincial procuratorship of Britain. There can be little doubt that the Wealden iron industry was considered of major strategic importance.

[1] I am most grateful to Mr Cleere for allowing me to use this material, at the time of writing (Spring 1980) as yet unpublished.

[2] Inscription from Beauport Park recording reconstruction of a bath-house by a civilian bailiff (*vilicus*).

Expansion of this south-coast industry seems to coincide with a similar development in the Forest of Dean, and the date for both appears to be Hadrianic. It is very tempting to link this, as in the case of the lead industry, with the Wall and the Hadrianic–Antonine impetus in the cities. This brings us to the figures Mr Cleere has managed to extract in a convincing manner from the large quantity of data available in the form of slag heaps. Very briefly, the method of analysis is based on the total amount of slag produced by a site during its life, the length of time and historical period when it was active dated by the usual types of archaeological find, and the probable consumption of iron by Britain under the various main headings such as buildings, weapons, tools, and—least easy to calculate of all—ships and boats. On any calculation, Mr Cleere suggests that by the end of the first century Britain was self-sufficient in iron production. He argues that a population of about 2 million in the second century would have required around 250,000 buildings, of which not more than 10 per cent would have needed replacement in any one year. This would have demanded about 200 tonnes of iron, out of about 1,000 tonnes from what appear to have been civilian iron works. Subtracting another 200 tonnes for civil trade and industry, something like 600 tonnes surplus remains. Similarly the eastern Wealden works under official control produced around 600 tonnes per annum, far too much for military consumption in Britain once the main constructions of the Hadrianic and Antonine periods were complete. The figures for home consumption need adjusting, of course, in the light of the much larger population now being postulated for Roman Britain. If the true number was somewhere between 4 and 6 million inhabitants, then most or all of the production from the civilian works could have been used in Britain. On the other hand, we are still left with the substantial surplus from the official factories.

The figures for the manpower required to produce the amounts calculated are probably the first for any Romano-British industry to have any degree of reliability, and are therefore in themselves of the first importance historically. Towards the end of the first century about 300 production workers were needed, rising to something over 1,400 in the early third and falling to around 200 by the end of Roman rule. To this Mr Cleere would add not more than 20 per cent to cover supervisory, clerical, and other categories of worker. As he remarks, 'It seems remarkable that the requirements for iron of an estimated total population in the second century of two million could have been satisfied, and a considerable surplus made available for export, by about 1500 craftsmen.' But perhaps even more revealing is the implication for the balance of occupations among that population. If this was a major industry—which it surely was —then we may begin to appreciate how few men had to be employed in industry to meet the needs of the ancient world compared with other forms of commerce, with administration and the armed forces, and most of all agriculture. It should prevent us from making facile comparisons with the modern economy, while alerting us to the efficiency with which a sophisticated society could be supplied with material goods of a high quality.

But to return to the surplus. There seems to be a strong case for supposing a considerable volume of iron exported from Britain. Where did it go? There is no evidence, but the army of the Rhine and the flourishing civil markets of Gaul seem very strong possibilities on general grounds.

That this may indeed have been so is supported by an important piece of negative evidence. Around the middle of the third century the official ironworks in the eastern Weald closed, apparently at the same time that the fleet base at Dover was demolished and the *classis Britannica* itself disappears from the record. One cannot help guessing that this may have something to do with the barbarian invasions of Gaul, the Imperium Galliarum and all the associated political and military upheavals of the second half of the century on the Continent. The devastation of the Gallic cities and the impoverishment of northern Gaul marked by the abandoned villa lands may indicate a collapse of the civil market for British iron abroad and the usurpation of Carausius may well have cut Britain off at a critical moment from the opportunities presented by the great reconstruction under the Tetrarchy. Another possibility, suggested by Mr Cleere, is that the south coast was becoming too vulnerable to pirates. It is perhaps not pressing speculation too far to suggest that the closing down of the eastern Wealden enterprises may be intimately connected with the development of the Saxon Shore system, which was perhaps drawn together into a coherent force for the first time under Probus. Naval resources could on this view no longer be spared for their old supply and transport function, supporting the Weald industry. Instead they were now needed in an attack role, perhaps under a new command headquarters on the Gallic side of the Channel. Moreover the Imperium Galliarum may have suggested that it was dangerous to leave the major source of a vital strategic material for the Continental armies across the sea in Britain. Exploitation of Gallic deposits of iron, even if more difficult to work, would be deemed safer in those suspicious times. The British sources of iron could be left to supply Britain alone.

In Britain itself after the loss of the eastern Weald the general level and pattern of production declined only slowly from the middle of the third century. One may reasonably assume that military requirements within Britain (now that their eastern Weald works were shut) and the revival in the building industry from the last quarter of the third century provided a very adequate market for the rest, and it is possible some export revived under the Tetrarchy. Around the middle of the fourth century the output from the main producers seems to have declined substantially, and it is reasonable to associate this with the troubles that hit Britain at that time. However, that this affected producers more than consumers is suggested by a notable increase in smaller-scale iron-working in towns and villas. We cannot, therefore, argue a collapse in demand. Moreover the main iron areas seem to have continued active to the end of the century, even if at a much reduced level. In the last quarter of the century there is much domestic production as most of the main works closed down. This process, and the point at which it became critical, remains to be charted in detail and much closer dating is required. It must be connected intimately with the breakdown of central administration and communications and perhaps most of all with the disintegration of the army and its procurement service. If in the future we can place this more accurately, we shall have a sharper insight into those critical periods 369 to 409 and the years immediately after the break with Roman rule.

We should now turn to the best-known class of artefact from Roman Britain—pottery. Here we have a different archaeological situation to consider.[1] Unlike the iron industry, the evidence comes chiefly from the product itself rather than the factory (though a growing amount of knowledge is being gained about the production sites themselves). This allows us to look at a different aspect of ancient life—the distribution of some of the most common articles of daily life and therefore by implication the shopping habits of the population and the success or failure of different commercial concerns competing for a mass market. Pottery, in fact, has survived in such enormous quantities and has such distinct forms and fabrics that it is possible to study the location and chronology of its manufacture and changes in style and taste with some hope of arriving at reliable answers to some of the questions one would ask in investigating a modern trade from manufacture to customer. A less satisfactory aspect is that so many scholars have specialized in the subject that there is much disagreement in detail, not untouched by *odium academicum*. However some general points can be made with more confidence than on any other ancient product. It is clear that there are two main markets, the one being direct supply to the army, the other sale to the general public. There had already been a flourishing trade in home-produced and imported wares in the south-east before the Conquest and this included products from the empire. The army seems to have started off with the stock it brought with it. Some potters obviously accompanied the invading troops or came soon after, but local skill was soon utilized. Apart from a relatively small amount of production by the Roman army itself, which hardly went beyond the early second century, we have to reckon with two major categories of pottery in use in Britain—that which was imported from factories abroad and that made in similar potteries in Britain. Both were in civilian hands. In addition there are certain special types of pot, notably the large jars or amphorae which contained oil or wine, that came in chiefly as containers.

---

[1] See particularly A. Detsicas (ed.), *Current Research in Romano-British Coarse Pottery*, CBA Research Report 10 (1973).

Their origin therefore reflects the trade in the commodity carried in them, not in pottery itself, and they were often reused for other purposes, like oil drums or plastic containers today.

A recent short survey by Vivien Swan neatly summarizes the arrangement of the home industry, after expressing her own view that the quantity and distribution of particular wares on military sites make it certain that there were large-scale contracts issued on behalf of the army, though none of these documents survive:

While the major industries were primarily concerned with supplying the army (sometimes from a considerable distance), and tended to concentrate on specialist vessels (for example mortaria and flagons), many smaller potteries of comparatively local significance flourished, and were the main suppliers of the civil markets. Some of these were probably initially set up to supply military units, and when the troops moved north, they were reduced to local status only; whatever the circumstances, most major settlements would have had their own local pottery. Their distinctive products, mostly kitchen wares, were often influenced by local Iron Age traditions and many items continued to be hand-made or partly hand-made throughout the Roman period. These workshops manufactured perhaps between 70 and 80 per cent of all the pottery in Roman Britain, and except in Wales and the north-west (where no native potting tradition existed), most probably never traded their wares more than ten to fifteen miles. This helps to explain the great diversity of wares from region to region.[1]

It was in the finer wares that imports dominated the longest. The two outstanding groups were the glossy red ware known generally as 'samian' or 'terra sigillata' and the black or dark brown pots from the Rhineland and central Gaul. In the earliest days the red pottery came from the Arretine works in Italy, but the market was soon captured by the great factories of southern Gaul. These sent huge quantities of their pottery to Britain till, towards the end of the first century, they were challenged by new factories producing a similar product in central Gaul. For most of the second century this new group supplied nearly all the samian for Britain, though yet another offshoot of the industry set itself up in eastern Gaul and was able to achieve some penetration of the British market. The central Gaulish

[1] Vivien G. Swan, *Pottery in Roman Britain*, Aylesbury (1975), 8.

industry subsequently contracted severely, at the end of the second century or some time in the early third, and hardly any pottery from there appears in Britain thereafter. Since the dating of the end of central Gaulish samian has largely depended on the assumption of a destruction of Hadrian's Wall in 197—and we have seen how thin the evidence for that is—we can no longer presume the cause was destruction of factories in Gaul during the war between Septimius Severus and Clodius Albinus. It is perfectly possible the end came as the result of political or commercial pressures, and at a slightly later date. The east Gaulish manufacturers managed to hold on to some of their gains overall, but little of their production is found in Britain. In the latter part of the second century the dark-finished fine pottery of the Rhineland and Gaul began to appear in Britain in considerable quantities. This seems to have managed to retain a substantial market in Britain in the third century. However, in the second half of the second century a flourishing British pottery industry had emerged that was producing not only coarse wares but also fine pottery ('Castor ware') that is remarkably like Rhenish. Thus by the end of the second century the British consumer of fine pottery had a choice of central or eastern Gaulish samian, Rhenish, Gaulish or British dark wares, and a number of lesser but good quality makes. The failure of the central Gaulish industry may indeed have been due to competition, British taste having been caught by the newer dark wares though other provinces continued to take the red pottery of east Gaul. There is no doubt that the British potters were not slow to take advantage of the collapse of the import trade in samian, though the difficulty in distinguishing Castor ware from the Continental types makes it impossible to know what proportion of the market they captured with any certainty.

Of the British groups of potteries producing both coarse and fine wares the most notable was that in the Nene valley around Peterborough. The area had great advantages—not only suitable raw materials but an excellent position in the communications system. In the first century it had been the site of the vexillation-fortress of Longthorpe. It lay on the edge of the enormous second-century development of the Fenland, with immediate access to the Fenland waterways and good river connections inland to carry away its products in bulk. It may have had one other advantage as well. Between the Roman town of Chesterton and the medieval village of Castor aerial photography shows an extraordinarily densely packed suburb which has every appearance of representing intensive industrial development. Overlooking that development was a very large villa, the fragments of which have been known for a long time in and around Castor churchyard. One cannot help suspecting that here lay the headquarters of a *procurator saltus* overseeing the Fenland development. The advantages to the new industry of being at the centre of communications to a very large local market on which to build its initial prosperity are obvious. One may perhaps speculate a little further that the early failure of part of the Hadrianic agricultural and salt-producing colonization of the Fenlands may have turned the attention of the procurator and his masters to new ways of exploiting the region. The encouragement of the pottery industry might have been one of those ways, particularly if the salt industry of the Fens proper had not grown quite as much as had been hoped. Around Chesterton we have the typical Romano-British industrial picture. Even the largest industries, like salt and pottery, were located in the countryside. The town has the characteristics of a small town, not a large one, and appears to be an appendage of the industries, rather than they of it. It was the raw materials, the fuel, and the communications that these industries needed to flourish, not a large urban work-force; and apart from the one great villa—which we have guessed was official—they did not attract the sort of wealthy benefactors or residents who could transform a small town into a city.

By the Severan period the Nene Valley potteries were in full production and other smaller centres of fine ware manufacture entered the market now being vacated by samian. Later on in the century an important fine pottery centre emerged, or rather re-emerged, in the Oxford region,[1] some of whose kilns were excavated on the Churchill Hospital site in Headington. These Oxford potters took a major share of

[1] There had been an earlier phase of production of fine wares in Oxfordshire from the middle of the second century to the early third: see C.J. Young, *Oxfordshire Roman Pottery*, Oxford (1977).

the market in the fourth century, and we shall shortly look a little closer at the distribution pattern. This pottery belongs to the group known as 'colour-coated', as do the wares made in the fourth century in Hampshire in the New Forest. Yet another good-quality southern producer in the fourth century was the Farnham group of potters, to whom we shall return.

In the troubles that struck Britain in the third quarter of the fourth century very serious damage seems to have been done to the general prosperity of the home pottery industry, and this extended to the great producers of coarse ware for the army as well as the fine ware producers. For a long time the origin of the so-called 'black-burnished ware' was entirely unknown. It is now thought there were two main centres, one in Dorset, the other somewhere in eastern England. From about AD 120 till the war of 367 the Dorset potters were major suppliers to the army and the north in general, and between about 140 and 250 they were joined by the eastern factories. There is a similar pattern for the large-scale production of mortaria or mixing-bowls in factories operating near Nuneaton at Mancetter and Hartshill that supplied the army in the north from around the beginning of the second century but also stopped with the war of 367. After the restoration of Britain by Theodosius a decision seems to have been taken to switch northern military orders to a pottery that had been operating since some time before the middle of the century near Malton. This 'Crambeck ware' factory expanded its production to take the large part of this market till it finally disappeared. The same market was also entered in quantity at about the same time by the manufacturer of the 'Huntcliff' cooking-pot from the east Yorkshire area. It is not known whether the war had largely destroyed the former main factories or whether costs were now being cut by reducing transport distances. It may indeed be that long-distance transport, especially by sea, was now much more risky, or that opportunity was taken to change an arrangement that had gone unchallenged for nearly three centuries, though there were now much more convenient sources of supply.

I have outlined some of the main trends in Roman pottery in Britain because of the great quantity in which it has survived and the detail in which it has been studied. For these reasons it is worth looking at certain recent studies of parts of the pottery industry, for they tell us much about what can and cannot be extracted from the evidence.

We noted earlier the Farnham group of potters who were active in the fourth century. However they were only part of a much larger industry which had been in operation for a long time. The whole complex centres on the medieval royal forest of Alice Holt, which helps to explain why the remains were undisturbed for so long after the Roman period. The discovery of more than eighty dumps of 'wasters' or rejects has permitted a stype of study hardly undertaken elsewhere in Britain, for it has been possible to construct a complete sequence of pot types from the first century to the fifth, obtaining their relative chronology from the dumps and their dating by comparison with finds from excavations where other forms of evidence are available. The fortunate chance that there were so many dumps and that many of them have been hardly disturbed since first deposited has established a sound basis for charting the development of an industry and its reactions to changing circumstances. By relating to this examination of the factory area discoveries of the finished product in the places where it actually ended up, historical dates have been assigned to the changes observable at the point of manufacture and the market distribution of the wares in different periods assessed.[1] The results show a successful but comparatively local sale of the output in the second half of the first century, the pot types being adapted from native British forms. In the second century the makers continued these types in production but seem to have been obliged to manufacture 'black-burnished' ware alongside them in order to compete with the newly emerged Dorset industry. This enabled the Alice Holt potters to avoid commercial extinction in the second century and to survive to take advantage of the changes in the market in the middle of the third century we have already observed in connection with other products. At that stage they come to the fore as a major producer. The turning-point in their career, in

---

[1] *Current Archaeology*, 54 (1976), 212 f. (on work in progress by Malcolm Lyne and Rosemary Jefferies).

fact, seems to be the winning of the London market for coarse pottery, which they dominated for much of the fourth century. In the late fourth century they once again took advantage of changes in the country-wide situation, and with new forms and fabrics maintained their success. Their market sensitivity is well illustrated by the way in which they picked up a general change in fashion from around AD 330 in Britain south of the Thames towards pottery in buff fabric; and even their very latest wares reflect the tastes of the close of the fourth century and the beginning of the fifth. They retained their flexibility to the end.

The study of the Alice Holt industry has been conducted on classic archaeological lines. It is worth contrasting certain other recent Romano-British pottery studies based on contemporary marketing theory and mathematical models. Here too the results seem promising, though at times more controversial. Ian Hodder's study 'Some Marketing Models for Romano-British Coarse Pottery' published in 1974[1] suggested that broadly speaking there were four categories of coarse pottery production, each of which displayed a different pattern of distribution. The first was the medium-scale producer, whose sales depended on easy access to a town as focus for distribution. The area reached in quantity was not regular around the town but elongated along any main roads radiating from it. These producers seem to have been able to sell around the factory, around a nearby town and along the main roads. This emphasizes the function of the town as a market and its link to the countryside—and it ought to be added that the pattern seems to hold good for the more substantial small towns as well as for the cities. I think Hodder is right in not trying to push the theory as far as saying with confidence that this means the potters were certainly sending their wares out by means of itinerant traders along the roads to minor markets, since the pattern may equally reflect the ease with which country shoppers could come into the town. Indeed, Hodder's study of Hampshire pottery apparently made adjacent to Chichester shows that the distribution extends markedly to the east and along Stane Street to the north-east, but falls off rapidly

---

[1] *Brit.* 5 (1974), 340 ff.

in the direction of Winchester. This is, as he points out, precisely what one would expect when there are competing centres of retailing; and it is a pattern more easily detected from artefacts in the ancient world, where different sources of supply are more likely to have been used by different towns, than in the modern, where products tend to be manufactured and distributed nationally. On the other hand, we can now substitute the marketing questionnaire and the traffic census for the statistical count of potsherds.

Hodder points out that the same sort of distribution pattern is also discernible in certain other products, such as roofing and flue tiles and other items that could normally be obtained locally only through a town. It also appears in the more expensive types of pottery, such as samian, mortaria, and to some extent the fine wares from the Oxford and New Forest factories. It is very interesting that one area study shows:

> In the late third and fourth centuries, finer wares were only found in large percentages (20 to 25 per cent) in the towns and in sites on or near the roads. These sites with high percentages of fine pottery are not all one class of important site, such as villas, but include small rural settlements . . . Thus, although the pattern may be partly due to the location of concentrations of consumer wealth, the main point of similarity between sites with high percentages of fine pottery is propinquity to the main roads where . . . a reasonable price for the pottery could be maintained.[1]

The second category is the very large producer of coarse pottery, such as Alice Holt or the coarse-ware production of Oxford. The distribution of these pots does not seem to be markedly affected by either towns or main roads, and the suggestion is that the initial cost of the product was kept so low by economy of scale that the cost added by transport was not sufficient to make the price prohibitive. It is therefore reasonable to assume that where the buyer was within easy reach of a town he had a choice of products, but where he was relatively remote only the coarse wares were available to him. There is, however, one particular exception which has also been studied by Hodder, the fine ware of the Oxford kilns, which seems not only to have overcome to some extent

---

[1] Ibid. 350 f.

this disadvantage and to have been sold throughout the region irrespective of urban centres or roads, but also competed successfully with the fine wares from the New Forest. Thus Hodder has been able to demonstrate that Oxford wares were sold much nearer to the New Forest than vice versa.[1] One reason for this is perhaps that the much larger production of fine wares from Oxford may have put it altogether on a closer footing with coarse pottery in price. It would thus have had a big advantage over the New Forest ware even on its own ground, though obviously this diminished in the districts very near to the New Forest factories and their main retailing points.

There is one aspect of the Oxford industry's distribution on which the pottery specialists disagree, and it is a particularly important one. Fulford and Hodder take as their starting-point a contention that certain sites far from the centre of production seem to have a much higher proportion of Oxford wares than their general distribution would make one expect. Since these sites are near good water communications with Oxford, then the cheapness of water transport is the likely cause. If this is true, then perhaps the reason why the Oxford industry grew so large in the first place and was thus able to compete exceptionally well was because cheap transport allowed it to build up an initial market on a large scale. This would provide working capital for further expansion. I have already suggested this as a possibility for the Nene Valley industry. Christopher Young,[2] however, disagrees with Fulford and Hodder: 'In fact, the Oxford kilns do not seem to have been much affected by the availability or non-availability of water routes since the distribution is as strong in areas not reachable by river as those that were.'

It is the middle zone between producers that is the most difficult to predict, since there both the availability of rival products and the cost of the transport are most delicately balanced. Speaking of the New Forest industry, Vivien Swan has summarized the commercial picture that emerges from the study of the larger pottery producers:

---

[1] M. Fulford and I. Hodder, 'A Regression Analysis of Some Late Romano-British Pottery: A Case Study', *Oxoniensia*, 39 (1974), 26 ff.

[2] A. Detsicas (ed.) op. cit. 111.

A highly industrialized organization is implied, whose mass-production was closely geared to pre-determined markets. Indeed, to suggest that something as up-to-date as 'market research' was a regular feature of the system, may well fall not far short of the truth.[1]

Hodder's third category of pottery producer is the very small business, which often does not seem to have been near a convenient market town and whose wares apparently had a very localized distribution. Nevertheless, as Hodder says, 'Although the evidence is slight it seems possible that there were quite a number of small-scale production concerns providing small overlapping areas of rural markets with many of the coarser wares.' They thus have to be taken into account when studying apparent anomalies in the distribution of the larger factories, and it may well be that in many places they could offer the local buyer a very competitive service, with a lower price for the same type of product or a better quality pot at the same price as the coarse wares from the larger concerns. This is the point at which the medium-sized factory probably could least well compete in the more remote districts, which is indeed reflected in the observed patterns of distribution we have been considering. Vivien Swan brings some of these ideas about pottery together in a general point that we may usefully extend to a much wider range of ancient trade and industry—that one may expect three main zones of distribution: one of near saturation around the point of manufacture, one of fairly frequent occurrence in towns and Romanized rural sites, and one where occurrence is rare, often so rare in fact as to be little more than accidental.

So far we have largely been considering the private sector of the buying public, where I have implicitly assumed a modicum of free play of market forces. The final category to consider was perhaps the most important, the requirements of the army and other parts of the government service for which official arrangements existed. It is indeed doubtful if some of the major producers would have survived, or operated on anything more than a local scale, without it; and we have already seen that this is an area where conscious decisions of officialdom, possibly (but by no means certainly)

[1] Ibid. 124.

including issuing of large-scale contracts, affect the pattern drastically. Ordinary 'commercial' considerations are not necessarily here the controlling factor, any more than in modern deals in military supplies. We saw Dorset as a major supplier for the Roman army in the north. If formal contracts did not exist, the manufacturer who transported his pots to the north and offered them to the military purchasers may have been able to overcome the cost of moving them simply by saturating the market and obtaining a virtual monopoly. On the other hand, if there were contracts, very large orders (with the assurance that everything produced would be bought) may have allowed the factories to offer exceptionally low prices that both were attractive to the army and allowed the manufacturer to offset the other advantages against his transport costs. Again, the army may have costed transport quite separately in its accounts or not at all, so that it did not have to appear in the price offered by the manufacturer. Nor can we rule out politics and personal influence as probable factors. In a Roman context it would be abnormal for them to be absent. It is therefore probably futile to expect ordinary market considerations to be dominant in the choice of supplier. Yet by allowing the growth of particular producers these official decisions must have immensely affected the rest of the industry. Thus we have to treat with great caution models that attempt to explain any pottery distribution beyond the most local on the assumption that an essentially free market was in operation. Equally, we may be sure that the Romans would not have understood the concepts of 'fair' and 'unfair' competition as we use them today.

In order to round off the picture I am attempting to form of the character of industry and trade in Roman Britain I propose now to move on from the potteries to look briefly at three other areas of commerical activity, each different from the other. They are the wine trade, the textile industry, and the workshops of the urban craftsmen. None of them escaped effects from the course of political events and in the first two at least we shall see evidence for government intervention, direct or indirect.

The import trade in wine was already, it appears, well established before the Roman Conquest, indeed even before

Caesar.[1] South Italian wine was coming in through the south coast of England in amphorae in the first half of the first century BC and possibly even earlier. One may perhaps imagine that among the agents from whom the Romans received intelligence of Britain were these wine merchants. It may have been unfriendly relations between Caesar and the southern Britons that caused an apparent shift in this trade eastwards to the Trinovantes around Colchester, but it is reasonable to assume that Cunobelinus and his court, once the Catuvellauni had defeated the pro-Roman Trinovantes, kept up the consumption of wine with the same fine disregard for nationalism in trade that is reflected in their conspicuous consumption of other luxury articles from the empire.

One problem in studying the wine trade is that amphorae were also used as containers for oil, fruit, and the fish-sauce that was very popular with Roman cooks. A study of the Roman amphorae from Spain has suggested that certain types were particularly used for the last commodity,[2] though, to quote a comment on one of the best-known Iron Age warrior burials 'not everyone may believe that the Snailwell chieftain went to the next world with jars of fish sauce'. However it now appears that oil amphorae can be identified by the use of gas chromatography and other techniques of analysis, and it should be possible (resources permitting) to eliminate these.[3] Spanish olive oil and sauce were certainly entering the country in this period, but it is possible that the Spanish amphorae of the first and second centuries found in Britain represent an extensive wine trade that was already taking over from the principal Italian shippers before the Conquest and expanded greatly under Roman rule. Imperial concern about competition outside Italy is indeed reflected in Domitian's edict ordering the destruction of vineyards beyond the Alps, but it seems to have had no practical effect. In Gaul in particular the

[1] See D.P.S. Peacock, in D. Hill and M. Jesson (eds.), *The Iron Age and its Hill-forts*, Southampton (1971), 161 ff.
[2] M.B. Lloris, *Anforas Romanas en España*, Monografías Arqueológicas (Anejos de *Caesaraugusta*), 8 (1970) and review article by A.J. Parker, *Int. Journ. Naut. Arch. and Underwater Explor.* 1 (1972), 225 ff.
[3] J. Condamin and others, *Archaeometry*, 18 (1976), 195 ff.

second century seems to be marked by more and more vine-growing. By the end of the century wine was certainly being transported on the Moselle, if not yet grown there.

The civil war between Septimius Severus and Clodius Albinus seems to have disrupted the wine trade very severely. After the Severan victory punitive action and confiscations in Spain resulted in Spanish wine no longer reaching Britain in anything but the tiniest quantities. Indeed, the presence of one of the very few Spanish amphora stamps of the period on a Fen Edge site near Mildenhall suggested that one of the Severan party was present there, possibly carrying out confiscation of properties and their incorporation in the imperial estates.[1] Nevertheless, this setback to one supplier was, as in other industries, apparently taken as an opportunity by others. The two main foreign suppliers were probably now Germany and the Gironde, and there is one clue that the two trades were linked. Rhenish amphorae attest wine from German vineyards, and we have two inscriptions relating to Bordeaux, one the stone of M. Aurelius Lunaris whom we have already met as a *sevir Augustalis* of both York and Lincoln,[2] and the other recording L. Solimarius Secundinus of Bordeaux[3] who is described as a merchant in the British trade (*negotiator Britannicianus*). The particularly interesting point about the latter man is that he originated from the Rhineland, suggesting either that he learnt his business there and then moved to Bordeaux or that like many present-day wine merchants he dealt in the products of more than one region. Oddly enough we do not have any indisputable evidence that the trade with the Gironde was in fact wine. There are something like fifty examples of wine-barrels known from the north-western provinces,[4] made from more than one type of wood, and it has been suggeseed that the famous barrels of silver fir from Silchester (barrels and tubs were reusable as well-linings) represent the Bordeaux trade, since that particular tree is not found closer than the southern part of France. One barrel from London and many in Belgium contain Alpine wood, suggesting shipment along

[1] Phillips (ed.), *Fenland*, 238 (site no. 6879, Holywell Drove, Mildenhall).
[2] Inscription dated AD 237, at Bordeaux (see p. 999 above).
[3] *CIL* XIII, 634.
[4] See G.C. Boon, *Arch. Cambr.* 124 (1975), 52 ff.

the Rhine, which would indeed be an easier route with much less mileage by sea. Less, in fact, is known about the *vignoble Bordelais* in the Roman period than one would wish.[1] Certainly vines seem to have been grown in districts that are no longer producers, as the extensive *cave* discovered at Allas-les-Mines in the deep valley of the upper reaches of the River Dordogne indicates. This may be due to climatic and landscape change; but if these upland vineyards were contributing to the export trade the prices must have been high, since the river is difficult. Indeed, in more recent times it was customary to break up the river craft when they reached Bordeaux, as the return journey against the current was too difficult. There is one possible line of research on contact with Britain suggested by medieval St. Emilion, where the streets are cobbled with stone alleged to have been brought as ballast in the empty wine ships from Britain. Similar petrological examination on Roman sites in the region might well yield significant results.

It is difficult to know what effect further government intervention later on in the third century had on the trade. In 277, shortly after the collapse of the Imperium Galliarum and immediately following the devastation of the economy of Gaul by the barbarian invasion of 276 the Emperor Probus[2] lifted the legal restrictions on the production of wine in Britain and Gaul. It ought to have invigorated the Gallic producers and one might expect the encouragement of new developments further north, where the impact of the German onslaught had first been felt. In the fourth century Ausonius praises the product of the Moselle, where local production was very probably stimulated by the presence of the imperial capital at Trier. The Loire would have been well placed to serve the British market, and the Emperor Julian's reference to vineyards in the neighbourhood of Paris may reflect an outlier of this region or of Champagne. The evidence for British vine-growing is so far exceedingly thin, though there is some reason to think this may partly be due

---

[1] The official Museum of Wine of the *Conseil Interprofessionel des Vins de Bordeaux* at St. Emilion is reduced to using a picture of the Silchester barrels to illustrate the Roman wine industry.

[2] SHA, *Probus*, xviii. 8.

to inadequate recording in past excavations.[1] Only at Gloucester is there anything remotely satisfactory, and that is from the report of a nineteenth-century find and has little detail.[2] If there were British vineyards, we do not know if their production went beyond the small-scale operation that has revived in this country in recent years, nor whether it extended beyond domestic consumption to the commercial market. As today, it had severe competition from British beer, a commodity important enough to be noted in Diocletian's Price Edict, where, as Professor Frere reminds us, its price was fixed at twice that of Egyptian beer, though whether that is much of a recommendation remains an open question.

Another British industry specifically noted in the Price Edict is textiles.[3] This included the British duffle coat (*byrrus Britannicus*) and a woollen rug (*tapete Britannicum*), indicating that by the beginning of the fourth century made-up garments from Britain were commonly enough known to be worth regulating. It is possible that earlier some British products had the exclusivity of Harris Tweed or Otterburn cloth, for in the early third century a garment called a *tossia Britannica* is recorded on an inscription as a present sent by a governor of Britannia Inferior to someone in Gaul.[4] As I have already noted, it was at one time thought that the great fourth-century villas were accompanied by a widespread replacement of labour-intensive arable farming by sheep ranches, partly influenced by the extreme shortage of labour then envisaged for the period. Yet we have already seen ample evidence for mixed farming on the best-investigated fourth-century villa and conversely the bone analysis from second-century Hockwold suggested strongly the keeping of beasts for wool in an area where the population seems to have been relatively dense on the land. Nor is it at all certain that all the wool used was produced inside the provinces of Britain. A Roman model of a bale of wool found in Skye

[1] D. Williams, 'A Consideration of the Sub-Fossil Remains of *Vitis vinifera L.* as Evidence for Viticulture in Roman Britain', *Brit.* 8 (1977), 327 ff.

[2] Gloucester, with its Italian legionary veterans, may anyhow represent the site of an exceptional and possibly short-lived experiment.

[3] For a technical study of the textile-producing industries see J.P. Wild, *Textile Manufacture in the Northern Roman Provinces,* Cambridge (1970).

[4] *CIL* XIII, 3162.

suggests that raw material was being imported into Roman territory for processing.[1] It could, too, explain other Roman objects found in Scotland, even the far north, which may have been bartered for wool.

Finished woollen products like those in the Price Edict were presumably exported to other parts of the Roman world as well as sold in Britain. It is interesting that two of the largest pieces of wool-processing equipment known in Britain do not come, as one might expect, from the countryside but from towns, Great Chesterford and Caistor-by-Norwich. Similarly the *Notitia* mentions one of the state weaving-mills that supplied the fourth-century army with uniforms as situated in Britain, listing the *procurator gynaecii in Britannis Ventensis*. This mill may have been at *Venta Belgarum* (Winchester) or *Venta Icenorum* (Caistor-by-Norwich) or even *Venta Silurum* (Caerwent), but it does suggest a site in or near a town, and a relatively important one. Similarly on the Continent there were such official mills at Trier, Rheims, and Tournai. Unlike the other industries so far considered, this seems to be an urban one.

Another trade centred on certain Romano-British towns, but carrying out much of its actual work in the villas, was the mosaic industry. It can be fairly described as industrial, because it is clear that there were at least four, possibly five, identifiable schools of mosaicists—whether large firms or groups of craftsmen working in a common style and using common pattern-books we do not know—centred on Cirencester, Chesterton (Water Newton), Dorchester (Dorset), Brough-on-Humber, and somewhere in the centre of the south.[2]

All were at their peak in the fourth century, laying pavements chiefly in the villas and clearly responding to the flowering of villa life in the first half of the century. There is some sign that the areas in which they operated were not mutually exclusive—in other words that there was an element of competition. Nevertheless, the Cirencester school, at the

---

[1] Wild, op. cit. 23 and plate XIIc.
[2] D.J. Smith, in A.L.F. Rivet (ed.), *Roman Villa*, 71 ff., especially 95 ff.; D.E. Johnston, in J. Munby and M. Henig (eds.), *Roman Life and Art in Britain*, Oxford (1977), 195 ff. For a list of mosaics see A. Rainey, *Mosaics in Roman Britain; a gazetteer*, Newton Abbot (1973).

centre of the richest villa area of the period, is among the greatest in the west and we may assume it earned a good deal of money for its proprietors. The schools may be classed as urban because there is good evidence that the more complicated sections of mosaic—especially pictorial roundels and the like—were made up by the leading craftsmen in their own workshops and transported out to the site. It seems likely, too, that stores and tools were held in the mosaic firms' yards and one may assume a drawing office or library of designs and some accommodation for the clerks who handled the accounts and other records. Though it is not possible yet to identify similar schools for earlier periods, there is no reason to suppose that at least from the second century similar British firms were not established in the towns, even if in the early years after the Conquest much work was carried out under the supervision of Continental master craftsmen. The output of the mosaic firms in terms of individual products was, of course, infinitesimal compared with the other industries we have so far considered, but it has to be remembered that each piece was a large-scale luxury item and one may fairly guess that the financial turnover of one of these businesses would bear comparison with the mass-producing manufacturers of more everyday goods. The impact of the mosaicists on their towns in terms of wealth generated ought thus not to be underrated, and we should remember that they were only one among a number of crafts probably in the same financial league that are implied by the prosperity of the building industry—for example the makers of decorative and architectural sculpture and the painters of murals, all of whom must, to a greater or lesser degree, have needed a working base in the cities.

Before closing this survey of trade and industry we should not pass over the contribution made to the economy of Roman towns by the smaller businesses represented in large numbers by the individual urban craftsmen and shops. Detailed remains of their establishments are of course well known from Pompeii, Herculaneum, and Ostia, and range from the purely retail and service trades like butchers, greengrocers, bars, and brothels to jewellers, smiths, and bronze-workers who made and sold goods direct. Some establishments, such as bakeries, could be on a substantial

scale, while still contained in city blocks, or *insulae*; and
Ostia in particular has a number of examples of warehouses
and safe-deposit buildings that must have served many trades.
In Britain the retail trade is well illustrated by a shop selling
samian which was destroyed by fire in the forum at Wroxeter
in the middle of the second century, its stock preserved in
the debris in the order in which it had fallen from the shelves.
At Verulamium extensive ranges of small shops, apparently
leased from larger landlords, were flourishing before the
Boudiccan sack of the town, and though it seems to have
taken something like fifteen years before they revived, they
then went on reconstructing themselves on the same lines
more or less unchanged for another three-quarters of a
century. Around AD 150 the shopkeepers seem to have
bought up their leases, for they were then rebuilding
separately. Nevertheless they retained what must have been a
pleasant covered arcade along the front.[1] Shortly afterwards
the whole area was destroyed by fire and subsequently much
of the town was occupied by large town houses. This, of
course, does not mean that retail trade dwindled. In fact it
probably increased as a direct consequence of the arrival of
the gentry, but one may imagine astute shopkeepers who had
acquired their leases now seeing an opportunity to sell out
prime sites at a much enhanced price.

As in the Italian cities, smiths, bronze-workers, and
jewellers are all attested in the shops at Verulamium,[2] and
the recent evidence for gold-smelting under the palace site
in London, though probably official, may have come from a
private jeweller. A particularly interesting luxury trade was in
the making of decorative pieces from Whitby jet. Evidence
for such manufacture is recorded at York and the objects
themselves are also surprisingly common in the Rhineland,
but there without any sign of waste material. It is therefore
almost certain that the jet ornaments were exported as
finished articles, probably from York. In the larger towns one
may expect a municipal market-building or *macellum*: such
buildings are already known at Cirencester, Leicester, and
Verulamium. We may have a suspicion that the much

[1] See Frere, op. cit. 282 for a summary of the evidence at Verulamium.
[2] Cf. *RIB* 712 (Malton).

disputed Site XI at Corbridge is neither an unfinished military headquarters building nor a projected forum for the civil town but a public market. It might even be, like the Piazzale delle Corporazioni at Ostia, a building providing guild-rooms for associations of merchants, in this case supplying the army and trading beyond the Wall. There is Barates of Palmyra, supplier of flags or standards, buried at Corbridge, and one can reasonably imagine the purveyors of black-burnished ware, for example, had accommodation somewhere in the north. We know altogether of five *collegia* or associations in Britain who may have been merchants or craftsmen,[1] but the actual trade is only specified in one case, the 'Cogidubnus' inscription at Chichester, where the donors specify themselves as 'the guild of smiths (*collegium fabrorum*) and its individual members'.[2]

The Chichester guild was prudently honouring the imperial house and had sought the permission of Cogidubnus in his role as local representative of the emperor. The dedication to Neptune and Minerva, deities of the sea and of skill, perhaps suggests they were primarily engaged in metal-work for ships, and the probability that there was a military stores-depot at Chichester in the first century suggests an official market for their craft. Prudence of another sort is demonstrated by the dedication by a trader at Bowness-on-Solway to an unknown deity, apparently as he was about to set out upon some commercial enterprise: 'And if my venture should prosper, then I promise to gild every letter of the verse inscribed on this stone.' To succeed in business in the ancient world one needed friends, the favour of officialdom, a record of loyalty to the state, and the good offices of the gods.

People also needed one other commodity—money. Senators were theoretically barred from engaging in commerce, hence both the emergence of the equestrian class as the greatest power in the world of finance and business and the extensive use of freedmen as agents to run concerns. Nevertheless, the involvement of the richest men in Rome in provincial business was often, as we have noted, hardly concealed, and Dio's statement that Seneca had ten million

---

[1] Caerwent, Bath, York, Silchester, and Chichester.
[2] *RIB* 91.

sesterces out on loan in Britain before the Boudiccan rebellion shows how large the investment could be.[1] However, despite large sums of money coming from private sources such as this in the first century, there is real doubt as to the extent to which Britain had a monetary economy in the first century. Though the evidence is unclear, it does appear that the total number of coins circulating was relatively smaller in Britain than in southern Gaul or Italy at the same time, and where they are found tends more often to be in towns than in the countryside. The relative rarity of coins of small denominations in Britain may also support the notion of the slow development of a fully money-based system, since army pay, the chief reason why coinage was imported in bulk, seems to have been issued in fairly large denominations. However, in the second century the quantity of coins in circulation rises to equal the other western provinces, which would be consistent with the Flavian impetus to urban life and the subsequent strengthening of the towns in the first half of the second century. There is considerable evidence in Britain, too, for widespread copying of coins. This may not always be a matter of forgery since there are signs that it was sometimes permitted because of a shortage of coinage.

The progressive debasement of the coinage was a method many emperors adopted to assist their financial difficulties, though there is no simple answer to the effect this may have had on real prices or ease of trade. Usurpers needed coinage to pay their troops and officials, and being cut off from central supplies often set up their own mints. These coins passed into general circulation. Such usurpers often sought popularity by increasing pay for the troops and, at least at first, improving the quality of the coins themselves. Thus the proclamation of a would-be emperor and an immediate payment of a donative to the troops with promise of more to come might stimulate trade. The earliest known Roman mint in Britain is of this kind. Carausius struck coins at London and at another site, probably Colchester. His successor Allectus continued the practice. The London mint was in fact kept working till around 326, and was for a short time revived by Magnus Maximus. Apart from these relatively

---

[1] Dio, LXII. ii.

brief periods, Britain relied for its supply of actual cash on Continental mints and on the copies already mentioned.

It is generally considered that under the Late Empire the importance of the money economy declined, for a number of reasons including the inflation and lack of confidence of the third century and the tendency to remunerate troops and officials (of whom there were more and more) increasingly by allowances in kind and in plate or bullion. This emphasizes the other side of the picture, that without the presence in Britain of the machinery of the Roman state there would have been no real money economy at all. Andrew Burnett has put the point clearly:

Coins had first entered Britain in large numbers with Claudius's army in 43 and coins had stopped entering Britain with the departure of the army with Constantine III. Mint location, coin production and supply had always been dictated by state expenditure, pre-eminent in which was the army, and this is perhaps the single and most important difference between Roman coin policy and the modern social policy of providing sufficient coinage for daily civilian needs.[1]

The great degree of wear on the latest Roman coins found in Britain makes it difficult to be sure how long they were in general circulation, but by 420 or 430 coinage seems to have no longer been a normal means of exchange. It seems not fanciful to link the collapse of mass-production industry with this phenomenon. The withdrawal or dissolution of the regular army probably dealt it a tremendous blow as contracts ceased to be honoured or large purchases made. Yet this does not wholly explain the end, since we have seen that towns survived at least till the middle of the century and there is little sign of an abrupt break in the countryside. It seems likely that among the major causes is that the distribution system on which the factories supplying the civilian market depended could not work without money, for except in the case of the smallest local concerns it is impossible to see how it could have worked without coinage.

We therefore have a notable paradox. There is real doubt whether before the Roman Conquest coins were used as currency to any significant degree: it is more than likely that the Celtic pieces and occasional Roman coins found in

[1] Burnett, *The Coins of Roman Britain* (1977), 15 f.

Iron Age contexts represent gifts or symbolic offerings, perhaps between potentates, rather than trade. It was the arrival of large numbers of soldiers and officials paid in cash that created the money economy. Thus the introduction of the vast superstructure of a Roman province, in theory a massive burden on a country that had managed to do without it, brought with it the money that made a very substantial network of industry and commerce, some of it on a considerable scale by any standard, both possible and profitable, and transformed the prospects of British agriculture. In Boudicca's time the advantages were certainly not apparent to the Britons, at least among their leaders. Cash tended to flow into the pockets of the small trader or producer and the humble provincial who was recruited into the Roman army or other branches of the government service. Wealth drained out of the estates of the British nobility, who were expected to bear the expense of civic and provincial display and suffered the depradations of corrupt Roman officials. It took the patient work of Flavian and subsequent administrations to bring them round. But by the late fourth century the army had become once more unpopular throughout the empire and its run-down in Britain may well not have been lamented, as we have seen, among leading Romano-British provincials. Central funds had probably already ceased to come in before the break with Roman rule, but the expulsion of Constantine III's officials finally demolished the edifice of provincial government. The Britons had thus knocked out the cornerstone of their own money economy. To many of the British landowners this may have mattered comparatively little compared with the relief from imperial taxation, whether by Arles or Ravenna, and the constant demand for recruits. The collapse of large-scale trade and industry probably hit some of those who had money invested in business. On the other hand, by the fifth century it was the state rather than private individuals that controlled much of industry in the empire, and many wealthy provincials probably welcomed the availability of cheap labour to serve on the land as men were thrown out of work. We have seen in Gaul the rich retiring not uncomfortably to their estates and in Italy the senate becoming more and more disenchanted with the imperial structure. In the first century the British aristocracy eventually accepted that the empire was in their interest. In the fifth century this was no longer axiomatic, and at least some of them were prepared to seize the opportunity to cut free.

From the days of Constantine the Great and Constantius II economic power in the west had become increasingly polarized, between the emperor and the state on one side and the greater landowning aristocracy on the other. First the pagan religious institutions and then the cities had lost their wealth. Spending by impoverished individual *curiales* and by the municipalities themselves was sharply reduced, with all that meant for the many trades that had flourished on it. In Britain the effect was not balanced by a rich Church, nor by the presence of large bodies of the best-paid troops and officials. It was not even softened, as it was on the Continent, by the establishment of barbarian kingdoms that continued to demand the output of long-established Roman factories. It is a transfer of wealth, not an economic collapse that we are witnessing in this period. The financial world may have disintegrated but not wealth based on land. The fifth-century revolt from Roman rule must have completed the process. It was the middle classes and the artisan whose occupations and prosperity were finally swept away as the basis of their commerical world dissolved.

The prospects for the Romano-British upper class may have appeared bright in 409, and it is not surprising that we heard of a period of great prosperity following the break. They might well have continued for a long time to live as well in many respects as before—if not better—had the relations between Roman and barbarian in fifth-century Gaul been paralleled in Britain. But the Saxons were to prove very different from the Visigoths, the Franks, or even the Huns. The political gamble failed and the economic pattern of Britain had been destroyed, with very little advantage to anyone, even the barbarians, for a very long time to come.

NOTE

Ancient crop yields. The figures in this chapter were based on work published before Mr P.J. Reynolds' work at Butser became available. (See particularly *Iron Age Farm*, 57 ff.) The latter is a much more sophisticated exercise than previous research, and is not based only on direct experiment but also consideration of different varieties of grain and other crops and on a number of variables in farming conditions. These results alone suggest that a radical reappraisal will be required—and that his work needs to be repeated on other soils and in other parts of the country.

The figures in the text are given in the light of the suggestions of S. Applebaum (*Brit.* 6 (1975), 121 f.) and of A.L.F. Rivet (Rivet (ed.), *Roman Villa*, 197). At Bignor Applebaum calculates 20 bushels of corn from the acre, but emphasizes the exceptionally favourable soil. Professor Rivet has suggested a minimum of 106,000 acres for grain alone to supply the annual first-century *official* requirements.

21

RELIGION AND SOCIETY

R ELIGION, in all its many aspects, was so embedded in the culture of the ancient world that it is impossible to consider one without the other. Already in the second century BC the Greek politician and historian Polybius had assessed the position of religion in Roman society as the cement of the Roman state.[1] But religion was much more than just a matter of public observance and political loyalty. It permeated every side of life and took many different forms. Our period saw the decline of the old public, formal Classical religion of the Olympian gods and the emergence of new religions demanding personal commitment. Some were based on private devotion; others evolved into highly organized societies of their own. At the same time, the equally personal and very ancient belief in the local deities of family, home and place retained an immense hold over the mind.

One of the reasons why religion in Roman Britain is both so confusing and often so difficult to interpret is the tendency in the Roman world to 'conflate' with Classical gods the deities of the peoples the Romans conquered or that were imported into the empire. This process greatly helped the integration of Roman and conquered, for the Romans were extremely tolerant of foreign religions provided there was no suspicion of political conspiracy (they strongly disliked closed groups and societies) and the rites were not so repugnant as to be intolerable (such as human sacrifice).[2] The fact that the native deities were often much less clearly defined or differentiated from one another than the Graeco-Roman gods meant that the identification could vary from place to place, and it is often difficult for us to determine precisely what deity is involved. There was a further reason for the distortion that often occurred in presenting native gods in Roman guise. Representational sculpture was more or

---

[1] Polybius, vi. 56.
[2] The Christians suffered both these allegations, as did the Jews in later history.

less unknown in pre-Roman Britain and, as far as we know, written dedications foreign to it. Thus when people came to imitate Roman ways by erecting statues and inscribed altars to local gods, this could only be done by means of Classical forms of expression, even though the deities and the ideas they represented might be quite alien.

It is possible to erect a framework to classify the cults found in Roman Britain, but it has to be understood that it is no more than a rough one and cannot become more precise. The first main group are the native cults, those already in Britain before the Conquest. They themselves were very mixed, having grown up locally or been imported from abroad in the pre-Roman period. Indeed it is highly probable that we are unwittingly including in this native or 'Celtic' group many cults that came in from other Celtic provinces *after* the Roman invasion but are more or less impossible to distinguish from those already here. One of the best examples of a goddess likely to have been purely native and local is Coventina, the water-goddess of Carrawburgh on Hadrian's Wall, to whom we shall return. As an instance of a Celtic import we may combine the 'Mars Lenus or Ocelus Vellaunus' who is found on one dedication at Caerwent[1] with 'Mars Ocelus' on another Caerwent stone[2] and look at them in the light of the great sanctuary of 'Lenus Mars' at Trier,[3] itself the site of a dedication by a man from Britain.[4] Here we have the identification of the Roman Mars with a Celtic deity under more than one name or possibly with more than one deity, and there is a strong probability that at Caerwent he is an import from the Rhineland.

The second main group is comprised of the purely Classical gods of the Graeco-Roman world, as for example appear on the Minerva and Neptune inscription at Chichester.[5] These are the deities of the Olympian pantheon. We have another normal form of Roman deity in dedications like those to Fortuna and Bonus Eventus honoured by a husband and wife at Caerleon.[6] Such 'personifications', of Rome herself, of

[1] *RIB* 309: statue base, dedicated by a Roman citizen, on behalf of a *collegium*, as a joint dedication to this deity and the Imperial Cult.
[2] *RIB* 310, dedication by an *optio* (the rank immediately junior to a centurion).
[3] *CIL* XIII, 3654 etc.   [4] *AE* 1915, no. 70.
[5] *RIB* 91.   [6] *RIB* 318.

provinces, cities, or regions are a regular Roman form of expression, though in the case of the goddesses of some of the British tribes, for example *Dea Brigantia*, one might suspect a pre-Roman tribal deity in Roman dress, though one could easily be wrong.[1] Also Graeco-Roman, but of more recent origin, was the Imperial Cult. Some of its roots lay in the 'ruler-cults' of non-Roman states, particularly Egypt and the east, but it was undoubtedly Mediterranean rather than north-western.

The third main group is made up of non-Roman cults that are pure imports and had no native counterparts. These make a very wide range. From the west, from inside other western provinces and beyond, came in particular some striking Germanic cults,[2] probably chiefly through soldiers of German origin. An example is recorded on the altar to the Imperial Cult and to 'the goddesses the Alaisiagae, Baudihillia and Friagabis' set up by the *numerus* of Hnaudifridus.[3] From the east were deities that had long been accepted by Rome, such as Isis (to whom there was a temple at London),[4] or Jupiter Dolichenus from Syria and Sol Invictus, the Un-conquered Sun, both apparently introduced into Britain in the second century and popular in the third, and both at one time or another patronized by the imperial family. Less common eastern deities such as Astarte[5] were probably the object of devotions by a small group of people or a single individual. In the long run much more important were the 'mystery-religions' imported from the east, in which initiation and membership of a congregation promised the worshipper a religious experi-ence particular to that religion and often associated with sacraments and beliefs in eternity or salvation. Among the most famous had been the mysteries of Eleusis in Attica, which was highly respectable and supported by Graecophile emperors,

---

[1] Brigantia: *RIB* 2091 (Birrens): a dedication by a legionary architect. The fact that the cult of Brigantia seems to be particularly strong in the third century rather than earlier may well argue *against* it being primarily native—see Salway, *Frontier People*, 192.

[2] The line between 'Germanic' and 'Celtic' is not easy to draw.

[3] *RIB* 1576 (Housesteads), cf. 1593 (also Housesteads) by the *Germani cives Tuihanti*.

[4] The inscription of the governor Martiannius Pulcher and a jug marked 'ad fanum Isidis'.

[5] *RIB* 1124 (Corbridge): an inscription in Greek by a man with a Latin name. Cf. *RIB* 1129 to Heracles of Tyre by Diodora 'the priestess'.

and the less publicly approved 'enthusiastic' cults that involved forms of religious hysteria, for example that of Cybele. But the greatest were Mithraism and Christianity. The religion of Mithras was a version of the Persian creed of Zoroaster. It became popular in the west among army officers and men of business[1] since it insisted on strict principles of discipline and integrity. It was exclusive in its membership, in direct contrast to Christianity which in some other ways it resembled.

We have noted the vast variety of ancient religion and the difficulty the Classical world itself had in equating Celtic religions neatly with its own cults. The 'Mars' we met at Caerwent and Trier, for example, is probably not simply the Roman god of war but covers a much wider Celtic concept of a 'high god'. For us the problem of interpretation is much worse, for we face the same fundamental problems in assessing the religious manifestations of Roman Britain itself as Professor Piggott describes in relation to what the Romans found when they arrived:[2]

Although we have literary evidence . . . it does not necessarily illuminate the archaeology. Not only may it be impossible to bring Diogenes and his tub together, or the Druid as known from the texts with the sanctuary identified by archaeology, but that other difficulty of inference, the interpretation of a structure in terms of function, confronts us recurrently. Even if one is reasonably certain in interpreting a structure as a temple or a shrine, or in inferring ritual from burial practices, one cannot then relate them to the beliefs held by the ministrants, nor the Order of the Office.

Accepting this admirable expression of methodological sanity—particularly appropriate in an area that has attracted more extravagant nonsense than most—we may go on like Professor Piggott to try to isolate in very general terms some broad features of Celtic religion. This must necessarily draw both on Britain and on the Continent and make use of material from different points in a wide period of time. One of our chief questions thereafter will be to what extent Britain conforms to the general picture that emerges, and to

[1] In Britain its chapels appear in London and alongside military stations, for example Rudchester and Carrawburgh on Hadrian's Wall.
[2] Stuart Piggott, *The Druids* (1975), 48.

what extent it seems to have been idiosyncratic. Another question is how far away native Celtic religion was in fact from Roman: in other words how great a gap had to be bridged to assimilate Celtic religious practices into the life of the empire.

The difficulty the Romans had in identifying specific Celtic deities with their own with consistency partly sprang from the fact that the native gods had less pronounced individual characteristics. Consequently a Celtic god may be identified as Mars in one place or at one time, as Mercury in another. Nevertheless it appears that there was a Celtic concept of a supreme or high god and a multitude of lesser deities, some widely worshipped, others very local indeed. Notable features are 'triads' or groups of three, some animal, others human, such as the very popular Matres or Mother-Goddesses particularly common in the Rhineland.[1] Also widely found are a horned god, sometimes named as Cernunnos,[2] and a god with a wheel. There is also a rider god, at times associated with Jupiter and appearing in the Rhineland on the so-called 'Jupiter Columns' of which the dedication at Cirencester of a column by a fourth-century provincial governor may be one British example.[3] Popular among the Celtic peoples was the equestrian goddess Epona, a cult apparently spreading out from the centre of Gallic resistance at Alesia, scene of Caesar's final victory and capture of Vercingetorix. Her cult spread widely under Rome, and she on occasion appears to merge with the Matres as a goddess of plenty.

Many of the native deities are associated with water, and in particular with springs (as Sulis Minerva at Bath) or sources of rivers (for example the Seine). Ritual pits or shafts also occur quite frequently, and there may be a close association with the water cult, as they often appear to have started life as wells. Indeed it is frequently difficult to be clear whether

[1] For example the Matres Aufaniae pictured on an elegant sculpture dedicated by Quettius Severus, *quaestor* of the colony of Cologne. For the important Matres sculpture found reused in the fourth-century Thames-side stretch of the walls of London see *Current Archaeology*, 57 (1977), 317; 58 (1977), 350; J. Munby and M. Henig (eds.), *Roman Life and Art in Britain*, British Archaeological Reports, 41 (2) (1977), 383 f.

[2] Sometimes alleged to be the origin of Herne the Hunter.

[3] *RIB* 103. There is another from Chichester.

a shaft that has been filled and contains large quantities of artefacts was originally dug as a well or as a ritual shaft, or combined these functions. Such shafts sometimes show signs of sacrifice. In addition there is, particularly in southern Gaul before the Roman conquest, a Celtic cult of the severed head, to which we shall return.

Burial rites in the Celtic world are varied, including both cremation and various forms of inhumation, and as in pre-Iron Age Britain the barrow or burial mound still persists in late pre-Roman times, though less commonly. Burial with weapons and other possessions also continues, though as we noted earlier the number of rich Iron Age 'warrior-graves' that have been found in Britain is very small. In certain areas, notably the 'Arras Culture' district of East Yorkshire, chariot burials occur, a tradition originating in Early Iron Age Europe, but they are rare and the culture is poorer than its Continental counterpart. Very common on the Continent are cemeteries in rectangular enclosures. A number have long been known in Britain, and there is no doubt we ought to take this phenomenon into account as a matter of course when considering the possible function of the very many rectangular and 'sub-rectangular' enclosures that are being discovered in larger and larger numbers in Iron Age and Roman contexts in Britain.

The form of the Celtic shrine is a subject much argued over. A notable feature of the north-western Roman provinces is the so-called 'Romano-Celtic' temple. These range in size, but are generally fairly small. They are characterized by a 'double-box' plan, with occasional variations in the form of concentric circles or polygons. What this implies by way of superstructure is uncertain: they may have been quite low, with a lean-to veranda surrounding a central *cella* or inner shrine, or they may have been towers with a much lower ambulatory. Sometimes the simpler versions have no veranda, and I see no reason at all to suppose any fundamental difference in religion between the Romano-Celtic temple and the simplest shrine, more or less indistinguishable from the native hut. It is indeed true that none of the pre-Roman shrines so far identified in Britain has a veranda and all are circular except the possible example at Heathrow (London Airport). It may well be that the veranda and the rectangular version are ideas that came in from the Continent with the Roman conquest, but the Romano-Celtic temple itself is a form that sprung from the fusion of Roman and native in the north-western provinces and is not found outside them,[1] and the types exist side by side, for example inside the old hill-fort of Maiden Castle in Dorset. Both Roman and German dedications are found in the circular shrines as well as purely native cults.[2] It is normal practice in the ancient world to find all sorts of shrine alongside one another, from the greatest Classical sanctuaries such as Delphi through extensive but unpretentious complexes such as Trier or Springhead in Kent to minor groups such as the adjoining shrines of Mithras, Coventina, and of the Nymphs and the Genius Loci outside the fort at Carrawburgh. The last example was unroofed, and it is likely that others among the simplest type were similarly open to the sky. It is, of course, perfectly possible that the simple types outlasted the more imposing into post-Roman times, when Roman building materials and architectural skills became scarce and wealthy patronage less available in an increasingly Christianized world. But I am certain that wealth and taste, rather than race or religion, determined the degree of architectural sophistication encountered.

Whether the Romano-Celtic type evolved from an Iron Age forerunner remains uncertain, though there are a few possible prototypes.[3] What is certain is that Roman-period shrines often overlie Iron Age predecessors. This occurs both for the simple type[4] and the sophisticated.[5] The Romano-Celtic type itself, despite its common occurrence, is almost uniformly modest in size throughout the Roman period by Classical standards.[6] Like the shrines of pre-Roman Gaul they often lie within enclosures, sometimes in pairs or

---

[1] For the Romano-Celtic temple see M.J.T. Lewis, *Temples in Roman Britain*, Cambridge (1966), 1 ff.; D.R. Wilson, *J. Brit. Arch. Ass.* 3rd ser. 38 (1975), 3 ff.

[2] e.g. *RIB* 733 (Scargill Moor) dedicated by a Roman unit commander to a Romano-Celtic god; *RIB* 1593-4 (Housesteads), dedications by German troops to Roman and German deities.

[3] See Piggott, op. cit. 52 ff.

[4] For example Frilford.

[5] Details of excavation on Hayling Island in 1976-7 were very kindly supplied to me by Mr Anthony King.

[6] Exceptions, such as those at Autun and Périgueux, stand out by virtue of their rarity.

greater numbers, and are frequently dwarfed by the size of the enclosure itself. Professor Piggott draws our attention to a striking characteristic of pre-Roman religious practice:[1]

The concept of the temple as an architectural civic monument, ancient in the Mediterranean and even older in the Near East, was as alien to the Celts as to their predecessors in barbarian Europe ... there are exceptions, mostly attributable to classical influence, but the archaeological evidence is here consonant with the texts in general. Sanctuaries in woodland clearings that might at most be ceremonial enclosures struck the Greek and Roman writers as something unusual, as did the heavy forests themselves. It looks as if much of the awe and horror expressed at the dim barbarian groves may have been inspired by the contrast between a rural continental world in which uncleared woodland still dominated the landscape, and the urban pattern of life in what were by then the increasingly open coastlands of the Mediterranean.

This contains a number of assumptions that we should question but much more importantly points to certain apparently fundamental aspects of Celtic religion. We may agree that the architectural pretensions of the native sanctuaries were small, but they do not seem to have been competing with much in the secular field (other than fortifications) and this need not diminish their importance in the eyes of their people as *monuments*. Secondly, perhaps unintentionally, Professor Piggott seems to equate the Classical temple solely with the imposing structures erected in the cities of the Mediterranean world. This omits the fact that some of the most revered features in the historic Mediterranean cities themselves were very simple, often natural in origin, like the rock fissures and the holy olive tree on the Acropolis at Athens[2] or the Lapis Niger, a black stone in the Forum at Rome.[3] It also ignores the fact that many of the greatest shrines of the Classical world were rural and extremely remote, like Bassae or Dodona in Greece. Thirdly it revives the notion of the overwhelming northern forest, which we have seen good reason to doubt for Roman Britain and probably for Iron Age Britain before it. Nevertheless these are reservations of detail. Forest certainly played a greater part in the landscape than today, and the apparent

---

[1] Piggott, op. cit. 48.
[2] See I.T. Hill, *The Ancient City of Athens* (1953), 174, 177.
[3] See D.R. Dudley, *Urbs Roma* (1967), 89 ff.

importance of the sacred grove in Celtic religion cannot be gainsaid.[1] Professor Piggott summarizes the evidence:

When we turn to open sanctuaries or sacral enclosures we encounter a complex and most intriguing series of sites. These must belong to the same early religious tradition that in Greece gave rise to the concept of the *temenos*, literally a 'cut' or share of land, here apportioned to the god, a 'consecrated and enclosed area surrounding the god's altar, which was the centre of worship and the only indispensable cult structure', and in the Roman world the same idea expressed in the original sense of the words *fanum* and *templum*. Whether the Celtic sanctuary-word *nemeton* . . . included such precincts as well as natural woodland clearings is uncertain, but it could have done . . .

There is a Gallo-Brittonic word *nemeton* which is used for a shrine or sanctuary in a sense that implies a sacred grove or clearing in a wood. The word is cognate with the Latin *nemus*, the primary sense of which (like that of *lucus*) is not so much a wood as a wood with a clearing in it, or the clearing itself within a grove. The most famous *nemus* was that of Diana at Aricia, where

> The priest who slew the slayer
> And shall himself be slain

held, uneasily, the title of *Rex Nemorensis*. Strabo records the name of the meeting-place of the council of the Galatians in Asia Minor as *Drunemeton*, the sacred oak-grove, and Fortunatus writes in the sixth century A.D. of a place *Vernemet*[*on*] 'which in the Gaulish language means the great shrine' (using here the word *fanum*). Many *nemeton* place-names existed in the Celtic world, from *Medionemeton* in Southern Scotland, *Vernemeton* itself between Lincoln and Leicester and in Gaul, *Nemetodurum*, the modern Nanterre, to *Nemetobriga* in Spain. *Aquae Arnemetiae*, the modern Buxton, appears to show how the thermal springs there were associated with a sacred grove. In the eighth century 'forest sanctuaries which they call *nimidae*' are listed as heathen abominations, and in the eleventh, a Breton 'wood called Nemet' is recorded. The word and the idea came through into Old Irish as *nemed*, a sanctuary, and *fidnemed*, a forest shrine or sacred grove.[2]

How far, then, are these characteristics of Celtic religion distant from the practices of the Classical world, in particular the traditions of Rome? Let us start with the idea of a

---

[1] These factors may possibly explain the popularity of the Roman god Silvanus in the northern provinces. For example on Scargill Moor we find Vinotonus Silvanus on one altar and Vinotonus alone on another in the same shrine (*RIB* 732, 733). However it is quite likely that Silvanus himself does not conceal a native god, but is the purely Roman god being equated with a local one.

[2] Piggott, op. cit. 62 ff.

sanctuary as essentially an enclosure rather than a building. Celtic and Classical are here a great deal closer than might at first appear. Nor is this surprising, considering their origins in a common if very distant past. In essence the temples to the deities of the Graeco-Roman pantheon were monuments attesting the honour in which the particular gods were held. Such a temple served as a symbol of the community or state the deity protected, housed his image, and sheltered the votive gifts of people and state. These buildings were *not* intended to house congregations of worshippers, though rites might be performed inside them by priests or magistrates. Public ceremonial and public worship were almost always concentrated on the altar of the god in the forecourt or enclosure of the temple, and in the open air. In Britain we have an outstanding example in the great altar of the Imperial Cult in front of the Temple of Claudius at Colchester, within its elaborately colonnaded courtyard.[1] This may look very different from the native-style sanctuary at Gosbecks Farm outside the same city, where a tiny temple lies in one corner of another large and elaborate walled enclosure, but the principle is essentially the same. The Gosbecks enclosure has, in fact, the same basic feature—a spacious enclosure— as the Classical *temenos* designed for processions, public sacrifices, and public worship, all in the open air. This same emphasis on the open air is of course apparent not only in the great public altars but the little unroofed shrines we noted earlier. But Gosbecks has a further feature, which almost certainly links it with the pre-Roman world. The temple itself is curiously offset in its enclosure, and it is extremely difficult to explain this unless one assumes that the placing was determined by the presence of a holy object such as a sacred tree or grove of trees.

Strabo's reference to the council of the Galatians[2] makes us look also at the Celtic sanctuary as a meeting-place or place of assembly. Two features are particularly noticeable

---

[1] M.R. Hull, *Roman Colchester*, Society of Antiquaries Research Report 20, Oxford, (1958), 175 f. For a reappraisal see D. Fishwick, *Brit.* 3 (1972), 164 ff., and *Brit.* 4 (1973), 264 f.; and for a review of the *colonia* and preceding fortress as a whole see P. Crummy, *Brit.* 8 (1977), 65 ff.

[2] Presumably the Gallic people settled in Asia Minor, though it may refer to the Gauls themselves.

in Gaul: the association of the temple or sanctuary with a theatre and also with a piazza, often conventionally called in the modern literature a forum. The association of temple and theatre is, of course, common in the Classical world, both in city and rural contexts. Urban examples include the proximity of the Theatre of Dionysus at Athens to the temples of the Acropolis, or in a Roman provincial setting the close architectural linking of a principal temple and the theatre in a single complex at Augst, a Roman *colonia* in Switzerland. At Verulamium there is the interesting juxta-position of an elaborated form of the Romano-Celtic temple in its own precinct immediately behind the theatre (itself of northern type) though not architecturally linked to it. For the rural equivalent the great theatre at the sacred site of Epidauros in Greece is perhaps the best known example; and in Gaul one may quote Sanxay south-west of Poitiers, where a theatre lies across a small river from the temple and 'forum' complex, or St. Cybardeaux near Angoulême with its massive theatre built into the hillside below a complicated group of small temples and other buildings. It is therefore very interesting that the example of a Romano-Celtic sanctuary we have already noted at Gosbeck's Farm outside Colchester also has a theatre alongside. It is much smaller in size, but not all Gallic sanctuaries were on the scale of Sanxay or St. Cybardeaux. A small stone theatre at Cherré[1] in a rural setting near Le Lude, approximately equidistant from Tours and Le Mans, lies close to the site of a temple and probably one of the so-called forums, the whole being much more comparable in size to Gosbecks.

The connection of drama with religion is very familiar to us from Classical Greece, but the smallness of the stage at Sanxay suggests that in its religious role it was perhaps more employed as a platform for ritual or speeches to the gathered multitude than for dramatic performances. Indeed we are familiar in modern times with the use of the stadium for the revivalist meeting, and one thinks of the meetings addressed by St. Paul and other leaders of the early Church.[2] The

[1] Excavation in progress, 1977.
[2] There is an interesting parallel in the timber 'theatre' at the Anglian royal site of Yeavering in Northumberland that may have been used by Paulinus in his successful mission to convert the Northumbrians in the seventh century.

'forum', too, would have allowed for the gathering of large groups of pilgrims and open-air ceremonial for those not permitted into the temple enclosure itself.

We have seen how the native religions of north-west Europe and the old Classical cults of the Graeco-Roman world shared the tradition of outdoor ritual. The introduction of congregational worship *inside* sacred buildings was largely the responsibility of the mystery-religions from the east.[1] While there were some fairly large buildings in the Greek world capable of holding congregations associated with mystery-cults, in the west the cults at first chiefly met in small buildings—in the case of Mithraism because the secrecy and the significance of the dark cave were themselves integral to the ritual; in the case of the Christians for safety against discovery and persecution. When Christianity became lawful and official, it was to the secular buildings of the Roman world that the Church looked for architectural models, not the Classical temple.

Another element in religion that became much more important in the Classical world with the spread of the mystery-religions was the concept of the professional priest. In traditional Roman religion every head of a household carried out priestly functions within his own home and family, and broadly speaking this was carried over into the public sphere, where the magistrate (and later the emperor) assumed priestly offices along with his political and military career. There were, of course, ancient rules and taboos affecting the choice and behaviour of the holders of these religious offices, but by and large there was not a separate priestly caste or profession. In many of the oriental religions this was not so, and the separation was made complete when Christianity became the official religion of the empire, however much state might interfere in Church and vice versa. The Greek world had long held the philosopher in high esteem. The wandering holy man is not unknown under the Empire, particularly in the east. However professional priests tended to be equated in the minds of Roman governments with magicians and other political and social undesirables, and

---

[1] For oriental religions see especially E. and J.R. Harris, *The Oriental Cults in Roman Britain*, Leiden (1965).

were from time to time expelled from Rome. Philosophy, morals, and ethics were a proper study for a Roman gentleman and it was held correct that they should inform his public and private life, but the professional priest as such, particularly preaching a moral code, was alien to the pre-Christian Empire, and when he appeared he was treated with suspicion. Since we are pursuing the study of a Roman province, this is the context in which it is appropriate to turn to the Celtic priesthood of the Druids. It is frequently alleged that a political role in focusing and uniting native resistance to Rome was one major reason for the determination of Rome to dispose of them, the savagery of their rites being the other. The Romans certainly took them seriously in Gaul. Claudius, for example, whose interest in history and ritual and whose enthusiasm for promoting the Gallic upper classes in other ways is well known, nevertheless attempted to exterminate the Druids in Gaul. It is difficult to explain this unless the reasons were pressing. Yet we do not have to assume the same was true in Britain. All the examples of the Druids as a major political force come from the Continent.[1] Claudius boasted of tribes and kings submitting to him in Britain but said nothing of Druids, nor do the other sources. Caesar, who could compare Britain—at least the powerful kingdoms of the south and east—with the political structure of Gaul, says of them: 'The Druidic religion is thought to have been found in existence in Britain and taken from there to Gaul. Nowadays those who want to study it deeply still go to Britain.'[2]

In Britain they do not reappear till the year of the Boudiccan rebellion, and then in the context of Suetonius Paulinus' attack on Anglesey, not specifically in connection with the uprising far away in East Anglia. Tacitus certainly describes Anglesey as 'a source of strength to rebels'[3] and 'heavily populated and a sanctuary for fugitives'[4] but the major reason given for Suetonius' assault on it is rivalry with Corbulo of whose recent spectacular victory in Armenia he

---

[1] In the revolt of Vercingetorix against Caesar and of Florus and Sacrovir under Tiberius and again in the native rebellions of the Year of the Four Emperors. Action was taken against them by Augustus, Tiberius, and Claudius.

[2] Caesar, *Bell. Gall.* vi. 13.   [3] Tacitus, *Agr.* xiv.

[4] Tacitus, *Ann.* xiv. 29.

was jealous. The extirpation of Druids is not given as an objective. Tacitus describes the defenders of Anglesey in the following terms:

The enemy was arrayed along the shore in a massive, dense and heavily-armed line of battle, but it was a strangely mixed one. Women, dressed in black like the Furies, were thrusting their way about in it, their hair let down and streaming, and they were brandishing flaming torches. Around the enemy host were Druids, uttering prayers and curses, flinging their arms towards the sky. The Roman troops stopped short in their tracks as if their limbs were paralysed. Wounds were received while they stood frozen to the spot by this extraordinary and novel sight. However in the end exhortations from their commander and an exchange among themselves of encouragement not to be scared of a womanish and fanatic army broke the spell. They overran those who resisted them and cast them into their own flames. Subsequently a garrison was imposed on the defeated enemy and the groves sacred to savage superstitions destroyed (these people regarded it as right (*fas*) to sprinkle their altars with the blood of prisoners and to consult the wishes of the gods by examining the entrails of humans).[1]

This is more or less the sum of our direct evidence for an active part played by the Druids in British resistance. Caesar, more than a century earlier, did not say that he had come across any Druids himself in Britain and leaves us with the impression that he considered Britain in his time as a repository of Druidic lore, giving no hint of contemporary political power or influence. Apart from this passage from Tacitus, Roman references to Druid savagery or subversion are reserved for Gaul and even in this account of Anglesey Tacitus does not actually associate them with the groves or human sacrifices, though it is reasonable to assume that they were.[2] But the most surprising feature of his account is that the Roman troops were amazed 'by this extraordinary and novel sight'. If the Druids were well known in Britain, particularly if they were a major element in British resistance to Rome, one can only wonder why the Roman army had not come across them previously in the years since the

[1] Ibid. 30.
[2] Dio's reference to atrocities carried out by Boudicca's followers on their prisoners in the 'grove of Andate' (whom he describes as the British goddess of victory) and 'other sacred spots' is in the context of the capture of Verulamium and London and his wording (though he seems to confuse the sequence of events) excludes the possibility of a reference to Anglesey (Dio, LXII. vii. 3). There is no mention of Druids.

Claudian invasion. We have no record that Claudius extended
his measures against the Druids to Britain; and if they had
become a significant force in the intervening period one
would have expected the Romans to have heard enough
about them not to be surprised when at last they came face
to face. There must have been Gauls and Germans—there
were almost certainly Batavians—amongst the auxiliary
troops included in the assault on Anglesey. Some of these
must have been acquainted with Druidic practices on the
Continent and been well aware of their reputation in Roman
circles there. The only reasonable explanation is that they
were not common in Britain—and probably had not been,
even in Caesar's time—and that the warlike part they played
on this occasion was totally unexpected. It may well have
been the 'Furies' that really frightened the Roman troops.
In Classical legend the Furies were, like the homicidal female
devotees of Bacchus, only too familiar. Moreover the soldiers
may have been more chilled by the curses directed at them
than by the appearance of Celtic priests themselves.
Barbarians were common enough, but ghosts, black magic,
and curses were taken seriously in the Classical world, and
are part of that darker side of Classical religion which we shall
briefly examine a little later. It is worth noting now that
Pliny the Elder, writing perhaps as late as AD 79 and certainly
revising his book as a whole well after the taking of Anglesey,
talks of the Emperor Tiberius' legislation to exterminate
Druidism in Gaul and then goes on to mention Britain
without saying anything about any subsequent action against
them there as well.[1] On the contrary, he emphasizes that
at the time of writing (*hodie*)[2] Britain was enthralled by
magic and so obsessed with the elaboration of its ritual that
one might suppose the Persians had learnt their practices
from the Britons. Throughout the meagre record of British
Druidism, then, we have this emphasis on Druidic lore and
ritual, not politics nor, with the exception of Anglesey, war.

One further piece of evidence is often quoted to support
the theory of wide Druid power in Britain. This is the great
hoard of Iron Age metalwork found in the bog of Llyn

---

[1] Pliny the Elder, *Nat. Hist.* XXX. xiii.
[2] I see no reason to ignore the plain meaning of the word and assume Pliny
must be referring to a period before 61.

Cerrig Bach on Anglesey itself, much of it apparently not originating from Wales but from different parts of south-eastern England.[1] The tradition of depositing votive objects in lakes and wells was certainly widespread in the Celtic world and water plays an important part in Celtic religion.[2] This find may therefore be evidence for the sacred fame of Anglesey having spread far in Britain. On the other hand, it may reflect the dedication to the gods of the place by local chieftains of fine possessions gained in trade, diplomacy, or war. But the most awkward feature when trying to associate this hoard with Tacitus' Druids is that the archaeological dating of the objects puts the hoard before the Claudian invasion. All in all, we cannot assume a political influence for the Druids in Britain anything like that in Gaul, at least by Roman times. On the other hand, as we shall see, there is every reason to believe Pliny's assertion of British addiction to magic and ritual and no reason to doubt that Druidic tradition played an important part in the mental climate in which Romano-British religion was to flourish.

It is revealing that Tacitus chooses to make a point of the ritual of human sacrifice in the groves destroyed on Anglesey and implies (without actually saying so) that it was a regular practice. This is clearly meant to shock the Roman reader and perhaps to justify the drastic Roman action, but the details described are in themselves significant. The central feature of the public ceremonial in official Roman religion was the sacrificing of *animals* at the altars of the gods. The future was predicted—especially in great matters of state—by the inspection of the entrails of the sacrificial animals by the official *haruspices*. On the other hand, both Greeks and Romans regarded *human* sacrifice as completely barbaric.[3] They could from time to time kill off prisoners of war in a way that most of us would consider unacceptable, but this was done for political or military, not religious reasons.[4]

[1] Sir Cyril Fox, *A Find of the Early Iron Age from Llyn Cerrig Bach, Anglesey* (Cardiff), 1946.

[2] There is the enormous collection of such objects, for example, from the source of the Seine.

[3] There are only two instances which might so be interpreted in the whole of known Roman history.

[4] For example, Julius Caesar's execution of Vercingetorix after displaying him in his triumph after the final victories in Gaul.

The especial horror of what was revealed on Anglesey was that it must have seemed an impious parody of Classical religion, perhaps comparable in its way with the revulsion felt by the Christians at the Mithraic rites, which they saw as a Satanic imitation of the Christian sacraments.

Tacitus does not mention the discovery of any severed heads in the groves of Anglesey. The cult of the severed head had been common in Iron Age Gaul, both sculptured and real. It is possible that Tacitus chose the other details as the most effective, for the reasons indicated above, but there are no other literary references either to suggest such a cult in Britain, though there is some archaeological evidence.[1] On the other hand when Tacitus describes what the army of Germanicus found in Germany when they arrived on the scene of Quinctilius Varus' defeat he goes out of his way to say that they saw human skulls fastened to the trunks of trees and that in the neighbouring woods were the 'barbaric altars' at which the tribunes and senior centurions captured by the Germans had been slaughtered.[2] The argument, from silence, for what it is worth, suggests that the severed head was not a prominent feature in the cult encountered by the Romans in Anglesey.

Traditional Roman religion, the ancient practice of the Roman state, still meant something in Tacitus' time. Under Trajan the *gravitas*, simplicity, and integrity which was associated with the aristocratic way of life of the earlier Republic and was inextricably bound up with the traditional religion seemed to be returning. It is easy to dismiss or deride Augustus' deliberate revival of the old state religion a century earlier as no more than a political sham that only lightly papered over the autocracy and cynicism of his own regime. Nevertheless, whatever Augustus' own inner beliefs may have been, it was part of his elaborate and calculated attempt to restore stability by reviving the outward forms of the Republic. By these means he hoped both to conciliate the remains of the old conservative aristocracy and to draw in the new men who had risen to senatorial or equestrian rank in the Civil Wars and were adopting the attitudes of the traditonal

---

[1] There is for example a coin of Cunobelinus showing a priest with a severed head (D. Allen, *Proc. Prehist. Soc.*, n.s. 24 (1958), 61, pl. viii, no. 68).

[2] Tacitus, *Ann.* i. 61.

upper classes. There were enough people ready to be persuaded of the reality of the restored Republic, or willing for the sake of the return of peace at last to go along with what they knew to be a façade, to make this a remarkable success.

It is a compliment both to the strength of Roman tradition and to the cunning with which Augustus went about laying the foundations of this new state that anything of this survived the appalling record of the succeeding Julio-Claudians long enough to revive in the second century. It is perhaps even more surprising that it came through Domitian's attempt to restore it by means of a bigoted savagery which did not shrink from burying an unchaste Vestal Virgin alive. Yet it still had a real existence as a symbol of the ancient decencies and the majesty of Rome, a function for which late fourth-century senators were still willing to fight when they struggled with Christian emperors over the Altar of Victory. But in many ways this is symbolic. The old religion was chiefly a symbol or talisman, and by the time Tacitus was writing personal spiritual needs were beginning to be met in other ways, a point to which we must later return.

In the last years of the old Republic the state religion had fallen into disrepute because of its blatant misuse by Caesar and other politicians to obstruct one another and to promote their own political manœuvres. Augustus used the machinery of the state religion and all the resources of art, architecture, and literature to promote an appearance of a return to the dignified and honest ways of the earlier Republican past. Linked with this was the close identification of himself and the imperial family with the state religion. This rapidly developed into the Imperial Cult, though it was, with perhaps rare exceptions, only in the eastern provinces that members of the imperial family were actually deified while still alive until well into the first century AD. As we have already seen, the provincial aristocracy played an important part in the official religion of the Capitoline triad—Jupiter, Juno, and Minerva—and in the Imperial Cult of the emperor and Rome. Even at times or in places where it was felt inappropriate to dedicate altars direct to the emperor or even to the emperor linked with Rome, it was very common to dedicate to the emperor's *numen* or *genius*, his presiding spirit,[1] or that of the imperial house as a whole. In fact it became common to add such a dedication to altars primarily set up to another deity.[2] It also became a frequent practice to erect altars 'for the welfare of the emperor' or in his honour, and a large number of these come from the army.[3] The deliberate cultivation of this devotion to the emperor by the army was one of the ways in which the imperial government tried to ensure the loyalty of the troops. Alongside the parade ground of the fort at Maryport on the Cumbrian coast have been found a whole series of altars to Jupiter Optimus Maximus deliberately buried, apparently representing the dedication, at a military ceremony held at regular intervals, of a new official altar by the current commanding officer. Closely linked with these cults were those of *Disciplina Augusta*, or imperial military discipline,[4] and of the *genius* of the particular unit.[5] The regimental standards were normally kept in a special chapel in the headquarters building, and themselves might be the subject of a cult marked by altars.[6] Dedications to Discipline and these other manifestations of loyalty were especially common at times of uncertainty and civil war, and underline the essentially political nature of official Roman religion.

The personal religion of Roman Britain can only be described by that overworked word, kaleidoscopic, for it was not only immensely varied and multi-hued but also changes shape each time one looks at it, making it exceptionally difficult to describe concisely. Some examples may give a better impression of the scene. On Bollihope Common, near Stanhope on the moors of County Durham, an altar of the Imperial Cult was found in 1747.[7] It had been reused in ancient times, and the following inscription (to which I have

---

[1] For example *RIB* 181 of AD 155 from Keynsham near Bristol. For early inhibitions about dedications directly to the living emperor see the discussion of the Imperial Cult at Colchester by D. Fishwick (*Brit.* 3 (1972), 164).

[2] e.g. *RIB* 1585 (Housesteads) to Jupiter Optimus Maximus and the Deities of the Emperors (*numinibus Augustorum*) by the First Cohort of Tungrians.

[3] e.g. *RIB* 897 (Old Carlisle), for the welfare of the Emperor Gordian, his wife, and all the imperial house, set up by a cavalry regiment.

[4] e.g. *RIB* 990 (Bewcastle).

[5] e.g. *RIB* 1083 (Lanchester); *RIB* 447 (Chester).

[6] e.g. *RIB* 1262, 1263 (High Rochester); cf. *RIB* 451 (Chester) to the *genius* of the standard-bearers of the Twentieth legion, erected by one of them as a gift to his colleagues.   [7] *RIB* 1041,

already referred in another context) cut on it: 'To the Unconquered Silvanus, Gaius Tetius Veturius Micianus, prefect of the *ala Sebosiana*, auxiliary cavalry, set up this altar in willing fulfilment of his vow, if he were to capture the remarkably fine boar which many predecessors had failed to catch.' In one sense this is remarkably familiar. It combines light-hearted triumph at a sporting victory with the sort of taste eighteenth-century gentlemen displayed in setting up memorial verses to their favourite hounds. On the other hand there is a distinct feeling that the power of Silvanus is very considerable: the adjective 'Unconquered' is frequently paralleled in dedications to Mithras[1] and in the imperial religion of the Unconquered Sun. One notes, too, the reference to a vow fulfilled, an extremely common feature. Prayer for a specific objective and to a specific god was a central feature of ancient life. It is very common indeed to find this in the context of closely localized gods. At Greta Bridge, in Yorkshire, for example, a Celtic lady called Brica and her daughter who bore the Roman name of Januaria and was perhaps the product of a marriage with a soldier in the nearby fort, dedicated an altar to the local Nymph by name, again in thanks for a prayer answered.[2] Often the deity has no name and is simply referred to as *genius loci*, the Spirit of the Place.[3] Sometimes one suspects the dedicator simply does not know the name of the local god and is playing safe, but one cannot escape the conviction that most people felt every spot had its own presiding spirit, just as every human being had his *numen*, and every enterprise deserved its prayer. Sometimes the *genius* is on a grand scale, scarcely distinguishable from the 'personification' deities of cities or provinces or tribes. Under this heading we may note the dedication to 'The Land of the Batavians' by Ateius Cocceianus, imperial slave, erected on being released from a vow at the fort site at Old Carlisle in the Cumbrian Plain.[4] Much more direct is the thankful dedication of Claudius Epaphroditus Claudianus, tribune of the First Cohort of Lingones, to 'the *genius* of the commandant's house.'[5] This is very close to the ancient Roman family cult

---

[1] e.g. *RIB* 1546 (Carrawburgh).   [2] *RIB* 744.
[3] e.g. *RIB* 646 (York).   [4] *RIB* 902.
[5] *RIB* 1075 (Lanchester).

of the *lares* and *penates*, the spirits of the home; but the wording once again suggests a specific prayer answered. It is akin to the obvious feeling of relief expressed by whoever set up an inscription at Moresby: 'to record the successful erection of the gable'.[1] One of the most endearing is from Malton: 'Good luck to the *genius loci*! Use this goldsmith's workshop with as much good fortune for yourself as you may, little slave!'[2] Many of these dedications are to deities that occur fairly widely over a particular geographical area, but are nevertheless clearly felt to be essentially of that region. Such, for example, are Cocidius, Belatucader, and Maponus who are common in the neighbourhood of Hadrian's Wall. In the last case there is good reason for guessing from the place-name Lochmaben in Dumfries and Galloway that there was a native cult-centre in the region before the Roman army arrived and it was felt wise to honour the local deity. At Ebchester we find Virilis, who describes himself as 'a German', fulfilling a vow to Cocidius, whom he describes as 'Vernostonus Cocidius', either a local version or a conflation with one of his own gods brought from home.[3]

One deity particularly often honoured by the commanders of army units is Fortuna, frequently enough to make it seem a semi-official cult. This may perhaps seem unsurprising in that context, particularly in view of the importance attached to Luck in Roman commanders by their troops and themselves. But these dedications occur unexpectedly often not on the parade ground or in the headquarters building, or even in extra-mural shrines, but in military bath-houses. At Bowes fort there is a particularly interesting example. It records the rebuilding of the bath-house for the First Cohort of Thracians under the supervision of the prefect of the *ala equitum Vettonum* (stationed at Ebchester) by the direct orders of the provincial governor, Virius Lupus.[4] It could thus hardly be more official. At Kirkby Thore another altar seems to have been even more specific about the deity, apparently describing her as *Fortuna Balnearis*.[5] It has been sometimes conjectured that the goddess thus commemorated in bath-

[1] *RIB* 799.   [2] *RIB* 712 (Malton).
[3] *RIB* 1102.   [4] *RIB* 730, dated to 197 or 198.
[5] *RIB* 764, now lost.

houses was not primarily the deity of good fortune in war, but more closely associated with the gaming which was a regular recreation practised both by soldiers and civilians in bathing establishments. Yet though this may be one aspect, it is difficult to associate it with the obviously official nature of many of the dedications. The Bowes inscription perhaps gives us a different clue. It states that the baths were rebuilt because 'they had been destroyed by the force of fire'. One reason why bath-houses were so often constructed outside forts rather than within is probably the risk of fire, with furnaces presumably being stoked every day even in summer, and one may suspect that Fortuna is being asked to oversee a potentially dangerous installation. In other words, the motive is fear.

Fear and gratitude are, of course, particularly evident in the healing cults. One finds represented in Britain as elsewhere altars to the Classical gods of medicine and health, notably Aesculapius,[1] but by far the most striking manifestations are the major centres presided over by native or Romano-native healing deities. The two most notable are Sulis Minerva around the hot springs at Bath, starting relatively early in the Roman period, and Nodens at Lydney in Gloucestershire, which in its fully developed form is remarkably late.[2] The latter was the site of an Iron Age hillfort and a Roman iron mine, and subsequent to AD 364 developed into a pagan pilgrimage centre to the native healing god Nodens, with temple, baths, extensive guesthouse for those seeking help from the god, and a series of rooms that may have been used by patients awaiting visitation by the deity in visions or dreams. Such healing cults, as at many modern saints' shrines, are often marked by votive models of the part needing cure. The best known of the great healing cults in Britain must be that of Sulis Minerva. The vast monumental complex of temple and baths came into use in the Flavian period[3] and is part of the flowering of urban culture in Britain in the later first century, and continued in use to the end of the fourth century or the

---

[1] e.g. *RIB* 1072 (Lanchester).

[2] There are some doubts on whether the religious complex is late fourth century in its entirety or may have had earlier phases as a sacred site.

[3] See, for example, *RIB* 172, dated to AD 76.

beginning of the fifth. Very briefly described, the sacred spring lay at the heart of the layout, linked on one side to an elaborate walled precinct with temple of Classical type and principal outdoor altar and on the other to the massive bathing establishment. Windows permitted a view directly across the spring from the baths to the main altar. At various points in its history the complex was extensively modified, the most dramatic change being the provision of a barrel-vaulted roof over the Great Bath, which may or may not have been covered in the earlier phases. This alteration, which necessitated massive strengthening of the structure, seems to have been carried out late in the second century or at the beginning of the third.

As usual, the conflation of Roman and native deities in Bath is unsure and ambivalent. A fine bronze head depicts the Classical Minerva, and symbols associated normally with her appear on the temple pediment. Yet the central feature of that pediment is a male gorgon-like head, whose closest parallel in Britain is the Oceanus on the great dish of the fourth-century Mildenhall Treasure. The importance of the complex as a religious centre is underlined by the discovery of a statue base standing in the temple enclosure dedicated to Sulis Minerva by L. Marcius Memor, *haruspex*.[1] The *haruspices* represent the Etruscan tradition in official Roman religion, and it is extremely interesting to find one in so distant a province as Britain, and dedicating to a conflated Romano-Celtic deity. Their function was divination by means of inspection of the entrails of sacrificial animals, by interpretation of prodigies (abnormal births and the like) and the observation of lightning. Not all Romans took the art seriously, but nevertheless like much in official Roman religion this did not prevent its acquiring considerable social and political weight. The *haruspices* chiefly operated at Rome and in the Italian cities, and this is a measure of the importance of the cult at Bath.

The general social level of Roman Bath, however, is better illustrated from the many dedications by middle-class army officers and the like. A typical example is that to Sulis for the good health and safety of Aufidius Maximus, centurion

---

[1] *JRS* 56 (1966), 217, no. 1.

of the Sixth legion, erected by his freedman Marcus Aufidius Lemnus.[1] Another similar inscription demonstrates again the linking of Roman and native and the practice of including a reference to the emperors: Gaius Curiatius Saturninus, centurion of the Second legion, erects a stone on behalf of himself and his family to Dea Sulis Minerva and to the *numina* of the emperors.[2] As usual, these are both in fulfilment of vows, and, one assumes, record a cure gained and the hope of future protection from illness and other misfortune. Centurions and their like one finds, but, with the possible exception of Marcius Memor, no one of more exalted rank. In Roman times the spa appears middle-class, respectable, and seriously dedicated to healing and recreation. The growth of a comfortable walled town round the great establishment at its centre indicates that these functions brought it solid good fortune.

The personal needs that took people to Bath in Roman days had their darker side. Curses and magic are not unknown in the material remains from Roman Britain,[3] often occurring at the same sites as the appeals for health. Forces that could bestow health could also withhold it. From the reservoir supplied by the sacred spring of Sulis Minerva came a lead sheet with an inscription in handwriting, each word being written backwards as is common both in Roman and other magic.[4] It curses someone unknown who has abducted or enticed a girl, and includes the names of the suspects: 'May he who carried off Vilbia from me become liquid as the water; May she who so obscenely ate her lose the power of speech; whether the culprit by Velvinna, Exsupereus, Severinus, Augustalis, Comitianus, Catusminianus, Germinilla or Jovina.'

The range of suspects seems large and is both male and female. It is a commonplace to make sure that a prayer or curse does not overlook the right target but the range of sexual practices that may have prompted the deed is interesting. At Lydney the target seems less in doubt. Another

---

[1] *RIB* 144.　　　　　　　　　　　[2] *RIB* 146 (AD 161 or later).
[3] Excavation on the temple site at Uley (Gloucestershire) has produced in the region of 200 'curse-tablets', increasing by about a half the total known from the whole of the Roman empire (excavation in progress; see *Brit.* 9 (1978), 457).
[4] *RIB* 154.

lead plate bears the inscription:[1] 'To the divine Nodens. Silvianus has lost his ring and given half what it is worth to Nodens. Among those who bear the name Senicianus let none enjoy health until he brings it to the temple of Nodens.'

This curse does not seem to have worked—at least not straightaway, for the plaque bears a second inscription: the single word 'renewed' (*rediviva*). More obscure ideas are hinted at by a strange inscription on a fragment of gold leaf found in York which has symbols of unknown significance, probably magical, and a Coptic phrase, written in Greek lettering and apparently meaning 'the lord of the gods'[2] A thoroughly unpleasant plaque from Clothall near Baldock bears the sentence:[3] 'Tacita is cursed by this and declared putrified like rotting blood.'

The Clothall plate had been nailed to some object, as were many of the others. However, not all these religious plaques bear such nasty messages. Many are similar to the stone inscriptions we have already considered, and were doubtless often put up by those who could not afford anything more expensive. However, even from rural shrines, they are often in precious metal, and one may imagine relatively simple structures decked with votive offerings, some individually quite costly. A group found at Barkway near Royston gives an idea of the contents of a rural shrine: a bronze statuette of Mars, seven silver plaques, six to Mars (one equated with a Celtic god as 'Mars Toutatis'), and one to Vulcan, and part of a bronze *patera* or handled bowl regularly used in ancient ritual.[4] From Stony Stratford comes another silver inscription with the familar theme of the vow fulfilled: 'To the divine Jupiter and Vulcan, I, Vassinus, their votary who vowed that if they brought me home safely I would pay six *denarii* now have remitted what I owed to the gods.' On this occasion, however, a new element is introduced into the archaeology, for the inscription was found along with two plaques to Mars and a number of other metal objects that included a ritual head-dress made up of chains and plates.[5]

---

[1] *RIB* 306. A gold ring (the privilege of the equestrian class) was found at Silchester and is now at the Vyne, Hampshire; it bears the name Senicianus: see notes in *RIB* for references to discussion on possible connections.

[2] *RIB* 706.   [3] *RIB* 221.

[4] See *RIB* 218, 219, 220.   [5] *RIB* 215, and see *RIB* 216, 217.

One recalls Pliny the Elder describing the Britons as obsessed with ritual.

This piece may be compared with the ceremonial crowns found at another rural shrine, at Wilton in the parish of Hockwold-cum-Wilton in Norfolk.[1] This lies east of the largest of the southern Fenland settlements and just across the river from one of the richest of the Fen Edge villa sites. The picture of a multiplicity of relatively small cult-centres in the countryside begins to sharpen, shrines that both acted as a focus for personal hopes and fears and, from the evidence of the ritual dress and equipment, were the scene of ceremonial worship as well as private devotions. There is a strong probability that at least some lay on villa estates. The deities are a mixture of Roman and native and the occurrence of votive offerings in silver and occasionally gold indicates the participation in the cults of people of means. We are not dealing merely with the religion of the humblest country folk. A second-century Roman writes to a friend, asking if he has ever visited the head of a certain river, named Clitumnus:

The source itself emerges at the bottom of a fair-sized hill, which bears a grove of ancient cypresses. It bubbles out in several separate springs of varying strength. These converge first into a broad still pool. There the water, clear as glass, allows you to see gleaming pebbles on the bottom and the coins that people have thrown in . . . The banks of the river are lined with ash and poplar, whose reflections appear like objects floating on the limpid surface. The water itself glitters like snow and is icy cold. Hard by stands the ancient, much-hallowed[2] temple. The image of Clitumnus within it is dressed in the official toga of a Roman magistrate, and from the number of oracular tablets[3] visible it is clear that a god is in truth in the place.[4] Many smaller shrines are dotted around the main one, each to a different deity. Each is named and has its own ceremonial, and some even have their own springs, for the main river is joined by lesser rivulets within the site. A bridge crosses below the point where the streams come together, and this marks the lower limit of the sacred water. Above the bridge only boats are allowed: below one may swim as well. The people of Hispellum, to whom the late deified Emperor Augustus gave the place, have provided public baths and an inn. There are a number of private villas as well which have taken advantage of the superb sites available fronting onto the

---

[1] J.M.C. Toynbee, *Art in Roman Britain* (1962), 178, no. 128: cf. 177, no. 127 (Cavenham, Suffolk).

[2] *priscum et religiosum*: compare the Cirencester column (*RIB* 103).

[3] Inscribed slips of wood were cast to foretell the future.

[4] *praesens numen.*

river. All in all, there is nothing that will not delight you. Indeed, you will even be able to indulge in a little studying, for you will see incriptions everywhere, emanating from a multitude of people and to be seen on every column and every wall. Many bear sentiments you will applaud, some will make you laugh—but I am being unfair: you are much too kind to make fun of anyone . . .

This could be a description of Roman Gaul or Britain, but in fact it is Pliny the Younger describing a stop on a journey in rural Italy.[1] The affinity between Roman religion and that of the Celtic areas under Roman rule becomes closer and closer the more one looks at the cults that appealed to the ordinary people of every class rather than the great public ceremonial of the Roman state. We can usefully turn back now, within this context, to the little Romano-British shrine of Coventina at Carrawburgh, and see how even in the far reaches of the frontier one of these local cults, outwardly humble in appearance, could attract large numbers of people over a long period. The shrine itself is the simplest type of structure, similar in plan to a small Romano-Celtic temple but with the well itself taking the place of the usual central chamber or *cella*. In this well were found more than 13,000 Roman coins and a mass of pots, altars, carved stones, incense-burners, pearls, a skull, and other objects. Some of these may have been cast in during a period of desecration, perhaps by Christians (the nearby chapel of Mithras was also destroyed) but much seems to have been deposited as votive offerings, and the association of water, a shaft, and possibly the human skull suggest strong links with some of the central characteristics of Celtic religion. Dedicators include officers, soldiers, and possibly civilians, and the coins continue down to the reign of Gratian.[2]

There is good reason, in fact, to suspect a continuation (or reimportation) of the cult of the ritual shaft in Roman Britain. At Ashill in Norfolk religious practices in association with a shaft were being carried out in the Flavian period[3] and at Cambridge a site that had previously been occupied

---

[1] Pliny, *Letters*, viii. 8.
[2] See *RIB* 1522-35 (especially 1526 to *Nimfae Coventine* by Mahudus, a German; 1529, with a representation of the goddess; and 1530, 1531—incense-burners 'to Coventina Augusta' made by Saturninus Gabinius with his own hands).
[3] *East Anglian Archaeology*, 5 (1977), 9 ff.

by a shrine, possibly going back to the Iron Age, produced nine shafts. In each shaft there was the burial of a dog and one or more babies. These shafts date from the late third century or early fourth. The children were buried with shoes (a practice to which we shall return when we consider burial in general), and the presumption is that they were children who had died in infancy, buried in holy ground, and in the most elaborate and sanctified manner in shafts to help them on their way into the next world, rather than the reverse purpose of their burial making the shafts sacred. On the other hand, in late pre-Roman times sacrifice may well have been employed in this connection, for the head of a woman, still attached to the neck, was buried behind the lining of a well at the rural settlement at Odell in Bedfordshire.[1]

For the survival of the severed head cult itself within the Roman period we have no certain evidence from Britain.[2] The skull from Coventina's well may be accidental, and it is probable that if there had been any such cult in an active form on such a site where it would be immediately detected by the Roman authorities it would have been promptly suppressed. The skulls from the Boudiccan destruction layers at London might at first suggest the Britons were still head-hunting in war, but the exhibition of the heads of executed traitors was after all normal in England as late as the seventeenth century and in that age had no religious significance.[3] Indeed, Tacitus' description of the massacres carried out by Boudicca in the captured Roman cities reads in its details like a savage parody of Roman criminal justice at its most cruel. Nevertheless, it is possible that some of the sculpture from Roman Britain—particularly the Towcester and Gloucester heads—records the survival of such cults in symbolic form under Roman rule.[4]

[1] *Current Archaeology*, 66 (1979), 217.

[2] See p. 706 below for decapitated skeletons in Late Roman cemeteries. At present these seem to be a purely funerary ritual, with no proven connection with the Iron Age cult. However, it is interesting to note decapitated skeletons also at Odell.

[3] The public display of gibbeted criminals, of course, survived into the nineteenth century.

[4] The Towcester head is probably funerary, but with a likely Gaulish connection (see J.M.C. Toynbee, op. cit. 148, no. 48). It has, however, been argued that the Gloucester head may not be Roman but Romanesque, in other words early medieval. (*Ant. J.* 55 (1975), 338 ff.)

Personal religion is, of course, a subject that cannot be separated from death and burial, and the range of burial customs displayed in Roman Britain is wide.[1] The two main rites were cremation and various forms of 'inhumation' or burial of the body unburnt; and there is no evidence known to me of exposure of bodies above ground during the Roman period as in certain eastern cultures. In very broad chronological terms cremation, the traditional Roman practice, was the dominant rite during the first and second centuries and inhumation in the third, fourth, and fifth. This seems to have been partially but not entirely due to the spread of Christianity and a literal belief in the resurrection of the body. At Chichester, the St. Pancras cemetery which was used from Flavian times till the fourth century (but less frequently after about AD 200) produced a total of 260 burials from the excavation of 1966-9, all but nine of which were cremations.[2] In contrast, a small rural cemetery at Martyr Worthy in Hampshire, which started in the second century and continued into the fourth, contained inhumations only.[3] There are exceptions to the pattern. The large cemetery at Guilden Morden in Cambridgeshire, for example, produced anomalies in the form of a fine first-century inhumation and a cremation of the late third century or early fourth. However, there is no doubt that pagan funerary fashion was moving in the direction of inhumation elsewhere in the Roman world concurrently with the rise of Christianity, but was already well established in Britain as part of this general trend before the Christian religion had any real hold here. The depositing of objects with the dead, either to help the soul on its journey to the other world, to comfort the dead in the grave, or as a mark of respect and adornment for the corpse at burial, may have become less common with Christian influence but did not die out. Their presence does not rule out a Christian burial nor their absence prove one: the elaborate accompaniments of the body of Maria, wife of the most

---

[1] See J.M.C. Toynbee, *Death and Burial in the Roman World* (1971), for a general survey. R. Reece (ed.), *Burial in the Roman World*, CBA Research Report 22 (1977) is a collection of papers containing much research on Britain or directly relevant to it. The scattered material from the important cemeteries in the Cambridge area has been collected by Miss Liversidge (*Proc. Camb. Ant Soc.* 67 (1977), 11 ff.).

[2] *Brit.* 1 (1970), 302.

[3] *Brit.* 7 (1976), 364.

Christian Emperor Honorius, could hardly make this point more strongly. Similarly, while there is a tendency to orientate Christian burials east–west it is by no means universal; and pagan cemeteries with regular orientation are not unknown.[1]

Under Roman law it was illegal to bury the dead within a town. At the same time there was a strong desire not to be overlooked after death and a fear of loneliness in the grave. Hence we find the main roads leading from cities lined with cemeteries. Here the dead could be sure that the passing traveller would notice their memorials and perhaps stop to read an inscription, and expect their family and friends to gather on certain festivals. At Winchester, where one of the major town cemeteries lay alongside the road to Mildenhall, the earliest graves lay closest to the city.[2] Sometimes cemeteries went out of use and were not always respected, but on the whole the pattern of cemeteries can be used by the historian to define the outer limits of settlement, particularly for periods when they can be proved to have been in use. Sometimes renewed urban growth was obliged to site itself beyond the earliest cemeteries. This is particularly true of civil settlements outside major military bases, where one may often suspect that very early army graves prevented civil development occurring close to the fortress itself, even if reasons of tactical prudence did not forbid it.

The same tendency for burial to occur near roads is also observable in the countryside, as, for example, the Martyr Worthy and Stanton Harcourt groups which lie alongside country lanes. A type of cemetery well known on the Continent and frequently recognized in a rural context seems to carry through from the pre-Roman Iron Age into the Roman period. These commonly take the form of a rectangular enclosure like those of the Iron Age mentioned earlier; usually marked by a ditch and bank.[3] Some of the

[1] All the graves in the inhumation cemetery excavated at Stanton Harcourt in Oxfordshire in 1978 were arranged north–south, apparently aligned on a lane, though the bodies themselves lay in no single manner. The presence of the decapitation rite among the burials suggests the cemetery was at least partly pagan.

[2] *Brit.* 7 (1976), 371.

[3] A British example at Puckeridge in Hertfordshire contained sixty cremations, and was apparently associated with a Roman settlement abandoned about AD 80 which had succeeded an Iron Age site. Most of the burials had 'three or more pots and a pair of hobnailed boots', some had glass containers or metal-fitted wooden caskets (*Brit.* 4 (1973), 299 f.).

66

Continental examples have evidence for wooden gates at the entrances, and an example from Würtemberg is particularly significant in that its bank overlay one of those shafts with a stake at the bottom noted as a feature of Celtic relgion.[1] A study by Dr Edith Wightman has indicated that in the part of the Rhineland around Bonn some of these enclosures seem to have gone out of use with the arrival of the Romans, but that others continued and that there was an apparent revival in the fourth century of some of those that had fallen out of use. She has also, most significantly, detected a relationship between the cemeteries and the distribution of Romano-Celtic temples in the region.[2]

While it might appear at first sight that some of the most ancient Christian churches and their associated cemeteries in Continental cities break the rule excluding burial within cities, which continued in force even when Christianity became the official religion of the empire, it becomes clear on closer examination that the churches usually originated from chapels set up in cemeteries that lay at the time outside Roman cities. In many cases these were over the graves of martyrs, and attracted subsequent burials of Christians who wanted to be as near as possible to the saint. The best known example is probably that of the Basilica of St. Peter at Rome, the result of an enormous engineering operation by Constantine to erect his church over the existing extra-mural cemetery on the Vatican hillside that was believed to contain the grave of St. Peter himself.

Only infant burials seem to have been exempted from the general prohibition, judging from their occurrence within towns and other settlements; and it may be that the Classical right of a father to decide whether or not the new-born child should be brought up or exposed affected belief about the necessity to bury outside the inhabited area.[3] Until the baby had been formally recognized by the father and taken into

[1] H. Zürn, *Proc. Prehist. Soc.* 37, 2 (1971), 218 ff. In Germany the larger versions of these enclosures (about which there has been much archaeological debate) are known as *Viereckschanzen*. See Piggott, op. cit. 67 ff. for a convenient account.

[2] E.M. Wightman, *Bonner Jahrb.* 170 (1970), 211 ff. At Litlington in Cambridgeshire and other British sites the enclosures are sometimes walled.

[3] There are even examples on military sites (e.g. barracks at Malton, a tower at Chesters).

the family its existence as an individual was perhaps un-confirmed. In country districts, too, where convention if not law excluded normal burial within farm or villa precincts, groups of infant burials are not uncommonly found in the corners of farmyards.[1] On the other hand, where adult remains are found in settlements there is a *prima facie* case for suspecting accident or murder. In the Fen Edge settle-ment at Hockwold the skeleton of a man was found buried in silt in a ditch, and it seemed probable that his presence was not known when the site was reoccupied briefly after a severe flood.[2] On the other hand, the couple buried under a new floor in one of the buildings of the civil settlement outside Housesteads, the man having a sword-point embedded in him, had obviously been concealed with intent.[3]

Ghosts were much feared and needed placating, but there was also a more friendly aspect to the cult of the dead. The famous 'pipe' cremation found at Caerleon, where a tube led from the canister holding the ashes to the surface, is an example of a Mediterranean practice rare in the northern part of the empire but underlines the very common Classical belief that the dead could benefit from libations offered at the tomb by the living. Fear that one would not receive proper burial and one's spirit wander unregarded encouraged the formation of burial clubs. These were not only responsible for arranging the funeral but also held regular meetings and commemorative meals, and often purchased plots reserved for the burial of their members and at which they could gather. These societies were particularly popular with slaves and the poor, who might be without means or surviving relatives to ensure a ritually complete funeral and commemorative rites on anniversaries thereafter. At Halton Chesters on Hadrian's Wall the tombstone of a slave named Hardalio was erected by an association set up

[1] The very large group from the villa at Hambleden is probably a special case.
[2] *Proc. Camb. Ant. Soc.* 60 (1967), 55. Dismembered skeletons found in Late Iron Age or early Roman ditches at Canterbury in an area later included in the town were, whatever the means they came by their deaths, probably not known to the subsequent Roman inhabitants.
[3] Cf. Canterbury, a very similar case (two soldiers). A different sort of irregular burial suggesting murder is the possible concealment of a body in an already occupied grave in the Roman cemetery at Dunstable (*Current Archaeology*, 69 (1979), 312; CBA Group 9 *Newsletter*, 9 (1979), 7).

by his fellows.[1] In such cases the association took the place
of the dead man's family. At Ostia a clearer picture of their
activities emerges when one contemplates the rows of tombs
fronting on to the main road into the city, some with neat
enclosures or gardens in front, where offerings might be
left, flowers grown and the funerary or commemorative
banquet held.[2] It is indeed not uncommon to portray the
dead man himself as present at the banquet. The tombstone
of the Moorish freedman Victor at South Shields shows him
lying comfortably on a dinner-couch, while a small figure
offers him wine from a bowl lying beneath the seat.[3] Such
representations cannot, of course, be dissociated from
ideas of the dead in paradise or from the ritual meal common
to several religions current at the time, though it is often
extremely difficult to know the meaning of the scenes
portrayed to the people who purchased the monuments,
since gravestones and sarcophagi were sometimes bought
from the ready-made stock kept in the mason's yard,
awaiting only the addition of a suitable inscription. It is
well-known that the iconography of one religion was often
adapted by another and given a new meaning, and this
practice in the funerary masons' trade can only have
encouraged the flexibility we so often encounter.

There is evidence, particularly from the higher levels of
society, that the family duty to bury and commemorate the
dead was conscientiously carried out generation after generation. In Britain the great earthen burial mounds—'barrows'
or *tumuli*—at Bartlow on the border of Essex and Cambridgeshire are perhaps the best known instances. There is a similar
set at Stevenage and both probably represent the same social
group, the Romano-British aristocracy. Indeed, it is possible
that both families were members of the same *civitas* and

---

[1] *RIB* 1436: the *collegium conservorum* recorded suggests a larger group of
slaves than one would expect to find as the domestic servants of a camp commandant or other soldier stationed there. They were perhaps employed in some
enterprise, private or official, unknown to us: the fact this fort lay closest to the
gate where Dere Street crosses the Wall may have some connection with this.

[2] The importance of flowers and tomb-gardens as representing the dead
reunited with the life of the Earth is emphasized by Richmond, *Archaeology and
the After-Life in Pagan and Christian Imagery*, Oxford (1950), 26 f.

[3] *RIB* 1064: the cup-bearer is perhaps his own slave-boy, though such figures
are often a conventional part of such a scene.

represented on its council. At Holborough in Kent there is a particularly interesting example of behaviour towards the dead. There a barrow had been constructed over an elaborately carried-out cremation, which can be dated to the beginning of the third century, and a secondary burial, this time the inhumation of a child, had been inserted into it within a few years. Both the initial Holborough burial and one of the Bartlow barrows contained a folding stool and it is clear that both stem from the same social class. The child's interment at Holborough was, it appeared, carefully inserted, probably with the intention of respecting the original burial. There is a strong chance that this reflects a deliberate family decision. Indeed, it is perhaps not completely fanciful to catch in the change from cremation to inhumation one of those rare echoes of family life; for there were signs that the original cremation had been considered already rather archaic when it was carried out, for the ashes were deposited in a curious mock-coffin, almost as if the wishes of an elderly and conservative member of the family to be buried in the old manner had been carried out by his heirs, but with an attempt to make the rite conform to more modern ideas. When the child died a little later, there was no need for such pretence.

The substitution of inhumation for cremation as the mostly commonly adopted form of burial went deeper than mere fashion, and we should not imagine that the family debate we have imagined at Holborough was about trivialities. Sir Ian Richmond considered that the change from cremation to inhumation reflected the triumph of Roman individualism over Greek conceptions of the merging of the soul after death in a universal godhead or divine force.[1] I do not think this can be sustained. Cremation was not only Greek, it was also the traditional Roman form of funeral. In point of time, the change overlaps with the period when Neoplatonic ideas were modifying traditional Roman philosophy and when the eastern mystery religions were winning converts in the west and affecting general ideas about death and the afterlife. It accords more easily with these facts to see Roman respect both for the family and the identity of the individual ancestor as providing an environment in which the new ideas could

[1] Cf. Richmond, op. cit. 41.

flourish. Christianity and to some extent the other religions which had been developing in the eastern part of the known world where Greek and oriental met offered individual contact with the divine, salvation, and a life after death. To many Romans this was a creed that was compatible with, indeed enhanced, their own ancestral notions of personality. However, there is no reason to think that without the arrival of these outside influences, predominantly eastern, the Romans would have changed their burial customs. Their innate conservatism, at its most intense in the religion of the family, would almost certainly have held them to their ancient practices to the end.

The emphasis on the individual is reflected more clearly by the obvious importance placed in Roman Britain on the grave, and the monuments by which the dead were recorded, however varied their form. They were normally inscribed, and the classic type is a dedication to the *manes* or spirit of the deceased. It records his name, parentage, voting tribe if a Roman citizen, his career and distinctions, and the name and relationship of the person or persons erecting the monument. Sometimes the dead person is portrayed in relief sculpture, ranging in style and competence from the splendid full-length relief of M. Favonius Facilis, a centurion of the Twentieth legion, erected around the middle of the first century at Colchester by his freedmen,[1] down to the very crude but touching stone commemorating Vacia, *infans*, aged three, buried at Carlisle.[2] It is common to find monuments being erected by the heirs of the dead, by spouses, parents, sons or daughters. Freedmen, too, often appear in this role, in many cases doubtless because they have been set free in their master's will—an accepted practice—but often as their late employer's closest associate or man of business. The exact age of the deceased at death is very frequently recorded, though there is a tendency in later inscriptions to adopt the formula 'lived for more or less so many years . . .' (*vixit plus minus*), a practice probably influenced by the spread of Christian notions of the relative unimportance of earthly life and its duration.[3]

[1] *RIB* 200: its excellent state of preservation is probably due to its being thrown flat during the Boudiccan rebellion.   [2] *RIB* 961.
[3] For example the tombstone of Flavius Antigonus Papias, a Greek (*RIB*

The tombstone of Favonius Facilis was originally plastered and painted, in the manner of much ancient sculpture whether of stone or wood, and it is probable that most of the carved lettering on stone inscriptions was similarly coloured. In areas where stone was scarce or where the family were too poor to afford stone there were doubtless very many wooden monuments with lettering that was either carved or sign-written. The ashes from cremation burials are in Britain generally found in pots or glass jars; inhumations were either in wooden, lead, or stone coffins or placed straight into the ground. Lead coffins are themselves found enclosed in stone outer cases, sometimes supplied from quarries far away. This could cause unfortunate mistakes. At the Arbury Road cemetery at Cambridge there were clearly some exceptionally incompetent undertakers. Among other errors the most spectacular resulted in the stone coffin having to be split across its middle to accept the lead inner coffin which was too long for it. The scene at the funeral can be left to the imagination. We cannot, however, always blame the undertaker, as there was much reuse of funerary monuments. One interesting practice, found for example at York and in the recently excavated Poundbury cemetery at Dorchester in Dorset,[2] is the pouring into the coffin of liquid gypsum. This set, leaving a mould of the body, and has proved efficient in preserving hair and other materials. In the Poundbury cemetery for example the gypsum filling of a stone coffin had kept the outline of a shroud edged with gold wire.[3]

The tomb itself, when it was more than a simple grave, could range from a small stone or tile structure, through unostentatious vaults to large buildings intended to mark the importance of the deceased or to provide accommodation for generations of dead from the same family or club. The Bartlow Hills, with their flat tops, are mounds closely connected in form with those common in Gallia Belgica and probably part of the same cultural tradition. There are

---

955, Carlisle): on this stone the pagan formula *Dis Manibus* is retained, though by the fourth century it seems to have become a formality employed by pagans and Christians alike.

   [2] *Brit.* 6 (1975), 277.   [3] *Brit.* 1 (1970), 299.

a few circular stone or partly stone tombs, such as that at High Rochester (Bremenium) in Redesdale,[1] which may be culturally associated with these barrows but are perhaps more likely to be derived from circular monuments fairly common in the Classical world. One of the grandest British monuments is the mausoleum on the plateau of Shorden Brae above the Tyne, which lies between the Roman town of Corbridge and the site of the Agricolan fort.[2] It consisted of a central structure, probably a tower, containing a pit, and lay within a large walled enclosure the corners of which seem to have been decorated with impressive stone lions. The monument was dated to the middle of the second century by one pot from the central building. It is not, in fact, absolutely certain that there was ever a body deposited in the monument, as there was no trace of a burial except for nails in the pit that might have come from a box or coffin. It is not impossible that it was a cenotaph for a very senior officer killed in the Antonine wars in the north.

One is reminded here at Shorden Brae of the monument to M. Caelius, centurion of the Eighteenth legion, lost in the disaster of AD 9 in Germany, on which his brother specifically states that the bones have not yet been recovered.[3] Great importance was attached by the Romans to the proper disposal of the body and heirs felt it incumbent upon them to make it clear that they were doing the best they could by erecting a cenotaph when an actual burial was impossible. Six years after the defeat Germanicus made it a particular point of honour to reach the camp of Varus where the bones of his men lay still unburied and to give them proper burial, marking the spot with a turf monument. The Emperor Tiberius subsequently disapproved, and one of the possible reasons given by Tacitus provides a sudden insight into Roman practices and beliefs:[4] 'It is possible that he felt a Roman commander-in-chief, invested with the powers of an

---

[1] I.A. Richmond, 'The Romans in Redesdale', *History of Northumberland*, Vol. 15, Newcastle upon Tyne (1940), 105.

[2] See J.P. Gillam and C.M. Daniels, *Arch. Ael.* 4th ser. 39 (1961), 37 ff. This was originally discovered on an air photograph and resembled a Romano-Celtic temple in shape. The tentative identification as a mausoleum was later confirmed by excavation.

[3] *CIL* XIII, 8648.   [4] Tacitus, *Ann.* i. 62.

augur and other most ancient religious roles, should not take part in funerary rites.' The underlying concepts are of the sanctity and purity of the priest and the ritual defilement associated with contact with death. These are found in many religions. The peculiarly Roman element is that the religious powers, like the secular ones, stem from the office: once the general or magistrate came to the end of his appointment he also laid down his priestly powers and the ritual restrictions they imposed upon his behaviour.

While the correct burial of the dead was felt a matter of great importance, a sacred trust laid upon the living, the elaborate precautions taken by some Romans to make sure that their tombs were not disturbed suggest that there was less respect for old graves than one might expect.[1] It is common to find threats against perpetrators of damage to the tomb or even secondary burial in it incorporated in funerary inscriptions. Such fears were not groundless. The Roman city walls of Chester, for example, show that in the fourth century large numbers of tombstones were uprooted to provide material for repairs; and even where one might least expect it, disturbance seems to have occurred. However there are sometimes signs that this was done with respect. The Corbridge mausoleum was demolished in the Late Roman period, but some of the sculptured stone was buried in a pit, like the annual altars on the parade ground at Maryport; and it is clear that for some unknown reason one of the burials in another important mausoleum was removed carefully.

This latter monument is in other ways in contrast to the Shorden Brae example, for it lies in the south, is associated with a villa and was certainly not a cenotaph. Its owners, however, may have been officials. Alongside the house at Lullingstone in Kent, this mausoleum matches both the pagan and Christian features of the villa itself in importance. It is graphically described by Joan Liversidge and tells us much about the importance attached by Romans to the housing of the dead:

[It] was at first believed to be a temple of normal Romano-Celtic type with a rectangular *cella* approached through a columned doorway with a wooden door. Fragments of wall-painting, some of them showing

---

[1] Reece (ed.), op. cit. 51: possible desecration of pagan cemetery at York.

the legs and feet of figures on a green background, occurred in the
cella with voussoirs of tufa covered with *opus signinum*.[1] The ambulatory outside had a floor and walls of pink cement and a recess for an
altar or possibly a funerary relief; for underneath the building the
excavators found a burial vault 10 feet square cut into the chalk. It
had contained two adult inhumations in lead coffins but one lead coffin
had been removed in the late fourth century; presumably without its
grave goods, as the vault still contained two identical groups, each with
a glass flask with dolphin-shaped handles, a knife and a spoon. The
bases of two glass bowls were also recovered and two flagons, one of
bronze, the other of colour-coated pottery. The surviving coffin was
decorated in relief with scallop shells and cable pattern and on its lid,
near the head, lay [a] games board and thirty gaming pieces . . . The
skeleton inside the coffin had been buried wearing some form of
leather clothing and pieces of linen were also identified. A pebble
with a hole in it lay by its left hand. Originally the two burials had
been enclosed in a wooden cist 7 feet square and 4 feet high which had
been bolted into the clay with eight heavy 9-inch bolts and angle-irons,
one of which was used as a wedge for levelling one corner. Above this
came layers of puddled chalk and gravel, the top layer forming the
cella floor.[2]

Sometimes, as here, the burial was intended to be hidden
from sight, and one may assume the decoration on the lead
coffin was for the purposes of the funeral and to please the
dead. Many stone sarcophagi also were clearly intended to
be buried. Others, however, were elaborately decorated and
meant to remain above ground or in a vault where they could
be seen. Sometimes they were free-standing, in other cases
they are undecorated on the back and intended to stand in a
niche or against a wall. Some bear inscribed panels very
similar to the free-standing tombstones;[3] and a fashion for
portrait busts of the deceased in low relief in a central *tondo*
or roundel, often of a married couple, has provided us with
some of our most important examples of Late Roman
portrait sculpture. The imperial families of the fourth and
fifth centuries indulged in the most extravagant and gigantic
sarcophagi of Egyptian porphyry, a stone both difficult to
transport and to work and a fitting monument to the
deliberate cult of personal grandeur practised by Diocletian
and his successors. These sarcophagi were often housed in
commissioned mausolea, an imperial taste going back to the

---

[1] A cement rendering incorporating crushed tile, also used for floors and walls.
[2] Joan Liversidge, *Britain in the Roman Empire* (1968), 479 f.
[3] e.g. *RIB* 16 (London); *RIB* 687 (York).

very foundation of the Empire. They are extreme examples of the enduring desire of the Roman and provincial nobility for their dignity to be remembered after death.[1]

The funeral itself had long been an important opportunity to display the family distinctions, and in upper-class families images of the ancestors were carried in procession. After the death of Septimius Severus in Britain an extraordinary ritual was carried out at Rome, where a full-sized image of the dead emperor was laid out in state for several days and paid honours as if still alive but dying, till the doctors declared the emperor officially dead. In most funerals the body was carried on a litter to the cemetery, where, if cremation was being practised, it was burnt on a pyre. The ashes were washed in wine and put into whatever container was being used. Sacrifices were offered to the *lares* or spirits, the mourners were purified from the defilement of contact with death and a wake held. The importance of wine in such ceremonial may suggest that the appearance of amphorae in burials even in pre-Roman Britain may not be mere ostentation or as drink for the dead. Certainly the jug and handled-bowl (*patera*)[2] which appear along with the sacrificial knife in relief on many Roman altars are also found in connection with the dead across the Roman world, including Britain. In the Holborough barrow, in association with the primary burial, several amphorae had been deliberately broken and wine poured over them. It was common to provide the deceased with a coin with which to pay Charon, the ferryman who carried the dead across the river of the Underworld to the realms of Hades in Classical mythology. The important cemetery found at Cirencester between the city and the amphitheatre has produced a number of skeletons with a coin in the mouth and one or more with a coin on each eye,[3] and the same provision of coins is found as late as the middle of the fourth century at Poundbury, despite the generally Christian ethos of that community.[4] We have already noted at several points the

---

[1] The Late Roman Poundbury cemetery at Dorchester has produced several probably Christian mausolea demonstrating the persistence of the practice of building such structures. (*Brit.* 1 (1970), 298 f.)

[2] See H.U. Nuber, *Bericht d. Röm.-Germ. Kommission*, 53 (1972), 1 ff. Amphora, jug, and *patera* occur, for example, on the Bartlow Hills.

[3] *Brit.* 4 (1973), 309.   [4] *Brit.* 6 (1975), 277.

placing of treasured objects in the grave. One particularly notable example from York is a folding fan,[1] similar to one held by an elegant Roman lady on a fine tomb-relief from Carlisle.[2] That the practice continued in Christian circles is demonstrated by another burial at York, a lady who went to her grave equipped with earrings, bracelets, armlets, a glass jug, a mirror, and a piece of bone strip pierced with the Christian motto: 'Sister, hail! May you live in God.'[3]

So far the funerary practices have been intelligible, either because they correspond with descriptions by classical authors or clearly stem from beliefs recorded by them, or because they seem to have a rational explanation. I deliberately say 'seem' because there are other practices known archaeologically that seem to have no literary parallels nor any likely explanation. This must make us think twice before attributing reasons to *any* funerary or religious practice from the ancient world for which we have no written evidence. However there are degrees of unintelligibility. For example the fairly common occurrence of pots that have been deliberately drilled or broken may indicate a ritual killing of the object that is to accompany the dead—or it may simply be a way of discouraging the reuse of utensils that have been associated with death and burial. More difficult to understand is the occurrence of hobnails for boots. These occurred in most of the graves of the first century found at Puckeridge and still appear in the cemetery at Curbridge in Oxfordshire which is probably Late Roman in date.[4] At Puckeridge it appeared that each person buried had been supplied with a pair of boots; in the second case—an inhumation cemetery—the nails were found around the feet of the skeletons. We may perhaps surmise that the dead were felt to need a good pair of boots for their journey to the Underworld. Indeed, the presence of a building at the cemetery near the amphitheatre outside Cirencester which contained a furnace and over 2,000 of these

---

[1] *Arch. J.* 103 (1946), 78 ff.; RCHM *Eburacum*, pl. 71.

[2] See Toynbee, *Art in Roman Britain*, pl. 86 and p. 161, no. 89; Salway, op. cit. 217, no. 22.

[3] *Soror, ave: vivas in Deo*: RCHM op. cit. 73.

[4] *Brit.* 7 (1976), 336; *Oxoniensia*, 41 (1976), 38 ff.

hobnails[1] makes one wonder whether footwear was specially made for funerary purposes—indeed whether on occasion a few nails may not have been placed in the grave as a symbolic gesture in place of an actual pair of boots.

A much odder practice is the beheaded skeleton. Three from the Guilden Morden cemetery and four from Dorset have long been known: Miss Liversidge points out that all but one were probably women.[2] It is now becoming clear that there were many more examples of this practice.[3] In many of the cases the head is placed at the feet or between the legs.[4] Of the examples quoted by Miss Liversidge only the male had the head detached but in its correct place in relation to the rest of the body. This man may, as she suggests, have been an executed criminal—and there was other evidence to support this. However it is difficult to assume this to apply to all the other cases as well.

The bodies were, we may therefore presume, dismembered soon after death: an unusual example from the Dunstable group proves that the limbs were still articulated at the time, for in that case the head had not only been placed between the legs but the latter had been cut off above the knee and arranged so that the feet lay on either side of the neck. It is interesting, though it may be no more than a coincidence, that the Curbridge cemetery which produced the shoe-nails round the feet also contained three skeletons with their heads between their feet, while Dunstable contained two burials which had had boots laid under the knees. For the present we seem to have in the decapitation burials a rite that has no easy explanation. The dating if anything makes it more difficult to hazard a guess than otherwise. Beginning in the late third century or early fourth and possibly continuing into the fifth, it is too late to be easily associated with the Iron Age severed head cult, yet too early to be obviously associated with *large-scale* arrival of barbarians

[1] *Brit.* 6 (1975), 273. 'Coffin-nails' are often reported from graves and presumed to imply wooden coffins that have perished. It would perhaps be worth re-examining some of these in the light of this practice.

[2] Liversidge, op. cit. 477.

[3] The rite is being studied by R.A. Chambers at Oxford (see *Current Archaeology*, 57 (1977), 319).

[4] For example, at Duston in Northamptonshire (*Brit.* 7 (1976), 334) and Stanton Harcourt in Oxfordshire (excavation, spring 1978).

in Roman service. The truth is, that we do not know either the origin of this rite nor what it meant. We can only record it, with the observation that it ought to remind us of just how much that is very alien to our ways of thinking lay beneath the superficially modern and familiar appearance of the Roman world. The sacrifices made to the *lares* at the traditional funeral reflect elements at the core of Roman private religion. But we encounter extreme difficulty if we try to define the precise meaning or origins of the underlying beliefs. It is clear that the centre of Roman religion in its strictest sense—the religion of Rome itself and thence Italy and the Roman communities abroad—is the cult of the household and the family, living and dead—or rather the spirits that oversee them and dwell within them. Writ large, the core of the state religion is exactly the same— the cults of Vesta, or the sacred hearth of the City and the Forum, and of even older deities. On to this the Graeco- Roman Olympian religion with all its myths was a subsequent graft. The central Roman cults have no such personified myths but only a presence and rituals, and are close to pure animism. From such beliefs the notions of the *numen* of an individual, particularly the emperor, and the cult of the *genius*, of which we have seen examples, could develop naturally and become infinitely flexible.

With this background of belief, it is not surprising that integral to the daily life of the traditional Roman family were the respects paid to the spirits of the family and household, most notably the *lares*, the *penates* or spirits of the larder, and frequently the slightly more personified Vesta or goddess of the hearth. There is much uncertainty as to the origin and meaning of the *lares familiares* themselves. There is some reason to think that they started as outdoor deities, and *lares* continued to be found as spirits of crossroads in Classical times. It is alternatively considered possible that they originated in the cult of the dead and were thought of as ghosts. Whatever their origin and content, their normal place as gods of the home was in the *lararium* or shrine within the house. There they could also be joined by images of other more personified deities particularly associated with family life and fortune such as Vesta herself, Venus, Juno Lupicina, goddess of childbirth, and any gods especially venerated by the particular family. The platform for such a household shrine was found at Silchester, a city which has also produced statuettes of a *lar* and of a *genius*. Various forms of the *genius* could represent different aspects of the family and household. Perhaps the most extreme official move made by the Christian emperors of the fourth century against paganism was Theodosius' prohibition of the customary respects paid in the home to the household gods and the celebration of their festivals. The imperial government was no longer simply requiring public observance of the new state religion, but struck at what a *paterfamilias* might do in his own house. The old gods of the Roman state had already been banished from public life. Now the divinities of the family itself were to be denied worship, and in the context of the central place of the family in Roman life, both private and political, the crucial nature of the prohibition becomes obvious. Theodosius was, of course, right in identifying the final target. Until the most ancient cults of the home could be stamped out there could be no hope of uniform adherence to Christianity in the empire at large nor could the eventual loyalty of the oldest senatorial families to the policy of the court be hoped for while their children continued to be brought up under the daily influence of the old religion in its most impressive form.

The association of other deities with the *lares* and *penates* in the *lararium* reminds us that Romans frequently included other gods in their family worship. Among the most striking of the local deities in Britain are the *Genii Cucullati*,[1] usually shown as small figures wearing heavy cloaks with hoods attached and worn in position, remarkably like representations of medieval peasants. They, like the *Matres*, often appear as a triad, and like most other religious reliefs in Roman Britain there is no reason to doubt that most came from temples or shrines in public places. However in the *vicus* outside the fort of Housesteads one of the excavated houses had tucked away in its interior a shrine with a relief depicting the *Genii Cucullati*.[2] It is, of course, possible that the 'house' was in

[1] See J.M.C. Toynbee, 'Genii Cucullati in Roman Britain', *Hommages à Waldemar Deonna*, Coll. Latomus 28 (1957), 456 ff.

[2] In House IX: the shrine seems from a deposit of coins to have been erected about AD 229—see Salway, op. cit. 87, footnotes, for references to the excavations in the *vicus*.

fact a chapel used by a group of devotees to this cult (which was popular in the Wall region) but the situation of the shrine suggests it was private to that particular family.

It is a moot point to what extent these family cults can be considered *personal* religion. They were certainly private in that they were inextricably bound up with the closed circle of the household and the family, living and departed. But were they personal, in the sense of communication between individual and deity, a religious experience peculiar to himself? To many ancients this might have seemed a meaningless question, in that family and state were everywhere involved with the divine. Yet the enormous number of dedications set up in recognition of a prayer answered demonstrate that the individual widely felt that his personal needs were noted and answered by particular pagan gods; and there are occasions where an even closer experience of the supernatural is recorded. An inscription from Bath, for example, quite clearly states that it was erected as the result of a vision (*ex visu*).[1] Other dedications are set up by order of the god (*ex iussu*), presumably the consequence of some similar occurrence, and the practice of the sick sleeping at the temples of the great healing gods was a logical extension of the same belief in the personal appearance of the divinity to an individual.

I noted above, in the context of the gradual change from cremation to inhumation, how Romans turned to the eastern mystery religions. This was already happening under the Late Republic and gained more and more momentum during the Early Empire. They seem to have felt a need for personal revelation which was lacking in the old rituals. At the same time philosophy, particularly among the senatorial class, helped to provide an intelligible basis for traditional moral standards and a consolation in the tribulations through which they passed under the Julio-Claudian and Flavian emperors, the memory of which remained a powerful force in the second century.

To understand Tacitus' historical writings, for example, we have to see him against the background of his personal experience of rising in a public career under Domitian and

---

[1] *RIB* 153: the actual name of the deity is lost.

the closely similar experiences of his relations, notably Agricola, and his circle of friends and acquaintances. He is not only excusing failure to resist tyranny: some senators had tried, with fatal consequences to themselves and little apparent effect on the course of events. He is also making the positive point that moral duty requires service to the state, however bad the emperor. Such endurance and persistence in duty was in line with the Stoic philosophy popular in his class; and one might argue that without the combination of this force with family ambition the mechanism of the Roman government could not have been carried on relatively undamaged for so long. At the same time, there was the countervailing influence of Epicurean philosophy that argued for the achievement of personal tranquillity by deliberate avoidance of situations that would lead to extremes of pleasure or pain. Epicureanism accorded well with that other powerful tendency we have noted in Roman upper-class attitudes, the desire to withdraw into private life, the high value placed on dignified leisure (*otium cum dignitate*). At its best this encouraged the quiet cultivation of the arts, friendship, and particularly the enjoyment of the countryside. At its extreme it fostered that unwillingness of the fourth-century senatorial class to become involved in the burdens of public service even when the opportunity was offered to them once more after the restrictions imposed by third-century emperors. It was a frame of mind that led to the holding of office for the briefest possible time necessary to fulfil family duty and the adoption of retirement as a way of life.

Philosophy, however, was not enough for a very large number of people, particularly in those classes where the conditions of life were a great deal harder, nor in the end was it sufficient for many of the senatorial class itself. For Marcus Aurelius the consolations of philosophy could sustain him to the highest degree as he sought to serve the state; but we already have Hadrian enthusiastically taking part in mystery religion. At the lowest end of society, among slaves and the urban poor, hope of a personal salvation and relief from this world were demanding something more, and Christianity fell on ready ground in the cities of the empire, not least among the city proletariat of Rome itself.

But as far as Britain is concerned the first of the major eastern mystery cults to gain a powerful hold was that of Mithras.[1]

We have already noted its attraction for soldiers and merchants. It was exclusively—or almost exclusively—confined to men, and the small size of its chapels underlines the fact that one of the consequences of the rigour of its seven grades of initiation was small congregations. On the other hand its devotees were persons of consequence: officers and business-men. It appealed to the same trait in Roman society as Stoicism, the life of discipline and action. One of the altars from the Mithraeum outside the fort at Carrawburgh[2] was dedicated between AD 198 and 211 by the prefect of the First Cohort of Batavians, Aulus Cluentius Habitus of Larinum in Italy.[3] It can hardly be coincidence that the man from Larinum who was defended by Cicero on a charge of murder in 66 BC with the speech known as the *Pro Cluentio* was also named Aulus Cluentius Habitus.[4] It is important and significant that this altar, which seems to come from the earliest phase of the temple, demonstrates that Mithraism could attract a member of one of those few families who still survived in public life from the old Italian upper class of the Republic. The well-known Temple of Mithras in London shows another aspect of Mithraism that may help to explain its popularity with the business com-munity, in addition to the obvious attractions of the cult's masonic secrecy and insistence on integrity. Some threat to the cult caused the deliberate concealment of a large group of sculpture within the London temple. Together with casual finds from the same site, these demonstrate vividly the ease with which Mithraism seems to have been able to absorb other religions or at least to offer them tolerant hospitality. As well as the indubitably Mithraic sculptures the London temple group included a river god, perhaps the Thames, a *genius*, a head of Minerva, another of the Graeco-Egyptian Serapis, a Bacchic scene reminding us of the popularity of

---

[1] See especially M.J. Vermaseren, *Mithras, the Secret God*, 1963.
[2] I.A. Richmond and J.P. Gillam, *Arch. Ael.* 4th ser. 29 (1951), 1 ff.
[3] *RIB* 1545.
[4] 'Integrity' is not perhaps the word one would use of the earlier members of the family.

the Dionysiac cult with its joyful afterlife, a circular relief
that seems to derive from a cult of Thracian origin, and a
fragment of one of the Dioscuri.[1] Such willingness to accommodate other cults may have made Mithraism particularly
acceptable to the cosmopolitan business community of
London, as well as to army officers who were themselves
gradually being drawn from a wider and wider background.

The evidence for deliberate destruction at both these
Mithraea, which are by no means alone in this respect,
raises the question of how a cult which had had such powerful
backing came to an end. At Carrawburgh there seem to be
two periods of destruction, the first about the end of the
third century, the second probably in the fourth after an
extensive refurbishing. It is possible that the first destruction
was by enemy action at the time of the fall of Allectus, but it
is not impossible that local Christians seized the opportunity
presented by the victory of the Caesar Constantius to attack
the detested rival religion. It is certainly very likely that the
second and final destruction was due to Christian action,
possibly on official orders. The London Mithraeum shows a
broadly similar pattern. The dating of its foundation is in
dispute, as the major sculptures have been dated on style to
the second century, but the pottery now suggests construction
around AD 240.[2] However it certainly stood intact till a
crisis occurred somewhere about the beginning of the fourth
century, when extensive dismantling of the structure took
place and the main pieces of sculpture were hidden. Indeed,
the head of Mithras seems to have been already damaged by
a blow from an implement before the concealment was
carried out.[3] Yet some time not long after the shrine was put
out of action, the building was brought back into use and
pagan worship revived, though we do not know whether

---

[1] See Toynbee, *Art in Roman Britain*, nos. 29, 32, 36, 37, 38, 61, 69, 110
for discussion and illustrations of material from this site.

[2] Pottery studies by Joanna Bird, kindly brought to my notice by Mr Ralph
Merrifield. It is, of course, entirely possible that the sculptures were brought from
an earlier temple elsewhere.

[3] Mr Merrifield has also drawn my attention to this feature (see also his
passage in J. Munby and M. Henig (eds.), *Roman Life and Art in Britain*, 376 ff.,
suggesting extensive vandalism while the sculptures were still exposed); and to the
fact that the objects that can be associated with the final phase of use are either
Bacchic or could be associated with the worship of Bacchus—none are Mithraic.

the congregation was aware of the hidden Mithraic objects beneath their new floor. In fact, it is quite likely that the cult practised when the temple reopened was one less objectionable than Mithraism to the Christians. It is not impossible that events connected with the arrival of Constantius in Britain in 296 had given the London Mithraists reason to believe a major Christian attack on their chapel was imminent, even though Christianity itself was still illegal. Equally the elevation of Constantine at York may have caused alarm, long before he himself began to take vigorous measures in favour of the Church. However it is the revival of both these chapels for pagan worship in the fourth century that reminds us of the very varying policies of Christian emperors in the fourth century towards pagan practices. It reminds us too both of the periods when Britain was under the control of pagans or pagan sympathizers and of the longevity of paganism in Britain as a whole to which I shall return.

While it is true that Mithraism presented an especial target for Christian fanatics and there are examples of Mithraic images being destroyed when others are untouched, it would be unfair (or too complimentary, depending on one's point of view) to attribute all such destruction to Christian fanatics. Sometimes one may suspect rivalry between other sects or mere vandalism. An altar from Bath leaves us completely in doubt about the circumstances—or indeed the exact religion— but emphasizes the horror felt at sacrilege:[1] 'This sacred spot which had been wrecked by insolent persons has been made ritually clean and re-dedicated to the virtue and *numen* of the emperor by C. Severius Emeritus, centurion in charge of a region.' Here it is possible that the place was sacred to the Imperial Cult, though the frequent association of the emperor's *numen* with other deities on inscriptions makes it impossible to be certain. Nevertheless the position of the dedicator as a *centurio regionarius* and the possibility that the area around Bath had a special status, at least till the late third century, make it feasible that the context is a local revolt in which rebels, like Boudicca, had attacked a shrine of the Imperial Cult. We should be very cautious before assuming

[1] *RIB* 152: it was found somewhere near an altar (*RIB* 140) by a citizen of the Treveri to Mars Loucetius and Nemetona, Celtic deities of the Rhineland, but need not have come from the same shrine or plot.

Christian responsibility for any wrecked pagan shrine. Even the famous Cirencester column and statue restored by the governor of Britannia Prima in the name of the 'ancient religion' (*prisca religione*) gives no hint that it has been deliberately damaged, let alone that Christians were responsible.

Not all fourth-century Christians indeed possessed the vigorous intolerance of St. Martin of Tours, a former imperial guardsman who was not above borrowing troops from the civil authorities in Gaul to assist in the demolition of temples; and even he felt Magnus Maximus was going too far when he proposed to send military forces to root out Christain heretics in Spain. The extremist Maximus, of course, had been raised to the throne in Britain: Britain as a diocese had been thoroughly overhauled and restored a few years earlier by the elder Theodosius, whose own family came from the Christian aristocracy of Spain which was already developing some extremely rigorous brands of Christianity in the later fourth century, and whose son was himself the emperor we have observed finally banning the household gods. Yet it is generally agreed that pagan religion survived strongly to the very end of Roman rule in Britain and probably beyond. This apparent contradiction obliges us to weigh the evidence for the strength and character of the Romano-British Church rather closely.

It is not the task of this volume to attempt the charting of the rise of the Celtic or 'insular' Church in Britain, which had its roots in Roman Britain but which, in the form it is encountered in the later fifth and sixth centuries, developed largely in parts of Britain which were either not part of the empire at all—or had not been within it for a very long time— or in the least Romanized regions of the Roman territory. But the enormous importance of Christianity in the life and politics of the Later Empire which we have already observed makes it unavoidable that we consider the evidence for the Church in Britain under Roman rule.

The increasing identification of the Roman state religion with the person of the emperor cannot have helped to maintain its credibility. In the course of the first century assumption of divine or quasi-divine honours had been accompanied by periods of ludicrous, scandalous, or downright abominable behaviour by emperor and imperial family.

The posthumous deification of Claudius was treated as a joke, yet Claudius had been one of those early emperors who resisted divinity for himself as far as possible. By the end of the first century Domitian had insisted on what amounted in practice, if not in law, to the assumption of divinity during his lifetime. This combined with his determined and brutal assault on the position, property, and even the lives of senators to confirm the Imperial Cult as a symbol of oppression and to strengthen, as we have seen, the hold of ethical philosophy, in so far as it can be dissociated from religion, as the creed of the upper-class opposition to the Principate. However, in the troubles of the later second century and the terrible events of the third something more than philosophy was widely felt to be needed. The popularity of the mystery religions increased, and the emergence of a new class of soldier-emperors drawn from the African and eastern provinces, from backgrounds more and more divorced from the traditional world of the aristocratic Roman west, meant that the court itself was ripe for experiments with new forms of official religion. At its worst this produced the excesses of the Emperor Elagabalus, who made prodigious efforts to introduce his own very peculiar version of sun-worship into Rome itself, but in general it produced a climate in which the eastern religions flourished. A foretaste of fourth-century religious absolutism was provided by the mighty Emperor Aurelian, significantly the restorer of the unity of the Empire, who from 274 seems to have intended the introduction of the worship of the Unconquered Sun as the exclusive religion of the state. At the time of his death in 275 he was apparently planning a new attack on the Christians, yet ironically his own policy encouraged monotheism. A victorious soldier-emperor was moving towards the enforcement of religious unity under his own version of its banner. Compulsory ideology, once confined to the brief reigns of a few eccentric if not positively mad emperors, was soon to become a commonplace policy among rational incumbents of the imperial throne.

The over-all story of the rise of Christianity is outside the scope of this book, but it should be noted that the periods of active persecution were only brief and the faith's own almost complete lack of discrimination as to whom it would admit to its number gave it great advantages over the exclusive cults. Emperors as early as Trajan avoided the deliberate hunting of Christians and the religion became increasingly respectable. Christian apologists took their faith into the area of philosophical debate and writing, an area traditionally acceptable for a Roman gentleman, even if he did not agree with the views being proffered. From the middle of the third century pagan philosophy also took a new and very important turn, which itself influenced Christian thinking. For a considerable time there had been moves towards bringing together the conservative Stoic creed with Aristotelian and Platonic concepts and the more visionary beliefs of the Pythagoreans. Embodied in the work of the philosopher Plotinus at Rome and others, this gave new strength to paganism and became the intellectual core of the opposition to official Christianity in the fourth century.

Diocletian's prolonged attempt to restore the respectable old religion, including a particular emphasis on Jupiter and Hercules with whom he identified the branches of his new imperial family, has to be seen as part of his general policy of national regeneration through the massive strengthening of the traditional institutions of the state. In this he was the true heir of Augustus rather than Aurelian. It was only at the very end of his reign that he initiated a new persecution of the Christians, for reasons that are uncertain but possibly because he felt their opposition to the state religion had now, because of their vastly increased numbers, become a real threat to his programme of restoration. In 313 Constantine's edict of toleration was the first step in the dramatic reversal of official policy towards the Church. For another dozen years Constantine himself combined Christianity with devotion to Sol Invictus, the sun-cult that we have seen was very closely associated with that of Mithras. However from 324, when the whole empire was at last under Constantine's control, monotheistic Christianity became dominant and thereafter rapidly assumed the place formerly occupied by the traditional Capitoline cults as the official religion.

We have earlier seen how for Christians in Britain the turning of the tide had probably already begun with the recovery of the island by Constantius I as Caesar in 296. There was probably little persecution of Christians in Britain after that date, and from 324 the boot was firmly on the other foot. Henceforth the struggle was on the one hand between the new imperial religion and paganism, increasingly illegal as the more extremist Christian emperors passed stricter and stricter measures, with only temporary respites, and on the other between the official version of Christianity and heresy, though how those were defined often depended on which emperor was in power. Both paganism and heresy put up a strong fight in the west, and we shall return to what this means in terms of Britain and Romano-British archaeology.

However, we have first to look at what evidence there is for Christianity in Britain *before* the end of the third century. The answer at present has to be that there is very little. Professor W.H.C. Frend has summarized the general state of knowledge, pointing out that while Christianity, like other eastern religions, was carried westward by individuals it seems to have been particularly strong where there were Jewish communities. Moreover, except when engaged in rebellion in Palestine or civil strife in Alexandria (where hatred between the large Greek and Jewish communities was endemic), the Jews and their faith were protected. Unlike the Christians the Jews hardly ever attempted to make converts, from the very nature of their religion, and so posed no threat to the state cults. To many Romans the Christians were seen as a Jewish sect, even if often disliked by orthodox Jew and Gentile alike. Nevertheless, the presence of Christians in a Jewish community established a potential of growth by conversion outside that may not in many cases have been recognized, but it existed. Conversely, where there were few Jews, there were likely to be few Christians:

In the West, apart from Rome and some of the larger towns in north Africa, there were few Jewish centres, and consequently few Christian centres in the first two centuries. The churches at Lyons and Vienne on the main trade routes leading northwards from Marseille seem to have been exceptional, and most of their members seem to have belonged to immigrant trading groups from Asia Minor. To these Christians the ordinary native provincials were 'wild and barbarous tribes' with whom they had little dealing.[1] Even in the next century when the Church was making great strides in the East, a foreign, Greek-speaking element seems to have played a considerable role in establish-

[1] Eusebius, *Hist. Eccl.* V. i. 57.

ing Christianity in western towns. Occasionally, as at Aquileia where the earliest church was built within a stone's throw of a large synagogue, association with Judaism may have assisted the process. In Britain the earliest references to Christianity found in Tertullian *c.* 200 and Origen *c.* 240 may be derived from travellers' tales. 'The parts of the island inaccessible to Rome have been subject to Christ'[1] has the sound of an exaggerated story circulated among the Christians of Carthage by some returning merchant. The name Aaron, however, as one of the two confessors allegedly martyred at Caerleon also suggests a Jewish influence on the mission to these islands. But Origen's suggestion *c.* 240 that 'Christianity was a unifying force among the Britons' could have had little basis in fact.[2] Christianity in Britain was not in the first place an indigenous movement.[3]

Though it is generally unsatisfactory to rely upon negative evidence, the archaeology bears this out. Even the famous 'word-square' from Cirencester need not detain us. It is an apparently nonsensical stanza scratched on Roman wall-plaster of uncertain date whose letters can be arranged to form a cross composed of the Latin words for Our Father (*Pater Noster*) and the Greek letters alpha and omega. However it has been demonstrated to be highly unlikely that this device (known also outside Britain) had a Christian origin and there is no independent evidence to indicate a Christian connection for the British example.[4] A much more important piece of evidence to be examined is the hoard of Christian plate found in 1975 within the walls of the small town at Chesterton (Water Newton) which we have already met as the urban centre dependent on the Nene Valley pottery industry. This hoard is certainly Christian and does contain pieces for which arguments can be produced suggesting a third century date.[5] It comprises nine vessels of various types, eighteen

---

[1] Tertullian, *Adversus Iudaeos*, vii, 4: *Britannorum inaccessa Romanis loca Christo vero subdita.* Frere suggests that merchants may have made converts on journeys along the Scottish and Irish coasts (*Britannia*, 371), which is consistent with a picture of a few scattered Christians.

[2] Origen, *Homil. iv in Ezekiel interp.* 1. (Migne, *Patrologia Latina*, xxxv. 723).

[3] W.H.C. Frend, 'The Christianization of Roman Britain', in Barley and Hanson (eds.), *Christianity in Britain 300–700*, 37 f.

[4] For the Cirencester inscription see *Archaeologia*, 69, 197; *J. Brit. Arch. Ass.* 3rd ser. 16 (1953), pl. 1; Frere, *Britannia*, 332. Francis Clark has most effectively undermined the argument for a Christian origin for this conceit in *The Rise of Christianity*, Open University A291 Units 13–16 (1974), 21 f.

[5] For a detailed interim publication see K.S. Painter, *The Water Newton Early Christian Silver*, British Museum (1977).

more or less complete votive plaques and fragments of a number of others. Many of the pieces bear Christian symbols or inscriptions, and one mentions the word *altare*, almost certainly 'sanctuary' rather than 'altar'. This latter, taken with the plaques which had, like the strikingly similar pagan plaques we considered earlier, been attached to some structure, make it clear that the whole group represents fittings and furnishings deliberately removed from a Christian shrine and carefully buried. The importance of this find is threefold. It is the earliest Church plate from the whole empire.[1] Secondly, it clearly came from an actual shrine, however small, and was not the travelling equipment of a priest. Finally, the votive plaques show the Christian worshippers adopting one of the commonest forms of religious practice in the ancient world.

Is this find evidence for a Christian community at Water Newton, and if so, can it be put into the third century? It has to be said first that the individual vessels themselves, if one ignored the Christian inscriptions on some of them, could all equally well be secular. There is no specifically Christian form about them. Only two of the vessels are arguably analogous in type with pieces dated elsewhere for the beginning of the third century, and most of them are apparently to be dated stylistically to the second half of the third century or the first half of the fourth. In the case of at least one the dating is probably after the Peace of the Church in 313. On the other hand, there seems nothing in the group that is paralleled in work of the later fourth century. It therefore seems on balance that the group as a whole ought to be put in the first half of the fourth century, bearing in mind that precious objects, especially Church plate, are likely to be kept and used long after their date of manufacture. The second question is whether the shrine was at Water Newton itself. Since Water Newton lies on major road and water routes and the material had to be removed from its home and hidden, there can be no certainty that it did not come from elsewhere. Nevertheless the unusual nature of Water Newton is worth remembering. In the

[1] There is nothing else earlier than the sixth century—see Painter, op. cit. 48, n. 51.

fourth century the walled town had suburbs covering 250 acres or more (100 ha.). The total complex was thus of the same order of magnitude as the walled area of Roman London—in effect a rural development amounting in area and perhaps population to an industrial 'city'. It is characteristic of the ancient world that this industrial city is without any sure sign of municipal organization. Even the existence of walls round its centre is no proof. Indeed, those walls may have been erected by the owner of the villa at Castor, whether imperial or private. It could reasonably be argued that the existence here of a Christian community based on and perhaps originating from the semi-urban industrial workers of the potteries is more likely than in a 'normal' Romano-British country town or among the agricultural peasantry. This is the sort of background that is consistent with much of the social pattern of the early Church before it became respectable and eventually compulsory. Water Newton, exceptional as it seems to be in Britain, is a reasonable setting for a third-century Christian community, but the evidence of the objects themselves, as we have seen, cannot be used to prove it.

There is stronger evidence of third-century Christianity in the story of the martyrdom of St. Alban. We have earlier observed Germanus visiting this saint's shrine in 429 after routing the Pelagians in public debate. St. Alban's judge is described as 'Caesar', which makes it highly likely that this trial took place when Geta was left in charge of affairs during Septimius Severus' Scottish war of 208-9. He is also reported as ordering the cessation of persecution because it was strengthening rather than weakening the Christians.[1] This may indeed have been a general observation, but would make sense in the particular context of a local Christian community. Moreover, if the great medieval abbey of St. Albans is really at the site of the shrine visited by Germanus, then its situation just outside the Roman city of Verulamium supports the notion of early Christianity in Britain as an urban phenomenon. Even so Verulamium may have been unusual—it is, after all, the first recorded British martyrdom and need not reflect the presence of a community founded

---

[1] See Frere, op. cit. 332.

any appreciable time before. Its members could well have arrived from abroad in the wake of the Severan victory over Clodius Albinus rather than represent an indigenous movement. Indeed, the only other pre-Constantinian martyrs of whom we know in Britain are the Julius and Aaron already mentioned, who may have been executed at Caerleon either in the persecution carried out in the short reign of Decius (249–51) or under the Emperor Valerian between 257 and 259. Once again the circumstances may have been exceptional. Legions had always attracted a cosmopolitan population,[1] particularly by the middle of the third century, and the unusually grand civil settlement alongside the base that may have had municipal pretensions is atypical of Roman Britain.

We have no martyrs at all recorded in the period of the last great assault on the Church which took place in the final years of Diocletian and under Galerius. The lack of bloodshed can certainly be attributed to the control of the north-western provinces exercised by Constantius I, and we have no stories of Christian communities broken up or driven underground. Constantius certainly permitted the destruction of Christian places of worship within his territories, while preventing the martyrdom of Christians themselves,[2] yet there is not any certain archaeological evidence for such destruction at this time in Britain.[3] All in all, the inference must be that, apart from individuals and perhaps a few scattered urban groups, Christianity had little hold in Britain before the elevation of Constantine. This is from negative evidence, but there is very little to set on the other side.

The Peace of the Church meant a revolutionary change in circumstances, and we need to look at the evidence for Christianity in Britain in the fourth century to see if this is reflected here. For background, it is convenient to quote the summary of Church organization by A.H.M. Jones:

The Church early evolved its basic unit, the bishopric. The bishopric usually corresponded to the city, the civil unit of administration, which

---

[1] Cf. the Caerleon 'pipe burial' discussed above.
[2] See Painter, op. cit. 21 and references.
[3] I think the burial of the Water Newton treasure is probably later still.

was also the natural social group. Administrative units which were not cities, such as independent villages, and *saltus, regiones* and *tractus* of imperial land, often had their own bishops, and so sometimes did centres of population within city territories—market towns, large villages and in particular military stations. In the east the rule, one city, one bishop, was by the fifth century strictly observed . . . In the west there was no special legislation, but the rule was generally accepted. We can test it precisely only in Gaul, where the exceptions are negligible . . . We have no evidence for Britain, but as its political structure corresponded to that of northern Gaul, with large predominantly rural *civitates*, it is probable that like Gaul it had a bishop for each of its 28 *civitates*,[1] and perhaps a few more for populous military stations which were not *civitates* . . .[2]

Up to the middle of the fourth century the army and the villas were flourishing, the latter particularly so, and the towns, if not so grand or playing such a central role in society as before, were at least still well founded. At this stage we might expect to find bishops, if any, based on the unit most generally preferred elsewhere in the empire, the city. But after the events of the forties, fifties, and sixties anything may have happened. The restoration of Britain by the elder Theodosius revived army and towns, but in the long run, in the course of the last quarter of the fourth century and the first half of the fifth, as the balance of economic and political power swung towards the surviving landed gentry, it is unlikely it did not affect the organization of the Church.

Jones goes on to explain how the bishops and clergy were appointed:

Bishops were elected by the clergy and people of their city . . . The people is specified to be the *ordo et plebs*, or the *honorati ordo et plebs* or *honorati et plebs*. On occasions the common people might have a decisive influence, but in the *Epistola ad Gallos* the pope condemns elections made '*favore populi*'; 'for what is sought for is not what the people wishes but what evangelical discipline desires; the plebs bears witness only as often as it regards the merit of some worthy man and so lends the ear of favour . . .'

The lower clergy were appointed and promoted by the bishop, but he was expected to pay due regard to the wishes of the founders of parish churches and their heirs . . . Bishops fall into three categories.

---

[1] The figure of 28 is taken from Gildas, whose source is unknown and uncheckable.

[2] A.H.M. Jones, in Barley and Hanson (eds.), op. cit. 9 ff.

The popes and the clergy naturally favoured regular promotion from the lower ranks of the clergy; Pope Zosimus thought that the civil service, with automatic promotion by seniority, should be a model for the church . . . But laymen often preferred a real holy man, whose *suffragia* would be effective with God, or an eminent layman, whose *suffragia* would be useful with the imperial or royal government . . . And despite the opposition of the imperial government and the disapproval of the popes a large number of the clergy seem to have been drawn from the middle class of landowners, the decurions of the cities. Such men naturally secured positions in episcopal or at any rate urban churches. The country clergy were normally peasants; if they were *coloni* their landlord's permission was required, if slaves they had to be manumitted first.

Where, then, the Church was predominantly urban we may expect to find both its bishops and its lower clergy men of good family and influence, where it is located in a predominantly rural setting, the priests are more likely to have been from the lower orders and at least in everyday affairs subject in practice to secular landowners. In the fourth and fifth centuries it could be very much in the interest of Christian landowners to have churches, even bishops, on their estates. This mattered less in the eastern empire, where the aristocracy was often absentee and closely associated with the emperor in the capital, than in the west where it was more and more divorced from the court and building its own separate 'power base', both in the City of Rome and on its estates. A different sort of Church is implied as between town and country, and in the west at least the weaker the city the stronger the power of the secular magnates over it.

Almost immediately the Church became legal, British bishops appear. In 314 three bishops attended the Council of Arles and it can be argued that these, together with a priest and a deacon, came from four sees based on the capital cities of the early fourth-century provinces.[1] However, if there were no more than four, and if they came from the four new capitals, I am inclined to suspect that the organized Church in Britain was only just being formed, perhaps by imperial command. Bishops from Britain appeared again at the Council of Rimini under Constantius II in 359, though their poverty was such that the emperor offered free transport

[1] J.C. Mann, *Antiquity*, 35 (1961), 316 ff.

via the Imperial Post. A numerous, powerful, and rich clergy is not the picture that emerges from the British church. Indeed, one wonders if by 359 the original episcopal organization was already in decline. If the cities were ruined by the troubles of the mid-fourth century and never recovered— as some would argue—or had only a partial recovery after the Theodosian reconstruction, then it would be possible to explain the non-appearance of later city bishops on this ground alone. But whether or not this happened, there may be another reason, inherent in the nature of the Romano-British Church.

The archaeology adds a little to the picture. Free-standing churches are almost non-existent. The building so identified at Silchester remains reasonably certain, but its date is extremely problematic: it may be early in the fourth century. This modest building is 'basilican' in form, and the evidence for its identification is convincing but not absolute.[1] In fact city churches are so far almost unrecognized in Britain, and there may be an archaeological reason for this— even if, indeed, they ever existed in substantial numbers. One has been tentatively identified at Caerwent, and the literary source for St. Augustine's arrival at Canterbury in AD 597 to convert the Saxons says that he found Queen Bertha already using an old Roman building as a church dedicated to St. Martin. This may or may not indicate a specific building that had already been dedicated as a church in the fourth century, though even then we cannot assume continuity of worship. The real difficulty of identifying churches inside Roman towns anywhere has been elucidated by Dr Ralegh Radford. He has made clear a fundamental architectural difference between the cemetery churches (the churches erected over important Christian graves) and the urban churches of the fourth and fifth centuries.[2] In cities, the basilican form, derived from the Roman civil basilica, was very rare. The normal type was a series of

---

[1] The evidence was reconsidered by Professor Frere: 'The Silchester Church: The Excavation by Sir Ian Richmond in 1961', *Archaeologia* 105 (1976), 277 ff.

[2] C.A. Ralegh Radford, in Barley and Hanson (eds.), op. cit. 19 ff. The most illustrious of the cemetery churches was perhaps Constantine's vast Vatican basilica, the old St. Peter's.

rooms set aside for the various different liturgical purposes within the bishop's house. This even happened, as at Trier, when a major cathedral was built under imperial patronage. The bishop's house or palace had become a separate complex, yet the pattern of a set of rooms or halls was retained. While the origins of this scheme may lie in the need for secrecy in the pre-Constantinian period, the practice continues late on the Continent. It implies that we should expect to find this type of structure, not basilicas, in provincial cities. Yet they are hardly distinguishable from private houses, except by some lucky find of furnishings or decoration, and this fact may go some way to explaining why we have so far no indisputable examples of city churches in Britain.

Another sort of church is represented by the timber structure provisionally identified in the Saxon Shore fort at Richborough.[1] This, however, seems very late in date, is paralleled by examples in Late Roman fortifications on the Continent and has nothing to do with urban Christianity in Britain, except in the sense that it *might* have served a refugee group from a former town community. Like Silchester, however, it is a very modest building. On the other hand, something very different is represented by the splendid chapel that replaced the pagan cult-room in the villa at Lullingstone, like it seemingly adorned with family portraits, though this time as wall-paintings rather than sculptured busts. Other wealthy villa-owners were also Christian—notably those who commissioned the great mosaics in the principal dining-rooms at Hinton St. Mary in Dorset[2] and Frampton in Gloucestershire.[3] One may perhaps reasonably suspect that strong Christian communities were found in pockets, rather than evenly distributed.[4] The occurrence in Dorset, for example, both of the Hinton St.

[1] P.D.C. Brown, *Brit.* 2 (1971), 225 ff. The date is uncertain, but probably the end of the fourth century or beginning of the fifth. The Second legion—or one of the new legions formed from it—is reported at Richborough in the fourth century, and one recalls the occasional association of bishops with military bases.

[2] J.M.C. Toynbee, *JRS* 54 (1964), 7 ff.: the interpretation of the centre roundel as a representation of Christ is probable, though a Christian emperor is a less likely possibility.

[3] Non-Christian motifs are also present, but probably with an allegorical or even syncretic purpose.

[4] See also p. 731 n. 2 below on villas and churches.

Mary villa and the massive Christian town cemetery at
Dorchester itself (to be discussed below) suggests strongly
that the religious colour of the most influential local landowners was a leading factor in the practices of the whole
neighbourhood, particularly where town and country were
closely integrated through these landowners being of the
curial class and therefore obliged to serve on the *civitas*
council or taking a direct interest in the town for other
reasons. The possibility begins to form that the core of
the Romano-British church may have lain in a section of the
fourth-century landed class. Apart from the occasional
third-century urban group whose existence I have conjectured, it seems increasingly likely that the Romano-British
Church hardly existed before Constantine. It may well have
flourished chiefly in the great new villas, perhaps brought
in then from Gaul and fostered among the supporters of the
House of Constantine. How much the older Romano-
British gentry was touched by this development is an open
question, and any development of urban bishoprics may well
have been more to do with imperial initiative and the arrival
of new officials in the reorganized provinces and their
administrative centres than the old interaction between
gentry and Romano-British town. Indeed, it is interesting to
speculate whether the concealment of the Water Newton
treasure was in the face of pagan reaction against the Church
under toleration during the short reign of Magnentius,
350–3. Certainly the violence of the subsequent punishment
of Britain by Paul the Chain indicates that the outbreak of
feeling against the ruling dynasty was regarded as serious. We
do not know how widespread it had been, but one may infer
that it had included a significant number of notables. It is
perhaps not a coincidence that Water Newton has also
produced an important hoard of secular plate and coins,[1]
probably buried in AD 350, perhaps by one side or the other
in fear of retribution to come. If Paul the Chain left the
Christian landowners more powerful but more isolated from
their peers and from the bulk of the common people, the
contrast between the occasional rich Christian villa and the

---

[1] C.M. Johns and R. Carson, in *Durobrivae: A Review of Nene Valley Archaeology*, 3 (1975), 10 ff.

general paucity of Christian evidence in Britain is more intelligible. We earlier traced the hypothesis that the main Pelagian oppostion to Germanus in 429 lay among a powerful faction within the surviving aristocracy of Roman Britain, and indeed compared the description of them with the people portrayed on the walls of Lullingstone. It will be remembered that one of the great Roman landowners who had estates in Britain was Melania, the benefactress of the Church who sold off all her lands for its benefit. She was tolerant of the Pelagian doctrine herself, and we know she was in possession of property in Britain prior to 404, the date when she decided to sell up, and therefore well before the series of revolts that were to sunder Britain from Rome. We may surmise a Pelagian land-owning group in Britain both before and after the break with the empire. Christianity, as we saw earlier, had become more acceptable to the western upper classes after the death of Valentinian I in 375 and there are likely to have been rather more Christians among the leading Romano-Britons in the last quarter of the century. On the other hand we hear no more of city bishops from Britain, and the Church was probably even more firmly in the hands of the landowning class in this period of revival than before, whether like St. Patrick's father of middle rank as municipal decurions or like Melania of much higher social status and wider possessions. This applies both to the official faith and the various heresies that from time to time flourished. In Spain in the fourth century heresy was rife among the aristocracy and Melania herself had an estate in Africa with two bishops professing different creeds. In the fourth and fifth centuries the battles were with heresy as well as paganism, and the existence of a Pelagian party may imply that by the early fifth century the British church had become strong enough to feel that unity in the face of paganism was not the only policy it could afford.

It is interesting to inquire whether we can infer from the behaviour of their Continental colleagues anything of how the adoption of Christianity is likely to have affected the behaviour of these aristocrats. Apart from influencing their stand in the various internal political and ideological struggles, one might expect it to change their conduct in the most critical area as far as the population at large was concerned—their reaction to the troubles of the times. Yet there is the paradoxical fact that the two main strains in Christian approaches to the barbarian threat and to public duty closely mirrored traditional Roman attitudes, in practice if not theory. One party in the Christian church regarded contemporary life as a lost cause—even illusory and unimportant—and advocated retreat from the world, the other, typified by the energetic St. Ambrose, urged on all Romans a duty to defend the empire and the Faith from the heathen or heretical barbarians. Thus we have the two contradictory tendencies in pagan tradition, the Epicurean retreat from the stresses of the world and the Stoic persistence in public duty, being reproduced in Christian attitudes. It is not therefore surprising to find relatively little difference in the behaviour of pagans and Christians where we can observe them in better-documented provinces. It may be that the strain in Christian thought that saw the contemporary world as evil and the barbarians as the wrath of God led some to abandon resistance and at the most extreme to disappear into one of the earliest monastic communities, which began to develop slowly in the west in the last quarter of the fourth century and spread rapidly in the fifth.[1] But in general we may expect no more than a continuation of the traditional dichotomy of behaviour. If there was avoidance of office in fourth-century Britain and an increased tendency for the nobility to live on their estates in relative ease it was no more than their contemporaries were practising on the Continent and a development of an old characteristic of their class. In the fifth century we may reasonably assume that there were men in Britain who reluctantly but stoically strove to maintain order and government, like Sidonius Apollinaris in Gaul, others who preferred to come to terms with the situation, retreating to their safest estates and carrying on the life of *otium cum dignitate* as well as they could, like Pontius Leontius under Visigothic rule, and yet others, who, having played a prominent part in public life, withdrew into fastnesses like

---

[1] The first monastic house in the west was founded by Martin of Tours in 372: Whithorn in Galloway may have been formed in imitation of this before the end of the fourth century. (See Thomas, *Britain and Ireland*, 78 ff. for a summary of the evidence.)

Cl. Postumus Dardanus, whether their motive was philosophical, religious, or self-preservation —in this world as well
as the next.[1] Precedents and moral support could be found
for any of these courses of action in both Christian and pagan
thought. Roman tradition, in short, once more proved
persistent and infinitely adaptable to circumstance.

The contrast in Britain between the occasional rich
Christian villa and the general paucity of evidence elsewhere,
especially for urban Christianity, does not of course mean
that there is no other sign of Christian observance at all.
The question is how much does it add up to; and to that
there is no clear answer. There is a scatter of small personal
objects such as finger-rings or lamps with certain or possible
Christian symbols or phraseology, and a few tombstones
similarly distinguished.[2] Then there are the spectacular
but rare finds of fourth-century plate such as Traprain,
Mildenhall, or Corbridge, which include some pieces
demonstrably of Christian origin. Next there is an interesting
group of lead tanks that have been plausibly identified as
fonts.[3] There are cemeteries and their associated structures.
And there is the destruction of pagan monuments.

Taking these categories of evidence one by one, it has first
to be said that the quantity of small objects, of graffiti and
of tombstones or other inscriptions is infinitesimal compared
with the vast amount that is undeniably pagan. The major
hoards can in none of the cases be with certainty associated
with persons certainly resident in Britain. They are most
probably either robbers' loot, for example Traprian, lost in
transit (as may have been the scattered pieces from the Tyne
at Corbridge, which also includes the pagan Lanx), or (as
perhaps in the case of the Mildenhall Treasure) personal
wealth accompanying a visiting imperial official normally
resident elsewhere, even though he may have had some
property in Britain.

The lead tanks or troughs are an interesting group. Of the

[1] See chapter 16 above.
[2] See J.D. Wall, *Arch. Ael.* 4th ser. 43 (1965), 201 ff.; 44 (1966), 147 ff., for
a survey of Christian evidence for the north in the Roman period.
[3] Wall, ibid. 44 (1966), 153 ff.: another such tank has come subsequently
from a Roman well at the small Roman town of Ashton near Oundle (*Current
Archaeology*, 56 (1976), 274).

ten now known only some bear Christian symbols, but they are sufficiently similar to suggest they all had the same purpose. Baptism is a reasonable hypothesis. In the early Church baptism was only performed by a bishop, but we cannot assume each of these objects marks the centre of a bishop's see. While their physical weight makes it obvious they are not part of a priest's portable equipment, the presence of light handles on the trough from Ireby in Cumbria indicate it could be dragged a short distance, for example into the body of a church, when the bishop arrived to conduct baptism. Only at the Silchester and Richborough sites is there any evidence at all for a permanent baptistry. Where these lead troughs or vats can be associated with a Roman settlement it seems either to be a small town, for example Ashton, in the Nene valley district, or a villa, such as Wiggonholt in Sussex.[1] Icklingham, just off the Fen Edge in Suffolk, has produced more than one such trough and is a site with very unusual characteristics. It covers an area of around 37 acres (about 15 ha.), the scale of a small town or of a villa with an exceptionally large group of associated buildings, like some of the great houses in Gaul. It also has an important group of cemeteries which contain features assumed to be of Christian type. There is some evidence that Icklingham had pagan religious significance before becoming Christian, and the changes may have included deliberate obliteration of its past. One wonders whether it may have been the centre of a Church estate, based on confiscated temple property or land given to the Church out of Fenland imperial domain. It will bear continued investigation and interpretation.[2]

We looked earlier at Roman attitudes to death and the way in which the mystery religions, including Christianity, seem to have influenced changes in burial rite. We have not, however, yet examined Romano-British cemeteries as such for evidence for Christianity in Britain. Of the various sources

---

[1] The Wiggonholt villa calls to mind the proximity of Castor to Water Newton since it lies within an extensive industrial area.

[2] For the 1974 excavations see *East Anglian Archaeology*, 3 (1976), 63 ff. The possibility that Icklingham might correspond to imperial land in the south-eastern Fenland as we have conjectured Castor did in the north-west is worth noting; as is its nearness to Mildenhall.

they are perhaps the most likely to produce new information on a substantial scale. I have noted some of the difficulties in distinguishing Christian from pagan burials, but there is no doubt there were certain practices widely adopted in Christian cemeteries in the Roman world: west–east orientation of the burials, avoidance of reuse of previous graves, lack of grave-goods, inhumation in place of cremation. There is sometimes an attempt to preserve the body as intact as possible[1] and a decided tendency for burials to cluster round a single grave or mausoleum, either that of a martyr, bishop, or other Christian of special significance or the vault of a family of prominence in the local Christian community. The shrine above a martyr's grave (*martyrium*) was of course a potent attraction for pilgrims. It is clear that many early churches on the Continent, especially those associated with cemeteries outside Roman cities, grew either out of shrines of this type or the mausolea (*memoriae*) of prominent Christian families at which communities gathered and like their pagan counter-parts remembered their dead. At Faversham, in Kent, a Roman mausoleum is incorporated into the chancel of the medieval church. This, and the many other examples where Roman buildings lie beneath later churches, may represent a significant continuity or memory of Christian sanctity. On the other hand, the abundance of ruined Roman buildings that could be reused or employed as quarries in the early medieval period must make us very wary of such speculation.[2] In Britain we are left with the curious situation, to quote Professor Rahtz, that 'of all late Roman cemeteries, only Poundbury has yielded unequivocal Christian evidence.'[3] This Dorchester cemetery can fairly be considered a major city graveyard. There are something like 4,000 burials known, apparently starting late in the third century or early fourth. The earliest area has a group of random burials,

---

[1] C.J.S. Green, in Reece, op. cit. 46 ff. argues for a probable Christian origin for the encasing of the body in gypsum or lime plaster already mentioned (as well as the sealing of coffins with lead).

[2] They often lie over villas—for example Widford (Oxfordshire) or Wood-chester (Gloucestershire)—and sometimes seem to follow on from very early in the Christian Saxon period. (Rivenhall, Essex: W. and K. Rodwell, *Brit.* 4 (1973), 115 ff.) It is just possible that some of these villas represent 'house-churches', but the caution is fully applicable.

[3] P. Rahtz, in Reece, op. cit. 54.

probably pagan, and a separate, deliberately orientated group lying around a single interment. This was followed in the course of the fourth century by a much larger cemetery with at least eight mausolea, including several decorated internally with paintings and one containing a coffin with an undoubted Christian inscription. This vast assemblage of burials presents a rare opportunity to study a Romano-British community dominated by Christian practices, though not necessarily all subscribing to Christian beliefs. We have to take into account the certain presence locally of powerful Christians. There were of course the general effects of Christian practices on the population at large, whether Christian or not, and there could also be an element of compulsion. The latter is particularly likely to have been applied on properties where the master was himself an enthusiastic Christian. The Theodosian Code suggests that an increase in the number of beatings on estates might help the workers to attend to their devotions more readily.[1]

Our last category of evidence is possible archaeological traces of the exercise of Christian power against the pagans. It is difficult to accept the reuse of second- and third-century coffins and a broken pagan altar in a cemetery at York as signs of Christian disrespect for pagan dead as has been on occasion argued, for we have seen that such disturbance was common in the ancient world. The destruction of Mithraea deserves closer attention. In the context of his excavation at Rudchester Mr J.P. Gillam wrote of the demolished Mithraea on Hadrian's Wall:

The parallels between the three are close, while there seem to be no close parallels to this precise kind of treatment elsewhere in the Empire. In all three the main relief was destroyed and largely or completely removed, . . . while the altars were left in position without desecration. Such uniform treatment implies a single wave of feeling along the line of the Wall, or a single general order.[2]

Mr Gillam's dating evidence pointed to destruction in the late third century or early fourth. It could thus be contemporary with the hiding of the main pieces of sculpture in the London Mithraeum. We have thus to reckon with a strong possibility that there was an order issued at one particular

[1] *Cod. Theod.* XVI. v. 52.
[2] J.P. Gillam and I. MacIvor, *Arch. Ael.* 4th ser. 32 (1954), 218.

moment by someone possessing authority throughout Britain, rather than any general upsurge of Christian violence. We cannot be sure when or by whom, though perhaps the most unlikely person is Constantine himself, since his personal devotion to the cult of the Unconquered Sun, very closely associated with Mithras, remained open for a long time and his exclusive adherence to the Christian faith was equivocal.

The military context of the Wall Mithraea must lead us to consider the position of the army in fourth-century religion. Constantine's order to his army at the Milvian Bridge to bear the Christian symbol and his subsequent victory there undoubtedly conferred immediate military prestige on Christianity. Later it was soldier-emperors, notably Valentinian I, and the Pannonian officers risen from the ranks who were rigid and enthusiastic Christians. Yet, for Britain, there is hardly any evidence at all for Christian sentiment in the Roman army.[1] In fact all we have is a few small objects, such as we have been considering in the general context, plus one Christain symbol on a single stone in the bath-house at Catterick, another from an unknown context at Maryport—and the desecration of the Mithraea. And, as Mr Watson reminds us in the context of the Carrawburgh Mithraeum:[2]

. . . it is as well to bear in mind what was going on at this time at the nearby Coventina's Well. Offerings continued to pour in. If they are not as numerous as in former times, that is probably rather an indication of economic conditions in the frontier zone than of a general conversion to Christianity.

This picture for the army is not out of line with the general pattern for fourth-century Britain. Not only do we find senior officers restoring monuments to the ancient religion at Cirencester or dedicating mosaics in the pagan complex at Lydney, but the evidence for the use of lesser pagan shrines goes as late as for other categories of Roman site—in other words to some unspecifiable period in the fifth century. Like, for example, the villas, the evidence from individual religious sites is very variable. Some pagan shrines

[1] See G.R. Watson, in Barley and Hanson op. cit. 51 ff.
[2] Ibid. 53.

go out of use in the early or mid fourth century, others continue throughout it, some are actually built after the war of 367 and some certainly continue in use well into the fifth century. The Carrawburgh Mithraeum was not repaired and had become a tip by about the middle of the fourth century; the rural shrine at Brean Down in Somerset was converted for some industrial purpose around AD 370 and the temple behind the theatre in the centre of Verulamium was abandoned about 380. Yet the coins do continue at many pagan shrines after that, and the economic explanation for the decline in quantity of offerings may be as good as the religious one. The Hockwold ritual crowns were hidden in a hole cut in the floor of the temple which had certainly remained in use to the very end of the fourth century. It would, of course, be very surprising if the general advance of Christianity had no effect on the popularity of the pagan cults, but none of this allows us to accept an overwhelming decline in pagan belief or, which is even more surprising, in pagan practices. Indeed, since we can find no evidence for a dominant observance of Christianity among the army, where as always the official religion was compulsory, we cannot be surprised if evidence for it elsewhere in Britain is sparse and for the collapse of paganism by AD 400 unconvincing.

This conclusion is quite contrary to the commonly held assumption that by the early fifth century Roman Britain was a Christian country in which paganism had largely ceased to be a real issue. That notion led to a view of Church history that includes a universally established Romano-British Church that was broken by the 'Arrival of the Saxons' or some other catastrophe in the middle of the century and forced back into the monasticism and tribal bishoprics of the Celtic hinterland. Yet such a picture of the Romano-British Church can only be built on implied evidence—the vigour with which neighbouring barbarians were converted (for example in Ireland by St. Patrick) or the emergence of Pelagianism as a formidable heresy—combined with an assumption that the empire at large was by now wholly Christian.

Both these arguments are weak. Neither St. Patrick nor Pelagius can be used to demonstrate a thoroughly Christian country. We have already touched on the possibility that

British Christianity was strong chiefly among a very influential but possibly quite small group in the Romano-British aristocracy. There were certainly heretics among this class: we may strongly suspect there were plenty of pagans as well. The empire in the west was in fact anything but solidly Christian. In Rome itself we have seen the struggle between senatorial pagans and Christian emperors symbolized by the disputes over the Altar of Victory continuing late in the fourth century. In 388 Theodosius the Great himself was formally met at the Balkan city of Aemona by pagan priests, the officials of the corporation.[1] Later, as we noted, Theodosius prohibited even the private celebration of pagan rites—but how successful was he? One may perhaps explain away an incident like the martyrdom of a Christian group in the Tyrol in about AD 400 for attempting to destroy a cult of Saturn at a holy well as being the exceptional result of rural isolation and superstition.[2] But how does one account for the fact that at Cosa in Italy a building in the decayed town-forum which had been taken over for use as a shrine of Dionysus in the course of the fourth century continued to house a flourishing cult apparently well into the fifth? If that could happen in Italy, is it surprising that pagan shrines survived to the end of Roman Britain?[3] In fact they fall into place in a much wider picture that is not difficult to substantiate.

In the Italian countryside paganism was still active in the second half of the fifth century.[4] Further north archaeological evidence in the intensely Romanized Rhineland indicates that the temple complex at Pesch was still in use under Honorius, and A.H.M. Jones draws on literary evidence to demonstrate a lively pagan survival at a much later date still in the western provinces at large:

There were still in the latter part of the sixth century a substantial number of rural pagans in the western provinces. Pope Gregory the

[1] See Ralegh Radford, op. cit. 25, and 35, n. 18 for references.
[2] Ralegh Radford, ibid. 25, and 36, n. 19.
[3] Even Dorchester in Dorset around where the Christian community was obviously strong and included men of property, there is no evidence for the destruction of pagan shrines (for example, at Maiden Castle).
[4] Bishop Maximus of Turin, describing the situation in 460. (See W.H.C. Frend, in Barley and Hanson, op. cit. 43 for reference and other material on this subject.)

Great found that in Sardinia many peasants, including tenants of church lands, were openly practising pagan worship, bribing the governor of the province to turn a blind eye. In 589 the Third Council of Toledo declared that 'the sacrilege of idolatry is rooted in almost the whole of Gaul and Spain,' and a series of Gallic Councils in 533, 541, 567, 578 and 625 denounced pagan practices, such as the worship of holy trees and holy springs. Martin of Bracara in the latter part of the sixth century wrote a tract *'de correctione rusticorum'*, in which he denounces among other pagan practices the observation of Thursday, the day of Jupiter, instead of Sunday. Anecdotes in Gregory of Tours show that the survivals of paganism were not merely witchcraft and superstition, but regular worship of the old pagan gods—Jupiter, Mercury, Minerva, Venus.[1]

There can be little doubt, of course, that Roman religious and political conservatism did much to prolong the life of the pagan cults. But there is a factor so far not introduced in this context, the increasing Germanic element in the Late Roman army. Doubtless many officers found it expedient to follow imperial Christianity from the days of Constantine on, though we should not forget the reign of Julian or the late interlude between AD 392 and 394 when the pagan *magister militum* Arbogast ruled with the Christian but compliant Eugenius and the temporary support of the Roman aristocracy. In the ranks, many Germanic troops must have remained pagan, if privately. They are likely to have found in Britain many of those Germanic and Celtic cults which had been long-established among the armies still actively being practised. As Roman armies came more and more to rely heavily on barbarian allies even the appearance of a religiously united army under the official imperial faith must have become less and less convincing, since barbarians, even if Christian, were likely to be Arian rather than Catholic.[2]

The replacement after AD 375 of Valentinian's crude Pannonian associates as dominant party at court by the Gallo-Roman aristocrats of Ausonius' circle not only helped the process of reconciling the western upper classes with the militant church but also must have greatly increased the prestige of the Christian provincial nobility at home. It is perhaps not entirely accidental that in the latter part of the

[1] A.H.M. Jones, in Barley and Hanson, op. cit. 15, with references.
[2] This was of course particularly true of the Visigoths.

fourth century these aristocrats felt able to indulge in the luxuries of ecclesiastical controversy. The most notable were perhaps the Priscillianists whom we saw Magnus Maximus pursuing in Spain, but in the 390s Victricius, bishop of Rouen and pupil of St. Martin, visited Britain to settle some unspecified ecclesiastical disputes. There is no evidence, however, to suggest that either St. Martin himself or Victricius carried out a programme of vigorous evangelization of the lower rural population in Britain as they did in northern Gaul.[1] In 429, we may recall, Germanus had to resort to mass baptism to acquire a Christian army. Yet, referring to the second quarter of the fifth century, Professor W.H.C. Frend has stated: 'At this period one senses rather than is able to prove that Britain was mainly as Christian a country as northern Gaul had become a generation before'.[2] By this, for he accepts Victricius' claim that the north-west of Gaul was more of less completely Christian, he implies that Britain was a Christian country so long as villa and town society survived. The claim is probably overstated for Gaul and I do not believe it for Britain. On the other hand, while agreeing with Professor Frere that pagan persistence and revival in the later fourth century had relatively little to do with the deliberate restoration of the old religion under Julian, we do not have to accept his notion that it was 'due to the insular character of Britain itself, and to its remoteness from the sources of power which were attempting to supplant paganism by the new official cult'.[3] Instead we have to see fourth and fifth-century paganism in Britain in the light of surviving paganism on the Continent. Indeed, the break with Rome may have given new opportunities to Romano-British pagans as much as to anti-imperial Christians.

The pagan persistence may explain two sorts of 'sub-Roman' cemeteries which occur mostly in the western parts of Roman Britain occupied late by the Saxons and to which attention has recently been drawn by Professor Rahtz.[4] One group seems to be associated with sites which had

---

[1] St. Martin: Sulpicius Severus, *Vita S. Martini*, 13–15; Victricius: Paulinus of Nola, *Letters*, xviii.4 and Victricius himself, *De Laude Sanctorum*, 1 ff.

[2] W.H.C. Frend, in Barley and Hanson, op. cit. 45.

[3] Frere, op. cit. 373.

[4] In Reece, (ed.), op. cit. 53 ff.: Type B and Type C.

certainly been religious (predominantly pagan) in the Roman
period and suggests that 'the possibility must be considered
that Roman religious sites may have continued as pagan
sacred sites well into the 5th and 6th centuries or even
later'.[1] The other seems to be associated with hill-top
occupation, mostly hill-forts, in the post-Roman period.
Professor Rahtz suggests that these hill-tops, too, may not
have been military sites in this period as generally assumed,
but religious. One must certainly agree that some Iron
Age hill-forts, such as Maiden Castle, became temple sites
in the Roman period when they had ceased to be native
military strongholds, and the religious associations may well
have lingered on, whether it was now with a pagan or a
Christian connotation.

There is, altogether, good reason to suppose that the pagan
Saxons encountered a strong indigenous pagan element
in Britain as well as the Christian Church, nor should we
forget the strong probability that religious beliefs among
the Germanic troops of Late Roman armies closely resembled
their own. We cannot simplify the conflicts around and
after the end of Roman rule in Britain in terms of Christian
against pagan any more than we can see it purely in terms of
Romano-Briton against barbarian. However, in the context
of the collapse of the structure of Roman Britain, it is
perhaps significant that the Britons who appear in Gaul in
the middle and later fifth century have come with their
bishops. Bishop Mansuetus is recorded at the council at
Tours in 461 and Riocatus is mentioned by Sidonius
Apollinaris about 476, in the very period when the imperial
court collapsed in Italy but independent Roman authority
remained firm in northern Gaul. With all its uncertainties,
the movement of a substantial population from Britain to the
Loire and Brittany in this period probably coincides with the
collapse of the Romano-British way of life in the major
part of the old province. This way of life had depended on
the provincial gentry and the system of landed estates and
towns, never so much as when the imperial government had
been expelled and the army disintegrated. Such evidence as
there is points to the organized Roman Church in Britain

[1] Ibid. 55.

having depended on the same structure. The Church that survived was very different, but one factor in its survival in the unconquered western parts of Britain may well have been that in the course of the fourth century its centre of gravity had already moved from the towns to the landed gentry and their estates. In the first half of the fifth century after the break with Roman rule it is not difficult to imagine bishops and clergy as clients of local 'tyrants' and lesser notables throughout the old provinces; after the collapse of order in the middle of the century some crossed to Gaul, others may well have retreated gradually westwards.

In western Britain itself it is reasonable to expect that something of the old pattern persisted for a long time, fading only gradually, particularly if estates themselves were undisturbed, as for example now appears likely in South Wales.[1] However the Church's survival probably owed just as much to the monastic groups existing in remote places and to the fact that it had proceeded far with the conversion of the barbarians of Ireland and Scotland. Some were settled in the western part of what had been Roman Britain but were not by any means necessarily (or even probably) in social and political sympathy with Rome. The British Church, we may conjecture, now contained highly disparate elements. As a distinctive political and social structure the old Church had gone down with the old Romano-British world.

NOTE

Religion in Roman Britain: addenda. A conference on 'Temples, Churches and Religion in Roman Britain' was held in Oxford in May 1979. A number of important papers were read, and it is expected that they will be published in due course. They are mostly not taken into account in the preceding chapter, but it has been possible to make one or two slight additions in the light of material presented then.

Note should also be taken under this heading of a publication edited by Julian Munby and Martin Henig: *Roman life and art in Britain: a celebration in honour of the 80th birthday of Jocelyn Toynbee*, British Archaeological Reports 41 (1977), collected papers based on an earlier conference.

---

[1] Important results are coming from the work of Dr Wendy Davies on Welsh charters. (See W. Davies, *Past and Present*, 81 (1978), 1 ff.)

APPENDIX I

A Note on Roman Names

UNDER the Republic and Early Empire it was customary for a Roman citizen to have at least three names—a forename (*praenomen*), used at home, a surname (*nomen*), indicating his family or *gens*, and one or more additional names (*cognomina*). Thus we find Gaius Julius Caesar or Marcus Tullius Cicero. The most common *praenomina* were often abbreviated in writing: M. for Marcus, for example, G. for Gaius, Sex. for Sextus, and so on. The *cognomen* was sometimes peculiar to an individual, sometimes an indication of one branch of a large *gens*. A few examples should make the system clear. The Emperor Vespasian was Titus Flavius Vespasianus, his younger son Titus Flavius Domitianus. Both had the same forename, Titus, and their membership of the Flavian *gens* was indicated by the middle name. It was the *cognomen* that distinguished them. A large *gens*, such as the Cornelii, posed problems. Thus the great Republican family of the Scipios were the Cornelii Scipiones, and many of them bore additional *cognomina*. Simple examples are Gnaeus Cornelius Scipio Calvus or Lucius Cornelius Scipio Barbatus. Often, additional *cognomina* were assumed to commemorate some success in public life: for example the general who defeated Hannibal in Zama in Africa became Publius Cornelius Scipio Africanus Major. Names could be further complicated by the process of adoption. Another Scipio, the intellectual and soldier Scipio Aemilianus, was born a son of Lucius Aemilius Paullus and adopted by Scipio Africanus' son. His full names eventually bore witness to his outstanding military career which included among other successes the capture of the city of Numantia. Hence his name became Publius Cornelius Scipio Aemilianus Africanus Numantinus.

In practice men were usually known by *nomen* and *cognomen*, sometimes reversed, or by *nomen* alone, and spelling varied. The governor of Britain Quintus Petillius Cerialis Caesius Rufus (as attested by an inscription) appears in our text of Tacitus as Petilius Cerialis (with one 'l' in the first name); the procurator Decianus Catus features as Catus Decianus (a stylistic device), and Gaius Suetonius Paulinus, conqueror of Boudicca, as Suetonius alone. Nevertheless the three names, the *tria nomina*, remained the prerogative of the Roman citizen and distinguished him from the non-citizen (*peregrinus*) and the slave. In formal documents he would give his father's *praenomen*, the Roman voting 'tribe' in which he was enrolled and frequently his place of origin as well, important evidence of his right to the citizenship.

Women were often not given a *praenomen*, even when they were citizens. Female *nomina* therefore came to be used familiarly as well as in public. Hence we find many Antonias in the imperial family, a name transmitted down from Mark Antony (Marcus Antonius). In other cases the *cognomen* was regularly employed. There were, for example, three ladies normally called Agrippina prominent in the Julio-Claudian House, all descended from Augustus' chief lieutenant, Marcus Vipsanius Agrippa. Two were named Vipsania Agrippina (one being Gaius' mother), the other Julia Agrippina, mother of Nero.

Slaves normally had a single name. If granted their freedom, they frequently adopted their former master's *praenomen* and *nomen*, retaining their own servile name as *cognomen*. Non-citizens granted citizenship (for example, soldiers discharged from auxiliary units at the end of their service) regularly took the *nomen* of the reigning emperor. Ulpii and Aelii of the mid-second century or later, for example, are therefore likely to be members of families first enfranchised under Trajan (Marcus Ulpius Traianus) and Hadrian (Publius Aelius Hadrianus) respectively.

From the time of the virtual extension of the citizenship to the whole empire under Caracalla, the *tria nomina* came to have less importance as a mark of distinction, though very elaborate names continued to appear. On the other hand there was concurrently a trend towards simplification. The rise of men of increasingly recent foreign origin to high positions in the Roman state seems to have encouraged the retention of names of 'ethnic' origin, often coupled with a Roman one. Thus at the end of the fourth century we have the two great *magistri militum*, Flavius Arbogastes and Flavius Stilicho, not bothering to disguise their barbarian antecedents by assuming more fully Romanized names.

One further practice is worth recording. Emperors adopted the name Caesar to underline their legitimacy even after the line of descent had died out with the end of the Julio-Claudians. However the title *imperator*, with which a victorious Roman general had been saluted under the Republic, was taken into the imperial nomenclature in a rather curious form. It was adopted as a *praenomen* by Augustus and by Otho, and then by Vespasian and all subsequent emperors. In this usage it was a name and not a title (a fact emphasized by the way emperors also used the word *after* their personal names when victories were won by their armies). Inscriptions and other formal references to emperors therefore commence the recitation with 'Imperator Caesar . . .' before continuing with their other names, their ancestry, titles, offices, and honours.

APPENDIX II

Roman Emperors from Augustus to Justinian

THE names of the emperors are given here in the forms under which they are commonly encountered in modern works in English. Fuller details of the names, offices, and families of the emperors from Augustus to Constantine III will be found in R.G. Collingwood and Ian Richmond, *The Archaeology of Roman Britain* (1969), 326 ff., and short biographies of many in *The Oxford Classical Dictionary*, 2nd. edn. Oxford (1970). This list does not attempt to differentiate between 'legitimate' emperors and 'usurpers' or to list every minor usurper, particularly after the end of Roman rule in Britain. Dates are those of the effective reign (many emperors designated their successors or others as co-emperors, but these are only shown when there was a real sharing of the supreme power).

Julio-Claudians
Augustus (Octavian) 27 BC–AD 14 (sole ruler from 30 BC)
Tiberius 14–37
Gaius (Caligula) 37–41
Claudius 41–54
Nero 54–68

Galba 68–69
Otho 69
Vitellius 69–70

Flavians
Vespasian 69–79
Titus 79–81
Domitian 81–96

Nerva 96–98
Trajan 98–117
Hadrian 117–138

Antonines
Antoninus Pius 138–161
Marcus Aurelius 161–180
Lucius Verus 161–169 (with M. Aurelius)
Commodus 180–192

Pertinax 193
Didius Julianus 193

742

Severan House & its rivals
Septimius Severus 193–211
Clodius Albinus 193–197
Pescennius Niger 193–194
Caracalla 211–217
Geta 211–212
Macrinus 217–218
Elagabalus 218–222
Severus Alexander 222–235

Maximinus ('Thrax') 235–238
Pupienus 238
Balbinus 238
Gordian I 238
Gordian II 238
Gordian III 238–244
Philip I ('the Arab') 244–249
Philip II 244–249
Uranius 248–253
Pacatianus 248
Jotapianus 249
Decius 249–251
Herennius Etruscus 250–251
Hostilianus 250–251
Gallus 251–253
Volusianus 251–253
Aemilianus 253
Valerian 253–259
Gallienus 253–268
Macrianus 260
Regalianus 261
Aureolus 267–268
Laelianus 268
Marius 268

 'Gallic emperors'
 Postumus 260–269
 Victorinus 269–271
 Tetricus 271–273

Claudius II ('Gothicus') 268–270
Quintillus 270
Aurelian 270–275
Domitian II uncertain
Vaballathus 270–271
Tacitus 275–276
Florianus 276
Probus 276–282
Saturninus 280
Carus 282–283

Julianus 283
Carinus 283–285
Numerian 283–284

The Tetrarchy
Diocletian 284–305
Maximian 286–305, 307–308
Constantius I ('Chlorus') 305–306 (*Caesar* 293–305)
Galerius 305–311 (*Caesar* 293–305)
Carausius 287–293
Allectus 293–296 (in Britain)
Achilles 296
Flavius Severus 306–307
Maximin Daia 310–313
Maxentius 307–312
Alexander 308–311
Licinius 308–324

House of Constantine & rivals
Constantine I ('Constantine the Great') 306–337
Valens 314
Martinianus 323
Constantine II 337–340
Constans 337–350
Constantius II 337–361
Nepotianus 350
Vetranio 350
Magnentius 350–353
Claudius Silvanus 355
Julian ('the Apostate') 360–363 (*Caesar* 355–360)

Jovian 363–364

House of Valentinian & rivals
Valentinian I 364–375
Valens 364–378
Gratian 367–383
Procopius 365–366
Valentinian II 375–392
Magnus Maximus 383–388
Flavius Victor 384–388
Eugenius 392–394

House of Theodosius & rivals
Theodosius I ('Theodosius the Great') 379–395

Western emperors	*Eastern emperors*
Honorius 395–423	Arcadius 395–408
Marcus 406? (in Britain)	Theodosius II 408–450
Gratian 407 (in Britain)	
Constantine III 407–411	

Western emperors	*Eastern emperors*
Maximus 409–411	
Jovinus 411–412	
Constantius III (Flavius Constantius) 421	
John (Johannes) 423–425	
Valentinian III 425–455	
	Marcian 450–457
Petronius Maximus 455	Leo 457–474
Avitus 455–456	Leo II 474
Majorian 457–461	Zeno 474–491
Libius Severus 461–465	Anastasius 491–518
Anthemius 467–472	
Olybrius 472	*House of Justin*
Glycerius 473	Justin I 518–527
Julius Nepos 473–480	Justinian 527–565
Romulus ('Augustulus') 475–476	etc.

APPENDIX III

Governors of the British Provinces

FROM the Claudian invasion till the recall of Julius Agricola the list of governors is complete and the time at which each took up office known within a margin of error of not more than one year. Thereafter there are gaps in the record and the dates of none of the governors are entirely reliable. From the division of Britain into two provinces in the early third century the record becomes increasingly patchy; and very little is known of the *vicarii* of the fourth-century diocese and the governors of the individual provinces into which it was subdivided.

Aulus Plautius AD 43–47
Publius Ostorius Scapula 47–52
Aulus Didius Gallus 52–57
Quintus Veranius 57/58
Gaius Suetonius Paulinus ?58–61
Publius Petronius Turpilianus 61–63
Marcus Trebellius Maximus 63–69
Marcus Vettius Bolanus 69–71
Quintus Petillius Cerialis 71–74
Sextus Julius Frontinus 74–77
Gnaeus Julius Agricola 78–84 (or 77–83)
Sallustius Lucullus perhaps 84–89
Publius Metilius Nepos ? by 96
Titus Avidius Quietus ?97/98–?100/101
Lucius Neratius Marcellus ?100/101–103 or later
Marcus Appius (*or* Atilius) Bradua perhaps 115–118
Quintus Pompeius Falco 118–122
Aulus Platorius Nepos 122–?125
Sextus Julius Severus *c.*131–132/133
Publius Mummius Sisenna ?131/132–?
Quintus Lollius Urbicus 138/139–?144
Gnaeus Papirius Aelianus by 146
Gnaeus Julius Verus by 158
— -anus Longus or Longinus 158/159–161
Marcus Statius Priscus 161/162
Sextus Calpurnius Agricola by 163/164–?166
Quintus Antistius Adventus in period 169–180
? Caerellius Priscus in period 169–180
Ulpius Marcellus by 180–?
Publius Helvius Pertinax 185–?187
Decimus Clodius Albinus 191/192–? (*Caesar* 193, died 197)
Virius Lupus 197–201/202

Marcus Antius Crescens Calpurnianus acting governor ?202
Gaius Valerius Pudens 202/203–205 or later
Lucius Alfenus Senecio 206/207–?

Britannia Superior
Gaius Junius Faustinus Postumianus ?
Titus Julius Pollienus Auspex
  ? in period *c.*223–226
Rufinus ?
Marcus Martiannius Pulcher ?
Titus Desticius Juba
  in period 253–255

Britannia Inferior
Gaius Julius Marcus by 213
? Marcus Antonius Gordianus
  ? by 216
Modius Julius by 219
Tiberius Claudius Paulinus 220
Marius Valerianus 221–222/223
Claudius Xenephon 223
Maximus by 225
Claudius Apellinus
  in period 222–235
Calvisius Rufus
  in period 222–235
Valerius Crescens Fulvianus
  in period 222–235
(T)uccianus by 237
Maecilius Fuscus
  in period 238–244
Egnatius Lucilianus
  in period 238–244
Nonius Philippus by 242
Octavius Sabinus
  in period 260–269

Diocese of the Britains
Vicarii
Pacatianus by 319
Flavius Martinus ? 353
Alypius (soon after Martinus)
Civilis 368
Victorinus probably in period 395–406
Chrysanthus probably in period 395–406

Governors
Aurelius Arpagius (? Britannia Secunda) in period 296–305
Flavius Sanctus mid fourth century
Lucius Septimius (Britannia Prima) ?

NOTE

This list assumes the final division into Britannia Superior and Inferior
was later than the governorship of Alfenus Senecio. It omits Geta (see
p. 228 above) and also assumes the Ulpius Marcellus of *RIB* 1463,
1464 is the same as the governor of that name in office in or before
180. For Rufinus, see p. 253 above.

APPENDIX IV

Tiberius Claudius Cogidubnus?

THE name of 'Tiberius Claudius Cogidubnus' was hardly known to the modern world outside the circle of Romano-British specialists —apart from the fleeting glance of schoolboy readers of the *Agricola*—till the discovery of the villa or 'palace' at Fishbourne and its attendant publicity. The enthusiasm of the newspapers and television overtook the rather more cautious approach of the excavator, and the absolute association of the man with the building entered popular historical mythology. To some extent we can separate the questions of the name and career of the man from the function of Fishbourne, yet I now think (after acute and long-maintained scepticism) that the association with the site, though not proven, is probable.

The identity and career of the man are historically the more important questions. The starting point must be the passage in the *Agricola* (the only literary reference): *quaedam civitates Cogidumno regi donatae* (*is ad nostram usque memoriam fidissimus mansit*).[1] This I have rendered as 'certain *civitates* were given to Cogidumnus to be king over them. He survived, ever most loyal, to within our own memory.' The first problem is that the Latin is ambiguous over his kingship: it is not clear whether he was already a king or (as I suspect) became a king by being put in charge of what looks like a number of separate British peoples grouped together by Claudius. It does, however, seem reasonable to assume that these particular *civitates* were existing local communities rather than new units artificially created by the Roman administration.

The second question is the correct form of his name. The state of the text of the *Agricola* as it has come down to us provides reason for caution. Our earliest manuscript dates from the time of Charlemagne in the ninth century. On that manuscript someone, who there is reason to think had access to a different manuscript of Tacitus, wrote a correction *in ninth-century handwriting*. His version therefore has equal authority as a source. He altered the name from *Cogidumnus* to *Togidumnus*. Dio does in fact tell us of a *Togodumnus* (the son of Cunobelinus who was killed in battle in AD 43) but we cannot reject the manuscript correction on the grounds that it is a false memory of Dio. We have no evidence that the corrector had seen Dio nor do we know what other sources he had. All Dio does in this context is to prove the existence of 'Togodumnus' or something like it as an aristocratic Celtic name in the first century AD.

At first sight this problem would seem to be solved by the inscription

---

[1] Tacitus, *Agr.* xiv.1.

748

found in Chichester in 1723[1] (which was, indeed, the chief reason for
associating our man with that area).[2] This records the dedication of a
temple to Neptune and Minerva for the good health of the imperial
family by a local guild of smiths (or possibly shipwrights), a dedication,
as the inscription says (in the accepted restoration of two badly
damaged lines) 'by authority of Tiberius Claudius Cogidubnus, king
and imperial legate in Britain.' Now 'Cogidubnus' is a perfectly acceptable variant spelling of Cogidumnus as a Celtic name, and although the
Latin for 'king' (*rex*) seems to be abbreviated to the single letter 'R'
no one has produced a satisfactory alternative explanation for that
feature of the inscription. There is therefore little doubt that we are
dealing with the same man. That, however, is the point at which reasonable certainty gives out. Of the name the damaged stone only preserves
. . . *Claud*(*ius*) . . . *gidubnus*. We therefore know no more about his last
name from the inscription than we do from the manuscript. In adopting
the name 'Cogidubnus' for this man, therefore, we do it only from
convenience and need to keep in mind the uncertainty. For his first
name the size of the gap on the stone and the existence of the
'Claudius' make it a reasonable supposition that it was Tiberius,
common in the Claudian family and quite likely here if citizenship
had been received from the emperor or through the agency of one of
his relatives or ancestors.

Two features about the site at Fishbourne have raised reasonable
doubts in the minds of some scholars about its identity as the palace
of the client king. One is the relatively late date of the complex in its
fully developed, grand phase (after AD 73 and probably around 80);
the other the highly sophisticated Mediterranean taste exhibited by its
form and decoration. The first objection does not seem to me to be
serious. The *Agricola* was published in 98. Tacitus himself was born
around AD 56 and was writing for his own generation and that of his
father-in-law, who had served first in Britain under Suetonius Paulinus
and again under Petillius Cerialis. If Cogidubnus had been put on his
throne by Claudius at the age of, say, 30 in AD 43 or soon after, he
would have been under 50 during the Boudiccan revolt, less than 60
during the Year of the Four Emperors, and still in his early seventies
at the end of Agricola's governorship of Britain.

As to the sophistication of Fishbourne, it has to be admitted that
even the forerunners to the great Flavian villa, though modest in
comparison, were very advanced in comparison with other country
houses in Britain in the mid-first century. The first probably non-
military structure was a particularly substantial and well-decorated
timber-framed house, built in the first ten years or so after the
Invasion. In the 60s this was replaced by an extensive complex in
stone, containing imported materials and almost certainly constructed

---

[1] *RIB* 91.
[2] The alleged place-name evidence for a kingdom centred on Chichester is
discounted by Professor K. Jackson. (Cf. Margaret Gelling, *Signposts to the Past*
(1978), 49 f.)

with the aid of men trained in the building trades elsewhere in the empire, a very unusual feature to be found this early in a civil building in Britain. The Flavian house itself, of course, is unparalleled in Britain both in size and style. If, for the sake of the present argument, we assume these buildings to represent successive rebuildings of the palace of the client-king rather than one of the other possibilities we rehearsed earlier in this book, then we have to consider what sort of patron this degree of awareness of the mainstream of Roman taste implies. It is perfectly possible for a British prince to have acquired such tastes—perhaps by being educated at Rome (such a practice, a form of taking hostages, not being uncommon in the relations between the emperors and foreign states). Nevertheless the total lack of evidence makes this no more than a guess, and certainly insufficient to make one prefer this theory to the alternatives. One of these is that Cogidubnus was a Briton, but that Fishbourne was entirely designed and decorated to Roman specifications and presented as a gift to the king by the emperor, reflecting the donor's tastes and not the occupant's.

There is a third possibility that has unexpectedly acquired real weight from a fresh piece of evidence. The remarkable stone circular temple on Hayling Island, close to Fishbourne, which replaced an Iron Age predecessor in the AD 50s or 60s has been very acutely observed by its excavators to be built in exactly the same technique as Fishbourne, a technique, moreover, paralleled not in Britain but in Gaul.[1] Now, there is nothing other than reasonable inference from silence to indicate that Cogidubnus was a *Briton*. Yet Caesar had made use of the Gaul Commius in Britain, and it might well have seemed sensible to Claudius to employ in this key role a man who was not a Briton but had a sound Romano-Celtic background. Claudius' fondness for the Gauls is, of course, well-known. His measure for the introduction of Gauls from 'long-haired' Gaul (*Gallia Comata*) into the senate was mocked but passed in AD 48:[2] indeed he pointed out at the time that there were already individual senators from the city of Lyons, situated in Gaul proper beyond the confines of the ancient, fully Romanized province of Gallia Narbonensis. In fact Claudius' own connections with Gallia Comata and that of his forebears went much further back. His beloved father, Nero Claudius Drusus (the Elder Drusus) was appointed governor of the whole of Gaul in 13 BC and conducted a census of the country in 12 BC. Claudius himself was born at Lyons in 10 BC, where his father had erected a famous altar to Rome and Augustus. His grandfather, Tiberius Claudius Nero, was not only made responsible for the establishment of citizen colonies in Narbonese Gaul; he had also done Caesar and Rome signal service during the Civil Wars that brought Caesar to supreme power by keeping Gaul peaceful and on the Caesarian side, when she might well have taken the opportunity to throw off the Roman yoke. It is therefore not beyond the bounds of possibility that

---

[1] For the excavation see R. Downey, A. King and G. Soffe, *The Hayling Island temple: third interim report on the excavation of the Iron Age and Roman temple 1976–78* (1979).   [2] *ILS* 212; Tacitus, *Ann.* xi. 23–5.

Cogidubnus was in fact a Gaul, perhaps from a family that had already received the citizenship under the emperor's father or grandfather. It is, of course, possible that Claudius advanced some Britons at the same time as he brought Gauls into the senate. Indeed, there is just a hint that he may have had such a move in mind, for grants of money to leading individuals (such as Dio tells us Claudius made to certain Britons)[1] were commonly made by emperors to allow men they wished to see hold office to possess the necessary property qualification. Yet the task of persuading the senate of the acceptability of Britons would have been an infinitely larger task than in the case of the Gauls. The substantial difficulty Claudius had in passing the latter proposal through the senate may well have deterred him from pressing on with any such plan for Britain, though he may have hoped the Britons would win the same privileges in the longer term. In fact, Britons are noticeable by their lack of representation in the senatorial order at all periods.

We have now to examine the rest of Cogidubnus' title on the Chichester inscription. He is there described as *rex et legatus Augusti in Britannia* (or so the only feasible restoration of the text has it). This is an unparalleled title, though 'kings and prefects' are known from areas like the Alpes Maritimes which were particularly difficult to control by ordinary military means. The post of *legatus Augusti* implies senatorial rank, and while I do not think—for the reasons above—that this is impossible under Claudius if he was a Gaul or less probably a Briton, I like Professor Eric Birley's suggestion that it was a reward for services in rallying support for Vespasian in AD 69.[2] It is, as he points out, in line with Vespasian's ready award of membership of the senate to others who had joined his cause. If, as we have seen, it is likely that Cogidubnus had played a vital role in much earlier days by ensuring the security of the bases from which Vespasian himself, as a legionary commander, had advanced westwards in Britain, then a close relationship may already have formed a quarter of a century before Vespasian's accession. Tacitus' description of Cogidubnus' loyalty 'to within our own memory' suits such a career perfectly.

There is a further implication if this interpretation is correct: Cogidubnus must have remained loyal to Rome throughout the rebellion of Boudicca, a circumstance which would be well known to Tacitus through Agricola's service with Suetonius Paulinus. It is now therefore possible to begin constructing a hypothetical historical framework for the archaeology. The starting-point is appointment under Claudius to form the client kingdom, and we can assume that in the first stage this was under the watchful eyes of the military. As soon as the main Roman forces were transferred permanently further west, part of one of their initial bases could be converted to provide a dignified residence for the king. The proximity of Fishbourne to the religious centre at Hayling Island—perhaps already a major focus for the native peoples of the region well before the arrival of the

[1] Dio, LXII. ii. 1.   [2] E. Birley, *Brit.* 9 (1978), 244 f.

Romans—was doubtless politically very convenient. The replacement of
the house by the first stone villa in the 60s was perhaps a reward for
loyalty during the rebellion. Anyone in authority who remained true
at this time could well have expected both tangible rewards and a great
increase in standing in the province. The reconstruction of the temple
could have been carried out at the same time: the Romans in Britain
and those provincials who had stood by Rome had escaped by the
skin of their teeth from a dreadful danger and it would be appropriate
both to thank the tribal gods and to emphasize the conflation of
Roman and Celtic in western provincial religion.[1] Less than a decade
later we may imagine Cogidubnus treading a wary path as the army in
Britain watched from the sidelines the rapidly changing fortunes of
the parties involved in the Year of the Four Emperors, itself divided
politically. His own probable past connections with Vespasian and
local prestige may have helped to hold the situation steady in the
province. Certainly it looks as if he had done enough to deserve extraordinary honours at the hands of Vespasian. The final scene in our
hypothesis would be the construction of the great villa in the governorships of Frontinus or Agricola. Could this mark an immensely
comfortable retirement for Cogidubnus and the end of the client
kingdom?[2]

---

[1] In this context we may note Plutarch (*De defectu oraculorum*, ii) who
mentions the return of the grammarian Demetrius of Tarsus from Britain.
Demetrius reports in AD 83 that there are a number of isolated islands around
Britain, several named after gods or heroes. On the orders of Domitian he had
sailed to the nearest to inspect it: he found few people there, all holy men whom
the Britons regarded as sacred. We do not know the location of this particular
island: Hayling Island, however, in the light of this evidence, fits into a tradition
still clearly alive in the late first century.

[2] This appendix was written before the publication of articles on Cogidubnus
by A.A. Barrett (*Brit.* 9 (1979), 227 ff.) and J.E. Bogaers (*ibid.* 243 ff.).

BIBLIOGRAPHY

THIS bibliography follows the pattern set by earlier volumes in *The Oxford History of England*. As Collingwood said of his bibliography, it is 'a review of the sources in general, not a collection of references for individual statements in the text.' It is hoped that the reader intent on pursuing the subject further will find here some guidance for reading on his particular interests. No attempt is made to list the enormous number of works, particularly articles in periodicals, that now exist on Romano-British and allied topics. The emphasis is on where the inquirer may best begin to look.

I have attempted to assess the relative value of certain of the sources, but only where this seemed particularly helpful to the general reader. I have not followed Collingwood in being so comprehensively or trenchantly critical of the works I have cited, partly out of deference for the greater willingness of the present generation of historians to admit to the validity of contrary views, partly because the huge increase in literature on our subject since Collingwood's day leaves no space to include works merely to dismiss them. This is not to say that such works no longer appear. Indeed, the proliferation of the poorer kind of archaeological journalism attests the popular interest in Roman Britain but on the whole offers little to the serious student. It is sadder that I have had to exclude for reasons of space and balance many works of excellence. Works cited in my footnotes have also for the most part been omitted, unless they have formed a major source frequently used. The footnotes themselves contain bibliographical details for each work on the first occasion it is cited: thereafter short titles are employed where those works are again cited in a later chapter or after a long interval of text. This is also perhaps the most convenient point to mention that for reasons of economy at the printers I have eliminated all but the bare minimum of the cross-references from one passage in my text to another that originally appeared in my manuscript footnotes. I apologize for any inconvenience to the reader and hope that the Index will serve his needs. Following Collingwood again, I have mostly not mentioned works more than once in this bibliography. It is therefore worth mentioning that many of them deal with many other aspects of the subject than that for which they are specifically included.

Collingwood rightly drew attention to the fact that unlike the later volumes in the series a very large proportion of the evidence on which his book was based came from archaeological rather than documentary sources. In this there is now less difference between Roman Britain and later periods of history than there was in 1937. The disciplines of medieval and post-medieval archaeology have made such enormous strides in the intervening years that they are now major tools of the historian. Moreover, there has been a growing realization that it is worth looking again and again at the ancient writers, both in the light of continuing work on the manuscript traditions and their interpretation, and in the context of the continuing discoveries of archaeology by which the texts are illuminated and which they in their turn illuminate. But, of course, the quantitative difference between the sources is still there. I have therefore included in this bibliography some information on the ways in which archaeological evidence of importance to the historian of the period is now being recorded, some of it in places and by methods not in use at the time this present book's predecessor was published.

ANCIENT AUTHORS

Standard texts of the majority of classical authors, accompanied by notes on the manuscript traditions, variant readings, and critical emendations are available in the Clarendon Press volumes known as the Oxford Classical Texts (OCT)—*Scriptorum Classicorum Bibliotheca Oxoniensis*—or in the German Teubner editions. The French Budé texts may also be found useful. Greek and Latin texts with parallel English translations are also commonly found in the Loeb Classical Library. Editions of the principal writings relevant to Roman Britain in general use include:

Ammianus Marcellinus (*c.*AD 330–95), ed. Clark (1910–15): cf. R. Syme, *Ammianus Marcellinus and the Historia Augusta*, Oxford (1968).

Antonine Itinerary (*Itinerarium Antoninianum*) (third century), ed. Cuntz, *Itineraria Romana*, 1 (Teubner, 1929).

Appian (*c.*90–160), ed. Mendelssohn (1879–81); White (Loeb, 1912–13).

Augustus, *Res Gestae* (as issued revised AD 14, possibly edited subsequently), ed. Gagé (1935): cf. P.A. Brunt and J.M. Moore, *Res Gestae Divi Augusti: The Achievements of the Divine Augustus*, Oxford (1967): text, translation, and notes.

Aurelius Victor (later fourth century), *Caesares* or *De Caesaribus*, ed. Pichlmayr (Teubner, 1911).

Caesar (100–44 BC), *Gallic War* (*De Bello Gallico*), ed. Rice Holmes (1914).

'Chronicler of 452' (previously attributed to Prosper Tiro), ed. Mommsen, *MGH (AA)*, 9 (1894–8), 615 ff.

Claudian (died *c.*404), ed. Koch (Teubner, 1893).

Cassius Dio (later second century to after 229), ed. Boissevain (1895–1931); Cary (Loeb, 1914–27): cf. Fergus Millar, *A Study of Cassius Dio*, Oxford (1964).

Code of Justinian (*Codex Justinianus*, issued 529, revised 534), ed. Krüger (1877).

Digest of Justinian (*Digesta seu Pandectae*, 533), ed. Mommsen (1870).

Eutropius (mid-fourth century), *Breviarium (ab urbe condita)*, ed. Rühl (Teubner, 1887).

Gildas (mid-sixth century), *De excidio et conquestu Britanniae*, ed.
Mommsen, *MGH (AA)*, 13, 1 ff. (1894–8); Williams, *Gildas* (1899–
1901).

Herodian (early third century), *Histories* (*Ab excessu Divi Marci*), ed.
Stavenhagen (Teubner, 1922); translation, E.C. Echols, Berkeley and
Los Angeles (1961).

Justinian (emperor): see under *Code* and *Digest* above.

Notitia Dignitatum (late fourth/early fifth century, dates disputed), ed.
Seeck (1896). The *Notitia* was in two sections, western (*Notitia
Dignitatum Occidentalis*) and eastern (*Notitia Dignitatum Orientalis*).
See A.H.M. Jones, *Later Roman Empire*, Oxford (1964), 3, 347 ff.
(with tables); R. Goodburn and P. Bartholomew, (ed.), *Aspects of
the Notitia Dignitatum*, British Archaeological Reports Supplementary Ser. 15, Oxford (1976) (reviewed J.D. Harries, *JRS* 67
(1977), 187 f.)

Orosius (early fifth century), *Historiae adversum paganos*, ed. Zang-
meister (Teubner, 1889).

Panegyrics (*Panegyrici Latini Veteres*), ed. R.A.B. Mynors (*XII Panegyrici
Latini*, OCT, 1964):

Anon. (formerly attributed to Eumenius), *Panegyric of Constantius
Caesar* (i.e. Constantius I) = *Pan. Lat. Vet.* VIII (V), delivered
AD 297.

Anon. *Panegyric of Constantine the Great* = *Pan. Lat. Vet.* VI (VII),
delivered 310.

Pacatus, *Panegyric of Theodosius the Great* = *Pan. Lat. Vet.* II (XII),
delivered 389.

Pausanias (mid-second century), *Description of Greece*, eds. Jones and
Wycherley (Loeb, 1918–35); Spiro (Teubner, 1903); Meyer (1954).

Procopius (sixth century), *History of the Wars of Justinian*, ed. Haury
(1905–13).

Ptolemy (first half of the second century), *Geography*, ed. Fischer
(1932).

Ravenna Cosmography (*Ravennatis Anonymi Cosmographia*), (seventh
century compilation), eds. Pinder and Parthey (1860): cf. I.A.
Richmond and O.G.S. Crawford, 'The British Section of the Ravenna
Cosmography', *Archaeologia*, 93 (1949), 1 ff. (text, maps, and
commentary).

Scriptores Historiae Augustae (dates disputed, probably late fourth
century), ed. Hohl (Teubner, 1927): cf. R. Syme, op. cit.

Strabo (mid-first century BC to early first century AD), *Geography*,
ed. Jones (Loeb, 1917–33).

Suetonius (later first century to early second century), *Lives of the
Caesars* (*Caesares*), ed. Ihm (Teubner, 1907–8).

Tacitus (mid-first century to early second century): cf. R. Syme,
Tacitus, Oxford (1958):

Agricola, ed. Ogilvie and Richmond, *Cornelii Taciti: De Vita
Agricolae*, Oxford (1967): text with extensive commentary.

Histories (*Historiae*), ed. Fisher (OCT, 1911).

Annals (*Annales*), ed. Fisher (OCT, 1907); Koestermann (Teubner,
1960).

Theodosian Code (*Codex Theodosianus*) (AD 438), ed. Mommsen and Meyer (1905): translation C. Pharr, Princeton (1952, reprint New York, 1969).

Vegetius (late fourth century), *Epitoma rei militaris*, ed. Lang (Teubner, 1885).

Verona List (AD 312–14), ed. Mommsen, *Gesammelte Schriften*, Berlin (1905–13), 5, 561 ff.; Seeck (see *Notitia Dignitatum* ed. 1876): cf. A.H.M. Jones, *JRS* 44 (1954), 21 ff., and *Later Roman Empire*, 3, 381 ff.

Zosimus (early sixth century), ed. Mendelssohn (1887).

There is one subject anthology which is particularly useful, a small book edited by J.C. Mann, *The Northern Frontier in Britain from Hadrian to Honorius: Literary and Epigraphic Sources*, Newcastle upon Tyne (n.d.). This contains the Latin sources in the original, the Greek in translation. It is convenient also to mention at this point the paper by Sir Ian Richmond 'Ancient Geographical Sources for Britain north of Cheviot' in *Roman and Native in North Britain*, Edinburgh (1958), which he edited and which contains the relevant texts as an appendix (p. 150 ff.).

Almost all the writings relating to Roman Britain (including a number of minor sources not listed above) are to be found translated in the excellent *Literary Sources for Roman Britain* (1977), edited for the London Association of Classical Teachers as 'Lactor 11' by J.C. Mann and R.G. Penman. The principal texts not included there because of their length are:

Caesar, *Gallic War*, iv. 20–38; v. 1–23.

Tacitus, *Annals*, xii. 31–40; xiv. 29–39.

Tacitus, *Agricola*.

'Lactor 11' incorporates a list of the documentary sources, with the compilers' assessment of their value as historical evidence and brief biographical notes on the ancient writers. There is also a collection of references to texts and inscriptions arranged under selected topics.

With all translations the reader should be warned of the convention that alternative interpretations of the original are rarely given, unless the text has obviously become corrupt in the process of copying and re-copying since ancient times (and not always then). The Penguin Classics (Harmondsworth) include translations of the three main sources omitted from 'Lactor 11':

S.A. Handford, *Caesar: The Conquest of Gaul* (1951).

Michael Grant, *Tacitus: The Annals of Imperial Rome* (1956).

H. Mattingly, *Tacitus: On Britain and Germany* (1948; revised S.A. Handford, 1970).

I have used one other ancient source extensively, the *Letters* of the Younger Pliny (*c.*AD 61–*c.*112). The standard edition is R.A.B. Mynors' Oxford Classical Text (2nd edition, 1966) and there is a massive commentary by A.N. Sherwin-White (*The Letters of Pliny: A Historical and Social Commentary*, Oxford (1966)) which does not, however, always discuss points of particular interest to archaeologists. The *Letters* are also available in a Penguin translation (B. Radice, *The Letters of the Younger Pliny* (1963)).

THE ROMAN EMPIRE

Within the space of this bibliography it is not feasible to explore the modern literature on the Roman Empire at large, but readers may like their attention drawn to one or two works of reference. At the head of any such list must come the second edition of *The Oxford Classical Dictionary*, eds. N.G.L. Hammond and H.H. Scullard, Oxford (1970, reprinted with corrections, 1972, 1973). Individual entries include their own bibliographies. Mention should also be made of a collection of sources in translation edited by N. Lewis and M. Reinhold (*Roman Civilization—Sourcebook II: The Empire*, New York (2nd edition, 1966)). The main collection of inscriptions relating to the western part of the empire is still the *Corpus Inscriptionum Latinarum*, Berlin (1863–), supplemented by the periodicals *Ephemeris Epigraphica* and *L'Année épigraphique* and notes on new discoveries and fresh inter-pretations in the *Journal of Roman Studies* and elsewhere. The most frequently encountered substantial selection of epigraphic material is H. Dessau, *Inscriptiones Latinae Selectae*, Berlin (1892-1916). For the history of the Roman world from the late third century onwards I have made extensive use of the late Professor A.H.M. Jones's *The Later Roman Empire 284-602*, Oxford (1964), as my footnotes testify. I mention it again here not only because of its importance but also to explain its unusual nature. Its author made the deliberate choice to base it on a complete reading of all the available ancient literary sources, made possible only by more or less ignoring other modern work on the subject and almost entirely excluding the archaeological evidence. Jones's self-imposed discipline produced a magisterial survey founded on a unique grasp of the written sources, a grasp recorded in the immense apparatus of notes, themselves a major work of reference.[1] How much was lost by the method is impossible to quantify. B.H. Warmington's important assessment of *The Later Roman Empire* (*History*, 50 (1965), 54 ff.) doubts if much was lost by omitting the archaeology, but extensive work has been done on the material remains of the Late Empire in the west since that review was written, and there are topics on which that judgement can no longer be upheld. On the other hand, it is at least arguable that Jones's volumes would form a lesser work if he had deflected from his austere path, certainly a less readable one. Comparable in scale is M. Rostovtzeff's survey *The Social and Economic History of the Roman Empire* (second edition edited by P.M. Fraser, Oxford (1957), and reprinted with corrections first in 1963). Another classic—concise and particularly useful to the general reader—is G.H. Stevenson's *Roman Provincial Administration till the Age of the Antonines*, Oxford (1949), a summary of the manner in

---

[1] Originally issued in 1964 with the pages of the third volume (notes and indexes) separately numbered from the rest of the book, continuous pagination was adopted when the work was reprinted.

which Rome's government of her possessions had evolved and an
outline of the system as it existed under the Principate. Finally, we
may note an intriguing collection of generalizations by prominent
historians from Gibbon onwards compiled by D. Kagan, whose title
itself perhaps begs the ultimate question for the ancient historian:
Decline and Fall of the Roman Empire: Why Did It Collapse? Boston
(1962).

ROMAN BRITAIN: BIBLIOGRAPHIES AND ABSTRACTS

Collingwood's bibliography surveyed the history of writing on Roman
Britain up to his own time, starting from its beginnings in the sixteenth
century and tracing its development in both general works and the
volumes on local history and topography in which Britain is particularly
rich. These works are themselves sources of major importance for the
modern student of the subject, since their authors often recorded finds
made in their own or earlier times and since lost, or described the
remains of monuments in the field which are no longer visible or have
been destroyed by subsequent changes in the landscape brought about
by natural agencies or the hand of man. Collingwood's bibliography
remains an excellent starting-point for the exploration of these earlier
works. It is when Collingwood reaches the twentieth century that we
can see most clearly how the bibliographical picture changed between
the 1930s and the present day. Apart from the sheer volume of material
now available, to which reference has already been made, the most
important development has been the appearance of specialized and
general bibliographies, classified indexes, gazetteers, topographical
surveys, and—a practice derived from the sciences—the regular publication of volumes of abstracts of current articles and books. These
and allied developments make it possible for the Romano-British
scholar to remain generally aware of what is going on in his field, even
though he can no longer hope to be acquainted with it all in any depth.
A working knowledge of these new guides is one of the most important
tools for any present-day inquirer in our subject to possess.

In many ways Wilfred Bonser's two volume *A Romano-British
Bibliography (55 BC–AD 449)*, Oxford (1964) marks the end of the
era in Romano-British studies characterized by Collingwood, and
summarizes the subject before the great changes in the quantity and
modes of publication set off in the 1960s and 1970s by the response
to the challenge of post-war redevelopment were much advanced.
Bonser searched a very large number of sources and include material
published down to the end of 1959. As a professional librarian, he
deliberately made no attempt at evaluation, and is particularly valuable
for obscure publications or material that will probably have been
rejected by other modern authorities, yet may in passing contain
information of importance.

The beginnings of more systematic publication and record-keeping
are to be found, however, well before Bonser's closing date. Among the
chief instigators of this change has been the Council for British

Archaeology, many of whose enterprises fall within the scope of this bibliography. As early as 1949 the CBA published the *Archaeological Bulletin for the British Isles, 1940-1946*, the first in a regular series of volumes that in 1954 reached its present form as the *Archaeological Bibliography for Great Britain and Ireland*. More recently the CBA— through its specialist sub-committees—has become particularly interested in education, and readers may find of wider use a booklet originally intended for that field alone entitled *British Archaeology: An Introductory Booklist*, first published in 1976 and currently issued with a supplement including relevant material which had appeared up to the end of the summer of 1977. It is also, while on the subject of booklists, worth drawing attention to another which also goes beyond Roman Britain, K.D. White's *A Bibliography of Roman Agriculture*, Reading (1970).

To return to the major publications of the CBA, perhaps the most influential has been the introduction of the volumes of *British Archaeological Abstracts*, which started with a pilot edition in 1967. The first of the regular volumes appeared in 1968, covering the period 1 July–31 December 1967, and they have been issued at half-yearly intervals since that date, with a coverage extending over both the British literature and a wide selection of foreign publications. A valuable supplement to each year's pair of volumes is the parallel annual CBA booklet earlier known as *Current and Forthcoming Offprints on Archaeology in Great Britain and Ireland* and now entitled *Current Archaeological Offprints and Reports*, which lists reprints currently available for sale to the general public (chiefly from the journals of archaeological and related societies) and the sources from which they can be obtained.

FINDS AND EXCAVATIONS

The principal annual record of finds and excavations in Roman Britain is the section entitled 'Roman Britain in 19..' which appeared in the *Journal of Roman Studies* from 1921 to 1969 and has continued in *Britannia* from the inception of that journal in 1970. That section is subdivided into 'Sites Explored' and 'Inscriptions'. The history of archaeological activity in Britain in a particular year can be supplemented by reading the CBA annual *Report* (which has become *Archaeology in Britain* since 1971-2) and the more ephemeral CBA *Calendar of Excavations*, published several times a year with a special number in more recent years summarizing the results of each season. This latter publication has expanded its function to contain editorials and general news, reflected in its new title as *C.B.A. Newsletter and Calendar*. Many of the CBA Regional Groups publish substantial annual records of activity in their own areas (for example, the *West Midlands Archaeological News Sheet*, whose name concealed a publication of around a hundred pages). This is a fairly recent development in England at large, but for Scotland *Discovery and Excavation in Scotland* is of relatively long standing.

Because the major learned journals (which I shall note below) appear at least a year after the event, and since the full reports of excavations are often not published till years after the digging has finished, it is not easy to keep abreast of current developments. For this reason we have particular cause to be grateful for the coverage given by broadcasting and the press, inaccurate in detail though it can often be. Some general magazines have a high standard. *The Illustrated London News* in particular built up a long tradition of archaeological articles, usually on the more prestigious excavations. Among newspapers *The Times* has most consistently provided coverage of archaeological news beyond the most obviously sensational. Finally mention must be made of the periodical *Current Archaeology* which appears six times a year, a publication often underrated by professional archaeologists but of prime importance in making up-to-date information on excavation and theory available in an attractive format both to professionals and a wider public. Much of the content takes the form of reportage of current events and book reviews and comment by the editors, but it also frequently includes articles by specialists on their latest work. This context does perhaps permit a greater freedom for the trying-out of hypotheses—not to mention the healthy airing of controversy and prejudice—than would normally be possible in the more weighty journals. But its most important function is the spreading of news about current work and its implications outside the increasingly narrow compartments into which specialist archaeology is being divided.

TOPOGRAPHY, REGIONAL AND LOCAL SURVEYS

An introduction to the history of work on topography and local history which has been actively pursued in Britain since the early part of the sixteenth century is to be found in Collingwood's bibliography; and in parenthesis it is worth noting the important contribution to making further practical use of the antiquarian sources (especially records of sites and finds since destroyed or lost) represented by the publication of M.W. Barley's *A Guide to British Topographical Collections* (1974).

Modern theory is still heavily influenced, as we have noted at various points in this book, by Sir Cyril Fox's *The Personality of Britain: Its Influence on Inhabitant and Invader in Prehistoric and Roman Times*, Cardiff (4th edn. 1943). His over-all distinction between highland and lowland is reflected in the titles of the two excellent collections of papers published by the CBA as *The effect of man on the landscape: the Highland Zone* (Research Report No. 11: ed. J.G. Evans, Susan Limbrey and Henry Cleere, 1975) and *The effect of man on the landscape: the Lowland Zone* (Research Report No. 21: ed. Susan Limbrey and J.G. Evans, 1978). Much of the modern work was also inspired by the first publication by the Ordnance Survey of the *Map of Roman Britain* in 1924. The fourth edition (Southampton, 1978) is in two sheets at a scale of 1: 625,000. Comparison between this and the first edition—or even the third (1956)—will demonstrate the enormous increase in sites known that has occurred in recent years. The original map and its successive revisions represent one of the greatest and most sustained achievements of British archaeology and the continuation of the project is central to the progress of our subject. In its book form, the 1978 edition incorporates a gazetteer and notes on sources for Roman place-names in Britain. The map itself, as its compilers declare, is deliberately conservative, omitting what has not been demonstrated with a high degree of certainty to be Roman. It retains one serious (though unavoidable) difficulty for the user, in that it does not differentiate between periods within Roman times.

Another work that will be of fundamental importance to students of the Roman geography of Britain appeared near the end of 1979. This is A.L.F. Rivet and Colin Smith's *The Place-Names of Roman Britain*. Half the book consists of an alphabetically arranged list of ancient names of places and peoples or tribes, each briefly discussed under sources of evidence, derivation or etymology, and identification or location on the present-day map of Britain. The other half first examines the languages of Britain relevant to place-names in the Roman period and the linguistic and textual problems facing the scholar, and then lists, discusses, and as necessary quotes the relevant texts of the sources. Those interested in Roman roads and communications will find the new and detailed examination of the ancient Itineraries (or road-books) particularly useful. This corpus of place-names will undoubtedly become one of the standard reference works on Roman Britain.

In many ways Fox's early book *The Archaeology of the Cambridge Region*, Cambridge (1923)—reissued in 1948 with a thoughtful appendix, 'Reflections on *The Archaeology of the Cambridge Region*'—has become, half a century later, the most significant part of his work, as the central importance of the *regional* study in the understanding of ancient cultures emerges more and more strongly. Generalizations become increasingly suspect and we await greater coverage of ancient Britain region by region and period by period. However, there are one or two works that, used with due caution, can be helpful in comprehending the over-all picture of man in the landscapes of the past. J.G. Evans's *The Environment of Early Man in the British Isles* (1975), for example, while still based on the inevitably fragmentary evidence (and allowing for reservations on the general views expressed on the Roman period), nevertheless draws on a wide range of sciences and makes a valuable contribution to our understanding of the environmental background to human activity.

Realization of the importance of landscape studies to the Roman period came particularly early in the study of the Romano-British countryside, and an influential collection of papers, edited by Charles Thomas, was published in 1966 as CBA Research Report No. 7, *Rural Settlement in Roman Britain*. This was the outcome of a conference which brought together people working on different aspects of the subject and in many cases more or less out of touch with their colleagues' researches. Such publications of the proceedings of conferences on a particular theme, within the general discipline of Roman Britain, have become an increasingly important source in recent years for the student of the period.

Local period studies have long formed part of the tradition notably represented by that monument to Victorian scholarly enterprise, *The Victoria History of the Counties of England* (or *VCH*). This latter work is still in progress, still of necessity based on the pre-1974 counties with which it started. Some counties have such extensive Roman remains that separate volumes for the period are now required. In 1963, for example, Volume III of the VCH *Essex* (ed. W.R. Powell) appeared as *Roman Essex*, including major contributions by Sir Ian Richmond and M.R. Hull. Richmond himself, long before, had pioneered this approach in part of a county in *The Romans in Redesdale*, a chapter in Volume 15 of *The History of Northumberland* (ed. Madeleine Hope Dodds), Newcastle upon Tyne (1940). With this in importance can be grouped O.G.S. Crawford's monograph, the *Topography of Roman Scotland North of the Antonine Wall*, Cambridge (1949).

Crawford himself was among the great pioneers of archaeological aerial photography, and but for the development of this technique by Crawford and a few contemporaries between the First and Second World Wars the magnitude of the threat to ancient remains posed by development after 1945 would never have been realized. The nature of the crisis was crystallized in the enormously influential occasional publication *A Matter of Time* issued in 1960 by the Royal Commission on Historical Monuments (England). This small book concentrated particularly on the river gravels, where the remains respond exceptionally well to aerial photography and where the threat from mineral extraction for the construction industry was (and is) most acute. *A Matter of Time* set the pattern both for rescue archaeology in the countryside and for a style of publication which together still account for a very significant proportion of the archaeological effort in Britain today. Among the earlier examples of such publication is the fifth volume in the Royal Geographical Society Research Series, *The Fenland in Roman Times* (1970), by P. Salway, S.J. Hallam, and J. l'anson Bromwich and edited by C.W. Phillips. This married the plotting of aerial photographs with fieldwork, analysis of the contents of museums, reports from a network of local correspondents and the records of earlier discoveries. It drew particularly heavily on contributions by sedimentologists and palaeobotanists, and touched on other environmental techniques that have since been taken much further by others. As a matter of archaeological record it attempted a complete gazetteer of all the sites and finds then known from the region, accompanied by a series of maps to the scale of 1:25,000 covering the areas for which there was the most extensive evidence from the air. On some of these maps it was possible to print geological information at the time exceptional in its detail and quality and generously made available by the Institute of Geological Sciences, permitting a new type of examination of settlement in its physical setting.

It is unlikely that resources of cartographic office man-power on the scale the Royal Geographical Society was able to devote to this project in the 1960s will ever be available again, but new techniques of map-making based on computers, both for the storage of information and through computer-graphics for the production of the maps them-selves, already in use for archaeology in Germany, ought to make similar projects possible by different methods. In the meantime *A Matter of Time* has borne other fruit. For many years the Ordnance Survey and the Royal Commissions built up for the purposes of their own publications what amounted to national archives of archaeological discovery, though in neither case was this their primary intention. The former in particular was seriously threatened by Government economies and neither was ideally suited to serve the needs of those local workers responding to the threat to sites. A new philosophy has replaced the objective of total publication. The trend nowadays is instead to attempt the comprehensive storage of data as accessibly as possible in 'Sites and Monuments Records', housed in a variety of institutions, such as County Museums, Archaeological Units, or Local Authority Planning Departments. Methods in use differ, but there is likely to be a growth of computer-based systems which permit rapid recording and ready recovery of information. At the centre of this largely informal network of archives—as yet not nationally organized—is the National Monuments Record in London, now a division of the English Royal Commission, and corresponding National Monuments Records within the Royal Commission on the Ancient and Historical Monuments of Scotland in Edinburgh and the Royal Commission on Ancient and Historical Monuments in Wales at Aberystwyth. The growth of these surveys in England and their lack of co-ordination has been charted at the instigation of the English Royal Commission by C.C. Taylor and F.A. Aberg and published by the Stationery Office as *Survey of Surveys 1978: a review of local archaeological field survey and recording*, not only a document of reference but also containing recommendations for the future organization of this fundamental archaeological activity from which changes may spring and of which active archaeologists should be aware.

Many of the most recent publications based on these records have come as a response to the realization that archaeological knowledge forms an important element in modern planning. We may take as an example a group of publications produced to a deliberately similar format by different bodies in a single region. The exemplar was Don Benson and David Miles's *The Upper Thames Valley: An Archaeological Survey of the River Gravels*, Oxford (1974). This was followed by Timothy Gates, *The Middle Thames Valley: An archaeological survey of the river gravels*, Reading (1975) and by Roger Leech, *The Upper Thames Valley in Gloucestershire and Wiltshire: An Archaeological Survey of the River Gravels*, Bristol (1977). All these included sites of various periods, but a large proportion are undoubtedly Iron Age or Romano-British. The Berkshire Archaeological Committee followed the gravels survey by Timothy Gates with an upland volume, Julian C. Richards on *The archaeology of the Berkshire Downs: an intro-ductory survey*, Reading (1978). To this we may add the much more ambitiously produced RCHM volume *Iron-Age and Romano-British Monuments in the Gloucestershire Cotswolds* (1976)—one of the special period volumes the Royal Commission, too, is now producing. Together all these works constitute a basis or starting-point for thematic studies of our period in a particular region in a way that has never previously existed.

No bibliography on sites and monuments should, of course, omit at least one general guide for the person anxious to see for himself those that still have enough visible to be worth a visit. Among a large number of such guides—many of poor quality—one stands out by itself: Roger J.A. Wilson, *A guide to the Roman Remains in Britain* (2nd edn. 1980), a book to be recommended to the serious student of the period and to the general visitor alike.

INSCRIPTIONS

The main collection of ancient inscriptions is R.G. Collingwood and R.P. Wright, *The Roman Inscriptions of Britain*, of which the first volume (*Inscriptions on Stone*) was published at Oxford in 1965. This contains text, translations, notes, and illustrations of all the inscriptions found before the end of 1954; as well as a general index and a concordance table linking the numbering in this volume to that of *CIL* VII. The second volume, not yet published at the time of writing, will include inscriptions on other materials found to the end of 1956 and classified indexes for the whole work. For inscriptions found in subsequent years, the relevant volumes of *JRS* or *Britannia* should be consulted.

Readers may also find useful a collection of epigraphical material edited by M.C. Greenstock (*Some Inscriptions from Roman Britain* (1971), published as 'Lactor 4'). Contrary to its title, this in fact includes a number of inscriptions found outside Britain but relevant to it, a helpful pointer to some important material excluded from *RIB* by its terms of reference.

GENERAL WORKS

The reader may welcome a longer perspective into the pre-Roman past than it has been possible to provide at the beginning of this book. Derek Roe's *Prehistory* (1970) can be particularly recommended and Richard Bradley, *The Prehistoric Settlement of Britain* (1978) is a pleasingly literate and quietly witty translation of otherwise indigestible modern theory into readable prose. The very difficult task of tackling the northern European background to the Roman expansion has hardly ever been better undertaken than by T.G.E. Powell in *The Celts* (1958), which, though in parts superseded by more recent work, remains as good an introduction as the general reader can find anywhere. The publication of a new edition, revised by Stuart Piggott, was imminent at the time of writing. Much more immediately concerned with our geographical area and up-to-date in detail—if more involved in current controversy—is Barry Cunliffe, *Iron Age Communities in Britain*

(2nd edn. 1978). A conspexus of the various views held by the participants in the debate about fundamental issues that make the Iron Age so difficult for the non-specialist is provided by the collection of papers edited by John Collis, *The Iron Age in Britain: A Review*, Sheffield (1977). As we have noted, much of the debate initially arose out of reaction against the picture of Iron Age Britain which relied too heavily on Bersu's brilliant excavation of Little Woodbury (G. Bersu, 'Excavations at Little Woodbury', *Proc. Prehist. Soc.* 6 (1940), 30 ff.); while the argument against successive invasions of Britain was sparked off by F.R. Hodson (see in particular Hodson, 'Cultures of Continental Type in Britain', ibid. 30 (1964), 100 ff.). In this context an article which helps to put into perspective the spectacular but rare warrior burials of the Late Iron Age is worth individual mention—John Collis, 'Burials with Weapons in Iron Age Britain', *Germania*, 51 (1973), i, 121 ff.

For the non-specialist a first impression of the artefacts of the Iron Age could very conveniently be gained from the unpretentious but well-illustrated *Later Prehistoric Antiquities of the British Isles* introduced in 1953 by the British Museum primarily as a guide to its own collections but of wider use. The Ordnance Survey *Map of Southern Britain in the Iron Age*, Chessington (1967) with its introductory booklet gives the general pattern, if now rather out of date, of the geographical distribution of Iron Age culture in the part of Britain where it can most clearly be distinguished. D.W. Harding in *The Iron Age in Lowland Britain* (1974), and S.S. Frere (ed.), *Problems of the Iron Age in Southern Britain* (1961, reprinted 1978), fill in more of the detail. The Iron Age in the north is more elusive. Papers in A.L.F. Rivet (ed.), *The Iron Age in Northern Britain*, Edinburgh (1966) attempted to come to terms with the issues, and we may expect important illumination to be shed on the idiosyncratic developments in east Yorkshire by I.M. Stead's forthcoming study under the joint aegis of the CBA and the Yorkshire Philosophical Society, *The Arras Culture*.

No discussion of the Iron Age cultures and their immediate predecessors can avoid the most prominent remains they have left in the landscape, the hill-forts. Two works need individual mention here— D.W. Harding (ed.), *Hillforts: Later Prehistoric Earthworks in Britain and Ireland* (1976), and Margaret Jesson and David Hill (eds.), *The Iron Age and its Hill-Forts: papers presented to Sir Mortimer Wheeler*, Southampton (1971)—and there are numerous reports on individual sites. Celtic coinage, whether or not it is a reliable indicator of political patterns, is an important study in itself, and mention must be made of at least one of D.F. Allen's works, for example his paper on 'The Origins of Coinage in Britain' in the volume edited by Frere cited above (pp. 61 ff.), and of Colin Haselgrove, *Supplementary gazetteer of findspots of Celtic coins in Britain* (1977).

Some indication of what Sir Ian Richmond's full-scale survey of Romano-British history might have been is preserved in his Penguin Press *Roman Britain*, 2nd edn. Harmondsworth (1963). In the event no book fully replaced Collingwood's Oxford History, but in 1967 S.S. Frere's *Britannia* provided an extremely well-documented account of the subject as it then stood. This book immediately became the standard work of reference. Frere's *Britannia* was extensively revised and brought up to date by its author for the 1974 paperback edition. Readers should, incidentally, note that the version issued in 1978 between hard covers is a reprint of the 1974 edition with slight corrections, not a further revision. The exceptional value of *Britannia* is in its very full footnotes (often lacking in Collingwood) and in its bibliography which is by far the best readily accessible guide to what is important among individual papers in the learned journals down to the early 1970s. Frere draws effectively on a wide appreciation of both literary and archaeological sources to build his own account of Roman Britain. A differently orientated book, much more weighted towards social and economic matters than narrative and more heavily dependent on the archaeology, is John Wacher's *Roman Britain* (1978). The reader will notice that these two authors diverge substantially from time to time in their interpretation of the evidence, both from one another and from this present book, demonstrating how different conclusions may validly be drawn from the material available to us in the present fragmentary state of knowledge. A slighter and older work than either Frere or Wacher, but one that ought to be mentioned because of both the influence it had in inspiring interest in the subject and the ideas it set in motion, is M.P. Charlesworth, *The Lost Province*, Cardiff (1948), which is of particular interest for what he had to say about the aftermath of the Roman period in Britain. Nor, in concluding this paragraph, should we omit a short work from another major authority on Roman Britain who, like Richmond, never produced a full-scale monograph but nevertheless has a claim to be considered the person who did most to establish the modern study of Roman Britain. This work is F.J. Haverfield, *The Romanization of Roman Britain*, originally delivered as a lecture in 1905 and whose fourth edition was revised by Sir George MacDonald (Oxford, 1923).

Few writers have equalled Richmond's felicitous blend of classical learning and archaeological expertise and none successfully imitated his style—though several have tried—but we may properly place alongside his best work A.L.F. Rivet's urbane and delightful *Town and Country in Roman Britain* (2nd edn. 1964). A different side of the subject, one in which both Collingwood and Richmond were distinguished, is seen in Richmond's revision of Collingwood's classification of Romano-British material remains which was issued in 1969 as R.G. Collingwood and Ian Richmond, *The Archaeology of Roman Britain*, having been finally prepared for the publisher by D.R. Wilson after Richmond's own death. The reader may, however, find it useful to see the austere flesh of this invaluable exercise in taxonomy filled out and put in context with other detail and comparative material in Joan Liversidge, *Britain in the Roman Empire* (1968).

Writers on the Post-Roman period in Britain have generally been obliged by the nature of the evidence to concentrate their attention either on the Celtic or the Anglo-Saxon aspects of the subject. A short but helpful guide through the complex secular and religious evidence for Late and Post-Roman Celtic Britain is provided by Charles Thomas, *Britain and Ireland in Early Christian Times, AD 400-800* (n.d.); and David Brown's excellently written *Anglo-Saxon England* (1978) can equally be recommended. Both differ from the present book in their interpretations of the end of Roman Britain. Leslie Alcock, a more cautious scholar than either the title of *Arthur's Britain: History and Archaeology AD 367-634* (1974) or the publicity that surrounded his excavations at South Cadbury might suggest, provides in that book the perspective on the period of one of its foremost students. Of the very few people at home in both the Late Roman Continental sources and the British literary tradition John Morris was in a class of his own. His major paper 'Dark Age Dates' (in the collection of essays presented to Eric Birley, *Britain and Rome* (1966), edited by Michael G. Jarrett and Brian Dobson, pp. 145 ff.) has been cited in the footnotes to this book. His larger-scale study, *The Age of Arthur*, appeared in 1973 and represents his developed views. The reader, however, needs to be warned that his ideas are not universally agreed with and his conclusions were often more stimulating to the student than likely to command general acceptance. While in this Post-Roman area one major work of classification should be included, J.N.L. Myres' *A Corpus of Anglo-Saxon Pottery of the Pagan Period*, Cambridge (1978), while mentioning that this, too, is a field not without controversy. The book is, however, without doubt a *magnum opus*, and it is useful to place beside it Myres's interpretative *Anglo-Saxon Pottery and the Settlement of England*, Oxford (1969). To some extent the divide in Early Anglo-Saxon studies has been about the interpretation of artefacts, largely from cemeteries or casual finds. Only recently have extensive excavations of settlements begun to give new perspectives, and it is interesting to observe Trevor Rowley, one of the exponents of the study of landscape history, editing the collection of papers entitled *Anglo-Saxon Settlement and Landscape*, British Archaeological Reports no. 6, Oxford (1974).

PERIODICALS

The learned periodicals that contain articles on our subject fall into three groups. First there are the journals of the national archaeological societies; then those of the main local societies (mainly, but not entirely, organized on a county basis and a substantial proportion of nineteenth-century origin) and finally the productions of a variety of bodies formed more recently, often in response to local or regional threats to antiquities. *The Journal of Roman Studies* and *Britannia* have already been mentioned. The Society for the Promotion of Roman Studies, which is responsible for both publications, produced a consolidated index for *JRS* nos. 41-60 (1951-70) in 1975. The *Antiquaries Journal*, issued in twice-yearly parts by the Society of Antiquaries of London, contains some of the most important articles and notes, and *Archaeologia*, an occasional series from the same source, publishes papers that require a large format and expensive illustration (for example, F.H. Thompson and J.B. Whitwell, 'The Gates of Roman Lincoln', *Archaeologia* 104 (1973), 129 ff.). An index to volumes 51-100 (1888-1966) was published as a special issue in 1970. The *Archaeological Journal* (from the Royal Archaeological Institute) and the *Journal of the British Archaeological Association* are also important. For Scotland the *Proceedings of the Society of Antiquaries of Scotland* should also be consulted and for Wales *Archaeologia Cambrensis* (the journal of the Cambrian Archaeological Association) and the *Bulletin of the Board of Celtic Studies*. From time to time there are articles of Romano-British interest in *Antiquity* (which has an exceptionally wide range in world archaeology) and often important items of report or discussion in its section of Notes.

Many of the annual publications of the county societies are notable learned journals in their own right, for example *Archaeologia Aeliana* (from the Society of Antiquaries of Newcastle upon Tyne), *Oxoniensia* (the Oxfordshire Architectural and Historical Society) or the *Proceedings of the Cambridge Antiquarian Society*. The third group ranges from a variety of intentionally ephemeral newsletters to substantial publications, often exploiting more unusual formats or unorthodox methods of production than the established county journals. We have already taken note of the reports of the CBA Groups, but we may take as examples of the substantial publications in this category *Durobrivae* (in which the important work in progress in the Nene Valley is reported) or the handsome *South Lincolnshire Archaeology*, whose first issue was published by the South Lincolnshire Archaeological Unit in 1977.

MONOGRAPHS AND SPECIAL SUBJECTS

A general observation that emerges from the compilation of a bibliography on Roman Britain is that there are still major aspects which, surprisingly, lack a major monograph. Thus, for example, we have no single, full-scale treatment of religion or, even more surprising, the Roman army in Britain. It is to be hoped that these gaps will in due time be filled in the manner in which we have Jocelyn Toynbee on art, John Wacher on towns, or Stephen Johnson on the Saxon Shore. Collections of papers given at conferences are of first-rate importance, but do not fulfil the same purpose as the comprehensive study by a single scholar.

When, however, we come to look at subdivisions of the major topics, the picture is different. Military history, to take our second example, is well served by its specialists, though both for the early period and the Late Empire there is less available than the central period. There is no modern full-length study of Caesar's campaigns in Britain. We do have Christopher Hawkes' 1975 Mortimer Wheeler Archaeological Lecture (*Proceedings of the British Academy*, 63 (1977), 125 ff.), which has an extensive bibliography. For the Invasion and the immediately succeeding decades there are two books for the general reader: Donald R. Dudley and Graham Webster *The Roman Conquest of Britain, AD 43–57* (1965), and the second edition of Webster's study of the rebellion of Boudicca (*Boudica: the British Revolt against Rome AD 60* (1978)). The frontiers, especially the northern, have received a great deal of attention. Many articles have been published over the years in the proceedings of the international Congresses of Roman Frontier Studies. The first of these congresses was held at Newcastle upon Tyne in 1949 and papers given at them have been published by the national organizing committees of the successive meetings. In passing we should also note the article by Professor J.C. Mann, 'The Frontiers of the Principate', in the enormous collection of essays being edited by H. Temporini and W. Haase under the general title *Aufstieg und Niedergang der römischen Welt* (Berlin and New York), appearing in numerous volumes and loosely arranged by theme within three major parts—I: from the foundation of Rome to the fall of the Republic; II: the Principate; and III: the Late and Post-Roman world. John Mann's thoughtful article appears in Part II, volume 1 (1974).

A particularly influential assemblage of articles on the north was edited by Sir Ian Richmond as *Roman and Native in North Britain*, Edinburgh (1958); and my own *The Frontier People of Roman Britain*, Cambridge (1965; reprinted with corrections and additions, 1967) remains the only full-length study of the Romanized civilian population of the frontier region, though supplanted in detail by more recent excavation and research. Visitors to Hadrian's Wall will need the Ordnance Survey map at a scale of two inches to one mile, *Hadrian's Wall*, 2nd edn. Southampton (1975), and C.M. Daniel's excellent thirteenth edition of J. Collingwood Bruce's Handbook, now entitled *Handbook to the Roman Wall with the Cumbrian Coast and Outpost Forts* (Newcastle upon Tyne, 1978). From the nineteenth century to the present day a tradition of periodic organized perambulations of the Wall by groups of scholars has been accompanied by handbooks specially prepared for these 'Pilgrimages', published under various imprints since 1849. Detailed documentation on individual sections of the Wall will be found listed in Collingwood Bruce or in E. Birley, *Research on Hadrian's Wall*, Kendal (1961), but the most modern survey of the general issues is David J. Breeze and Brian Dobson *Hadrian's Wall*, 2nd edn. Harmondsworth (1978), which takes a forthright but fair and balanced line on the many controversial matters that are still the subject of lively debate. Modern work on the Antonine Wall is less easily accessible, much of it being scattered in the learned journals. The Ordnance Survey '2½ Inch' (1:25,000) map, *The Antonine Wall*, Southampton (1969), however, provides an excellent start. Sir George Macdonald's *The Roman Wall in Scotland*, 2nd edn. Oxford (1934), must be mentioned as a classic of its kind; and Anne S. Robertson's brief *The Antonine Wall: A Handbook to the Roman Wall between Forth and Clyde and a Guide to its surviving remains*, Glasgow (1960; 3rd edn. 1979, which takes into account recent work) is an admirable introduction. We may supplement this with a collection of papers published as *Scottish Archaeological Forum*, 7, Edinburgh (1975). The military history of Roman Wales is splendidly surveyed for us in Michael G. Jarrett's largely rewritten second edition of V.E. Nash Williams, *The Roman Frontier in Wales*, Cardiff (1969). More recently, there has been considerable attention paid to the Saxon Shore and allied topics. The most satisfactory single work is Stephen Johnson's book already mentioned above, *The Roman Forts of the Saxon Shore* (1976) and other specialists' work is well represented in the CBA Research Report no. 18, *The Saxon Shore* (ed. D.E. Johnston, 1977). D.A. White, *Litus Saxonicum*, Madison, Wisconsin (1961) needs mention, if only because often referred to in other books. Major monographs on individual sites may be represented by, for example, B. Cunliffe (ed.), *Excavations at the Roman Fort at Richborough, Kent, No. 5*, Oxford (1968), continuing a series of Society of Antiquaries reports on earlier excavations on that site, and note should be taken of S.S. Frere's important review (in *Antiquity*, 51 (1977), 163 f., of Cunliffe's Portchester excavation report) which incidentally comments on and agrees with Stephen Johnson's main thesis.

Lacking, as we have noted, an up-to-date monograph on the army in Britain, nevertheless readers will find useful material on individual topics in many places, including Eric Birley's *Roman Britain and The Roman Army: Collected Papers*, Kendal (1961)—which also touches on other areas of our subject—and on the Late army and the *Notitia Dignitatum* in reviews published in *JRS* 67 (1977), 186 f. and 187 respectively. An antidote to the many popular misconceptions on the appearance and composition of the Roman army in Britain is contained in an unassuming but valuable and well-produced booklet, H. Russell Robinson's *What the Soldiers Wore on Hadrian's Wall*, Newcastle upon Tyne (1976), which carries its subject unusually but helpfully through into the fourth century.

Roads were, of course, of importance not only to the army but to all aspects of Romano-British life. The second edition of Ivan D. Margary's *Roman Roads in Britain* (1967) is a monument to an outstanding lifetime's work on a major aspect of our subject. On another major aspect, the towns, we may start with John Wacher, *The Towns of Roman Britain* (1975), and remember the influential earlier collection of conference papers edited by the same writer, *The Civitas Capitals of Roman Britain*, Leicester (1966). Another important set of papers has been edited by W. Rodwell and T. Rowley as *The Small Towns of Roman Britain*, Oxford (1976). For a monograph on a single town we may select G.C. Boon, *Silchester, the Roman Town of Calleva*, Newton Abbot (1974). The results of one of the largest and most important of modern excavations of a town are now appearing, marked by S.S. Frere's *Verulamium, I*, Oxford (1972), and we may note also in this context his article 'Verulamium and the Towns of Britannia' in Temporini and Haase, II, 3 (1975). Barry Cunliffe has usefully adopted a practice of making his excavation results more accessible by supplementing his major reports by more popular, lower-priced books, and under this heading we should note here that his *Roman Bath* (1969), in the Society of Antiquaries Research Reports series, was followed by *Roman Bath discovered* in 1971.

A number of works are relevant to the historically important subject of sites with both military and civil occupation. W.F. Grimes described in *The Excavation of Roman and Mediaeval London* (1968) the rescue work in the City that revealed among other important results the existence of the Trajanic fort and the relationship to it of the later city wall. Colchester has been well-served by major publications (C.F.C. Hawkes and M.R. Hull, *Camulodunum: First Report on the Excavations at Colchester 1930-1939*, Oxford (1947); M.R. Hull, *Roman Colchester*, Oxford (1958)); and the work is by no means finished. The Royal Commission's *Eburacum: Roman York* (1962) appeared as volume I of *An Inventory of the Historical Monuments in the City of York* and was a model in its time; and we should note Paul T. Bidwell's forthcoming *The Legionary Bath-House and Basilica and Forum at Exeter*, the publication of one of the most recently excavated and important examples of a city succeeding a legionary base.

Some aspects of the study of the Romano-British countryside we have noted earlier in this bibliography. The papers edited by A.C. Thomas, *Rural Settlement in Roman Britain* (1966), record some of the first results of modern work in this area. A.L.F. Rivet's essay 'The Rural Economy of Roman Britain', in Temporini and Haase, II, 3 may appropriately be recorded here, and the same author also edited the papers entitled *The Roman Villa in Britain* (1969), which was the first modern attempt to bring together thought on this much debated subject. A new collection of essays has supplemented this: Malcolm Todd (ed.), *Studies in the Romano-British Villa*, Leicester (1978). As a study of a single villa, seen by its excavator, there is, of course, Cunliffe on Fishbourne—in detail in *Excavations at Fishbourne*, i-ii, Leeds (1971) and in a book for the non-specialist as *Fishbourne: A Roman Palace and Its Garden* (1971). Similarly there is the long series of reports on the Shakenoak villa in Oxfordshire by A.C.C. Brodribb, A.R. Hands, and D.R. Walker, published in Oxford from 1968—very different in style and format but from the same viewpoint. By contrast, John Percival, in *The Roman Villa: An Historical Introduction* (1976), takes the vast theme of the villa in the western part of the empire. In the strictest sense, therefore, his book is not for inclusion in a Romano-British bibliography, but the extremely uneven state of knowledge about villas made it inevitable that much of his material should be drawn from Britain and Gaul.

The subject of religion in Roman Britain may properly commence with the Celts. Stuart Piggott's *The Druids* (1968, revised edition 1975), cited in the text of this book, is an admirable study, much wider than its title may suggest. M.J.T. Lewis, *Temples in Roman Britain*, Cambridge (1966) remains the standard work on structures, particularly on the Romano-Celtic shrines, though much work has been done since. An early monograph on a single site had much influence on many aspects of thinking on Romano-British religion. This was

Sir Mortimer Wheeler's *Report on the Excavations of the Prehistoric, Roman, and Post-Roman Site in Lydney Park, Glos.* published with his wife, T.V. Wheeler (Oxford, 1932), and almost as important were the religious aspects of his work at the great hill-fort of Maiden Castle, near Dorchester (*Maiden Castle, Dorset*, Oxford (1943)). E. and J.R. Harris's *The Oriental Cults in Roman Britain*, Leiden (1965) approaches a different but also important aspect of the subject. Christianity is, like other areas we have examined, a field in which a collection of papers represents the only substantial book ranging over the subject at large. M.W. Barley and R.P.C. Hanson (eds.), *Christianity in Britain, 300–700*, Leicester (1968) performs this role. Two short but important publications have been included in my footnotes but should be particularly noted here: K.S. Painter, *The Mildenhall Treasure: Roman Silver from East Anglia*, British Museum (1977) and the same author's *The Water Newton Early Christian Silver* (1977), also from the British Museum. We ought to note an early example of the modern publication of Roman cemeteries, L.P. Wenham, *The Romano-British Cemetery at Trentholme Drive, York* (1968). The CBA Research Report (no. 22) edited by Richard Reece and entitled *Burial in the Roman World* (1977) contains much from Roman Britain or of direct relevance to it and brings the picture up to date.

Art in Britain is better served by major monographs. E.M. Jope and P. Jacobsthal, *Early Celtic Art in the British Isles* (Oxford, forthcoming) promises to provide us with a standard work for the Celtic background (the reader may also care to note Stuart Piggott and Glyn Daniel's pleasing *Picture Book of Ancient British Art*, Cambridge (1951)). For the Roman period we are splendidly provided by J.M.C. Toynbee's *Art in Britain under the Romans*, Oxford (1964), superbly supplemented by her Phaidon Press illustrated catalogue of the 1961 Exhibition of Art in Roman Britain at the Goldsmith's Hall, London, entitled *Art in Roman Britain* and published in 1962 with detailed comments on each piece. We should also note here a massive project intended to record the sculpture of the empire, the *Corpus Signorum Imperii Romani* (or *CSIR*), of which volume I, 1, by E.J. Phillips (covering Corbridge and Hadrian's Wall east of the North Tyne) was published at Oxford in 1977.

Pottery has long been at the centre of Romano-British archaeology. Introductory guides include Vivien G. Swan, *Pottery in Roman Britain*, Princes Risborough (2nd edn. 1978) and Graham Webster, *Romano-British Coarse Pottery: A Students' Guide*, CBA Research Report no. 6 (1963). J.P. Gillam, 'Types of Roman Coarse Pottery Vessels in Northern Britain', first published as an article in *Arch. Ael.* 4th ser. 35 (1957), 180 ff. and reprinted with renumbered pages, was a pioneering work of the first importance. Those interested in samian wares will need to have by them the fundamental book in English, F. Oswald, and T.D. Pryce, *An Introduction to the Study of Terra Sigillata* (1920) and the more modern J.A. Stanfield and G. Simpson, *Central Gaulish Potters*, Oxford (1958). There are many specialist works, but B.R. Hartley has added to his more technical studies the brief *Notes on the*

Roman Pottery Industry in the Nene Valley, Peterborough (1960) which is of particular interest for the general reader. Two collections of papers permit one to gain a view of investigation and the movement of ideas in this field in general over recent years: Alec Detsicas (ed.), *Current Research in Romano-British Coarse Pottery*, CBA Research Report no. 10 (1973); and John Dore and Kevin Greene (eds.), *Roman pottery studies in Britain and beyond: papers presented to John Gillam, July 1977*, British Archaeological Reports Supplementary Ser., 30, Oxford (1977). For the many other products of industry found in Britain we may note as examples—though none are as extensively published as pottery—J.P. Wild on *Textile Manufacture in the Northern Roman Provinces* (including Britain) or Joan Liversidge, *Furniture in Roman Britain* (1955).

Coins are almost as frequently used by Romano-British archaeologists as dating evidence and in 'economic' analysis as pottery; and in addition their political significance is endlessly discussed. Andrew Burnett's British Museum booklet, *The Coins of Roman Britain* (n.d.) is an excellent starting-point for the beginner: C.H.V. Sutherland, *Coinage and Currency in Roman Britain*, Oxford (1937) is the standard work. Modern methods of analysing the distribution of coins and its significance may be represented here by John Casey and Richard Reece (eds.), *Coins and the Archaeologist*, British Archaeological Reports, 4, Oxford (1974), though it should be noted that there is general agreement neither on methods nor conclusions in this field.

Theory and methodology in fact provide the areas in which there is perhaps the greatest degree of dispute in archaeology today. Oddly enough, however, the basic principles on which archaeology proceeds are still as well expressed in Sir Mortimer Wheeler's *Archaeology from the Earth*, Oxford (1954; reissued, Penguin Press 1956) as anywhere else, though many of the individual techniques have advanced or been superseded since he wrote. It is useful to bear in mind five main areas: excavation; out-of-doors archaeology *not* involving excavation and often referred to by professional archaeologists rather confusingly as 'field archaeology'; typology and the study of small finds; theoretical archaeology; and the effects of the techniques available on the theory and philosophy of archaeology itself. Peter J. Fowler has conveniently brought together and discussed many of the issues involved in the differing ways in which archaeology is now understood and practised in *Approaches to archaeology* (1977).

In excavation itself, Wheeler's methods have been supplemented and modified by many subsequent excavators. One of the most painstaking and subtle exponents of the art of excavation is Philip Barker, whose book *Techniques of Archaeological Excavation* (1977) and Graham Webster's review of it in *The Antiquaries Journal* (*Ant. J.* 58 (1978) 391 f.) should be mentioned here. Methods adopted by different excavators and under different conditions, however, vary widely. A straightforward guide to modern archaeological practice for those without a prior archaeological background is conveniently contained in David Miles' *An Introduction to Archaeology* (1978). Miles is himself a

distinguished practitioner of fieldwork (or 'non-destructive archaeology')
as well as excavation—we have already noted above his important
collaboration with Benson in the first Thames Valley survey—and the
techniques used in this latter branch of archaeology are well illustrated
in the CBA volume edited by Elizabeth Fowler, *Field Survey in British
Archaeology* (1972). Equally useful is D.R. Wilson (ed.), *Aerial reconnaissance for archaeology*, CBA Research Report no. 12 (1975), based
on a symposium held in 1974. This is, of course, not only one of the
most important tools of the modern archaeologist; it is also a field in
which technical developments and new applications are particularly
likely to occur.

Various other techniques have been mentioned from time to time
in this book and will have been noted by the reader. However I should
not close without mentioning a few of the major publications in the
field of 'analytical archaeology'. In part, recent importations into
archaeological technique have come from the Social Sciences. On the
whole the concepts here are not difficult for the general reader to
grasp, though the jargon is often almost impenetrable. Other techniques
are much more purely mathematical, and are less easily accessible to
the general reader without a mathematical background. The chief
credit for drawing the attention of archaeologists dramatically to new
methods must go to David L. Clarke, whose sadly early death prevented
him from developing his theme fully. His *Analytical Archaeology* has
been revised by B. Chapman (1978), a volume edited by him entitled
Spatial Archaeology came out in 1977, and a collection of his papers
has been published, but his work ended too soon. It ought to be
mentioned that a number of archaeologists—including some with
experience of the Social Sciences and of computer applications in other
fields—doubted the practicability within the limitations of archaeology
of some of the methods advocated, and I was one of them and remain
so. The matter is fraught with controversy, and a browse through the
pages of *Antiquity* in the past few years will give the reader an idea of
what is involved. Another publication to be noted in this general
context is Ian Hodder and Clive Orton, *Spatial Analysis in Archaeology*,
Cambridge (1976). Moving into the more purely mathematical, we
should note J.E. Doran and F.R. Hodson, *Mathematics and Computers
in Archaeology*, Edinburgh (1975). This is an introduction to an area
in which the authors were pioneers, largely as applied to prehistory.
These mathematical techniques have been comparatively slow to enter
Romano-British studies, yet in many ways the mass of material finds
from our period makes it potentially a very promising field in which to
practise mathematical methods of analysis. There can be little doubt
that the next generation of publications on Roman Britain will take the
use of these techniques for granted, with a clearer view of their value
in attacking particular problems, of their various advantages and limitations. There should be no clash with the more traditional skills of the
historian. Together with the longer-established forms of archaeology
the new techniques must be used alongside the critical analysis of the
written sources. We shall not be surprised on those occasions when

the results of our different approaches to a problem fail to agree. There is no prospect that we shall ever have all the information necessary to form a final or complete picture of any aspect of the past, even for recent periods. For Roman Britain our evidence is so fragmentary that we shall always have to be satisfied with the best impression we can gain by using all the approaches available to us. Future work on Roman Britain must be judged not only on the range of approaches it employs and how judiciously it has employed each of them, but on its degree of understanding of what it is and is not possible to know.

INDEX

compiled by Eileen Powell

Bruce-Mitford, R., 136

Brunnus, 270

Bruttium, 443

Buckinghamshire, 43, 484

Buckland, P.C., 551

building: industry, 302, 390, 422, 514, 629, 638; materials, 562–3, 602–3, 609, *and see* timber, stone, etc.; programmes, 112, 117, 124, 138, 142, 232, 576; Wroxeter, 185, 584; Flavian, 156–163; third century, 265–7; Constantinian, 325–8; fourth century, 372; late use of Roman buildings, 495

Bulgaria, villa and village, 610

Burdur, inscription, 566

bureaucracy, 332, 336–9, 346: attempt to reduce, 360; increase, 371, 535; affecting access, 519; in kingdoms and prefecture, 450–1

Burgh Castle, fort, 281, 300

Burgh-by-Sands, fort, 166

Burgundians: prisoners of war, 282; settled in Roman territory, 433, 446, 453, 477, 491, 499; some expelled, 490; in Britain, 549

Burgus (Bourg-sur-Gironde), 450

burials, 358–9, 375, 514, 520–1, 522, 526, 693–703: Iron Age, 10, 46, 670; aristocratic, 56, 417, 461, 471, 494; live, 682; sacred objects, 683, 702, 712, 719, *and see* cemeteries, grave goods; Christian, 731 ff.

Burnett, A., 425, 661

Burrus, Sex. Afranius, 116, 119

Burton Down, 627

Bury, J.B., 433

butchers, 657

Brythonic (Brittonic) language, 17

Butler, R.M., 174

Butser, farm project, 554, 663

Buxton, 673

Buzenol, relief, 623

Byzantine emperors, 325

Byzantium, 521; *and see* Constantinople

Cadbury Congresbury, hill-fort, 453

Caecina Alienus, A., 128–9

Caelius, M. (centurion), 701

Caerellius Priscus, 210

Caerleon: legionary fortress, 98, 137, 152, 231, 255; rebuilding, 163, 256; *canabae*, 575, 583; status, 512, 583; inscriptions from, 250, 512; amphitheatre, 579; martyrs?, 718, 721

Caernarvon: waterside fortifications, 384; troops from, 404

Caerwent, 138, 185, 186, 586: inscriptions, 251, 534, 659; gates, 262; plague, 552; weaving-mill?, 656; pagan gods, 666, 668; church, 724

Caesar, C. Julius: state of Britain and Gaul in his time, 1–18; constitutional position and motives for invasion, 22–5, 38–9, 396; invasion of Britain, 25–38; relations with British tribes, 42, 57; handling of resistance, 102, 106, 126, 669, 680; contrast with period of Claudian invasion, 75–84; example and source of *auctoritas*, to Augustus, 48–50, to Claudius, 71, to Julian, 359–363; as military historian, 304; Julian family, 68, 71, 155, 291; Druids, 24, 677; economic factors and the invasion, 41, 37, 630, 652

Caesar (title), 516, and *passim*

Caesarea, title for London?, 328

Caesennius Paetus, L., 117

Caister-by-Yarmouth, military?, 258

Caistor-by-Norwich (Venta Icenorum); forum and *civitas*, 156, 593; weaving-mill? 696

Caledonia, 147, 229; *and see* Scotland

Caledonians, 225–7, 230, 241, 318

Calgacus, 146–8

Caligula (emperor), *see* Gaius

Calpurnius (St. Patrick's father), 463

Calpurnius Agricola, Sex., 203, 205, 207, 635

Calpurnius Piso, C., 128

Calvisius Rufus, 251

Cambrai, 493

Cambridge: Iron Age shaft, 692; cemeteries, 693, 700

Cambridgeshire, 12, 43, 101: river communications, 252, 562

Camelon, fort, 144, 205

Camelot, *see* South Cadbury

Ouse, river, Cambs., 268, 564
ovation, 97, 394
oxen, 563, 627; *and see* cattle, stock-raising
Oxford, kilns, 644
Oxfordshire, 43, 68: pottery, 644-9; cemeteries, 694, 705-6
oyster shells, 565, 630

Pacatianus, 345
pagan cults, 666-70: stripped of wealth, 341, 577, 663; tolerated by Christian emperors, 341, 354-6; outlawed, 356, 370, 401, 408-10; revived, 362-3, 409, 443; family gods, 408, 707-8; altar of 671, 712-13, 730; Celtic cults, 669-70, 691; ritual shafts, 680, 691-2, 735; springs and water cults, 666, 669, 680, 686, 688, 690-1, 735, 736; trees, 672-4, 736; severed head, 670, 681, 691-2, 706; Mithras, 711-12; Bath, 686-8; Coventina, 691-2, 733; Lydney, 362, 686; Springhead, 596; *and see* mystery religions, *nemus*, Mithraism, shrines
pagan culture, 665-714: among senatorial class, 341, 365, 370, 401, 409; political importance, 582; attacks on, 356, 401, 408-10, 443; Britain, 470-1, 713, 726-7, 730, 733-7; burial practices, 693, 702; philosophy, 709-10; *and see* Christian culture, Druidism, religion
pagus, 535
Painter, K.S., 373, 431, 532, 718-19, 721
paintings: wall, 465, 725, 732; plaster, 233, 603, 609, 703; civilian in military uniform, 410
palaces: Nero's Golden House, 156, 161; Diocletian, 325, 452; Cologne, 456, 493; Trier, 325; governor's at London, 112, 156-7, 161, 530-1, 658; York?, 229, 328, 583; bishop's at Trier, 725; *and see* Fishbourne, official residences
palaeobotany, *see* scientific analysis
Palatine Hill, Rome, 161

palatine troops (*palatini*), 375, 366-7, 404
Palestine, 75, 131, 717
palisades, 175
Palladius, 395
Palmyra, Barates, 514, 659
Pamphylia, 109
panegyrics: Constantine, 315, 326; Constantius, 303-4, 314, 318, 319, 630; Theodosius, 378
Pannonia: revolts, 49, 273; legions from, 72-3, 217; Pannonians in Britain, 394, 522; defeat of Magnus Maximus, 404; municipal organization, 537; support for Christianity, 733; *ala II Pannoniorum*, 510-1
Papinian, 229
parasitology, 551
Paris, 360, 590: naval unit, 384; wine, 654
Parisi, 10: British, 46, 135; Gallic, 590
Park Street, Hertfordshire, villa, 605
Parthia, 239
Parthians, 272-3; *and see* Persians
Pater Noster, 718
pater patriae, 177
patera, 689, 704
patrician: status, 155; Late Roman military title, 475-6, 486, 488-9
Patrick, Saint, 462-3, 727, 734
patronage, 616-17: imperial, 49-50, 78-80, 518-19; army, 21, 164-5, 212; legal remedies from, 143, 527, 533-4; of local communities, 143, 153-5, 251, 279, 534; of Christians, 342-3, 462, 725; and doctrine of Grace, 462, 466; display of status, 465-6, 469; and see *clientela*
pattern construction, 541, 615
Paul, Saint, 675
Paul the Chain, Paulus *Catena*, 357-8, 532, 726
Paulinus, *see* Suetonius Paulinus
Paulinus of Nola, 737
Paulinus, Saint, 675
Paulus (*comes*), 491
Pausanias, 194, 199, 200-1
Peacock, D.P.S., 57, 636, 652
Peak District, 4
Peal, C.A., 636